Contents

Appendices

Index

FOREWORD

This Report is the outcome of a successful collaboration between the Ministry of Agriculture, Fisheries and Food and the Department of Health with the Office of Population Censuses and Surveys in the important and topical area of nutrition. It is the first ever dietary and nutritional survey of a nationally representative sample of adults aged 16 to 64 in Great Britain, and it will provide a sound basis for the development of future food and health policy, and for measuring its success.

We warmly welcome the Report, and hope that it will be a foundation on which future collaborative ventures can be built.

BARONESS HOOPER
Parliamentary Under-Secretary
    of State
Department of Health

DAVID MACLEAN
Parliamentary Secretary
Ministry of Agriculture,
    Fisheries and Food

Preface

This Dietary and Nutritional Survey of British Adults, the first collaborative survey of this kind undertaken by the Social Survey Division of OPCS, on behalf of MAFF and the Department of Health, has produced an enormous volume of data on the food and nutrient intake, nutritional status, and anthropometric and blood pressure measurements of the British population, aged between 16 and 64. This Report presents only the initial findings of the survey. These data are presented in the knowledge that they represent only a fraction of what could be derived from the database. In view of the likely public and scientific interest in the survey and the length of time that would be needed fully to explore, and to comment upon, the wealth of data generated by the survey, both the Steering Group on Food Surveillance and the Committee on Medical Aspects of Food Policy recommended that these initial findings should be published as soon as possible. They are therefore presented with limited commentary and interpretation to avoid any delay in publication and to stimulate the widest possible discussion and further inquiry among professional bodies and interested individuals.

The Departments plan to undertake further analyses and to prepare a more detailed commentary and interpretation of the findings during the forthcoming year, with a view to publishing a report under the auspices of the Committee on Medical Aspects of Food Policy and the Steering Group on Food Surveillance. To this end we would welcome comment on the data published so far and suggestions for further analyses.

The database will be deposited with the ESRC Data Archive at the University of Essex and independent researchers may therefore carry out their own analyses of any aspects of the survey.

We would like to thank the Social Survey Division of OPCS for the way they have carried out this survey. We would also like to thank the doctors and respondents who took part, all of whom made an indispensable contribution to the survey.

SIR DONALD ACHESON
Chief Medical Officer
Department of Health

Chairman, Committee on
Medical Aspects of Food Policy

DR M E KNOWLES
Chief Scientist
Ministry of Agriculture,
Fisheries and Food

Chairman, Steering Group
on Food Surveillance

Authors' acknowledgements

We would like to thank everybody who contributed to the survey and the production of this Report. We were supported by the specialist staff in Social Survey Division who carried out the sampling, fieldwork, primary analysis and editing stages, and particular thanks are due to the interviewers who showed such commitment and enthusiasm to a survey which placed considerable demands on their skills.

We would also like to record our gratitude to the following people for their support, technical advice and assistance at various stages of the survey;

- the professional staff at the Ministry of Agriculture, Fisheries and Food, the Department of Health and the Scottish Home and Health Department, in particular Helen Crawley (formerly of MAFF) and Mr R W Wenlock (Department of Health);

- Ann Wheeler-Clarke and Katrine Sutherland, consultant nutritionists;

- Professor J V G A Durnin, for his advice on the anthropometric measurements;

- the staff at the Wolfson Research Laboratories, for their advice and work on the analysis of the biochemical specimens;

- Dr B Cox, for the loan of the Accutorr sphygmomanometers;

- Dr A Leeds and Dr R Skinner, formerly of the Department of Health's Nutrition Unit;

- Dr S Bingham, for her advice on the 24-hour collection of urine;

- the doctors and other personnel recruited to collect the specimens of blood.

Most importantly, we would like to thank all those people who gave up so much of their time to take part in this survey, made the interviewers very welcome in their homes and showed such interest in the aims of the research.

Notes

Tables showing percentages
Where percentages have been rounded to the nearest whole number they may not always add up to 100%.

Values of less than 0.5% are represented in tables by a zero. A dash (–) indicates that there were no cases in the cell concerned.

Tables showing mean and median values
Values for means, medians, percentiles and standard errors (SE) are shown to an appropriate number of decimal places. A dash (–) indicates a zero value.

Significant differences
Differences which are commented on in the text are shown as being significant at the 0.01 or 0.05 levels. Throughout the report we use the terms 'significant' and 'statistically significant' interchangeably. Differences which were not significant (shown in the tables as NS) are those where $p > 0.05$.

Where the differences between subgroups are compared for a number of variables, for example, differences between men and women in the consumption of wine, fortified wine and beer, the significance level shown ($p < 0.01$ or $p < 0.05$) applies to *all* comparisons unless otherwise stated.

Standard errors for estimates have been calculated as if the sample had been drawn as a simple random sample.

For a proportion (p) of a sample of n cases the standard error is given by:

$$se(p) = \sqrt{\frac{p(1-p)}{n}}$$

Standard errors for estimates of mean values are shown in the tables.

The standard error of the difference between two proportions or means (a and b) for different subgroups of the sample is given by:

$$se(a - b) = \sqrt{[se(a)]^2 + [se(b)]^2}$$

Summary

Introduction

This report contains the initial findings of the Dietary and Nutritional Survey of British Adults which was carried out between October 1986 and August 1987. The survey aimed to recruit a nationally representative sample of adults aged 16 to 64 living in private households in Great Britain. Pregnant women were excluded from the sample.

The sample was recruited using a multi-stage random probability design. A total of 2197 people completed a full seven-day dietary record. This represented 70% of the eligible sample. A 24-hour urine collection was made by 77% of people who co-operated with some aspect of the survey and 76% of responders aged 18 to 64 gave a specimen of blood. Comparison of the characteristics of the responding sample with those of the total population and other large surveys showed good general agreement, although there were indications that the 16 to 24 age group may have been underrepresented (*Chapter 5*).

National averages
Foods

A wide range of foods was consumed by the informants. Broad categories of foods consumed by 75% of the sample included whole milk, cheese, eggs and egg dishes, beef and veal dishes, bacon and ham, white bread, biscuits, potatoes, potato chips, and coffee and tea. There were differences between men and women in both the types and quantities of foods consumed. Men generally consumed larger quantities of foods during the seven-day recording period. A larger proportion of women than men consumed wholemeal bread, reduced fat milks, salad vegetables, fresh fruit and confectionery. Conversely men were more likely than women to have eaten fried white fish, sausages, meat pies and chips. Older informants were more likely than younger informants to have eaten potatoes, milk puddings, butter, preserves and fresh fruit and vegetables. Younger adults more commonly ate savoury snacks and takeaway items, such as meat pies, burgers and kebabs than those aged 35 and over (*Chapter 6*).

Energy intakes and body mass index

The average daily recorded energy intake for men was 2450kcal (10.3MJ) and 1680kcal (7.05MJ) for women. These recorded energy intakes were similar to those reported in other large population studies. There was little variation in the average recorded energy intake up to the age of 50, but recorded energy intakes were lower in the 50 to 64 year age group. Exclusion of people on slimming diets and those who were unwell during the recording period and who reported that their eating had been affected gave recorded average energy intakes of 2480kcal (10.4MJ) for men and 1750kcal (7.3MJ) for women. The relatively low ratios of recorded energy intakes to calculated basal metabolic rate (27% of men and 40% of women less than 1.2) suggested that the recorded intakes may not have represented habitual intakes (*Chapter 7*). Average energy intakes were below the current recommended daily amounts (RDAs), particularly for women. On average, however, no group was underweight, although overweight was common.

The Quetelet or Body Mass Index was used as a measure of body fatness. Average body mass index was 24.9 in men and 24.6 in women, and tended to be higher in older groups. Although in those aged 16 to 49 body mass index was higher in men, in the 50 to 64 year olds, it was higher in women. Compared with a larger survey of heights and weights using similar methodology carried out in 1980, median body mass index was similar for both sexes, but average body mass index was higher in both men and women at all ages. The prevalence of obesity, defined as body mass index of 30 or more, was 12% in women, compared with 8% in 1980. This increase was less marked in men (8% compared to 6%) (*Chapter 14*).

The average height of men was 174.5cm, and of women 161.7cm. Average height was less in older age groups in both sexes. These recorded heights were higher than in the 1980 study which recorded 173.9cm for men and 160.9cm for women (*Chapter 14*).

Fat intakes and blood lipids

Average daily recorded fat intake was 102.3g for men and 73.5g for women. This represented 37.6% of total energy for men and 39.2% for women. Fat provided 40.4% and 40.3% of food energy (that is, excluding alcohol) for men and women respectively. The percentage of food energy derived from fat was similar across all age groups. Only 12% of men and 15% of women had fat intakes which met the Committee on Medical Aspects of Food Policy (COMA) target of 35% or less of food energy from fat.

Men consumed on average 42.0g of saturated fatty acids and 5.6g of trans fatty acids compared with 31.1g and 4.0g respectively for women. Intake of saturated fatty acids did not vary by age. Saturated fatty acids contributed 16.5% and 17.0% of food energy in men and women respectively. Only 11% of men and 12% of women derived less than the COMA target of 15%

of food energy from saturated plus trans fatty acids, and only 6% of men and 8% of women met both targets. Thirty per cent of men and 27% of women obtained 15% or less of their food energy from saturated fatty acids alone. Saturated fatty acids provided a greater proportion of food energy for the oldest group compared with the youngest group.

The average ratio of polyunsaturated to saturated fatty acids (P:S) was similar for men and women (0.40 and 0.38 respectively; medians 0.35 and 0.34). However, both men and women over the age of 50 had lower average P:S ratios than the younger age groups. The major sources of fat were meat and meat dishes (24%), cereal products (19%), fat spreads (16%), milk and milk products (15%) and vegetables (11%). For saturated fatty acids, meat and meat dishes provided 23% of the total, as did milk and milk products. Cereal products (18%) and fat spreads (17%) were also major sources (*Chapter 9*).

Blood samples were analysed for total and high density lipoprotein (HDL) cholesterol. Low density lipoprotein (LDL) cholesterol was not measured directly but was estimated as total minus HDL cholesterol. No correction was applied for triglycerides, which were not measured as samples were not collected while fasting. Average serum total cholesterol concentration was 5.8mmol/l in men, and was higher in older age groups. Overall only 32% of men had serum total cholesterol less than 5.2mmol/l, and that proportion fell with age so that 13% of men aged 50 to 64 had serum total cholesterol below this level. Conversely 6% of men had serum total cholesterol of 7.8mmol/l or greater, and this rose to 10% in those aged 50 to 64. In women, average serum total cholesterol was also 5.8mmol/l, but the rise with age was especially marked over 50 years of age. Only 36% of all women, and 10% of those aged 50 to 64, had serum total cholesterol less than 5.2mmol/l. Overall, 8% of women had serum total cholesterol of 7.8mmol/l or more, but in those aged 50 to 64 this proportion rose to 21%.

Apart from age the main predictor of serum total cholesterol for both sexes was body mass index. Serum total cholesterol increased with increasing body mass index, but the relationship with other variables was less marked. Both the proportion of food energy derived from saturated fatty acids, and dietary cholesterol intake, but not total fat intake, were associated with total serum cholesterol. In contrast the proportion of food energy derived from total fat showed an association with HDL cholesterol. Average HDL cholesterol concentration was 1.2mmol/l in men and 1.4mmol/l in women. Although not consistently associated with age, HDL cholesterol tended to be lower in those of both sexes who smoked or had higher body mass index, and rose with the amount of alcohol consumed (*Chapter 17*).

Carbohydrate and dietary fibre
On average men consumed 272g and women 193g of carbohydrate per day. This represented 44.7% and

44.2% of food energy respectively. Total sugars provided 42% of the carbohydrate for men (115g) and 45% for women (86g). Carbohydrate intake was lower for the older informants (age 50 to 64) than the youngest group. Intakes of total sugars decreased through the age range for women but not for men. The major sources of carbohydrate were cereal products (46%), vegetables (16%) and sugar, confectionery and preserves (13%). For sugars the major sources were cereal products (23%), sugar, confectionery and preserves (29%), beverages (17%), and milk and milk products (13%).

The average intake of dietary fibre (modified Southgate method) was 24.9g (10.3g per 1000kcal) for men and 18.6g (11.2g per 1000kcal) for women. On average, older women consumed more dietary fibre than younger women, particularly when expressed per 1000kcal. Forty-five per cent of men and 16% of women consumed 25g or more dietary fibre per day while 25% of men and 6% of women had daily intakes of at least 30g. Almost half the dietary fibre was derived from cereal products, wholemeal and other non-white bread providing 17% and white bread a further 13%. Vegetables provided 38% of the total of which potatoes provided 12% (*Chapter 8*).

Protein
On average the daily intake of protein was 84.7g for men and 62.0g for women. The current RDAs for protein are based on protein providing 10% of energy. In this study protein provided 15.2% of total energy for women and 14.1% for men, well in excess of the RDA. The main sources of protein were meat and meat products (36%), cereal products (23%), milk and milk products (17%) and vegetables (9%) (*Chapter 8*).

Vitamins and minerals
Intakes of a wide range of vitamins, minerals and trace elements were calculated from the food consumption data. They have been compared with the UK RDAs where these exist. Average intakes of vitamins from food (excluding dietary supplements) were well above RDA levels for all the age groups studied (*Chapter 10*). For most vitamins men had higher total intakes than women but when expressed per 1000kcal women had higher intakes. Younger informants tended to have lower vitamin intakes per unit energy. Within the sample 17% of women and 9% of men took dietary supplements (*Chapter 5*). A wide range of dietary supplements were taken. The most common categories were multivitamins, cod and halibut liver oils, vitamin C and B complex vitamins. Informants who took dietary supplements had higher intakes of vitamins from food than informants who did not take supplements (*Chapter 10*). The dietary supplements increased these differences further. However, the average intakes from food for both groups were above the RDAs.

Average intakes of pre-formed retinol were 1277μg (median 618μg) for men and 1133μg (491μg) for women. Average intakes of carotene were 2414μg (median

1895µg) in men and 2129µg (1696µg) in women. There was a tendency for consumption of both retinol and carotene to rise through the age range for both men and women (*Chapter 10*).

Plasma levels of retinol (vitamin A) do not reflect short-term dietary intake. No values below 10µg/100ml (0.03µmol/l), suggestive of long-term dietary deficiency, were found. Of the carotenoids, only β-carotene is an important precursor of retinol, but all the carotenoids have been shown to contribute to antioxidant status.

Circulating levels of β-carotene, α-carotene, and β-cryptoxanthin all tended to increase with age in both men and women, and women had higher levels than men of all these substances. Circulating levels of lycopene tended to decrease with age in both men and women, and men had higher average levels than women. In both sexes dietary intake of carotene was positively associated with circulating α-carotene and β-carotene (*Chapter 17*).

Average daily intakes of vitamin E from all sources were 11.7mg (median 9.3mg) in men and 8.6mg (6.8mg) in women. Average plasma levels of tocopherol (vitamin E) were 27.1µmol/l in men and 26.2µmol/l in women. The levels increased with age in both sexes, being about 50% higher among 50 to 64 year olds than 18 to 24 year olds. Plasma tocopherol can also be expressed as the ratio of tocopherol to cholesterol. This averaged 4.65 for men and 4.58 for women and did not vary significantly with age. Both plasma tocopherol concentration and tocopherol:cholesterol ratio were positively related to dietary intake of vitamin E (*Chapter 17*).

Average riboflavin intake was 2.29mg (median 2.03mg) for men, and 1.84mg (1.56mg) for women (*Chapter 10*). Riboflavin status was assessed as the activity coefficient in erythrocytes of the enzyme glutathione reductase, which requires riboflavin as a cofactor. The higher this activity coefficient (EGRAC) the lower the levels of riboflavin available. A value of less than 1.30 is generally regarded as normal. The mean values for men and women were 1.09 and 1.10 respectively. One per cent of men and 2% of women had EGRAC of 1.3 or greater (*Chapter 17*).

Average intakes of calcium (940mg for men, and 730mg for women) were well above the RDA. For both sexes calcium intake increased through the age groups. The main sources of calcium were milk and milk products (48%), cereal products (25%) and vegetables (7%).

Average intake of iron from food for men was 13.7mg (median 13.2mg) and 14.0mg (13.2mg) from all sources. This compares with the RDA of 10mg for men. Average intake of iron from food for women was 10.5mg (median 9.8mg). This increased to 12.3mg (10.0mg) when dietary supplements were included. Iron intakes were lower in younger women (median 9.5mg and 9.6mg in the 16 to 24 and 25 to 34 age groups respectively) compared with 10.3mg in the 35 to 49 and 50 to

64 age groups. Median intakes for women under the age of 50 were below the RDA of 12mg. The main dietary sources of iron were cereal products (42%), meat and meat products (23%) and vegetables (15%) (*Chapter 11*).

Four per cent of all women, but virtually no men, had haemoglobin concentrations below 11g/dl. There was no relationship between haemoglobin concentration and age in either sex. Serum concentrations of ferritin were measured to assess iron stores. A value below 25µg/l is generally considered to indicate low iron stores. Average ferritin concentration in men was 106.9µg/l, and rose steadily with age. Average ferritin concentration in women was 46.8µg/l, being 35.3µg/l in those aged 18 to 49, but 76.2µg/l in those aged 50 to 64. Overall, 4% of men and 33% of women had serum ferritin concentration less than 25µg/l, but this proportion rose from 12% in women aged 50 to 64 to 42% in women aged 18 to 49. For men, both serum ferritin and haemoglobin rose with increasing alcohol consumption. For women, only serum ferritin was associated with drinking behaviour. Neither haemoglobin nor ferritin showed a consistent linear relationship with total dietary iron intake (*Chapter 17*).

Average daily intakes of potassium were 3187mg and 2434mg in men and women respectively. Estimated average daily food sodium (that is, making no allowance for salt added during cooking or at the table) was 3376mg for men and 2351mg for women (*Chapter 11*).

Urine collections were assayed for their potassium and sodium content. Potassium excretion averaged 77mmol/24h (3000mg/24h) in men and 62mmol/24h (2610mg/24h) in women, and this was unrelated to age. Average sodium excretion was 173mmol/24h (3980mg/24h) in men and 132mmol/24h (3040mg/24h) in women, tending to decrease in both sexes with age. Dietary intake of potassium and of sodium were positively related to their 24-hour urinary excretion both in men and in women (*Chapter 16*).

Blood pressure
Blood pressure was measured using an automated technique which had been used in previous large scale studies. However, the particular instruments used have been reported to overestimate pressures below, and to underestimate those above, 80mm Hg, whether systolic or diastolic. It is therefore possible that the use of these instruments may have affected the results. Of those on no medications which might have affected their blood pressure, average blood pressure was 125/77mm Hg among men, and 118/73mm Hg among women, and tended to rise with age in both sexes. Overall, 3% of untreated men had systolic blood pressure of 160 mm Hg or more, though this proportion was 6% in those aged 50 to 64. Six per cent of all men, and 9% of those aged 50 to 64, had diastolic blood pressure of 95mm Hg or more. Systolic blood pressure of 160mm Hg or more was almost confined to those aged 50 to 64; 6% of men and 8% of women were in that

category. Overall, 3% of women had diastolic blood pressure of 95mm Hg or more, and the proportion rose with age, to 6% in those aged 50 to 64. In men, but not women, both systolic and diastolic blood pressure rose consistently with increasing alcohol consumption. Higher body mass index was consistently associated in both sexes with higher blood pressure. Diastolic blood pressure was not associated with urinary sodium or potassium excretion in either sex (*Chapter 15*).

Alcohol and smoking

Twenty-one per cent of men and 35% of women were classified as non-drinkers on the basis of the seven-day dietary record. In the youngest group these figures were 32% and 46% for men and women respectively. For those informants who recorded alcohol consumption during the survey week, mean daily intakes were 31.5g (median 23.2g) for men and 10.6g (6.8g) for women. Among consumers, those over the age of 50 recorded lower alcohol intakes on average than younger informants. On average the proportion of energy provided by alcohol for consumers was 8.7% (median 6.9%) for men and 4.3% (3%) for women. For the total diary sample 7% of women and 28% of men had intakes of 10% or more of their energy from alcohol. Twenty-one per cent of women and 47% of men obtained 5% or more of their energy from alcohol.

Body mass index, blood pressure and serum total cholesterol were significantly higher among men but not among women who drank alcohol. HDL cholesterol showed a consistent trend in both sexes to rise with increasing recorded alcohol consumption. γ-glutamyl transpeptidase and ferritin concentrations as well as mean corpuscular volume (MCV) were higher in both men and women who drank alcohol and increased with increasing intake. Plasma concentrations of carotenes except lycopene fell with increasing alcohol intake in men, but there was no similar consistent trend in women (*Chapters 14 and 17*).

Approximately two thirds of the total responding sample described themselves as non-smokers; the proportion was similar for the diary sample. Women who smoked were more likely to be light smokers (fewer than 20 cigarettes a day) than men (22% and 17% respectively). Smoking was more prevalent in women below the age of 50 compared with older women. For both sexes smoking was less common in Social Classes I and II (*Chapter 5*).

Classification of individuals by smoking and alcohol consumption was included with a number of other characteristics in analysis of variance (*Chapter 12*). After allowing for other characteristics included in the analyses, in both men and women energy intake rose with increasing alcohol consumption. The proportion of food energy from saturated fatty acids was lower for non-drinkers compared with drinkers. Intakes of protein, sugars and dietary fibre were higher in non-drinkers than drinkers.

For women but not for men, energy intake was significantly lower in smokers. The proportion of energy provided by alcohol was higher in smokers than in non-smokers. The diets of male smokers contained less fibre, iron, vitamin C, folate, protein, thiamin and niacin equivalents, and more sugars, than non-smokers. The proportion of food energy they derived from saturated fatty acids was higher, and their P:S ratio lower, than non-smokers. For women, differences reached statistical significance for fibre, iron, vitamin C, folate, riboflavin and calcium.

In men body mass index fell with increasing numbers of cigarettes smoked. Serum total cholesterol levels were not related to smoking behaviour but serum HDL cholesterol showed a consistent trend to decline with increasing numbers of cigarettes smoked in both sexes. Potassium excretion in both men and women, and sodium excretion in men, were lower in smokers. EGRAC rose and plasma carotenoids and tocopherol:cholesterol ratio fell with increasing number of cigarettes smoked among both men and women.

Region

Average recorded energy intake was lower for those men living in Scotland (2240kcal/day) compared with 2450kcal/day for all men. On average, Scottish men and women were shorter and had lower body mass index than those from other parts of Great Britain (*Chapters 7 and 12*). Men in Scotland and the Northern region consumed more alcohol on average, and derived a greater proportion of their energy from alcohol, than men in other regions (*Chapter 7*). However after allowing for other factors this difference no longer reached statistical significance (*Chapter 12*). Serum ferritin and γ-glutamyl transpeptidase concentrations and MCV were all on average higher in Scottish men than in men elsewhere, but a similar trend was not seen for women. Men and women in Scotland had lower intakes of fibre and lower values per unit energy. After allowing for other factors men, but not women, in Scotland and London and the South East had lower fibre intakes than men in other regions.

Although men in Scotland consumed less fat and both saturated and polyunsaturated fatty acids than men in other regions, these differences were not apparent when expressed in terms of percentage of food energy. However, after allowing for other factors included in the analyses, men in Scotland and London and the South East derived a significantly higher proportion of food energy from fat and saturated fatty acids than men in other regions. The average P:S ratio did not vary significantly between regions.

Although Scottish men had lower intakes of a number of vitamins and minerals these differences were not apparent when expressed per 1000kcal. Plasma carotenoids tended to be higher in London and the South East for both men and women. In Scotland, urinary sodium excretion in men was higher, and urinary potassium excretion in both men and women was lower, than in other regions. There were no significant regional differences in blood pressure, in total serum cholesterol or in HDL cholesterol concentration.

Socio-economic characteristics

Recorded energy intake was lower for unemployed men than for other men. Recorded energy intakes were also lower for both men and women living in households receiving benefits. For women there was a trend towards lower average recorded energy intake in lower social classes (*Chapter 7*). Women from Social Classes IV and V had the highest body mass index but there was no consistent trend with social class in men. Men and women from Social Classes IV and V were found to be 1.8cm and 2.8cm shorter respectively than those from Social Classes I and II. These differences were less than in the 1980 survey, particularly in men (*Chapter 14*).

A higher proportion of both men and women who were working consumed alcohol during the recording week. However, on average those unemployed men who did consume alcohol had higher intakes than other men. Unemployed men and informants living in households receiving benefits had lower intakes of protein and carbohydrate but there was no difference in the proportion of energy derived from either. Among men and women intakes of sugars and fibre tended to be higher among those in Social Classes I and II than those in Social Classes IV and V (*Chapter 8*). Unemployed men and those living in households receiving benefits had lower intakes of fat and fat as a percentage of food energy (*Chapter 9*). These differences persisted after allowing for other factors (*Chapter 12*). The intake of polyunsaturated fatty acids was higher for men in Social Classes I and II and the P:S ratio tended to be lower for lower social classes, but these differences were no longer apparent when allowance was made for other factors. Blood pressure and serum total and HDL cholesterol concentrations were not significantly related to social class in either men or women (*Chapter 17*).

Unemployed men and women had lower intakes of many vitamins and minerals. These differences were not explained totally by their lower recorded energy intakes. However, average intakes of the unemployed met the RDAs. Informants in households receiving benefits showed a similar pattern. Potassium excretion in both men and women, and sodium excretion in men, were lower in the unemployed. There were no significant differences in height, body mass index, blood pressure,

or serum total or HDL cholesterol between those working and those unemployed for either sex. Plasma carotenoid levels and the tocopherol:cholesterol ratio tended to be lower among the unemployed, especially men (*Chapter 17*).

The recorded intakes of many vitamins and minerals were lower for informants classified to Social Classes IV and V than for Social Classes I and II. In women there was a linear trend for consumption of most vitamins and minerals to decline with social class. With the exception of iron, average intakes by all social classes met the RDAs.

Serum concentrations of all carotenoids were consistently lower among both men and women from Social Classes IV and V compared with I and II. Tocopherol:cholesterol ratio also tended to fall with social class. EGRAC tended to be higher in those from Social Classes IV and V, especially in men (*Chapter 17*).

Slimmers

At the time of the dietary record 12% of women and 4% of men reported that they were on a slimming diet. The average length of dieting was 6.5 and 10 weeks for women and men respectively. Informants who reported that they were on a slimming diet recorded lower energy intakes than other informants and had higher body mass index. After allowing for other factors slimmers had higher intakes of protein and most minerals and vitamins, and for women higher fibre intakes. Male and female slimmers derived a lower proportion of energy from fat and saturated fatty acids (*Chapter 12*).

Consumption of food outside the home

Over 90% of informants recorded consumption of some food outside the home during the seven-day recording period. On average men consumed 34% of their total energy (31% of food energy) outside the home compared with 24% (23%) for women. Both men and women consumed a smaller proportion of their fibre, protein, iron, carotene and thiamin intake than of food energy outside the home. For both sexes a greater proportion of alcohol than of food energy was consumed outside the home. Men consumed 55%, and women 36%, of their alcohol intake outside the home. Men, but not women, consumed a greater percentage of their sugars than of food energy outside the home. Younger informants consumed a greater proportion of their food energy outside the home than did older informants (*Chapter 14*).

1 Background, purpose and research design

This chapter describes the background to the request for this survey, its main aims and the overall research design and methodologies. Subsequent chapters and appendices to the report give more detailed accounts of the methodologies used in the various components which together made up the 'Dietary and Nutritional Survey of British Adults'.

1.1 The need for a survey

Over the past few years it has been apparent, even to the lay observer, that there have been considerable changes in the eating habits of adults in Great Britain. With changes in lifestyle, including more women working outside the home, greater numbers of people travelling and taking holidays abroad, and a larger immigrant population with different foods and methods of food preparation and cooking, there has been a demand for a greater variety of foods and far wider availability of pre-prepared and convenience foods. With greater affluence many people are also eating outside their own home, in restaurants, pubs and at the homes of their friends and relations; eating out has become an important social and recreational event.[1]

Against this background there has been an apparent increasing awareness among the general population of the importance of a healthy lifestyle—stopping or cutting down cigarette smoking, taking regular exercise and eating what is perceived as a 'healthy diet'. The concern with a healthy diet has, in itself, led to an increasing consumer demand for so-called 'healthy foods', which in turn has led to the introduction and wide availability of, for example, lower fat products, (such as skimmed and semi-skimmed milks, low fat spreads and lower fat meat products), high fibre cereals and bread, and foods with a lower salt content.

Relationships between diet and health are widely accepted; in the past, and currently in other, less industrialised, parts of the world, concern has been mainly with the effects on health of undernutrition. For example, during the Second World War the effects of rationing and food shortages on the nation's health, and, in particular on the health of children, were carefully monitored.[2] Nowadays, in the western world and in other industrialised countries, concern with diet is mainly in relation to what have been called 'the diseases of affluence'. Much work has been done to try to explain changes in the mortality and morbidity rates of, for example, certain cancers, cardiovascular disease and diabetes, and, in noting the variation between countries in death and morbidity rates from such diseases, considerable attention has been paid to the possible role of diet.

The causes of cardiovascular disease and its possible relationship to diet have been of great concern. In 1984, the Committee on Medical Aspects of Food Policy (COMA) published a report on diet and cardiovascular disease which included recommendations on dietary changes to decrease the incidence of coronary heart disease and cerebrovascular disease.[3]

In England and Wales in 1982 the cause of death for 40% of men and 38% of women was recorded as coronary heart disease or cerebrovascular disease. These were the most frequently certified causes of death compared with any other group of diseases. Within Great Britain mortality rates from coronary heart disease were higher for all age groups and for both men and women in Scotland and Northern Ireland than in England and Wales. Moreover, whereas in many countries, for example, USA, Belgium, Finland, Australia and Canada, deaths from coronary heart disease had been declining quite sharply, in the United Kingdom until quite recently the reduction had not been nearly as marked. In 1978 for men, only in Finland were death rates for coronary heart disease higher than in Scotland, Northern Ireland, Ireland and England and Wales. Among women, Scotland and Northern Ireland had the highest rates.

However, recent figures show a marked downward trend in the rates of death from coronary heart disease for men and women between the ages of 35 and 64 in England and Wales, in Scotland and in Northern Ireland.[4]

(Figs 1.1 to 1.4)

In an attempt to reduce these mortality rates, COMA in its report on diet in relation to cardiovascular disease made a number of recommendations specifically aimed at the general public as dietary advice.[3] The main recommendation was that the consumption of saturated fatty acids and fat in the United Kingdom should be reduced; no more than 15% of energy should come from saturated plus trans fatty acids, or 35% from total fat.

They also recommended that:

(i) the consumption of fibre-rich carbohydrates should increase to compensate for the reduction in dietary energy;

(ii) the intake of simple sugars should not increase; and

Figure 1.1 Death rates from coronary heart disease/100,000 for males and females aged 35–44, 45–54 and 55–64 in England and Wales in the years 1950–51 to 1986–87 (1950–67: ICD(7) 420–422; 1968–78: ICD(8) 410–414; 1979–87: ICD(9) 410–414)*

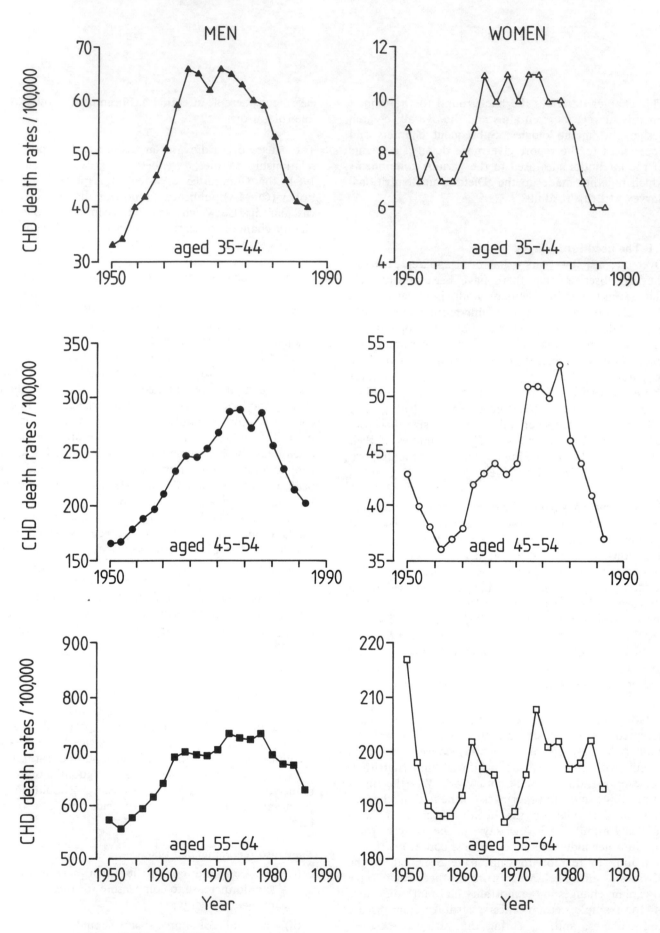

*Source: Office of Population Censuses and Surveys

Figure 1.2 Death rates from coronary heart disease/100,000 for males and females aged 35–44, 45–54 and 55–64 in Scotland in the years 1950–51 to 1986–87 (1950–67: ICD(7) 420–422; 1968–78: ICD(8) 410–414; 1979–87: ICD(9) 410–414)*

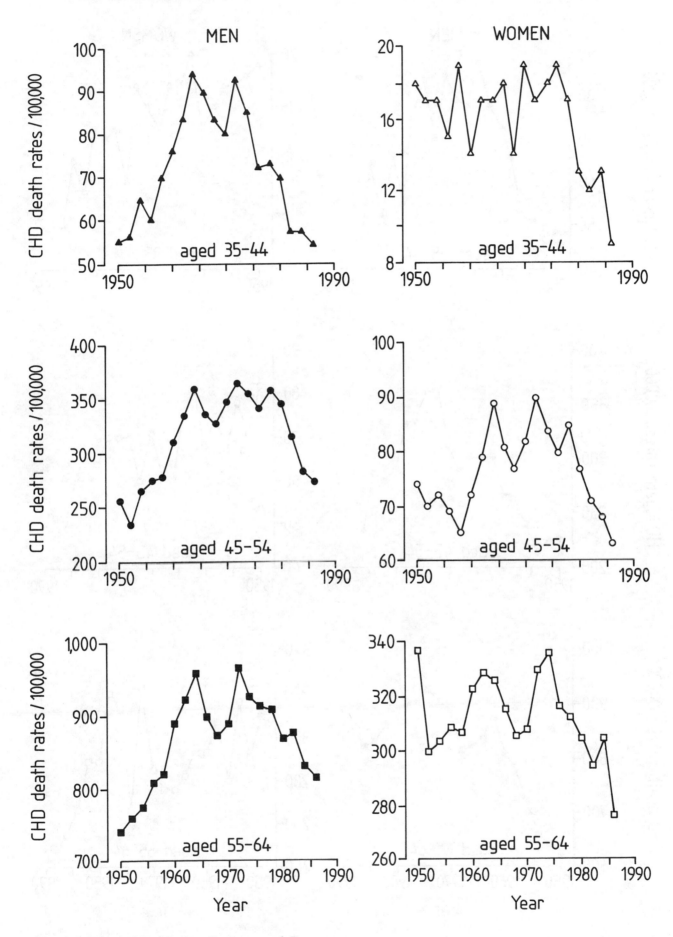

*Source: Office of Population Censuses and Surveys

Figure 1.3 Death rates from coronary heart disease/100,000 for males and females aged 35–44, 45–54 and 55–64 in Northern Ireland in the years 1950–51 to 1986–87 (1950–67: ICD(7) 420–422; 1968–78: ICD(8) 410–414; 1979–87: ICD(9) 410–414)*

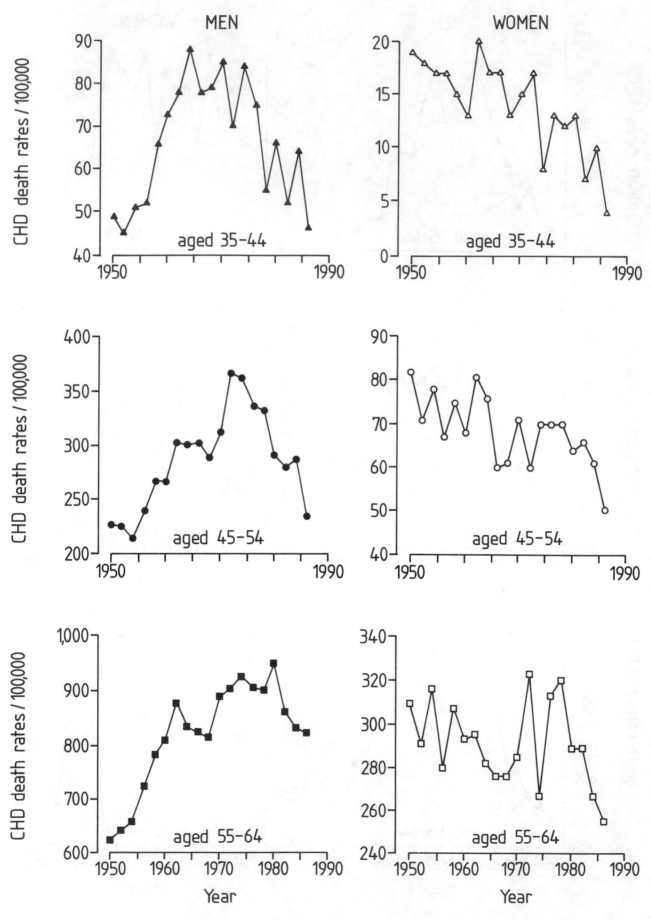

*Source: Office of Population Censuses and Surveys

Figure 1.4   Death rates from coronary heart disease for men and women aged 35–44, 45–54, 55–64 in England and Wales in the years 1950–51 to 1986–87 plotted as a percentage of the rate in 1950–51*

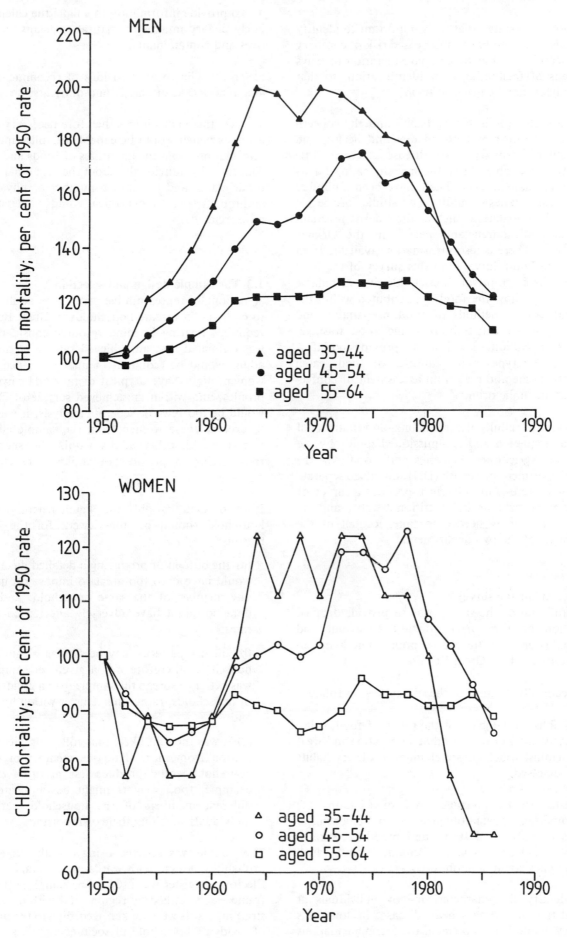

*Source: Office of Population Censuses and Surveys

(iii) the dietary intake of common salt should not increase and that consideration should be given to decreasing it.

The Report also stated that 'it is important to identify individuals . . . (who have an increased risk of coronary heart disease) . . . and to give consideration to ways and means of facilitating their identification, so that special advice may be given to them'.

Despite the changes in eating habits and the concern about the relationships between diet and health, and in particular, coronary heart disease, there is little information available about the current eating habits of adults in Great Britain. There have been a number of small scale studies of adults, and studies of specific groups in the population, such as the elderly, pregnant women, schoolchildren and people in the Orkney Islands.[5, 6, 7, 8] There is also information available from the National Food Survey, but this survey of the food purchasing habits of private households gives no reliable information on how the food is distributed within the household, about methods of food preparation and cooking or about actual intakes and food wastage. Moreover the National Food Survey provides no information on the types and quantities of foods eaten outside the home and makes no assessment of confectionery or alcoholic drinks.[9]

This survey of adult dietary habits and nutritional status was requested and commissioned jointly by the Ministry of Agriculture, Fisheries and Food (MAFF) and the Department of Health (DH). Each had separate and mutual interests in different aspects of a survey of adult dietary behaviour and nutritional status, and the design of the survey needed to take account of the requirements of the two departments.

1.2 The aims of the survey

The overall aim of the survey was to provide detailed information on the current dietary behaviour and nutritional status of the adult population living in private households in Great Britain.

More specifically the aims of the survey were as follows.

1. To establish a database of the range of food, drink and nutrient intakes of the adult population in Great Britain, against which future changes in dietary habits could be assessed.

2. To establish the average, and distributions of, anthropometric, haematological, and biochemical measures of nutritional status and blood pressure in the adult population in Great Britain, against which future changes could be monitored.

3. To identify the characteristics of individuals at increased risk of coronary heart disease. In doing this the survey would help implement the recommendations made in the Report of the Committee on Medical Aspects of Food Policy (COMA) on diet and cardiovascular disease.

4. To provide information to enable the calculation of likely dietary intakes of natural toxicants, food additives and contaminants.

5. To assist in future revisions of recommended daily amounts (RDA) of energy and nutrients.

To meet these aims it was therefore necessary to design a survey which would be capable of collecting detailed information about the quantities of foods and nutrients consumed by individuals, about the brand names of the foods eaten, and to make a number of physiological, anthropometric, biochemical and haematological measurements.

1.3 The sample design and selection

A nationally representative sample of adults aged 16 to 64 living in private households in Great Britain was required. Bearing in mind resource considerations, it was estimated that an achieved sample of about 2000 adults would be required for analysis. Since pregnant women might have atypical dietary and physiological profiles, and within an achieved sample of 2000 there would be too few for separate analysis, it was decided to exclude these women from the sample eligible for interview. All other adults within the specified age range living in private households were eligible for interview.

It was decided that only one eligible person per selected household should be interviewed, for the following reasons:

(a) the burden of producing a detailed dietary record would have been too great to impose on more than one member of the same household, and to have done so might have adversely affected co-operation rates;

(b) dietary patterns may be similar within the same household; therefore, for a given set sample size it was better to spread the sample over a greater number of households, rather than cluster within households; and

(c) it was thought likely that collecting dietary information from more than one member of the same household would produce less accurate data. For example, food weights might be duplicated across different members of the household, rather than individuals weighing their own portion.

The sample was selected using a multi-stage random probability design, with wards as first stage units. The Electoral Register was used as the sampling frame. The frame was stratified by region, and within each major stratum, wards were ranked according to the proportion of heads of household in socio-economic groups 1 to 5 and 13, using census data.

A total of 120 wards was selected as first stage units, with probability proportionate to the total electorate in the ward, and from each ward 33 addresses were selected. At the fieldwork stage interviewers were instructed to select one individual from the selected household, the selection being predetermined by the number of eligible persons in the household. This method of selection, which avoids the response difficulties associated with the selection of a 'named person sample', is based on a technique developed by Kish.[10]

Since the requirement was for a sample of adults living in private households, institutions were excluded at the sample selection phase wherever possible; institutions identified by interviewers at the fieldwork stage were excluded from the set sample of addresses.

At the selection of the first stage units, that is the 120 wards, 30 wards were systematically allocated to each of four fieldwork waves. Fieldwork was distributed over four waves to allow for seasonality. The fieldwork starting dates were October 1986, and January, April and July 1987.

A letter was sent to each selected address in advance of the interviewer calling; interviewers reported that it was well received by informants, and helped in gaining co-operation.

A more detailed account of the sample design and selection is given in Appendix B.

1.4 The elements of the survey

To meet the several aims of the research, it was necessary to design a study which would incorporate both dietary and physiological elements.

This was achieved by asking each individual to:

—answer a short interview questionnaire, giving personal and household information, and general information on dietary habits;

—keep a record for seven days of weighed intakes of all food and drink consumed both in and out of the home;

—provide information on any dietary supplements, for example, vitamin tablets, and on all prescribed medicines being taken;

—agree to certain body measurements being taken—height, weight, wrist diameter, mid-upper arm circumference, and, for males only, calf circumference;

—have three consecutive measurements taken of their blood pressure and heart rate;

—provide a 20ml specimen of blood by venepuncture (subjects aged 18 and over only)[11];

—make a 24-hour collection of urine.

Copies of the fieldwork documents are provided in Appendix A.

As a result of pilot and feasibility work, where response rates were lower than hoped for, it was decided at the main stage of the survey to make an incentive payment of £10 to informants who completed the seven-day weighed dietary record. This payment was made regardless of whether they co-operated with any other aspect of the survey.

All the interviewers working on the survey were experienced interviewers who had been fully trained by the Social Survey Division of OPCS. In addition to their routine training, each interviewer attended a personal briefing (over 3½ days) conducted by research and professional staff from Social Survey Division, the two client departments, and two professional nutritionists recruited to work on the survey. These residential briefings covered how to complete the weighed intake record, techniques for checking and detailed probing of the dietary record, training on how to code the entries in the diaries for food and brand, training on how to take the anthropometric and blood pressure measurements, and the procedures for obtaining the urine and blood specimens.[12] Emphasis was placed on the accuracy of recording and coding the dietary information and of the measurement techniques.

In addition to the personal briefings written instructions were provided for interviewers and personnel taking the blood samples, and a training video was produced which interviewers were able to borrow for private study. Any interviewer working on more than one fieldwork wave of the study was recalled between waves for a one-day refresher course in the techniques being used on the survey.

In Chapter 2 the reasons for the choice of a seven-day weighed intake methodology for obtaining the dietary information are discussed, and full details of the dietary methodology, the recording and weighing procedures for foods eaten in and out of the home, and the food and brand coding and editing procedures carried out on the completed dietary records are given there and in Appendix D.

Chapter 3 and its associated appendices describe the methodologies for the anthropometric and blood pressure measurements. The purpose of these measurements, the choice of anthropometric measurements to be made and the techniques and instruments used are reported in detail.

Chapter 4 deals with the methods used to obtain a sample of urine from a 24-hour collection, and the venepuncture procedure. The chapter describes the purpose of obtaining these specimens, the techniques and equipment used, and the analyses carried out on the specimens. Appendix J gives an account of the procedures used by the laboratories for analysing the specimens and quality control data.

1.5 Response to the survey

Informants could have completed any combination of the elements of the survey, and the data in the various chapters are based on those completing that element (rather than on those persons who completed all aspects of the survey). Response rates were therefore calculated separately for the individual elements—interview, dietary record, the various anthropometric measurements, blood pressure measurements, the blood and urine samples. In respect of these last two elements, the base figures in the tables vary, since in some cases the samples obtained had deteriorated by the time they reached the laboratories and were unfit for analysis, and it was not always possible to obtain the 20ml of blood required for the full range of analyses to be carried out.

In addition to calculating response rates for the individual elements in the survey, rates for each fieldwork round were calculated, as well as the total for all rounds. Chapter 5 gives the detailed response rates and provides data on the characteristics of the interviewed sample.

Overall, 70% of the eligible sample completed a full seven-day dietary record, and a further 14% co-operated with some other aspect of the survey. Of the total eligible sample, 76% co-operated with each of the anthropometric and blood pressure measurements; this represents more than 90% of those co-operating with any aspect of the survey. The response rates for the blood sample and urine collection were calculated on the total number of cases in which a sample was analysed, which as noted above, underestimates the proportion of the sample who provided specimens. Urine samples available for analysis were obtained from 65% of the total eligible sample (77% of those co-operating with any aspect of the survey) and 76% of respondents aged between 18 and 64 who co-operated with some aspect of the survey gave a blood specimen.

In Chapter 5 the characteristics of the responding samples are compared; there was little difference in the characteristics of the samples, and no evidence of bias in response to the dietary record. Checks on the validity of the sample are also reported in that chapter, and it is concluded that the dietary sample accurately reflected the regional distribution of the population, and the population according to the number of adults in the household. There was however some evidence that people aged between 16 and 24 were underrepresented in the dietary sample, but the difference was relatively small, and reweighting was not carried out.

1.6 Plan of the report

As noted above, Chapters 2, 3 and 4 describe in detail the methodologies of the various elements in the survey, and Chapter 5 reports on the response analysis.

Subsequent chapters form the substantive part of the report and deal separately with the results from the different elements in the survey. Thus Chapters 6 to 14 are devoted to results based on the data collected in the dietary records. They cover the quantities of foods consumed (*Chapter 6*), nutrient intakes (*Chapters 7 to 11*), and nutrient intakes from foods eaten outside the home (*Chapter 14*). Chapters 12 and 13 report on the results of using multivariate techniques of analysis on the food and nutrient data, and include an attempt to characterise different types of diet in a useful way. Chapters 15 to 17 give the results of the physiological, biochemical and haematological measurements made, that is, the anthropometry (*Chapter 15*), the blood pressure measurements (*Chapter 16*), and the analysis of the blood specimens (*Chapter 17*). Data on urinary sodium and urinary potassium are presented in Chapter 11 where dietary intakes of these minerals are discussed; data on urinary creatinine are given in Chapter 15 together with the data on fat free mass and other anthropometric measures and the data on urinary urea are given in Chapter 8 where protein intakes are shown.

This Report is largely concerned with providing basic descriptive statistics for the variables measured and information on their associations with demographic, social and behavioural characteristics of the sample population. However, one of the aims in the analysis was to relate the dietary and the biological data. Some preliminary work has been done in this area and the results are presented in the body of the Report.

1.7 Summary

The dietary and nutritional survey of British adults was requested and commissioned jointly by the Ministry of Agriculture, Fisheries and Food and the Department of Health.

The main aim of the study was to provide detailed information on the current dietary behaviour and nutritional status of the adult population living in private households in Great Britain. Additionally the survey was intended to provide a database of the food, drink and nutrient intake of the population against which future changes in dietary behaviour could be measured; to provide anthropometric, haematological and biochemical measures of nutritional status which could also subsequently be used to monitor changes; to identify the characteristics of individuals at increased risk of coronary heart disease (as a response to the recommendations made by the Committee on Medical Aspects of Food Policy in its report on diet and cardiovascular disease); to estimate the dietary intakes of natural toxicants, food additives and contaminants; and to assist in future revisions of recommended daily amounts (RDA) of energy and nutrients.

A nationally representative sample of adults aged 16 to 64 living in private households in Great Britain was required. Pregnant women and people living in institutions were ineligible to take part in the survey.

It was estimated that an achieved sample of about 2000 adults would be adequate for analysis purposes. A stratified, multi-stage sample design with wards as primary sampling units was used. Stratification was by region and a socio-economic indicator and 120 wards were selected as first stage units with probability proportionate to their total electorate. From each first stage unit 33 addresses were selected from the Electoral Register with probability proportionate to the number of electors at the address. From each selected address one adult in the eligible age range was selected at random for interview; the chance of selection was determined by reference to the number of eligible adults in the household.

Fieldwork was distributed in four waves over a 12-month period, to allow for seasonality, and at the first stage of sample selection the wards were systematically allocated to the four fieldwork periods. Interviewing was carried out over the period October 1986 to August 1987.

The survey comprised a short interview; a seven-day weighed dietary record; anthropometric and blood pressure measurements; the taking and analysis of a 20ml sample of blood; and the analysis of a specimen of urine taken from a 24-hour collection. A letter was sent to selected addresses in advance of the interviewer calling and an incentive payment of £10 was paid to informants who kept the weighed dietary record for the full seven days.

Interviewers working on the survey were given intensive face-to-face training in all aspects, as well as written instructions, and two professional nutritionists were contracted to assist on the study.

The response to the various elements of the survey is detailed in Chapter 5; full dietary records were obtained from 70% of the eligible sample and a further 14% of the sample gave partial co-operation with some aspects of the survey; 77% of those who co-operated fully or partially made a 24-hour urine collection and 76% of those aged 18 to 64 who co-operated with some aspect of the survey gave a specimen of blood. Chapter 5 also compares the characteristics of the responding samples; there was little difference in the characteristics and no evidence of bias in response to the dietary record.

The Report presents basic descriptive statistics for the variables measured and their associations with demographic, social and behavioural characteristics of the achieved sample. Some preliminary analysis relating the dietary variables and the physiological measures is also presented.

References and notes

1. Data from the General Household Survey show, for example, that in 1986 47% of persons aged 16 and over had, in the four weeks before the date of interview, gone out for a meal; in 1980 the comparable figure was 40%. *General Household Survey 1986.* HMSO (London, 1989) Table 13.25.

2. For example, *The feeding of young workers* (1941), *Food problems* (1941), *Typical wartime meals* (1942/3), *The Stoke and Salford dietary survey* (1943/4), *Domestic food production* (1944) and *Vegetable consumption* (1944). All these surveys were carried out by the Government Social Survey.

3. Committee on Medical Aspects of Food Policy. *Diet and cardiovascular disease. Report of the Panel on diet in relation to cardiovascular disease.* Department of Health and Social Security. Report on Health and Social Subjects, No 28. HMSO (London, 1984).

4. Office of Population Censuses and Surveys. Deaths from coronary heart disease/100,000 for males and females aged 35–44, 45–54 and 55–64 in England and Wales, in Scotland and in Northern Ireland in the years 1950–51 to 1986–87.

5. Department of Health and Social Security. *A nutrition survey of the elderly. Report by the Panel on nutrition of the elderly.* Report on Health and Social Subjects, No 3. HMSO (London, 1972).

6. Schofield C, Wheeler E, Stewart J. The diets of pregnant and post pregnant women in different social groups in London and Edinburgh: energy, protein, fat and fibre. *Br J Nutr* 1987; 58: 3. pp 369–381.

7. Committee on Medical Aspects of Food Policy. Sub-committee on nutritional surveillance. *The diets of British schoolchildren.* Department of Health. Report on Health and Social Subjects, No 36. HMSO (London, 1989).

8. Barber S A, Bull N L, Cameron A M. A dietary survey of an isolated population in the UK: the islanders of Orkney. *Hum Nutr: Appl Nutr* 1986; 40A: pp 462–469.

9. Ministry of Agriculture, Fisheries and Food. *Household food consumption and expenditure.* Annual reports of the National Food Survey Committee. HMSO (London).

10. Kish L. *Survey sampling.* J Wiley & Sons Ltd. (London, 1965) pp 398–401.

11. Since the written consent of the parent or guardian would have been required if a blood sample was taken from a minor, it was decided to restrict the taking of blood to subjects aged 18 to 64.

12. Blood specimens were not taken by the interviewers but by recruited doctors or other appropriately qualified personnel, who were accompanied on their visits to the subjects' homes by the interviewers.

2 Methodology for the dietary record

2.1 Choice of methodology

A number of different survey techniques are available for collecting data on food consumption. These include duplicate diet studies, recall methods and record keeping. The methods have different advantages and disadvantages and several factors affect the final choice of method. These include the objectives of the study, the detail and the precision needed to study the problem effectively, the population group to be studied and the scientific and financial resources available. This dietary survey was designed with aims both of investigating possible relationships between nutrient intake and selected health measures, and also of providing detailed information on the range and distribution of intakes of foods and nutrients within the adult population of Great Britain. Because of the detail and precision needed a weighed inventory method was chosen. Although the method is known to be onerous for the informant, is labour intensive and costly, requires high motivation and may interfere with eating habits, it has the outright advantage over other methods of being the most precise method available for accurately recording the amounts of food consumed.[1,2] Also, this method does not have the disadvantage of inaccuracies due to errors in recall and errors involved in estimating portion sizes are also minimised.

The length of time over which a weighed inventory is kept can vary. The recording period should be long enough to give reliable information on normal food consumption and it is important adequately to represent both weekdays and weekends in the record because of possible variations in eating patterns; this can be achieved either by sampling various days of the week on different individuals, or by collecting information from each individual for a complete week. The latter solution was chosen since it requires a smaller sample of individuals to achieve a given level of precision, and allows a simpler sampling pattern.

2.2 Outline of the methodology

The main aspects of the dietary methodology are described in this chapter, but additional details of the recording and coding procedures are given in Appendix D.

Informants on the survey were issued with accurately calibrated scales and asked to keep a weighed record of all foods consumed both in and out of the home over a seven-day period. For each item of food consumed they were asked to record a description of the food and its brand, the weight served, and the weight and description of any leftovers on each plate or container of food. Where an item could not be weighed, for example because it was consumed away from home and the scales were not available, informants recorded a description of the portion size; descriptions included approximations to standard measures such as tablespoons, numbers of slices of bread, numbers of potatoes and whether they were small, medium or large.

In order to analyse the nutrient content of an individual's food intake, the component nutrients in each item consumed must first be calculated. Each food was allocated a code number which enabled the food to be linked to the relevant nutrient information on the computerised databank. It was necessary for informants to weigh the basic components of foods separately so that individual food items could be coded; for example a cup of coffee was split to coffee powder, water, milk and sugar, and a sandwich was split to bread, spread and filling.

The nutrients within different types of foods obviously vary, but the nutrient content of items within the same general type of food can also differ considerably depending on the precise nature of the food: for example, *frozen crinkle-cut* potato chips fried in blended vegetable oil are different from *fresh straight-cut* potato chips fried in blended vegetable oil. In order to allow for these sources of variation the food code list needed to be an extensive document and, in total, nutrient information was provided for about 5000 separate food items including recipes.

A considerable amount of information was needed in order accurately to code each item of food consumed, and the nature of the detail required differed to some extent between food groups. For this reason it was necessary for coding to take place as soon as possible after the food was consumed, and that the coder should be able to contact the informant to probe for any missing details of the food. Coding was therefore carried out by interviewers who had been trained in use of the food code list, and advice was given by two consultant nutritionists appointed to work full time during the fieldwork period.

2.3 The recording process

At the first call to the selected household the interviewer carried out the sampling procedure, as described in Chapter 1, to determine which member of the household was to be approached, and then made an appointment to interview the selected person and to place the diary. At this placing call the interviewer completed a short questionnaire covering background information on the informant's personal circumstances and dietary habits, and then went on to explain the procedure for the dietary record and to demonstrate the use of the food scales.

2.3.1 The questionnaire

The short questionnaire was designed to provide basic classificatory data about the informant and his or her household, to collect information on the informant's dietary habits which might be of use when coding the dietary record, and to provide some details of the individual's diet which could not be derived from the seven-day record. Topics covered included their use of salt and artificial sweeteners, whether they were dieting, and details of dietary supplements. A record was also made of each informant's pattern of eating for a typical day, which gave interviewers an indication of the number and type of meals and snacks that they might expect to find in the dietary record.

At the end of the seven-day period a record was made of any unusual circumstances or illness during the previous week which might have affected the dietary record. All informants who completed either a dietary record or any of the physical measurements were also asked for information on any prescribed medicines that they were taking.

2.3.2 The dietary record

Each informant was issued with a set of food scales and two recording documents; a detailed record book for use with foods eaten or prepared at home and a small pocket book for recording information about foods eaten outside the home.

The scales used for the survey were lightweight, battery-powered Soehnle scales which give a digital display of weight, which could be zeroed after each item was weighed; the scales were calibrated in 2 gram units.

The home record book was the main recording and coding document and in it the informant was asked to write down a description of each food item consumed or prepared at home on each day of the recording period, together with the weight served and the weight of any leftovers. For each entry information was also collected on the time that the food was eaten and whether the item was eaten at home or away from home.

Informants were given a small pocket book to carry whenever they were away from home, and in which they could record information about any food and drink at the time that it was consumed. They were asked to give a full description of each item, including its price, a description of the quantity served and of the amount that was not eaten. For foods which were not pre-packaged they were also asked to record the name of the outlet where the food was purchased.

Where possible, duplicate items of foods eaten away from home were purchased by interviewers; this enabled more accurate weight information to be used in the food record, and also provided more detailed descriptions for coding the items. Duplicates were not purchased for meals eaten at restaurants but, for these items, weights were allocated by the nutritionists based on the descriptions of the portions eaten and on their knowledge of likely portion sizes.

2.3.3 The recording procedure

Informants were asked to weigh and record all foods consumed, both in and out of the home, over a complete week starting on the day after the interviewer's placing call; all recording days started at midnight. During the seven days informants recorded every item consumed, including medicines, food supplements and drinks of water; where items were too small to be weighed, such as artificial sweeteners, a description of the quantity was recorded. Informants were not, however, asked to describe the amount of salt used in cooking or added at the table since a more accurate representation of total sodium intake could be inferred from the amount of sodium excreted in the 24-hour urine collection.

The interviewer called back approximately 24 hours after the placing call in order to check that the informant was recording items correctly, to probe for further details, to give encouragement and to remotivate where appropriate. Most informants who completed the first day of recording went on to make a full seven-day record.

During the recording period the interviewer visited the informant as many times as was thought to be necessary and on at least one occasion other than the 24-hour checking call. At these visits the interviewer checked for inadequate descriptions of foods and removed any completed pages of the home record book which were ready for coding.

Where survey information is collected by diary methods there is some evidence of a reduction in the amount of information given as the recording period progresses. In order to guard against this occurrence the interviewer completed a meals check sheet for each informant, summarising the number of meals, snacks and drinks consumed each day. This check sheet gave an indication of days on which eating habits differed from the normal pattern, particularly showing whether the number of drinks and snacks recorded had declined; interviewers were then able to probe any inconsistencies.

2.4 Coding and editing the food record

Interviewers were trained to recognise the detail required for coding foods of different types by means of a personal briefing and exercises completed at home.

2.4.1 Food and brand coding

The food code list and associated nutrient databank used on the survey were compiled by the Nutrition

Branch of the Ministry of Agriculture, Fisheries and Food; (details are given in Appendix E).

A basic food code list giving the code number and a full description of each item was prepared for use by interviewers, and this list contained approximately 2500 codes. The list was organised into sections by food type, for example milk and cream, puddings, vegetables, fruit, beverages and types of meat. Interviewers were also provided with an alphabetical index to foods to help them in finding food items in the main code list.

A separate list of raw foods and extra recipe codes was provided for the consultant nutritionists and, as fieldwork progressed, further codes were added to the list for recipes found in the dietary records. By the end of fieldwork there were approximately 5000 separate codes for food items, and corresponding entries on the nutrient databank.

The brand of foods was collected to enable appropriate coding for nutritional purposes and to provide information about additives. Informants were asked to record the brand name of all foods which were pre-packaged. Interviewers were again responsible for the brand coding of items, and were each issued with a brand list organised into similar sections to the food code list, but including a separate section for 'own brands'.

After interviewers had coded the entries in the dietary records the documents were checked by office coders. The consultant nutritionists working on the survey dealt with specific queries, advised on coding and checked the quality of the coding. During this check they dealt with missing weights, for example by converting descriptions of portion sizes to weights, and checked that the appropriate code was used for each recipe item.

2.4.2 Editing—leftovers and food supplements
Computer edits were run on the dietary and questionnaire data to check for completeness and consistency of information. At this stage the weight of each food item eaten was calculated by subtracting the weight of leftovers from the served weight of the item; where a combined weight was given for a number of leftover items the total weight of leftovers was divided amongst the food items in proportion to the served weights of those items. Information on the quantity and frequency of use of food supplements was used to calculate the nutrient intake from these sources, and this was added to the appropriate diary records.

Following completion of these checks and calculations the information from the dietary record was linked to the nutrient databank and food items were converted to their constituent nutrients. Edit checks were run to identify cases where the intake of any nutrient was outside the specified range for normal intakes (in most cases only a maximum value could be specified); such

cases were individually checked and coding errors were corrected.

Most of the dietary analysis presented in this report is based on the average daily intake of nutrients from all sources, either including or excluding food supplements. Each food code used was, however, also allocated to one of 51 main food groups which were further divided to a number of subgroups (Appendix H). Information on the quantity of food consumed from each subgroup is tabulated in Chapter 6, and data on the contribution of the main food groups to intake of specific nutrients are included at relevant points in Chapters 7 to 11.

2.5 Summary
This chapter describes the methodology for the seven-day dietary record, including the recording and weighing procedures, the food and brand coding and an outline of the computer editing of the dietary data. Appendix D gives more detail on the recording and coding procedures, and Appendix E describes the nutrient databank.

The weighed inventory method for obtaining dietary information was chosen for this study as being the most precise method available for recording the amounts of foods eaten. A seven-day recording period was selected as being both practicable and long enough to give reliable information on food consumption and adequately covering weekdays and weekends.

Having selected an individual for participation in the survey, at the first call the interviewer conducted a short interview which collected information on the subject's basic dietary behaviour and some information which could not be obtained from the weighed dietary record; this information was of help in coding the dietary record. The food scales were demonstrated and the recording procedures explained.

Soehnle electronic scales, calibrated in 2 gram units, which could be zeroed after each item was weighed were left with the informant. In a home record book the informant was asked to write down details of every food eaten or prepared at home. For every food item information was required on the component weights served and left over; a detailed description of the item, including the cooking method, if appropriate, was needed together with the brand name for pre-packaged items. It was also recorded whether the item was eaten at home or away from home.

Details of items consumed out of the home were recorded in a small pocket book and the information was subsequently transcribed to more detailed recording sheets by the interviewer. If it was not possible to weigh the item or record the weight from information on the packaging, then the informant was asked to provide as detailed a description as possible of the amount consumed. Descriptions of the nature of the item and brand information were also recorded and in order to allow interviewers to purchase a duplicate of some of the items that could not be weighed, and subsequently determine the weight, the price and place of purchase were recorded.

The interviewer was required to call back on the informant 24 hours after the diary had been placed—mainly to encourage continued co-operation—and thereafter every two or three days during the recording period, to check for inadequate descriptions and missing weight information and to collect completed diary pages for coding.

The food code list was compiled by the Ministry of Agriculture, Fisheries and Food and contained over 5000 codes, including additions during the fieldwork period for recipe items. The food code list corresponded to a nutrient databank, which held, in computerised form, nutrient quantities for each of the food codes.

Brand information was collected mainly to provide information for later calculation of intakes of food additives, and a brand code list was compiled for the brands of all pre-packaged items, including 'own label' brands.

The first stage of coding was carried out by the interviewers; this allowed the speedy identification of missing information and the facility for the interviewer to ask for the detail at the next call made on the informant. Coding was checked by office coders and nutritionists and at this stage any descriptive information on quantities was converted to weights.

The first stage of the computer edit converted the weight of a served portion to the weight of the food eaten, by subtracting the weight of leftovers. After converting the food data to nutrient data, by linking the food codes to the nutrient databank, the computer edit then checked for intakes outside specified ranges. Identified cases were inspected and identifiable errors corrected.

The Report gives information on the average daily intakes of nutrients from all sources, including and excluding nutrients from food supplements, information on the quantity of food consumed from food subgroups, and on the contribution of the main food groups to specific nutrient intakes.

References
1. Marr J W. Individual dietary surveys: purposes and methods. *Wld Rev Nutr Diet* 1971; 13: 105–164.
2. Pekkarine M. Methodology of the collection of food consumption. *Wld Rev Nutr Diet* 1970; 12: 145–171.

3 Anthropometric measurements and blood pressure: purpose and methodology

This chapter explains the reasons for including anthropometric and blood pressure measurements in the survey, why certain body measurements were selected and describes the equipment and methodologies used to take them. Response rates for the various measurements are given in Chapter 5 and the results are given in Chapters 15 and 16.

3.1 Purpose of the measurements

As has already been noted, one of the aims of this study was to relate dietary intakes to physiological measurements, to help implement some of the recommendations contained in the COMA report on diet and cardiovascular disease.[1] In particular it was thought that this aspect of the study might help facilitate the identification of individuals at increased risk of coronary heart disease.

Body measurements themselves provide health indicators which can be compared over time for different groups of the population. It was considered most important to have some measure of fatness in view of the established relationship between obesity and increased morbidity and mortality.[2,3]

A measure of blood pressure was considered necessary since blood pressure and mortality from cardiovascular disease and stroke are also strongly related.[4]

3.2 Choice of anthropometric measurements

In a laboratory or clinical setting, body composition can be assessed by elaborate techniques such as measurement of total body water, body density and total potassium. However, for this study a method was needed which would provide an accurate assessment of fatness in the population which was simple, relatively inexpensive, and which could be used with reasonable technical accuracy by non-professional operators.

Measuring skinfold thickness at several sites on the body has a close enough relationship with direct techniques to be able to provide a sufficiently accurate predictor of body fat.[5]

It was therefore decided to take measurements of skinfold thickness in the pilot study. This showed that taking these measurements required considerable skill and experience if they were to be valid and reliable. Inter-observer variation could be kept to an acceptable level only with a small number of trained observers. It was not possible to give the large number of interviewers

allocated to work on the main stage of this study sufficient training and experience to produce acceptable precision. Moreover pilot work also showed that the skinfold thickness techniques were unacceptable to a significant proportion of informants. It was therefore decided not to attempt to make these measurements on the main stage of the survey but instead to make other measurements which can also predict fat free mass.

Height and weight were measurements for which the techniques and instruments had previously been used on surveys carried out by OPCS,[6] and these measurements could also be used to calculate the Quetelet or Body Mass Index (weight(kg)/height(m)^2) which allows for the effect of height on weight. However although commonly used as a measure of body fatness, it is not ideal and therefore mid-upper arm circumference, wrist diameter, and, for males, calf circumference were also measured.[7] Taking all these measurements accurately and reliably in a non-clinical setting was felt likely to be practicable and acceptable to informants.

The equations used to calculate fat free mass for men and women in different age groups based on these body measurements are given in Appendix F.

3.3 Techniques and instruments used

All the interviewers working on the survey were trained in taking the measurements reproducibly at personal briefings. Once trained, any interviewer working on a subsequent fieldwork round of the survey attended a one-day refresher briefing where the measurement techniques were checked and further exercises conducted. A training video was produced to demonstrate the techniques and copies were loaned to interviewers for private study and revision.

As noted earlier all the measurements were made after the end of the seven-day dietary recording period. Detailed descriptions of the techniques used to make each measurement are given in Appendix G.

Height: the techniques and instruments used for measuring height were the same as those used on the survey of 'The heights and weights of adults in Great Britain'.[6] The measurement was taken using a portable stadiometer, positioning the subject's head such that the Frankfort plane was horizontal, and while maintaining this position, stretching to the maximum unsupported height. The stadiometers were calibrated in millimetre units, and the reading taken to the nearest millimetre.

Weight: Soehnle digital personal weighing scales, calibrated in 200 gram units were used, and placed on a hard level surface for making the measurement. All the scales were checked and calibrated by a specialist contractor prior to each fieldwork round before being issued to interviewers.

Subjects were asked to remove shoes, any outer or heavy clothing and empty their pockets of coins and keys. All remaining items of clothing being worn were recorded by the subject on a self-completion form; this was intended to allow for an estimate of the total weight of clothing worn to be made and deducted from the recorded weight to give estimated nude weight. The weight data used in this first report of the survey have made no allowance for clothing; other researchers have taken estimated values of 0.9kg for males in light clothing and 1.5kg for males in heavier clothing. For females the corresponding estimates are 0.6kg and 0.9kg.[8]

Measurement was not made at a standard time of day.

Wrist diameter, mid-upper arm circumference and calf circumference: these measurements were taken from the left side of the subject's body, although it has been shown that there are no significant differences between the right and left sides of the body in arm and leg measurements.[9] If for any reason the interviewer was unable to make any of the measurements on the left side, then measurements were made on the right side and an explanation given on the interview questionnaire. Any unusual circumstances which might have affected a measurement were also recorded. At the end of fieldwork all comments were examined by an official at the Department of Health who advised on any cases to be excluded from the analysis because of unusual circumstances such as deformities.

Wrist diameter was measured using specially modified vernier callipers calibrated in millimetre units. The measurement was made across the styloid processes with pressure applied to the jaws of the callipers to compress the tissues. The position of the lower arm and hand was standardised to take this measurement.

Mid-upper arm circumference was measured in two stages using a conventional measuring tape to identify the mid-point of the upper arm, and a specially modified insertion tape to measure the horizontal circumference at the mid-point.

Interviewers were instructed to take the measurement under clothing, preferably with the arm removed from any sleeve. Where the subject was unable or unwilling to comply with this request the measurement was only included in the analysis if a shirt or thin blouse was being worn; measurements taken over jumpers or similar garments were excluded.

The position of the subject's arm was standardised for each stage of the measurement. The mid-point of the

upper arm was identified as halfway between the inferior border of the acromion process and the tip of the olecranon process. In taking the circumference measurement care was taken to ensure that a horizontal measurement was taken and that the tissues were not compressed.

The insertion tape used to make the circumference measurement was calibrated in such a way as readings to the nearest millimetre could be taken.

Calf circumference was measured for male subjects only.

The measurement was made using the specially modified insertion tape; readings were taken to the nearest millimetre. Wherever possible the measurement was made under clothing or with clothing removed. The few cases where the subject was unable or unwilling to comply with this protocol were excluded from the analysis.

The position of the subject's leg and foot was standardised and the maximum horizontal circumference measured.

3.3.1 The importance of measurement error in the calculation of fat free mass

In general, it would appear that only quite large errors, above those expected from even relatively inexperienced operators, are likely to have a significant effect on the estimate of fat free mass.[10] For example, an error in body weight of 1kg would affect the value for fat free mass by 0.48kg. An error of 5cm in height affects the predicted fat free mass for men by 0.85kg, and a 2cm error by 0.34kg. An error of as much as 2cm in calf circumference affects the prediction by only 0.4kg, and of 1cm by 0.22kg. For wrist diameter, where the technique is relatively easily learnt, an extreme error of 0.2cm would affect the value by 0.44kg.

The personal weighing scales used on the study were of high quality, were calibrated in 200g units and were checked and recalibrated before each round of fieldwork.

At the end of each training session all the interviewers in the group were asked to make one measurement each of wrist diameter, calf circumference and mid-upper arm circumference on the same two subjects. Inter-observer coefficients of variation between groups of observers ranged from 0.87% to 2.70% for wrist diameter, from 0.04% to 1.25% for mid-upper arm circumference and from 0.25% to 0.68% for calf circumference. *(Table 3.1)*

After the single measurement had been made those interviewers with the largest 'errors' were given further training and practice. At the rebriefings, where the measurement techniques were monitored and the exercise repeated all interviewers generally performed better, taking more reproducible measurements.

Durnin, McKay and Webster, in conclusion to their work on the importance of measurement error state that 'small measurement errors would not be likely to alter greatly the accuracy of any prediction of FFM (*Fat Free Mass*), particularly since there is no obvious reason why these errors would be biased in one direction. It is highly probable that many measurement errors cancel each other out, making the error in prediction probably of little account.'[11]

3.4 Blood pressure: equipment used and techniques for measurement

In a clinical situation, blood pressure is usually measured using a mercury sphygmomanometer and listening for the characteristic Korotkoff sounds as the pressure in the inflatable cuff is released. Correct positioning of the cuff is important and to the untrained ear detection and correct interpretation of these sounds can be difficult and hence errors can be made. Thus for use by non-clinically trained interviewers a simple, accurate and reliable means of measuring blood pressure, which was automatic and hence would eliminate, as far as possible, observer bias, was required.

At the feasibility and pilot stages of the survey interviewers were supplied with and trained in the use of two types of automatic, battery operated sphygmomanometers, the Copal UA-231 and DS-175 monitors.[12]

Both operated on the principle of automatic inflation of the cuff, (to a level set by the operator) automatic and controlled release of the pressure in the cuff, and the electronic detection of the characteristic sounds by a microphone. Both monitors gave a digital reading of systolic and diastolic pressures and the heart rate, and one, the DS-175, also gave a paper printout of the readings. Each separate cycle of measurement had to be initiated by the operator.

Although other researchers had found the Copal UA-231 monitor reliable and accurate,[13] during the planning stages of the main survey it was withdrawn by the manufacturers, and replaced with the DS-175 monitor. The performance of this monitor was poor, with 'rogue'

measurements, variable levels of inflation and problems in operation. Moreover the fact that the cuff inflated slowly, being dependent on battery power, meant that the procedure was uncomfortable, and often painful for subjects.

For the main stage of the survey portable, mains operated automatic sphygmomanometers—'Accutorr' monitors—were borrowed.[14] Although heavy to transport these monitors are easy to operate—inflation is automatic to an automatically determined appropriate pressure (hence the cuff is comfortable and quickly inflated to maximum pressure), repeated measurements can be carried out automatically at pre-set intervals, and the detection of the systolic and diastolic pressures is not dependent on a microphone system (important when being used in a domestic setting) but is by means of an oscillator and transducer.

3.4.1 Accuracy and reliability of the Accutorr sphygmomanometers

Before being issued to interviewers all the monitors were calibrated against a standard mercury column.

The manufacturers of the Accutorr quote the accuracy of the monitor, based on tests which compared systolic and diastolic pressures from the monitor to auscultatory measurements, as follows:[15]

systolic error = − 3.9mm Hg, standard
  deviation ± 7.7mm Hg;
diastolic error = 2.5mm Hg, standard
  deviation ± 6.5mm Hg;
number of measurements = 181;
range of pressures included in
  study = 52mm Hg–180mm Hg.

Other researchers have compared blood pressure measured by oscillometry, using the Accutorr monitor, with direct intra-arterial blood pressure monitoring in 21 patients.[16]

They report that the Accutorr overestimated blood pressures below 80mm Hg, and conversely underestimated readings above about 80mm Hg, whether sys-

Table 3.1 **Mean values and standard deviations for wrist diameter, mid-upper arm circumference and calf circumference taken by groups of interviewers on two subjects**

(a) Wrist diameter

No of interviewers	12	14	13	12	12	12	12	11
Mean measurement for subject (cm)	5.74	4.73	5.55	6.21	4.74	4.80	4.79	6.19
Standard deviation (cm)	0.05	0.06	0.06	0.06	0.05	0.13	0.09	0.13
Standard deviation/mean × 100 (%)	0.87	1.27	1.08	1.29	1.05	2.70	1.88	2.10

(b) Mid-upper arm circumference

No of interviewers	11	11	11	12	12	12	12	10
Mean measurement for subject (cm)	30.5	30.0	25.8	25.6	33.1	25.6	26.2	28.1
Standard deviation (cm)	0.11	0.22	0.11	0.11	0.26	0.01	0.26	0.35
Standard deviation/mean × 100 (%)	0.36	0.73	0.43	0.43	0.79	0.04	0.99	1.25

(c) Calf circumference

No of interviewers	11	11	11	12	12	12	12	10
Mean measurement for subject (cm)	38.3	37.6	36.7	35.6	41.6	35.8	37.4	37.4
Standard deviation (cm)	0.20	0.16	0.25	0.09	0.14	0.14	0.19	0.17
Standard deviation/mean × 100 (%)	0.52	0.43	0.68	0.25	0.34	0.39	0.51	0.45

tolic, diastolic or mean, by up to 20mm Hg. There are other reports that oscillometric methods generally underestimate at hypertensive readings when compared with direct radial pressure techniques,[17] and this may have affected the results. However, this method has been used successfully in other large scale surveys.[18]

3.4.2 Fieldwork techniques for measuring blood pressures

Since blood pressure is not only variable within an individual, but may also be subject to systematic bias— observer bias, instrument bias, seasonal effects and the effects of the physical and psychological circumstances in which the measurement was made—it was important for us to attempt to standardise the procedures as far as possible in a domestic setting.[19,20,21] Extensive training in the use of the Accutorr monitors was therefore given to interviewers at the briefings, and was covered at the one-day refresher meetings and demonstrated in the training video.

It has been reported that repeating the measurement of blood pressure at each occasion reduces the bias of a single measurement.[21] Interviewers were therefore instructed to take three consecutive blood pressure measurements at pre-set intervals of one minute. They were also instructed to try to ensure that the environment in which the measurements were made were controlled as far as possible. Quiet surroundings were sought, and the subject was asked not to drink, talk or smoke during the measurements, and, preferably not recently to have eaten or smoked. Two different size cuffs were supplied with the Accutorr monitor, a standard adult size and large adult size, and interviewers were instructed in their appropriate use.

All measurements were made with the subject seated and the forearm supported at heart level.

Systolic, diastolic and mean blood pressure readings are displayed by the monitor and these together with displayed heart rate readings were recorded on the questionnaire for the three measurements on each subject. Any unusual circumstances were noted by the interviewer (for example, cuff too large, noisy or stressful environment); these notes were examined and any readings thought likely to be invalid were excluded from the analysis.

3.4.3 Ethical issues

Interviewers were not qualified to judge whether or not a blood pressure reading was normal, or to give an opinion to a subject. Moreover, if an interviewer commented on, or reacted to, a particular reading this may have affected the subsequent reading. Nevertheless subjects have a right to know their pressures and there was an ethical responsibility to act if a reading was high.

Therefore, with the subject's written consent, interviewers immediately sent a copy of the blood pressure readings, with a covering letter, to the subject's general practitioner (GP) in order that he or she could make the clinical judgement whether action might be necessary. As a further precautionary measure an anonymised copy of each blood pressure reading was scrutinised by a Senior Medical Officer at the Department of Health. If the reading was judged to be high, then, by reference to the serial number, the research officer at OPCS was alerted and sent a further letter to the subject's GP, drawing attention to the reading. In cases where the subject was not registered with a GP, or refused consent for us to contact their GP, a letter suggesting they might seek medical advice was sent direct to the subject.

3.5 Summary

The anthropometric and blood pressure measurements were included in the survey as part of the requirement to provide information on the relationship between dietary intakes and physiological measurements. Since both obesity and high blood pressure are strongly related to excess mortality, measures of these were required.

It has been reported that measurements of height, weight, mid-upper arm circumference, wrist diameter and calf circumference (males only) in combination, provide good estimators of fat free mass (and hence fatness). Taking these measurements had several advantages over other, more sophisticated, measures of fatness and it was decided that they should be included as part of the survey.

Interviewers were fully trained in the techniques for making these measurements and were provided with equipment which was regularly checked and accurately calibrated. The body positions for making the measurements were standardised, but it was not possible to control other external factors, such as the time of day the measurement was made. Any unusual circumstances that might have affected the measurement were reported by the interviewers and specialist advice was taken as to whether such measurements should be excluded from the analysis.

Interviewers were supplied with fully automatic monitors for taking blood pressure readings; these reduced the likelihood of observer bias and error due to the incorrect identification and interpretation of Korotkoff sounds that might have occurred had conventional mercury sphygmomanometers been used. Interviewers were fully trained in the use of the monitors, and used a standard protocol for making the measurements. As with the anthropometric measurements it was not possible to control fully external factors, but unusual circumstances that may have affected the measurement were reported. Three measurements were made at pre-set intervals of one minute.

Each subject's GP was routinely informed, with consent, of the blood pressure readings, and for readings judged to be clinically high a further letter of notification was sent to the subject's GP.

It is unlikely that any errors in the anthropometric measurements might cause a systematic bias, or generally that they would result in significant errors in the prediction of fat-free mass. No allowance was made for the weight of clothing or for physiological changes, such as fluid balance, in the data that used weight information.

It has been reported that there is a threshold of about 80mm Hg above which oscillometric blood pressure monitors of the type used on this study tend to underestimate pressure and below which the tendency is to overestimate the pressure.

References and notes

1. Committee on Medical Aspects of Food Policy. *Diet and cardiovascular disease. Report of the Panel on diet in relation to cardiovascular disease.* Department of Health and Social Security. Report on Health and Social Subjects, No 28. HMSO (London, 1984).
2. Royal College of Physicians of London. Obesity. Report. *J R Coll Physicians Lond* 1983; 17: 5–65.
3. Garrow J S. *Treat Obesity Seriously.* Churchill Livingstone. (Edinburgh, 1981).
4. Pickering G W. *High Blood Pressure.* Churchill (London, 1968).
5. Durnin J V G A, Womersley J. Body fat assessed from total body density and its estimation from skinfold thickness: measurements of 481 men and women aged from 16 to 72 years. *Br J Nutr.* 1974; 32: 77–97.
6. Knight I. *The heights and weights of adults in Great Britain.* HMSO (London, 1984).
7. Durnin J V G A, McKay F C, Webster C I. A new method of assessing fatness and desirable weight, for use in the armed services. (University of Glasgow, 1985) Unpublished paper.
8. Barker M E, McClean S I, McKenna P G et al. *Diet, Lifestyle and Health in Northern Ireland.* Centre for Applied Health Studies, University of Ulster, Coleraine, NI. (1988).
9. Durnin J V G A, McKay F C, Webster C I. op cit. p 10.
10. Durnin J V G A, McKay F C, Webster C I. op cit. pp 79–85.
11. Durnin J V G A, McKay F C, Webster C I. op cit. p 85.
12. Copal UA-231 monitors were available from Andrew Stephens Co, Blackpool, Lancashire. The DS-175 monitor was supplied by John Bell and Croyden, 50 Wigmore Street, London W1.
13. Gallacher J, Yarnell J W G, Rogers S, Sweetman P. Automatic measurement of blood pressure: evaluation of the Copal UA-231 automatic sphygmomanometer. *J Epidemiol Community Health* 1985; 39: 220–223.
14. Accutorr 2A monitor; manufactured by Datascope Corporation, Paramus, New Jersey. UK distributor: Datascope Medical Co Ltd, Cambridge Science Park, Cambridge CB4 4WE.
15. Datascope Corporation. *Results of testing Accutorr 1A to the AAMI standard for electronic or automated sphygmomanometers* (proposed). Datascope Corporation, Paramus, New Jersey, US.
16. Gourdeau M, Martin R, Lamarch Y, Tetreault L. Oscillometry and direct blood pressure; a comparative clinical study during deliberate hypotension. *Can Anaesth Soc J* 1986; 33: 300–307.
17. Johnson C J H, Kerr J H. Automatic blood pressure monitors. *Anaesthesia* 1985; 39: 261–267 Quoted in Gourdeau M *et al.*
18. Cox B D, Blaxter M, Buckle A L J *et al. The health and lifestyle survey: preliminary report of a nationwide survey of the physical and mental health, attitudes and lifestyle of a random sample of 9003 British adults.* Health Promotion Research Trust (London, 1987).
19. Evans G J, Rose G. Hypertension. *Br Med Bull* 1971; 27: 37–42.
20. Brennan P, Greenberg G, Miall W, Thompson S. Seasonal variation in arterial blood pressure. *Bri Med J* 1982; 285: 919–923.
21. Petrie J C, O'Brien E T, Littler W A, de Swiet M. Recommendations on blood pressure measurement. *Bri Med J* 1986; 293: 611–615.

4 The collection and analysis of urine and blood specimens: purpose and methodology

This chapter gives the reasons for collection and analysis of specimens of urine and blood from co-operating subjects, and gives details of the techniques and equipment used to obtain the specimens and the biochemical analyses performed on them. In Chapter 5 the response rate achieved in obtaining the specimens is given; Chapter 17 gives the results of the analyses of the blood specimens and the results from the analysis of the samples of urine are included in Chapter 8 (urinary urea), Chapter 11 (urinary sodium and potassium), and Chapter 15 (urinary creatinine). Appendix J contains a technical report on the analytic procedures used by the laboratory which received the specimens, and quality control data.

4.1 The purpose of obtaining urine specimens

It is currently a matter of controversy whether or not dietary intake of common salt or sodium is related to blood pressure. The relevance of hypertension to the aims of this study and the requirement to obtain measurements of blood pressure for the survey population have been explained elsewhere in this report (*Chapter 3*).

It is not possible to obtain reliable estimates of the dietary intakes of salt (sodium) from information on weighed intakes of foods, because existing food tables are not comprehensive, and, more importantly, because no allowance can be made for the amounts of salt added during cooking and at the table. Moreover it is not possible to weigh these additions accurately.[1] However it is possible to estimate intakes of sodium and potassium, assuming the body is in balance for the minerals, by measuring their urinary excretion.[2]

Since sodium and potassium are excreted in the urine at a rate which varies with intake, it is necessary to obtain a complete collection of urine over a 24-hour period to allow for fluctuations. A specimen from the collection (adequately mixed) can then be analysed, and provided the total volume excreted over the 24-hour period is known, the total excretion of sodium and other analytes can be calculated.

4.2 Techniques and equipment for the 24-hour urine collection

All subjects selected for inclusion in the survey were asked to make a 24-hour urine collection as soon as possible after the end of the seven-day dietary recording period. Interviewers avoided reference to any interest in dietary salt intake when explaining the purpose and methods of making the urine collection, so as to minimise any changes in normal dietary behaviour.

Interviewers were trained in all the techniques associated with obtaining the specimens of urine, including obtaining information on the total volume of urine passed, taking the samples from the complete collection, and packaging them for despatch to the laboratory for analysis. All these techniques were also demonstrated in a training video prepared for the interviewers.

The equipment for making the 24-hour urine collection was left with the subject at the end of the dietary recording period together with a leaflet explaining the procedures to be followed. Although the collection could be made over any 24-hour period, in practice most subjects found it more convenient over a weekend, when they would not have to take the collection equipment to work.

The equipment comprised:

—a collection container—the *Rolon 24-hour specimen storage container*[3]—a purpose designed, polythene-lined cardboard box with a plastic closure clip and a capacity of approximately 2500ml which packs flat, and was assembled in the subject's home. In general, one collection container was left with female subjects and two with males;

—a polypropylene jug (500ml capacity), kept inside a resealable plastic bag when not being used;

—a preservative (thymol). A small amount was added from a plastic spatula to the collection container by the interviewer before the collection was started. Thymol was chosen as it was known not to interfere with any of the analyses;

—a plastic carrier bag, for transporting the collection equipment away from home;

—a safety pin, for the informant to pin under- and outer-garments together during the period of the collection, and thus act as an *aide-memoire* that the specimen of urine about to be passed should be collected;

—a Salter spring balance (5kg × 25g) for weighing the total amount of urine collected (see later);

—3 × 5ml and 1 × 10ml specimen tubes, labelled with the subject's unique survey identifier (serial number), a plastic Pasteur pipette, disposable polythene gloves, polystyrene container and packing material for despatching the samples and a laboratory analysis request card.[4]

4.2.1 Making a 24-hour collection

Subjects were asked to make the 24-hour collection in accordance with the protocol described in the explanatory leaflet left with them (Appendix A). Subjects were instructed to keep the collection in a cool place, out of sunlight, and the presence of the preservative was explained. If the jug was used to collect the urine and transfer it to the container, rather than passing the urine direct, it was explained that this should be rinsed only with clean water, and kept in the sealed polythene bag.

4.2.2 Obtaining a measure of the total volume of urine collected

Interviewers were instructed to call back on subjects as soon as possible after the collection had been made.

Weighing the urine collected was found to be more reproducible than measurement of volume.[5] The total collection, which in some cases comprised three containers, was weighed using the spring balance. To compensate for the weight of the container, the balance was tared using an empty container, ensuring that the reading was taken with the scale at eye level. Interviewers recorded on the questionnaire the total weight of urine collected, the date and time the collection started and finished, the period of collection, and whether any voidings were lost.

The urine in the collection container was then well mixed; if more than one container was used then the contents of all the containers were mixed.

Samples of urine were then pipetted into the sample tubes, the caps secured and the samples packed in the boxes ready for despatch. A urine analysis request card was completed for the specimens from each subject, and this together with the samples was sent by first class post, at the earliest opportunity, to the Wolfson Research Laboratories in Birmingham, where the analyses were carried out.[6]

4.2.3 Analyses

The urine samples were analysed for concentrations of sodium, potassium, urea and creatinine. Weekly lists of results were provided by the laboratories and any result of potential clinical significance was immediately referred by the laboratories to OPCS, and to a Senior Medical Officer at the Department of Health, who scrutinised the anonymised data. Where a result was judged potentially clinically significant, the research officer at OPCS was alerted and a letter sent to the subject's general practitioner.

4.3 Validation of the 24-hour urine collection

As explained above, the accuracy of the results from the analysis of a specimen of urine is dependent on the completeness of the 24-hour collection. There is a technique for checking for completeness, which requires the subject to take three 80mg tablets of *p*-amino benzoic acid (PABA) during the period of the collection. Completeness is verified by measuring the recovery of PABA in the collected urine.

As paracetamol and sulphonamide drugs interfere with the analysis used to estimate recovery of the marker, subjects taking these preparations must be excluded from the validation.[7] Moreover, subjects under the age of 18 would have required the written consent of a parent or guardian. These procedures would have added to the administrative burden of an already complex survey package, have raised issues of confidentiality and ethics, and would probably have resulted in a much higher level of non-co-operation in making 24-hour urine collections. For these reasons it was decided not to use the PABA marker technique in this survey.

The completeness of the 24-hour collections made by co-operating subjects on this survey has therefore not been validated. Williams and Bingham reported, in a study designed to validate the completeness of 24-hour urine collections, that 17% of collections from their sample population were incomplete as validated using the PABA marker technique, of which 14% would have been detected as incomplete by measurement of creatinine and 29% from self-reporting.[8]

The analysis of data from the present study excludes all results from subjects who reported failing to collect one or more voidings, and all cases where the period of collection was less than 18 hours or greater than 30 hours. For periods between 18 and 30 hours, volumes collected have been standardised to 24 hours.

Inconsistencies between the total volume recorded on the interview questionnaire and the laboratory analysis request card also resulted in a few cases being excluded from the analysis of results.

4.4 The purpose of obtaining a specimen of venous blood

One of the aims of this study was to identify the types of individuals at increased risk of coronary heart disease by relating dietary intakes to physiological and biochemical measures with health relevance, such as serum cholesterol and serum ferritin. In section 4.6 the various analyses performed on the blood specimens are described and in Chapter 17 their particular relevance in terms of dietary behaviour and health is explained.

4.5 Techniques and equipment used for obtaining a specimen of venous blood

Having completed a dietary record and co-operated with the anthropometric and blood pressure measurements, subjects aged 18 and over were asked to agree to a venepuncture procedure to obtain 20ml of blood.[9] It should be noted that although co-operation with this aspect of the survey was specifically sought, independent of agreement to any of the other elements in the survey, payment of £10 for completing a dietary record was not withheld if a subject declined to give a specimen of blood.

An appointment was made for an appropriately qualified person, usually a doctor, recruited by the Department of Health, to call with the interviewer to take, process, pack and despatch the specimen of blood. These people were given an *ex gratia* payment of £10 per specimen obtained.

All the specimens were sent to the Wolfson Research Laboratories in Birmingham for analysis.[6]

All the procedures associated with obtaining a sample of venous blood were tested rigorously pre-mainstage to ensure they were safe and acceptable to subjects, interviewers and the medical profession; ethical approval for this aspect of the study was sought and obtained from the Ethical Committee of the British Medical Association. All local Family Practitioner Committees were notified of the study; in only one case was there a referral to a local ethical committee and approval was given in this case.

The point during the survey at which the blood sampling procedure was mentioned to the subject was left to the interviewer's discretion; some preferred to do so at the beginning when introducing the survey, and thought it might encourage co-operation, while others preferred to wait until a good rapport had been established. There was no evidence that the point at which the topic was introduced affected the likelihood of obtaining co-operation. Response rates for co-operation with the taking of the blood specimen are given in Chapter 5.

Interviewers were provided with special sterile unit packs of equipment to hand to the doctor taking the sample. Again strict procedures were specified to ensure that the specimen was obtained in a standardised way, and both doctors and interviewers were given written instructions. All the techniques for taking, processing, and packing the samples were demonstrated at the interviewer briefings and in the training video.

The equipment comprised:
—an individual equipment pack containing 2 × graduated Pasteur pipettes, 1 × 20ml sterile disposable syringe, 1 standard 21 gauge hypodermic needle, an alcohol sterilizing swab, cotton swabs, and an adhesive dressing;[4]
—a despatch pack containing 1 × 5ml EDTA tube, 1 × 5ml and 1 × 2ml lithium heparin tube, 1 × 10ml beaded tube, 1 × 5ml plain tube, 2 × sealable plastic bags, 2 × laboratory analysis request cards;[4]
—a tourniquet;
—a selection of hypodermic needles of various sizes, including a small 'butterfly' needle and flexible connector.[10]

It was emphasised to the doctors that to ensure standardisation only the equipment provided should be used.

4.5.1 Taking the specimen of blood

The specimen of blood was taken in the subject's home. As it was not possible to control the time of day at which it was taken, the specimen was not necessarily from a fasting subject.

The subject's left arm was wiped with the sterile swab and then the doctor attempted to obtain 20ml of venous blood. Doctors were asked to avoid using a tourniquet if possible, but if it had to be used, to release it before the blood was withdrawn. With subjects who were difficult to bleed, a maximum of two attempts were made to obtain a specimen, before abandoning the procedure.

Having removed the hypodermic needle from the syringe the specimen was then syringed into the specimen tubes in the following order: 5ml into the EDTA tube, 4ml into the 5ml lithium heparin tube, 2ml into the 2ml lithium heparin tube and the remainder into the 10ml plain beaded tube.

The order in which the specimen of blood was to be syringed into the various tubes was decided on the basis of a priority order for the various analyses being carried out, bearing in mind that it was not always possible to obtain the full 20ml sample of whole blood.

Each tube was labelled with a unique subject identifier (serial number), the cap secured and the tube inverted several times to mix the contents. The two analysis request cards were completed and the relevant section of the interview questionnaire completed giving the time and date the specimen was taken and noting any difficulties experienced in obtaining the specimen.

The specimen in the 5ml EDTA tube was wrapped in packing material, sealed in a plastic bag, and despatched in a polystyrene box, with one of the analysis request cards, by first class post *immediately* to the laboratory.

Within three hours of the sample being obtained the specimen in the 10ml beaded tube was centrifuged (usually at the doctor's surgery or local hospital) and all the available serum pipetted into the 5ml plain tube. The tube containing the serum and the two lithium heparin tubes were then packed, sealed in a plastic bag and despatched, in a polystyrene box with the other analysis request card, by first class post to the laboratory.

At all times the samples were kept out of direct sunlight, and in a cool place, but not frozen.

The doctors were responsible for appropriate disposal of all the used equipment and waste materials.

4.6 Analyses carried out on the whole blood, serum and plasma samples

1. *Whole blood:*

1(*a*) *haematological profile:* haemoglobin; haematocrit; mean corpuscular volume; mean corpuscular haemoglobin concentration;

1(*b*) red cell folic acid;

1(*c*) erythrocyte glutathione reductase activation coefficient (EGRAC).

2. *Serum:*

calcium; creatinine; albumin; total protein; alkaline phosphatase; total cholesterol; high density lipoprotein (HDL) cholesterol; ferritin; γ-glutamyl transpeptidase; vitamin B12.

3. *Plasma:*

retinol; α-carotene; ß-carotene; lycopene; ß-cryptoxanthin, α-tocopherol.

The laboratory calculated globulin as (total protein minus albumin), non-HDL cholesterol as (total serum cholesterol minus HDL cholesterol), and the tocopherol:cholesterol ratio.

The samples were not analysed for any variables which were not nutritionally relevant. This was explained to subjects as it was felt to be of importance in gaining their co-operation.

The significance of the various analytes in relation to health, nutritional status and dietary behaviour is explained in Chapter 17 and Appendix J gives a technical report on the analytic procedures used by the laboratory and quality control data.

4.7 Summary

This chapter describes the reasons for obtaining and analysing specimens of urine and blood, and the techniques and equipment used to obtain the specimens.

The main reason for requiring a specimen of urine was to allow an estimate to be made of sodium intake; it has been suggested that dietary intakes of sodium are related to hypertension. Reliable estimates of intakes of sodium cannot be obtained from information on weighed intakes of food because existing food tables are not comprehensive and because no allowance can be made for the amount of salt added in cooking or at the table.

Estimates of sodium intake from specimens of urine must be made by taking a sample of urine from a complete 24-hour collection, since excretion fluctuates with intake.

All subjects in the study were asked to make a 24-hour collection of urine after the end of the dietary recording period. Informants were supplied with all the necessary equipment and with written instructions on the procedure. At the end of the collection interviewers weighed the total amount of urine collected (as a proxy for a volume measurement), and, having ensured that the collection was well mixed, took samples for analysis. The samples were packed and despatched with details of the date and time the collection started and finished, the total weight of the collection and details of any collections lost during the 24 hours, to the Wolfson Research Laboratories, in Birmingham, where they were analysed for concentrations of sodium, potassium, urea and creatinine.

The completeness of the 24-hour collections was not validated but excluded from the analysis are all cases where the subject reported failing to collect one or more voidings, and all cases where the period of collection was less than 18 hours or more than 30 hours. In the analyses, the volumes collected have been standardised to 24 hours.

Subjects aged 18 and over were asked to co-operate with a venepuncture procedure to obtain 20ml of blood. Subjects aged 16 and 17 were excluded from this part of the survey because of the administrative difficulties associated with obtaining consent in relation to minors. A sample of blood was required for analysis of constituents with health relevance related to nutrition, for example, cholesterol and iron status.

Appropriately qualified personnel were recruited by the Department of Health to take the blood samples and they were accompanied on a visit to the informant's home after the completion of the seven-day dietary recording period. All the procedures associated with taking the blood samples were rigorously tested prior to the mainstage of the survey to ensure that they were safe and acceptable to subjects, interviewers and the medical profession. Ethical approval for this part of the study was obtained from the Ethical Committee of the British Medical Association.

The specimen was obtained in a standardised way, using equipment provided and in accordance with written instructions; however, since it was not possible to control the time of day that the blood sample was taken, the specimens are not necessarily from fasting subjects.

For the full range of analyses to be carried out 20ml of whole blood was required; in some cases it was not possible to obtain the full 20ml, and guidance was given on how the sample was to be allocated to specimen tubes on the basis of priorities for analysis. One part of the 20ml was centrifuged within three hours of being collected and the serum was sent for analysis. All the samples were packed and despatched, at the earliest possible opportunity, to the Wolfson Laboratories for analysis.

In section 4.6 details are given of the analyses carried out on the samples of whole blood, serum and plasma.

Appendix J gives a technical report on the analytic procedures carried out by the laboratories and quality control data.

Weekly listings of results from the analysis of both the blood and urine specimens were sent by the laboratories and any result of potential clinical significance was immediately referred to OPCS and to a Senior Medical Officer at the Department of Health. All the weekly listings, which were anonymised, were scrutinised and any result of potential clinical significance was referred to the subject's general practitioner by the research officer at OPCS.

References and notes

1. Paul A A, Southgate D A T. *McCance and Widdowson's The Composition of Foods,* 4th edition. HMSO (London, 1978).
2. Schacter J, Harper P H, Radin M E, Caggiula A W, McDonald R H, Diven W F. *Hypertension* 1980; 2: 695–699.
3. The Rolon 24-hour specimen storage container is available from Rocket of London, Imperial Way, Watford WD2 4XX.
4. Unit packs containing these items were specially designed and prepared for the survey by the Wolfson Research Laboratories, Queen Elizabeth Medical Centre, Edgbaston, Birmingham B15 2TH.
5. It has been assumed that 1g of urine is equivalent to 1ml; no adjustment has been made to the data to allow for the specific gravity of urine.
6. The Wolfson Research Laboratories, Queen Elizabeth Medical Centre, Edgbaston, Birmingham B15 2TH.
7. Bingham S A, Cummings J H. The use of creatinine output as a check on the completeness of 24-hour urine collections. *Hum Nutr: Clin Nutr* 1985; 39C(5): 343–353.
8. Williams D R R, Bingham S A. Sodium and potassium intakes in a representative population sample: estimation from 24h urine collections known to be complete in a Cambridgeshire village. *Br J Nutr* 1986; 55: 1; 13–22.
9. Since the written consent of a parent or guardian would have been required if a blood sample had been taken from a minor, it was decided to restrict the taking of blood to subjects aged 18 and over.
10. The Miniven Small Vein Luer Set—21GTW, OD 0.8mm.

5 Response to the survey and characteristics of the interviewed sample

This chapter gives details of the response achieved for each of the main elements of the survey package and describes the main characteristics of the total responding sample (those who co-operated with any combination of survey elements), and of the diary sample (those who completed a full seven-day dietary record). Where possible the characteristics of the sample are compared with those of the population as a whole or of larger samples from general population surveys.

A more detailed description of the characteristics of the sample is shown only for those who completed the dietary record, since this is the sample to which much of the Report refers. Information is first presented on a number of characteristics, either of the respondent or of his or her household, which are commonly used in social research, and then on characteristics related to the individual's diet and health status, including whether he or she was on a slimming diet, and the informant's smoking behaviour.

5.1 Response and non-response

The level of response on the dietary and nutritional survey of British adults can be presented in a variety of ways since informants could have completed any combination of the elements of the survey: interview, dietary record, the various anthropometric measurements, blood pressure measurements, the blood sample and the urine sample. The following tables summarise response to each of these individual elements for each round separately, as well as the total for all rounds.

Table 5.1 shows the outcome for the set sample of addresses issued to interviewers in each round of fieldwork. About one fifth (21%) of the total set sample were ineligible for the survey. The high rate of ineligibility was chiefly due to the exclusion from the scope of the survey of elderly households, where all members were aged 65 or over. The total of ineligible cases includes refusals and cases of non-contact where the interviewer was able to establish that all members of the sampled household were outside the eligible age range.

Another group excluded from the sample was pregnant women; their dietary needs and physiological status differ from those of other women and, in a sample of this size, they would not form a large enough group for separate analysis. Elderly households and pregnant women together accounted for 80% of ineligible cases. The remaining one fifth of ineligible addresses were either institutions, business addresses, or demolished or empty premises. *(Table 5.1)*

For those who took part in the survey a distinction is made between those who completed a full seven-day dietary record and those who partially co-operated, that is completed a combination of elements of the survey but did not complete a dietary record. Overall, 70% of the eligible sample completed a full seven-day dietary record, and a further 14% co-operated with some other aspects of the survey. There was no significant difference between fieldwork rounds in the overall response rate although response to the seven-day diary was lowest in the final round of fieldwork, carried out in July and August.

Refusals to all aspects of the survey accounted for 13% of the eligible sample; this included fewer than 1% which were refusals made to the OPCS head office in response to the advance letter. The remaining refusals were made at the time of the interviewer's visit and included refusals made both by the household as a whole and by the selected individual.

Only 3% of the set sample were not contacted. This low level of non-contacts in part reflects that it was not a named person sample, so it was not necessary to trace individuals who had moved from the sampled address. In addition, the field periods for the survey were relatively long, with interviewing spread over a two-month period for each round.

5.1.1 Response to the measurements

Response rates for the anthropometric and blood pressure measurements are shown in Table 5.2. The response stated is based on the number of measurements that were recorded; this may be slightly lower than the number of cases in which informants were willing to co-operate due to cases where there were difficulties in actually taking the measurements. Response rates are expressed both as a proportion of the total eligible sample and as a proportion of the total responding sample (those who co-operated with any aspect of the survey). Since calf circumference was measured only for men, response to this measurement is shown only as a percentage of eligible male respondents.

(Table 5.2)

Three quarters (76%) of the eligible sample co-operated with each of the individual measurements; this corresponds to at least 90% of the responding sample. Few informants refused individual measurements having agreed in principle to the anthropometric measurements.

In some cases a measurement was recorded but was later excluded from the analysis on the basis of difficulties reported by the interviewer in taking the measurement accurately. These included cases where, for example, the wrist had been fractured, or where the informant's hair style or posture had interfered with the measurement of height. Full details of the reasons for excluding each type of measurement are given in the relevant sections of the Report.

5.1.2 Response to blood and urine samples
Response rates for the blood sample and the urine collection are based on the number of cases in which a sample was analysed (Table 5.3). This slightly understates the proportion of the eligible sample who were willing to co-operate with these aspects of the survey, because samples were sometimes damaged in transit or insufficient for the analysis, and because the doctor was occasionally unable to take a blood sample. A urine collection was made by 77% of the responding sample (65% of the eligible sample) and 76% of eligible respondents (that is, those aged between 18 and 64 who co-operated with any aspect of the survey) gave a blood sample. Response to both of these aspects of the survey was lowest in the summer fieldwork period.

(*Table 5.3*)

The figures in Table 5.3 show the proportion of informants for whom a sample of blood or urine was analysed, but the number of cases for whom any individual analysis was performed could vary according to how large a sample was obtained and the priority order of the analyses that were carried out. Further details of the number of cases for which results for each analyte was obtained are given in the relevant sections of the Report.

5.1.3 Response to measurements among fully and partially co-operating informants
Table 5.4 shows response to the various measurements separately for those who had kept a full seven-day dietary record and the partially co-operating sample. Respondents who had completed the dietary record showed their commitment to all aspects of the survey by almost total co-operation with the anthropometric measurements. As expected there were lower levels of response among the partially co-operating sample but, even so, almost half of this group of informants co-operated with the anthropometric and blood pressure measurements. For both groups, more respondents co-operated with the measurement of height and weight than the other measurements, but response declined only slightly for these and for the measurement of blood pressure.

(*Table 5.4*)

A similar pattern was seen for co-operation with the blood and urine samples, with respondents to the dietary record being more likely than partially co-operating respondents to give samples. Response among the record keeping sample continued at a very high level; 88% made a 24-hour urine collection and 86% of those who were eligible gave a blood sample. There was a more marked decline in response amongst those who did not keep a dietary record with only 22%

making a urine collection and 25% of those who were eligible giving blood. The lower level of response among partially co-operating respondents would be expected given that the samples could not be taken at the same visit as the anthropometric measurements.

5.2 Characteristics of the responding sample

5.2.1 Sex and age
The sex and age distribution of the responding and diary samples are compared in Table 5.5 with the age and sex distribution of adults in private households according to the 1986 General Household Survey and the 1987 population estimates for Great Britain.[1] The total responding sample appears to underrepresent individuals in the 16 to 24 age group, and particularly women of that age. This underrepresentation of younger people may in part be explained by the exclusion from the sampling frame of institutional addresses, such as educational establishments. The use of the Electoral Register as a sampling frame and the ineligibility for the survey of pregnant women may also contribute to the shortfall. It is, however, acknowledged that there are particular difficulties in contacting and gaining co-operation for surveys from young adults whose life-style may be less settled than that of older people.

At the second stage of response to the seven-day dietary record, the distribution for this sample is closer to that of the larger General Household Survey sample and to population estimates. This is, however, achieved because of a slightly lower response to the dietary record among the oldest age group contacted (aged 50 to 64 years). Once they had agreed to the preliminary interview young people (aged 16 to 24 years) were no less likely than other age groups to go on to keep a dietary record. (*Table 5.5*)

5.2.2 Region
Respondents to the dietary survey were coded according to the standard region in which they lived, and the distributions for the total responding sample and the diary sample are compared in Table 5.6 with population figures for 1986. There was no significant difference between the regional distributions of the responding and diary samples and both were similar to the total population figures.

The sample size within each of the standard regions shown was too small to allow significant differences to be identified in results presented at this level of disaggregation. The analyses presented in this Report distinguish four broad regions: Scotland; Northern; Central, South West and Wales; and London and South East. In spite of its small size (9% of the sample), Scotland was separately identified because of the region's particularly high rate of mortality from heart disease, and the interest in possible links between dietary intakes and health indicators. Each of the other three broad regions contained between one quarter and one third of the diary sample. (*Table 5.6*)

The age distributions for men and women differed to some degree between the broad regions identified in the analyses. Younger men (16 to 24) made up a larger proportion of the sample in the Northern region than in the Central and South West regions and Wales, or London and the South East regions, but there were fewer men aged 35 to 49 in the North than in London and the South East. The proportion of men in the sample aged 35 and over and living in Scotland was smaller than elsewhere. The age distribution of women differed little between regions; there were, however, fewer older women (aged 50 to 64) in London and the South East than in the Central and South West regions and Wales. (*Table 5.7*)

5.2.3 Social class

In order to code social class, informants were asked to give details of their current or most recent job or, if retired, of their main job during their working life. Similar information was also collected for the head of household. The information both for the informant and for the head of household was coded to six social class groups according to the Registrar General's classification of occupations.

A substantial number of informants could not themselves be allocated to a social class because they had never been in paid employment; most of these were full-time students or women who were keeping house. Throughout this Report the social class of the head of household has been used as a characteristic of the sample. This is available in a larger number of cases than is the informant's own social class, it is less dependent on sex and age differences between informants, and it is more useful as a generalised indicator of the economic position of a household.

Table 5.8 shows social class of head of household by sex of informant for the responding and diary samples. Because of the small numbers of respondents in Social Classes I and V, these cases were combined with Social Classes II and IV respectively to give a four-fold classification for use in the analysis. Comparison of the diary sample with the total responding sample shows that there was no significant difference by social class in the likelihood that respondents would go on to complete a dietary record. In a small number of cases (1% of the diary sample) it was not possible to assign a social class coding, and these cases are excluded from subsequent analyses by social class. The social class distributions for men and women did not differ significantly. (*Table 5.8*)

Table 5.9 shows the social class distribution by sex and age of respondent for the diary sample. Among women, younger respondents, under the age of 35, were more likely than older women to be classified as Social Class III manual. (*Table 5.9*)

The social class distribution of men and women in the diary sample did not differ markedly between regions. Men in Scotland and the North were less likely than men in London and the South East to be classified to Social Classes I and II. (*Table 5.10*)

5.2.4 Employment status

Respondents to the survey were asked whether they were working either full time or part time at the time of the interview. Those who were not in paid employment were asked further questions about their current status and the responses were categorised to identify the unemployed and those who were in full-time education, keeping house or retired. Similar questions about current employment status were also asked of the head of household.

The analyses in this Report are based on the informant's own employment status. The possible financial effect of the head of household being unemployed is reflected by whether anyone in the informant's household was in receipt of benefits, rather than by employment status (see section 5.2.5).

Informants who were in paid employment were also asked if they did shiftwork at all; if so, they were asked to describe the type of shifts worked and details were taken of the actual hours worked during the week in which they kept the dietary record. Analysis of the dietary habits of shiftworkers is therefore possible but has not been undertaken in this Report. The numbers of informants who ever worked shifts was relatively small (only 9% of the dietary sample) and these covered a variety of types of shiftwork.

Table 5.11 shows the employment status of the responding and diary samples, and indicates that there was no difference in the likelihood that respondents of any particular group would go on to complete the dietary record. Overall, 80% of men and 60% of women respondents were working at the time of the survey. As would be expected, part-time work was more common amongst women than men (25% of women compared to 2% of men); students who had a part-time job were classified as students rather than as being in part-time employment.

Some 7% of the diary sample were unemployed; the unemployed were defined as those who were looking for work, were intending to look for work but who were prevented by sickness, and those who were waiting to take up a job that they had already obtained. The remainder of the sample were classed as economically inactive; most women in this category were looking after the home and family (23% of the sample). Within the category of the economically inactive, the retired comprised 8% of the total diary sample. (*Table 5.11*)

The analyses in the Report distinguish between those in employment, the unemployed and others. The numbers of students and retired people were too small to allow separate analysis of these subgroups. The unemployed, although only a relatively small group within the sample, were separately identified because of interest in whether their food and nutrient intake differed from that of other groups; another approach to identifying possible groups who were 'at risk' was by focusing on households in receipt of state benefits, as discussed in the next section.

Table 5.12 shows that the employment status of both younger and older men in the diary sample differed from that of men in the middle of the age range. Less than 70% of men in the 16 to 24 and 50 to 64 age groups were working at the time of the survey, compared to more than 90% of men between the ages of 25 and 49. Most of this difference is accounted for by higher proportions of economically inactive men (see Glossary) in these age groups, but younger men (aged less than 25) were also more likely than others to have been unemployed at the time of the survey (13% compared to 9% overall). For women, unemployment was also higher for those aged less than 25 (11% compared to 5% overall). The proportion of women who were working was greatest in the 35 to 49 age group and least amongst those over the age of 50 (73% compared to 45%); participation in the labour force of those aged less than 35 would be influenced both by the number of younger women in full-time education and by women having moved out of the labour force to look after young children. (Table 5.12)

The employment status of informants differed both according to region and social class (Tables 5.13 and 5.14). The largest proportion of male respondents in paid employment was in London and the South East, while Scotland had a higher proportion of unemployed men than other regions (21% compared to 5% in London and the South East). London and the South East also had the highest proportion of working women. Differences in the proportion of women who were unemployed were less marked than for men, but the proportion in the Northern region was slightly higher than the overall figure. (Table 5.13)

Differences in employment status according to social class were again more marked for men than for women. Men in Social Classes IV and V were the least likely group to be working, and the proportion unemployed was higher for men classified to the manual social classes (Social Classes III manual, IV and V) than for non-manual social classes. Similar trends were evident for women but the absolute differences were smaller. (Table 5.14)

5.2.5 Receipt of state benefits

The composition of an individual's diet is influenced by a variety of factors, but it might be expected that the household's disposable income would be an important influence, particularly where financial resources are limited. In order to collect income data in sufficient detail for use in the analysis it would have been necessary to include a series of detailed questions in the interview; collecting complete information on a household's sources and amounts of income is generally recognised as difficult, and it was also thought that the inclusion of such a sensitive topic might have jeopard-

ised response to other elements of the survey. In recognition of these potential difficulties income data were not collected but informants were asked if they, or anyone in their household, were currently receiving unemployment benefit, supplementary benefit, or family income supplement.[2]

In order to improve the effectiveness of the benefits variable as an indicator of relative deprivation, cases where unemployment or supplementary benefit was being received by someone in the household, but where the head of household was in full-time work, were excluded from the 'receiving benefits' category. All cases where family income supplement was received were included as benefit households.

Table 5.15 shows the proportions of the responding and the diary samples where a member of the household was in receipt of each of these individual benefits, after exclusion of the cases where the head of household was in full-time work. Overall, about 12% of respondents to the dietary record were in households receiving one or other benefit; this provides sufficient numbers to analyse benefit receivers as a separate group. Women were more likely than men to be in households receiving benefits, whilst informants aged between 35 and 49 were least likely to live in benefit households (9% compared to 14% for the other age groups). (Tables 5.15 and 5.16)

5.2.6 Household size and type

At the time that an individual was selected from the household a record was made of the number of adults aged 16 or over in the sampled household. Table 5.19 shows the number of adults per household for the responding and diary samples compared to the distribution of adults by size of household for the 1987 General Household Survey (GHS). Comparison cannot be made with the proportion of households of each size included in the GHS sample since the dietary sample was designed to select households with probability proportional to their size and so was not designed to be a representative sample of households.

There was no significant difference between the distributions for the responding and diary samples; both showed a smaller proportion of informants in one-person households than did the GHS. The proportions of the sample in households of different sizes might be expected to differ from that of nationally based statistics because of the exclusion from this sample of elderly households, which are particularly likely to be single-person households. Women in this sample were more likely than men to be living in one or two-adult households; consequently a higher proportion of men than of women were living in households containing a large number of adults. (Table 5.19)

At the initial interview, details of all members of the informant's household were collected and used to classify respondents according to their household composition into four household types for men, and five for women, based on the presence or absence of a spouse or partner and of dependent children. Dependent children were defined as children of the informant who were under the age of 16, or aged 16 to 18 and in full-time education. A spouse includes a non-married partner in the household where the informant described him or herself as married or living together as married.

The four main household types for men and women were: informants who were living alone; those living with a spouse or partner but with no dependent children; those living with other adults but with no spouse and no dependent children; and those with dependent children in their household, with or without a spouse. In addition, there were sufficient women, but not men, living with dependent children but without a spouse or partner to be separately identified.

Table 5.20 shows the household classification of men and women in the responding and the diary samples, and indicates that respondents who were living with a spouse and with dependent children were more likely than other groups to go on to complete a dietary record. Most of the sample were married or living as married, either with or without dependent children; 34% of the diary sample were living with a partner but without children whilst 35% were living with a partner and with dependent children. Lone parents represented 4% of the sample, and were predominantly women. Seven per cent of informants lived alone. The remaining 16% of the diary sample were living with other adults but not with a spouse; this category includes those informants who were living with their parents and those living with other unrelated adults. *(Table 5.20)*

As might be expected there were differences in the distribution of household types by age of the respondent. Young people (aged less than 25) were more likely than other informants to be living with other adults but with neither a spouse nor dependent children; older people (aged 50 or more) were more likely than others to be living with their spouse but with no dependent children. *(Table 5.21)*

Tables 5.22 and 5.23 show household composition for men and women by region and by the social class of the head of household. More men in the Northern region were living with other adults but not with a spouse (32% compared to 25% overall), but this was not the case for women. Women in Social Classes IV and V were more likely than other women to be lone parents (17% of the group compared to 7% overall). *(Tables 5.22 and 5.23)*

5.3 Medical and dietary variables
A number of questions on dietary practice were included in the interview schedule in order to provide classificatory information which could not easily be derived from the food record. The most important of these questions concerned slimming diets, the taking of food supplements, smoking and whether the respondent's eating had been affected by their being unwell

during the period of record keeping. All respondents to the diary and to the physical measurements were also asked about any prescribed medicines which they were taking, since it was important to be able to exclude from the analysis those cases where a measurement might have been affected by drugs.

5.3.1 Slimming diets
At the time of completing the dietary record 12% of women and 4% of men reported that they were on a slimming diet. There was little variation according to the age of respondent in the proportion who were dieting. For women the average length of the slimming diet was 6.5 weeks, compared to an average of almost 10 weeks for dieting men. *(Table 5.24)*

5.3.2 Food supplements
Food supplement taking was rather more common than being on a slimming diet. As with dieting, women were more likely to be taking supplements (17% of women compared to 9% of men). Supplement taking was most frequent among older women, with almost a quarter (23%) of the 50 to 64 age group taking supplements. Amongst men, the incidence of supplement taking did not increase consistently with age. *(Table 5.25)*

Supplement taking was found to be related to the social class of the head of the informant's household. Men in Social Classes I and II were more likely than other men to be taking supplements (12% of the group compared to 7% of others); women in Social Classes I and II were more likely than those in manual social classes to be taking supplements (21% compared with 15%). *(Table 5.26)*

The supplements identified covered more than 25 types of product, and Table 5.27 identifies the most commonly used supplements; it should be noted that any one individual could be taking more than one type of product. Multivitamins with or without iron were the two most common groups, followed by cod liver and halibut liver oil, and vitamin C. More men than women were taking vitamin C and vitamin E, whilst vitamin B6 and iron were more commonly taken by women. *(Table 5.27)*

5.3.3 The unwell
At the end of the seven-day recording period respondents to the dietary record were asked whether they had been unwell during the period of the record, and whether this had affected their eating habits. Table 5.28 shows that 13% of men and 20% of women had been unwell during the week, but only 5% of men and 10% of women claimed that their eating had been affected. The average length of illness for all who were unwell during the dietary recording week was 3.2 days; those whose eating had been affected were unwell for an average of 2.8 days. *(Table 5.28)*

Younger men (under the age of 35) were more likely to have been unwell and their eating affected than were men aged 35 or more. A similar age effect is also seen for women with those aged 25 to 34 years being most likely to report that their eating was affected by their being unwell. *(Table 5.29)*

5.3.4 Smoking

All respondents were asked whether they smoked cigarettes and, if so, how many they smoked daily. On the basis of these questions individuals were classified as non-smokers, light smokers (smoking fewer than 20 cigarettes daily) and heavy smokers (smoking 20 or more cigarettes daily). The prevalence of smoking was of particular interest in relation to blood pressure and to the results of the analyses of the blood and urine samples; results are therefore presented for the total responding sample.

Approximately two thirds of all informants were non-smokers; 66% of men and 65% of women, and these proportions were not significantly different for the diary sample. Women who smoked were more likely than men to be light smokers; 22% of women were light smokers compared to 17% of men. In Table 5.30 these are compared to figures from the 1986 General Household Survey (GHS); the dietary sample included a slightly smaller proportion of male light smokers than the larger GHS sample. The average number of cigarettes smoked daily by smokers in the responding sample was 18 for men and 14 for women.

(Table 5.30)

Smoking amongst women was most prevalent among those aged 25 to 34, where 39% were smokers, but there was little variation by age for men. For both sexes smoking was more common amongst the lower social classes; 78% of men and 77% of women in Social Classes I and II were non-smokers compared to 54% of men and only 51% of women in Social Classes IV and V. Heavy smokers were also more likely to be in the manual social classes. *(Tables 5.31 and 5.32)*

5.3.5 Alcohol

A classification of alcohol drinking behaviour based on the amount of alcohol recorded in the seven-day dietary record was derived for use in analysis. Individuals who consumed no alcohol during the recording week were classed as non-drinkers, and drinkers were divided into three categories on the basis of recommended weekly limits for men and women and using an 8 gram per unit conversion for alcohol intake.[3]

Table 5.33 shows the distribution of drinking behaviour by age and sex of the diary sample. Men of all ages were less likely than women to be non-drinkers, and they were more likely than women to have alcohol intakes at the upper end of the range. People under the age of 25 were more likely to be non-drinkers than those in the older age groups. For women there was little variation by age in the proportion with higher intakes (more than 112g) but older men, aged 35 or over, were more likely than younger men to have intakes of more than 168g per week. *(Table 5.33)*

Due to the small numbers in the category of greatest alcohol intake (more than 440g for men and more than 280g for women), the two categories of heavier drinkers were combined for some of the later analyses. Further information on the alcohol intake of the diary sample is presented in Chapter 7.

5.3.6 Prescribed medicines

Almost one quarter of the total responding sample was taking a prescribed medicine, including the contraceptive pill; the comparative figures for men and women were 18% and 35% respectively. Table 5.34 indicates the different proportions of men and women in each group who were taking one or more prescribed medicines. For men there was a significant increase in the proportion of respondents taking prescribed medicines between the youngest age groups (under 35) and the 35 to 49 age group, and a further sharp increase amongst the 50 to 64 age group. A larger proportion of women than men in each age group were taking prescribed medicines, even when those women taking the oral contraceptive are excluded. Prevalence of prescribed medicine taking, excluding oral contraceptives, was lowest among women in the 16 to 24 age group.

(Table 5.34)

The names of any prescribed medicines being taken were noted on the interview schedule and each was coded by a medical practitioner to one of 20 groups. The prevalence of drugs in the most common groups is shown in Table 5.35. The two most common drug types for men were anti-hypertensives and analgesics. After excluding oral contraceptives, the most common drug types for women were analgesics and diuretics. Women were much less likely than men to be taking anti-hypertensive drugs. *(Table 5.35)*

5.4 Summary

A total of 2,635 individuals co-operated with one or more aspects of the survey, which represented 84% of the eligible sample; a full seven-day dietary record was completed by 70% of the eligible sample. Response to the anthropometric and blood pressure measurements was high (90% of all responders), and more than three quarters of eligible responders gave samples of blood and urine (76% and 77% respectively).

There was little difference in the characteristics of the responding and diary samples, and no evidence of bias in response to the dietary record.

A limited number of checks on sample validity were possible by comparing the characteristics of the achieved sample with those of the total population, or with those of larger samples on general population surveys; there are some difficulties in drawing comparisons because of the exclusion from this sample of households where all members were aged 65 or over. The dietary sample reflected the regional distribution of population and, insofar as it could be compared, the distribution of the population according to the number of adults in the household. The percentages of smokers in this sample did not differ from those recorded for the General Household Survey.

There is some evidence that this sample underrepresented people in the 16 to 24 age group according to the age distribution of 1987 population estimates, but the shortfall was less in comparison with the General Household Survey. The shortfall in the number of young people might be related in part to the use of the Electoral Register as a sampling frame, and to the exclusion from the sample of the institutional population. It was not considered necessary to reweight the sample to the age distribution of the population since the difference was relatively small, and since many of the analyses in this Report take account of the age of the respondent.

References and notes

1. OPCS. *General Household Survey, 1986*. HMSO (London, 1989).
2. In 1988, as part of changes to the system of Social Security payments, Family Income Supplement was replaced by Family Credit, and Supplementary Benefit by Income Support.
3. Royal College of Physicians of London. *A great and growing evil: the medical consequences of alcohol abuse*. Tavistock Publications (London, 1987).

Table 5.1   Response rates by fieldwork round

	Round of fieldwork									
	Autumn		Winter		Spring		Summer		Total	
Set sample = 100%	**990**		**990**		**990**		**990**		**3960**	
Ineligible	198	*20%*	219	*22%*	205	*21%*	200	*20%*	822	*21%*
Eligible sample = 100%	**792**		**771**		**785**		**790**		**3138**	
Full seven-day diary	555	*70%*	548	*71%*	568	*72%*	526	*67%*	2197	*70%*
Partial co-operation*	115	*15%*	101	*13%*	97	*12%*	125	*16%*	438	*14%*
Refusals	104	*13%*	100	*13%*	100	*13%*	118	*15%*	422	*13%*
Non-contacts	18	*2%*	22	*3%*	20	*3%*	21	*3%*	81	*3%*

* *Partial or no seven-day diary, and co-operation with any other aspects of survey*

Table 5.2   Co-operation with anthropometric and blood pressure measurements by fieldwork round

	Round of fieldwork										
	Autumn	Winter	Spring	Summer	Total		Autumn	Winter	Spring	Summer	Total
Height:						**Mid-upper arm circumference:**					
measurements made	**608**	**585**	**601**	**593**	**2387**	measurements made	**605**	**584**	**600**	**589**	**2378**
as % of eligible sample	77%	76%	77%	75%	76%	as % of eligible sample	76%	76%	76%	75%	76%
as % of responders	91%	90%	90%	91%	91%	as % of responders	90%	90%	90%	90%	90%
Weight:						**Calf circumference:**					
measurements made	**608**	**585**	**600**	**594**	**2387**	measurements made	**311**	**283**	**299**	**296**	**1189**
as % of eligible sample	77%	76%	76%	76%	76%	as % of eligible responders	91%	87%	92%	91%	90%
as % of responders	91%	90%	90%	91%	91%						
Wrist diameter:						**Blood pressure:**					
measurements made	**606**	**584**	**600**	**591**	**2381**	measurements made	**602**	**584**	**596**	**589**	**2371**
as % of eligible sample	77%	76%	76%	75%	76%	as % of eligible sample	76%	76%	76%	75%	76%
as % of responders	90%	90%	90%	91%	90%	as % of responders	90%	90%	90%	90%	90%

Table 5.3 Co-operation with blood sample and urine collection by round of fieldwork

| | Round of fieldwork | | | | |
	Autumn	Winter	Spring	Summer	Total
Urine sample:					
samples analysed	**528**	**494**	**534**	**484**	**2040**
as % of eligible sample	67%	64%	68%	61%	65%
as % of responders	79%	76%	80%	74%	77%
Blood sample:					
samples analysed	**499**	**465**	**499**	**455**	**1919**
as % of eligible responders*	79%	75%	77%	72%	76%

* Eligible responders = responders aged 18 to 64

Table 5.4 Response to the measurements by whether informants had kept a dietary record

All rounds

| | Co-operation with dietary record | | |
	Full dietary record	No dietary record	Total
	%	%	%
Height and/or weight	99	48	91
Some or all of other anthropometric measurements	99	47	90
Blood pressure	99	47	90
Blood sample*	86	25	76
Urine sample	88	22	77
Both blood and urine samples*	83	21	73
Base:	2197	438	2635

* As % of eligible responders (aged 18 to 64)

Table 5.5 Sex and age of responding and diary samples compared to 1986 General Household Survey and 1987 population estimates

| Age group | Responding sample | | | Diary sample | | | 1986 GHS sample | | | 1987 population estimates * | | |
	Men	Women	Total	Men	Women	Total	Men	Women	Total	Men	Women	Total
	%	%	%	%	%	%	%	%	%	%	%	%
16–24	19	16	17	20	17	18	21	20	21	23	22	23
25–34	23	22	23	23	23	23	22	23	23	22	22	22
35–49	31	34	32	32	35	33	31	30	31	30	30	30
50–64	27	28	28	25	25	25	25	26	26	24	25	25
Base = 100%	*1320 (49%)*	*1315 (51%)*	*2635*	*1087 (49%)*	*1110 (51%)*	*2197*	*8078 (49%)*	*8331 (51%)*	*16409*	*17822 (50%)*	*17761 (50%)*	*35583*

* Base figures in thousands

Table 5.6 Regional distribution of responding and diary samples compared to 1986 population estimates

Region	Responding sample	Diary sample	1986 population*
	%	%	%
Scotland	**9**	**9**	**9**
North	6	6	6
Yorkshire & Humberside	8	8	9
North West	12	11	12
Northern	**26**	**25**	**26**
East Midlands	8	9	7
East Anglia	3	3	4
West Midlands	9	9	9
South West	8	8	8
Wales	5	5	5
Central, South West and Wales	**33**	**33**	**33**
Inner London	4	4	} 12
Outer London	8	8	
Rest of South East	20	20	19
London and South East	**32**	**32**	**31**
Base = 100%	*2635*	*2197*	*55,196,400*

* Regional Trends 1988; estimates for population of all ages

31

Table 5.7 Age of diary sample by sex and region
Diary sample

Age of informant	Region									
	Men					Women				
	Scotland	Northern	Central, South West and Wales	London and South East	Total	Scotland	Northern	Central, South West and Wales	London and South East	Total
	%	%	%	%	%	%	%	%	%	%
16–24	24	25	17	18	20	17	20	15	17	17
25–34	30	22	24	22	23	30	20	21	26	23
35–49	25	28	33	36	32	32	33	35	36	35
50–64	21	26	27	24	25	22	27	29	21	26
Base = 100%	*96*	*274*	*364*	*353*	*1087*	*95*	*290*	*368*	*357*	*1110*

Table 5.8 Social class of head of household by sex of informant for responding and diary samples

Social class of head of household	Responding sample			Diary sample		
	Men	Women	Total	Men	Women	Total
	%	%	%	%	%	%
I and II	33	34	34	35	35	35
III non-manual	12	13	13	13	13	13
III manual	36	31	33	35	31	33
IV and V	17	20	19	16	20	18
Never worked/ inadequate information	2	2	2	2	1	1
Base = 100%	*1320*	*1315*	*2635*	*1087*	*1110*	*2197*

Table 5.9 Social class of head of household by sex and age of informant
Diary sample

Social class of head of household	Sex and age of informant									
	Men				All ages 16–64	Women				All ages 16–64
	16–24	25–34	35–49	50–64		16–24	25–34	35–49	50–64	
	%	%	%	%	%	%	%	%	%	%
I and II	30	35	39	34	35	28	34	41	33	35
III non-manual	12	12	13	14	13	15	8	14	14	13
III manual	41	36	32	35	35	39	37	29	26	32
IV and V	17	16	16	17	17	18	21	16	26	20
Base = 100%	*206*	*249*	*344*	*271*	*1070*	*186*	*250*	*380*	*280*	*1096*

Table 5.10 Social class of head of household by sex of informant and region
Diary sample

Social class of head of household	Region									
	Men					Women				
	Scotland	Northern	Central, South West and Wales	London and South East	Total	Scotland	Northern	Central, South West and Wales	London and South East	Total
	%	%	%	%	%	%	%	%	%	%
I and II	30	29	37	40	35	32	36	32	39	35
III non-manual	18	12	11	13	13	14	13	11	15	13
III manual	33	38	36	33	35	36	30	34	30	32
IV and V	18	21	16	14	17	19	22	24	16	20
Base = 100%	*93*	*268*	*360*	*349*	*1070*	*95*	*287*	*365*	*349*	*1096*

Table 5.11 Employment status of informant by sex for responding and diary samples

Employment status of informant	Responding sample			Diary sample		
	Men	Women	Total	Men	Women	Total
	%	%	%	%	%	%
Working full time	77	34	56	78	35	56
Working part time	2	24	13	2	25	14
Total working	80	59	70	80	60	70
Unemployed	9	5	7	9	5	7
Total economically active	88	64	76	90	65	77
In full-time education	3	2	2	3	2	3
Keeping house	0	24	12	0	23	12
Retired and other	8	9	9	7	8	8
Total economically inactive	11	35	23	10	34	22
Not known	0	1	1	0	1	1
Base = 100%	*1320*	*1315*	*2635*	*1087*	*1110*	*2197*

Table 5.12 Employment status of informant by sex and age
Diary sample

Employment status of informant	Sex and age of informant									
	Men				All ages 16–64	Women				All ages 16–64
	16–24	25–34	35–49	50–64		16–24	25–34	35–49	50–64	
	%	%	%	%	%	%	%	%	%	%
Working	69	90	91	68	81	63	59	73	45	61
Unemployed	13	9	8	9	9	11	6	3	3	5
Economically inactive	18	1	2	23	10	26	36	24	51	34
Base = 100%	*213*	*254*	*346*	*272*	*1085*	*187*	*251*	*384*	*278*	*1100*

Table 5.13 Employment status of informant by region and sex
Diary sample

Employment status of informant	Region									
	Men					Women				
	Scotland	Northern	Central, South West and Wales	London and South East	Total	Scotland	Northern	Central, South West and Wales	London and South East	Total
	%	%	%	%	%	%	%	%	%	%
Working	67	77	80	88	81	54	57	60	67	61
Unemployed	21	9	10	5	9	7	9	4	3	5
Economically inactive	12	14	10	7	10	39	34	36	30	34
Base = 100%	*95*	*274*	*363*	*353*	*1085*	*95*	*287*	*365*	*353*	*1100*

Table 5.14 Employment status of informant by sex of informant and social class of head of household
Diary sample

Employment status of informant	Sex of informant and social class of head of household							
	Men				Women			
	I and II	III non-manual	III manual	IV and V	I and II	III non-manual	III manual	IV and V
	%	%	%	%	%	%	%	%
Working	88	84	81	67	62	67	61	55
Unemployed	4	4	11	19	3	4	6	8
Economically inactive	9	12	8	14	35	29	33	37
Base = 100%	*377*	*138*	*377*	*176*	*384*	*140*	*345*	*217*

Table 5.15 Households in receipt of selected benefits where head of household was not working full time, for responding and diary samples

Type of benefit	Responding sample	Diary sample
	% in receipt of named benefit	% in receipt of named benefit
	%	%
Unemployment benefit	3	3
Family income supplement	1	1
Supplementary benefit	10	9
One or more of above benefits	**13**	**12**
Base = 100%	*2624*	*2190*

Table 5.16 Households in receipt of selected benefits by age and sex of informant

Diary sample

Age of informant	Sex of informant					
	Men		Women		Total	
	%	Base	%	Base	%	Base
16–24	14	213	16	189	15	402
25–34	10	253	18	253	14	506
35–49	8	345	10	384	9	729
50–64	14	271	14	282	14	553
All ages	11	1082	14	1108	12	2190

Table 5.17 Households in receipt of selected benefits by region and sex of informant

Diary sample

Region	Sex of informant					
	Men		Women		Total	
	%	Base	%	Base	%	Base
Scotland	23	96	17	95	20	191
Northern	14	272	18	289	16	561
Central, South West and Wales	11	363	17	367	14	730
London and South East	6	351	6	357	6	708
All regions	11	1082	14	1108	12	2190

Table 5.18 Households in receipt of selected benefits by social class of head of household and sex of informant

Diary sample

Social class of head of household	Sex of informant					
	Men		Women		Total	
	%	Base	%	Base	%	Base
I and II	4	377	5	384	4	761
III non-manual	6	138	14	141	10	279
III manual	12	376	11	347	11	723
IV and V	27	175	32	222	30	397
Not known	38	16	36	14	37	30
All cases	11	1082	14	1108	12	2190

Table 5.19 Number of adults per household by sex of informant for responding and diary samples and compared to 1987 General Household Survey sample

Number of adults in informant's household	Responding sample			Diary sample			1987 GHS*
	Men	Women	Total	Men	Women	Total	Total
	%	%	%	%	%	%	%
One	8	13	10	7	12	10	14
Two	52	54	53	52	55	54	53
Three	25	21	23	25	20	23	20
Four or more	15	12	14	16	12	14	14
Base = 100%	*1320*	*1315*	*2635*	*1087*	*1110*	*2197*	*20764***

* *General Household Survey 1987; proportion of adults aged 16 and over in households of different sizes*
** *General Household Survey 1987; total number of adults aged 16 and over*

Table 5.20 Household type by sex of informant for responding and diary samples

Household type	Responding sample			Diary sample		
	Men	Women	Total	Men	Women	Total
	%	%	%	%	%	%
Informant alone	8	8	8	7	8	7
Informant and spouse, no dependent children	34	36	35	33	34	34
Informant and parents, no spouse, no dependent children	21	12	16	20	11	16
Informant and others, no spouse, parents or dependent children	4	5	5	5	5	5
Informant and spouse with dependent children	33	32	32	34	35	35
Informant, no spouse, with dependent children	1	7	4	1	7	4
Base = 100%	*1320*	*1315*	*2635*	*1087*	*1110*	*2197*

Table 5.21 Household composition by age and sex of informant
Diary sample

Household composition	Sex and age of informant									
	Men				All ages 16–64	Women				All ages 16–64
	16–24	25–34	35–49	50–64		16–24	25–34	35–49	50–64	
	%	%	%	%	%	%	%	%	%	%
Informant alone	1	10	6	8	7	6	7	5	13	8
Informant and spouse, no dependent children	5	26	22	76	33	10	13	29	77	34
Informant and others, no spouse, no dependent children	85	19	7	6	25	62	9	6	6	16
Informant and spouse with dependent children	10	45	64	10	35	13	60	53	3	35
Informant, no spouse, with dependent children*	–	–	–	–	–	9	11	8	1	7
Base = 100%	214	254	346	273	1087	189	253	385	283	1110

* Due to small numbers in the sample, men living with dependent children are all included in the category 'Informant and spouse with dependent children'

Table 5.22 Household composition by sex of informant and region
Diary sample

Household composition	Sex of informant and region									
	Men					Women				
	Scotland	Northern	Central, South West and Wales	London and South East	Total	Scotland	Northern	Central, South West and Wales	London and South East	Total
	%	%	%	%	%	%	%	%	%	%
Informant alone	12	6	7	5	7	10	9	6	8	8
Informant and spouse, no dependent children	31	33	35	32	33	30	35	36	34	34
Informant and others, no spouse, no dependent children	28	32	21	22	25	22	16	13	18	16
Informant and spouse with dependent children	29	29	37	41	35	35	30	38	35	35
Informant, no spouse, with dependent children*	–	–	–	–	–	4	10	7	5	7
Base = 100%	96	274	364	353	1087	95	290	368	357	1110

* Due to small numbers in the sample, men living with dependent children are all included in the category 'Informant and spouse with dependent children'

Table 5.23 Household composition by sex of informant and social class of head of household
Diary sample

Household composition	Sex of informant and social class of head of household							
	Men				Women			
	I and II	III non-manual	III manual	IV and V	I and II	III non-manual	III manual	IV and V
	%	%	%	%	%	%	%	%
Informant alone	3	9	8	10	7	21	1	10
Informant and spouse, no dependent children	37	40	29	29	39	26	34	33
Informant and others, no spouse, no dependent children	20	20	27	29	14	23	16	14
Informant and spouse with dependent children	40	31	36	32	36	23	46	25
Informant, no spouse, with dependent children*	–	–	–	–	4	8	3	17
Base = 100%	377	138	378	177	386	141	347	222

* Due to small numbers in the sample, men living with dependent children are all included in the category 'Informant and spouse with dependent children'

Table 5.24 Percentage of diary sample who were on a slimming diet by age and sex of informant
Diary sample

Age	Percentage who were on a slimming diet					
	Men		Women		Total	
	%	Base	%	Base	%	Base
16–24	3	214	12	189	7	403
25–34	4	254	10	253	7	507
35–49	5	346	14	385	10	731
50–64	4	273	13	283	8	556
All ages	4	1087	12	1110	8	2197

Table 5.25 Percentage of diary sample who were taking food supplements by age and sex of informant
Diary sample

Age	Percentage who were taking food supplements					
	Men		Women		Total	
	%	Base	%	Base	%	Base
16–24	6	214	10	189	7	403
25–34	11	254	15	253	13	507
35–49	8	346	19	385	14	731
50–64	9	273	23	283	16	556
All ages	9	1087	17	1110	13	2197

Table 5.26 Percentage of diary sample who were taking food supplements by sex of informant and social class of head of household
Diary sample

Social class	Percentage who were taking food supplements					
	Men		Women		Total	
	%	Base	%	Base	%	Base
I and II	12	377	21	386	16	763
III non-manual	7	138	19	141	13	279
III manual	8	378	14	347	11	725
IV and V	6	177	16	222	11	399
All cases	9	1070	17	1096	13	2166

Table 5.27 Most common types of food supplement by sex of informant
Supplement takers in diary sample

Type of food supplement	Percentage of supplement takers using specified supplement		
	Men	Women	Total
	%	%	%
Multivitamins (without iron)	26	22	23
Multivitamins (with iron)	19	18	19
Cod/halibut liver oil	16	20	19
Vitamin C	26	13	17
Vitamin E	9	3	5
Vitamin B6	1	9	7
B complex vitamins	10	11	11
Iron	2	9	7
Calcium	3	6	5
Yeast	4	8	7
Base	93	194	287

Table 5.28 Whether informant was unwell during seven-day recording period by sex of informant for responding and diary samples

Whether unwell	Responding sample			Diary sample		
	Men	Women	Total	Men	Women	Total
	%	%	%	%	%	%
Unwell and eating affected	4	8	6	5	10	7
Unwell but eating not affected	6	9	8	8	10	9
Not unwell	72	68	70	87	80	84
No dietary record	18	16	17			
Base = 100%	*1320*	*1315*	*2635*	*1087*	*1110*	*2197*

Table 5.29 Percentage of diary sample whose eating was affected by their being unwell by age and sex of informant
Diary sample

Age	Percentage whose eating was affected by being unwell					
	Men		Women		Total	
	%	Base	%	Base	%	Base
16–24	10	214	10	189	10	403
25–34	7	254	14	253	11	507
35–49	2	346	9	385	6	731
50–64	2	273	7	283	4	556
All ages	5	1087	10	1110	7	2197

Table 5.30 Smoking behaviour by sex of informant for responding and diary samples

Smoking behaviour	Responding sample			Diary sample			GHS 1986*	
	Men	Women	Total	Men	Women	Total	Men	Women
	%	%	%	%	%	%	%	%
Non-smoker	66	65	65	67	66	66	66	69
Light smoker—fewer than 20 cigarettes per day	17	22	20	17	22	20	20	21
Heavy smoker—20 or more cigarettes per day	17	12	15	16	12	14	15	10
Base = 100%	*1318*	*1314*	*2632*	*1085*	*1109*	*2194*	*8874*	*10304*

* General Household Survey 1986; respondents aged 16 and over

Table 5.31 Smoking behaviour by sex and age of informant
Responding sample

Household type	Sex and age of informant									
	Men				All ages 16–64	Women				All ages 16–64
	16–24	25–34	35–49	50–64		16–24	25–34	35–49	50–64	
	%	%	%	%	%	%	%	%	%	%
Non-smoker	65	64	66	67	66	67	61	63	71	65
Light smoker	25	16	15	15	17	26	26	21	19	22
Heavy smoker	10	20	19	19	17	7	13	16	11	12
Base = 100%	*244*	*307*	*406*	*361*	*1318*	*214*	*287*	*447*	*366*	*1314*

Table 5.32 Smoking behaviour by sex of informant and social class of head of household
Responding sample

Smoking behaviour	Sex of informant and social class of head of household							
	Men				Women			
	I and II	III non-manual	III manual	IV and V	I and II	III non-manual	III manual	IV and V
	%	%	%	%	%	%	%	%
Non-smoker	78	68	59	54	77	71	59	51
Light smoker	11	17	20	23	19	18	25	28
Heavy smoker	11	15	22	23	5	11	16	21
Base = 100%	436	163	469	226	448	174	404	266

Table 5.33 Alcohol intake by sex and age of informant
Diary sample

Alcohol intake in dietary recording week	Sex and age of informant									
	Men				All ages 16–64	Women				All ages 16–64
	16–24	25–34	35–49	50–64		16–24	25–34	35–49	50–64	
	%	%	%	%	%	%	%	%	%	%
None	32	17	17	21	21	46	29	31	38	35
Less than 168 g (men); 112 g (women)	34	42	40	44	40	40	54	51	52	50
168 g to 400 g (men); 112 g to 280 g (women)	22	28	28	25	26	12	16	16	8	13
400 g or more (men); 280 g or more (women)	12	13	15	10	13	2	1	2	1	2
Base = 100%	214	254	346	273	1087	189	253	385	283	1110

Table 5.34 Percentage of total responding sample who were taking prescribed medicines by age and sex of informant
Responding sample

Age	Percentage taking prescribed medicines						Percentage taking prescribed medicines other than oral contraceptives					
	Men		Women		Total		Men		Women		Total	
	%	Base	%	Base	%	Base	%	Base	%	Base	%	Base
16–24	9	244	37	214	2	458	9	244	12	214	9	458
25–34	7	308	36	287	2	595	7	308	16	287	11	595
35–49	17	407	29	448	2	855	17	407	26	448	20	855
50–64	35	361	41	366	3	727	35	361	39	366	33	727
All ages	18	1320	35	1315	2	2635	18	1320	25	1315	20	2635

Table 5.35 Main types of prescribed medicines being taken by sex of informant
Responding sample and prescribed medicine takers

Drug type	Responding sample			Medicine takers			Medicine takers, excl. oral contraceptives**		
	Men	Women	Total	Men	Women	Total	Men	Women	Total
	%	%	%	%	%	%	%	%	%
Sex hormones*	–	11	5	–	34	22	n/a	n/a	n/a
Anti-hypertensives	6	4	5	36	8	20	36	17	25
Analgesics	4	6	5	22	12	20	22	26	24
Diuretics	3	4	3	16	8	14	16	18	17
Antibiotics	2	3	3	15	7	12	15	14	14
Antacids	1	1	1	8	2	5	8	5	6
Antidiabetics	1	1	1	9	2	5	9	3	6
Corticosteroids	1	1	1	4	2	3	4	4	4
Vitamin supplements	0	1	1	2	3	3	2	5	4
Drugs for anaemia	0	1	1	1	3	3	1	5	4
Total taking prescribed medicines	18%	35%	24%	219	421	640	219	300	519

* includes oral contraceptives
** includes sex hormones
n/a not applicable

6 Quantities of foods consumed

Information on the weights of individual foods eaten was collected in the dietary record, but in order to analyse patterns of food consumption it was necessary to simplify the data by grouping foods. Each food on the code list was allocated to one of 51 main groups which were further divided to 84 subgroups; the complete list of food groups is shown in Appendix H(i), and examples of the types of food included in each of the main food groups are given in Appendix H(ii).

For each member of the sample the quantity of food (grams) consumed during the recording week from each of the defined subgroups was calculated. It is therefore possible to show both the percentage of informants who consumed foods from each group, and the average amount of each food type consumed weekly by various groups within the sample.

6.1 Quantities of foods consumed by men and women

Table 6.1 shows the mean and median amounts of each food type consumed by the total sample and by those people within the sample who consumed the food. Also shown separately for men and women are the mean and median intakes of each food type for the consumers only. (*Table 6.1*)

For many of the food types listed, there was no difference in the proportion of men and of women eating the food during the recording week; however, the average amounts of each food type eaten by consumers was generally greater for men than for women.

Among cereal products white bread was the most commonly consumed item, eaten by 88% of men and 86% of women, and the average amount eaten by men who were consumers was 75% greater than that eaten by women. Women were more likely than men to have eaten wholemeal bread, 55% compared to 49%, (p<0.05) and other non-white breads, 50% to 39%, (p<0.01) but there was no clear evidence that women were more likely than men to have eaten the other high fibre products identified. In general, high fibre breakfast cereals were more popular than other breakfast cereals, eaten by 40% and 30% of the sample respectively.

About a quarter of the sample (26%) ate pasta during the week, and one third (33%) ate rice. On the other hand, biscuits and cakes, buns and pastries were eaten by about three quarters of the sample.

The proportion of the sample consuming whole milk was 88%, compared to 23% who consumed some semi-skimmed milk and 18% who consumed some skimmed milk. The mean amount of reduced fat milk drunk during the week was less than the mean amount of full fat milk consumed; this result is, however, difficult to interpret because of the possibility that individuals used more than one type of milk during the week.

A higher percentage of women than of men ate cottage cheese (10% compared to 4%), yoghurt (33% compared to 21%) and drank skimmed milk (21% compared to 15%), (p<0.01). The median quantities of cottage cheese and yoghurt consumed during the week were greater for women than for men.

Of the types of fat spreads identified, butter was the single most popular spread; it was eaten by 60% of the sample as a whole. There were few significant differences between men and women in the type of fat spreads consumed, although women were more likely to have eaten butter, 62% compared to 57%, (p<0.05) and men were more likely to have eaten 'other soft margarines', 30% compared to 23%, (p<0.01).

The types of meat consumed by the largest proportion of the sample were 'beef, veal and beef and veal dishes' (which includes minced beef, stews, casseroles, lasagne, etc) and bacon and ham (eaten by 76% and 77% respectively); 66% of the sample ate chicken or turkey during the week. Lamb and pork were less common (32% and 42% of the sample), and only a quarter of the sample (24%) had eaten liver or liver products during the week. The greater average weights of beef and poultry consumed does not necessarily indicate that larger quantities of meat were consumed but may reflect the inclusion of stews and casseroles in these meat categories. Men were more likely than women to have eaten most types of meat during the week and particularly burgers, sausages, meat pies and other meat products (p<0.05).

Fried white fish was the most commonly consumed type of fish, eaten by 48% of men and 40% of women (p<0.05). Other (non-fried) white fish was, however, eaten by a greater proportion of women than men, 28% compared to 23% (p<0.01). About one third (35%) of the total sample ate oily fish during the seven-day recording period.

Salad vegetables were eaten by a higher proportion of women than men, and the average amounts eaten by consumers were similar for both sexes. The most commonly consumed vegetables were peas, eaten by 72% of the sample, with carrots and leafy green vegetables each eaten by at least 60% of the sample. More men than women ate baked beans during the recording week, 51% compared to 44%, (p<0.01).

Potatoes were coded to three main groups: chips; other fried and roast potatoes; and other potatoes, chiefly boiled and mashed potato. The category of 'other potato products' included potato waffles and croquettes which were grilled or baked with no additional fat; these were consumed only rarely. Potatoes, other than roast or fried, were the most commonly consumed single food type, eaten by 90% of the sample. Three quarters of the sample, but more men than women, ate chips (p<0.01), and more than half (52%) ate roast or fried potatoes. On average, men consumed larger quantities than women both of fried or roast potatoes and of savoury snacks and crisps.

Women were more likely than men to have eaten all types of fresh fruit; 59% of women had eaten apples and pears and 31% had eaten oranges or related fruits, compared to 51% and 24% respectively of men, (p<0.01). The difference in the amount of fruit consumed by men and women was also less than for other products, suggesting that fruit was a more important part of the diet of women than of men. Canned fruit was not widely eaten, and twice as many informants ate fruit in syrup as fruit in juice, 18% compared to 9%, (p<0.01).

More men than women consumed table sugar during the week, 73% compared to 58%, (p<0.01). Women were, however, more likely than men to have eaten chocolate, 58% compared with 50%, or sugar confectionery, 25% compared with 17%, (p<0.01).

Fruit juice was, like fresh fruit, consumed by more women than men, 47% compared to 37%, (p<0.01). Amongst alcoholic beverages, wine and fortified wine were more likely to have been drunk by women than men, but beer was much more commonly drunk by men, 64% of men compared to 22% of women, (p<0.01). Overall, tea was more popular than coffee, consumed 88% of the sample compared to 80% who drank coffee; the average amount of tea drunk by consumers was greater than the average consumption of coffee by coffee-drinkers.

6.2 Variation by age group in the foods eaten
The proportion of consumers in each age group who ate foods of various types, and the mean and median amounts eaten by consumers are shown in Table 6.2.

(*Table 6.2*)

In general there are indications that the oldest age group had a more traditional diet; for example, people aged 50 to 64 were more likely than those aged 16 to 24 to have eaten non-fried potatoes and less likely to have eaten pasta or rice (p < 0.01). The oldest group was also more likely than the youngest to have eaten milk puddings, ice cream, cheese, canned fruit in juice and preserves (p < 0.01), and butter and canned fruit

in syrup (p < 0.05). On the other hand, more older informants had eaten a range of fresh foods, such as salad and green vegetables and fresh fruit, and also both oily fish and non-fried white fish (p < 0.01).

A number of snack and convenience items were less likely to have been eaten by older informants than by those aged under 35 years; for example, burgers and kebabs, savoury snacks, non-diet soft drinks and chocolate confectionery, were less likely to have been consumed by those aged 35 to 49 than by those aged 25 to 34 (p < 0.01). For most of these food types the amount eaten by the younger consumers was also larger than for the older age group, and this reinforces the variation in the diets of different age groups.

The youngest age group (aged 16 to 24) were the least likely group to have eaten many of the reduced fat or higher fibre food types. For example, foods such as wholemeal bread, high fibre breakfast cereals, semi-skimmed milk, and 'polyunsaturated' margarine were consumed less often by those aged 16 to 24 than by those aged 25 to 34 (p < 0.01). The youngest people were, conversely, more likely than the older group to have eaten other breakfast cereals and other soft magarines (p < 0.01).

The proportions consuming fortified wine and spirits all increased through the age range; the percentage who drank beer was greatest in the 25 to 34 age group, but the amount drunk by consumers was greatest amongst those aged 16 to 24 years. Those in the youngest age groups were significantly less likely than informants aged 25 to 34 to have drunk tea, coffee, spirits and wine (p < 0.01); they did, however, drink fruit juice more frequently than people aged 35 or over and they consumed non-diet soft drinks more frequently than any other group (p < 0.01).

The quantities of food eaten by consumers varied little across the age range and no systematic trend was evident. Older people tended on average to eat a larger amount of most fat spreads (except polyunsaturated margarine where there was little difference) and of salad vegetables, tomatoes, carrots, leafy green vegetables, apples and pears. The youngest age group consumed the greatest quantities of chips, meat pies, burgers and kebabs, non-diet soft drinks and beer.

6.3 Variation by region in the foods eaten
Table 6.3 gives similar information on the types of food eaten for informants in each of the four main regions identified throughout this Report. There was some variation between regions in the percentage of informants who consumed items of a particular type, but few clear trends emerge.

(*Table 6.3*)

There are some indications of a more traditional pattern of foods in the Northern region compared to the Central and South Eastern regions. In comparison with people in other regions in England and Wales, Northerners were less likely to eat pasta and rice and more likely to eat fried white fish and potato chips ($p < 0.01$). They were also less likely to consume salad vegetables and more likely to eat meat pies, with the greatest differences in consumption being between Northern England and the South East and London ($p < 0.01$).

Informants in Scotland were markedly less likely than informants living elsewhere to have eaten lamb, oily fish, skimmed milk, carrots, peas and leafy green vegetables, ($p < 0.01$); the likelihood of their eating polyunsaturated margarine was also somewhat less than for other informants ($p < 0.05$), and, compared with informants living in the Central region and in the South East and London, the Scots were significantly less likely to have eaten salad vegetables ($p < 0.01$). The data show that informants living in Scotland were more likely than others to have consumed semi-skimmed milk and non-diet soft drinks, and more likely than those in the Central and South Eastern regions of Great Britain to have eaten fried white fish ($p < 0.01$).

There are some differences between regions in the type of alcoholic drinks consumed. Informants in the Northern region were more likely than those in Scotland to have drunk beer, ($p < 0.01$), and the average amount consumed by drinkers was also greatest in this region; wine was drunk by a larger proportion of informants in London and the South East than elsewhere ($p < 0.01$). The percentage of the sample who drank spirits was similar in Scotland and the South East, and lower elsewhere, ($p < 0.05$), but consumers in Scotland on average drank almost twice as much during the week as did those in the South East.

6.4 Summary

Data have been presented on the average weekly consumption of foods in more than 80 food groups; variation in the proportion of the sample who consumed foods of each type and in the average amounts consumed according to the informant's sex and age, and the region in which he or she lived has also been considered.

There are indications that women were more likely than men to have chosen food items which have a 'healthy image'; more women ate wholemeal bread, reduced fat milk, salad vegetables and fresh fruit. A similar influence may be seen in that women were less likely to have eaten fried white fish, sausages, meat pies, and chips but, on the other hand, more women than men had eaten confectionery during the week. Men consumed greater amounts of most foods than did women, but women ate relatively large amounts of vegetables, other than potatoes, and of fruit.

The main difference in the consumption of food types by age of informant was between the extremes of the age range. Older people were more likely to have eaten traditional foods such as potatoes, milk puddings, butter, and preserves, and also to have eaten fruit and vegetables. Younger adults were more likely than those aged 35 and over to have eaten savoury snacks and foods often associated with 'take-away' meals such as meat pies, burgers and kebabs.

Some regional differences emerged in the types of foods consumed. There are indications of a more traditional pattern of eating in Northern England. Beer drinking was also more prevalent in the North whereas informants in the South East were more likely to have drunk wine during the recording week.

All foods contain nutrients, but the range and amount of nutrients vary from food to food and it is the intake of nutrients which plays an important role in the functioning of body systems. In the following chapters the nutrient intake of the sample is examined in detail, but the subject of food consumption is returned to in Chapter 13 where a classification of dietary types within the sample is presented.

Reference

1. Ministry of Agriculture, Fisheries and Food. *Household Food Consumption and Expenditure: 1986.* Annual report of the National Food Survey Committee, HMSO (London, 1987).

Table 6.1 Total quantities (grams) of food consumed during seven-day recording period by sex of informant

Type of food	Men			Women			Total				
	Consumers only		% who ate	Consumers only		% who ate	Consumers only		% who ate	Total sample	
	Mean	Median		Mean	Median		Mean	Median		Mean	Median
	(g)	(g)	%	(g)	(g)	%	(g)	(g)	%	(g)	(g)
Pasta	271	224	25	218	186	27	243	204	26	63	0
Rice	353	241	35	241	194	30	301	218	33	98	0
Other cereals	181	122	47	140	102	46	161	114	46	74	0
White bread	668	580	88	381	331	86	524	421	87	458	360
Wholemeal bread	514	404	49	310	241	55	405	296	52	209	40
Other bread	245	159	39	189	131	50	213	141	45	96	0
High fibre bkfast cereals	290	194	39	219	161	42	253	171	40	102	0
Other breakfast cereals	161	119	31	112	82	28	138	96	30	41	0
Biscuits	141	102	74	121	88	80	131	93	77	100	64
Fruit pies	180	150	23	139	116	18	162	132	20	33	0
Buns, cakes & pastries	289	216	72	230	188	77	258	200	75	193	129
Milk puddings	278	240	14	225	192	14	251	212	14	35	0
Ice cream	148	110	34	112	84	36	129	98	35	45	0
Sponge type puddings	189	150	12	150	137	9	171	149	10	18	0
Other puddings	303	224	48	247	185	46	276	209	47	129	0
Whole milk	1440	1218	89	1166	949	87	1303	1083	88	1148	897
Semi-skimmed milk	1324	1068	21	953	736	24	1122	892	23	254	0
Skimmed milk	1036	802	15	951	744	21	986	759	18	181	0
Other milk and cream	127	60	41	137	60	45	132	60	43	56	0
Cottage cheese	104	88	4	127	87	10	120	87	7	8	0
Other cheese	160	129	80	118	96	79	139	108	80	111	84
Yoghurt	288	232	21	311	242	33	303	239	27	82	0
Eggs and egg dishes	227	181	82	172	140	78	200	166	80	160	123
Butter	88	65	57	69	47	62	78	54	60	47	15
Polyunsaturated margarine	98	73	34	67	55	32	82	61	33	27	0
Low fat spread	99	73	18	67	49	21	82	58	19	16	0
Block margarine	54	28	23	44	20	20	49	22	21	11	0
Other soft margarine	95	62	30	58	41	23	78	50	26	21	0
Yellow spreads	95	66	10	60	46	12	76	53	11	8	0
Other spreads & fats	16	15	5	15	10	4	15	12	5	1	0
Bacon & ham	171	133	82	114	90	73	144	112	77	111	80
Beef & veal	388	314	79	291	234	72	341	278	76	258	191
Lamb	227	149	34	160	112	31	195	128	32	63	0
Pork	188	136	44	130	100	40	160	116	42	67	0
Coated chicken	167	136	9	142	119	9	154	128	9	14	0
Chicken & turkey	275	214	68	223	169	63	250	194	66	164	108
Liver	127	106	23	114	90	24	120	100	24	29	0
Burgers & kebabs	197	140	31	142	106	26	171	118	28	48	0
Sausages	168	126	58	110	92	48	142	112	54	75	32
Meat pies & pastries	298	221	60	198	155	47	253	183	53	134	60
Other meat products	231	158	48	166	104	42	200	128	45	91	0
Fried white fish	205	175	48	162	139	40	185	162	44	82	0
Other white fish	182	155	23	162	139	28	171	146	26	44	0
Shellfish	138	79	12	73	50	15	101	57	14	14	0
Oily fish	164	119	34	107	85	36	135	99	35	47	0
Raw carrots	73	46	12	72	48	17	72	46	15	10	0
Raw tomatoes	162	124	66	150	119	71	156	122	69	107	63
Other salad vegetables	168	113	70	167	117	75	168	115	72	121	66
Peas	179	148	73	131	102	71	155	121	72	111	78
Green beans	123	96	22	98	75	21	111	86	22	24	0
Baked beans	249	192	51	171	138	44	212	166	48	101	0
Leafy green vegetables	198	154	62	161	128	62	179	138	62	110	68
Carrots	131	100	61	109	84	58	120	92	60	71	42
Fresh tomatoes (not raw)	102	71	21	78	60	18	91	65	19	18	0
Other vegetables	341	251	88	289	221	88	315	237	88	277	200
Potato chips	458	372	81	311	245	69	389	306	75	291	207
Fried/roast potatoes	238	188	55	154	124	49	198	150	52	103	41
Other potato products	116	110	3	111	102	4	113	106	4	4	0
Other potatoes	643	556	90	435	383	91	538	462	90	486	419
Savoury snacks	93	65	49	70	55	52	81	56	51	41	7
Apples & pears	381	266	51	336	244	59	356	252	55	195	75
Oranges & other citrus	248	183	24	265	192	31	258	188	28	71	0
Bananas	212	150	26	194	144	37	201	148	32	64	0
Canned fruit in juice	147	121	8	184	114	10	167	115	9	15	0
Canned fruit in syrup	168	134	18	135	108	17	152	122	18	27	0
Unsalted nuts & mixes	60	29	12	66	26	13	63	28	12	8	0
Other fruit	284	190	38	308	182	49	298	184	44	131	0

Table 6.1 (*continued*)   **Total quantities (grams) of food consumed during seven-day recording period by sex of informant**

Type of food	Men			Women			Total				
	Consumers only		% who ate	Consumers only		% who ate	Consumers only		% who ate	Total sample	
	Mean	Median		Mean	Median		Mean	Median		Mean	Median
	(g)	(g)	%	(g)	(g)	%	(g)	(g)	%	(g)	(g)
Sugar	227	179	73	150	90	58	193	136	65	126	35
Preserves	88	58	47	64	38	50	76	48	48	37	0
Other sugars	27	20	5	28	22	6	28	20	6	2	0
Sugar confectionery	57	28	17	46	27	25	50	28	21	10	0
Chocolate confectionery	126	77	50	111	75	58	118	77	54	64	18
Fruit juice	691	483	37	586	440	47	631	457	42	267	0
Diet soft drinks	928	372	11	793	420	20	842	403	16	131	0
Other soft drinks	1230	748	61	955	600	62	1090	672	61	669	240
Liqueurs	60	46	2	84	50	7	78	48	5	4	0
Spirits	176	92	24	107	69	21	143	84	22	32	0
Wine	562	362	30	485	327	36	520	350	33	172	0
Fortified wine	266	122	10	183	120	20	211	120	15	31	0
Beers	5148	3731	64	1352	726	22	4154	2490	43	1785	0
Cider, perry, etc	1158	574	10	836	574	8	1006	574	9	92	0
Coffee	3251	2222	79	3537	2294	82	3398	2232	80	2725	1616
Tea	4280	3826	88	4019	3710	88	4147	3741	88	3651	3299
Miscellaneous	462	339	96	395	301	95	429	317	95	409	302

Table 6.2   Total quantities (grams) of food consumed during seven-day recording period by age of informant
Consumers only

Type of food	Age of informant											
	16–24			25–34			35–49			50–64		
	Mean	Median	% who ate	Mean	Median	% who ate	Mean	Median	% who ate	Mean	Median	% who ate
	(g)	(g)	%	(g)	(g)	%	(g)	(g)	%	(g)	(g)	%
Pasta	266	220	28	253	206	35	236	202	26	209	182	16
Rice	334	244	34	290	230	42	301	207	34	281	198	21
Other cereals	204	153	51	175	122	50	148	109	47	123	80	39
White bread	578	465	92	497	408	89	523	419	86	510	410	83
Wholemeal bread	392	230	40	385	296	50	400	296	55	433	316	57
Other bread	191	136	35	217	140	46	201	135	45	235	154	51
High fibre bkfast cereals	204	138	27	223	176	40	288	193	43	254	176	46
Other breakfast cereals	159	105	43	130	92	32	128	89	26	133	112	22
Biscuits	126	92	65	127	89	78	137	89	79	129	101	82
Fruit pies	150	120	14	152	124	16	152	120	23	183	150	25
Buns, cakes & pastries	227	173	66	208	158	69	289	217	79	276	233	81
Milk puddings	249	199	11	211	202	12	276	210	14	252	229	19
Ice cream	128	100	27	143	100	32	122	96	38	128	92	39
Sponge type puddings	186	140	10	155	130	9	167	150	11	179	150	11
Other puddings	276	209	42	250	172	45	284	220	48	286	226	51
Whole milk	1370	1075	87	1279	1100	89	1251	1013	88	1344	1154	87
Semi-skimmed milk	1127	717	17	985	744	24	1169	897	25	1187	1018	22
Skimmed milk	623	465	14	921	594	18	1159	930	20	997	915	20
Other milk and cream	141	47	31	146	60	42	100	54	44	155	63	50
Cottage cheese	185	148	3	84	74	8	129	98	6	124	85	10
Other cheese	131	98	71	138	112	77	144	105	82	140	116	84
Yoghurt	305	168	27	292	239	29	310	247	27	301	244	26
Eggs and egg dishes	201	152	73	207	179	78	201	166	83	191	163	83
Butter	66	42	54	71	44	61	76	54	60	94	73	63
Polyunsaturated margarine	71	50	26	80	59	35	89	64	35	81	66	34
Low fat spread	78	53	17	73	45	22	75	57	17	101	77	21
Block margarine	44	20	23	46	26	25	52	26	23	54	22	15
Other soft margarine	72	45	38	72	53	28	77	55	25	98	71	18
Yellow spreads	76	47	10	63	52	9	74	52	13	89	71	9
Other spreads & fats	16	10	5	18	15	4	15	13	5	13	11	5

Table 6.2 (*continued*) **Total quantities (grams) of food consumed during seven-day recording period by age of informant**
Consumers only

Type of food	Age of informant											
	16–24			25–34			35–49			50–64		
	Mean	Median	% who ate	Mean	Median	% who ate	Mean	Median	% who ate	Mean	Median	% who ate
	(g)	(g)	%	(g)	(g)	%	(g)	(g)	%	(g)	(g)	%
Bacon & ham	142	102	72	133	112	74	141	109	79	156	124	82
Beef & veal	323	265	72	404	330	73	345	298	78	294	228	77
Lamb	195	114	31	204	124	26	175	126	34	211	140	38
Pork	148	114	41	173	116	43	155	117	40	163	121	44
Coated chicken	168	138	10	148	132	12	161	124	8	134	111	6
Chicken & turkey	259	200	63	262	207	66	247	190	69	235	183	62
Liver	117	100	16	123	96	20	120	98	28	119	102	28
Burgers & kebabs	218	170	45	185	143	35	133	103	26	120	106	13
Sausages	162	114	54	147	116	52	131	105	55	137	101	49
Meat pies & pastries	316	236	61	246	180	54	240	178	52	223	180	49
Other meat products	254	166	39	188	120	46	202	145	44	178	113	50
Fried white fish	195	169	42	188	150	43	181	158	45	182	166	46
Other white fish	160	123	18	157	130	20	164	138	28	189	160	34
Shellfish	104	76	10	82	57	14	121	56	17	85	57	13
Oily fish	118	99	24	120	94	33	140	102	36	145	102	42
Raw carrots	78	60	10	65	42	13	76	45	17	70	53	15
Raw tomatoes	121	85	53	143	115	67	159	130	73	181	136	76
Other salad vegetables	125	83	64	168	117	72	177	119	76	181	125	74
Peas	154	118	73	153	122	74	162	130	71	150	117	69
Green beans	92	70	18	97	78	20	119	93	23	121	92	25
Baked beans	248	182	56	235	188	52	199	155	47	167	145	38
Leafy green vegetables	145	122	49	166	124	53	171	134	68	214	165	71
Carrots	105	88	52	118	87	55	121	92	63	129	105	65
Fresh tomatoes (not raw)	70	62	10	77	62	16	77	61	21	117	84	27
Other vegetables	265	186	80	304	223	86	331	244	92	333	267	91
Potato chips	544	439	85	416	327	77	345	290	75	278	223	64
Fried/roast potatoes	220	152	51	198	150	50	195	150	55	184	147	50
Other potato products	118	100	4	118	112	4	109	107	3	111	106	4
Other potatoes	497	412	88	503	414	85	532	446	93	603	556	93
Savoury snacks	106	83	70	85	61	61	68	53	48	59	40	31
Apples & pears	286	204	41	351	224	49	351	242	61	402	319	61
Oranges & other citrus	252	190	21	253	180	26	260	187	27	261	198	35
Bananas	190	146	23	195	143	31	211	150	32	200	151	38
Canned fruit in juice	123	112	6	141	128	10	207	121	8	165	101	12
Canned fruit in syrup	132	110	14	130	109	15	150	124	20	178	140	20
Unsalted nuts & mixes	47	26	7	59	30	14	73	30	13	61	25	13
Other fruit	232	147	30	245	150	39	299	183	49	358	246	53
Sugar	163	122	72	189	140	67	216	162	65	188	101	58
Preserves	66	36	32	60	38	43	75	48	53	91	66	58
Other sugars	22	22	4	33	25	6	26	20	7	28	24	6
Sugar confectionery	69	40	26	44	25	20	40	19	21	54	30	18
Chocolate confectionery	162	124	64	123	77	61	102	70	52	90	60	44
Fruit juice	676	447	46	665	474	48	604	434	40	591	486	37
Diet soft drinks	778	399	18	1039	639	17	743	423	16	837	283	12
Other soft drinks	1689	1083	82	1073	690	68	889	525	56	667	446	47
Liqueurs	110	46	6	61	46	5	77	48	4	64	50	5
Spirits	95	48	13	106	69	20	164	92	25	162	98	27
Wine	462	277	19	496	362	36	575	375	39	480	313	32
Fortified wine	161	100	8	189	100	12	246	166	15	203	123	21
Beers	5081	3444	39	3926	2399	51	4163	2403	44	3709	2009	37
Cider, perry etc	1512	736	12	1029	574	12	835	574	8	555	426	6
Coffee	2225	1515	67	3149	2299	82	4119	2626	86	3325	2222	81
Tea	2740	2111	77	3907	3619	86	4507	4054	90	4726	4454	96
Miscellaneous	408	286	94	433	332	95	441	340	97	423	312	95

Table 6.3 Total quantities (grams) of food consumed during seven-day recording period by region
Consumers only

Type of food	Region											
	Scotland			Northern			Central, South West and Wales			London and South East		
	Mean	Median	% who ate	Mean	Median	% who ate	Mean	Median	% who ate	Mean	Median	% who ate
	(g)	(g)	%	(g)	(g)	%	(g)	(g)	%	(g)	(g)	%
Pasta	247	218	37	242	200	18	220	183	30	259	220	32
Rice	265	207	35	300	217	28	310	218	37	304	221	40
Other cereals	186	152	30	170	120	52	146	100	45	162	116	47
White bread	564	488	86	537	464	89	545	439	86	483	381	88
Wholemeal bread	331	227	46	408	281	53	456	358	53	363	274	50
Other bread	217	160	45	221	156	44	205	122	44	215	151	46
High fibre bkfast cereals	244	180	35	243	159	38	254	160	44	262	194	40
Other breakfast cereals	122	101	34	133	90	29	147	95	29	136	96	29
Biscuits	149	102	79	120	86	77	140	98	77	125	89	75
Fruit pies	145	120	16	151	121	18	164	139	22	169	140	22
Buns, cakes & pastries	208	160	69	261	213	73	274	210	77	251	193	75
Milk puddings	261	214	13	251	214	12	257	220	14	244	201	15
Ice cream	123	100	36	124	93	30	127	96	36	136	100	38
Sponge type puddings	143	114	7	184	156	8	159	138	13	184	150	10
Other puddings	225	160	41	260	204	40	286	216	51	286	220	49
Whole milk	1204	1086	84	1237	1039	87	1331	1084	89	1350	1099	89
Semi-skimmed milk	1189	1001	37	1147	888	21	1135	898	21	1057	821	22
Skimmed milk	575	570	5	998	790	17	1060	882	24	906	612	18
Other milk and cream	76	47	27	131	60	40	112	57	45	161	60	47
Cottage cheese	99	91	7	139	92	8	107	85	7	123	83	6
Other cheese	128	87	84	126	97	72	142	110	83	148	121	81
Yoghurt	274	247	20	306	226	26	299	242	28	310	240	28
Eggs and egg dishes	210	173	83	203	167	81	200	165	81	194	164	77
Butter	69	47	63	78	53	56	84	57	57	76	55	65
Polyunsaturated margarine	87	61	26	84	69	35	89	65	34	73	54	32
Low fat spread	51	46	18	93	69	17	80	55	19	84	59	22
Block margarine	30	20	19	37	16	20	61	28	22	50	26	23
Other soft margarine	85	64	34	82	48	35	76	50	22	73	50	22
Yellow spreads	73	42	8	76	47	9	76	56	14	76	54	9
Other spreads & fats	21	23	5	15	15	5	16	12	4	13	10	4
Bacon & ham	136	112	82	154	116	80	137	110	77	144	108	75
Beef & veal	351	305	81	342	265	76	319	259	76	362	296	74
Lamb	211	120	17	179	120	30	204	128	35	193	136	35
Pork	147	110	36	153	113	44	157	116	42	172	126	42
Coated chicken	159	123	10	161	133	7	128	119	7	165	143	12
Chicken & turkey	266	199	61	239	182	63	245	181	69	260	208	65
Liver	109	90	18	129	112	25	122	102	23	113	90	26
Burgers & kebabs	170	129	29	166	126	29	139	105	26	205	150	30
Sausages	147	115	51	136	111	49	142	110	52	143	112	56
Meat pies & pastries	251	180	52	284	198	59	243	180	54	237	180	48
Other meat products	170	105	53	201	118	49	197	132	46	215	150	39
Fried white fish	189	152	52	186	160	51	177	155	41	192	180	40
Other white fish	179	132	22	165	143	29	163	140	24	181	164	26
Shellfish	82	50	14	120	76	13	88	50	11	103	57	17
Oily fish	147	106	29	142	102	39	115	90	48	144	106	36
Raw carrots	64	38	15	68	53	13	73	51	15	76	45	15
Raw tomatoes	149	114	66	139	108	66	164	132	70	162	124	70
Other salad vegetables	140	95	63	162	108	68	167	110	74	178	133	77
Peas	114	86	59	155	122	77	167	140	74	151	114	68
Green beans	93	81	13	106	80	13	113	89	28	113	85	25
Baked beans	201	159	45	209	171	50	227	164	48	203	160	46
Leafy green vegetables	165	137	42	155	128	60	178	140	64	199	150	65
Carrots	103	90	39	123	94	65	120	96	63	120	90	57
Fresh tomatoes (not raw)	78	58	18	90	63	18	86	65	19	98	70	22
Other vegetables	288	167	83	288	220	88	305	240	88	353	259	89
Potato chips	415	333	80	445	369	81	390	300	73	329	254	70
Fried/roast potatoes	171	141	30	179	137	43	202	150	57	208	170	59
Other potato products	125	108	7	121	102	3	107	106	2	107	106	4
Other potatoes	478	417	92	524	438	89	582	504	92	518	438	90
Savoury snacks	86	55	53	78	53	47	85	56	55	77	58	49

Table 6.3 (*continued*) **Total quantities (grams) of food consumed during seven-day recording period by region**
Consumers only

Type of food	Region											
	Scotland			Northern			Central, South West and Wales			London and South East		
	Mean	Median	% who ate	Mean	Median	% who ate	Mean	Median	% who ate	Mean	Median	% who ate
	(g)	(g)	%	(g)	(g)	%	(g)	(g)	%	(g)	(g)	%
Apples & pears	313	219	49	305	213	51	377	277	58	381	265	56
Oranges & other citrus	320	224	34	242	194	26	262	180	27	244	182	28
Bananas	220	151	31	200	148	27	203	141	35	195	150	32
Canned fruit in juice	112	98	8	157	101	9	145	117	9	211	126	9
Canned fruit in syrup	148	122	23	133	102	16	154	124	18	165	132	18
Unsalted nuts & mixes	46	20	14	69	30	9	83	35	11	52	30	16
Other fruit	253	148	43	291	179	37	288	195	45	321	185	50
Sugar	151	102	61	189	130	67	200	138	67	198	150	63
Preserves	96	66	46	71	43	49	77	50	49	73	45	48
Other sugars	19	8	3	27	26	4	31	23	6	26	20	7
Sugar confectionery	43	27	17	55	30	23	44	24	21	54	30	20
Chocolate confectionery	122	72	55	112	72	53	110	73	53	129	88	56
Fruit juice	584	409	43	599	442	40	635	440	41	663	510	45
Diet soft drinks	969	530	20	969	424	14	795	372	16	754	402	15
Other soft drinks	1144	708	72	1227	660	61	1001	640	60	1056	684	61
Liqueurs	64	56	5	88	50	6	70	46	4	79	49	5
Spirits	244	141	27	121	70	19	147	89	19	127	75	27
Wine	545	280	26	507	350	29	471	350	29	556	354	43
Fortified wine	312	126	13	187	106	12	193	114	15	218	137	17
Beers	4175	2583	35	4849	3211	47	4254	2540	43	3432	2023	42
Cider, perry etc	1316	764	6	1422	720	9	759	574	11	953	574	8
Coffee	3560	2258	75	3345	2121	78	3312	2222	80	3484	2502	83
Tea	3523	3041	84	4208	4049	88	4316	3894	90	4082	3680	87
Miscellaneous	607	489	93	414	306	96	443	342	97	378	279	94

7 Nutrient intake: energy and alcohol

7.1 Introduction

As explained in Chapter 2, all foods consumed during the seven-day recording period were assigned a code number from a detailed coding list of foods; this code number allowed cross-reference to a computerised databank on which each food was defined in terms of its energy content and 35 nutrients. In this and the following four chapters data are presented on the intakes of each of these nutrients for men and women separately, looking at variation in intake according to the main characteristics of the sample. Results are presented both as absolute intakes and as percentages of energy (or per 1000kcal). For selected nutrients the percentage of total intake derived from different food groups is also shown.

Chapter 12 looks in greater detail at variation in nutrient intake and dietary patterns, using analysis of variance to identify those characteristics of the sample which explain most variance in nutrient and food intake. The final aspect of the discussion of nutrient intake concerns foods eaten outside the home, and in Chapter 14 data are presented on the proportion of recorded intake of the major nutrients which was derived from 'eating out'.

The recorded nutrient intakes of the sample have, where appropriate, been compared with existing guidelines and recommendations on intake. Recommendations on levels of fat and fibre in the diet published in recent reports by COMA[1] and NACNE[2] are used. More generally, the Department of Health defines recommended daily amounts (RDAs) for intakes of a range of nutrients,[3,4] and these are quoted at the relevant points in the text. These are currently under review.

The recommended daily amount of food energy is equivalent to the estimated average requirement for groups of people. The energy requirement of individuals will vary according to differences in basal metabolic rate and voluntary activity. The RDAs for nutrients are not minimum requirements. They are derived from estimates of nutrient requirements together with a considerable margin of safety. They are defined as 'the average amount of the nutrient which should be provided per head in a group of people if the needs of practically all members of the group are to be met'. Nearly all individuals would be expected to have requirements below these amounts, and a nutrient intake below the RDA should not therefore be taken to imply dietary deficiency. However, the greater the proportion of people with intakes below the RDA, the greater the possibility that some individuals may be undernourished.

7.2 Intake of energy

Energy intake is conventionally expressed either in kilocalories (kcal) or megajoules (MJ); throughout the text of this Report kilocalories are primarily referred to, but the conversion to megajoules is given in brackets. The values for energy shown are the combined intakes from food and alcohol and, unless otherwise stated, proportions of energy derived from different parts of the diet are calculated using energy from all sources, including alcohol.

The average energy intake recorded for men in the sample was about 46% higher than that for women; the average for men was 2450kcal (10.3MJ), and that for women was 1680kcal (7.05MJ) (p < 0.01). The median values for recorded intakes were close to mean values, indicating that the distribution of intakes was not very skewed. *(Table 7.1)*

For both sexes, average intake was similar for all ages up to 49 years, but decreased among the oldest group of respondents; mean intakes were significantly lower among men and women aged 50 to 64 compared with those aged 35 to 49 (p < 0.01). Less than a quarter (22%) of men recorded an average daily intake below 2000kcal (8.4MJ). At the other end of the range of energy intakes, 16% of men consumed more than 3000kcal (12.6MJ), but men at the top of the age range covered by the survey were less likely (7%) than all men to have an intake of this size (p < 0.01). In comparison, some 34% of the sample of women recorded a daily intake of less than 1500kcal (6.3MJ), and only 23% of women recorded more than 2000kcal (8.4MJ) daily.

In order to compare recorded energy intakes with the RDAs for energy, it is necessary to make some assumptions about the level of activity of this sample. Assuming that the majority of individuals in the sample were in the range from sedentary to moderately active gives an RDA for men aged 18 to 34 of between 2510kcal (10.5MJ) and 2900kcal (12.1MJ), and between 2400kcal (10.1MJ) and 2750kcal (11.5MJ) for men aged 35 to 64. The RDA for most women aged 18 to 54 is 2150kcal (9.0MJ), reducing to 1900kcal (7.9MJ) for women aged 55 or over.

The RDAs for energy differ from those for nutrients in that they are defined as the mean estimated requirement; thus it would be expected that roughly half of a group of individuals would have requirements greater, and roughly half lower, than the RDA. There are, however, practical difficulties in defining average requirements and there is some evidence that requirements are declining with time.

Recorded energy intakes were also compared with those reported by other recent studies in Great Britain and Northern Ireland, and the results are shown in Table 7.2. It can be seen that, both for men and women, the energy intakes recorded in this survey were similar to those in the only other surveys of large samples, carried out in Northern Ireland[5], in South Wales[7,8] and in Ipswich, Stoke and Wakefield.[9] The average energy intake recorded for women was, however, lower than that reported for the smaller sample in the Cambridge study.[6] Average energy intakes were also low in comparison with accepted values for habitual intakes. This is a common result for dietary surveys of the general population.   (*Table 7.2*)

7.2.1 Dieters and the unwell

Informants who were slimming or whose eating was affected by their being unwell during the recording period would be expected to have lower energy intakes than the rest of the sample.

Four per cent of men and 12% of women in the diary sample said that they were on a slimming diet at the time of the interview (see Chapter 5). Table 7.3 shows that average and median intakes were consistently lower for dieting than for non-dieting informants, although the sample of dieting men was relatively small. Both men and women who were on a slimming diet had an average reported energy intake which was about one fifth lower than that of non-dieting informants ($p < 0.01$). Self-defined slimmers were a varied group who recorded a wide range of energy intakes; the upper 2.5 percentile values for dieting men and women were no less than 90% of the equivalent values for non-dieting informants.   (*Table 7.3*)

Table 7.4 shows the energy intake for men and women who said that their eating had been affected by their being unwell during the recording period. Energy intakes were lower both for men and women ($p < 0.01$), although, as with dieters, there were again very few men in the unwell category. The difference between the average daily energy intakes of those whose eating was affected by their being unwell and others was greater for women than for men. As for slimmers, the unwell had a wide range of intakes, and the upper 2.5 percentile values were only 10% lower than those of informants who were not unwell.   (*Table 7.4*)

Although dieters and the unwell had lower energy intakes than other members of the sample they have not been excluded from the analyses in this Report since, at any time, there will be a number of individuals in the population who are either dieting or unwell. The figures for nutrient intakes presented are therefore based on the total diary sample, which represents a

cross-section of the population in Great Britain aged 16 to 64 years.

7.2.2 Quality of data for recorded energy intake

Although low in comparison with RDAs, the average values for energy intake recorded for this sample were similar to those reported by other surveys using either a weighed inventory or other method.[5,7,8,9] In assessing the quality of data from any study of dietary intake it may be helpful to distinguish between the precision and validity of the recording method used. Precision relates to whether the dietary intake in the specific period of the study has been accurately measured, while validity reflects whether the measured intake is an accurate record of an individual's habitual diet.

Sources of imprecision in weighed records include the choice of foods included in the code list, the choice of the food composition information used and, more importantly, the process of recording by the individual.[10] For foods eaten outside the home there is also possible error due to estimation of portion sizes. As outlined in Chapter 2, attempts were made to minimise possible inaccuracy in the process of recording in a number of ways. Interviewers made frequent checking calls to each informant, they collected information in the interview on the informant's usual eating pattern, checked for consistency in the pattern of eating during the week, and asked specifically about any meals or snacks which appeared to have been missed from the record.

The comparison of energy intake over a specified period to a reliable measure of energy expenditure can help to indicate whether the energy recorded is likely to represent habitual intake. The dietary energy intake of an individual who is neither gaining nor losing weight is, over a period of days, equal to the energy expended on maintenance and physical activity. An individual's particular energy requirements are dependent both on his or her basal metabolism, which is the energy required to maintain life, and on the level of physical activity undertaken. Although it was possible only to make an approximate assessment of, rather than measure, basal metabolic rate, the ratio of energy intake to calculated basal metabolic rate can be compared with values for this ratio compiled by the World Health Organisation.

Approximate values for the basal metabolic rate of individuals in this sample were calculated using simple regression equations based on body weight and the age and sex of the informant.[11] Table 7.5 shows the distributions for the ratio of energy intake to calculated basal metabolic rate for the total sample of men and women; average values for the ratio were 1.39 for men and 1.22 for women. Studies by the World Health Organisation have shown that values below 1.2 for this ratio are rare, and habitual intakes of this order are unlikely to meet requirements. Values of less than 1.2 were calculated for 30% of men and 47% of women in this sample. Extreme low values of this order are possible over a short period but could not be maintained over a long period as habitual intake. *(Table 7.5)*

It has been seen that informants who were on a slimming diet and those whose eating was affected by their being unwell had lower average energy intakes than the rest of the sample; for these groups recorded energy intake would not be expected to represent habitual intake. The exclusion both of dieters and of those who were unwell from the sample gives average values for energy intake of 2480kcal (10.4MJ) for men and of 1750kcal (7.3MJ) for women; average values for the ratio of energy intake to basal metabolic rate increase slightly to 1.41 for men and 1.28 for women. Some 40% of non-dieting, well women, and 27% of men had ratios with a value of less than 1.2.

The low average recorded energy intakes of this sample may have arisen for a number of reasons. It could be that the sample had genuinely low habitual intakes, but the evidence presented on the ratio of energy to calculated basal metabolic rate suggests this is unlikely. Other than this, there are two main possible reasons for the low energy intakes. It is not possible to draw conclusions as to which of these is the most likely, nor are they mutually exclusive, but it appears that the effect is stronger for women than for men.

First, the recorded intake may not reflect habitual intake because of conscious or subconscious underrecording or omission by members of the sample. If this were the reason for the low recorded energy intakes, then the intake reported would be an accurate record neither of habitual diet nor of the diet during the recording week.

An alternative explanation is that individuals taking part in the survey modified their diet. This might have taken the form of simplification of the diet so that it was easier to record, or individuals might have taken the opportunity, while recording the food that they were eating, to restrict their intake in some way, for example to aid weight control. In both cases the modified diet could be an accurate record of food eaten during the recording week, but would not correspond to the informant's habitual diet.

It is concluded that the level of energy intake recorded for both men and women is broadly consistent with other dietary surveys of the general population, either using weighed inventories or other techniques, but there is evidence that the recorded intake underrepresents habitual intakes. This is more apparent in women than in men, perhaps because women tend to be more sensitive about the issues of food consumption and weight. There is, however, no evidence from the data that underreporting or modified diets are confined to particular subgroups of the sample.

7.2.3 Contribution of main food types to total energy intake

Table 7.6 shows the contribution of major food types (see Appendix H(i)) to total energy intake for men and women, and for the sample as a whole. The largest contribution to recorded energy intake was from cereal products, which provided 30% of the overall average energy intake. Within the cereal products category bread provided 13% of total energy intake, and biscuits, buns, cakes and pastries together provided 9% of the total. Meat and meat products, vegetables (including potatoes) and milk and milk products were the next largest contributors to energy intake, providing 16%, 12% and 11% respectively of average energy intake. *(Table 7.6)*

There was little variation between men and women in the sources of energy, except that men derived a significantly larger proportion of their energy intake from beverages than did women (p<0.01); this is related to the greater consumption of beer and cider by men, which provided 7% of their total energy intake.

Figures 7.1 to 7.6 show the contribution of the main food groups to total energy intake of men and women by age of informant, social class of head of household and regional classification.

The contribution of cereal products to energy intake increased markedly with increasing age of informant and, to a lesser extent, the contribution of milk and fats was also greater among older groups. There was a marked decline with age in the percentage of energy provided by vegetables. The percentage of energy provided by meat and meat products, sugars and beverages also decreased with increasing age of informant. *(Figs 7.1 & 7.2)*

There were some differences in the sources of energy according to social class grouping. Meat and meat products and vegetables made a greater contribution to the energy intake of informants in Social Classes III manual, IV and V; these groups derived rather less of their total energy from cereal products and milk than did those in higher social classes. *(Figs 7.3 & 7.4)*

There was little variation between regions in the sources of energy. Among men, however, it appears that informants in Scotland and Northern England derived more of their energy from beverages, including alcoholic beverages, and less from cereal products than did those in the Central and Southern regions. *(Figs 7.5 & 7.6)*

7.2.4 Variation in energy intake

Tables 7.7 to 7.12 show the distribution of energy intake according to the round of fieldwork and the main characteristics of the sample.

Seasonal effects

Fieldwork for the survey was conducted in four rounds at equal intervals through the year in order to allow for seasonal patterns in dietary intake and the seasonal availability of particular foods. As shown in Table 7.7, there was little difference in men's total energy intake between autumn, winter and spring, although average intake was significantly lower in the summer quarter (p<0.05). The difference in average values was not, however, reflected in the lower and upper 2.5 percentiles which were similar for each round of fieldwork. The average energy intake of women showed no significant seasonal variation. *(Table 7.7)*

Region
Among men, energy intake was significantly lower for those living in Scotland, where the mean recorded intake was 2240kcal (9.4MJ) compared to 2450kcal (10.3MJ) overall (p<0.01); 32% of Scottish men had an average daily calorie intake of less than 2000kcal (8.4MJ), compared to 22% of all men (p<0.05). There was, however, no significant difference in energy intake of women according to the region in which they lived.
(Table 7.8)

Socio-economic characteristics
Table 7.9 indicates that men who were working had the highest average energy intake and the unemployed had the lowest intake; averages were 2520kcal (10.5MJ) for working men, 2230kcal (9.3MJ) for the economically inactive, and 2060kcal (8.6MJ) for the unemployed (p<0.01). For women there was no clear difference in average intake according to employment status.
(Table 7.9)

A classification based on whether informants lived in households in receipt of selected state benefits was used as a crude indicator of relative deprivation (see Chapter 5; 5.2.5). Table 7.10 shows that recorded energy intake was lower for both men and women living in households receiving benefits, and the difference was particularly marked for men (an average intake of 2210kcal, 9.2MJ, compared to 2480kcal, 10.4MJ, for others) (p<0.01).
(Table 7.10)

Table 7.11 shows recorded energy intake according to the sex of informant and social class of the head of the household in which he or she lived. For men there was no systematic difference in energy intake through the social class scale; men in Social Class III non-manual had the lowest calorie intake (2230kcal, 9.7MJ, compared to 2450kcal, 10.3MJ, overall) (p<0.05). Among women in the sample there was a clearer trend with lower recorded energy intake among lower social classes; the average intake for those in Social Classes I and II was 1740kcal (7.3MJ) compared to 1580kcal (6.6MJ) for those in Social Classes IV and V (p<0.01).
(Table 7.11)

Household composition
Among men there was no significant difference in energy intake according to household type classification. A greater range of average intakes was evident for women; lone mothers had the lowest average recorded energy intake (1580kcal, 6.6MJ) compared to an energy intake of 1720kcal (7.2MJ) among other women with dependent children (p<0.01).
(Table 7.12)

7.3 Alcohol
Average daily intakes of alcohol by age group for men and women are shown in Table 7.13.

The average alcohol consumption of the total sample was between three and four times higher for men than women, an average of 25.0g for men and 6.9g for women (p<0.01). For both sexes consumption was greatest in the middle of the age range, from 25 to 49. Median values for the total samples of men and women were considerably lower than mean values. These figures on alcohol intake for the sample as a whole can be compared with the results of the Northern Ireland survey of adult diets[5] which reported average alcohol intakes of 15.3g for men and 4.8g for women.
(Table 7.13)

Some 21% of men and 35% (p<0.01) of women consumed no alcohol during the recording period, but the proportions of respondents in the youngest age group who had not drunk alcohol during the recording week were greater (32% of men and 46% of women) (p<0.01). The incidence of drinking during the week was therefore 79% among men aged 16 to 64 and 65% among women in this age range, which corresponds closely with figures reported for the 1987 OPCS survey of drinking;[12] this survey found that 80% of men and 66% of women aged 16 to 64 had drunk alcohol in the previous week.

Alcohol differed from other nutrients measured in the survey in that a considerable number of informants recorded a zero intake. Data are therefore presented for the average intakes both of the total sample and of consumers only.

The second section of Table 7.13 shows the average daily alcohol intake for consumers only, by age and sex of informant. The distributions were positively skewed and average consumption for women was about one third of the average value for men (10.6g compared to 31.5g). As for the alcohol intake of the sample as a whole, average consumption declined for both sexes above the age of 50, (p<0.05), but the alcohol intake of consumers under the age of 25 was comparable to that of those aged 25 to 49.

Table 7.14 shows the percentage of total energy derived from alcohol by age and sex of informant. This reinforces the pattern seen for absolute intake of alcohol; men obtained 6.9% of total energy from alcohol compared to 2.8% for women, (p<0.01), but men and women who were consumers obtained somewhat higher percentages of energy (8.7% for men and 4.3% for women) (p<0.01). For the sample as a whole the proportion of energy obtained from alcohol was highest for those aged between 25 and 49 years; however, for consumers only, the proportion was similar for all ages up to age 50. In spite of the lower total energy intake of the oldest group, the proportion of energy provided by alcohol was still lower than for other age groups. *(Table 7.14)*

The NACNE report[2] recommended a reduction in alcohol intake towards 5% of total energy. On average, women consumers within this sample had intakes below this level, and 86% of all women were within this guideline. Men who consumed alcohol derived, on average, 8.7% of their energy from alcohol, and only 59% of the total sample of men were below the NACNE guidelines.

7.3.1 Variation in alcohol intake
Tables 7.15 to 7.21 show the mean and median intake of alcohol, for the total sample and for consumers only, according to the main characteristics of the sample.

Dieters and the unwell
Men who were on a slimming diet were less likely to have consumed alcohol during the recording week than were non-dieting men, (p < 0.05), but there was no difference for consumers either in the absolute amount of alcohol consumed or in the percentage of total energy intake which was derived from alcohol. Dieting women were no less likely to have consumed alcohol than were other women and for both men and women there was no difference in alcohol intake for consumers according to whether they were slimmers or not.
(Table 7.15)

It appears from Table 7.16 that informants who were unwell were less likely to have drunk alcohol during the week, and those who did consume alcohol also drank a smaller amount. Due to the small size of the unwell sample the differences are not, however, significant. *(Table 7.16)*

Region
The main difference by region in alcohol intake is seen for men who were consumers; men in the North consumed a significantly greater absolute amount of alcohol than men in the South East and London, (p < 0.01), and men in Scotland and the North derived a greater proportion of their total energy intake from alcohol than other men (p < 0.01). There were, however, no differences in the alcohol intake of women according to region. *(Table 7.17)*

Socio-economic characteristics
Men and women who were working were more likely to have consumed alcohol during the recording week than those who were unemployed or economically inactive (p < 0.01). Working women who did consume alcohol were also likely to have a higher alcohol intake than other women who consumed alcohol and to obtain a greater proportion of their total energy intake from alcohol (p < 0.05). However, among men the small number of unemployed who consumed alcohol consumed significantly greater amounts than working men (p < 0.05), and also derived a greater proportion of their energy intake from alcohol (p < 0.01). *(Table 7.18)*

Informants who were in households in receipt of selected benefits were less likely than others to have consumed alcohol (p < 0.01). Among consumers, men in households receiving benefits had a higher average intake that did other men (p < 0.05), but there was no difference between the average intakes of the two groups of women. *(Table 7.19)*

The proportion of the sample who consumed alcohol during the week was least for those in Social Classes IV and V. Thus 67% of men and 47% of women in Social Classes IV and V consumed alcohol, compared with 86% of men and 75% of women in Social Classes I and II (p < 0.01). Among female consumers there was little variation in alcohol intake across the social classes, but male consumers in the lower social classes had higher intakes of alcohol. For example, male consumers in Social Class III manual drank, on average, 35.6g of alcohol, compared with 26.9g for those in Social Class III non-manual (p < 0.05). *(Table 7.20)*

Household composition
Table 7.21 shows that men who were either living on their own or in households with other adults, but without a spouse, were less likely than those with a spouse to have consumed any alcohol, (p < 0.01), but the consumers among these two groups had higher absolute intakes of alcohol than did men in other household types (p < 0.05). This effect may in part be a reflection of the different age structure of the household type categories; a greater proportion of the youngest age group lived with other adults than in other household types. Among women there was a trend to higher average consumption of alcohol by women living with their spouse or other adults, but with no dependent children. *(Table 7.21)*

7.4 Summary
The recorded energy intakes of this sample were similar to those reported by other surveys using either weighed inventories or other techniques. A comparison of recorded intake to calculated basal metabolic rate suggests, however, that recorded energy intake may not have represented habitual intake for many of the sample. This possible shortfall was more pronounced for women than men, but there was no evidence of particular bias within the sample of men or women.

The energy intakes of slimmers and those whose eating was affected by their having been unwell during the recording period were significantly lower than the intakes of the non-dieting, and well groups. There was, however, little variation in energy intake according to season or region, although men in Scotland recorded a lower average intake than those in other regions.

There was little variation in the average recorded energy intake of informants up to the age of 50, but the 50 to 64 year age group had lower average intakes. Intakes were also lower for informants living in households receiving benefits, among unemployed men, and for women in lower social classes. The strength of these relationships is investigated further in Chapter 12.

The mean alcohol consumption of this sample was greater than that recorded in Northern Ireland.[5] For those who consumed alcohol during the recording week, the proportion of total energy obtained from alcohol was, on average, above the guidelines proposed by NACNE[2] for men in the sample, but within the guideline level for women.

Patterns of alcohol consumption between different subgroups of the sample are difficult to summarise because of the combined effect of the proportion who consumed alcohol and the amount drunk. Among the total sample, consumption of alcohol was highest in the middle of the age range covered by the survey; there were fewer consumers in the youngest age group, and older informants drank less on average.

Dieting men had a lower alcohol intake overall than non-slimmers, but this difference was not seen for women, and both men and women who were unwell drank less on average than other informants who had not been unwell or whose eating was not affected. Among men, those living in Northern England, those in Social Class III manual, and informants who were living without a spouse had higher intakes than others. Among women, consumption was higher for those who were working.

References and notes
1. Committee on Medical Aspects of Food Policy. *Diet and cardiovascular disease. Report of the Panel on diet in relation to cardiovascular disease.* Department of Health and Social Security. Report on Health and Social Subjects, No 28. HMSO (London, 1984).
2. National Advisory Committee on Nutrition Education. *A discussion paper on proposals for nutritional guidelines for health education in Britain.* Health Education Council (London, 1983).
3. Department of Health and Social Security. *Recommended daily amounts of food energy and nutrients for groups of people in the United Kingdom.* Report on Health and Social Subjects, No 15. HMSO (London, 1979).
4. The RDA for groups of people in the UK were last reviewed in 1979. In 1987 COMA set up an expert panel to review the recommended daily amounts of food energy and nutrients for groups of people in the UK. COMA will review the existing RDA for nutrients and look at the available scientific evidence relating to human requirements for other nutrients for which RDAs have not so far been set. At the time of writing this review is still underway.
5. Barker M E, McLean S I, McKenna P G *et al. Diet, Lifestyle and Health in Northern Ireland.* Centre for Applied Health Studies, University of Ulster, Coleraine, NI. 1989.
6. Bingham S A, McNeil N I, and Cummings J H. The diet of individuals: a study of randomly chosen cross section of British adults in a Cambridgeshire village, England, UK. *Br J Nutr* 1981; 45(1): 23–35.
7. Fehily A M and Bird G. The dietary intakes of women in Caerphilly, South Wales: A weighed and photographic method compared. *Hum Nutr: Applied Nutr* 1986; 40A(4): 300–307.
8. Barasi M E, Phillips K M, and Burr M L. A weighed dietary survey of women in South Wales. *Hum Nutr: Applied Nutr* 1985; 39A: 189–194.
9. Cade J E, Barker D J P, Margetts B M, Morris J A. Diet and inequalities in health in three English towns. *BMJ* 1988; 296: 1359–1362.
10. Stockley L. Direct measurents of intake. In *The dietary assessment of populations.* MRC Environmental Epidemiology Unit: Scientific Report no 4, 1984; 1–4.
11. Equations for calculation of approximate basal metabolic rate*:

Age	Men	Women
16–18	$2.72 + 0.0732(wt)$	$3.12 + 0.0510(wt)$
19–30	$2.84 + 0.0640(wt)$	$2.08 + 0.0615(wt)$
31–60	$3.67 + 0.0485(wt)$	$3.47 + 0.0364(wt)$
61–64	$2.04 + 0.0565(wt)$	$2.49 + 0.0439(wt)$

wt = weight in kg

*World Health Organisation. *Energy and protein requirements. Report of a joint FAO/WHO/UNU expert consultation.* Technical Report Series 724 WHO (Geneva, 1985).
12. Goddard E and Ikin C. *Drinking in England and Wales in 1987.* HMSO (London, 1988).

Table 7.1 Average daily energy intake (kcals) by age and sex

Energy intake (kcals)	Age 16–24	Age 25–34	Age 35–49	Age 50–64	All ages 16–64
	cum %	*cum %*	*cum %*	*cum %*	*cum %*
Men					
Less than 1500	8	6	3	4	5
Less than 2000	27	22	20	22	22
Less than 2500	50	53	54	60	55
Less than 3000	79	85	78	93	84
All	100	100	100	100	100
Base	*214*	*254*	*346*	*273*	*1087*
Mean (average) value	2460	2440	2500	2380	2450
Median value	2490	2470	2460	2380	2440
Lower 2.5 percentile	1190	1270	1380	1370	1330
Upper 2.5 percentile	3820	3700	3620	3420	3620
Standard error of the mean	47	38	32	31	18
	cum %	*cum %*	*cum %*	*cum %*	*cum %*
Women					
Less than 1500	31	38	29	40	34
Less than 1750	56	56	52	63	56
Less than 2000	74	79	73	82	77
Less than 2250	91	89	89	94	91
Less than 2500	97	95	96	99	97
All	100	100	100	100	100
Base	*189*	*253*	*385*	*283*	*1110*
Mean (average) value	1700	1670	1730	1610	1680
Median value	1690	1670	1740	1620	1690
Lower 2.5 percentile	740	790	800	810	800
Upper 2.5 percentile	2610	2580	2620	2340	2580
Standard error of the mean	32	29	23	23	13

Table 7.2 Comparison of energy intakes in Great Britain with other studies

Study	Energy intake for men (kcal per day)	Energy intake for women (kcal per day)
Great Britain	2450 *(n = 1087)*	1680 *(n = 1110)*
Northern Ireland (*Barker et al, 1988*) [5]	2526 *(n = 258)*	1670 *(n = 334)*
Cambridge (*Bingham et al, 1984*) [6]	2395 *(n = 32)*	1955 *(n = 31)*
Caerphilly (*Fehily et al, 1984*) [7]	2412 *(n = 493)*	—	—
Llantwit Major (*Barasi et al, 1985*) [8]	—	—	1760 *(n = 101)*
Ipswich, Stoke and Wakefield (*Cade et al, 1988*) [9]	2541 *(n = 1115)*	1642 *(n = 1225)*

Table 7.3 Average daily energy intake (kcals) for dieting and non-dieting informants by sex

Energy intake (kcals)	Men Dieting	Men Not dieting	Men Total	Women Dieting	Women Not dieting	Women Total
	cum %	*cum %*	*cum %*	*cum %*	*cum %*	*cum %*
Less than 1500	24	5	5	61	30	34
Less than 1750	33	11	12	78	53	56
Less than 2000	48	21	22	91	75	77
Less than 2500	72	54	55	99	97	97
Less than 3000	96	83	84	100	100	100
All	100	100	100	100	100	100
Base	*46*	*1041*	*1087*	*138*	*972*	*1110*
Mean (average) value	2050	2470	2450	1400	1720	1680
Median value	2030	2450	2440	1340	1720	1690
Lower 2.5 percentile	600	1350	1330	620	920	800
Upper 2.5 percentile	3420	3640	3620	2320	2590	2580
Standard error of the mean	100	18	18	39	14	13

Table 7.4 Average daily energy intake (kcals) by sex and whether informants eating was affected by their being unwell

Energy intake (kcals)	Men			Women		
	Unwell and eating affected	Not unwell/ eating not affected	Total	Unwell and eating affected	Not unwell/ eating not affected	Total
	cum %	*cum %*	*cum %*	*cum %*	*cum %*	*cum %*
Less than 1500	22	5	5	60	31	34
Less than 1750	37	10	12	75	54	56
Less than 2000	47	21	22	90	76	77
Less than 2500	71	54	55	99	97	97
Less than 3000	88	84	84	100	100	100
All	100	100	100			
Base	*51*	*1036*	*1087*	*106*	*1004*	*1110*
Mean (average) value	2130	2470	2450	1400	1710	1680
Median value	2030	2450	2440	1340	1710	1690
Lower 2.5 percentile	1240	1330	1330	590	890	800
Upper 2.5 percentile	3530	3640	3620	2330	2590	2580
Standard error of the mean	91	18	18	46	13	13

Table 7.5 Ratio of energy intake (MJ) to calculated basal metabolic rate for men and women

Energy intake (MJ)/calculated basal metabolic rate	Men	Women
	cum %	*cum %*
Total sample		
Less than 1.0	13	26
Less than 1.2	30	47
Less than 1.4	51	71
Less than 1.6	73	87
All	100	100
Base	*1076*	*1102*
Mean (average) value	1.39	1.22
Median value	1.39	1.23
Lower 5 percentile	0.83	0.66
Upper 5 percentile	1.93	1.78
Standard error of the mean	0.01	0.01
	cum %	*cum %*
Non-dieting informants who were not unwell		
Less than 1.0	11	18
Less than 1.2	27	40
Less than 1.4	49	66
Less than 1.6	72	85
All	100	100
Base	*983*	*873*
Mean (average) value	1.41	1.28
Median value	1.41	1.28
Lower 5 percentile	0.90	0.77
Upper 5 percentile	1.94	1.80
Standard error of the mean	0.01	0.01

Figure 7.1   Men: Percentage of energy from main food groups by age

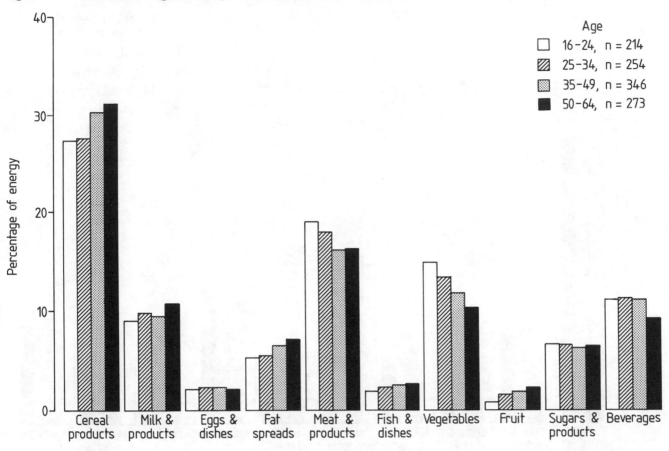

Figure 7.2   Women: Percentage of energy from main food groups by age

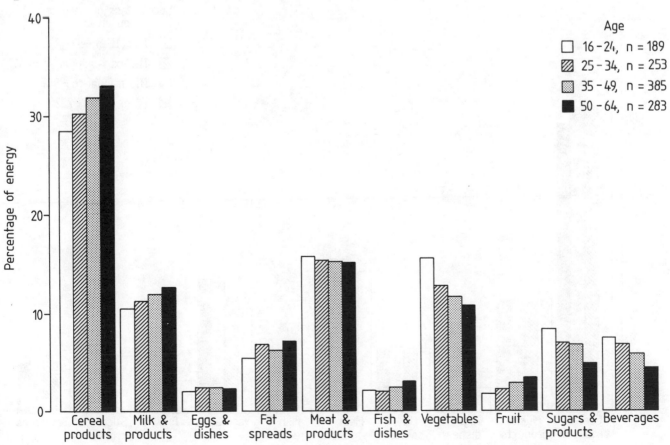

Figure 7.3   Men: Percentage of energy from main food groups by social class of head of household

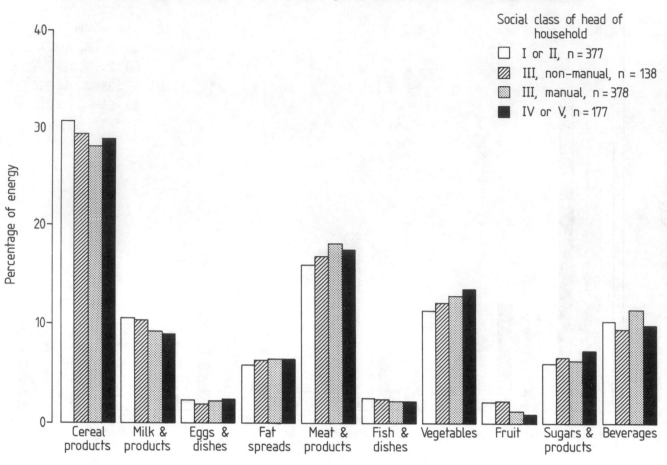

Figure 7.4   Women: Percentage of energy from main food groups by social class of head of household

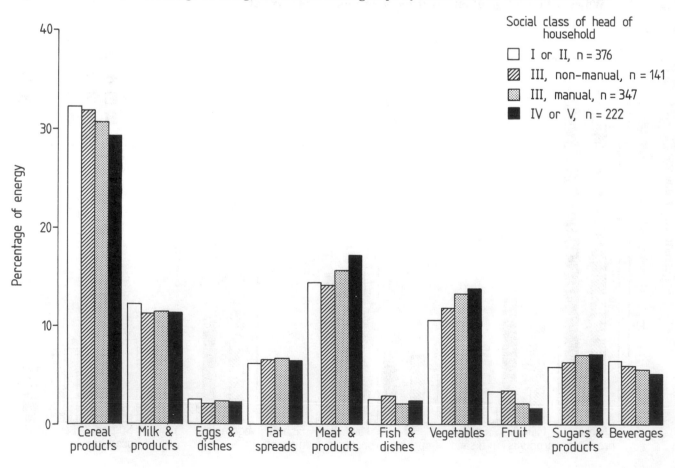

Figure 7.5   Men: Percentage of energy from main food groups by region

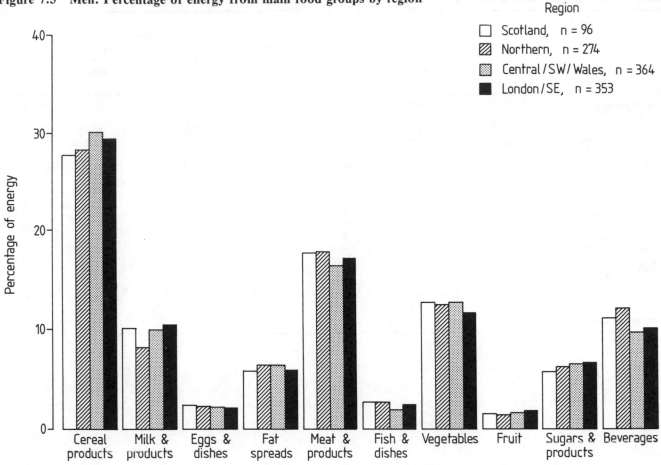

Figure 7.6   Women: Percentage of energy from main food groups by region

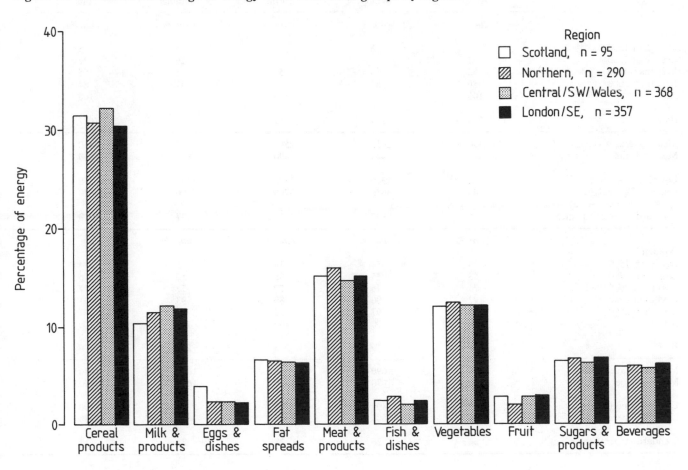

Table 7.6 Average daily energy intake (kcals) from main food types by sex of informant

Food type	Sex of informant					
	Men		Women		Total	
	Amount	% of total	Amount	% of total	Amount	% of total
Cereal products	715	29	524	31	619	30
of which						
—bread	*318*	*13*	*204*	*12*	*260*	*13*
—biscuits, buns, cakes, pastries	*200*	*8*	*170*	*10*	*185*	*9*
Milk and products	238	10	197	12	218	11
Eggs and egg dishes	54	2	39	2	47	2
Fat spreads	151	6	108	6	129	6
Meat and products	420	17	259	15	338	16
Fish and fish dishes	57	2	40	2	49	2
Vegetables	302	12	206	12	253	12
Fruit and nuts	39	2	44	3	42	2
Sugar, confectionery and preserves	157	6	111	7	133	6
Beverages	259	11	100	6	179	9
Miscellaneous	57	2	53	3	55	3
TOTAL	2450	100	1680	100	2060	100
Number of cases	*1087*		*1110*		*2197*	

Table 7.7 Average daily energy intake (kcals) by fieldwork round and sex of informant

Energy intake (kcals)	Round of fieldwork				
	Autumn	Winter	Spring	Summer	Total
	cum %	*cum %*	*cum %*	*cum %*	*cum %*
Men					
Less than 1500	6	6	5	5	5
Less than 2000	21	22	18	29	22
Less than 2500	53	55	51	61	55
Less than 3000	80	85	82	87	84
All	100	100	100	100	100
Base	*278*	*269*	*285*	*255*	*1087*
Mean (average) value	2490	2450	2500	2350	2450
Median value	2460	2440	2490	2320	2440
Lower 2.5 percentile	1270	1300	1400	1320	1330
Upper 2.5 percentile	3580	3620	3760	3600	3620
Standard error of the mean	35	37	35	37	18
	cum %	*cum %*	*cum %*	*cum %*	*cum %*
Women					
Less than 1500	34	34	34	35	34
Less than 1750	53	55	58	59	56
Less than 2000	75	76	79	77	77
Less than 2250	92	90	89	93	91
Less than 2500	97	97	95	98	97
All	100	100	100	100	100
Base	*277*	*279*	*283*	*271*	*1110*
Mean (average) value	1700	1690	1680	1660	1680
Median value	1700	1670	1690	1670	1690
Lower 2.5 percentile	770	800	740	790	800
Upper 2.5 percentile	2510	2600	2600	2440	2580
Standard error of the mean	26	26	28	25	13

Table 7.8 Average daily energy intake (kcals) by region and sex

Energy intake (kcals)	Region				
	Scotland	Northern	Central, South West and Wales	London and South East	Total
	cum %	*cum %*	*cum %*	*cum %*	*cum %*
Men					
Less than 1500	14	4	4	6	5
Less than 2000	32	23	22	20	22
Less than 2500	68	53	54	53	55
Less than 3000	93	81	82	85	84
All	100	100	100	100	100
Base	*96*	*274*	*364*	*353*	*1087*
Mean (average) value	2240	2460	2490	2450	2450
Median value	2220	2450	2460	2470	2440
Lower 2.5 percentile	1230	1350	1400	1320	1330
Upper 2.5 percentile	3560	3640	3820	3560	3620
Standard error of the mean	62	37	32	30	18
	cum %	*cum %*	*cum %*	*cum %*	*cum %*
Women					
Less than 1500	35	35	32	35	34
Less than 1750	57	60	54	56	56
Less than 2000	78	78	77	76	77
Less than 2250	92	91	90	91	91
Less than 2500	97	97	96	97	97
All	100	100	100	100	100
Base	*95*	*290*	*368*	*357*	*1110*
Mean (average) value	1650	1670	1700	1680	1680
Median value	1600	1660	1710	1700	1690
Lower 2.5 percentile	800	780	780	840	800
Upper 2.5 percentile	2530	2560	2670	2510	2580
Standard error of the mean	45	25	24	22	13

Table 7.9 Average daily energy intake (kcals) by employment status and sex

Energy intake (kcals)	Employment status		
	Working	Unemployed	Economically inactive
	cum %	*cum %*	*cum %*
Men			
Less than 1500	4	13	10
Less than 2000	18	45	33
Less than 2500	50	80	72
Less than 3000	81	97	95
All	100	100	100
Base	*875*	*99*	*111*
Mean (average) value	2520	2060	2230
Median value	2510	2080	2300
Lower 2.5 percentile	1360	1200	1190
Upper 2.5 percentile	3700	3070	3150
Standard error of the mean	20	51	49
	cum %	*cum %*	*cum %*
Women			
Less than 1500	32	42	37
Less than 1750	55	67	58
Less than 2000	76	79	77
Less than 2250	91	88	91
Less than 2500	97	95	97
All	100	100	100
Base	*670*	*57*	*373*
Mean (average) value	1700	1640	1650
Median value	1710	1570	1650
Lower 2.5 percentile	850	830	770
Upper 2.5 percentile	2600	2540	2530
Standard error of the mean	16	59	24

Table 7.10 Average daily energy intake (kcals) by sex of informant and whether benefits received

Energy intake (kcals)	Whether benefits received	
	Received	Not received
	cum %	*cum %*
Men		
Less than 1500	10	5
Less than 2000	33	21
Less than 2500	71	53
Less than 3000	94	82
All	100	100
Base	*119*	*963*
Mean (average) value	2210	2480
Median value	2190	2470
Lower 2.5 percentile	1200	1340
Upper 2.5 percentile	3140	3650
Standard error of the mean	49	19
	cum %	*cum %*
Women		
Less than 1500	43	33
Less than 1750	68	55
Less than 2000	80	76
Less than 2250	94	90
Less than 2500	98	97
All	100	100
Base	*153*	*955*
Mean (average) value	1560	1700
Median value	1600	1700
Lower 2.5 percentile	590	880
Upper 2.5 percentile	2460	2600
Standard error of the mean	39	14

Table 7.11 Average daily energy intake (kcals) by sex of informant and social class of head of household

Energy intake (kcals)	Social class of head of household			
	I and II	III non-manual	III manual	IV and V
	cum %	*cum %*	*cum %*	*cum %*
Men				
Less than 1500	4	7	6	7
Less than 2000	18	28	22	28
Less than 2500	56	59	51	58
Less than 3000	85	91	81	82
All	100	100	100	100
Base	*377*	*138*	*378*	*177*
Mean (average) value	2470	2330	2490	2410
Median value	2440	2370	2480	2350
Lower 2.5 percentile	1400	1320	1330	1230
Upper 2.5 percentile	3540	3490	3760	3960
Standard error of the mean	27	46	32	52
	cum %	*cum %*	*cum %*	*cum %*
Women				
Less than 1500	28	31	36	44
Less than 1750	50	52	60	64
Less than 2000	73	75	79	81
Less than 2250	87	92	92	93
Less than 2500	95	97	97	99
All	100	100	100	100
Base	*386*	*141*	*347*	*222*
Mean (average) value	1740	1710	1670	1580
Median value	1750	1740	1640	1600
Lower 2.5 percentile	920	800	790	690
Upper 2.5 percentile	2640	2560	2530	2430
Standard error of the mean	22	35	23	30

Table 7.12 Average daily energy intake (kcals) by sex of informant and household composition

Energy intake (kcals)	Household composition			
	Informant alone	With others, no dependent children		With dependent child
		With spouse	No spouse	
Men	cum %	cum %	cum %	cum %
Less than 1500	11	6	6	4
Less than 2000	31	21	25	19
Less than 2500	57	58	51	54
Less than 3000	82	89	81	81
All	100	100	100	100
Base	*71*	*360*	*271*	*385*
Mean (average) value	2380	2410	2470	2490
Median value	2430	2420	2490	2440
Lower 2.5 percentile	1230	1360	1190	1350
Upper 2.5 percentile	3560	3520	3960	3650
Standard error of the mean	80	28	40	29

	Informant alone	With others, no dependent children		With dependent child	
		With spouse	No spouse	With spouse	Lone mother
Women	cum %	cum %	cum %	cum %	cum %
Less than 1500	37	36	31	32	41
Less than 1750	63	59	54	52	65
Less than 2000	83	79	77	74	78
Less than 2250	90	91	91	89	95
Less than 2500	96	98	97	95	99
All	100	100	100	100	100
Base	*84*	*382*	*182*	*386*	*76*
Mean (average) value	1630	1660	1710	1720	1580
Median value	1650	1650	1710	1740	1610
Lower 2.5 percentile	750	860	950	790	590
Upper 2.5 percentile	2510	2460	2590	2620	2460
Standard error of the mean	50	21	31	24	57

Table 7.13 Average daily alcohol intake (g) of total sample and consumers only by age and sex

Alcohol intake (grams)	Age				All ages 16–64
	16–24	25–34	35–49	50–64	
a) Total sample	cum %	cum %	cum %	cum %	cum %
Men					
Zero	32	17	17	21	21
Less than 5	45	33	30	36	35
Less than 10	51	40	40	47	44
Less than 20	60	55	53	60	57
Less than 40	75	77	77	77	76
All	100	100	100	100	100
Base	*214*	*254*	*346*	*273*	*1087*
Mean (average) value	22.2	25.9	27.9	22.5	25.0
Median value	8.9	16.7	18.3	11.1	14.4
Standard error of the mean	1.97	1.95	1.91	1.68	0.95
	cum %	cum %	cum %	cum %	cum %
Women					
Zero	46	29	31	38	35
Less than 5	65	53	59	69	61
Less than 10	77	68	74	82	75
Less than 20	89	90	86	94	89
All	100	100	100	100	100
Base	*189*	*253*	*385*	*283*	*1110*
Mean (average) value	6.4	7.7	7.7	5.3	6.9
Median value	0.6	4.4	3.0	1.6	2.3
Standard error of the mean	0.79	0.59	0.56	0.54	0.31
b) Consumers only					
Men					
Mean (average) value	32.8	31.2	33.5	28.4	31.5
Median value	24.6	23.2	25.4	20.3	23.2
Upper 2.5 percentile	107.3	107.7	128.3	109.6	110.7
Standard error of the mean	2.46	2.17	2.14	1.93	1.10
Base	*145*	*211*	*288*	*216*	*860*
Women					
Mean (average) value	11.9	10.8	11.3	8.6	10.6
Median value	7.1	8.4	7.0	5.0	6.8
Upper 2.5 percentile	41.6	39.5	39.5	35.8	39.7
Standard error of the mean	1.22	0.72	0.72	0.79	0.41
Base	*102*	*179*	*264*	*175*	*720*

Table 7.14 Percentage of energy from alcohol by age and sex for total sample and consumers only

Percentage of energy from alcohol	Age				All ages 16–64
	16–24	25–34	35–49	50–64	
a) Total sample	cum %	cum %	cum %	cum %	cum %
Men					
Zero	32	17	17	21	21
Less than 2%	47	36	34	40	39
Less than 5%	56	50	49	59	53
Less than 10%	78	70	70	74	72
All	100	100	100	100	100
Base	*214*	*254*	*346*	*273*	*1087*
Mean (average) value	5.9	7.3	7.6	6.4	6.9
Median value	2.5	5.0	5.1	3.4	4.2
Standard error of the mean	0.51	0.50	0.45	0.47	0.24
	cum %	cum %	cum %	cum %	cum %
Women					
Zero	46	29	31	38	35
Less than 2%	63	52	58	68	60
Less than 5%	79	75	77	86	79
Less than 10%	92	93	91	95	93
All	100	100	100	100	100
Base	*189*	*253*	*385*	*283*	*1110*
Mean (average) value	2.5	3.1	3.2	2.2	2.8
Median value	0.2	1.7	1.1	0.8	1.0
Standard error of the mean	0.29	0.23	0.23	0.22	0.12
b) Consumers only					
Men					
Mean (average) value	8.7	8.7	9.1	8.1	8.7
Median value	7.4	6.7	7.2	5.5	6.9
Upper 2.5 percentile	26.9	27.0	30.6	27.5	28.4
Standard error of the mean	0.63	0.55	0.50	0.53	0.27
Base	*145*	*211*	*288*	*216*	*860*
Women					
Mean (average) value	4.7	4.3	4.6	3.5	4.3
Median value	3.3	3.6	3.0	2.1	3.0
Upper 2.5 percentile	15.4	14.7	18.6	13.7	15.8
Standard error of the mean	0.43	0.28	0.30	0.31	0.16
Base	*102*	*179*	*264*	*175*	*720*

Table 7.15 Average daily intake of alcohol (g) and percentage of energy from alcohol by sex of informant and whether on a slimming diet

Alcohol intake (grams)	Whether on a slimming diet					
	Dieting			Not dieting		
	Mean	Median	SE	Mean	Median	SE
Men						
i. Total sample						
Alcohol intake (g)	19.3	9.7	3.84	25.2	15.1	0.98
Alcohol as % energy	5.8	2.9	1.15	6.9	4.3	0.25
% consuming alcohol		65%			80%	
Base		46			1041	
ii. Consumers only						
Alcohol intake (g)	29.6	20.5	4.96	31.6	23.2	1.12
Alcohol as % energy	8.9	6.8	1.48	8.7	6.9	0.28
Base		30			830	
Women						
i. Total sample						
Alcohol intake (g)	7.5	2.9	0.96	6.8	2.3	0.32
Alcohol as % energy	3.3	1.3	0.37	2.7	1.0	0.13
% consuming alcohol		68%			64%	
Base		138			972	
ii. Consumers only						
Alcohol intake (g)	10.9	6.3	1.26	10.5	6.9	0.43
Alcohol as % energy	4.9	3.2	0.47	4.2	3.0	0.17
Base		94			626	

Table 7.16 Average daily intake of alcohol (g) and percentage of energy from alcohol by sex of informant and whether eating affected by being unwell

Alcohol intake (grams)	Whether eating affected by being unwell					
	Eating affected			Not unwell/eating not affected		
	Mean	Median	SE	Mean	Median	SE
Men						
i. Total sample						
Alcohol intake (g)	17.9	5.5	3.28	25.3	14.9	0.98
Alcohol as % energy	5.1	2.5	0.81	7.0	4.3	0.25
% consuming alcohol		67%			80%	
Base		51			1036	
ii. Consumers only						
Alcohol intake (g)	26.8	21.5	4.15	31.7	23.4	1.13
Alcohol as % energy	7.7	8.1	0.95	8.7	6.8	0.28
Base		34			826	
Women						
i. Total sample						
Alcohol intake (g)	5.5	1.0	0.99	7.0	2.4	0.32
Alcohol as % energy	2.4	0.5	0.37	2.8	1.1	0.13
% consuming alcohol		58%			65%	
Base		106			1004	
ii. Consumers only						
Alcohol intake (g)	9.4	5.8	1.51	10.7	6.9	0.43
Alcohol as % energy	4.1	3.2	0.55	4.3	3.0	0.17
Base		62			658	

Table 7.17 Average daily intake of alcohol (g) and percentage of energy from alcohol by sex of informant and region

Alcohol intake (grams)	Region											
	Scotland			Northern			Central, South West and Wales			London and South East		
	Mean	Median	SE	Mean	Median	SE	Mean	Median	SE	Mean	Median	SE
Men												
i. Total sample												
Alcohol intake (g)	24.8	11.4	3.66	29.0	18.4	2.15	23.2	10.9	1.49	23.7	15.3	1.55
Alcohol as % energy	7.4	4.0	0.95	7.7	5.2	0.52	6.3	3.2	0.39	6.7	4.5	0.41
% consuming alcohol		72%			78%			79%			82%	
Base		96			274			364			353	
ii. Consumers only												
Alcohol intake (g)	34.5	26.2	4.60	37.3	29.3	2.49	29.3	21.3	1.71	28.8	21.3	1.75
Alcohol as % energy	10.3	7.4	1.15	10.0	7.9	0.58	8.0	5.8	0.44	8.1	6.3	0.45
Base		69			213			288			290	
Women												
i. Total sample												
Alcohol intake (g)	6.1	1.7	0.91	7.1	2.6	0.59	6.6	2.1	0.56	7.2	3.1	0.53
Alcohol as % energy	2.4	0.7	0.35	2.9	1.1	0.23	2.7	0.9	0.23	2.9	1.3	0.21
% consuming alcohol		55%			64%			64%			69%	
Base		95			290			368			357	
ii. Consumers only												
Alcohol intake (g)	11.1	9.2	1.30	11.0	7.2	0.78	10.3	6.0	0.78	10.4	7.0	0.68
Alcohol as % energy	4.4	4.1	0.48	4.5	3.3	0.31	4.2	2.5	0.32	4.2	3.1	0.26
Base		52			187			236			245	

Table 7.18 Average daily intake of alcohol (g) by sex and employment status of informant

Alcohol intake (grams)	Employment status of informant								
	Working			Unemployed			Economically inactive		
	Mean	Median	SE	Mean	Median	SE	Mean	Median	SE
Men									
i. Total sample									
Alcohol intake (g)	25.7	16.4	1.04	25.3	7.9	3.23	18.9	3.0	3.26
Alcohol as % energy	6.9	4.6	0.25	8.4	2.8	1.04	5.6	0.8	0.84
% consuming alcohol		83%			65%			64%	
Base		875			99			111	
ii. Consumers only									
Alcohol intake (g)	31.1	23.0	1.16	39.1	36.8	4.07	29.5	21.4	4.65
Alcohol as % energy	8.3	6.7	0.28	12.9	11.3	1.28	8.7	7.1	1.17
Base		725			64			71	
Women									
i. Total sample									
Alcohol intake (g)	8.1	3.7	0.42	5.5	1.1	1.09	5.1	0.5	0.47
Alcohol as % energy	3.3	1.5	0.17	2.3	0.5	0.43	2.0	0.1	0.19
% consuming alcohol		72%			58%			54%	
Base		670			57			373	
ii. Consumers only									
Alcohol intake (g)	11.3	7.3	0.51	9.4	6.7	1.56	9.4	5.6	0.76
Alcohol as % energy	4.6	3.2	0.20	3.9	3.2	0.60	3.7	2.4	0.30
Base		480			33			202	

Table 7.19 Average daily intake of alcohol (g) by sex of informant and whether benefits received

Alcohol intake (grams)	Whether benefits received					
	Received			Not received		
	Mean	Median	SE	Mean	Median	SE
Men						
i. Total sample						
Alcohol intake (g)	25.3	8.1	2.97	24.9	15.4	1.01
Alcohol as % energy	7.9	3.0	0.90	6.8	4.3	0.25
% consuming alcohol		64%			81%	
Base		*119*			*963*	
ii. Consumers only						
Alcohol intake (g)	39.6	37.5	3.77	30.6	22.4	1.14
Alcohol as % energy	12.4	11.2	1.13	8.3	6.7	0.28
Base		*76*			*782*	
Women						
i. Total sample						
Alcohol intake (g)	4.5	0.0	0.76	7.2	3.0	0.33
Alcohol as % energy	1.8	0.0	0.29	2.9	1.2	0.13
% consuming alcohol		45%			68%	
Base		*153*			*955*	
ii. Consumers only						
Alcohol intake (g)	10.0	4.9	1.45	10.6	6.9	0.43
Alcohol as % energy	4.1	2.6	0.54	4.3	3.0	0.17
Base		*69*			*649*	

Table 7.20 Average daily intake of alcohol (g) and percentage of energy from alcohol by sex of informant and social class of head of household

Alcohol intake (grams)	Social class of head of household											
	I and II			III non-manual			III manual			IV and V		
	Mean	Median	SE	Mean	Median	SE	Mean	Median	SE	Mean	Median	SE
Men												
i. Total sample												
Alcohol intake (g)	24.1	14.1	1.41	20.7	9.3	2.25	28.3	18.5	1.88	22.7	9.3	2.31
Alcohol as % energy	6.7	4.5	0.37	6.1	2.5	0.65	7.6	5.4	0.43	6.4	2.7	0.67
% consuming alcohol		86%			77%			80%			67%	
Base		*377*			*138*			*378*			*177*	
ii. Consumers only												
Alcohol intake (g)	28.1	20.4	1.54	26.9	18.1	2.64	35.6	27.1	2.17	33.8	26.3	2.94
Alcohol as % energy	7.8	6.0	0.40	8.0	5.4	0.75	9.5	7.4	0.49	9.5	6.8	0.86
Base		*323*			*106*			*301*			*119*	
Women												
i. Total sample												
Alcohol intake (g)	8.4	4.4	0.54	6.9	2.4	0.91	6.1	2.2	0.51	5.0	0	0.62
Alcohol as % energy	3.4	1.8	0.22	2.7	1.1	0.32	2.5	0.9	0.21	2.0	0	0.24
% consuming alcohol		75%			72%			62%			47%	
Base		*386*			*141*			*347*			*222*	
ii. Consumers only												
Alcohol intake (g)	11.2	7.6	0.64	9.6	6.3	1.15	9.9	6.1	0.71	10.5	6.4	1.07
Alcohol as % energy	4.5	3.2	0.26	3.7	2.8	0.40	4.1	2.6	0.30	4.3	3.2	0.40
Base		*290*			*102*			*216*			*105*	

Table 7.21 Average daily intake of alcohol (g) and percentage of energy from alcohol by sex of informant and household composition

Men

Alcohol intake (grams)	Informant alone			With others, no dependent children						With dependent child		
				With spouse			No spouse					
	Mean	Median	SE	Mean	Median	SE	Mean	Median	SE	Mean	Median	SE
i. Total sample												
Alcohol intake (g)	33.1	12.3	6.46	24.4	13.6	1.60	26.3	12.3	1.92	23.0	16.1	1.32
Alcohol as % energy	8.6	4.3	1.40	6.8	4.0	0.41	7.2	4.3	0.53	6.4	4.5	0.34
% consuming alcohol		73%			82%			71%			83%	
Base		71			360			271			385	
ii. Consumers only												
Alcohol intake (g)	45.2	31.5	8.22	29.6	20.4	1.80	37.0	30.0	2.28	27.9	21.8	1.46
Alcohol as % energy	11.8	8.9	1.71	8.2	5.9	0.45	10.2	8.1	0.63	7.7	6.5	0.38
Base		52			297			193			318	

Women

Alcohol intake (grams)	Informant alone			With others, no dependent children						With dependent child					
				With spouse			No Spouse			With spouse			Lone mother		
	Mean	Median	SE	Mean	Median	SE	Mean	Median	SE	Mean	Median	SE	Mean	Median	SE
i. Total sample															
Alcohol intake (g)	5.7	2.1	1.02	7.6	3.1	0.55	7.1	1.9	0.79	6.4	2.1	0.49	6.2	2.1	1.25
Alcohol as % energy	2.4	0.8	0.42	3.1	1.4	0.21	2.8	0.7	0.31	2.6	0.8	0.20	2.6	0.9	0.49
% consuming alcohol		64%			70%			59%			65%			54%	
Base		84			382			182			386			76	
ii. Consumers only															
Alcohol intake (g)	8.9	6.0	1.42	10.9	6.9	0.69	11.9	8.7	1.10	9.9	6.7	0.65	11.4	6.4	1.98
Alcohol as % energy	3.7	2.3	0.57	4.4	3.1	0.26	4.7	3.3	0.43	4.0	2.6	0.28	4.8	3.2	0.75
Base		54			267			108			250			41	

8 Protein intake, urinary urea and carbohydrate intake

In this and the following chapter data are presented on total intakes of protein, carbohydrate and fat and fatty acids, and on the percentage of total energy provided by each. Protein and carbohydrate are considered in this chapter, looking separately at starch, sugars and fibre, and results for urinary urea are also given.[1]

The urinary excretion of urea was expressed as a rate per 24 hours, calculated from the concentration in the urine aliquot, the total urine volume and the time period of collection.

8.1 Protein

Average protein intake was 37% higher for men than for women; the average intake for men was 84.7g (median 84.0g) compared to 62.0g (median 61.8g) for women. Average protein intake was lower among women aged 16 to 34 than for those aged 35 or over (p < 0.01), and among men aged 16 to 24 compared with those aged 35 and over (p < 0.05). *(Table 8.1)*

The Department of Health recommended daily amount (RDA) for protein varies according to sex, age and level of activity, based on the calculation that protein should provide about 10% of the energy requirement of each group.[2] Assuming that most of the general population would be classified somewhere between sedentary and moderately active, the RDA for protein is between 62g and 72g for men aged 18 to 34, and between 60g and 69g for men aged 35 to 64. The RDA for women aged 18 to 54 in most occupations is 54g of protein, reducing to 47g for women aged 55 or over. Average intakes recorded on the survey were well in excess of these figures.

As shown in Table 8.2 protein provided a significantly greater percentage of the total energy intake of women (15.2%) than of men (14.1%) (p < 0.01). This difference in part reflects the greater alcohol consumption of men than of women. However, even after the exclusion of energy derived from alcohol protein still contributed a higher percentage of the food energy of women (15.6%) than of men (15.2%) (p < 0.01). For both men and women protein provided a greater percentage of the total energy intake of the oldest age group compared to the youngest group (p < 0.01); for women the percentages were 16.1% and 14.0% respectively. *(Table 8.2)*

More than three quarters of the protein consumed was derived from three main food types. Meat and meat products were the major source, providing 36% of total protein intake. Cereal products provided a further 23% of protein, with more than half of this (14% of total intake) derived from bread. Milk and milk products provided 17% of total intake. There was no difference between men and women in the importance of the main food types as sources of protein. *(Table 8.3)*

8.2 Urinary urea

Urea is the principal nitrogenous constituent of urine, and is an end product of protein metabolism in the body. Dietary protein intake is the major, but not only, determinant of urinary urea excretion.

The mean urea excretion for men was 387mmol/24h, and for women 298mmol/24h and showed no systematic association with age. *(Table 8.4)*

8.3 Carbohydrate

The average intake of total available carbohydrate recorded by the sample was 272g for men (median 268g) and 193g (median 192g) for women. Total carbohydrate intake was markedly lower for informants aged 50 to 64 than those aged 16 to 24 (p < 0.01), but there was not a clear trend between these ages. *(Table 8.5)*

Table 8.6 shows the percentage of total energy intake derived from carbohydrate. As for protein, carbohydrate provided a lower proportion of the total energy intake of men than of women, 41.6% compared to 43.0% (p < 0.01), but this difference largely reflected the greater contribution of alcohol to men's total energy intake. If the energy derived from alcohol is excluded, carbohydrate represented 44.7% and 44.2% of the food energy of men and women respectively, a difference which was not statistically significant. The percentage of total energy provided by carbohydrate decreased with age, particularly among women; carbohydrate provided 44.9% of the total energy of women aged 16 to 24, compared to 42.3% for women aged 50 to 64 (p < 0.01). *(Table 8.6)*

The main sources of carbohydrate did not differ for men and women. Almost half (46%) of total carbohydrate intake was derived from cereal products, with bread contributing 22% of total intake. The second major source was vegetables, (16% of the total), and two thirds of this was from potatoes (11% of the total). Sugars, confectionery and preserves provided 13% of total intake. *(Table 8.7)*

8.3.1 Sugars

Average intake of total sugars was 34% higher for men than women; the average daily intake for men was 115g (median 109g) compared to an average of 86g for women (median 84g). Among the women in the sample average intakes decreased through the age range, and Table 8.14 shows a similar downward trend for the average intake of sugars per 1000kcal of energy consumed. Thus the oldest women had significantly lower absolute average daily intakes and intakes per 1000kcal than women aged 16 to 24 (p<0.01). For men there was no signficant difference in either average daily intake or intake per 1000kcal by age.

(Tables 8.8 & 8.14)

As well as occurring naturally in fruit, vegetables and milk, sugars are used in a variety of products; the sources of sugars in the diet are therefore spread across a number of food types. The category of sugar, confectionery and preserves was the main contributor, providing 31% of men's intake and 26% of women's intake (p<0.01). Cereal products contributed 23% of total intake, largely in biscuits and cakes, and puddings; these foods together provided 16% of the intake of sugars. Sizeable amounts of sugars were also provided by beverages, 18% of the total for men and 14% for women (p<0.01), and milk and milk products (13% of the overall total). *(Table 8.9)*

Information about the use of sugar and artificial sweeteners in tea and coffee was collected in the interview, which was carried out before the start of the dietary recording period. The results in Table 8.10 show that sugar was more commonly used in coffee than in tea (p<0.01), and men in all age groups were more likely than women to use sugar in drinks (p<0.01). The use of sugar in tea and coffee was more prevalent among younger informants, with men and women aged 16 to 24 being more likely than those aged 50 to 64 to use sugar (p<0.01, except for the use of sugar in coffee by men, where p<0.05). Artificial sweeteners were used, in total, by 10% of men and 12% of women; in the majority of cases (92%) the sweetener used was a 'non-calorie' type. *(Table 8.10)*

8.3.2 Starch

The average intake of starch recorded by men was 47% higher than that recorded by women; this is a greater difference than in total food energy consumed.[3] Men had an average intake of 156g (median 152g) compared to an average of 106g (median 106g) for women. Average consumption of starch decreased with age both for men and women, and was markedly higher in the youngest age group compared with those aged 50 to 64 (p<0.01). Starch intake per 1000kcal total energy was also significantly higher for men aged 16 to 24 than for any other group of men (p<0.01), but this pattern was not true for women where there were no significant differences associated with age. *(Tables 8.11 & 8.14)*

8.3.3 Dietary fibre

The COMA report on diet and cardiovascular disease[4] makes no specific recommendations about the intake of dietary fibre, but 'sees advantages in compensating for a reduced fat intake with increased fibre-rich carbohydrate provided that this can be achieved without increasing total intake of common salt or sugar'. NACNE[5] recommended that the average intake of dietary fibre among adults should be increased to 30g per day, with a short term aim for the 1980s of increasing average daily intake to 25g. The average intakes recorded by the sample were 24.9g for men (median 23.8g) and 18.6g for women (median 17.9g). Only 25% of men and 6% of women had an average fibre intake of 30g or more daily; 45% of men but only 16% of women had an average intake of 25g or more of fibre per day. The fibre intake of men varied little with age, but there was a trend to increasing fibre consumption among older women, with the oldest group having a significantly higher intake than those aged 16 to 24 (p<0.01). This difference was also seen in the fibre intake per 1000kcal energy of women, (p<0.01), as seen in Table 8.14. *(Tables 8.12 & 8.14)*

About half (47%) of the fibre consumed was derived from cereal products; white bread contributed 13% of total fibre intake and wholemeal and other non-white bread a further 17%. Vegetables were the next most important category (38% of fibre intake); potatoes were the most important individual vegetable contributing 12% of total fibre. Only 8% of total fibre intake was derived from the third most important food type, fruit and nuts. *(Table 8.13)*

8.4 Variation in intake of protein and carbohydrate

Tables 8.15 to 8.21 show the mean and median intakes of protein and carbohydrate, the contribution of these nutrients to total energy intake, and the average intakes of sugars, starch and fibre per 1000kcal total energy, for different groups within the sample.

Dieters and the unwell

As shown in the previous chapter, both dieters and the unwell had lower energy intakes than others within the sample. Table 8.15 shows that those on a slimming diet had lower average intakes of total available carbohydrate (p<0.01), but the percentage of total energy derived from carbohydrates was significantly lower only for women (p<0.01). These differences in carbohydrate intake were the result of lower intakes of both sugars and starch by those on a slimming diet (p<0.01). However intakes of sugars per 1000kcal were similar for women slimmers and other women. The average intake of dietary fibre was similar in slimmers and others within the sample; slimmers therefore had higher fibre intakes per 1000kcal total energy. This was true for men and women (p<0.01). *(Table 8.15)*

The similar absolute level of protein consumed did not differ according to whether the respondent was on a slimming diet or not, so protein provided a greater percentage of the total energy intake of slimmers than non-slimmers (p<0.01).

Informants whose eating was affected by their being unwell showed a different pattern to slimmers. The absolute amounts of protein and of the various types of carbohydrate consumed were lower for the unwell than for the remainder of the group (p<0.01), but the proportions of total energy provided by protein and carbohydrate were similar for both groups. This implies that those who were unwell had a similar pattern of eating to the healthy group, although consuming less food energy in total, whereas the diet of slimmers was qualitatively different to that of non-slimmers.

(*Table 8.16*)

Region
In general there were few differences between informants in different regions in the intake of protein and carbohydrate. Men in Scotland had lower absolute intakes both of protein and carbohydrate than men elsewhere (p<0.01), but the percentage of energy derived from protein and carbohydrate was not lower for Scottish men because of their lower recorded energy intake. Men living in Scotland also had lower average intakes of fibre than men in other regions (p<0.01), but their fibre intake per 1000kcal total energy was only significantly lower than that of men in the Central and South West regions and Wales (p<0.01).

(*Table 8.17*)

Socio-economic characteristics
Unemployed men had the lowest absolute intakes of protein although the percentage of energy they derived from protein was not significantly different from that of working or economically inactive men. Unemployed men also had the lowest absolute intakes of carbohydrate and both they and economically inactive men had intakes significantly below those of working men (p<0.01). However working men derived a lower proportion of their total energy from carbohydrate than economically inactive men (p<0.01). For women there were no significant differences in carbohydrate intake between the three groups, but unemployed women had a lower intake of protein than working women and derived a smaller proportion of their total energy from protein than did other women (p<0.01). (*Table 8.18*)

Lower average intakes of protein were recorded by men and women living in households receiving benefits (p<0.01), but the proportions of total energy provided by protein did not differ significantly. The absolute intake of carbohydrate by men in households receiving benefits was also below that of other men (p<0.01), but women in benefit households obtained a higher proportion of total energy from carbohydrate than other women (p<0.01). Both men and women in benefit households had lower average intakes of sugars (p<0.01) and fibre (p<0.01 for women, p<0.05 for men), but intakes per 1000kcal total energy did not differ significantly. (*Table 8.19*)

Some differences in intake of protein and carbohydrate were apparent according to the social class of the head of the household in which the informant was living,

but there was rarely a smooth trend across the groups. Men and women in Social Classes I and II had a higher absolute intake of protein (men: p<0.05; women: p<0.01), and of sugars and fibre (p<0.05) than men and women in Social Classes IV and V. Women in the non-manual groups also had a higher carbohydrate intake than women in the manual groups (p<0.05). Intakes of sugars and fibre per 1000kcal of energy showed similar differences (p<0.05), and the percentage of total energy provided by carbohydrate was lower for men and women (p<0.01) in Social Classes I and II than for those in Social Classes IV and V. The proportion of total energy provided by protein showed no association with social class. (*Table 8.20*)

Household composition
The lowest intakes were recorded by men who were living alone; highest intakes were recorded by men living with a wife and dependent child or children, except for protein where the highest intake was for married men without children. However, the differences between the highest and lowest intakes were only statistically significant for carbohydrate (p<0.05), starch and fibre (p<0.01). Married men obtained a markedly higher proportion of their total energy from protein and had a higher fibre intake per 1000kcal than men who were living with other adults, but not a spouse (p<0.01). Among women, lone mothers had the lowest average daily intakes of protein, carbohydrate, sugars and fibre; the highest daily intakes of protein and fibre were by married women without dependent children and of carbohydrate and sugars by women living with other adults but no spouse. The differences between the highest and lowest intakes were all statistically significant (protein and fibre: p<0.01; carbohydrate and sugars: p<0.05). Despite their relatively low absolute intakes, the proportion of total energy derived from carbohydrate and the intake of sugars per 1000kcal by lone mothers were not lower than for other women. Lone mothers did, however, obtain a lower proportion of their total energy from protein than either married women with no dependent children (p<0.01) or women living alone (p<0.05). Their intake of fibre per 1000kcal was also significantly lower than for any other group of women (p<0.05). (*Table 8.21*)

8.5 Variation in urinary urea
There were no differences for either men or women in urea excretion associated with whether or not the subject was on a slimming diet. (*Table 8.22*)

Men who were unwell and whose eating had been affected had a lower mean urea excretion than men who had not been unwell (p<0.01), but there were no similar differences among women. (*Table 8.23*)

There were no differences for either men or women in urea excretion associated with region. (*Table 8.24*)

Among men the mean excretion of urea was markedly lower for the unemployed compared with those who were working (p<0.01), and to a lesser extent the same was true for women (p<0.05). (*Table 8.25*)

The data also showed that mean excretion of urea was lower for subjects from households in receipt of certain state benefits, and again the association was more marked for men (p<0.01), than for women (p<0.05). (*Table 8.26*)

Mean excretion of urea also decreased with decreasing social class for both men and women. Among men mean excretion ranged for 410.2mmol/24h for those in Social Classes I and II, to 362.7mmol/24h for those in Social Classes IV and V (p<0.01). Among female subjects mean excretion ranged from 319.9mmol/24h to 280.3mmol/24h (p<0.01). (*Table 8.27*)

Male informants living in households without a spouse had a significantly lower mean urea excretion than married men, both with and without children (p<0.05). Women living with other adults but not a spouse similarly had lower urea excretion than married women (p<0.05). (*Table 8.28*)

Male and female non-smokers had a higher mean excretion of urea than those who smoked cigarettes (p<0.01), but there was little effect associated with the number of cigarettes smoked a day. (*Table 8.29*)

Alcohol consumption and urea excretion showed no apparent relationship for either men or women.
(*Table 8.30*)

8.6 Summary
Average intakes of protein recorded by men and women in the sample were well above current RDAs, with protein providing 14% and 15% of the total energy of men and women respectively. Carbohydrate provided 42% and 43% of total energy for men and women respectively. Average intakes of fibre were below the NACNE guidelines; men were closer to achieving the targets than women.

Recorded intakes of protein and carbohydrate were relatively consistent across all of the groups identified within the sample, and the percentages of energy they provided varied little between groups.

Protein provided a greater percentage of the energy intake of older people, and the percentage of energy they derived from carbohydrate was slightly lower for younger women than older women. Sugars and starch

intake also showed a reduction with age among women, but intake of fibre was higher among older women.

There is evidence that people who were unwell during the period of the dietary record consumed less protein and carbohydrate but the percentage of energy provided by protein and carbohydrate was similar to the rest of the sample. Slimmers, on the other hand, obtained a greater percentage of their energy from protein. Their fibre consumption per 1000kcal total energy was higher than that of non-slimmers.

Protein provided a lower percentage of the energy intake of unemployed women, but there was no association with social class or receipt of benefits. Carbohydrate provided a higher percentage of energy for women in households receiving benefits. In absolute terms intakes of sugars and fibre were lower for both men and women in households receiving benefits, but there was no significant difference between groups in average intakes of sugars and fibre per 1000kcal total energy.

Mean urea excretion was lower for unemployed men and women, for those in households receiving benefits, for those in the lower social classes and for smokers, as compared with the rest of the sample.

References
1. Chapter 4 describes the purpose of the urine analyses, and the methods and equipment used to obtain a 24-hour collection of urine and specimens from this total collection. Chapter 4 also describes some of the methodological problems associated with obtaining a complete 24-hour collection, and the possible effects on the results.
2. Department of Health and Social Security. *Recommended daily amounts of food energy and nutrients for groups of people in the United Kingdom.* Report on Health and Social Subjects No 15. HMSO (London, 1979).
3. The data show that the average daily reported intake of food energy by men was 2275kcal and by women, 1633kcal.
4. Committee on Medical Aspects of Food Policy. *Diet and cardiovascular disease. Report of the Panel on diet in relation to cardiovascular disease.* Department of Health and Social Security. Report on Health and Social Subjects No 28. HMSO (London, 1984).
5. National Advisory Committee on Nutrition Education. *A discussion paper on proposals for nutrition guidelines for health education in Britain.* Health Education Council (London, 1983).

Table 8.1 Average daily protein intake (g) by age and sex

Protein intake (grams)	Age				All ages
	16–24	25–34	35–49	50–64	16–64
	cum %	cum %	cum %	cum %	cum %
Men					
Less than 55	9	6	5	5	6
Less than 65	22	18	17	13	17
Less than 75	39	34	29	27	31
Less than 85	60	55	47	50	52
Less than 95	77	71	69	73	72
All	100	100	100	100	100
Base	*214*	*254*	*346*	*273*	*1087*
Mean (average) value	81.6	84.3	86.0	86.0	84.7
Median value	80.2	82.8	86.3	84.9	84.0
Lower 2.5 percentile	42.1	50.6	48.7	47.1	47.1
Upper 2.5 percentile	128.4	131.1	129.8	129.1	129.1
Standard error of the mean	1.48	1.31	1.11	1.21	0.63
	cum %	cum %	cum %	cum %	cum %
Women					
Less than 45	17	17	7	12	12
Less than 55	43	39	30	24	33
Less than 65	67	64	50	56	58
Less than 75	85	82	78	81	81
Less than 85	96	95	93	94	94
All	100	100	100	100	100
Base	*189*	*253*	*385*	*283*	*1110*
Mean (average) value	58.5	59.5	64.3	63.4	62.0
Median value	57.1	57.8	65.0	62.9	61.8
Lower 2.5 percentile	29.3	30.2	33.2	33.7	31.8
Upper 2.5 percentile	88.5	89.0	95.8	91.8	92.3
Standard error of the mean	1.09	0.98	0.78	0.87	0.46

Table 8.2 Percentage of total energy from protein by age and sex

Percentage of total energy from protein	Age				All ages
	16–24	25–34	35–49	50–64	16–64
	cum %	cum %	cum %	cum %	cum %
Men					
Less than 12%	29	21	20	16	21
Less than 14%	59	51	57	43	52
Less than 16%	87	82	83	71	81
Less than 18%	96	93	95	90	94
All	100	100	100	100	100
Base	*214*	*254*	*346*	*273*	*1087*
Mean (average) value	13.7	14.1	13.9	14.7	14.1
Median value	13.2	14.0	13.6	14.5	13.8
Lower 2.5 percentile	9.1	9.6	9.4	10.0	9.4
Upper 2.5 percentile	19.9	19.6	19.3	21.5	19.9
Standard error of the mean	0.25	0.20	0.14	0.17	0.09
	cum %	cum %	cum %	cum %	cum %
Women					
Less than 12%	19	21	10	6	13
Less than 14%	59	49	40	30	43
Less than 16%	83	74	68	56	69
Less than 18%	90	87	83	75	83
All	100	100	100	100	100
Base	*189*	*253*	*385*	*283*	*1110*
Mean (average) value	14.0	14.6	15.4	16.1	15.2
Median value	13.6	14.1	14.5	15.6	14.5
Lower 2.5 percentile	9.4	10.4	10.5	11.5	10.4
Upper 2.5 percentile	22.2	22.8	24.9	23.4	23.4
Standard error of the mean	0.21	0.20	0.19	0.19	0.10

Table 8.3 Contribution of main food types to average daily protein intake (g) by sex of informant

Food type	Men		Women		Total	
	Amount (g)	% of total	Amount (g)	% of total	Amount (g)	% of total
Cereal products	19.8	23	14.2	23	17.0	23
of which						
—bread	*11.7*	*14*	*7.6*	*14*	*9.6*	*14*
Milk and products	13.3	16	11.2	18	12.2	17
Eggs and egg dishes	3.5	4	2.5	4	2.9	4
Fat spreads	.1	0	.0	0	.0	0
Meat and products	31.6	37	20.9	34	26.2	36
Fish and fish dishes	5.2	6	4.0	6	4.6	6
Vegetables	8.0	9	5.7	9	6.9	9
Fruit and nuts	.6	1	.7	1	.6	1
Sugar, confectionery and preserves	.6	1	.6	1	.6	1
Beverages	.7	1	.7	1	.7	1
Miscellaneous	1.4	2	1.4	2	1.4	2
TOTAL	84.7	100	62.0	100	73.2	100
Number of cases		*1087*		*1110*		*2197*

Table 8.4 Percentage distribution of total urinary urea by age and sex

Total urinary urea (mmol/24h)	Age				All ages
	16–24	25–34	35–49	50–64	16–64
	cum %	*cum %*	*cum %*	*cum %*	*cum %*
Men					
Less than 200	7	8	7	11	8
Less than 275	22	21	21	18	20
Less than 350	44	36	39	37	39
Less than 425	68	61	64	69	65
All	100	100	100	100	100
Base	*144*	*192*	*280*	*225*	*841*
Mean (average) value	379	394	391	381	387
Median value	365	392	379	381	381
Lower 5.0 percentile	194	177	173	149	167
Upper 5.0 percentile	601	622	598	586	612
Standard error of the mean	11.16	9.66	8.29	8.79	4.65
	cum %	*cum %*	*cum %*	*cum %*	*cum %*
Women					
Less than 200	18	17	14	17	16
Less than 275	50	43	34	45	42
Less than 350	83	73	64	73	71
Less than 425	93	93	88	92	91
All	100	100	100	100	100
Base	*136*	*213*	*293*	*223*	*865*
Mean (average) value	283	291	315	292	298
Median value	276	287	308	282	293
Lower 5.0 percentile	147	128	152	138	146
Upper 5.0 percentile	466	446	465	443	457
Standard error of the mean	8.46	6.44	6.02	6.89	3.43

Table 8.5 Average daily carbohydrate intake (g) by age and sex

Carbohydrate intake (grams)	Age				All ages
	16–24	25–34	35–49	50–64	16–64
	cum %	*cum %*	*cum %*	*cum %*	*cum %*
Men					
Less than 200	19	20	16	20	18
Less than 250	35	42	37	44	40
Less than 300	59	66	65	72	66
Less than 350	80	79	82	90	84
All	100	100	100	100	100
Base	*214*	*254*	*346*	*273*	*1087*
Mean (average) value	282	267	277	263	272
Median value	281	266	269	262	268
Lower 2.5 percentile	136	117	131	142	131
Upper 2.5 percentile	471	464	434	406	435
Standard error of the mean	6.0	5.2	4.2	4.1	2.4
	cum %	*cum %*	*cum %*	*cum %*	*cum %*
Women					
Less than 150	17	23	23	29	24
Less than 200	46	57	53	63	55
Less than 250	79	84	80	90	83
Less than 300	96	96	94	99	96
All	100	100	100	100	100
Base	*189*	*253*	*385*	*283*	*1110*
Mean (average) value	204	192	197	182	193
Median value	204	188	196	178	192
Lower 2.5 percentile	77	87	76	84	83
Upper 2.5 percentile	326	308	324	285	314
Standard error of the mean	4.3	3.7	3.3	3.0	1.8

Table 8.6 Percentage of total energy from carbohydrate by age and sex

Percentage of total energy from carbohydrate	Age				All ages 16–64
	16–24	25–34	35–49	50–64	
	cum %	cum %	cum %	cum %	cum %
Men					
Less than 35%	10	17	16	16	15
Less than 40%	33	43	39	41	40
Less than 45%	63	72	71	70	70
Less than 50%	86	94	92	93	91
All	100	100	100	100	100
Base	*214*	*254*	*346*	*273*	*1087*
Mean (average) value	42.9	40.9	41.5	41.4	41.6
Median value	42.9	41.0	41.8	42.0	41.9
Lower 2.5 percentile	31.1	27.3	27.2	29.2	29.1
Upper 2.5 percentile	55.6	51.5	53.5	53.8	53.8
Standard error of the mean	0.45	0.40	0.36	0.39	0.20
	cum %	cum %	cum %	cum %	cum %
Women					
Less than 35%	5	7	11	10	9
Less than 40%	21	32	33	31	30
Less than 45%	51	62	66	69	64
Less than 50%	82	89	87	93	88
All	100	100	100	100	100
Base	*189*	*253*	*385*	*283*	*1110*
Mean (average) value	44.9	43.0	42.5	42.3	43.0
Median value	44.8	42.6	42.7	42.4	43.1
Lower 2.5 percentile	31.8	32.3	29.1	32.4	30.3
Upper 2.5 percentile	55.9	56.1	56.3	52.7	55.5
Standard error of the mean	0.44	0.38	0.34	0.31	0.19

Table 8.7 Contribution of main food types to average daily carbohydrate intake (g) by sex of informant

Food type	Men		Women		Total	
	Amount (g)	% of total	Amount (g)	% of total	Amount (g)	% of total
Cereal products	125.2	46	89.2	46	107.0	46
of which						
—*white bread*	*42.9*	*16*	*24.3*	*13*	*33.5*	*14*
—*wholemeal & other bread*	*22.1*	*8*	*17.3*	*9*	*19.7*	*8*
—*breakfast cereals*	*13.8*	*5*	*10.4*	*5*	*12.1*	*5*
Milk and products	13.5	5	12.4	6	12.9	6
Eggs and egg dishes	.6	0	.7	0	.7	0
Fat spreads	.0	0	.0	0	.0	0
Meat and products	14.2	5	8.3	4	11.2	5
Fish and fish dishes	2.6	1	1.7	1	2.2	1
Vegetables	44.4	16	29.6	15	36.9	16
of which						
—*potatoes*	*32.5*	*12*	*20.3*	*11*	*26.3*	*11*
Fruit and nuts	8.1	3	9.3	5	8.7	4
Sugar, confectionery and preserves	35.8	13	23.5	12	29.6	13
Beverages	21.5	8	13.0	7	17.2	7
Miscellaneous	6.1	2	5.5	3	5.8	3
TOTAL	272.1	100	193.3	100	232.3	100
Number of cases	*1087*		*1110*		*2197*	

Table 8.8 Average daily sugars intake (g) by age and sex

Sugars intake (grams)	Age				All ages 16-64
	16-24	25-34	35-49	50-64	
	cum %	cum %	cum %	cum %	cum %
Men					
Less than 60	16	13	12	12	13
Less than 80	31	28	21	26	26
Less than 100	43	46	39	41	42
Less than 120	56	60	59	59	59
Less than 150	76	80	76	80	78
All	100	100	100	100	100
Base	214	254	346	273	1087
Mean (average) value	114	112	117	114	115
Median value	109	105	111	111	109
Lower 2.5 percentile	34	38	38	39	37
Upper 2.5 percentile	227	234	222	216	224
Standard error of the mean	3.7	3.0	2.6	2.9	1.5
	cum %	cum %	cum %	cum %	cum %
Women					
Less than 60	21	25	24	33	26
Less than 80	37	47	45	52	46
Less than 100	60	70	65	74	68
Less than 120	83	84	78	89	83
Less than 150	95	94	92	98	95
All	100	100	100	100	100
Base	189	253	385	283	1110
Mean (average) value	92	85	89	79	86
Median value	91	83	85	78	84
Lower 2.5 percentile	27	29	23	25	25
Upper 2.5 percentile	176	167	180	147	171
Standard error of the mean	2.7	2.3	2.1	1.9	1.1

Table 8.9 Contribution of main food types to average daily sugars intake (g) by sex of informant

Food type	Men		Women		Total	
	Amount (g)	% of total	Amount (g)	% of total	Amount (g)	% of total
Cereal products	26.0	23	20.6	24	23.3	23
of which						
—*biscuits*	*3.7*	*3*	*3.3*	*4*	*3.5*	*3*
—*buns, cakes & pastries*	*9.2*	*8*	*7.5*	*9*	*8.3*	*8*
—*puddings & ice cream*	*6.0*	*5*	*4.7*	*5*	*5.3*	*5*
Milk and products	13.4	12	12.3	14	12.9	13
Eggs and egg dishes	.1	0	.1	0	.1	0
Fat spreads	0	0	0	0	0	0
Meat and products	1.5	1	.9	1	1.2	1
Fish and fish dishes	.2	0	.1	0	.2	0
Vegetables	6.4	6	4.9	6	5.6	6
Fruit and nuts	7.8	7	8.9	10	8.4	8
Sugar, confectionery and preserves	35.1	31	22.8	26	28.9	29
of which						
—*confectionery*	*6.2*	*5*	*6.4*	*7*	*6.3*	*6*
Beverages	21.0	18	12.5	14	16.7	17
Miscellaneous	3.1	3	3.0	3	3.0	3
TOTAL	114.6	100	86.1	100	100.2	100
Number of cases	*1087*		*1110*		*2197*	

Table 8.10 Use of sugar or artificial sweeteners in tea and coffee by sex and age

Use of sugar or sweetener	Sex and age of informant									
	Men					Women				
	16–24	25–34	35–49	50–64	All ages 16–64	16–24	25–34	35–49	50–64	All ages 16–64
	%	%	%	%	%	%	%	%	%	%
Tea										
Uses sugar	57	52	46	40	48	44	30	26	17	28
Uses artificial sweetener	1	4	8	12	7	5	8	8	10	8
Uses neither	32	38	40	45	39	34	54	58	71	56
Does not drink tea	10	6	6	3	6	16	8	8	3	8
Base = 100%	214	254	346	272	1086	189	253	385	283	1110
	%	%	%	%	%	%	%	%	%	%
Coffee										
Uses sugar	61	56	50	52	54	45	36	35	25	35
Uses artificial sweetener	1	6	11	15	9	5	9	12	14	11
Uses neither	19	31	28	24	26	28	41	44	52	43
Does not drink coffee	19	8	11	9	11	22	14	9	10	12
Base = 100%	214	254	346	272	1086	189	252	384	283	1108

Table 8.11 Average daily starch intake (g) by age and sex

Starch intake (grams)	Age				All ages 16–64
	16–24	25–34	35–49	50–64	
	cum %	cum %	cum %	cum %	cum %
Men					
Less than 90	6	9	6	8	7
Less than 120	18	23	21	24	22
Less than 150	39	49	46	55	48
Less than 180	64	75	71	83	74
All	100	100	100	100	100
Base	214	254	346	273	1087
Mean (average) value	165	153	158	147	156
Median value	165	150	155	147	152
Lower 2.5 percentile	77	58	78	68	69
Upper 2.5 percentile	279	254	263	242	258
Standard error of the mean	3.4	2.9	2.5	2.5	1.4
	cum %	cum %	cum %	cum %	cum %
Women					
Less than 90	25	30	30	34	30
Less than 120	64	69	68	78	70
Less than 150	88	92	92	95	92
All	100	100	100	100	100
Base	189	253	385	283	1110
Mean (average) value	111	106	107	102	106
Median value	112	104	106	102	106
Lower 2.5 percentile	38	46	39	46	42
Upper 2.5 percentile	178	170	174	169	172
Standard error of the mean	2.5	2.0	1.7	1.7	1.0

Table 8.12 Average daily fibre intake (g) by age and sex

Fibre intake (grams)	Age				All ages 16–64
	16–24	25–34	35–49	50–64	
	cum %	cum %	cum %	cum %	cum %
Men					
Less than 15	15	13	11	8	12
Less than 20	35	33	28	29	31
Less than 25	58	57	52	56	55
Less than 30	75	74	71	80	75
All	100	100	100	100	100
Base	214	254	346	273	1087
Mean (average) value	23.9	24.5	25.8	24.8	24.9
Median value	23.1	23.4	24.1	23.8	23.8
Lower 2.5 percentile	9.6	10.7	11.1	10.4	10.3
Upper 2.5 percentile	41.7	45.9	47.0	44.7	44.8
Standard error of the mean	0.56	0.57	0.50	0.53	0.27
	cum %	cum %	cum %	cum %	cum %
Women					
Less than 15	40	33	27	24	30
Less than 20	70	68	64	57	64
Less than 25	87	85	83	83	84
Less than 30	95	95	94	94	94
All	100	100	100	100	100
Base	189	253	385	283	1110
Mean (average) value	17.4	18.2	18.9	19.3	18.6
Median value	16.2	17.9	18.2	18.8	17.9
Lower 2.5 percentile	6.8	7.5	8.1	8.6	7.5
Upper 2.5 percentile	34.4	31.5	34.0	32.9	33.5
Standard error of the mean	0.47	0.41	0.34	0.38	0.20

Table 8.13 Contribution of main food types to average daily fibre intake (g) by sex of informant

Food type	Men Amount (g)	Men % of total	Women Amount (g)	Women % of total	Total Amount (g)	Total % of total
Cereal products	11.8	47	8.6	46	10.2	47
of which						
—white bread	*3.6*	*14*	*2.1*	*11*	*2.8*	*13*
—wholemeal & other bread	*4.1*	*16*	*3.1*	*17*	*3.6*	*17*
—high fibre breakfast cereals	*1.4*	*6*	*1.3*	*7*	*1.3*	*6*
Milk and products	–	–	–	–	–	–
Eggs and egg dishes	.0	0	.1	0	.1	0
Fat spreads	–	–	–	–	–	–
Meat and products	1.3	5	.8	4	1.1	5
Fish and fish dishes	.2	1	.1	1	.1	1
Vegetables	9.5	38	6.8	37	8.1	38
of which						
—potatoes	*3.1*	*12*	*1.9*	*10*	*2.5*	*12*
Fruit and nuts	1.5	6	1.8	9	1.7	8
Sugar, confectionery and preserves	.2	1	.2	1	.2	1
Beverages	–	–	–	–	–	–
Miscellaneous	.3	1	.3	2	.3	1
TOTAL	24.9	100	18.6	100	21.7	100
Number of cases	*1087*		*1110*		*2197*	

Table 8.14 Nutrient intake per 1000 kcal total energy by age and sex

Nutrient (units) per 1000 kcal total energy	Age of informant 16–24 Mean	Median	SE	25–34 Mean	Median	SE	35–49 Mean	Median	SE	50–64 Mean	Median	SE	All ages 16–64 Mean	Median	SE
Men															
Sugars (g)	45.8	45.8	1.1	45.4	45.1	0.9	46.3	45.8	0.8	47.5	47.4	0.9	46.3	47.4	0.9
Starch (g)	67.8	67.0	0.9	62.9	62.2	0.8	63.6	63.7	0.7	62.3	62.1	0.8	63.9	63.8	0.4
Fibre (g)	9.9	9.7	0.2	10.1	9.4	0.2	10.4	9.9	0.2	10.5	10.0	0.2	10.3	9.8	0.1
Base	*214*			*254*			*346*			*273*			*1087*		
Women															
Sugars (g)	53.6	53.1	1.1	50.1	48.8	1.0	50.9	49.1	0.8	48.2	47.4	0.9	50.5	49.4	0.9
Starch (g)	65.2	65.6	1.0	63.8	62.2	0.7	61.8	61.3	0.6	63.9	63.4	0.8	63.4	62.9	0.4
Fibre (g)	10.4	9.8	0.2	11.1	10.4	0.2	11.1	10.6	0.2	12.1	11.9	0.2	11.2	10.7	0.1
Base	*189*			*253*			*385*			*283*			*1110*		

Table 8.15 Average daily intake of protein and carbohydrate by sex of informant and whether on a slimming diet

| Average daily intake (units) | Whether on a slimming diet | | | | | |
| | Dieting | | | Not dieting | | |
	Mean	Median	SE	Mean	Median	SE
Men						
Protein (g)	85.6	86.6	3.42	84.7	83.9	0.64
Protein as % total energy	18.3	16.3	1.16	13.9	13.7	0.08
Carbohydrate (g)	219	226	12.0	275	271	2.4
Carbohydrate as % total energy	40.0	41.5	1.10	41.7	41.9	0.20
Sugars (g)	89	81	6.0	116	111	1.5
Starch (g)	128	128	8.0	157	153	1.4
Fibre (g)	24.6	23.7	1.31	24.9	23.8	0.28
Sugars (g per 1000kcal)	44.4	43.3	2.3	46.4	46.0	0.5
Starch (g per 1000kcal)	61.3	62.1	2.1	64.0	63.9	0.4
Fibre (g per 1000kcal)	12.3	12.0	0.5	10.2	9.7	0.1
Base		46			1041	
Women						
Protein (g)	61.1	61.0	1.35	62.1	61.9	0.49
Protein as % total energy	18.4	17.2	0.43	14.7	14.2	0.09
Carbohydrate (g)	155	150	4.5	199	197	1.9
Carbohydrate as % total energy	41.6	41.6	0.53	43.2	43.3	0.20
Sugars (g)	70	64	2.5	88	86	1.2
Starch (g)	84	83	2.9	109	108	1.0
Fibre (g)	18.0	17.7	0.60	18.7	17.9	0.21
Sugars (g per 1000kcal)	50.7	48.4	1.4	50.5	49.6	0.5
Starch (g per 1000kcal)	59.3	61.3	1.3	63.9	63.2	0.4
Fibre (g per 1000kcal)	13.0	12.3	0.4	11.0	10.5	0.1
Base		138			972	

Table 8.16 Average daily intake of protein and carbohydrate by sex of informant and whether eating affected by being unwell

| Average daily intake (units) | Whether eating affected by being unwell | | | | | |
| | Eating affected | | | Not unwell/eating not affected | | |
	Mean	Median	SE	Mean	Median	SE
Men						
Protein (g)	77.4	72.9	2.95	85.1	84.2	0.64
Protein as % total energy	14.9	14.7	0.34	14.1	13.8	0.10
Carbohydrate (g)	229	224	10.3	274	270	2.4
Carbohydrate as % total energy	40.7	39.9	0.91	41.7	42.0	0.20
Sugars (g)	87	81	6.1	116	111	1.5
Starch (g)	139	132	5.6	156	153	1.4
Fibre (g)	21.0	20.4	0.93	25.1	24.0	0.28
Sugars (g per 1000kcal)	40.2	37.8	1.9	46.6	46.1	0.5
Starch (g per 1000kcal)	67.3	67.2	2.0	63.8	63.8	0.4
Fibre (g per 1000kcal)	10.2	10.0	0.4	10.3	9.8	0.1
Base		51			1036	
Women						
Protein (g)	52.2	49.7	1.72	63.0	62.4	0.46
Protein as % total energy	15.4	14.5	0.40	15.1	14.4	0.11
Carbohydrate (g)	164	166	5.6	196	194	1.9
Carbohydrate as % total energy	44.1	43.6	0.68	42.9	43.0	0.19
Sugars (g)	75	74	3.4	87	84	1.1
Starch (g)	88	90	3.0	108	107	1.0
Fibre (g)	15.7	14.9	0.69	18.9	18.2	0.20
Sugars (g per 1000kcal)	52.4	49.8	1.8	50.3	49.3	0.5
Starch (g per 1000kcal)	64.3	63.2	1.5	63.3	62.9	0.4
Fibre (g per 1000kcal)	11.5	10.6	0.4	11.2	10.7	0.1
Base		106			1004	

Table 8.17 Average daily intake of protein and carbohydrate by sex of informant and region

Average daily intake (units)	Region											
	Scotland			Northern			Central, South West and Wales			London and South East		
	Mean	Median	SE	Mean	Median	SE	Mean	Median	SE	Mean	Median	SE
Men												
Protein (g)	78.8	79.6	2.10	84.3	82.3	1.28	85.9	85.8	1.08	85.6	85.1	1.08
Protein as % total energy	14.3	14.4	0.26	14.1	13.7	0.22	14.1	13.8	0.16	14.1	14.0	0.14
Carbohydrate (g)	245	244	8.1	273	270	4.7	283	278	4.3	269	269	4.0
Carbohydrate as % total energy	41.1	41.2	0.74	41.5	41.5	0.40	42.5	42.6	0.34	41.0	41.8	0.34
Sugars (g)	96	84	5.0	112	109	2.9	119	111	2.6	117	114	2.5
Starch (g)	145	144	4.4	159	158	2.8	161	158	2.6	150	149	1.5
Fibre (g)	21.4	20.2	0.82	24.8	23.6	0.54	26.4	25.1	0.50	24.3	23.3	0.44
Sugars (g per 1000kcal)	42.4	41.4	1.6	44.9	44.3	0.9	47.4	47.5	0.7	47.3	47.7	0.8
Starch (g per 1000kcal)	65.5	65.5	1.3	64.8	65.2	0.8	65.1	64.4	0.7	61.6	61.1	0.7
Fibre (g per 1000kcal)	9.7	9.4	0.3	10.2	9.6	0.2	10.7	10.2	0.2	10.0	9.6	0.2
Base	*96*			*274*			*364*			*353*		
Women												
Protein (g)	61.3	61.8	1.38	62.5	62.4	0.97	61.5	61.5	0.77	62.2	61.3	0.81
Protein as % total energy	15.6	14.3	0.43	15.3	14.7	0.19	15.0	14.1	0.18	15.2	14.6	0.17
Carbohydrate (g)	190	196	6.1	192	189	3.4	198	198	3.3	190	188	2.9
Carbohydrate as % total energy	43.1	42.8	0.68	43.0	43.1	0.35	43.5	43.6	0.32	42.5	42.7	0.33
Sugars (g)	81	78	3.8	84	81	2.2	88	86	2.0	88	85	1.9
Starch (g)	106	109	3.3	107	106	1.9	110	108	1.8	101	102	1.5
Fibre (g)	17.4	16.5	0.64	18.2	16.9	0.36	19.4	18.5	0.37	18.5	18.4	0.33
Sugars (g per 1000kcal)	48.3	46.7	1.7	49.4	48.1	0.9	50.7	49.6	0.8	51.7	50.8	0.8
Starch (g per 1000kcal)	64.9	64.2	1.3	64.3	62.6	0.8	64.5	64.7	0.6	61.0	60.7	0.7
Fibre (g per 1000kcal)	10.7	10.1	0.3	11.1	10.5	0.2	11.5	10.9	0.2	11.2	10.7	0.2
Base	*95*			*290*			*368*			*357*		

Table 8.18 Average daily intake of protein and carbohydrate by sex and employment status of informant

Average daily intake (units)	Employment status of informant								
	Working			Unemployed			Economically inactive		
	Mean	Median	SE	Mean	Median	SE	Mean	Median	SE
Men									
Protein (g)	87.0	86.1	0.67	71.7	67.9	2.13	79.1	79.6	2.07
Protein as % total energy	14.1	13.8	0.10	14.1	13.8	0.29	14.4	14.0	0.30
Carbohydrate (g)	279	276	2.7	230	239	6.8	256	254	6.6
Carbohydrate as % total energy	41.4	41.7	0.22	42.0	41.3	0.75	43.3	43.8	0.7
Sugars (g)	119	114	1.7	86	82	4.0	107	105	4.4
Starch (g)	158	155	1.6	142	140	4.6	146	144	4.2
Fibre (g)	25.5	24.3	0.30	21.5	20.1	0.89	22.9	22.7	0.71
Sugars (g per 1000kcal)	46.5	45.9	0.5	41.7	41.3	1.6	48.0	48.4	1.5
Starch (g per 1000kcal)	63.0	63.1	0.4	69.4	68.7	1.6	66.4	64.9	1.5
Fibre (g per 1000kcal)	10.2	9.7	0.1	10.4	10.0	0.3	10.4	10.2	0.3
Base		875			99			*373*	
Women									
Protein (g)	62.9	62.4	0.56	56.5	53.5	2.29	61.1	62.0	0.84
Protein as % total energy	15.2	14.5	0.14	14.0	13.4	0.40	15.2	14.6	0.17
Carbohydrate (g)	194	194	2.2	195	189	7.3	192	188	3.3
Carbohydrate as % total energy	42.5	42.8	0.24	44.9	44.0	0.83	43.5	43.4	0.32
Sugars (g)	88	85	1.4	84	83	4.6	83	82	2.0
Starch (g)	105	105	1.2	110	108	4.5	107	107	1.8
Fibre (g)	18.5	17.9	0.24	17.7	16.6	0.85	18.9	18.1	0.38
Sugars (g per 1000kcal)	50.8	49.6	0.6	51.8	48.1	2.3	49.7	49.1	0.8
Starch (g per 1000kcal)	61.8	61.3	0.5	67.2	67.7	1.6	65.5	64.8	0.6
Fibre (g per 1000kcal)	11.1	10.6	0.1	10.9	10.0	0.4	11.5	10.8	0.2
Base		670			57			*373*	

Table 8.19 Average daily intake of protein and carbohydrate by sex of informant and whether benefits received

Average daily intake (units)	Whether benefits received						
	Received				Not received		
	Mean	Median	SE		Mean	Median	SE
Men							
Protein (g)	75.4	73.5	2.01		86.0	85.0	0.66
Protein as % total energy	13.8	13.2	0.27		14.2	13.9	0.10
Carbohydrate (g)	251	251	7.3		275	271	2.5
Carbohydrate as % total energy	42.5	42.1	0.68		41.5	41.8	0.21
Sugars (g)	96	89	4.5		117	112	1.6
Starch (g)	153	151	4.7		156	152	1.5
Fibre (g)	22.9	22.3	0.84		25.1	24.0	0.29
Sugars (g per 1000kcal)	43.2	41.4	1.6		46.6	46.3	0.5
Starch (g per 1000kcal)	69.2	68.2	1.5		63.2	63.3	0.4
Fibre (g per 1000kcal)	10.4	9.8	0.3		10.2	9.8	0.1
Base		*119*				*963*	
Women							
Protein (g)	55.6	53.9	1.41		63.0	62.6	0.48
Protein as % total energy	14.6	14.3	0.27		15.2	14.5	0.11
Carbohydrate (g)	186	187	5.5		194	193	1.9
Carbohydrate as % total energy	44.5	44.0	0.53		42.8	42.8	0.20
Sugars (g)	78	73	3.4		87	85	1.2
Starch (g)	108	108	3.0		106	106	1.0
Fibre (g)	16.8	15.6	0.55		18.9	18.2	0.21
Sugars (g per 1000kcal)	48.2	47.0	1.4		50.8	49.6	0.5
Starch (g per 1000kcal)	69.6	69.8	1.0		62.4	61.9	0.4
Fibre (g per 1000kcal)	10.9	10.4	0.3		11.3	10.7	0.1
Base		*153*				*955*	

Table 8.20 Average daily intake of protein and carbohydrate from all sources by sex of informant and social class of head of household

Average daily intake (units)	Social class of head of household											
	I and II			III non-manual			III manual			IV and V		
	Mean	Median	SE	Mean	Median	SE	Mean	Median	SE	Mean	Median	SE
Men												
Protein (g)	87.0	85.6	0.95	81.9	82.8	1.60	84.9	83.9	1.13	81.6	80.3	1.79
Protein as % total energy	14.4	14.0	0.14	14.3	14.2	0.20	14.0	13.6	0.19	13.8	13.6	0.22
Carbohydrate (g)	272	271	3.8	261	256	6.6	274	268	4.1	275	269	6.7
Carbohydrate as % total energy	41.4	42.0	0.34	42.0	42.3	0.60	41.3	41.4	0.34	42.7	42.6	0.45
Sugars (g)	121	117	2.4	113	105	4.3	111	105	2.5	111	103	3.9
Starch (g)	150	148	2.1	146	147	3.7	161	160	1.7	161	163	3.9
Fibre (g)	26.0	24.8	0.45	23.7	22.9	0.79	24.6	23.8	0.45	24.2	22.8	0.69
Sugars (g per 1000kcal)	48.4	47.9	0.7	47.7	45.7	1.3	44.3	44.5	0.8	45.5	44.7	1.1
Starch (g per 1000kcal)	61.2	60.1	0.6	63.6	62.6	1.2	64.9	65.2	0.7	67.4	67.7	1.1
Fibre (g per 1000kcal)	10.7	10.2	0.2	10.2	9.7	0.3	10.0	9.5	0.1	10.1	9.5	0.2
Base	*377*			*138*			*378*			*177*		
Women												
Protein (g)	65.8	65.8	0.77	63.3	62.0	1.16	60.2	59.6	0.79	57.3	57.2	1.00
Protein as % total energy	15.5	14.7	0.16	15.4	14.8	0.35	14.8	14.2	0.17	15.0	14.3	0.23
Carbohydrate (g)	197	197	3.0	199	198	4.7	192	189	3.2	185	181	4.1
Carbohydrate as % total energy	42.3	42.5	0.31	43.5	43.7	0.50	43.0	43.1	0.32	43.8	43.5	0.42
Sugars (g)	91	89	1.8	91	90	2.9	84	81	2.1	78	72	2.6
Starch (g)	105	105	1.7	106	107	2.7	107	107	1.7	106	105	2.2
Fibre (g)	19.9	19.0	0.36	19.8	19.8	0.53	17.8	17.1	0.34	16.9	16.4	0.40
Sugars (g per 1000kcal)	51.8	51.5	0.7	53.1	52.1	1.2	49.2	48.8	0.9	48.5	46.4	1.2
Starch (g per 1000kcal)	60.3	59.9	0.6	62.3	62.1	1.0	64.6	64.1	0.7	67.3	68.3	0.8
Fibre (g per 1000kcal)	11.5	10.9	0.2	11.9	11.4	0.3	10.8	10.4	0.2	10.9	10.0	0.2
Base	*386*			*141*			*347*			*222*		

Table 8.21 Average daily intake of protein and carbohydrate by sex and household composition

Average daily intake (units)	Household composition											
	Informant alone			With others, no dependent children						With dependent child		
				With spouse			No spouse					
	Mean	Median	SE	Mean	Median	SE	Mean	Median	SE	Mean	Median	SE
Men												
Protein (g)	81.5	75.1	2.90	87.1	85.9	1.04	81.7	80.1	1.36	85.4	85.9	1.00
Protein as % total energy	14.2	13.4	0.46	14.8	14.4	0.18	13.5	13.2	0.17	14.0	13.7	0.14
Carbohydrate (g)	253	249	9.9	264	261	3.8	277	279	5.2	280	279	4.0
Carbohydrate as % total energy	40.4	40.8	0.92	41.0	41.5	0.34	42.1	41.7	0.42	42.2	42.4	0.32
Sugars (g)	110	103	6.4	113	108	2.4	115	110	3.3	117	111	2.4
Starch (g)	142	129	5.6	149	147	2.3	160	159	3.1	161	157	2.3
Fibre (g)	22.9	21.2	1.11	25.2	24.2	0.47	23.5	22.8	0.52	25.9	24.6	0.46
Sugars (g per 1000kcal)	45.4	47.1	2.0	46.4	46.1	0.8	45.9	45.9	1.0	46.7	45.8	0.7
Starch (g per 1000kcal)	60.7	59.6	1.8	62.2	62.9	0.7	65.3	64.8	0.9	65.2	64.3	0.6
Fibre (g per 1000kcal)	9.9	9.4	0.4	10.6	9.9	0.2	9.6	9.2	0.2	10.5	10.1	0.2
Base		*71*			*360*			*271*			*385*	

	Informant alone			With others, no dependent children						With dependent child					
				With spouse			No spouse			With spouse			Lone mother		
	Mean	Median	SE	Mean	Median	SE	Mean	Median	SE	Mean	Median	SE	Mean	Median	SE
Women															
Protein (g)	62.4	63.7	1.83	63.8	63.2	0.75	60.1	59.6	1.07	62.1	61.8	0.78	56.3	55.9	2.02
Protein as % total energy	15.7	15.0	0.40	15.7	15.2	0.16	14.4	13.8	0.24	14.9	14.2	0.19	14.6	14.2	0.36
Carbohydrate (g)	186	186	6.3	187	184	2.7	201	200	4.2	200	196	3.3	183	183	7.4
Carbohydrate as % total energy	42.8	43.1	0.68	42.0	42.0	0.29	44.1	44.4	0.47	43.4	43.0	0.32	43.4	43.9	0.80
Sugars (g)	83	85	3.8	83	80	1.8	89	87	2.7	90	86	2.1	77	70	4.3
Starch (g)	101	101	3.4	103	104	1.5	110	107	2.4	108	108	1.7	105	108	4.3
Fibre (g)	18.1	16.6	0.72	19.1	18.3	0.32	18.7	17.4	0.47	18.7	18.2	0.34	16.1	15.7	0.78
Sugars (g per 1000kcal)	50.8	50.0	1.6	49.1	47.7	0.7	51.9	51.5	1.2	51.6	51.5	1.2	48.1	48.1	2.0
Starch (g per 1000kcal)	62.8	62.9	1.3	62.1	61.3	0.6	65.0	63.8	1.0	63.3	63.1	0.6	66.7	67.2	1.5
Fibre (g per 1000kcal)	11.4	11.0	0.4	11.7	11.1	0.2	11.2	10.5	0.3	11.0	10.5	0.2	10.3	9.6	0.3
Base		*84*			*382*			*182*			*386*			*76*	

Table 8.22 Urinary urea by sex and whether informant was on a slimming diet during the seven-day dietary recording period

Urine analytes (units)	Whether on a slimming diet							
	Dieting				Not dieting			
	Mean	Median	SE	*Base*	Mean	Median	SE	*Base*
Men								
Urine volume (ml/24h)	1650	1525	133.8	*36*	1630	1513	25.2	*805*
Total urinary urea (mmol/24h)	415.8	384.8	27.62	*36*	385.4	381.0	4.70	*805*
Women								
Urine volume (ml/24h)	1525	1500	60.3	*106*	1416	1350	21.4	*759*
Total urinary urea (mmol/24h)	305.7	310.5	10.25	*106*	296.5	290.1	3.63	*759*

Table 8.23 Urinary urea by sex of informant and whether unwell during seven-day dietary recording period

Urine analytes (units)	Whether unwell during seven-day dietary recording period											
	Completed food diary									No food diary		
	Not unwell			Unwell								
				Eating affected			Eating not affected					
	Mean	Median	SE	Mean	Median	SE	Mean	Median	SE	Mean	Median	SE
Men												
Urine volume (ml/24h)	1650	1525	27.6	1389	1267	107.0	1622	1500	88.6	1535	1425	89.6
Total urinary urea (mmol/24h)	390.3	385.1	5.09	347.2	345.0	18.34	385.0	378.0	16.09	361.9	342.2	23.49
Base		695			32			67			48	
Women												
Urine volume (ml/24h)	1425	1350	23.2	1390	1260	65.3	1564	1463	60.7	1218	950	95.6
Total urinary urea (mmol/24h)	300.2	294.6	3.90	289.1	288.0	11.87	296.7	298.2	9.83	267.7	240.9	20.83
Base		657			81			96			31	

Table 8.24 Urinary urea by sex of informant and region

Urine analytes (units)	Region											
	Scotland			Northern			Central, South West and Wales			London and South East		
	Mean	Median	SE	Mean	Median	SE	Mean	Median	SE	Mean	Median	SE
Men												
Urine volume (ml/24h)	1480	1400	68.4	1604	1550	44.5	1651	1525	44.4	1674	1525	46.5
Total urinary urea (mmol/24h)	373.8	378.0	16.38	373.7	366.3	9.39	390.5	383.5	8.10	396.4	392.0	7.88
Base		77			212			276			277	
Women												
Urine volume (ml/24h)	1351	1225	74.4	1388	1312	40.8	1507	1400	34.5	1398	1375	34.3
Total urinary urea (mmol/24h)	279.1	275.4	13.46	296.3	292.9	6.98	304.6	305.5	5.30	295.8	285.9	6.30
Base		71			210			302			282	

Table 8.25 Urinary urea by sex and employment status of informant

Urine analytes (units)	Employment status of informant								
	Working			Unemployed			Economically inactive		
	Mean	Median	SE	Mean	Median	SE	Mean	Median	SE
Men									
Urine volume (ml/24h)	1643	1525	27.1	1638	1500	100.3	1539	1400	73.4
Total urinary urea (mmol/24h)	397.1	393.0	5.03	307.8	309.5	13.82	365.8	366.7	16.42
Base		688			68			85	
Women									
Urine volume (ml/24h)	1427	1375	24.8	1242	1152	86.6	1461	1350	37.9
Total urinary urea (mmol/24h)	301.8	298.9	4.15	273.7	279.8	13.38	291.7	283.0	6.57
Base		527			40			289	

Table 8.26 Urinary urea by sex of informant and whether benefits received

Urine analytes (units)	Whether benefits received							
	Receiving				Not receiving			
	Mean	Median	SE	*Base*	Mean	Median	SE	*Base*
Men								
Urine volume (ml/24h)	1632	1500	89.5	*85*	1627	1513	25.5	*753*
Total urinary urea (mmol/24h)	315.4	315.0	13.44	*85*	394.9	389.2	4.88	*753*
Women								
Urine volume (ml/24h)	1335	1250	53.7	*121*	1445	1375	21.8	*743*
Total urinary urea (mmol/24h)	278.9	279.6	10.70	*121*	300.7	296.0	3.58	*743*

Table 8.27 Urinary urea by sex of informant and social class of head of household

Urine analytes (units)	Social class of head of household											
	I and II			III non-manual			III manual			IV and V		
	Mean	Median	SE	Mean	Median	SE	Mean	Median	SE	Mean	Median	SE
Men												
Urine volume (ml/24h)	1709	1580	42.1	1632	1462	73.9	1606	1475	42.6	1486	1500	48.7
Total urinary urea (mmol/24h)	410.2	402.9	6.88	387.9	384.0	12.73	372.8	362.0	8.43	362.7	357.0	13.16
Base		*314*			*114*			*273*			*128*	
Women												
Urine volume (ml/24h)	1520	1450	33.7	1365	1275	56.6	1356	1300	35.2	1419	1325	45.7
Total urinary urea (mmol/24h)	319.9	318.3	6.16	293.0	288.0	8.46	285.1	280.0	5.93	280.3	280.0	6.93
Base		*311*			*101*			*271*			*174*	

Table 8.28 Urinary urea by sex of informant and household composition

Urine analytes (units)	Household composition											
	Informant alone			With others, no dependent children						With dependent child		
				With spouse			No spouse					
	Mean	Median	SE	Mean	Median	SE	Mean	Median	SE	Mean	Median	SE
Men												
Urine volume (ml/24h)	1562	1525	86.5	1731	1625	42.8	1462	1375	46.6	1654	1500	42.5
Total urinary urea (mmol/24h)	349.9	343.5	17.73	398.3	387.7	7.64	368.1	360.5	10.27	393.2	397.1	7.64
Base		*50*			*290*			*192*			*309*	

	Informant alone			With others, no dependent children						With dependent child					
				With spouse			No spouse			With spouse			Lone mother		
	Mean	Median	SE	Mean	Median	SE	Mean	Median	SE	Mean	Median	SE	Mean	Median	SE
Women															
Urine volume (ml/24h)	1504	1500	76.0	1561	1500	35.1	1158	1050	44.6	1414	1350	31.7	1347	1175	88.9
Total urinary urea (mmol/24h)	285.3	282.9	14.56	304.7	296.5	5.90	274.3	271.1	7.80	300.8	300.5	5.38	308.4	293.2	16.72
Base		*62*			*298*			*126*			*326*			*53*	

Table 8.29 Urinary urea by sex of informant and smoking behaviour

Urine analytes (units)	Smoking behaviour											
	None				Fewer than 20 cigarettes a day				20 or more cigarettes a day			
	Mean	Median	SE	*Base*	Mean	Median	SE	*Base*	Mean	Median	SE	*Base*
Men												
Urine volume (ml/24h)	1618	1500	29.0	*578*	1554	1463	56.9	*137*	1771	1563	75.1	*126*
Total urinary urea (mmol/24h)	405.4	403.0	5.39	*578*	345.1	333.0	12.71	*137*	345.9	350.8	11.13	*126*
Women												
Urine volume (ml/24h)	1410	1350	24.6	*562*	1453	1350	45.5	*194*	1527	1500	54.8	*109*
Total urinary urea (mmol/24h)	309.3	302.5	4.16	*562*	283.5	279.1	7.36	*194*	262.7	264.0	9.39	*109*

Table 8.30: Urinary urea by sex of informant and alcohol consumption during seven-day dietary recording period

Urine analytes (units)	Alcohol consumption during seven-day dietary recording period (g/week)											
	Nil			Less than 168g			168g—less than 400g			400g or more		
	Mean	Median	SE	Mean	Median	SE	Mean	Median	SE	Mean	Median	SE
Men												
Urine volume (ml/24h)	1455	1338	46.6	1564	1500	34.3	1705	1588	51.8	2114	1875	106.3
Total urinary urea (mmol/24h)	382.5	360.5	11.40	399.4	399.0	6.74	382.1	377.0	9.44	368.5	365.5	14.69
Base		*162*			*344*			*202*			*86*	
	Nil			Less than 112g			112g—less than 280g			280g or more		
	Mean	Median	SE	Mean	Median	SE	Mean	Median	SE	Mean	Median	SE
Women												
Urine volume (ml/24h)	1328	1250	35.0	1470	1390	28.4	1559	1500	58.1	1700	1600	146.1
Total urinary urea (mmol/24h)	284.5	278.5	6.54	309.5	306.4	4.56	295.0	300.7	8.50	281.8	233.8	32.52
Base		*280*			*432*			*108*			*14*	

9 Nutrient intake: fat and fatty acids

This chapter presents the results for intakes of total fat, saturated, polyunsaturated, monounsaturated and trans fatty acids and of cholesterol. Total fat and fatty acid intakes as percentages both of total and of food energy intake, and the ratio of polyunsaturated to saturated fatty acids (P:S ratio) consumed are also reported.

9.1 Total fat intake and fat as a percentage of energy intake

The average daily intake of total fat was 102.3g for men (median 101.8g) and 73.5g for women (median 73.3g). There was no significant difference in the average daily intake of total fat between different age groups.

(Table 9.1)

Tables 9.2 and 9.3 show the distributions and main statistics for total fat as a percentage of food energy and total energy, by age and sex of informant. Since men derived more of their total energy intake from alcohol than women there was a greater difference for men than for women in the two proportions tabulated. On average, men derived 37.6% of their total energy intake from fat, which represented 40.4% of their food energy intake; women derived 39.2% of their total energy intake from fat but, like men, derived 40.3% of their food energy from fat. The percentages of food energy derived from fat were also similar across all age groups.

(Tables 9.2 & 9.3)

The COMA Panel on diet and cardiovascular disease recommended that individuals' total fat intake should not exceed 35% of their *food* energy.[1] Only 12% of men and 15% of women in this sample had total fat intakes which provided 35% or less of their food energy, thus falling within the COMA recommendations. There was no significant variation in the proportion of informants in different age groups who achieved this target.

9.2 Saturated fatty acids

Comparative studies between countries have shown a strong positive relationship between the proportion of energy derived from saturated fatty acids and mortality from coronary heart disease.[1]

The average intakes of saturated fatty acids by age and sex are shown in Table 9.4. Men consumed, on average, 42.0g of saturated fatty acids (median 40.7g) compared to 31.1g (median 30.5g) for women. Intakes of saturated fatty acids did not vary by age of informant.

(Table 9.4)

Tables 9.5 and 9.6 show the distributions by age and sex for saturated fatty acids as a percentage of total energy and of food energy.

NACNE proposed the long term target of average intake of 10% of *total* energy from saturated fatty acids.[2] On average, saturated fatty acids contributed 15.4% to the total energy intake of men in the sample, and 16.5% of the total energy intake of women (p<0.01). Men derived an average of 16.5% and women 17.0% of their food energy from saturated fatty acids (p<0.01).

Saturated fatty acids represented a greater percentage of food energy for the oldest age group compared to the youngest group considered; saturated fatty acids represented 17.2% of the food energy of men aged 50 to 64 compared to 16.1% of those aged 16 to 24 (17.5% compared to 16.4% for women) (p<0.01). A quarter of men (25%) and only 22% of women in the 50 to 64 age group derived 15% or less of their food energy from saturated fatty acids, compared to 33% of men and 31% of women in the 16 to 24 age group (p<0.05).

(Tables 9.5 & 9.6)

9.2.1 Saturated plus trans fatty acids

Tables 9.7 and 9.8 show statistics for the percentages of total energy and of food energy derived from saturated plus trans fatty acids. COMA recommended that individuals' intakes of saturated fatty acids plus trans fatty acids should not exceed 15% of food energy;[1] only 11% of men and 12% of women were within the COMA recommendations.

(Tables 9.7 & 9.8)

9.3 Polyunsaturated and monounsaturated fatty acids

Polyunsaturated fatty acids are commonly divided into two groups, n-3 and n-6 polyunsaturates. Fish oils are the richest source of n-3 polyunsaturates; n-6 polyunsaturates include linoleic acid and are found mainly in plants, including soya, maize and sunflower oils.

The average daily intake of n-3 polyunsaturates recorded by the sample was 1.95g for men (median 1.83g) and 1.35g for women (median 1.26g). The average daily intakes of n-6 polyunsaturates recorded by the sample were considerably higher (p<0.01); an average of 13.8g for men (median 12.6g) and 9.6g for women (median 8.8g). The average daily intakes of n-6 polyunsaturated fatty acids were significantly lower among men and women aged 50 to 64 compared with the average values for the whole sample (p<0.01).

Intakes of n 3 polyunsaturated fatty acids were also significantly lower in the oldest men (p<0.01), but less markedly lower in the oldest group of women (p<0.05). *(Tables 9.9 to 9.13)*

The average daily intake of monosaturated fatty acids recorded for men was 31.4g (median 30.9g) and for women 22.1g (median 21.8g). Among men, intake did not vary significantly with age, but women aged 50 years or over had a lower intake than did younger women (p<0.01). *(Tables 9.14 to 9.16)*

The COMA Report on diet and cardiovascular disease made no specific recommendations for change in the consumption of polyunsaturated and monounsaturated fatty acids but, in order to facilitate the reduction of saturated fatty acids intake, it recommended that the ratio of polyunsaturated to saturated (including trans) fatty acids may increase to about 0.45.[1]

Table 9.17 shows the distribution for the ratio of polyunsaturates to saturates only, and Table 9.18 statistics for the ratio using saturates plus trans fatty acids. The same pattern is seen for both ratios. A higher value for the P:S ratio indicates a more favourable balance between polyunsaturated and saturated fatty acids in respect of cardiovascular disease.

The average P:S ratio was higher for men than women (p<0.05), with an average value of 0.40 for men (median 0.35) and of 0.38 for women (median 0.34). The ratio varied with age for both sexes. Men and women in the oldest age group had a lower average P:S ratio than did those below the age of 50 (p<0.01). *(Tables 9.17 & 9.18)*

9.4 Cholesterol

The effect of dietary cholesterol on serum concentrations varies with other aspects of the diet. The major dietary influence on serum cholesterol concentrations is the intake of saturated fatty acids. COMA reported in 1984 that the then current intakes of cholesterol (approximately 350mg to 450mg per day) were not excessive, and expected that these intakes would fall with implementation of the recommendation for intake of saturated fatty acids.[1] The data for an effect on serum cholesterol of dietary cholesterol are less secure than for that of saturated fatty acids. A significant effect appears to be seen mainly in individuals with a particular sensitivity. Dietary cholesterol, in a high fibre, low fat, low saturated fatty acids diet, has no effect on serum cholesterol.[3]

Table 9.19 shows that the intake of cholesterol was about 40% higher for men than for women (p<0.01); the average intake for men was 390mg (median 375mg) and that of women was 280mg (median 269mg). For both sexes, informants aged 50 to 64 had a significantly higher intake of cholesterol than the youngest group (p<0.01), in spite of the lower total energy intake amongst the oldest group. *(Table 9.19)*

9.5 Trans fatty acids

The average intakes of trans fatty acids by age and sex of the sample are shown in Table 9.20. As expected, men had greater average intakes than women; men consumed, on average, 5.6g of trans fatty acids (median 5.2g) compared to 4.0g (median 3.7g) for women (p<0.01). Men aged 50 to 64 had lower intakes of trans fatty acids than did men aged 16 to 24 (p<0.01). *(Tables 9.20 to 9.22)*

9.6 Sources of fat in the diet

Tables 9.23 to 9.28 show the contribution of the main food types to the intake of total fat and fatty acids in the diet.

Almost one quarter of total fat intake was derived from meat and meat products, and these were of greater importance for men (26% of total fat) than for women (22%) (p<0.05). A variety of meat products contributed to this total but the main groups were meat pies (5% of total fat), bacon and ham (4%), and beef and veal (4%). Almost one fifth (19%) of total fat was derived from cereal products; most of this was provided by biscuits, cakes and puddings. Milk and milk products and fat spreads also contributed significantly to fat intake; fat spreads provided 16% of the total, and milk and milk products 15%. The only other large contribution was from vegetables (11%) of which about half (5% of total intake) was provided by roast and fried potatoes, including chips, while savoury snacks contributed 2% of total intake. *(Table 9.23)*

Figures 9.1 to 9.6 compare the sources of total fat for men and women within the sample by age, social class and region. Meat and meat products, and vegetables (including roast and fried potatoes) were more important sources of the fat intakes of younger men and women, and they obtained less fat from cereal products. A similar pattern was seen according to the social class of the informant; those in lower social classes derived more of their fat intake from meat and meat products and vegetables and less from cereal products than did informants in higher social classes. Differences between regions were, however, less marked and tended to vary between men and women. *(Figs 9.1 to 9.6)*

The foods which contributed most to the intake of saturated fatty acids were broadly similar to those contributing towards total fat intake. Milk and milk products were, however, of greater relative importance than for total fat intake, and vegetables of lesser importance; both the meat and meat products and milk and milk products groups provided 23% of saturated fatty acids. Cereal products provided 18% of intake and fat spreads 17%, of which butter contributed most (10% of total intake). *(Table 9.24)*

Trans fatty acids were derived chiefly from fat spreads (30%), but a range of different types of spreads contributed; these were a more important source for men than for women (p<0.05). Cereal products were also important, providing 27% of the intake of trans fatty acids, and they contributed more of the total for women than for men (p<0.01). Meat and products contributed 18% of the total, with 7% from meat pies. Milk and products provided 10% of the intake of trans fatty acids. *(Table 9.25)*

Vegetables contributed 22% of the total intake of n–3 polyunsaturated fatty acids, with 13% provided by roast and fried potatoes. Meats, cereal products and fat spreads each contributed between 15% and 20% of total intake, but fish provided 14% of the total, and oily fish provided about half of this. Milk and milk products were a less important source of n–3 polyunsaturated fatty acids, providing only 6% of the total. *(Table 9.26)*

To a large extent n–6 polyunsaturated fatty acids were also derived from vegetables (24%) with 12% of total intake from roast and fried potatoes. Fish was not an important source. Cereal products and fat spreads each provided about one fifth of the total intake. Polyunsaturated margarine was the most important single food group within the fat spreads category (13%). Meat and meat products contributed 17% of the total. *(Table 9.27)*

Meat and meat products were the major sources of monounsaturated fatty acids (31%). Cereal products (18%), milk and milk products (12%), fat spreads (11%), and vegetables (12%) were also significant sources. *(Table 9.28)*

9.7 Variation in intake of fat
Dieters and the unwell
Respondents who were on a slimming diet during the dietary recording period had a lower intake of total fat than non-slimmers (p<0.01). Women on a slimming diet also had lower intakes of all fatty acids (p<0.01), but not of cholesterol; male slimmers reported consuming significantly less saturated, trans and monounsaturated fatty acids (p<0.01), but there was no difference in their consumption of polyunsaturated fatty acids or cholesterol. *(Table 9.29)*

Although slimmers consumed less fat than non-slimmers, the average percentage of food energy from fat for both male and female slimmers was still in excess of the COMA recommendations (38.6% and 38.2%).

Female slimmers consumed lower percentages of their total and food energy intake from fat and from saturated fatty acids than did non-slimmers (p<0.01), but there was no difference in the P:S ratio between these two groups of women. In contrast, although male slimmers obtained lower percentages of their total and food energy from saturated fatty acids and had a higher P:S ratio than male non-slimmers (p<0.05, p<0.01 and p<0.01 respectively), there was no significant

difference in percentage of either total or food energy obtained from total fat. *(Table 9.30)*

Respondents whose eating was affected by their being unwell during the recording period also tended to have lower intakes of fat than did the well group. Men whose eating was affected by their having been unwell had an average daily total fat intake of 93.7g compared to 102.7g (p<0.05); the comparable figures for women were 59.8g and 75.0g respectively (p<0.01). However, for men, but not women the proportion of total energy intake obtained from fat was higher among those who were unwell compared with others (p<0.01), but there were no other significant differences between the groups. *(Tables 9.31 & 9.32)*

Region
Compared with average values for all men in the sample, men in Scotland consumed less total fat and all types of fatty acids (p<0.01), except n–3 polyunsaturated fatty acids. There was no similar trend for women. Men in London and the South East derived a greater percentage of food energy from saturated fatty acids and from saturates plus trans fatty acids than did men in the Northern region, 17.0% and 19.2% compared to 16.2% and 18.4%, (p<0.01), but other percentages did not differ significantly. There were no significant differences between regions for women. Average values for the P:S ratio did not vary between regions either for men or for women.
(Tables 9.33 & 9.34)

Socio-economic characteristics
There were few significant differences according to employment status in women's intake of fat; compared with working women economically inactive women, on average, consumed less polyunsaturated fatty acids (n–3 polyunsaturates: p<0.01; n–6 polyunsaturates: p<0.05). For men, the pattern was similar to that seen for the intake of proteins and carbohydrates. Working men had the highest absolute intakes of all fatty acids, and unemployed men had the lowest intakes (p<0.01). Unemployed men had lower average values for the percentage of total and food energy from fat, saturated fatty acids, and saturated plus trans fatty acids (p<0.01). For example, unemployed men derived 39.0% of their food energy from fat compared to 40.7% for working men. There was however no significant difference in the average P:S ratio of men according to their employment status. *(Tables 9.35 & 9.36)*

Those informants living in households in receipt of benefits had significantly lower intakes of fat and all types of fatty acids (p<0.01, except for trans fatty acids where p<0.05). The percentage of total and food energy provided by fat, saturated fatty acids and saturated plus trans fatty acids was markedly lower for men in households receiving benefits (p<0.01); their average P:S ratio was also lower than for other men (p<0.05). For women there were no differences between those in households receiving benefits and others either in the percentage of energy from total fat or fatty acids, or in the P:S ratio. *(Tables 9.37 & 9.38)*

The intake of n–3 and n–6 polyunsaturated fatty acids was higher for men in Social Classes I and II than for men in manual social classes (p<0.01), but intake of other fatty acids and cholesterol did not differ significantly between men on the basis of social class. Among women consumption of fat, saturated fatty acids, n–3 and n–6 polyunsaturated fatty acids and cholesterol was significantly lower for those in Social Classes IV and V compared with women in Social Classes I and II (p<0.01). For both sexes, the percentage of total or food energy provided by fat and by saturated fatty acids did not differ significantly according to social class. The ratio of polyunsaturated fatty acids to saturated fatty acids was significantly lower for both men and women in Social Classes IV and V compared to those in the non-manual social classes (p<0.01). *(Tables 9.39 & 9.40)*

Household composition

Intakes of total fat, saturated and trans fatty acids, monounsaturated fatty acids and cholesterol by men showed no consistent trend according to household composition. Intakes of polyunsaturated fatty acids did however show some association. Consumption of n–3 polyunsaturated fatty acids was significantly higher among men with dependent children and those living with other adults compared with men living with a spouse but no dependent children (p<0.01). Intakes of n–6 polyunsaturated fatty acids were again higher among men with dependent children (p<0.01) and, less markedly, among those living with other adults (p<0.05) than for those living alone or with a spouse but no dependent children.

Compared to all men in the sample, men living with a spouse but no dependent children obtained significantly higher percentages of both total and food energy from saturated fatty acids and from saturated plus trans fatty acids (p<0.01). This group also had significantly lower P:S ratios compared with all men (p<0.01). Compared with lone mothers, consumption of trans fatty acids was higher for those women living with a spouse and dependent children (p<0.01), and for those living with a spouse but no dependent children (p<0.05). The percentage of total and food energy derived from fat was broadly consistent across all groups of women. Compared with all women those who were living with others but neither with a spouse nor with dependent children obtained a lower percentage of their total and food energy from saturated and saturated plus trans fatty acids (p<0.05). This group also had a higher than average P:S ratio (p<0.05). *(Tables 9.41 & 9.42)*

9.8 Individuals meeting the COMA recommendations for fat intake

During the week of the dietary record about 12% of men and 15% of women met the COMA recommendation that the food energy derived from fat should not exceed 35% of their food energy, whilst 11% of men and 12% of women had saturated plus trans fatty acid intakes equivalent to 15% or less of their food energy. Only 65 men and 90 women in the sample met both of the COMA recommendations during the recording week; this represents 6% of men and 8% of women interviewed. *(Tables 9.3 & 9.7)*

The informants meeting one or other of the COMA recommendations were not an easily identifiable group in terms of the main characteristics of the sample considered in this chapter. Slimmers and the unemployed were, however, more likely than non-slimmers or working informants respectively to have derived less than 35% of their food energy from fat; 28% of slimmers and 20% of the unemployed met this recommendation compared to 13% of the total sample.

9.9 Summary

Average values for the percentage of energy from fat and from saturated fatty acids were well above those levels recommended by COMA and NACNE. Average values for the P:S ratio were below the levels suggested by these reports.

Meat and meat products were the major source of dietary fat, but cereal products, milk and milk products, fat spreads and vegetables also made large contributions.

There was little difference between men and women in the percentages of food energy provided by fat, although men had lower values for fat as a percentage of total energy because of their greater average intake of alcohol. Saturated fatty acids provided, on average, a higher percentage of the food energy of women than of men, and women had lower values for the ratio of polyunsaturated to saturated fatty acids.

Intakes of fat and the percentages of total and food energy from fat did not differ significantly across the age groups. However older informants had lower intakes of polyunsaturated fatty acids and older women also had lower intakes of monounsaturated fatty acids. This resulted in older people having higher percentages of total and food energy from saturated fatty acids, and lower values for the P:S ratio. The oldest informants also had significantly higher intakes of cholesterol than the youngest group.

Female slimmers derived lower percentages of energy from fat and saturated fatty acids than non-slimmers which suggests that, as well as having lower absolute energy intakes, there was a qualitative difference in the diets of these women. Men and women who were unwell during the recording period also had lower absolute intakes of fat than others but among men the percentage of total energy they derived from fat was higher.

Men in Scotland consumed less than the overall average amounts of fat and all types of fatty acids except n–3 polyunsaturated fatty acids. There was little variation between regions in the intakes of women. Unemployed men and men in households receiving benefits recorded lower intakes and derived smaller percentages of their food energy from fat; they also had lower P:S ratios. Similar differences were not seen for women. Informants in Social Classes IV and V had lower P:S ratios than those in the non-manual social classes. Women in Social Classes IV and V consumed on average less fat and most fatty acids than women in Social Classes I and II. These differences were not observed for men.

References

1. Committee on Medical Aspects of Food Policy. *Diet and cardiovascular disease. Report of the Panel on diet in relation to cardiovascular disease.* Department of Health and Social Security. Report on Health and Social Subjects, No 28. HMSO (London, 1984).
2. National Advisory Committee on Nutrition Education. *A discussion paper on proposals for nutritional guidelines for health education in Britain.* Health Education Council (London, 1983).
3. Edington JD, Geekie M, Carter R *et al.* Serum lipid response to dietary cholesterol in subjects fed a low-fat, high fiber diet. *Am J Clin Nutr* 1989; 50: 58–62.

Table 9.1   Average daily total fat intake (g) by age and sex

Fat intake (grams)	Age				All ages
	16–24	25–34	35–49	50–64	16–64
	cum %	cum %	cum %	cum %	cum %
Men					
Less than 60	8	6	6	5	6
Less than 80	23	19	21	22	21
Less than 100	46	45	47	50	47
Less than 120	73	74	74	81	75
All	100	100	100	100	100
Base	*214*	*254*	*346*	*273*	*1087*
Mean (average) value	103.5	103.1	103.3	99.4	102.3
Median value	103.4	103.0	102.3	100.3	101.8
Lower 2.5 percentile	43.8	51.3	50.4	47.6	49.8
Upper 2.5 percentile	171.0	159.6	154.4	146.9	155.8
Standard error of the mean	2.14	1.79	1.51	1.51	0.85
	cum %	cum %	cum %	cum %	cum %
Women					
Less than 60	27	31	24	29	27
Less than 80	63	64	59	70	63
Less than 100	88	87	88	92	89
Less than 120	96	95	96	99	96
All	100	100	100	100	100
Base	*189*	*253*	*385*	*283*	*1110*
Mean (average) value	73.6	73.6	75.5	70.9	73.5
Median value	72.8	73.1	75.5	70.2	73.3
Lower 2.5 percentile	30.2	33.8	31.3	32.3	31.3
Upper 2.5 percentile	124.1	126.0	127.2	112.5	124.5
Standard error of the mean	1.61	1.51	1.19	1.21	0.68

Table 9.2   Percentage of total energy from fat by age and sex

Percentage of total energy from fat	Age				All ages
	16–24	25–34	35–49	50–64	16–64
	cum %	cum %	cum %	cum %	cum %
Men					
30% or less	6	6	8	8	7
33% or less	19	15	19	17	17
35% or less	29	24	30	26	27
38% or less	47	47	54	54	51
40% or less	64	64	71	70	68
42% or less	80	79	85	83	82
45% or less	94	94	95	93	94
All	100	100	100	100	100
Base	*214*	*254*	*346*	*273*	*1087*
Mean (average) value	37.9	37.9	37.1	37.6	37.6
Median value	38.3	38.4	37.5	37.6	37.9
Lower 2.5 percentile	27.4	28.2	25.0	27.0	26.6
Upper 2.5 percentile	47.6	46.0	46.8	47.6	47.1
Standard error of the mean	0.36	0.32	0.28	0.32	0.16
	cum %	cum %	cum %	cum %	cum %
Women					
30% or less	3	3	6	3	4
33% or less	11	11	14	8	11
35% or less	20	20	23	16	20
38% or less	41	39	39	36	39
40% or less	60	52	55	55	55
42% or less	78	67	71	70	71
45% or less	89	89	88	88	89
All	100	100	100	100	100
Base	*189*	*253*	*385*	*283*	*1110*
Mean (average) value	38.7	39.4	39.0	39.5	39.2
Median value	39.0	39.9	39.5	39.6	39.4
Lower 2.5 percentile	29.1	28.9	27.5	30.4	28.3
Upper 2.5 percentile	47.7	48.8	50.3	48.3	48.6
Standard error of the mean	0.33	0.33	0.29	0.29	0.16

Table 9.3 Percentage of food energy from fat by age and sex

Percentage of food energy from fat	Age				All ages
	16–24	25–34	35–49	50–64	16–64
	cum %	cum %	cum %	cum %	cum %
Men					
30% or less	2	1	1	3	2
35% or less	14	9	13	11	12
38% or less	29	26	29	29	28
40% or less	45	37	46	46	44
42% or less	63	55	67	67	64
45% or less	85	80	87	87	85
All	100	100	100	100	100
Base	*214*	*254*	*346*	*273*	*1087*
Mean (average) value	40.2	41.0	40.2	40.2	40.4
Median value	40.7	41.2	40.3	40.2	40.5
Lower 2.5 percentile	30.3	31.7	30.7	28.4	30.6
Upper 2.5 percentile	49.9	49.5	49.6	49.0	49.5
Standard error of the mean	0.34	0.31	0.24	0.28	0.14
	cum %	cum %	cum %	cum %	cum %
Women					
30% or less	2	3	5	2	3
35% or less	16	15	17	12	15
38% or less	33	31	30	29	30
40% or less	51	43	43	47	45
42% or less	66	57	61	63	61
45% or less	87	77	82	86	83
All	100	100	100	100	100
Base	*189*	*253*	*385*	*283*	*1110*
Mean (average) value	39.8	40.7	40.3	40.3	40.3
Median value	39.8	41.1	40.8	40.4	40.5
Lower 2.5 percentile	30.8	29.5	27.5	30.7	28.7
Upper 2.5 percentile	49.0	49.9	51.4	49.4	50.1
Standard error of the mean	0.35	0.34	0.30	0.29	0.16

Table 9.4 Average daily intake of saturated fatty acids (g) by age and sex

Saturated fatty acids intake (grams)	Age				All ages
	16–24	25–34	35–49	50–64	16–64
	cum %	cum %	cum %	cum %	cum %
Men					
Less than 25	11	8	9	7	9
Less than 30	21	16	19	18	19
Less than 35	32	34	30	30	31
Less than 40	50	50	48	41	47
Less than 50	75	78	74	71	74
All	100	100	100	100	100
Base	*214*	*254*	*346*	*273*	*1087*
Mean (average) value	41.6	41.7	42.0	42.7	42.0
Median value	39.8	40.1	40.6	43.0	40.7
Lower 2.5 percentile	16.2	19.3	19.3	20.1	19.1
Upper 2.5 percentile	73.7	73.4	69.0	69.3	69.4
Standard error of the mean	0.97	0.86	0.70	0.77	0.40
	cum %	cum %	cum %	cum %	cum %
Women					
Less than 25	31	33	26	32	30
Less than 30	53	50	45	49	49
Less than 35	71	68	63	70	67
Less than 40	82	81	80	83	81
Less than 50	96	94	94	96	95
All	100	100	100	100	100
Base	*189*	*253*	*385*	*283*	*1110*
Mean (average) value	30.4	30.9	31.7	30.8	31.1
Median value	29.3	29.9	31.2	30.6	30.5
Lower 2.5 percentile	10.9	11.0	11.5	14.3	11.8
Upper 2.5 percentile	53.5	55.2	55.8	50.6	54.6
Standard error of the mean	0.74	0.73	0.57	0.59	0.32

Table 9.5 Percentage of total energy from saturated fatty acids by age and sex

Percentage of total energy from saturated fatty acids	Age				All ages
	16–24	25–34	35–49	50–64	16–64
	cum %	cum %	cum %	cum %	cum %
Men					
12% or less	14	12	16	9	13
15% or less	47	45	50	37	45
18% or less	84	84	84	71	81
20% or less	96	93	96	89	94
All	100	100	100	100	100
Base	*214*	*254*	*346*	*273*	*1087*
Mean (average) value	15.2	15.3	15.1	16.1	15.4
Median value	15.2	15.4	15.0	16.1	15.4
Lower 2.5 percentile	9.9	9.6	9.4	9.8	9.6
Upper 2.5 percentile	21.0	21.6	21.0	22.7	21.7
Standard error of the mean	0.19	0.18	0.16	0.20	0.09
	cum %	cum %	cum %	cum %	cum %
Women					
12% or less	7	8	9	5	7
15% or less	35	33	33	25	31
18% or less	75	70	71	59	69
20% or less	94	86	85	80	86
All	100	100	100	100	100
Base	*189*	*253*	*385*	*283*	*1110*
Mean (average) value	16.0	16.4	16.4	17.1	16.5
Median value	16.2	16.2	16.3	17.2	16.4
Lower 2.5 percentile	10.9	10.1	9.5	11.2	10.4
Upper 2.5 percentile	21.4	22.3	23.5	23.2	22.9
Standard error of the mean	0.21	0.21	0.17	0.19	0.10

Table 9.6 Percentage of food energy from saturated fatty acids by age and sex

Percentage of food energy from saturated fatty acids	Age				All ages
	16–24	25–34	35–49	50–64	16–64
	cum %	cum %	cum %	cum %	cum %
Men					
12% or less	7	4	6	4	5
15% or less	33	30	32	25	30
18% or less	76	74	74	56	70
20% or less	94	89	89	81	88
All	100	100	100	100	100
Base	*214*	*254*	*346*	*273*	*1087*
Mean (average) value	16.1	16.5	16.3	17.2	16.5
Median value	16.2	16.6	16.1	17.3	16.5
Lower 2.5 percentile	10.9	11.2	10.6	10.2	10.6
Upper 2.5 percentile	21.9	22.1	22.1	23.4	22.4
Standard error of the mean	0.19	0.18	0.16	0.19	0.09
	cum %	cum %	cum %	cum %	cum %
Women					
12% or less	5	6	7	3	5
15% or less	31	27	28	22	27
18% or less	70	65	64	56	63
20% or less	91	82	82	77	82
All	100	100	100	100	100
Base	*189*	*253*	*385*	*283*	*1110*
Mean (average) value	16.4	16.9	16.9	17.5	17.0
Median value	16.5	16.8	16.8	17.4	16.9
Lower 2.5 percentile	10.9	10.7	10.0	11.9	10.7
Upper 2.5 percentile	22.1	22.7	23.9	23.4	23.4
Standard error of the mean	0.21	0.21	0.18	0.19	0.10

Table 9.7   Percentage of food energy from saturated plus trans fatty acids by age and sex

Percentage of food energy from saturated plus trans fatty acids	Age				All ages
	16–24	25–34	35–49	50–64	16–64
	cum %	cum %	cum %	cum %	cum %
Men					
15% or less	13	8	13	8	11
18% or less	40	41	45	32	40
20% or less	71	69	67	56	66
22% or less	92	88	87	81	87
All	100	100	100	100	100
Base	*214*	*254*	*346*	*273*	*1087*
Mean (average) value	18.4	18.6	18.5	19.4	18.7
Median value	18.6	18.7	18.5	19.7	18.9
Lower 2.5 percentile	12.6	12.8	12.0	11.3	12.3
Upper 2.5 percentile	23.9	24.6	24.3	25.0	24.7
Standard error of the mean	0.20	0.19	0.17	0.20	0.09
	cum %	cum %	cum %	cum %	cum %
Women					
15% or less	15	11	14	7	12
18% or less	43	38	37	33	37
20% or less	66	60	60	53	59
22% or less	87	79	83	73	79
All	100	100	100	100	100
Base	*189*	*253*	*385*	*283*	*1110*
Mean (average) value	18.5	19.1	19.1	19.6	19.1
Median value	18.7	19.1	19.2	19.6	19.2
Lower 2.5 percentile	12.6	12.0	11.2	13.4	11.7
Upper 2.5 percentile	24.5	25.2	27.0	25.2	25.5
Standard error of the mean	0.23	0.22	0.19	0.20	0.11

Table 9.8   Percentage of total energy from saturated plus trans fatty acids by age and sex

Percentage of total energy from saturated plus trans fatty acids	Age				All ages
	16–24	25–34	35–49	50–64	16–64
	cum %	cum %	cum %	cum %	cum %
Men					
15% or less	22	22	25	18	22
18% or less	56	61	60	47	56
20% or less	82	82	81	71	79
All	100	100	100	100	100
Base	*214*	*254*	*346*	*273*	*1087*
Mean (average) value	17.3	17.3	17.1	18.1	17.4
Median value	17.6	17.2	17.3	18.3	17.6
Lower 2.5 percentile	11.8	11.3	10.5	11.0	11.2
Upper 2.5 percentile	22.7	24.0	23.4	24.6	23.8
Standard error of the mean	0.21	0.21	0.17	0.21	0.10
	cum %	cum %	cum %	cum %	cum %
Women					
15% or less	18	14	17	10	15
18% or less	49	44	43	37	43
20% or less	70	67	68	58	65
All	100	100	100	100	100
Base	*189*	*253*	*385*	*283*	*1110*
Mean (average) value	18.1	18.5	18.5	19.2	18.6
Median value	18.3	18.4	18.6	19.1	18.6
Lower 2.5 percentile	12.1	11.2	10.7	12.6	11.5
Upper 2.5 percentile	23.7	24.7	26.0	25.0	25.1
Standard error of the mean	0.23	0.22	0.19	0.20	0.11

Table 9.9 Average daily intake of n-3 and n-6 polyunsaturated fatty acids (g) by age and sex

	Age				All ages
	16–24	25–34	35–49	50–64	16–64
a) Intake of n-3 poly-unsaturated fatty acids (g)					
Men					
Mean (average) value	2.00	2.02	2.00	1.78	1.95
Median value	1.95	1.93	1.88	1.70	1.83
Lower 2.5 percentile	0.73	0.85	0.81	0.61	0.79
Upper 2.5 percentile	3.71	3.82	4.28	3.45	3.74
Standard error of the mean	0.05	0.05	0.04	0.04	0.02
Base	*214*	*254*	*346*	*273*	*1087*
Women					
Mean (average) value	1.41	1.35	1.37	1.28	1.35
Median value	1.28	1.26	1.33	1.13	1.26
Lower 2.5 percentile	0.51	0.53	0.56	0.55	0.53
Upper 2.5 percentile	2.99	2.60	2.70	2.44	2.68
Standard error of the mean	0.05	0.04	0.03	0.03	0.02
Base	*189*	*253*	*385*	*283*	*1110*
b) Intake of n-6 poly-unsaturated fatty acids (g)					
Men					
Mean (average) value	14.2	14.3	14.3	12.1	13.8
Median value	13.7	13.2	12.9	11.1	12.6
Lower 2.5 percentile	5.3	5.7	5.4	3.7	5.1
Upper 2.5 percentile	29.4	28.5	34.5	24.3	29.0
Standard error of the mean	0.40	0.38	0.40	0.33	0.19
Base	*214*	*254*	*346*	*273*	*1087*
Women					
Mean (average) value	9.9	9.9	9.9	8.8	9.6
Median value	9.1	8.9	8.9	7.9	8.8
Lower 2.5 percentile	3.4	3.3	3.1	2.9	3.1
Upper 2.5 percentile	21.3	21.6	21.9	20.0	21.3
Standard error of the mean	0.32	0.30	0.25	0.25	0.14
Base	*189*	*253*	*385*	*283*	*1110*

Table 9.10 Percentage of total energy from n-3 polyunsaturated fatty acids by age and sex

Percentage of total energy from n-3 polyunsaturated fatty acids	Age				All ages
	16–24	25–34	35–49	50–64	16–64
	cum %	cum %	cum %	cum %	cum %
Men					
0.4% or less	4	3	4	7	5
0.6% or less	30	28	34	41	34
0.8% or less	68	67	70	74	70
1.0% or less	85	87	87	93	88
All	100	100	100	100	100
Base	*214*	*254*	*346*	*273*	*1087*
Mean (average) value	0.74	0.75	0.73	0.68	0.72
Median value	0.70	0.70	0.68	0.64	0.68
Lower 2.5 percentile	0.36	0.37	0.38	0.34	0.36
Upper 2.5 percentile	1.33	1.39	1.38	1.29	1.34
Standard error of the mean	0.02	0.02	0.01	0.02	0.01
	cum %	cum %	cum %	cum %	cum %
Women					
0.4% or less	2	2	2	4	2
0.6% or less	36	30	33	39	34
0.8% or less	65	72	73	71	71
1.0% or less	84	87	89	88	88
All	100	100	100	100	100
Base	*189*	*253*	*385*	*283*	*1110*
Mean (average) value	0.75	0.74	0.72	0.72	0.73
Median value	0.68	0.68	0.67	0.66	0.67
Lower 2.5 percentile	0.40	0.41	0.41	0.39	0.40
Upper 2.5 percentile	1.45	1.43	1.31	1.56	1.40
Standard error of the mean	0.02	0.02	0.01	0.02	0.01

Table 9.11 Percentage of food energy from n-3 polyunsaturated fatty acids by age and sex

Percentage of food energy from n-3 polyunsaturated fatty acids	Age				All ages
	16–24	25–34	35–49	50–64	16–64
	cum %	*cum %*	*cum %*	*cum %*	*cum %*
Men					
0.4% or less	2	2	1	4	2
0.6% or less	22	19	26	32	25
0.8% or less	62	57	61	69	62
1.0% or less	82	80	83	91	84
All	100	100	100	100	100
Base	*214*	*254*	*346*	*273*	*1087*
Mean (average) value	0.79	0.81	0.79	0.73	0.78
Median value	0.75	0.76	0.73	0.68	0.73
Lower 2.5 percentile	0.40	0.42	0.43	0.38	0.41
Upper 2.5 percentile	1.33	1.51	1.48	1.52	1.46
Standard error of the mean	0.02	0.02	0.02	0.02	0.01
	cum %	*cum %*	*cum %*	*cum %*	*cum %*
Women					
0.4% or less	2	2	1	3	2
0.6% or less	32	26	29	35	30
0.8% or less	64	66	67	68	67
1.0% or less	87	87	86	87	86
All	100	100	100	100	100
Base	*189*	*253*	*385*	*283*	*1110*
Mean (average) value	0.77	0.77	0.74	0.74	0.75
Median value	0.69	0.71	0.69	0.67	0.69
Lower 2.5 percentile	0.40	0.42	0.43	0.39	0.41
Upper 2.5 percentile	1.45	1.50	1.31	1.62	1.45
Standard error of the mean	0.02	0.02	0.01	0.02	0.01

Table 9.12 Percentage of total energy from n-6 polyunsaturated fatty acids by age and sex

Percentage of total energy from n-6 polyunsaturated fatty acids	Age				All ages
	16–24	25–34	35–49	50–64	16–64
	cum %	*cum %*	*cum %*	*cum %*	*cum %*
Men					
3% or less	5	6	11	9	11
4% or less	24	28	30	44	32
5% or less	54	50	57	68	58
6% or less	74	70	75	80	75
All	100	100	100	100	100
Base	*214*	*254*	*346*	*273*	*1087*
Mean (average) value	5.21	5.28	5.17	4.62	5.07
Median value	4.89	4.99	4.71	4.24	4.72
Lower 2.5 percentile	2.78	2.53	2.22	2.12	2.27
Upper 2.5 percentile	9.43	9.78	10.16	9.15	9.78
Standard error of the mean	0.12	0.11	0.13	0.12	0.06
	cum %	*cum %*	*cum %*	*cum %*	*cum %*
Women					
3% or less	6	8	8	11	9
4% or less	24	28	32	39	32
5% or less	56	53	55	61	57
6% or less	72	72	75	77	74
All	100	100	100	100	100
Base	*189*	*253*	*385*	*283*	*1110*
Mean (average) value	5.17	5.32	5.14	4.88	5.12
Median value	4.82	4.86	4.81	4.36	4.73
Lower 2.5 percentile	2.59	2.45	2.56	2.32	2.43
Upper 2.5 percentile	9.52	10.57	9.87	9.42	9.92
Standard error of the mean	0.13	0.13	0.10	0.12	0.06

Table 9.13 Percentage of food energy from n-6 polyunsaturated fatty acids by age and sex

Percentage of food energy from n-6 polyunsaturated fatty acids	Age				All ages
	16–24	25–34	35–49	50–64	16–64
	cum %	*cum %*	*cum %*	*cum %*	*cum %*
Men					
3% or less	3	4	6	15	7
4% or less	18	19	23	36	24
5% or less	46	41	49	60	49
6% or less	69	62	69	75	69
All	100	100	100	100	100
Base	*214*	*254*	*346*	*273*	*1087*
Mean (average) value	5.54	5.72	5.58	4.94	5.44
Median value	5.19	5.35	5.03	4.60	5.03
Lower 2.5 percentile	2.97	2.78	2.75	2.18	2.57
Upper 2.5 percentile	10.29	10.57	10.78	9.70	10.35
Standard error of the mean	0.12	0.12	0.13	0.12	0.06
	cum %	*cum %*	*cum %*	*cum %*	*cum %*
Women					
3% or less	5	7	8	11	8
4% or less	23	25	28	36	29
5% or less	52	50	51	60	54
6% or less	70	67	72	76	72
All	100	100	100	100	100
Base	*189*	*253*	*385*	*283*	*1110*
Mean (average) value	5.31	5.50	5.32	4.99	5.27
Median value	4.95	4.99	4.94	4.49	4.88
Lower 2.5 percentile	2.71	2.59	2.61	2.37	2.47
Upper 2.5 percentile	10.20	10.84	10.22	9.69	10.27
Standard error of the mean	0.13	0.13	0.11	0.12	0.06

Table 9.14 Average daily intake of monounsaturated fatty acids (g) by age and sex

Intake of monounsaturated fatty acids (grams)	Age				All ages
	16–24	25–34	35–49	50–64	16–64
Men					
Mean (average) value	32.4	32.0	31.5	29.9	31.4
Median value	31.4	31.3	31.0	30.0	30.9
Lower 2.5 percentile	13.8	17.0	15.8	14.9	15.6
Upper 2.5 percentile	55.8	52.6	48.2	46.8	49.5
Standard error of the mean	0.70	0.55	0.48	0.49	0.27
Base	*214*	*254*	*346*	*273*	*1087*
Women					
Mean (average) value	22.7	22.2	22.6	21.0	22.1
Median value	22.4	21.7	22.4	20.5	21.8
Lower 2.5 percentile	10.0	11.2	9.5	10.1	10.0
Upper 2.5 percentile	38.2	37.3	38.3	35.5	37.1
Standard error of the mean	0.50	0.45	0.37	0.37	0.21
Base	*189*	*253*	*385*	*283*	*1110*

Table 9.15 Percentage of total energy from monounsaturated fatty acids by age and sex

Percentage of total energy from monounsaturated fatty acids	Age				All ages
	16–24	25–34	35–49	50–64	16–64
	cum %	cum %	cum %	cum %	cum %
Men					
10.5% or less	29	21	33	32	29
11.5% or less	46	43	56	60	52
12.5% or less	65	68	76	76	72
13.5% or less	78	82	95	88	84
All	100	100	100	100	100
Base	*214*	*254*	*346*	*273*	*1087*
Mean (average) value	11.9	11.8	11.3	11.3	11.6
Median value	11.8	11.9	11.2	11.0	11.4
Lower 2.5 percentile	8.3	8.2	7.7	8.0	8.1
Upper 2.5 percentile	16.5	15.4	15.7	15.5	15.7
Standard error of the mean	0.15	0.12	0.10	0.11	0.06
	cum %	cum %	cum %	cum %	cum %
Women					
10.5% or less	21	22	26	27	25
11.5% or less	41	41	46	46	44
12.5% or less	61	62	67	66	64
13.5% or less	81	79	83	83	82
All	100	100	100	100	100
Base	*189*	*253*	*385*	*283*	*1110*
Mean (average) value	12.0	12.0	11.8	11.7	11.8
Median value	12.0	11.9	11.7	11.7	11.8
Lower 2.5 percentile	8.6	8.2	7.6	8.2	8.1
Upper 2.5 percentile	16.4	16.2	16.3	15.3	16.1
Standard error of the mean	0.14	0.13	0.11	0.11	0.06

Table 9.16 Percentage of food energy from monounsaturated fatty acids by age and sex

Percentage of food energy from monounsaturated fatty acids	Age				All ages
	16–24	25–34	35–49	50–64	16–64
	cum %	cum %	cum %	cum %	cum %
Men					
10.5% or less	16	10	17	15	15
11.5% or less	30	25	34	39	33
12.5% or less	50	44	58	62	54
13.5% or less	67	65	75	87	73
All	100	100	100	100	100
Base	*214*	*254*	*346*	*273*	*1087*
Mean (average) value	12.6	12.8	12.3	12.1	12.4
Median value	12.6	12.8	12.0	12.0	12.3
Lower 2.5 percentile	8.42	9.12	8.87	8.56	8.76
Upper 2.5 percentile	17.4	16.6	16.6	15.9	16.6
Standard error of the mean	0.15	0.13	0.10	0.11	0.06
	cum %	cum %	cum %	cum %	cum %
Women					
10.5% or less	16	20	20	22	20
11.5% or less	34	34	38	40	37
12.5% or less	53	53	56	61	56
13.5% or less	77	74	76	79	76
All	100	100	100	100	100
Base	*189*	*253*	*385*	*283*	*1110*
Mean (average) value	12.3	12.4	12.2	12.0	12.2
Median value	12.4	12.4	12.2	12.0	12.2
Lower 2.5 percentile	8.59	8.61	7.94	8.55	8.39
Upper 2.5 percentile	17.4	16.5	16.6	15.5	16.4
Standard error of the mean	0.15	0.13	0.11	0.11	0.06

Table 9.17 Ratio of polyunsaturated to saturated fatty acids by age and sex

Ratio of polyunsaturated to saturated fatty acids	Age				All ages
	16–24	25–34	35–49	50–64	16–64
	cum %	cum %	cum %	cum %	cum %
Men					
0.25 or less	11	15	18	33	20
0.3 or less	25	28	33	46	33
0.35 or less	43	42	48	61	49
0.4 or less	59	53	58	69	60
0.5 or less	79	75	75	84	78
All	100	100	100	100	100
Base	*214*	*254*	*346*	*273*	*1087*
Mean (average) value	0.41	0.43	0.42	0.35	0.40
Median value	0.38	0.39	0.36	0.31	0.35
Lower 2.5 percentile	0.19	0.17	0.17	0.13	0.16
Upper 2.5 percentile	0.86	0.81	1.03	0.84	0.87
Standard error of the mean	0.011	0.018	0.013	0.011	0.007
	cum %	cum %	cum %	cum %	cum %
Women					
0.25 or less	19	21	25	32	25
0.3 or less	35	37	39	48	40
0.35 or less	47	48	54	62	53
0.4 or less	62	61	63	71	64
0.5 or less	80	76	80	84	80
All	100	100	100	100	100
Base	*189*	*253*	*385*	*283*	*1110*
Mean (average) value	0.40	0.39	0.38	0.35	0.38
Median value	0.36	0.36	0.34	0.31	0.34
Lower 2.5 percentile	0.17	0.16	0.16	0.14	0.15
Upper 2.5 percentile	0.91	0.83	0.89	0.77	0.85
Standard error of the mean	0.015	0.011	0.009	0.010	0.006

Table 9.18 Ratio of polyunsaturated to saturated plus trans fatty acids by age and sex

Ratio of polyunsaturated to saturated plus trans fatty acids	Age				All ages
	16–24	25–34	35–49	50–64	16–64
Men					
Mean (average) value	0.36	0.38	0.37	0.31	0.35
Median value	0.33	0.34	0.31	0.27	0.31
Lower 2.5 percentile	0.17	0.16	0.15	0.12	0.14
Upper 2.5 percentile	0.71	0.72	0.90	0.74	0.75
Standard error of the mean	0.010	0.016	0.012	0.010	0.006
Base	*214*	*254*	*346*	*273*	*1087*
Women					
Mean (average) value	0.35	0.35	0.34	0.31	0.33
Median value	0.32	0.31	0.30	0.27	0.30
Lower 2.5 percentile	0.15	0.14	0.15	0.13	0.14
Upper 2.5 percentile	0.77	0.73	0.77	0.69	0.76
Standard error of the mean	0.012	0.010	0.008	0.009	0.005
Base	*189*	*253*	*385*	*283*	*1110*

Table 9.19 Average daily intake of cholesterol (mg) by age and sex

Cholesterol intake (mg)	Age				All ages
	16–24	25–34	35–49	50–64	16–64
Men					
Mean (average) value	362	383	398	407	390
Median value	343	371	381	383	375
Lower 2.5 percentile	132	167	163	166	151
Upper 2.5 percentile	752	659	722	755	741
Standard error of the mean	10.6	8.4	8.0	9.3	4.5
Base	*214*	*254*	*346*	*273*	*1087*
Women					
Mean (average) value	247	264	295	294	280
Median value	240	256	281	288	269
Lower 2.5 percentile	91	92	120	113	98
Upper 2.5 percentile	430	483	532	515	511
Standard error of the mean	7.1	6.7	5.4	6.2	3.2
Base	*189*	*253*	*385*	*283*	*1110*

Table 9.20 Average daily intake of trans fatty acids (g) by age and sex

Trans fatty acids intake (grams)	Age				All ages
	16–24	25–34	35–49	50–64	16–64
	cum %	cum %	cum %	cum %	cum %
Men					
less than 3	15	14	13	15	14
less than 4	28	31	30	32	30
less than 5	41	44	46	52	46
less than 6	58	62	62	70	63
less than 8	79	85	81	88	83
All	100	100	100	100	100
Base	*214*	*254*	*346*	*273*	*1087*
Mean (average) value	5.9	5.5	5.7	5.3	5.6
Median value	5.5	5.3	5.2	4.9	5.2
Lower 2.5 percentile	2.0	1.7	1.9	1.8	1.9
Upper 2.5 percentile	11.6	10.3	11.4	11.8	11.3
Standard error of the mean	0.18	0.15	0.15	0.15	0.08
	cum %	cum %	cum %	cum %	cum %
Women					
less than 2	13	11	12	12	12
less than 3	32	34	30	36	33
less than 4	60	58	51	60	56
less than 5	76	78	71	78	76
less than 6	86	87	85	90	87
All	100	100	100	100	100
Base	*189*	*253*	*385*	*283*	*1110*
Mean (average) value	4.0	4.0	4.1	3.8	4.0
Median value	3.7	3.7	3.9	3.5	3.7
Lower 2.5 percentile	1.1	1.1	0.8	1.0	1.0
Upper 2.5 percentile	9.1	9.1	8.8	7.5	8.8
Standard error of the mean	0.14	0.12	0.10	0.11	0.06

Table 9.21 Percentage of total energy from trans fatty acids by age and sex

Percentage of total energy from trans fatty acids	Age				All ages
	16–24	25–34	35–49	50–64	16–64
	cum %	cum %	cum %	cum %	cum %
Men					
1.3% or less	11	15	16	14	14
1.6% or less	25	33	33	30	30
1.9% or less	43	47	49	53	48
2.2% or less	59	64	64	69	64
2.5% or less	74	78	77	81	77
All	100	100	100	100	100
Base	*214*	*254*	*346*	*273*	*1087*
Mean (average) value	2.13	2.00	2.05	2.00	2.04
Median value	2.04	1.95	1.92	1.87	1.93
Lower 2.5 percentile	0.95	0.87	0.82	0.97	0.89
Upper 2.5 percentile	3.84	3.71	4.08	3.96	3.84
Standard error of the mean	0.05	0.05	0.04	0.05	0.02
	cum %	cum %	cum %	cum %	cum %
Women					
1.3% or less	11	10	13	11	11
1.6% or less	25	27	27	27	26
1.9% or less	51	46	41	45	45
2.2% or less	66	63	58	61	61
2.5% or less	74	77	73	77	75
All	100	100	100	100	100
Base	*189*	*253*	*385*	*283*	*1110*
Mean (average) value	2.10	2.10	2.11	2.08	2.10
Median value	1.89	1.98	2.06	2.00	1.99
Lower 2.5 percentile	0.88	1.04	0.74	0.84	0.88
Upper 2.5 percentile	3.97	3.84	3.84	3.95	3.88
Standard error of the mean	0.06	0.05	0.04	0.05	0.02

Table 9.22 Percentage of food energy from trans fatty acids by age and sex

Percentage of food energy from trans fatty acids	Age				All ages
	16–24	25–34	35–49	50–64	16–64
	cum %	cum %	cum %	cum %	cum %
Men					
1.3% or less	9	10	8	9	9
1.6% or less	21	24	24	24	23
1.9% or less	35	40	41	45	41
2.2% or less	53	56	56	63	57
2.5% or less	66	71	72	77	72
All	100	100	100	100	100
Base	*214*	*254*	*346*	*273*	*1087*
Mean (average) value	2.27	2.15	2.20	2.13	2.19
Median value	2.14	2.11	2.11	2.02	2.09
Lower 2.5 percentile	1.10	1.03	1.02	1.07	1.06
Upper 2.5 percentile	4.05	3.81	4.14	4.14	4.08
Standard error of the mean	0.05	0.05	0.05	0.05	0.02
	cum %	cum %	cum %	cum %	cum %
Women					
1.3% or less	11	7	10	10	9
1.6% or less	23	23	23	25	23
1.9% or less	47	41	37	42	41
2.2% or less	62	61	54	59	58
2.5% or less	73	74	70	75	73
All	100	100	100	100	100
Base	*189*	*253*	*385*	*283*	*1110*
Mean (average) value	2.15	2.17	2.18	2.13	2.16
Median value	1.99	2.05	2.12	2.05	2.07
Lower 2.5 percentile	0.95	1.07	0.77	0.95	0.92
Upper 2.5 percentile	4.10	3.87	3.91	4.06	3.91
Standard error of the mean	0.06	0.05	0.04	0.05	0.02

Table 9.23: Average daily fat intake (g) from main food types by sex of informant

Food type	Men		Women		Total	
	Amount	% of total	Amount	% of total	Amount	% of total
Cereal products	18.9	18	14.9	20	16.9	19
of which						
—*biscuits*	*3.2*	*3*	*2.9*	*4*	*3.1*	*4*
—*buns, cakes & pastries*	*6.1*	*6*	*5.0*	*7*	*5.5*	*6*
—*puddings and ice cream*	*2.8*	*3*	*2.2*	*3*	*2.5*	*3*
Milk and products	15.0	15	11.8	16	13.4	15
of which						
—*whole milk*	*7.1*	*7*	*5.7*	*8*	*6.4*	*7*
—*cheese*	*6.0*	*6*	*4.3*	*6*	*5.2*	*6*
Eggs and egg dishes	4.2	4	3.0	4	3.6	4
Fat spreads	16.6	16	11.8	16	14.1	16
of which						
—*butter*	*5.9*	*6*	*5.1*	*7*	*5.5*	*6*
—*polyunsaturated margarine*	*3.8*	*4*	*2.5*	*3*	*3.2*	*4*
—*low fat spreads*	*1.0*	*1*	*.8*	*1*	*.9*	*1*
—*other margarine & spreads*	*5.8*	*6*	*3.4*	*6*	*4.6*	*6*
Meat and products	26.9	26	16.2	22	21.5	24
of which						
—*bacon and ham*	*4.1*	*4*	*2.2*	*3*	*3.1*	*4*
—*beef and veal*	*4.3*	*4*	*2.9*	*4*	*3.6*	*4*
—*meat pies*	*5.3*	*5*	*2.8*	*4*	*4.0*	*5*
Fish and fish dishes	2.9	3	2.0	3	2.5	3
Vegetables	11.4	11	8.0	11	9.7	11
of which						
—*roast and fried potatoes (inc. chips)*	*5.9*	*6*	*3.5*	*5*	*4.7*	*5*
—*savoury snacks*	*2.2*	*2*	*1.8*	*2*	*2.0*	*2*
Fruit and nuts	.7	1	.7	1	.7	1
Sugar, confectionery and preserves	2.2	2	2.3	3	2.3	3
Beverages	.2	0	.1	0	.2	0
Miscellaneous	3.2	3	2.9	4	3.1	3
TOTAL	102.3	100	73.5	100	87.8	100
Number of cases	*1087*		*1110*		*2197*	

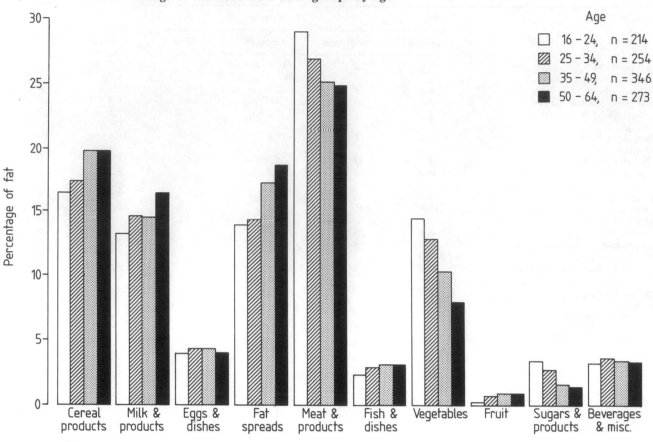

Figure 9.1   Men: Percentage of fat from main food groups by age

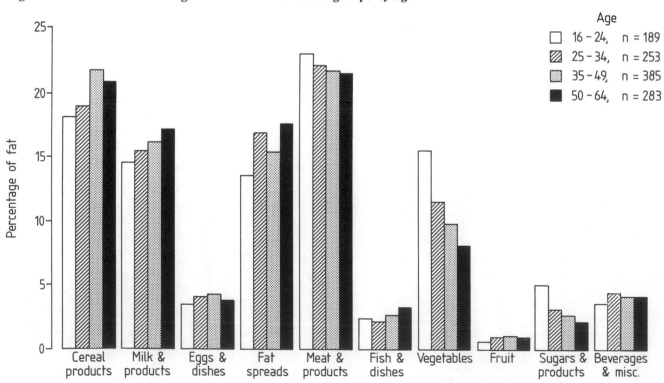

Figure 9.2   Women: Percentage of fat from main food groups by age

Figure 9.3   Men: Percentage of fat from main food groups by social class of head of household

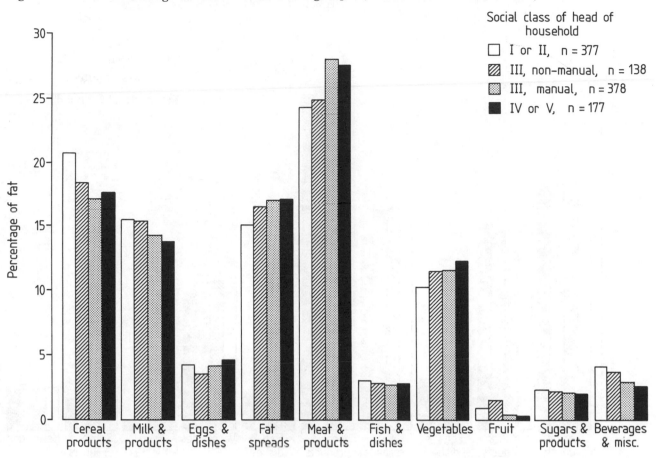

Figure 9.4   Women: Percentage of fat from main food groups by social class of head of household

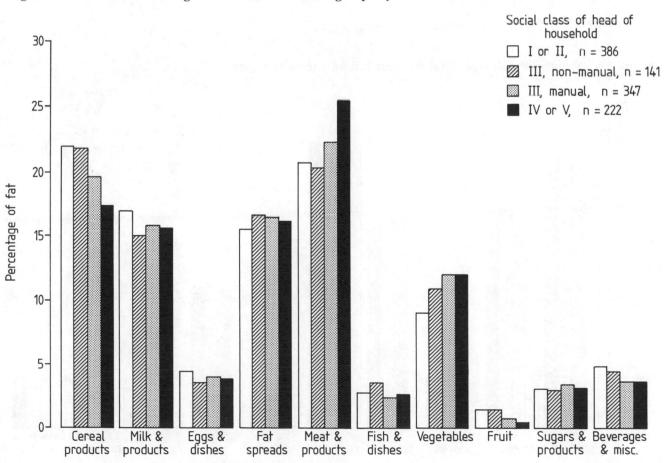

Figure 9.5   Men: Percentage of fat from main food groups by region

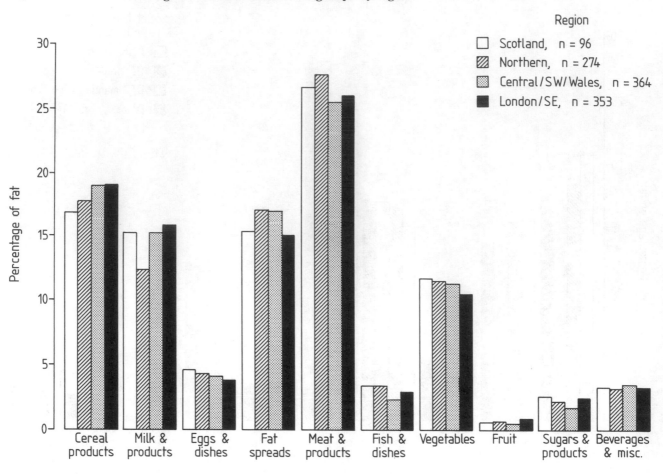

Figure 9.6   Women: Percentage of fat from main food groups by region

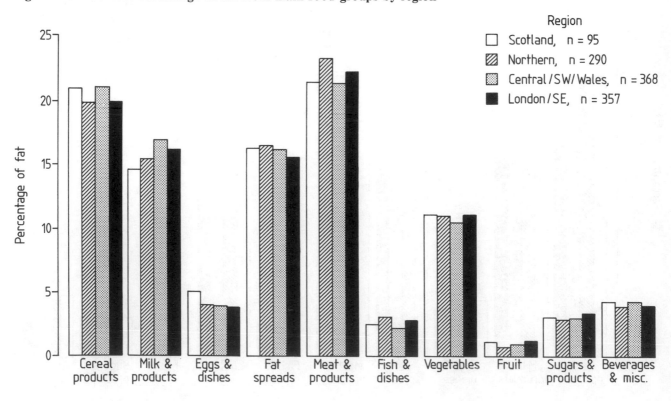

Table 9.24 Average daily intake of saturated fatty acids (g) from main food types by sex of informant

Food type	Men Amount	Men % of total	Women Amount	Women % of total	Total Amount	Total % of total
Cereal products	7.3	17	5.8	19	6.6	18
of which						
—*biscuits*	*1.5*	*4*	*1.3*	*4*	*1.4*	*4*
—*buns, cakes & pastries*	*2.2*	*5*	*1.9*	*6*	*2.0*	*6*
—*puddings & ice cream*	*1.6*	*4*	*1.2*	*4*	*1.4*	*4*
Milk and products	9.5	23	7.5	24	8.5	23
of which						
—*whole milk*	*4.5*	*11*	*3.6*	*12*	*4.1*	*11*
—*cheese*	*3.8*	*9*	*2.7*	*9*	*3.3*	*9*
Eggs and egg dishes	1.3	3	1.0	3	1.1	3
Fat spreads	7.1	17	5.4	17	6.2	17
of which						
—*butter*	*4.0*	*9*	*3.4*	*11*	*3.7*	*10*
Meat and products	10.4	25	6.2	20	8.3	23
of which						
—*bacon and ham*	*1.5*	*4*	*.8*	*3*	*1.2*	*3*
—*beef and veal*	*1.6*	*4*	*1.1*	*4*	*1.4*	*4*
—*meat pies*	*2.1*	*5*	*1.1*	*4*	*1.6*	*4*
Fish and fish dishes	.7	2	.5	2	.6	2
Vegetables	2.7	6	2.0	6	2.4	6
Fruit and nuts	.1	0	.1	0	.1	0
Sugar, confectionery and preserves	1.3	3	1.4	4	1.3	4
Beverages	.2	1	.1	0	.2	0
Miscellaneous	1.3	3	1.2	4	1.2	3
TOTAL	42.0	100	31.1	100	36.5	100
Number of cases	*1087*		*1110*		*2197*	

Table 9.25 Average daily intake of trans fatty acids (g) from main food types by sex of informant

Food type	Men Amount	Men % of total	Women Amount	Women % of total	Total Amount	Total % of total
Cereal products	1.42	25	1.21	30	1.31	27
of which						
—*biscuits*	*.34*	*6*	*.31*	*8*	*.32*	*7*
—*buns, cakes & pastries*	*.75*	*13*	*.64*	*16*	*.69*	*14*
—*puddings & ice cream*	*.19*	*3*	*.13*	*3*	*.16*	*3*
Milk and products	.51	9	.40	10	.46	10
of which						
—*whole milk*	*.24*	*4*	*.19*	*5*	*.21*	*4*
—*cheese*	*.21*	*4*	*.15*	*4*	*.18*	*4*
Eggs and egg dishes	.12	2	.10	3	.11	2
Fat spreads	1.76	31	1.08	27	1.42	30
of which						
—*butter*	*.27*	*5*	*.23*	*6*	*.25*	*5*
—*polyunsaturated margarine*	*.31*	*6*	*.20*	*5*	*.25*	*5*
—*block margarine*	*.24*	*4*	*.16*	*4*	*.20*	*4*
—*other margarine & spreads*	*.82*	*15*	*.40*	*10*	*.60*	*13*
Meat and products	1.08	19	.65	16	.86	18
of which						
—*meat pies*	*.44*	*8*	*.25*	*6*	*.34*	*7*
Fish and fish dishes	.06	1	.05	1	.06	1
Vegetables	.35	6	.25	6	.30	6
Fruit and nuts	.01	0	.01	0	.01	0
Sugar, confectionery and preserves	.17	3	.15	4	.16	3
Beverages	0.0	0	0.0	0	0.0	0
Miscellaneous	.12	2	.11	3	.11	2
TOTAL	5.60	100	4.00	100	4.79	100
Number of cases	*1087*		*1110*		*2197*	

Table 9.26 Average daily intake of n-3 polyunsaturated fatty acids (g) from main food types by sex of informant

Food type	Men Amount	% of total	Women Amount	% of total	Total Amount	% of total
Cereal products	.31	16	.24	18	.28	17
of which						
—*pasta, rice & grains*	*.08*	*4*	*.06*	*4*	*.07*	*4*
—*buns, cakes & pastries*	*.07*	*4*	*.06*	*4*	*.07*	*4*
Milk and products	.12	6	.09	7	.10	6
Eggs and egg dishes	.05	3	.03	2	.04	2
Fat spreads	.31	16	.20	15	.25	15
of which						
—*butter*	*.05*	*3*	*.04*	*3*	*.05*	*3*
—*polyunsaturated margarine*	*.09*	*5*	*.06*	*4*	*.07*	*4*
Meat and products	.38	19	.24	18	.31	19
of which						
—*chicken & turkey dishes*	*.08*	*4*	*.05*	*4*	*.06*	*4*
Fish and fish dishes	.27	14	.20	15	.23	14
of which						
—*fried white fish*	*.10*	*5*	*.07*	*5*	*.08*	*5*
—*oily fish*	*.14*	*7*	*.10*	*7*	*.12*	*7*
Vegetables	.44	23	.28	21	.36	22
of which						
—*roast & fried potatoes (inc. chips)*	*.29*	*15*	*.16*	*12*	*.22*	*13*
Fruit and nuts	.01	1	.01	1	.01	1
Sugar, confectionery and preserves	.01	1	.01	1	.01	1
Beverages	0.0	0	0.0	0	0.0	0
Miscellaneous	.04	2	.04	3	.04	2
TOTAL	1.95	100	1.35	100	1.63	100
Number of cases	*1087*		*1110*		*2197*	

106

Table 9.27 Average daily intake of n-6 polyunsaturated fatty acids (g) from main food types by sex of informant

Food type	Men		Women		Total	
	Amount	% of total	Amount	% of total	Amount	% of total
Cereal products	2.97	22	2.21	23	2.59	22
of which						
—white bread	.59	4	.31	3	.45	4
—wholemeal & other bread	.47	3	.37	4	.42	4
—buns, cakes & pastries	.73	5	.58	6	.66	6
Milk and products	.27	2	.22	2	.24	2
Eggs and egg dishes	.54	4	.37	4	.45	4
Fat spreads	2.87	21	1.86	19	2.36	20
of which						
—polyunsaturated margarine	1.82	13	1.19	12	1.51	13
Meat and products	2.43	18	1.48	15	1.95	17
of which						
—bacon and ham	.38	3	.21	2	.29	2
—beef and veal	.34	2	.23	2	.28	2
—meat pies	.45	3	.24	2	.34	3
Fish and fish dishes	.57	4	.36	4	.47	4
of which						
—fried white fish	.43	3	.28	3	.36	3
Vegetables	3.28	24	2.29	24	2.78	24
of which						
—roast & fried potatoes (inc. chips)	1.77	13	1.03	11	1.40	12
—savoury snacks	.68	5	.55	6	.62	5
Fruit and nuts	.21	2	.20	2	.21	2
Sugar, confectionery and preserves	.08	1	.08	1	.08	1
Beverages	.00	0	.00	0	.00	0
Miscellaneous	.53	4	.55	6	.54	5
TOTAL	13.76	100	9.63	100	11.67	100
Number of cases	1087		1110		2197	

Table 9.28 Average daily intake of monounsaturated fatty acids (g) from main food types by sex of informant

Food type	Men Amount	Men % of total	Women Amount	Women % of total	Total Amount	Total % of total
Cereal products	5.34	17	4.15	19	4.74	18
of which						
—pasta, rice & grains	.90	3	.63	3	.76	3
—biscuits	.85	3	.79	4	.82	3
—buns, cakes & pastries	1.72	5	1.39	6	1.55	6
Milk and products	3.70	12	2.90	13	3.30	12
of which						
—whole milk	1.76	6	1.40	6	1.58	6
—cheese	1.49	5	1.07	5	1.28	5
Eggs and egg dishes	1.65	5	1.12	5	1.38	5
Fats and spreads	3.53	11	2.55	12	3.03	11
of which						
—butter	1.27	4	1.08	5	1.17	4
Meat and products	10.46	33	6.27	28	8.34	31
of which						
—bacon and ham	1.73	6	.95	4	1.33	5
—beef and veal	1.69	5	1.13	5	1.41	5
—sausages	1.36	4	.74	3	1.05	4
—meat pies	1.90	6	.98	4	1.43	5
Fish and fish dishes	1.05	3	.69	3	.87	3
Vegetables	3.79	12	2.62	12	3.20	12
of which						
—roast & fried potatoes (inc. chips)	2.13	7	1.26	6	1.69	6
—savoury snacks	.73	2	.59	3	.66	2
Fruit and nuts	.31	1	.30	1	.31	1
Sugar, confectionery and preserves	.57	2	.59	3	.58	2
Beverages	.00	0	.01	0	.01	0
Miscellaneous	.95	3	.87	4	.91	3
TOTAL	31.35	100	22.07	100	26.66	100
Number of cases	*1087*		*1110*		*2197*	

Table 9.29 Average daily intake of fatty acids by sex of informant and whether on a slimming diet

Average daily intake (units)	Whether on a slimming diet					
	Dieting			Not dieting		
	Mean	Median	SE	Mean	Median	SE
Men						
Total fat (g)	84.1	85.7	4.80	103.1	102.5	0.86
Saturated fatty acids (g)	33.1	31.9	2.04	42.4	41.2	0.41
Saturated plus trans fatty acids (g)	37.1	37.5	2.27	48.1	47.1	0.46
Trans fatty acids (g)	4.05	3.87	0.30	5.67	5.26	0.08
n-3 polyunsaturated fatty acids (g)	1.77	1.69	0.13	1.95	1.84	0.02
n-6 polyunsaturated fatty acids (g)	12.8	12.6	0.91	13.8	12.6	0.20
Monounsaturated fatty acids (g)	25.9	27.0	1.56	31.6	31.1	0.27
Cholesterol (mg)	379	377	20.2	390	375	4.6
Base		*46*			*1041*	
Women						
Total fat (g)	58.5	55.9	1.96	75.7	74.8	0.70
Saturated fatty acids (g)	24.0	22.9	0.87	32.1	31.4	0.34
Saturated plus trans fatty acids (g)	26.9	25.5	0.99	36.2	35.5	0.38
Trans fatty acids (g)	2.97	2.79	0.15	4.14	3.81	0.06
n-3 polyunsaturated fatty acids (g)	1.20	1.13	0.05	1.37	1.28	0.02
n-6 polyunsaturated fatty acids (g)	7.9	6.6	0.39	9.9	9.0	0.15
Monounsaturated fatty acids (g)	18.0	17.0	0.60	22.7	22.2	0.22
Cholesterol (mg)	267	242	9.9	281	274	3.4
Base		*138*			*972*	

Table 9.30 Percentage of total and food energy from fatty acids by sex of informant and whether on a slimming diet

Proportion or ratio	Whether on a slimming diet					
	Dieting			Not dieting		
	Mean	Median	SE	Mean	Median	SE
Men						
Total fat as % total energy	36.2	37.0	1.05	37.6	38.0	0.16
Total fat as % food energy	38.6	39.0	1.04	40.5	40.5	0.14
Saturated fatty acids as % total energy	14.1	14.3	0.53	15.4	15.4	0.09
Saturated fatty acids as % food energy	15.1	15.6	0.54	16.6	16.6	0.09
Saturated plus trans fatty acids:						
as % total energy	15.9	16.1	0.59	17.5	17.6	0.10
as % food energy	16.9	17.3	0.59	18.8	18.9	0.09
Trans fatty acids as % total energy	1.72	1.74	0.10	2.05	1.94	0.02
Trans fatty acids as % food energy	1.83	1.77	0.11	2.20	2.10	0.02
n-3 polyunsaturated fatty acids:						
as % total energy	0.78	0.73	0.04	0.72	0.68	0.01
as % food energy	0.83	0.79	0.05	0.78	0.72	0.01
n-6 polyunsaturated fatty acids:						
as % total energy	5.48	5.34	0.27	5.05	4.70	0.06
as % food energy	5.84	5.72	0.28	5.43	5.00	0.07
Monounsaturated fatty acids as % total energy	11.2	11.0	0.38	11.6	11.4	0.06
Monounsaturated fatty acids as % food energy	12.0	11.7	0.39	12.5	12.3	0.06
Ratio of:						
polyunsaturated to saturated fatty acids	0.54	0.44	0.08	0.40	0.35	0.01
polyunsaturated to saturated plus trans fatty acids	0.48	0.38	0.08	0.35	0.31	0.01
Base		46			1041	
Women						
Total fat as % total energy	36.9	37.2	0.52	39.5	39.6	0.16
Total fat as % food energy	38.2	39.3	0.54	40.6	40.8	0.16
Saturated fatty acids as % total energy	15.1	15.1	0.29	16.7	16.5	0.10
Saturated fatty acids as % food energy	15.6	15.7	0.30	17.2	17.1	0.10
Saturated plus trans fatty acids:						
as % total energy	16.9	17.1	0.33	18.8	18.8	0.11
as % food energy	17.5	17.6	0.33	19.4	19.3	0.11
Trans fatty acids as % total energy	1.83	1.78	0.07	2.14	2.03	0.02
Trans fatty acids as % food energy	1.89	1.83	0.07	2.19	2.09	0.02
n-3 polyunsaturated fatty acids:						
as % total energy	0.78	0.73	0.03	0.72	0.66	0.01
as % food energy	0.81	0.76	0.03	0.74	0.68	0.01
n-6 polyunsaturated fatty acids:						
as % total energy	4.86	4.52	0.16	5.16	4.78	0.06
as % food energy	5.05	4.67	0.17	5.31	4.90	0.07
Monounsaturated fatty acids as % total energy	11.4	11.5	0.19	11.9	11.9	0.06
Monounsaturated fatty acids as % food energy	11.8	11.9	0.19	12.2	12.3	0.07
Ratio of:						
polyunsaturated to saturated fatty acids	0.40	0.35	0.02	0.38	0.34	0.01
polyunsaturated to saturated plus trans fatty acids	0.36	0.32	0.01	0.33	0.29	0.01
Base		138			972	

Table 9.31 Average daily intake of fatty acids by sex of informant and whether eating affected by being unwell

Average daily intake (units)	Whether eating affected by being unwell					
	Eating affected			Not unwell/eating not affected		
	Mean	Median	SE	Mean	Median	SE
Men						
Total fat (g)	93.7	95.1	4.15	102.7	102.0	0.87
Saturated fatty acids (g)	37.9	34.2	2.08	42.2	40.9	0.41
Saturated plus trans fatty acids (g)	42.7	40.7	2.29	47.9	46.7	0.46
Trans fatty acids (g)	4.86	4.57	0.32	5.64	5.25	0.08
n-3 polyunsaturated fatty acids (g)	1.86	1.81	0.09	1.95	1.84	0.02
n-6 polyunsaturated fatty acids (g)	13.3	11.6	0.77	13.8	12.6	0.20
Monounsaturated fatty acids (g)	28.9	28.1	1.26	31.5	31.0	0.28
Cholesterol (mg)	347	348	18.1	392	376	4.6
Base		51			1036	
Women						
Total fat (g)	59.8	55.7	2.26	75.0	74.2	0.70
Saturated fatty acids (g)	25.2	24.0	1.04	31.7	31.0	0.34
Saturated plus trans fatty acids (g)	28.3	26.7	1.16	35.8	35.1	0.38
Trans fatty acids (g)	3.10	2.90	0.16	4.09	3.77	0.06
n-3 polyunsaturated fatty acids (g)	1.10	1.01	0.05	1.38	1.29	0.02
n-6 polyunsaturated fatty acids (g)	7.9	6.7	0.46	9.8	8.9	0.14
Monounsaturated fatty acids (g)	18.1	16.8	0.69	22.5	22.0	0.21
Cholesterol (mg)	238	218	11.0	284	273	3.3
Base		106			1004	

Table 9.32 Percentage of total and food energy from fatty acids by sex of informant and whether eating affected by being unwell

Proportion or ratio	Whether eating affected by being unwell					
	Eating affected			Not unwell/eating not affected		
	Mean	Median	SE	Mean	Median	SE
Men						
Total fat as % total energy	39.6	39.9	0.62	37.5	37.7	0.16
Total fat as % food energy	41.9	42.3	0.67	40.3	40.5	0.15
Saturated fatty acids as % total energy	15.7	15.6	0.40	15.4	15.3	0.09
Saturated fatty acids as % food energy	16.7	16.8	0.44	16.5	16.5	0.09
Saturated plus trans fatty acids:						
as % total energy	17.8	17.8	0.44	17.4	17.5	0.10
as % food energy	18.8	18.9	0.48	18.7	18.8	0.10
Trans fatty acids as % total energy	2.06	1.91	0.11	2.04	1.93	0.02
Trans fatty acids as % food energy	2.16	2.06	0.11	2.19	2.09	0.03
n-3 polyunsaturated fatty acids:						
as % total energy	0.81	0.74	0.04	0.72	0.68	0.01
as % food energy	0.85	0.80	0.04	0.77	0.72	0.01
n-6 polyunsaturated fatty acids:						
as % total energy	5.71	5.44	0.28	5.04	4.70	0.06
as % food energy	6.01	5.74	0.28	5.41	5.00	0.07
Monounsaturated fatty acids as % total energy	12.4	12.4	0.29	11.5	11.4	0.06
Monounsaturated fatty acids as % food energy	13.1	12.9	0.31	12.4	12.3	0.06
Ratio of:						
polyunsaturated to saturated fatty acids	0.44	0.41	0.03	0.40	0.35	0.01
polyunsaturated to saturated plus trans fatty acids	0.39	0.36	0.03	0.35	0.31	0.01
Base		51			1036	
Women						
Total fat as % total energy	38.2	39.3	0.55	39.3	39.4	0.17
Total fat as % food energy	39.1	40.1	0.56	40.4	40.6	0.17
Saturated fatty acids as % total energy	16.1	16.4	0.36	16.5	16.4	0.10
Saturated fatty acids as % food energy	16.5	16.5	0.36	17.0	16.9	0.10
Saturated plus trans fatty acids:						
as % total energy	18.1	18.4	0.38	18.7	18.7	0.11
as % food energy	18.5	18.8	0.39	19.2	19.2	0.11
Trans fatty acids as % total energy	1.95	1.88	0.07	2.11	1.99	0.02
Trans fatty acids as % food energy	2.00	1.96	0.07	2.17	2.08	0.02
n-3 polyunsaturated fatty acids:						
as % total energy	0.71	0.63	0.03	0.73	0.67	0.01
as % food energy	0.73	0.66	0.03	0.75	0.69	0.01
n-6 polyunsaturated fatty acids:						
as % total energy	4.95	4.57	0.20	5.14	4.76	0.06
as % food energy	5.07	4.67	0.20	5.29	4.90	0.06
Monounsaturated fatty acids as % total energy	11.6	11.6	0.22	11.9	11.9	0.06
Monounsaturated fatty acids as % food energy	11.9	12.0	0.22	12.2	12.2	0.06
Ratio of:						
polyunsaturated to saturated fatty acids	0.39	0.34	0.02	0.38	0.34	0.01
polyunsaturated to saturated plus trans fatty acids	0.34	0.30	0.02	0.33	0.30	0.01
Base		106			1004	

Table 9.33 Average daily intake of fatty acids by sex and region

Average daily intake (units)	Scotland			Northern			Central, South West and Wales			London and South East		
	Mean	Median	SE	Mean	Median	SE	Mean	Median	SE	Mean	Median	SE
Men												
Total fat (g)	93.4	94.6	2.88	100.8	99.7	1.70	103.7	102.0	1.51	104.5	105.0	1.43
Saturated fatty acids (g)	38.5	36.2	1.27	40.8	39.5	0.78	42.6	41.3	0.72	43.4	42.4	0.71
Saturated plus trans fatty acids (g)	43.7	41.3	1.48	46.5	45.2	0.88	48.2	47.9	0.80	48.9	47.9	0.78
Trans fatty acids (g)	5.18	4.35	0.30	5.73	5.27	0.16	5.65	5.27	0.13	5.56	5.25	0.13
n-3 polyunsaturated fatty acids (g)	1.83	1.69	0.09	1.92	1.82	0.04	1.93	1.84	0.04	2.01	1.85	0.04
n-6 polyunsaturated fatty acids (g)	12.0	10.7	0.61	13.6	12.6	0.36	14.2	12.8	0.36	14.0	12.9	0.34
Monounsaturated fatty acids (g)	29.1	28.4	0.90	31.2	30.2	0.56	31.6	30.9	0.48	31.8	31.7	0.46
Cholesterol (mg)	367	354	17.2	386	376	9.2	393	374	7.8	396	385	7.5
Base		96			274			364			353	
Women												
Total fat (g)	72.9	71.8	2.36	72.5	71.1	1.24	74.2	74.3	1.25	73.9	73.6	1.18
Saturated fatty acids (g)	30.6	31.5	1.03	30.6	29.3	0.60	31.4	30.2	0.60	31.2	31.0	0.57
Saturated plus trans fatty acids (g)	34.4	35.3	1.18	34.5	33.5	0.67	35.5	34.4	0.67	35.2	35.0	0.64
Trans fatty acids (g)	3.89	3.87	0.20	3.96	3.73	0.11	4.10	3.85	0.10	3.93	3.56	0.10
n-3 polyunsaturated fatty acids (g)	1.35	1.27	0.06	1.35	1.27	0.03	1.31	1.21	0.03	1.39	1.31	0.03
n-6 polyunsaturated fatty acids (g)	9.5	8.3	0.57	9.4	8.5	0.26	9.7	8.9	0.23	9.9	9.0	0.25
Monounsaturated fatty acids (g)	22.3	21.8	0.73	21.9	21.8	0.38	22.2	21.9	0.38	22.2	21.5	0.36
Cholesterol (mg)	292	287	10.7	284	278	6.3	275	260	5.6	277	265	5.5
Base		95			290			368			357	

Table 9.34 Percentage of total and food energy from fatty acids by sex and region

Proportion or ratio	Scotland			Northern			Central, South West and Wales			London and South East		
	Mean	Median	SE	Mean	Median	SE	Mean	Median	SE	Mean	Median	SE
Men												
Total fat:												
as % total energy	37.7	38.7	0.61	37.0	37.5	0.34	37.4	37.5	0.28	38.3	38.6	0.24
as % food energy	40.7	40.9	0.52	40.1	40.2	0.29	39.9	40.3	0.26	41.1	41.0	0.23
Saturated fatty acids:												
as % total energy	15.5	15.2	0.31	14.9	14.8	0.18	15.3	15.2	0.16	15.8	16.0	0.16
as % food energy	16.8	16.7	0.27	16.2	16.0	0.17	16.3	16.4	0.16	17.0	17.0	0.16
Saturated plus trans fatty acids:												
as % total energy	17.6	17.5	0.33	17.0	17.0	0.20	17.3	17.4	0.17	17.9	18.1	0.17
as % food energy	19.0	18.9	0.29	18.4	18.3	0.18	18.5	18.6	0.17	19.2	19.3	0.17

Table 9.34 (*continued*)   **Percentage of total and food energy from fatty acids by sex and region**

Proportion or ratio	Region											
	Scotland			Northern			Central, South West and Wales			London and South East		
	Mean	Median	SE	Mean	Median	SE	Mean	Median	SE	Mean	Median	SE
Trans fatty acids:												
as % total energy	2.02	1.91	0.08	2.10	1.93	0.05	2.01	1.91	0.04	2.03	1.95	0.04
as % food energy	2.19	2.03	0.09	2.26	2.12	0.05	2.15	2.05	0.04	2.16	2.11	0.04
n-3 polyunsaturated fatty acids:												
as % total energy	0.74	0.66	0.03	0.71	0.68	0.01	0.70	0.66	0.01	0.74	0.69	0.01
as % food energy	0.80	0.75	0.03	0.78	0.73	0.01	0.75	0.72	0.01	0.80	0.73	0.02
n-6 polyunsaturated fatty acids:												
as % total energy	4.84	4.50	0.21	4.99	4.73	0.11	5.12	4.64	0.11	5.14	4.79	0.11
as % food energy	5.23	4.82	0.22	5.40	5.09	0.12	5.47	4.97	0.12	5.51	5.13	0.11
Monounsaturated fatty acids:												
as % total energy	11.8	11.8	0.24	11.5	11.3	0.12	11.4	11.3	0.10	11.7	11.5	0.10
as % food energy	12.8	12.8	0.23	12.4	12.4	0.12	12.2	12.1	0.11	12.6	12.3	0.10
Ratio of:												
polyunsaturated to saturated fatty acids	0.38	0.33	0.02	0.40	0.37	0.01	0.42	0.35	0.02	0.40	0.35	0.01
polyunsaturated to saturated plus trans fatty acids	0.33	0.28	0.02	0.35	0.32	0.01	0.37	0.31	0.01	0.35	0.31	0.01
Base		96			274			364			353	
Women												
Total fat:												
as % total energy	39.4	39.9	0.62	39.1	39.4	0.29	39.0	39.2	0.28	39.5	39.7	0.27
as % food energy	40.4	41.2	0.63	40.2	40.4	0.29	40.0	40.2	0.28	40.7	40.7	0.28
Saturated fatty acids:												
as % total energy	16.5	16.3	0.34	16.4	16.1	0.18	16.4	16.5	0.17	16.6	16.5	0.17
as % food energy	16.9	16.9	0.34	16.9	16.6	0.19	16.9	16.9	0.17	17.1	17.0	0.18
Saturated plus trans fatty acids:												
as % total energy	18.6	18.6	0.39	18.5	18.5	0.19	18.6	18.7	0.19	18.7	18.7	0.19
as % food energy	19.0	19.3	0.38	19.1	19.1	0.20	19.1	19.1	0.18	19.2	19.3	0.19
Trans fatty acids:												
as % total energy	2.06	1.98	0.09	2.10	1.96	0.05	2.13	2.06	0.04	2.07	1.97	0.04
as % food energy	2.11	2.06	0.09	2.16	2.05	0.05	2.19	2.13	0.04	2.13	2.05	0.04
n-3 polyunsaturated fatty acids:												
as % total energy	0.75	0.67	0.03	0.73	0.68	0.02	0.70	0.65	0.01	0.75	0.70	0.01
as % food energy	0.76	0.70	0.03	0.75	0.70	0.02	0.72	0.67	0.01	0.78	0.72	0.02
n-6 polyunsaturated fatty acids:												
as % total energy	5.03	4.52	0.21	5.01	4.57	0.11	5.08	4.70	0.10	5.28	4.88	0.11
as % food energy	5.17	4.71	0.22	5.17	4.81	0.12	5.23	4.85	0.10	5.44	4.98	0.11
Monounsaturated fatty acids:												
as % total energy	12.1	12.2	0.23	11.9	11.8	0.11	11.7	11.7	0.11	11.9	11.9	0.10
as % food energy	12.4	12.5	0.24	12.2	12.2	0.12	12.0	12.1	0.11	12.3	12.3	0.12
Ratio of:												
polyunsaturated to saturated fatty acids	0.37	0.32	0.02	0.37	0.34	0.01	0.37	0.33	0.01	0.39	0.34	0.01
polyunsaturated to saturated plus trans fatty acids	0.33	0.28	0.02	0.33	0.30	0.01	0.33	0.29	0.01	0.34	0.30	0.01
Base		95			290			368			357	

Table 9.35 Average daily intake of fatty acids (g) by sex and employment status of informant

Average daily intake (units)	Employment status of informant								
	Working			Unemployed			Economically inactive		
	Mean	Median	SE	Mean	Median	SE	Mean	Median	SE
Men									
Total fat (g)	106.0	105.3	0.93	82.0	81.0	2.57	92.2	96.8	2.44
Saturated fatty acids (g)	43.5	42.4	0.44	33.0	31.7	1.20	38.6	39.6	1.19
Saturated plus trans fatty acids (g)	49.3	48.0	0.50	37.5	37.1	1.31	43.6	44.4	1.32
Trans fatty acids (g)	5.81	5.36	0.09	4.47	3.97	0.21	4.97	4.72	0.22
n-3 polyunsaturated fatty acids (g)	2.02	1.88	0.03	1.57	1.50	0.06	1.75	1.65	0.07
n-6 polyunsaturated fatty acids (g)	14.4	13.1	0.22	10.4	9.5	0.50	11.8	11.5	0.48
Monounsaturated fatty acids (g)	32.4	31.8	0.30	26.0	25.9	0.83	28.3	28.9	0.78
Cholesterol (mg)	402	386	5.0	334	295	15.8	348	339	12.7
Base		*875*			*99*			*111*	
Women									
Total fat (g)	74.4	74.5	0.85	71.9	65.8	3.23	72.2	70.8	1.20
Saturated fatty acids (g)	31.2	30.5	0.41	29.8	27.2	1.37	30.9	30.9	0.57
Saturated plus trans fatty acids (g)	35.3	34.6	0.46	33.8	30.3	1.59	34.9	34.9	0.65
Trans fatty acids (g)	4.02	3.74	0.07	4.00	3.75	0.28	3.96	3.65	0.11
n-3 polyunsaturated fatty acids (g)	1.39	1.32	0.02	1.35	1.21	0.09	1.29	1.19	0.03
n-6 polyunsaturated fatty acids (g)	9.8	9.0	0.17	9.9	8.3	0.76	9.2	8.3	0.24
Monounsaturated fatty acids (g)	22.5	22.1	0.26	21.9	20.6	1.02	21.5	21.2	0.36
Cholesterol (mg)	285	273	4.1	257	237	15.1	273	268	5.5
Base		*670*			*57*			*373*	

Table 9.36 Percentage of total and food energy from fatty acids by sex and employment status of informant

Proportion or ratio	Employment status of informant								
	Working			Unemployed			Economically inactive		
	Mean	Median	SE	Mean	Median	SE	Mean	Median	SE
Men									
Total fat as % total energy	37.8	38.1	0.17	35.8	36.3	0.67	37.1	37.7	0.53
Total fat as % food energy	40.7	40.7	0.15	39.0	39.7	0.57	39.2	39.4	0.45
Saturated fatty acids:									
as % total energy	15.5	15.5	0.10	14.4	14.3	0.33	15.4	15.8	0.30
as % food energy	16.7	16.7	0.10	15.7	15.1	0.32	16.4	16.4	0.29
Saturated plus trans fatty acids:									
as % total energy	17.6	17.6	0.11	16.3	15.9	0.36	17.4	17.7	0.33
as % food energy	18.9	19.0	0.10	17.8	17.3	0.33	18.5	18.5	0.32

Proportion or ratio	Employment status of informant								
	Working			Unemployed			Economically inactive		
	Mean	Median	SE	Mean	Median	SE	Mean	Median	SE
Trans fatty acids:									
as % total energy	2.06	1.95	0.26	1.95	1.78	0.08	2.00	1.90	0.08
as % food energy	2.20	2.11	0.03	2.12	1.94	0.08	2.11	1.97	0.08
n-3 polyunsaturated fatty acids:									
as % total energy	0.73	0.69	0.01	0.69	0.63	0.03	0.71	0.66	0.02
as % food energy	0.79	0.73	0.01	0.76	0.71	0.03	0.75	0.70	0.02
n-6 polyunsaturated fatty acids:									
as % total energy	5.16	4.79	0.07	4.57	4.10	0.19	4.82	4.48	0.18
as % food energy	5.54	5.14	0.07	4.98	4.61	0.19	5.08	4.68	0.18
Monounsaturated fatty acids:									
as % total energy	11.6	11.4	0.06	11.4	11.3	0.24	11.4	11.3	0.19
as % food energy	12.5	12.3	0.07	12.4	12.5	0.22	12.0	11.9	0.17
Ratio of:									
polyunsaturated to saturated fatty acids	0.41	0.36	0.01	0.38	0.34	0.02	0.38	0.33	0.02
polyunsaturated to saturated plus trans fatty acids	0.36	0.31	0.01	0.34	0.30	0.02	0.33	0.30	0.02
Base		*875*			*99*			*111*	
Women									
Total fat as % total energy	39.1	39.5	0.20	39.1	39.2	0.73	39.3	39.4	0.29
Total fat as % food energy	40.4	40.8	0.20	40.0	39.9	0.74	40.1	40.2	0.28
Saturated fatty acids:									
as % total energy	16.3	16.2	0.12	16.3	15.9	0.39	16.8	16.9	0.18
as % food energy	16.9	16.7	0.12	16.6	16.5	0.39	17.2	17.2	0.18
Saturated plus trans fatty acids:									
as % total energy	18.4	18.4	0.13	18.4	18.1	0.44	18.9	19.0	0.19
as % food energy	19.1	19.1	0.13	18.8	18.9	0.44	19.3	19.3	0.19
Trans fatty acids:									
as % total energy	2.09	1.99	0.03	2.13	2.07	0.11	2.11	1.98	0.04
as % food energy	2.16	2.08	0.03	2.17	2.07	0.11	2.16	2.05	0.04
n-3 polyunsaturated fatty acids:									
as % total energy	0.74	0.68	0.01	0.74	0.67	0.04	0.71	0.65	0.01
as % food energy	0.77	0.71	0.01	0.75	0.71	0.04	0.72	0.67	0.01
n-6 polyunsaturated fatty acids:									
as % total energy	5.19	4.81	0.08	5.30	4.83	0.29	4.98	4.53	0.10
as % food energy	5.37	4.95	0.08	5.42	4.83	0.30	5.09	4.64	0.10
Monounsaturated fatty acids:									
as % total energy	11.9	11.9	0.07	11.9	11.8	0.28	11.8	11.6	0.11
as % food energy	12.3	12.3	0.08	12.2	12.1	0.29	12.0	12.0	0.11
Ratio of:									
polyunsaturated to saturated fatty acids	0.39	0.35	0.01	0.39	0.33	0.03	0.36	0.32	0.01
polyunsaturated to saturated plus trans fatty acids	0.34	0.31	0.01	0.35	0.29	0.02	0.32	0.28	0.01
Base		*670*			*57*			*373*	

Table 9.37 Average daily intake of fatty acids (g) by sex of informant and whether benefits received

Average daily intake (units)	Whether benefits received					
	Received			Not received		
	Mean	Median	SE	Mean	Median	SE
Men						
Total fat (g)	88.1	91.1	2.26	104.2	103.5	0.90
Saturated fatty acids (g)	35.8	36.2	1.04	42.9	41.8	0.43
Saturated plus trans fatty acids (g)	40.9	41.2	1.15	48.5	47.7	0.48
Trans fatty acids (g)	5.11	4.55	0.23	5.66	5.28	0.08
n-3 polyunsaturated fatty acids (g)	1.67	1.62	0.06	1.98	1.86	0.03
n-6 polyunsaturated fatty acids (g)	11.2	10.6	0.47	14.1	13.0	0.21
Monounsaturated fatty acids (g)	27.6	28.3	0.71	31.9	31.3	0.29
Cholesterol (mg)	337	299	14.0	397	381	4.7
Base		*119*			*963*	
Women						
Total fat (g)	67.7	67.9	1.81	74.5	73.9	0.73
Saturated fatty acids (g)	28.7	28.1	0.85	31.4	30.9	0.35
Saturated plus trans fatty acids (g)	32.4	31.7	0.96	35.5	34.9	0.39
Trans fatty acids (g)	3.76	3.51	0.15	4.03	3.74	0.06
n-3 polyunsaturated fatty acids (g)	1.22	1.16	0.04	1.37	1.28	0.02
n-6 polyunsaturated fatty acids (g)	8.4	7.6	0.32	9.8	8.9	0.15
Monounsaturated fatty acids (g)	20.7	20.5	0.56	22.3	21.9	0.22
Cholesterol (mg)	254	242	9.1	283	274	3.4
Base		*153*			*955*	

Table 9.38 Percentage of total and food energy from fatty acids by sex of informant and whether benefits received

Proportion or ratio	Whether benefits received					
	Received			Not received		
	Mean	Median	SE	Mean	Median	SE
Men						
Total fat as % total energy	36.1	36.3	0.59	37.8	38.1	0.16
Total fat as % food energy	39.2	39.4	0.50	40.6	40.6	0.15
Saturated fatty acids as % total energy	14.6	14.4	0.28	15.5	15.5	0.10
Saturated fatty acids as % food energy	15.9	15.5	0.27	16.6	16.6	0.10
Saturated plus trans fatty acids:						
as % total energy	16.7	16.9	0.30	17.5	17.7	0.11
as % food energy	18.1	18.1	0.28	18.8	19.0	0.10
Trans fatty acids as % total energy	2.09	1.89	0.80	2.04	1.93	0.03
Trans fatty acids as % food energy	2.26	2.05	0.08	2.18	2.09	0.03
n-3 polyunsaturated fatty acids:						
as % total energy	0.69	0.65	0.02	0.73	0.68	0.01
as % food energy	0.75	0.73	0.02	0.78	0.73	0.01
n-6 polyunsaturated fatty acids:						
as % total energy	4.58	4.23	0.17	5.13	4.77	0.07
as % food energy	4.95	4.76	0.17	5.50	5.10	0.07
Monounsaturated fatty acids:						
as % total energy	11.4	11.1	0.21	11.6	11.4	0.06
as % food energy	12.3	12.4	0.19	12.5	12.3	0.06
Ratio of:						
polyunsaturated to saturated fatty acids	0.38	0.33	0.02	0.41	0.36	0.01
polyunsaturated to saturated plus trans fatty acids	0.33	0.29	0.01	0.36	0.31	0.01
Base		*119*			*963*	
Women						
Total fat as % total energy	39.2	39.5	0.45	39.2	39.4	0.17
Total fat as % food energy	39.9	40.2	0.45	40.4	40.6	0.17
Saturated fatty acids as % total energy	16.5	16.5	0.26	16.5	16.4	0.11
Saturated fatty acids as % food energy	16.8	16.9	0.25	17.0	16.9	0.11
Saturated plus trans fatty acids:						
as % total energy	18.7	18.8	0.27	18.6	18.6	0.11
as % food energy	19.0	19.2	0.27	19.2	19.1	0.12
Trans fatty acids as % total energy	2.15	1.98	0.07	2.09	1.99	0.02
Trans fatty acids as % food energy	2.18	1.99	0.07	2.15	2.57	0.02
n-3 polyunsaturated fatty acids:						
as % total energy	0.71	0.65	0.02	0.73	0.67	0.01
as % food energy	0.73	0.66	0.02	0.75	0.69	0.01
n-6 polyunsaturated fatty acids:						
as % total energy	4.85	4.52	0.13	5.17	4.77	0.07
as % food energy	4.95	4.60	0.14	5.33	4.91	0.07
Monounsaturated fatty acids:						
as % total energy	12.1	12.0	0.18	11.8	11.8	0.06
as % food energy	12.3	12.1	0.19	12.2	12.2	0.07
Ratio of:						
polyunsaturated to saturated fatty acids	0.36	0.32	0.01	0.38	0.34	0.01
polyunsaturated to saturated plus trans fatty acids	0.31	0.28	0.01	0.34	0.30	0.01
Base		*153*			*955*	

Table 9.39 Average daily intake of fatty acids (g) by sex of informant and social class of head of household

Average daily intake (units)	Social class of head of household											
	I and II			III non-manual			III manual			IV and V		
	Mean	Median	SE	Mean	Median	SE	Mean	Median	SE	Mean	Median	SE
Men												
Total fat (g)	103.6	103.0	1.4	98.0	100.1	2.2	103.4	102.2	1.5	100.1	99.9	2.4
Saturated fatty acids (g)	42.5	41.7	0.64	40.3	38.7	1.07	42.5	41.1	0.71	41.2	39.2	1.10
Saturated plus trans fatty acids (g)	48.0	46.6	0.72	45.5	44.3	1.22	48.3	47.2	0.79	46.8	44.8	1.22
Trans fatty acids (g)	5.53	5.25	0.13	5.27	4.82	0.24	5.78	5.37	0.13	5.54	5.18	0.21
n-3 polyunsaturated fatty acids (g)	2.03	1.87	0.04	1.89	1.74	0.07	1.90	1.83	0.04	1.85	1.76	0.06
n-6 polyunsaturated fatty acids (g)	14.5	13.2	0.34	13.7	12.2	0.58	13.5	12.6	0.31	12.6	11.7	0.48
Monounsaturated fatty acids (g)	31.3	30.8	0.42	29.7	30.0	0.69	32.0	31.5	0.48	31.3	30.3	0.77
Cholesterol (mg)	396	385	6.9	367	350	11.6	391	376	7.7	390	375	13.4
Base		*377*			*138*			*378*			*177*	
Women												
Total fat (g)	75.8	74.7	1.2	73.9	75.6	1.8	73.7	71.8	1.2	69.6	70.5	1.5
Saturated fatty acids (g)	31.9	30.7	0.58	31.2	31.5	0.91	31.2	30.2	0.55	29.7	29.4	0.71
Saturated plus trans fatty acids (g)	35.9	34.7	0.65	35.2	35.5	1.02	35.3	34.3	0.62	33.5	33.5	0.80
Trans fatty acids (g)	3.99	3.77	0.09	3.99	3.77	0.16	4.10	3.74	0.11	3.85	3.38	0.13
n-3 polyunsaturated fatty acids (g)	1.38	1.33	0.03	1.39	1.27	0.05	1.35	1.25	0.03	1.25	1.14	0.04
n-6 polyunsaturated fatty acids (g)	10.4	9.5	0.26	10.0	9.0	0.41	9.4	8.6	0.23	8.4	7.8	0.26
Monounsaturated fatty acids (g)	22.5	21.9	0.36	21.9	22.4	0.56	22.3	21.6	0.36	21.4	21.1	0.48
Cholesterol (mg)	296	281	5.5	271	279	7.3	278	263	5.7	262	251	7.0
Base		*386*			*141*			*347*			*222*	

Table 9.40 Percentage of total and food energy from fatty acids by sex of informant and social class of head of household

Proportion or ratio	Social class of head of household											
	I and II			III non-manual			III manual			IV and V		
	Mean	Median	SE	Mean	Median	SE	Mean	Median	SE	Mean	Median	SE
Men												
Total fat:												
as % total energy	37.8	38.2	0.24	37.9	38.0	0.42	37.4	37.6	0.29	37.4	38.1	0.45
as % food energy	40.5	40.8	0.23	40.4	40.4	0.41	40.5	40.5	0.25	39.8	40.1	0.36
Saturated fatty acids:												
as % total energy	15.5	15.5	0.14	15.5	15.4	0.27	15.3	15.2	0.16	15.4	15.5	0.25
as % food energy	16.6	16.6	0.15	16.6	16.4	0.26	16.5	16.5	0.15	16.4	16.4	0.23
Saturated plus trans fatty acids:												
as % total energy	17.5	17.4	0.16	17.6	17.8	0.30	17.4	17.6	0.17	17.4	17.8	0.27
as % food energy	18.8	18.8	0.16	18.7	18.7	0.29	18.8	19.0	0.16	18.6	18.7	0.24

Table 9.40 (*continued*) **Percentage of total and food energy from fatty acids by sex of informant and social class of head of household**

Proportion or ratio	Social class of head of household											
	I and II			III non-manual			III manual			IV and V		
	Mean	Median	SE	Mean	Median	SE	Mean	Median	SE	Mean	Median	SE
Trans fatty acids:												
as % total energy	2.00	1.90	0.04	2.03	1.91	0.07	2.08	1.98	0.04	2.06	1.95	0.07
as % food energy	2.14	2.06	0.04	2.15	2.09	0.07	2.24	2.12	0.04	2.18	2.08	0.07
n-3 polyunsaturated fatty acids:												
as % total energy	0.75	0.70	0.01	0.73	0.70	0.02	0.70	0.65	0.01	0.70	0.66	0.02
as % food energy	0.80	0.75	0.01	0.78	0.76	0.02	0.76	0.71	0.01	0.74	0.70	0.02
n-6 polyunsaturated fatty acids:												
as % total energy	5.30	4.93	0.11	5.30	5.08	0.18	4.93	4.43	0.11	4.68	4.52	0.14
as % food energy	5.69	5.38	0.11	5.66	5.37	0.18	5.33	4.81	0.11	4.99	4.71	0.15
Monounsaturated fatty acids:												
as % total energy	11.4	11.4	0.09	11.5	11.3	0.16	11.6	11.4	0.11	11.7	11.7	0.16
as % food energy	12.3	12.2	0.09	12.3	12.1	0.18	12.6	12.4	0.11	12.5	12.3	0.15
Ratio of:												
polyunsaturated to saturated fatty acids	0.41	0.38	0.01	0.42	0.39	0.02	0.40	0.33	0.02	0.37	0.34	0.01
polyunsaturated to saturated plus trans fatty acids	0.36	0.33	0.01	0.37	0.34	0.02	0.35	0.29	0.01	0.32	0.29	0.01
Base		*377*			*138*			*378*			*177*	
Women												
Total fat:												
as % total energy	38.9	39.0	0.27	38.5	39.3	0.47	39.8	40.0	0.27	39.4	39.6	0.37
as % food energy	40.3	40.4	0.27	39.6	40.0	0.48	40.8	41.0	0.27	40.2	40.4	0.37
Saturated fatty acids:												
as % total energy	16.3	16.3	0.17	16.2	16.1	0.30	16.8	16.8	0.16	16.8	16.6	0.21
as % food energy	16.9	16.8	0.17	16.7	16.7	0.30	17.2	17.1	0.17	17.1	16.8	0.21
Saturated plus trans fatty acids:												
as % total energy	18.3	18.3	0.18	18.3	18.1	0.32	19.0	19.0	0.17	18.9	18.8	0.23
as % food energy	19.0	18.9	0.18	18.8	18.8	0.32	19.4	19.5	0.17	19.3	19.1	0.23
Trans fatty acids:												
as % total energy	2.02	1.98	0.03	2.05	2.49	0.06	2.18	2.02	0.04	2.16	1.99	0.06
as % food energy	2.09	2.08	0.03	2.10	2.03	0.06	2.24	2.09	0.04	2.20	2.03	0.06
n-3 polyunsaturated fatty acids:												
as % total energy	0.72	0.67	0.01	0.74	0.68	0.02	0.74	0.67	0.02	0.71	0.65	0.02
as % food energy	0.74	0.69	0.01	0.76	0.69	0.02	0.76	0.69	0.02	0.73	0.67	0.02
n-6 polyunsaturated fatty acids:												
as % total energy	5.33	5.00	0.10	5.22	4.90	0.18	5.09	4.72	0.10	4.70	4.35	0.11
as % food energy	5.52	5.15	0.11	5.38	5.04	0.18	5.23	4.84	0.11	4.81	4.43	0.11
Monounsaturated fatty acids:												
as % total energy	11.6	11.6	0.10	11.5	11.5	0.18	12.1	12.1	0.10	12.2	12.2	0.14
as % food energy	12.0	12.0	0.10	11.8	11.7	0.19	12.4	12.5	0.11	12.4	12.5	0.14
Ratio of:												
polyunsaturated to saturated fatty acids	0.40	0.35	0.01	0.40	0.37	0.02	0.37	0.33	0.01	0.34	0.31	0.01
polyunsaturated to saturated plus trans fatty acids	0.35	0.31	0.01	0.35	0.32	0.02	0.32	0.29	0.01	0.30	0.27	0.01
Base		*386*			*141*			*347*			*222*	

Table 9.41 Average daily intake of fatty acids (g) by sex and household composition

Average daily intake (units)	Household composition											
	Informant alone			With others, no dependent children						With dependent child		
				With spouse			No spouse					
	Mean	Median	SE	Mean	Median	SE	Mean	Median	SE	Mean	Median	SE
Men												
Total fat (g)	97.2	95.1	3.6	100.9	100.3	1.4	102.9	103.0	1.9	104.2	103.8	1.4
Saturated fatty acids (g)	39.6	38.4	1.63	42.8	42.3	0.67	41.3	39.7	0.84	42.3	41.1	0.68
Saturated plus trans fatty acids (g)	45.2	45.1	1.89	48.1	47.2	0.74	47.1	45.8	0.95	48.1	46.6	0.76
Trans fatty acids (g)	5.64	4.81	0.42	5.24	4.91	0.11	5.75	5.34	0.16	5.82	5.46	0.14
n-3 polyunsaturated fatty acids (g)	1.91	1.73	0.09	1.85	1.74	0.04	2.01	1.93	0.05	2.00	1.90	0.04
n-6 polyunsaturated fatty acids (g)	12.5	11.9	0.68	12.9	11.8	0.33	14.1	13.4	0.38	14.6	13.2	0.34
Monounsaturated fatty acids (g)	30.4	28.9	1.10	30.5	30.0	0.44	32.1	31.5	0.60	31.9	31.2	0.45
Cholesterol (mg)	404	407	20.8	397	381	6.8	377	349	10.2	390	373	7.4
Base	*71*			*360*			*271*			*385*		

	Informant alone			With others, no dependent children						With dependent child					
				With spouse			No spouse			With spouse			Lone mother		
	Mean	Median	SE	Mean	Median	SE	Mean	Median	SE	Mean	Median	SE	Mean	Median	SE
Women															
Total fat (g)	71.2	70.3	2.6	72.8	70.9	1.1	74.0	73.5	1.6	75.3	75.8	1.2	69.9	70.4	2.78
Saturated fatty acids (g)	30.9	30.8	1.30	31.0	30.1	0.52	30.6	29.6	0.74	31.7	31.5	0.58	29.2	28.3	1.23
Saturated plus trans fatty acids (g)	34.7	34.7	1.45	34.9	33.8	0.59	34.6	33.9	0.84	35.9	35.6	0.65	32.8	31.9	1.36
Trans fatty acids (g)	3.77	3.33	0.22	3.90	3.66	0.09	3.98	3.67	0.14	4.21	4.01	0.10	3.61	3.38	0.19
n-3 polyunsaturated fatty acids (g)	1.35	1.19	0.06	1.35	1.25	0.03	1.43	1.31	0.05	1.33	1.25	0.03	1.27	1.26	0.06
n-6 polyunsaturated fatty acids (g)	8.6	8.3	0.46	9.4	8.5	0.23	10.1	9.4	0.32	10.0	9.0	0.25	8.9	7.9	0.48
Monounsaturated fatty acids (g)	21.3	20.4	0.80	21.7	21.1	0.33	22.5	22.4	0.50	22.5	22.4	0.36	21.9	21.5	0.93
Cholesterol (mg)	286	284	11.9	294	286	5.3	255	250	7.4	280	267	5.6	258	257	11.7
Base	*84*			*382*			*182*			*386*			*76*		

Table 9.42 Percentage of total and food energy from fatty acids by sex and household composition

Proportion or ratio	Household composition											
	Informant alone			With others, no dependent children						With dependent child		
				With spouse			No spouse					
	Mean	Median	SE	Mean	Median	SE	Mean	Median	SE	Mean	Median	SE
Men												
Total fat:												
as % total energy	37.2	38.9	0.81	37.7	37.7	0.27	37.6	37.9	0.33	37.6	37.8	0.24
as % food energy	40.7	40.4	0.61	40.4	40.5	0.24	40.5	40.8	0.30	40.3	40.4	0.24
Saturated fatty acids:												
as % total energy	15.1	15.2	0.41	16.0	15.9	0.17	15.0	15.0	0.18	15.2	15.2	0.14
as % food energy	16.5	16.3	0.35	17.1	17.0	0.16	16.2	16.3	0.17	16.2	16.3	0.15
Saturated plus trans fatty acids:												
as % total energy	17.2	17.7	0.47	17.9	18.0	0.18	17.1	17.3	0.19	17.3	17.4	0.16
as % food energy	18.8	19.2	0.39	19.2	19.4	0.17	18.4	18.6	0.18	18.5	18.6	0.16
Trans fatty acids:												
as % total energy	2.12	1.95	0.14	1.95	1.88	0.03	2.07	1.99	0.05	2.09	1.95	0.04
as % food energy	2.30	2.12	0.14	2.09	2.03	0.04	2.23	2.13	0.05	2.22	2.14	0.04
n-3 polyunsaturated fatty acids:												
as % total energy	0.74	0.70	0.03	0.70	0.66	0.01	0.74	0.70	0.02	0.73	0.69	0.01
as % food energy	0.81	0.75	0.03	0.75	0.71	0.01	0.80	0.74	0.02	0.78	0.73	0.01
n-6 polyunsaturated fatty acids:												
as % total energy	4.81	4.64	0.23	4.82	4.38	0.11	5.16	4.85	0.11	5.28	4.81	0.11
as % food energy	5.25	4.96	0.23	5.17	4.77	0.11	5.56	5.20	0.12	5.65	5.22	0.12
Monounsaturated fatty acids:												
as % total energy	11.7	11.7	0.28	11.4	11.2	0.10	11.8	11.7	0.13	11.5	11.5	0.09
as % food energy	12.8	12.8	0.26	12.2	12.0	0.10	12.7	12.7	0.13	12.4	12.2	0.10
Ratio of:												
polyunsaturated to saturated fatty acids	0.38	0.38	0.02	0.37	0.33	0.01	0.41	0.37	0.01	0.43	0.38	0.02
polyunsaturated to saturated plus trans fatty acids	0.34	0.33	0.02	0.33	0.29	0.01	0.36	0.32	0.01	0.38	0.33	0.01
Base		71			360			271			385	

Proportion or ratio	Household composition														
	Informant alone			With others, no dependent children						With dependent child					
				With spouse			No spouse			With spouse			Lone mother		
	Mean	Median	SE	Mean	Median	SE	Mean	Median	SE	Mean	Median	SE	Mean	Median	SE
Women															
Total fat:															
as % total energy	39.2	39.4	0.61	39.3	39.5	0.25	38.8	39.0	0.38	39.2	39.8	0.29	39.6	39.7	0.59
as % food energy	40.1	40.7	0.61	40.6	40.6	0.25	40.0	39.9	0.39	40.2	40.8	0.29	40.7	40.8	0.61
Saturated fatty acids:															
as % total energy	16.9	16.4	0.37	16.7	16.6	0.16	16.0	16.0	0.24	16.4	16.4	0.17	16.5	16.5	0.31
as % food energy	17.3	17.1	0.37	17.3	17.1	0.16	16.5	16.4	0.24	16.9	16.8	0.17	17.0	16.9	0.34
Saturated plus trans fatty acids:															
as % total energy	18.9	18.7	0.39	18.8	18.8	0.17	18.1	18.1	0.26	18.6	18.7	0.19	18.6	18.7	0.33
as % food energy	19.4	19.3	0.39	19.4	19.3	0.17	18.6	18.6	0.27	19.1	19.2	0.19	19.1	19.3	0.35
Trans fatty acids:															
as % total energy	2.02	1.86	0.08	2.08	1.99	0.04	2.07	1.90	0.06	2.16	2.09	0.04	2.04	1.87	0.08
as % food energy	2.07	1.95	0.08	2.14	2.06	0.04	2.12	2.01	0.06	2.22	2.16	0.04	2.10	1.91	0.08
n-3 polyunsaturated fatty acids:															
as % total energy	0.75	0.67	0.03	0.74	0.68	0.01	0.76	0.68	0.02	0.70	0.65	0.01	0.73	0.67	0.03
as % food energy	0.77	0.69	0.03	0.76	0.71	0.01	0.78	0.71	0.02	0.72	0.67	0.01	0.75	0.70	0.03
n-6 polyunsaturated fatty acids:															
as % total energy	4.79	4.35	0.21	5.03	4.61	0.10	5.31	5.02	0.14	5.21	4.78	0.11	4.99	4.76	0.19
as % food energy	4.91	4.57	0.21	5.21	4.77	0.10	5.47	5.13	0.14	5.36	4.91	0.11	5.12	4.82	0.19
Monounsaturated fatty acids:															
as % total energy	11.8	11.5	0.25	11.8	11.8	0.10	11.9	11.9	0.14	11.8	11.7	0.10	12.5	12.2	0.26
as % food energy	12.1	11.8	0.26	12.2	12.2	0.10	12.2	12.3	0.15	12.1	12.3	0.11	12.8	12.6	0.27
Ratio of:															
polyunsaturated to saturated fatty acids	0.35	0.32	0.02	0.37	0.33	0.01	0.41	0.37	0.02	0.38	0.34	0.01	0.36	0.33	0.02
polyunsaturated to saturated plus trans fatty acids	0.31	0.28	0.02	0.32	0.29	0.01	0.36	0.32	0.01	0.34	0.30	0.01	0.32	0.29	0.02
Base		84			382			182			386			76	

10 Nutrient intake: vitamins

Vitamins are organic substances required in small amounts for growth and metabolism. They are essential substances which (with the exception of vitamin D) cannot be synthesised in the body and are therefore required in the diet.

From the record of foods consumed the quantity of a range of vitamins consumed by individuals in the sample was calculated, although it was necessary when compiling the nutrient databank to make assumptions about average vitamin losses in preparation and cooking of foods. This chapter presents the recorded average daily intakes of vitamins for men and women and for various subgroups of the sample. Food supplements may have a sizeable effect on the intake of some vitamins and where this is the case intakes are presented both inclusive and exclusive of supplements; these are referred to respectively as intakes from all sources and from food sources. For a number of vitamins data are also presented on the food groups which contributed to recorded intakes from food sources.

Further information on those characteristics of the sample which explained a significant amount of the total variance in vitamin intake are included in Chapter 12, where the results of an analysis of variance for selected nutrients are given.

10.1 Vitamin A (retinol and carotene)
Vitamin A as pre-formed retinol is present only in animal products, especially liver, kidney, fish oils and dairy produce. However, a number of carotenoids (mainly β-carotene) can also be converted to retinol in the body, and these are found chiefly in the yellow and orange pigments of vegetables; carrots and dark green vegetables are rich sources.

10.1.1 Pre-formed retinol
Table 10.1 shows the intake of pre-formed retinol for men and women within this sample by age of informant, showing both the intake from all sources (including supplements) and that from food sources only. Men had an average intake from all sources of 1277μg (median value of 618μg) compared to an average value for women of 1133μg (median 491μg).

On average, food supplements were not a major source of pre-formed retinol; they raised the average intakes for men and women above the average from food sources alone by 4% and 7% respectively; mean intakes of pre-formed retinol from food sources were 1226μg for men and 1058μg for women. The average intake from food sources was 16% higher for men than for women, although the averge energy intake of men in the sample was about 46% higher than that of women. The amount of pre-formed retinol per 1000kcal energy was, therefore, higher for women than men, as shown in Table 10.23, (p<0.01).

The average intake of pre-formed retinol increased steeply with age for both men and women. Intakes from food and from all sources were significantly lower in the 16 to 24 age group compared with the 25 to 34 age group for men (p<0.05), and compared with the 35 to 49 age group for women (p<0.01). (*Table 10.1*)

The range of pre-formed retinol intakes within the sample was wide and there was a marked skewness in the distribution, with median intakes only about half mean intakes.

Three fifths (61%) of the intake of pre-formed retinol by the sample was derived from meat and meat products, and almost all of this was from liver and products; women derived slightly more of their pre-formed retinol from liver products than did men, 61% compared to 55% (p<0.05). Milk and milk products contributed 14% of the intake of pre-formed retinol, and fat spreads a further 13%. Other food types contributed only a very small proportion of total intake.
(*Table 10.2*)

10.1.2 Carotene
The figures presented in Table 10.3 refer only to the recorded intake of carotene from all sources, since average daily intakes were not significantly affected by vitamin supplements. The average daily intake for men was 2414μg (median 1895μg) which was only 13% above that recorded for women (mean 2129μg, median 1696μg). As for pre-formed retinol, average intakes increased with the age of the informant both for men and women. (*Table 10.3*)

Table 10.4 underlines the importance of vegetables as the main source of carotene; 70% of the intake recorded by the sample was derived from vegetables. The only other significant contribution came from meat and meat products (12% of the total), which includes meat dishes containing vegetables. (*Table 10.4*)

10.1.3 Retinol equivalents
The total vitamin A content of the diet is usually expressed as retinol equivalents using the conversion factor for carotene that 6μg is equivalent to 1μg of retinol.

Table 10.5 reinforces the pattern already seen for intakes of pre-formed retinol and carotene, with increasing intakes among older groups within the sample. The overall average intake for men was 1679µg (median 1033µg) which was about 13% higher than that of women (mean 1488µg, median 849µg). These compare with an RDA[1] for both men and women of 750µg. *(Table 10.5)*

The contribution of food supplements increased the average intake of retinol equivalents from food sources by only 3% for men and 5% for women.

10.2 B-vitamins

10.2.1 Thiamin (vitamin B1)
The average intake of thiamin from all sources was 2.01mg for men (median 1.67mg) and 1.61mg for women (median 1.26mg). Food supplements raised the average intake of thiamin by 18% for men and 30% for women above the average from food sources. Thiamin intake, either including or excluding supplements, did not vary significantly with age. *(Table 10.6)*

Since thiamin requirements are related to energy and carbohydrate intakes, the RDA for thiamin varies according to sex, age, and level of activity of the individual. On the assumption that most people fall between the categories of sedentary and moderately active, the RDAs implied are about 1.1mg for men, 0.9mg for women aged less than 55 years, and 0.8mg for women aged 55 or over.

The most important food type in the provision of thiamin was cereal products (37% of total intake); within this group breakfast cereals provided 12% of the total, white bread 10% and wholemeal and other non-white breads a further 10%. After cereal products, vegetables were the next most important source of thiamin, providing a quarter of intake; within this group potatoes made the largest contribution with 17% of total intake. Meat and meat products provided 18% and milk and milk products 9% of total intake, but no other food type contributed more than 5% of the total. *(Table 10.7)*

10.2.2 Riboflavin (vitamin B2)
The average intakes of riboflavin from all sources for the sample were 2.29mg for men (median 2.03mg) and 1.84mg for women (median 1.56mg). This compares with an RDA for riboflavin of 1.6mg for men and 1.3mg for women. In the sample, supplements increased average intakes above those from food by 10% for men and 17% for women. Again there was little variation in intake by age for men, although the oldest women had significantly higher intakes than women aged 16 to 24 both from food sources and after the inclusion of riboflavin from food supplements (p<0.01). *(Table 10.8)*

Milk and milk products provided more than a quarter of the total riboflavin intake of the sample (26% for men and 30% for women). Meat and meat products (21%) and cereal products (22%) were also important sources, as they were for thiamin. Within the cereal products category, half of the riboflavin recorded came from breakfast cereals (11% of total intake), which are commonly fortified with the vitamin. Beverages contributed 11% of total riboflavin intake but were a more important source for men than for women, 13% compared to 8%, (p<0.01); this was due to the contribution of beer which was a more important part of the diet of men than of women. This difference was compensated for by women deriving more of their riboflavin than men from milk and milk products, 30% compared to 26%, (p<0.05). *(Table 10.9)*

10.2.3 Niacin equivalents
The niacin content of the foods consumed by respondents is expressed in the form of niacin equivalents, defined as the total amount of niacin consumed plus one sixtieth of the weight (in mg) of tryptophan. The average daily intake of niacin equivalents from all sources was 40.9mg for men (median 39.6mg) and 30.3mg for women (median 28.6mg). These averages compare with an RDA for niacin equivalents of 18mg for men and 15mg for women of all ages.

Supplements were proportionately less important than for the intakes of thiamin and riboflavin; average intakes from all sources were only 3% higher for men and 6% higher for women than the average intakes from food sources only. The average intake of niacin equivalents did not differ with age for male informants, but intakes from food sources were significantly lower in women under 35 compared with older women (p<0.01). *(Table 10.10)*

One third of the total intake of niacin equivalents was derived from meat and meat products; within this category poultry, and beef and veal were the two most important groups. Cereal products contributed a further 28% of total intake, 14% from bread and 8% from breakfast cereals, which may be fortified with the vitamin. Vegetables, milk and milk products and beverages each contributed about one tenth of total niacin equivalents. There was no difference between men and women in the importance of different food types. *(Table 10.11)*

10.2.4 Vitamin B6 (pyridoxine)
Within this sample average recorded intakes of vitamin B6 from all sources were 2.68mg for men (median 2.40mg) and 2.84mg for women (median 1.57mg). Vitamin supplements made a very large contribution to women's intake of vitamin B6, increasing the average daily intake above that from food sources alone by 81%; however the median intake for vitamin B6 from all sources was only 2% higher than the median intake from food sources alone. Men's average daily intake was raised by only 8% by the addition of food supplements. Average intakes from food sources for men were significantly lower in those aged 50 to 64 compared with those aged under 35 (p<0.01), but there were no

age-related differences in the average intakes from food sources for women. However, intakes including supplements were higher for women aged 35 and over than for those aged 16 to 24 (p < 0.01). *(Table 10.12)*

10.2.5 Vitamin B12 and folate
Average daily intakes of vitamin B12 are shown in Table 10.13. The average intake for men was 7.3μg (median 5.7μg), which was 35% above the average for women of 5.4μg (median 3.9μg). Only a small proportion of total intake was derived from vitamin supplements. Intakes both from food sources and from all sources were higher among older people (aged 35 or over) than for those in the 16 to 24 age group (p < 0.01). *(Table 10.13)*

The intake of folate showed little variation with age of respondent and vitamin supplements contributed little to total intake. The average recorded intake from all sources for men was 312μg (median 300μg), which was 42% above that for women (mean 219μg, median 209μg). *(Table 10.14)*

10.2.6 Biotin and pantothenic acid
Tables 10.15 and 10.16 show average daily intakes of these vitamins from all sources and from food only. Intakes of biotin tended to increase with age, with the youngest age group having lower intakes than men and women aged 25 and over (p < 0.01). Little biotin was derived from supplements. *(Table 10.15)*

Vitamin supplements were of more importance for intakes of pantothenic acid, raising the mean intake for women by 13% above that from food sources only. Average intakes from all sources were 6.6mg for men (median 6.1mg) and 5.1mg for women (median 4.5mg). There were no significant differences in intake according to the age of the respondent. *(Table 10.16)*

10.3 Vitamin C
Unlike most other vitamins considered there was no significant difference between men and women in the average intake of vitamin C from all sources. Average intakes from all sources for men and women in the sample were 74.6mg and 73.1mg (medians of 58.5mg and 54.1mg). There were no age-related differences for men in intakes of vitamin C from all sources, but women aged 16 to 24 had intakes markedly lower than the overall average for women (p < 0.01); however even these women had intakes above the RDA for vitamin C of 30mg.

The inclusion of supplements raised average intakes above those for vitamin C derived from food sources by 12% for men and 18% for women. Thus intakes from food sources were higher in men than women (p < 0.01). There was no significant difference by age in men's intakes of vitamin C derived from food sources, but women aged between 25 and 34 had intakes from food sources which were markedly lower than the average intake for women (p < 0.01), but again they were well above the RDA. *(Table 10.17)*

For this sample, vitamin C from food sources was derived largely from three food types: vegetables (46%), beverages (22%), which include fruit juices, and fruit and nuts (17%). Within the vegetable category potatoes were the most important single source, but more so for men than women, providing 19% of total intake compared to 13% for women, (p < 0.01). More than three quarters of the vitamin C derived from beverages was from fruit juice (18% of total intake), and most of the remainder in this category was from soft drinks (4%). Men derived more of their vitamin C intake from vegetables than did women (p < 0.01), which reflects their greater consumption of potatoes and, to some extent, other vegetables. This was balanced by women deriving a greater proportion of vitamin C from fruit and nuts (p < 0.01), and beverages (p < 0.05). *(Table 10.18)*

10.4 Vitamin D
Most of the normal adult requirements of vitamin D are obtained from sunlight. The few foods which naturally contain vitamin D are all animal products, but margarine and some other foods are fortified with the vitamin.

Average intakes of vitamin D from all sources were 3.78μg for men (median 2.95μg) and 3.09μg for women (median 2.27μg). Vitamin D from food supplements raised intakes above those from food sources by 10% for men and 23% for women. Average recorded intakes, both inclusive and exclusive of supplements, increased with age, and were markedly higher for men and women aged 35 and over compared with younger informants (p < 0.01). *(Table 10.19)*

The dietary vitamin D consumed by the sample was chiefly derived from fats and spreads (30%), cereal products (24%) and fish and fish dishes (22%). Margarine and various spreads other than butter provided most of the first, while oily fish provided the majority of the last. *(Table 10.20)*

10.5 Vitamin E
Average daily intakes of vitamin E are shown in Table 10.21; the average intake from all sources was 11.7mg for men (median 9.3mg) and 8.6mg for women (median 6.8mg). Supplements of this vitamin were, unlike other vitamins, equally important for men and women, raising average intakes by 18% and 19% respectively. Intakes of vitamin E from food sources and all sources did not vary significantly with age for men. Among women intakes from food sources were higher than the overall average in those aged 35 to 49 (p < 0.05), and intakes from all sources were significantly below the overall average for women aged 16 to 24 (p < 0.01). *(Table 10.21)*

10.6 Vitamin intakes of informants taking food supplements
So far in this chapter data has been presented on the average vitamin intake of the sample both from food

sources only and from all sources including supplements, with comment on the effect of supplements on average intakes. Vitamins derived from food supplements will, however, be a much more important source for the small group within the sample who were themselves taking a food supplement during the recording period. (The characteristics of this group are discussed in Chapter 5.)

Table 10.22 shows average daily intakes of vitamins from all sources for informants who were taking any food supplement compared to the average intakes of those who were not taking a food supplement. Vitamin intake from food sources only of men and women who were taking supplements are also shown. (*Table 10.22*)

Intakes of *all* vitamins recorded were higher in supplement takers, even when supplements were excluded. These differences, between those not taking supplements and intakes from food sources for those taking supplements were statistically significant for men and women for thiamin, niacin equivalents, folate, biotin and vitamin C, (p < 0.01), for pantothenic acid, (p < 0.05), for vitamins D and E, (men: p < 0.05; women: p < 0.01) and for retinol equivalents (men only: p < 0.05).

Average intakes of vitamins of both supplement and non-supplement users were above UK RDAs.

10.7 Variations in vitamin intake
In this section variation in the average intake of vitamins from all sources for men and women in the sample according to the main characteristics of the sample is considered. Since total vitamin consumption may be related to energy intake, the quality of the diet of different groups is compared by looking at vitamin intake from food sources per 1000kcal energy.

Age of informant
Table 10.23 shows the average vitamin density of the diet (that is, the vitamin intake from food sources per 1000kcal) for men and women by age group. Women had significantly higher intakes per 1000kcal of all nutrients except folate, vitamin B12 and vitamin B6 (p < 0.01, except for vitamin D, where p < 0.05); men had higher vitamin B6 intakes per unit of energy than women (p < 0.01). These differences in part reflect the higher alcohol consumption by men than women. Generally there was evidence of increasing vitamin density through the age range, with informants in the youngest age group (16 to 24 years) having lower vitamin intakes per unit of energy. Vitamin B6, thiamin and, for men, pantothenic acid, did not show this association. The age effect is more clearly seen for women than men, and is particularly marked for both sexes for intakes for retinol equivalents, carotene, biotin, vitamin B12 and vitamin D, where those aged 16 to 24 had intakes per 1000kcal significantly lower than the overall mean (p < 0.01). (*Table 10.23*)

Dieters and the unwell
Table 10.24 shows vitamin intakes from all sources for those informants who reported that they were on a slimming diet as compared to the non-dieting sample. It would appear that dieting informants generally had higher absolute intakes, but, with the exception of biotin intakes by women, (p < 0.01), the differences between the dieting and non-dieting samples were not significant; this is probably due to the variability in intake and the small size of the dieting sample, especially men. (*Table 10.24*)

Since informants on slimming diets had lower absolute energy intakes than the rest of the sample it would be expected that they would have higher levels of vitamins per unit of energy consumed. Table 10.25 confirms that women who were slimming had markedly higher intakes from food sources of all vitamins per 1000kcal except pre-formed retinol (p < 0.01, except retinol equivalents where p < 0.05). Among men, slimmers had significantly higher intakes per unit of energy than non-slimmers of pre-formed retinol, carotene, riboflavin, niacin equivalents, vitamins C and B12, and pantothenic acid (p < 0.01), and also of thiamin, folate and vitamins D and E (p < 0.05). Slimmers were also more likely than the rest of the sample to be taking food supplements; 22% of slimmers were taking food supplements, compared to 12% of non-slimmers (p < 0.01).
(*Table 10.25*)

Informants whose eating was affected by their being unwell during the recording period were a relatively small group, but they had significantly lower absolute intakes from all sources of many of the vitamins. The most marked differences, (p < 0.01), for both men and women were in intakes of niacin equivalents, folate, biotin and pantothenic acid. Additionally, unwell men had lower intakes of vitamins B6, C and E, and unwell women significantly lower intakes of thiamin, retinol equivalents, and vitamins B12 and D. However as the average values for vitamin intakes from food sources per 1000kcal for those who were unwell and the rest of the sample did not differ significantly, the differences between the groups in the absolute intake of the vitamins were, therefore, largely a reflection of differences in total energy intake. (*Tables 10.26 & 10.27*)

Region
In Table 10.28 average intakes from all sources are shown according to the sex of informant and the broad regional grouping used elsewhere in the Report. There is evidence of men in Scotland having lower intakes of many vitamins than men in the other regions, in particular, of folate and pantothenic acid (p < 0.01), and of biotin and retinol equivalents (p < 0.05). A similar pattern was not seen for women. Differences in the vitamin intakes of Scottish men reflected their lower energy intakes, and Table 10.29 shows that their average vitamin intakes from food sources per 1000kcal energy did not differ from those of men in other regions.
(*Tables 10.28 & 10.29*)

Socio-economic characteristics
Table 10.30 shows that men who were unemployed had significantly lower intakes than working men of all vitamins from all sources (p < 0.01), except pre-formed

retinol, retinol equivalents and vitamins B6 and B12. In respect of carotene, thiamin, and vitamins C and E their intakes were also markedly lower than those of economically inactive men (p<0.01). The intakes of niacin equivalents, folate, biotin, pantothenic acid, and vitamins B6 and C of men who were economically inactive were significantly lower than those of working men (p<0.01).

A similar pattern is seen for unemployed women who had lower intakes than working women of all vitamins, except carotene and vitamins C and D (p<0.01, except thiamin and vitamin E, where p<0.05). However, apart from a higher intake of biotin (p<0.01), the intakes of working and economically inactive women were not significantly different.

These differences in average vitamin intake between the unemployed and other groups were not explained totally by the lower energy intakes of the unemployed, as shown by the comparison of vitamin intake from food sources per 1000kcal in Table 10.31. Compared with working men, unemployed men had lower intakes per unit energy of carotene and vitamins C, D and E, and unemployed women had lower values for pre-formed retinol, retinol equivalents, riboflavin, niacin equivalents, biotin, pantothenic acid, vitamin B12, and folate (p<0.01). *(Tables 10.30 & 10.31)*

There were also signs of a possible income effect on women's intake of vitamins in that women in households receiving one of the specified benefits had markedly lower average intakes from all sources of carotene, riboflavin, niacin equivalents, folate, biotin, pantothenic acid and vitamins B6, C and D (p<0.01). Men in households receiving benefits also recorded significantly lower intakes than did other men of carotene (p<0.05), thiamin, riboflavin, niacin equivalents, folate, biotin, pantothenic acid, and vitamins C, D and E (p<0.01). *(Table 10.32)*

Table 10.33 shows the comparable figures for vitamin intake from food sources per 1000kcal energy. Women in households receiving benefits had lower values than other women for a range of vitamins including carotene, riboflavin, niacin equivalents, vitamins C and E, biotin and folate (p<0.01); for men, the only significant differences were in the intakes of vitamins C, D and E (p<0.01), and niacin equivalents and biotin (p<0.05). *(Table 10.33)*

Table 10.34 shows average vitamin intakes from all sources according to the social class of the head of household. For women the recorded intakes of all vitamins except pantothenic acid and vitamins D and E were lower for informants classified to Social Classes IV and V than for those classified to Social Classes I and II, (p<0.01, except for thiamin, where p<0.05). Among men the pattern was not as marked; intakes of pre-formed retinol, retinol equivalents, thiamin and vitamins B6, B12 and E were not significantly different for those in Social Classes IV and V as compared to those in Social Classes I and II. Moreover even when there were such differences there was not a linear trend between these extremes of the scale. The clearest trend across all four groups was for vitamin C intake; men in Social Classes I and II had an average daily intake of 96.8mg compared to an intake of 53.8mg for men in Social Classes IV and V (p<0.01). Women in Social Classes I and II had an average daily intake of 96.2mg compared to an intake of 55.8mg for women in Social Classes IV and V (p<0.01). *(Table 10.34)*

The differences observed for women in the average daily intakes of particular vitamins between those in Social Classes I and II and those in Social Classes IV and V were generally evident when intakes from food sources per 1000kcal were compared. However, intakes per 1000kcal of pre-formed retinol, thiamin and vitamins B12, D and E were not markedly different in women from these social classes. Differences in intakes per 1000kcal of retinol equivalents, riboflavin, and vitamin B12 were less marked (p<0.05), than the differences observed in the absolute intakes of these vitamins (p<0.01). For men, the same differences were found in intakes per 1000kcal between those in Social Classes I and II and those in Social Classes IV and V as were found for absolute daily intakes. *(Table 10.35)*

Household composition
Men's intakes of vitamins from all sources did not vary consistently according to the composition of the household in which they lived, and for women there is also no consistent pattern for all vitamins. Lone mothers had lower intakes of many vitamins as compared with all women, for example, niacin equivalents, biotin, pantothenic acid and vitamin D, (p<0.01), and also carotene and riboflavin, (p<0.05). Women living with others but neither with a spouse nor dependent children also had lower than average intakes of carotene and retinol equivalents, (p<0.01), and of vitamin B6 and biotin, (p<0.05). Women living with a spouse but no dependent children had higher than average intakes of carotene and vitamin D (p<0.01). *(Table 10.36)*

10.8 Summary
Average intakes of vitamins, both from food sources only and from all sources, were well above RDA levels, which confirms that vitamin intakes are likely to be adequate for most people's needs. Intakes of all recorded vitamins were higher for informants taking supplements than for non-supplement takers, even when intakes from supplements were excluded. However, average intakes by informants who did not take supplements were still above the RDAs.

Men had higher absolute average intakes of all vitamins but women had greater intakes per 1000kcal of most vitamins consumed. There was little variation by age in the absolute intakes of most vitamins but, where an effect was seen, intakes increased with age of informant; this was the case for the intakes of pre-formed retinol, carotene, retinol equivalents, biotin, vitamin B12 and vitamin D. In spite of the similarity in the absolute vitamin intakes of different age groups, there is evidence that older informants had higher levels of nutrients per 1000kcal of food consumed.

Informants who were slimming managed to maintain their absolute intake of vitamins and had higher intakes from food sources per 1000kcal of most vitamins than non-slimmers. Those who were unwell consumed smaller quantities of most vitamins, but the quality of their diet, expressed as vitamins per unit of energy, was similar to that of other members of the sample. The only strong regional effects in vitamin intake were the lower average intakes for men in Scotland, but this group showed no differences to men in other regions in average vitamin intake per 1000kcal energy.

There is evidence of differences in vitamin intakes both according to social class and indicators of household income; informants in lower social classes, the unemployed and those in households receiving benefits tended to have lower intakes of many vitamins, but even for these groups average intakes met the UK RDAs. A similar effect was also seen for lone mothers and for women living without a spouse or dependent children, although differences in intake between informants in other household types were not significant. The social class and income effects were generally still evident for intakes of these vitamins per 1000kcal total energy.

References

1. Department of Health and Social Security. *Recommended amounts of food energy and nutrients for groups of people in the United Kingdom*. Report on Health and Social Subjects No 15. HMSO (London, 1979).

Table 10.1 Average daily intake of pre-formed retinol (µg) by age and sex

	Sex and age of informant									
	Men				All ages 16–64	Women				All ages 16–64
	16–24	25–34	35–49	50–64		16–24	25–34	35–49	50–64	
a) Intake from all sources (µg)										
Mean (average) value	877	1216	1408	1481	1277	829	945	1215	1391	1133
Median value	494	600	647	683	618	401	456	519	562	491
Lower 2.5 percentile	163	194	232	212	194	119	106	136	192	135
Upper 2.5 percentile	5788	6671	7510	7405	6671	5896	6056	5699	5487	5779
Standard error of the mean	82.2	119.6	99.4	117.2	54.3	98.4	98.2	84.9	101.7	48.5
Base	*214*	*254*	*346*	*273*	*1087*	*189*	*253*	*385*	*283*	*1110*
b) Intake from food sources (µg)										
Mean (average) value	848	1184	1333	1425	1226	788	906	1140	1263	1058
Median value	487	584	633	670	602	389	438	481	516	463
Lower 2.5 percentile	163	188	232	212	190	114	106	136	192	134
Upper 2.5 percentile	5788	6671	7427	6793	6564	5896	6056	5654	5487	5698
Standard error of the mean	82.0	119.4	96.4	114.2	53.2	97.5	97.7	83.2	98.8	47.5
Base	*214*	*254*	*346*	*273*	*1087*	*189*	*253*	*385*	*283*	*1110*

Table 10.2 Average daily intake of pre-formed retinol (µg) from main food types by sex of informant

Food type	Men		Women		Total	
	Amount	% of total	Amount	% of total	Amount	% of total
Cereal products	74	6	62	6	68	6
Milk and products	175	14	138	13	156	14
Eggs and egg dishes	52	4	37	3	44	4
Fat spreads	167	14	118	11	143	13
Meat and products	720	59	670	63	695	61
of which						
—liver and products	*680*	*55*	*644*	*61*	*662*	*58*
Fish and fish dishes	17	1	13	1	15	1
Vegetables	12	1	9	1	10	1
Fruit and nuts	0	0	0	0	0	0
Sugar, confectionery and preserves	0	0	0	0	0	0
Beverages	0	0	0	0	0	0
Miscellaneous	9	1	11	1	10	1
TOTAL	1226	100	1058	100	1141	100
Number of cases	*1087*		*1110*		*2197*	

Table 10.3 Average daily intake of carotene (μg) by age and sex

Intake from all sources (μg)	Sex and age									
	Men				All ages 16–64	Women				All ages 16–64
	16–24	25–34	35–49	50–64		16–24	25–34	35–49	50–64	
Mean (average) value	1893	2211	2555	2833	2414	1576	1965	2344	2353	2129
Median value	1229	1676	1999	2360	1895	1179	1567	1934	1848	1696
Lower 2.5 percentile	175	212	332	421	247	166	173	353	214	197
Upper 2.5 percentile	6488	7971	7563	8361	7563	5671	6449	6746	7121	6523
Standard error of the mean	118.2	122.2	101.5	132.0	59.9	101.5	104.9	98.5	119.1	55.0
Base	*214*	*254*	*346*	*273*	*1087*	*189*	*253*	*385*	*283*	*1110*

Table 10.4 Average daily intake of carotene (μg) from main food types by sex of informant

Food type	Men		Women		Total	
	Amount	% of total	Amount	% of total	Amount	% of total
Cereal products	51	2	44	2	47	2
Milk and products	81	3	65	3	73	3
Eggs and egg dishes	3	0	4	0	4	0
Fat spreads	56	2	44	2	50	2
Meat and products	312	13	231	11	271	12
Fish and fish dishes	6	0	4	0	5	0
Vegetables	1668	69	1499	70	1583	70
Fruit and nuts	62	3	78	4	70	3
Sugar, confectionery and preserves	5	0	5	0	5	0
Beverages	5	0	5	0	5	0
Miscellaneous	166	7	149	7	157	7
TOTAL	2414	100	2129	100	2270	100
Number of cases	*1087*		*1110*		*2197*	

Table 10.5 Average daily intake of retinol equivalents (μg) by age and sex

	Sex and age of informant									
	Men				All ages 16–64	Women				All ages 16–64
	16–24	25–34	35–49	50–64		16–24	25–34	35–49	50–64	
a) Intake from all sources (μg)										
Mean (average) value	1192	1585	1834	1953	1679	1091	1273	1606	1784	1488
Median value	805	995	1118	1144	1033	658	738	926	1024	849
Lower 2.5 percentile	224	279	389	369	300	226	177	309	330	250
Upper 2.5 percentile	5962	7529	8136	7801	7042	6159	6700	6461	5891	6326
Standard error of the mean	86.1	127.2	102.2	122.2	56.9	99.4	102.1	87.7	104.0	50.1
Base	*214*	*254*	*346*	*273*	*1087*	*189*	*253*	*385*	*283*	*1110*
b) Intake from food sources (μg)										
Mean (average) value	1164	1552	1759	1897	1628	1051	1234	1531	1655	1413
Median value	786	965	1084	1132	1012	633	719	884	951	810
Lower 2.5 percentile	224	269	389	369	290	221	177	309	330	249
Upper 2.5 percentile	5962	7257	8024	7335	6964	6159	6700	6116	5875	6159
Standard error of the mean	85.8	127.0	98.9	119.2	55.7	98.7	101.5	85.6	100.7	49.0
Base	*214*	*254*	*346*	*273*	*1087*	*189*	*253*	*385*	*283*	*1110*

Table 10.6 Average daily thiamin intake (mg) by age and sex

	Sex and age of informant									
	Men				All ages 16–64	Women				All ages 16–64
	16–24	25–34	35–49	50–64		16–24	25–34	35–49	50–64	
a) Intake from all sources (mg)										
Mean (average) value	1.93	2.28	1.95	1.87	2.01	1.46	1.32	1.56	2.05	1.61
Median value	1.72	1.62	1.65	1.69	1.67	1.26	1.21	1.29	1.27	1.26
Lower 2.5 percentile	0.76	0.90	0.79	0.78	0.79	0.54	0.55	0.58	0.70	0.56
Upper 2.5 percentile	3.92	3.13	3.25	3.13	3.29	2.42	2.73	3.18	4.49	3.09
Standard error of the mean	0.13	0.57	0.18	0.15	0.15	0.16	0.04	0.12	0.54	0.15
Base	*214*	*254*	*346*	*273*	*1087*	*189*	*253*	*385*	*283*	*1110*
b) Intake from food sources (mg)										
Mean (average) value	1.72	1.66	1.71	1.70	1.70	1.26	1.21	1.25	1.25	1.24
Median value	1.68	1.57	1.65	1.69	1.65	1.23	1.18	1.24	1.23	1.22
Lower 2.5 percentile	0.72	0.85	0.79	0.78	0.79	0.52	0.55	0.57	0.70	0.55
Upper 2.5 percentile	2.85	2.96	2.85	2.83	2.87	2.30	2.02	1.98	2.05	2.06
Standard error of the mean	0.04	0.03	0.03	0.03	0.02	0.03	0.03	0.02	0.02	0.01
Base	*214*	*254*	*346*	*273*	*1087*	*189*	*253*	*385*	*283*	*1110*

Table 10.7 Average daily intake of thiamin (mg) from main food types by sex of informant

Food type	Men		Women		Total	
	Amount	% of total	Amount	% of total	Amount	% of total
Cereal products	.64	38	.46	37	.55	37
of which						
—white bread	*.18*	*11*	*.10*	*8*	*.14*	*10*
—wholemeal & other bread	*.16*	*9*	*.12*	*10*	*.14*	*10*
—breakfast cereals	*.19*	*11*	*.14*	*11*	*.17*	*12*
Milk and products	.13	8	.12	10	.13	9
Eggs and egg dishes	.02	1	.02	2	.02	1
Fat spreads	–	–	–	–	–	–
Meat and products	.32	19	.21	17	.26	18
of which						
—bacon and ham	*.10*	*6*	*.06*	*5*	*.08*	*5*
Fish and fish dishes	.03	2	.02	2	.03	2
Vegetables	.44	26	.30	24	.37	25
of which						
—potatoes	*.32*	*19*	*.19*	*15*	*.25*	*17*
Fruit and nuts	.03	2	.04	3	.04	3
Sugar, confectionery and preserves	.01	1	.01	1	.01	1
Beverages	.02	1	.03	2	.03	2
Miscellaneous	.05	3	.05	4	.05	3
TOTAL	1.70	100	1.24	100	1.47	100
Number of cases	*1087*		*1110*		*2197*	

Table 10.8 Average daily intake of riboflavin (mg) by age and sex

	Sex and age of informant									
	Men				All ages 16–64	Women				All ages 16–64
	16–24	25–34	35–49	50–64		16–24	25–34	35–49	50–64	
a) Intake from all sources (mg)										
Mean (average) value	2.18	2.43	2.24	2.33	2.29	1.53	1.67	1.98	2.00	1.84
Median value	1.93	2.00	2.05	2.08	2.03	1.37	1.47	1.61	1.63	1.56
Lower 2.5 percentile	0.85	0.92	1.00	0.92	0.92	0.58	0.52	0.66	0.70	0.59
Upper 2.5 percentile	4.56	4.02	4.28	4.32	4.32	3.07	3.46	4.16	5.19	4.04
Standard error of the mean	0.14	0.29	0.05	0.19	0.09	0.05	0.10	0.14	0.11	0.06
Base	*214*	*254*	*346*	*273*	*1087*	*189*	*253*	*385*	*283*	*1110*
b) Intake from food sources (mg)										
Mean (average) value	1.96	2.08	2.14	2.11	2.08	1.45	1.50	1.64	1.63	1.57
Median value	1.91	1.95	2.03	2.08	2.00	1.33	1.41	1.54	1.59	1.50
Lower 2.5 percentile	0.83	0.92	1.00	0.92	0.92	0.57	0.52	0.66	0.68	0.59
Upper 2.5 percentile	3.66	3.54	3.69	3.59	3.65	2.79	2.96	3.05	2.77	2.94
Standard error of the mean	0.05	0.04	0.04	0.04	0.02	0.04	0.04	0.03	0.03	0.02
Base	*214*	*254*	*346*	*273*	*1087*	*189*	*253*	*385*	*283*	*1110*

Table 10.9 Average daily intake of riboflavin (mg) from main food types by sex of informant

Food type	Men		Women		Total	
	Amount	% of total	Amount	% of total	Amount	% of total
Cereal products	.44	21	.35	22	.40	22
of which						
—breakfast cereals	*.23*	*11*	*.19*	*12*	*.21*	*11*
Milk and products	.54	26	.47	30	.50	27
Eggs and egg dishes	.11	5	.08	5	.09	5
Fat spreads	–	–	–	–	–	–
Meat and products	.46	22	.33	21	.39	21
of which						
—beef and veal	*.10*	*5*	*.07*	*4*	*.09*	*5*
—liver and products	*.12*	*6*	*.11*	*7*	*.11*	*6*
Fish and fish dishes	.04	2	.03	2	.04	2
Vegetables	.13	6	.10	6	.12	7
Fruit and nuts	.02	1	.03	2	.02	1
Sugar, confectionery and preserves	.02	1	.02	1	.02	1
Beverages	.28	13	.12	8	.20	11
of which						
—beer and cider	*.17*	*8*	*.02*	*1*	*.09*	*5*
Miscellaneous	.05	2	.05	3	.05	3
TOTAL	2.08	100	1.57	100	1.83	100
Number of cases	*1087*		*1110*		*2197*	

Table 10.10 Average daily intake of niacin equivalents (mg) by age and sex

	Sex and age of informant									
	Men				All ages 16–64	Women				All ages 16–64
	16–24	25–34	35–49	50–64		16–24	25–34	35–49	50–64	
a) Intake from all sources (mg)										
Mean (average) value	40.0	41.0	42.0	39.9	40.9	28.4	28.5	30.9	32.2	30.3
Median value	38.7	40.1	40.0	38.9	39.6	27.3	27.7	29.8	28.8	28.6
Lower 2.5 percentile	19.7	22.8	21.9	20.3	21.6	12.3	13.2	15.4	14.7	13.9
Upper 2.5 percentile	65.5	65.3	69.8	65.6	67.4	45.6	46.8	52.4	55.0	51.2
Standard error of the mean	0.93	0.76	0.99	0.68	0.44	0.85	0.54	0.53	2.24	0.63
Base	*214*	*254*	*346*	*273*	*1087*	*189*	*253*	*385*	*283*	*1110*
b) Intake from food sources (mg)										
Mean (average) value	39.0	40.2	40.5	39.5	39.9	27.3	27.7	29.5	28.7	28.5
Median value	38.3	39.8	39.7	38.9	39.2	27.1	27.3	28.9	28.3	28.1
Lower 2.5 percentile	19.7	22.8	21.9	20.3	21.6	12.3	13.2	14.7	14.7	13.7
Upper 2.5 percentile	60.5	62.2	65.8	61.9	62.2	42.3	45.2	47.4	47.4	46.4
Standard error of the mean	0.77	0.67	0.58	0.62	0.33	0.54	0.49	0.42	0.48	0.24
Base	*214*	*254*	*346*	*273*	*1087*	*189*	*253*	*385*	*283*	*1110*

Table 10.11 Average daily intake of niacin equivalents (mg) from main food types by sex of informant

Food type	Men		Women		Total	
	Amount	% of total	Amount	% of total	Amount	% of total
Cereal products	10.8	27	8.1	28	9.5	28
of which						
—white bread	*2.9*	*7*	*1.6*	*6*	*2.2*	*7*
—wholemeal & other bread	*2.7*	*7*	*2.1*	*7*	*2.4*	*7*
—breakfast cereals	*3.0*	*8*	*2.5*	*9*	*2.8*	*8*
Milk and products	3.4	9	2.9	10	3.1	9
Eggs and egg dishes	1.0	3	.7	3	.9	3
Fat spreads	.0	0	.0	0	.0	0
Meat and products	13.5	34	9.1	32	11.3	33
of which						
—beef and veal	*3.2*	*8*	*2.2*	*8*	*2.7*	*8*
—chicken and turkey	*2.7*	*7*	*2.1*	*8*	*2.4*	*7*
Fish and fish dishes	2.1	5	1.6	5	1.8	5
Vegetables	4.1	10	3.0	10	3.5	10
Fruit and nuts	.4	1	.4	2	.4	1
Sugar, confectionery and preserves	.1	0	.1	0	.1	0
Beverages	3.8	9	1.9	7	2.8	8
Miscellaneous	.7	2	.7	2	.7	2
TOTAL	39.9	100	28.5	100	34.1	100
Number of cases	*1087*		*1110*		*2197*	

Table 10.12 Average daily vitamin B6 intake (mg) by age and sex

	Sex and age of informant									
	Men				All ages 16–64	Women				All ages 16–64
	16–24	25–34	35–49	50–64		16–24	25–34	35–49	50–64	
a) Intake from all sources (mg)										
Mean (average) value	2.75	2.92	2.59	2.53	2.68	1.68	2.90	3.48	2.68	2.84
Median value	2.49	2.48	2.41	2.18	2.40	1.65	1.55	1.63	1.52	1.57
Lower 2.5 percentile	1.15	1.29	1.17	1.21	1.20	0.81	0.64	0.81	0.70	0.71
Upper 2.5 percentile	5.67	4.63	5.94	4.94	5.35	2.90	7.26	16.00	12.96	10.46
Standard error of the mean	0.14	0.30	0.06	0.16	0.09	0.05	0.60	0.62	0.42	0.28
Base	*214*	*254*	*346*	*273*	*1087*	*189*	*253*	*385*	*283*	*1110*
b) Intake from food sources (mg)										
Mean (average) value	2.57	2.53	2.49	2.34	2.48	1.63	1.54	1.60	1.53	1.57
Median value	2.47	2.48	2.39	2.17	2.38	1.63	1.53	1.57	1.47	1.54
Lower 2.5 percentile	1.15	1.24	1.17	1.21	1.20	0.73	0.64	0.76	0.70	0.71
Upper 2.5 percentile	5.15	4.18	4.60	4.47	4.47	2.83	2.56	2.74	2.53	2.62
Standard error of the mean	0.07	0.05	0.05	0.05	0.03	0.04	0.03	0.03	0.03	0.02
Base	*214*	*254*	*346*	*273*	*1087*	*189*	*253*	*385*	*283*	*1110*

Table 10.13 Average daily vitamin B12 intake (μg) by age and sex

	Sex and age of informant									
	Men				All ages 16–64	Women				All ages 16–64
	16–24	25–34	35–49	50–64		16–24	25–34	35–49	50–64	
a) Intake from all sources (μg)										
Mean (average) value	6.3	7.1	7.7	8.0	7.3	4.4	4.6	5.9	5.9	5.4
Median value	5.1	5.7	6.0	5.9	5.7	3.4	3.5	4.1	4.4	3.9
Lower 2.5 percentile	1.9	2.7	2.4	2.6	2.4	1.3	1.1	1.6	1.6	1.3
Upper 2.5 percentile	19.7	24.7	26.7	23.7	23.0	17.4	16.4	19.6	17.2	18.2
Standard error of the mean	0.29	0.34	0.31	0.41	0.17	0.28	0.25	0.27	0.28	0.14
Base	*214*	*254*	*346*	*273*	*1087*	*189*	*253*	*385*	*283*	*1110*
b) Intake from food sources (μg)										
Mean (average) value	6.2	7.1	7.6	7.8	7.2	4.4	4.5	5.6	5.8	5.2
Median value	5.1	5.7	5.9	5.9	5.7	3.4	3.5	4.1	4.3	3.9
Lower 2.5 percentile	1.7	2.7	2.4	2.6	2.4	1.3	1.1	1.5	1.6	1.3
Upper 2.5 percentile	19.8	24.7	26.7	23.6	22.9	17.4	16.4	18.6	16.4	17.8
Standard error of the mean	0.29	0.34	0.31	0.35	0.17	0.28	0.25	0.24	0.28	0.13
Base	*214*	*254*	*346*	*273*	*1087*	*189*	*253*	*385*	*283*	*1110*

Table 10.14 Average daily folate intake (μg) by age and sex

	Sex and age of informant									
	Men				All ages 16–64	Women				All ages 16–64
	16–24	25–34	35–49	50–64		16–24	25–34	35–49	50–64	
a) Intake from all sources (μg)										
Mean (average) value	302	319	322	301	312	217	208	224	222	219
Median value	285	303	310	289	300	198	198	213	214	209
Lower 2.5 percentile	140	164	138	156	145	91	84	106	102	95
Upper 2.5 percentile	600	563	555	569	562	343	349	410	402	385
Standard error of the mean	7.6	6.7	5.7	5.9	3.2	17.0	4.6	4.1	4.2	3.6
Base	*214*	*254*	*346*	*273*	*1087*	*189*	*253*	*385*	*283*	*1110*
b) Intake from food sources (μg)										
Mean (average) value	302	317	321	300	311	198	206	220	218	213
Median value	285	303	308	289	300	194	198	212	214	208
Lower 2.5 percentile	140	164	138	156	145	85	84	105	101	91
Upper 2.5 percentile	600	549	555	545	555	330	348	383	354	368
Standard error of the mean	7.6	6.4	5.6	5.7	3.1	4.7	4.4	3.7	3.9	2.1
Base	*214*	*254*	*346*	*273*	*1087*	*189*	*253*	*385*	*283*	*1110*

Table 10.15 Average daily biotin intake (μg) by age and sex

	Sex and age of informant									
	Men				All ages 16–64	Women				All ages 16–64
	16–24	25–34	35–49	50–64		16–24	25–34	35–49	50–64	
a) Intake from all sources (μg)										
Mean (average) value	35.1	40.5	40.8	38.8	39.1	23.7	26.6	32.0	29.4	28.7
Median value	33.5	39.1	39.5	37.4	37.8	23.6	24.9	28.8	27.3	26.5
Lower 2.5 percentile	12.8	15.7	16.2	14.1	15.1	8.1	8.3	11.8	11.0	9.9
Upper 2.5 percentile	66.6	70.8	72.1	71.1	71.4	42.6	56.7	72.8	55.1	58.1
Standard error of the mean	1.05	1.09	0.76	0.85	0.46	0.66	0.72	0.95	0.82	0.45
Base	*214*	*254*	*346*	*273*	*1087*	*189*	*253*	*385*	*283*	*1110*
b) Intake from food sources (μg)										
Mean (average) value	34.6	40.2	40.8	38.6	38.9	23.7	26.6	31.4	28.8	28.3
Median value	33.5	39.1	39.3	37.4	37.8	23.6	24.9	28.6	27.1	26.4
Lower 2.5 percentile	12.8	15.7	16.2	14.1	15.1	8.1	8.3	11.4	11.0	9.8
Upper 2.5 percentile	64.9	70.6	72.1	67.4	69.7	42.6	56.7	69.5	51.1	56.3
Standard error of the mean	0.99	1.05	0.76	0.81	0.45	0.66	0.72	0.91	0.69	0.42
Base	*214*	*254*	*346*	*273*	*1087*	*189*	*253*	*385*	*283*	*1110*

Table 10.16 Average daily pantothenic acid intake (mg) by age and sex

| | Sex and age of informant | | | | | | | | | |
| | Men | | | | All ages 16–64 | Women | | | | All ages 16–64 |
	16–24	25–34	35–49	50–64		16–24	25–34	35–49	50–64	
a) Intake from all sources (mg)										
Mean (average) value	6.5	6.9	6.6	6.3	6.6	4.4	4.7	5.3	5.6	5.1
Median value	6.1	6.1	6.2	5.8	6.1	4.3	4.6	4.6	4.4	4.5
Lower 2.5 percentile	2.7	3.3	2.9	3.2	2.9	2.1	2.0	2.5	2.1	2.1
Upper 2.5 percentile	14.8	11.2	10.7	10.6	11.2	7.5	8.5	9.1	11.1	9.1
Standard error of the mean	0.25	0.45	0.13	0.22	0.14	0.10	0.15	0.25	0.69	0.20
Base	*214*	*254*	*346*	*273*	*1087*	*189*	*253*	*385*	*283*	*1110*
b) Intake from food sources (mg)										
Mean (average) value	6.3	6.4	6.4	6.1	6.3	4.4	4.5	4.7	4.4	4.5
Median value	6.0	6.1	6.2	5.8	6.1	4.3	4.5	4.5	4.3	4.4
Lower 2.5 percentile	2.7	3.3	2.9	3.2	2.9	2.1	2.0	2.5	2.1	2.1
Upper 2.5 percentile	11.7	10.5	10.4	10.2	10.5	7.4	7.5	8.2	7.0	7.7
Standard error of the mean	0.17	0.15	0.10	0.10	0.06	0.10	0.09	0.08	0.08	0.04
Base	*214*	*254*	*346*	*273*	*1087*	*189*	*253*	*385*	*283*	*1110*

Table 10.17 Average daily vitamin C intake (mg) by age and sex

| | Sex and age of informant | | | | | | | | | |
| | Men | | | | All ages 16–64 | Women | | | | All ages 16–64 |
	16–24	25–34	35–49	50–64		16–24	25–34	35–49	50–64	
a) Intake from all sources (mg)										
Mean (average) value	70.9	79.8	77.9	68.5	74.6	61.5	66.0	81.8	75.5	73.1
Median value	53.1	60.5	59.0	60.2	58.5	49.2	50.0	56.8	62.0	54.1
Lower 2.5 percentile	19.1	22.0	19.4	17.7	19.1	12.0	11.8	16.2	17.9	14.4
Upper 2.5 percentile	246.5	236.0	235.7	151.7	227.3	188.8	170.8	285.5	191.8	209.2
Standard error of the mean	4.45	5.94	5.38	2.42	2.45	3.34	6.71	6.42	3.59	2.91
Base	*214*	*254*	*346*	*273*	*1087*	*189*	*253*	*385*	*283*	*1110*
b) Intake from food sources (mg)										
Mean (average) value	64.9	69.7	65.0	66.5	66.5	60.4	55.9	62.7	67.6	62.0
Median value	52.6	59.3	58.3	60.2	57.6	48.8	48.5	54.8	58.8	52.6
Lower 2.5 percentile	19.1	21.2	19.4	17.7	19.1	12.0	11.8	15.6	17.9	13.6
Upper 2.5 percentile	183.6	171.8	150.2	151.2	170.9	182.2	141.2	157.7	169.0	161.4
Standard error of the mean	3.26	2.64	1.97	2.04	1.20	3.27	2.08	1.96	2.42	1.18
Base	*214*	*254*	*346*	*273*	*1087*	*189*	*253*	*385*	*283*	*1110*

Table 10.18 Average daily intake of vitamin C (mg) from main food types by sex of informant

Food type	Men Amount	Men % of total	Women Amount	Women % of total	Total Amount	Total % of total
Cereal products	2.4	4	2.1	3	2.2	3
Milk and products	3.7	6	3.1	5	3.4	5
Eggs and egg dishes	.1	0	.1	0	.1	0
Fat spreads	.0	0	.0	0	.0	0
Meat and products	3.3	5	2.2	4	2.7	4
Fish and fish dishes	.2	0	.2	0	.2	0
Vegetables	33.0	50	25.6	41	29.3	46
of which						
—salad vegetables	5.2	8	5.3	9	5.3	8
—potatoes	12.7	19	7.9	13	10.3	16
—other vegetables	13.0	20	10.8	17	11.9	19
Fruit and nuts	9.4	14	12.8	21	11.1	17
Sugar, confectionery and preserves	.4	1	.3	1	.4	1
Beverages	13.3	20	14.9	24	14.1	22
of which						
—fruit juice	11.2	17	11.7	19	11.5	18
—soft drinks	1.8	3	3.1	5	2.5	4
Miscellaneous	.7	1	.7	1	.7	1
TOTAL	66.5	100	62.0	100	64.2	100
Number of cases	1087		1110		2197	

Table 10.19 Average daily vitamin D intake (μg) by age and sex

	Sex and age of informant Men 16–24	25–34	35–49	50–64	All ages 16–64	Women 16–24	25–34	35–49	50–64	All ages 16–64
a) Intake from all sources (μg)										
Mean (average) value	3.02	3.40	4.17	4.24	3.78	2.44	2.59	3.20	3.81	3.09
Median value	2.48	2.69	3.36	3.29	2.95	1.92	2.14	2.31	2.60	2.27
Lower 2.5 percentile	0.39	0.61	0.64	0.37	0.51	0.34	0.41	0.44	0.55	0.43
Upper 2.5 percentile	9.82	10.36	14.00	17.86	12.72	8.60	9.90	12.59	14.60	12.64
Standard error of the mean	0.17	0.16	0.20	0.23	0.10	0.16	0.14	0.16	0.22	0.09
Base	214	254	346	273	1087	189	253	385	283	1110
b) Intake from food sources (μg)										
Mean (average) value	2.81	3.16	3.71	3.80	3.43	2.10	2.30	2.61	2.82	2.51
Median value	2.39	2.64	3.23	3.24	2.87	1.86	2.05	2.25	2.34	2.17
Lower 2.5 percentile	0.39	0.61	0.64	0.37	0.51	0.34	0.41	0.43	0.55	0.43
Upper 2.5 percentile	8.08	9.80	11.01	10.67	9.92	5.17	6.35	7.15	7.13	6.89
Standard error of the mean	0.14	0.15	0.14	0.17	0.08	0.09	0.10	0.09	0.12	0.05
Base	214	254	346	273	1087	189	253	385	283	1110

Table 10.20 Average daily intake of vitamin D (μg) from main food types by sex of informant

Food type	Men		Women		Total	
	Amount	% of total	Amount	% of total	Amount	% of total
Cereal products	.77	22	.65	26	.71	24
of which						
—breakfast cereals	*.27*	*8*	*.23*	*9*	*.25*	*8*
—buns, cakes, pastries	*.35*	*10*	*.29*	*12*	*.32*	*11*
Milk and products	.20	6	.17	7	.19	6
Eggs and egg dishes	.33	10	.23	9	.28	9
Fat spreads	1.09	32	.70	28	.89	30
Meat and products	.13	4	.10	4	.11	4
Fish and fish dishes	.78	23	.52	21	.65	22
of which						
—oily fish	*.75*	*22*	*.50*	*20*	*.62*	*21*
Vegetables	.06	2	.04	2	.05	2
Fruit and nuts	0.0	0	0.0	0	0.0	0
Sugar, confectionery and preserves	0.0	0	0.0	0	0.0	0
Beverages	0.0	0	0.0	0	0.0	0
Miscellaneous	.06	2	.10	4	.08	3
TOTAL	3.43	100	2.51	100	2.96	100
Number of cases	*1087*		*1110*		*2197*	

Table 10.21 Average daily vitamin E intake (mg) by age and sex

	Sex and age of informant									
	Men				All ages 16–64	Women				All ages 16–64
	16–24	25–34	35–49	50–64		16–24	25–34	35–49	50–64	
a) Intake from all sources (mg)										
Mean (average) value	10.7	13.0	12.2	10.6	11.7	7.0	8.1	8.5	10.2	8.6
Median value	9.2	9.6	9.4	8.9	9.3	6.1	7.0	7.1	6.8	6.8
Lower 2.5 percentile	4.0	3.8	3.8	2.6	3.7	2.4	2.1	3.2	2.5	2.6
Upper 2.5 percentile	18.7	20.3	27.0	20.7	23.4	16.9	20.0	19.7	43.9	20.4
Standard error of the mean	0.91	2.42	1.17	0.90	0.74	0.24	0.51	0.48	1.16	0.36
Base	*214*	*254*	*346*	*273*	*1087*	*189*	*253*	*385*	*283*	*1110*
b) Intake from food sources (mg)										
Mean (average) value	9.7	10.2	10.4	9.2	9.9	6.8	7.3	7.6	7.0	7.2
Median value	9.2	9.6	9.4	8.8	9.3	6.1	7.0	7.0	6.6	6.7
Lower 2.5 percentile	3.5	3.8	3.8	2.6	3.5	2.4	2.1	3.0	2.4	2.5
Upper 2.5 percentile	18.6	18.2	24.0	18.1	19.5	13.8	15.1	16.1	14.1	15.2
Standard error of the mean	0.26	0.26	0.31	0.25	0.14	0.22	0.22	0.17	0.18	0.10
Base	*214*	*254*	*346*	*273*	*1087*	*189*	*253*	*385*	*283*	*1110*

Table 10.22 **Average daily intake of vitamins by sex of informant and whether taking any food supplement**

Vitamin (units)	Whether taking any food supplement								
	Not taking supplements			Taking food supplements					
	Intake from all sources			Intake from all sources			Intake from food only		
	Mean	Median	SE	Mean	Median	SE	Mean	Median	SE
Men									
Retinol (μg)	1186	596	54	2244	1440	240	1648	695	225
Carotene (μg)	2380	1858	62	2780	2210	216	2780	2210	216
Retinol equivalents (μg)	1583	997	57	2707	1827	249	2112	1227	234
Thiamin (mg)	1.7	1.6	0.02	5.5	2.4	1.73	1.9	1.8	0.07
Riboflavin (mg)	2.1	2.0	0.02	4.8	2.9	0.97	2.3	2.1	0.08
Niacin equivalents (mg)	39.5	38.9	0.3	55.0	49.9	3.3	43.6	41.6	1.13
Vitamin B6 (mg)	2.5	2.4	0.03	5.0	2.9	0.96	2.6	2.6	0.08
Vitamin B12 (μg)	7.14	5.62	0.17	9.34	6.44	0.90	8.2	6.2	0.65
Folate (μg)	308	297	3.3	355	339	12.5	340	332	10.4
Biotin (μg)	38.5	37.5	0.47	45.3	42.1	1.92	43.0	41.8	1.47
Pantothenic acid (mg)	6.2	6.0	0.06	10.2	7.5	1.39	7.0	6.5	0.34
Vitamin C (mg)	64.8	56.5	1.2	179.6	110.0	22.9	87.2	68.9	5.3
Vitamin D (μg)	3.4	2.8	0.08	8.1	6.6	0.66	4.1	3.4	0.29
Vitamin E (mg)	9.7	9.2	0.13	32.4	12.0	8.23	11.8	10.2	0.87
Base		994			93			93	
Women									
Retinol (μg)	1054	458	53	1505	856	115	1086	482	105
Carotene (μg)	2026	1571	58	2618	2201	147	2618	2201	147
Retinol equivalents (μg)	1391	787	55	1942	1272	119	1522	943	110
Thiamin (mg)	1.2	1.2	0.01	3.4	1.7	0.82	1.3	1.2	0.03
Riboflavin (mg)	1.6	1.5	0.02	3.2	2.3	0.33	1.7	1.6	0.04
Niacin equivalents (mg)	28.2	27.9	0.3	40.0	34.6	3.3	30.1	29.4	0.58
Vitamin B6 (mg)	1.7	1.5	0.11	8.4	1.9	1.44	1.7	1.6	0.04
Vitamin B12 (μg)	5.1	3.8	0.15	6.4	4.7	0.41	5.5	4.2	0.30
Folate (μg)	212	204	4.0	251	233	6.9	232	226	5.6
Biotin (μg)	27.5	25.9	0.42	34.6	30.3	1.55	32.4	29.9	1.31
Pantothenic acid (mg)	4.5	4.4	0.05	7.8	4.9	1.11	4.8	4.5	0.12
Vitamin C (mg)	59.2	49.9	1.2	139.0	85.6	14.8	75.5	70.5	3.2
Vitamin D (μg)	2.4	2.1	0.06	6.3	4.4	0.36	3.1	2.5	0.16
Vitamin E (mg)	7.0	6.5	0.10	16.1	9.1	1.92	8.2	7.6	0.27
Base		916			194			194	

Table 10.23 Vitamin intake (excluding supplements) per 1000kcal total energy by age and sex

Vitamin (units) per 1000kcal total energy	Age 16–24			25–34			35–49			50–64			All ages 16–64		
	Mean	Median	SE	Mean	Median	SE	Mean	Median	SE	Mean	Median	SE	Mean	Median	SE
Men															
Retinol (µg)	350	198	35.3	523	239	66.4	545	258	40.0	589	272	44.9	513	246	24.1
Carotene (µg)	794	523	49.7	965	650	67.7	1043	837	42.9	1223	979	58.9	1021	783	27.7
Retinol equivalents (µg)	483	316	37.3	684	381	71.8	719	427	40.9	793	486	46.7	683	408	25.5
Thiamin (mg)	0.71	0.69	0.01	0.70	0.66	0.02	0.69	0.68	0.01	0.72	0.69	0.01	0.70	0.68	0.01
Riboflavin (mg)	0.80	0.76	0.02	0.88	0.82	0.02	0.86	0.82	0.01	0.90	0.85	0.02	0.86	0.82	0.01
Niacin equivalents (mg)	16.3	15.9	0.34	16.9	16.3	0.28	16.4	15.8	0.18	16.9	16.2	0.25	16.6	16.0	0.13
Vitamin B6 (mg)	1.05	1.02	0.02	1.04	1.02	0.02	1.00	0.96	0.02	0.99	0.94	0.02	1.02	0.98	0.01
Vitamin B12 (µg)	2.56	2.09	0.13	3.04	2.33	0.18	3.10	2.40	0.13	3.26	2.51	0.13	3.02	2.33	0.07
Folate (µg)	123	122	2.2	135	124	4.8	129	126	1.8	127	121	2.0	129	123	1.4
Biotin (µg)	14.1	13.5	0.31	18.8	16.0	2.40	16.4	15.8	0.25	16.4	15.7	0.31	16.5	15.4	0.58
Pantothenic acid (mg)	2.58	2.44	0.06	2.72	2.54	0.08	2.58	2.49	0.03	2.58	2.46	0.04	2.61	2.48	0.03
Vitamin C (mg)	26.8	21.0	1.25	29.4	25.8	1.23	26.8	23.0	0.85	28.5	25.2	0.89	27.9	23.3	0.52
Vitamin D (µg)	1.14	0.97	0.05	1.38	1.06	0.13	1.49	1.23	0.06	1.61	1.38	0.08	1.42	1.17	0.04
Vitamin E (mg)	3.97	3.83	0.08	4.26	4.02	0.13	4.17	3.94	0.11	3.87	3.62	0.09	4.08	3.83	0.05
Base		214			254			346			273			1087	
Women															
Retinol (µg)	468	222	57.9	582	254	77.3	688	273	57.8	795	308	61.4	654	267	32.6
Carotene (µg)	937	687	59.2	1185	983	61.6	1401	1103	58.6	1484	1146	77.5	1294	1022	33.7
Retinol equivalents (µg)	624	364	58.7	780	432	80.0	921	517	59.7	1043	579	62.2	869	485	33.6
Thiamin (mg)	0.75	0.71	0.01	0.74	0.71	0.01	0.74	0.70	0.01	0.79	0.77	0.01	0.76	0.72	0.01
Riboflavin (mg)	0.87	0.78	0.02	0.91	0.85	0.02	0.98	0.88	0.02	1.04	0.98	0.02	0.96	0.88	0.01
Niacin equivalents (mg)	16.4	15.5	0.28	17.1	16.1	0.30	17.7	16.4	0.28	18.2	17.5	0.27	17.5	16.4	0.15
Vitamin B6 (mg)	0.98	0.91	0.02	0.94	0.90	0.02	0.95	0.89	0.01	0.97	0.93	0.01	0.96	0.91	0.01
Vitamin B12 (µg)	2.62	2.02	0.16	2.90	2.08	0.22	3.38	2.34	0.17	3.73	2.63	0.18	3.23	2.24	0.09
Folate (µg)	119	111	2.6	126	116	2.7	133	123	3.0	139	132	2.6	130	122	1.5
Biotin (µg)	14.2	13.6	0.43	16.2	15.3	0.44	19.5	16.3	1.17	18.4	17.3	0.57	17.6	15.7	0.45
Pantothenic acid (mg)	2.61	2.51	0.05	2.77	2.58	0.06	2.83	2.60	0.05	2.82	2.60	0.03	2.78	2.65	0.05
Vitamin C (mg)	37.0	28.2	2.28	34.2	29.0	1.33	37.9	32.4	1.26	42.9	35.5	1.58	38.2	31.9	0.78
Vitamin D (µg)	1.24	1.11	0.05	1.42	1.19	0.07	1.58	1.32	0.08	1.78	1.47	0.08	1.54	1.29	0.04
Vitamin E (mg)	4.00	3.70	0.10	4.31	3.97	0.10	4.41	4.10	0.09	4.28	4.02	0.09	4.29	3.98	0.05
Base		189			253			385			283			1110	

Table 10.24 Average daily intake of vitamins from all sources by sex of informant and whether on a slimming diet

Vitamin (units)	Whether on a slimming diet					
	Dieting			Not dieting		
	Mean	Median	SE	Mean	Median	SE
Men						
Retinol (μg)	1247	585	237	1278	621	56
Carotene (μg)	3245	2551	367	2377	1878	60
Retinol equivalents (μg)	1788	1172	254	1675	1028	58
Thiamin (mg)	1.9	1.5	0.15	2.0	1.7	0.16
Riboflavin (mg)	2.4	2.2	0.18	2.3	2.0	0.09
Niacin equivalents (mg)	43.2	40.2	2.32	40.7	39.6	0.45
Vitamin B6 (mg)	2.5	2.4	0.13	2.7	2.4	0.09
Vitamin B12 (μg)	8.6	6.1	1.0	7.3	5.7	0.18
Folate (μg)	329	303	16.2	311	300	3.23
Biotin (μg)	44.2	39.7	4.33	38.9	37.7	0.45
Pantothenic acid (mg)	6.7	6.1	0.45	6.6	6.1	0.14
Vitamin C (mg)	85.6	77.7	7.0	74.1	57.7	2.5
Vitamin D (μg)	5.3	3.3	0.94	3.7	2.9	0.10
Vitamin E (mg)	10.2	10.0	0.68	11.7	9.3	0.77
Base		46			1041	
Women						
Retinol (μg)	1184	482	155	1125	491	51
Carotene (μg)	2296	1733	169	2106	1696	58
Retinol equivalents (μg)	1567	879	160	1476	845	53
Thiamin (mg)	1.5	1.2	0.12	1.6	1.3	0.17
Riboflavin (mg)	2.2	1.6	0.20	1.8	1.6	0.07
Niacin equivalents (mg)	30.5	30.7	0.85	30.3	28.4	0.71
Vitamin B6 (mg)	3.6	1.5	1.01	2.7	1.6	0.28
Vitamin B12 (μg)	5.5	4.2	0.41	5.3	3.9	0.15
Folate (μg)	226	215	6.8	218	208	4.0
Biotin (μg)	35.1	29.4	2.38	27.8	26.3	0.37
Pantothenic acid (mg)	5.0	4.7	0.19	5.1	4.5	0.23
Vitamin C (mg)	83.3	67.6	5.2	71.7	52.6	3.2
Vitamin D (μg)	3.5	2.4	0.27	3.0	2.3	0.09
Vitamin E (mg)	8.7	6.1	0.98	8.6	7.0	0.39
Base		138			972	

Table 10.25 Vitamin intake (excluding supplements) per 1000kcal total energy by sex of informant and whether on a slimming diet

Vitamin (units) per 1000kcals total energy	Whether on a slimming diet					
	Dieting			Not dieting		
	Mean	Median	SE	Mean	Median	SE
Men						
Retinol (μg)	570	281	109	510	245	25
Carotene (μg)	1693	1239	211	991	776	27
Retinol equivalents (μg)	852	562	115	675	402	26
Thiamin (mg)	0.90	0.79	0.09	0.70	0.68	0.01
Riboflavin (mg)	1.16	1.02	0.10	0.85	0.81	0.01
Niacin equivalents (mg)	22.3	19.0	1.63	16.3	15.9	0.10
Vitamin B6 (mg)	1.22	1.18	0.06	1.01	0.97	0.01
Vitamin B12 (μg)	4.21	2.95	0.45	2.97	2.31	0.07
Folate (μg)	185	145	24.0	127	122	1.0
Biotin (μg)	33.8	18.0	13.1	15.7	15.3	0.1
Pantothenic acid (mg)	3.49	2.75	0.31	2.57	2.47	0.02
Vitamin C (mg)	45.5	37.9	4.5	27.1	23.0	0.5
Vitamin D (μg)	2.69	1.49	0.70	1.37	1.17	0.03
Vitamin E (mg)	5.33	4.26	0.60	4.02	3.78	0.05
Base		46			1041	
Women						
Retinol (μg)	876	284	146	622	266	31
Carotene (μg)	1718	1342	126	1234	981	34
Retinol equivalents (μg)	1162	563	152	828	474	32
Thiamin (mg)	0.89	0.83	0.03	0.74	0.71	0.01
Riboflavin (mg)	1.24	1.07	0.05	0.92	0.86	0.01
Niacin equivalents (mg)	21.9	20.8	0.64	16.8	16.1	0.13
Vitamin B6 (mg)	1.16	1.10	0.03	0.93	0.78	0.01
Vitamin B12 (μg)	4.34	2.69	0.43	3.07	2.20	0.09
Folate (μg)	171	151	7.7	125	119	1.1
Biotin (μg)	27.4	19.8	3.3	16.2	15.3	0.2
Pantothenic acid (mg)	3.53	3.04	0.13	2.67	2.54	0.02
Vitamin C (mg)	58.2	46.5	3.5	35.3	30.4	0.7
Vitamin D (μg)	2.33	1.56	0.23	1.42	1.27	0.03
Vitamin E (mg)	4.75	4.27	0.19	4.22	3.92	0.05
Base		138			972	

Table 10.26 Average daily intake of vitamins from all sources by sex of informant and whether eating affected by being unwell

Vitamin (units)	Whether eating affected by being unwell					
	Eating affected			Not unwell/eating not affected		
	Mean	Median	SE	Mean	Median	SE
Men						
Retinol (μg)	1288	650	373	1276	618	54
Carotene (μg)	2005	1284	314	2434	1921	61
Retinol equivalents (μg)	1622	932	410	1682	1040	56
Thiamin (mg)	1.6	1.4	0.08	2.0	1.7	0.16
Riboflavin (mg)	1.9	1.8	0.12	2.3	2.0	0.09
Niacin equivalents (mg)	36.6	34.8	1.60	41.1	39.8	0.45
Vitamin B6 (mg)	2.1	1.8	0.12	2.7	2.4	0.09
Vitamin B12 (μg)	7.0	5.1	1.05	7.4	5.7	0.18
Folate (μg)	265	256	13.6	314	303	3.3
Biotin (μg)	32.8	30.2	2.42	39.4	38.1	0.47
Pantothenic acid (mg)	5.6	5.6	0.26	6.6	6.1	0.14
Vitamin C (mg)	56.3	44.8	4.4	75.5	58.9	2.6
Vitamin D (μg)	3.4	2.0	0.55	3.8	3.0	0.10
Vitamin E (mg)	9.3	8.9	0.58	11.8	9.3	0.77
Base		*51*			*1036*	
Women						
Retinol (μg)	823	372	127	1165	503	52
Carotene (μg)	1876	1648	162	2156	1696	58
Retinol equivalents (μg)	1135	664	133	1525	869	53
Thiamin (mg)	1.2	1.0	0.11	1.7	1.3	0.16
Riboflavin (mg)	1.5	1.4	0.08	1.9	1.6	0.07
Niacin equivalents (mg)	25.0	25.0	0.99	30.8	29.0	0.69
Vitamin B6 (mg)	2.5	1.3	0.96	2.9	1.6	0.29
Vitamin B12 (μg)	4.4	3.4	0.42	5.5	4.0	0.15
Folate (μg)	176	169	7.5	223	213	3.8
Biotin (μg)	24.0	22.3	1.42	29.2	27.0	0.47
Pantothenic acid (mg)	3.9	4.0	0.16	5.2	4.5	0.22
Vitamin C (mg)	58.2	43.2	6.0	74.7	55.5	3.2
Vitamin D (μg)	2.3	1.6	0.22	3.2	2.3	0.10
Vitamin E (mg)	5.9	5.4	0.32	8.9	7.0	0.40
Base		*106*			*1004*	

Table 10.27 Vitamin intake (excluding supplements) per 1000kcal total energy by sex of informant and whether eating affected by being unwell

Vitamin (units) per 1000kcal total energy	Whether eating affected by being unwell					
	Eating affected			Not unwell/eating not affected		
	Mean	Median	SE	Mean	Median	SE
Men						
Retinol (μg)	708	243	266	503	246	22
Carotene (μg)	1044	551	203	1029	795	27
Retinol equivalents (μg)	882	388	293	673	413	23
Thiamin (mg)	0.72	0.70	0.03	0.70	0.68	0.01
Riboflavin (mg)	0.87	0.80	0.06	0.86	0.82	0.01
Niacin equivalents (mg)	17.2	16.4	0.56	16.6	16.0	0.13
Vitamin B6 (mg)	0.98	0.99	0.03	1.02	0.98	0.01
Vitamin B12 (μg)	3.62	2.31	0.75	2.99	2.33	0.07
Folate (μg)	126	118	5.2	129	123	1.5
Biotin (μg)	15.4	13.9	1.0	16.5	15.5	0.6
Pantothenic acid (mg)	2.68	2.44	0.12	2.61	2.49	0.03
Vitamin C (mg)	26.7	22.7	2.3	27.9	23.4	0.5
Vitamin D (μg)	1.31	0.97	0.24	1.43	1.19	0.04
Vitamin E (mg)	4.29	4.07	0.20	4.07	3.81	0.06
Base	*51*			*1036*		
Women						
Retinol (μg)	603	246	109	659	271	34
Carotene (μg)	1311	1045	101	1292	1008	36
Retinol equivalents (μg)	822	438	112	875	491	35
Thiamin (mg)	0.77	0.74	0.02	0.75	0.72	0.01
Riboflavin (mg)	0.97	0.89	0.04	0.96	0.88	0.01
Niacin equivalents (mg)	18.0	16.5	0.61	17.4	16.4	0.15
Vitamin B6 (mg)	0.99	0.92	0.03	0.95	0.91	0.01
Vitamin B12 (μg)	3.12	2.10	0.30	3.24	2.26	0.10
Folate (μg)	127	120	4.6	131	122	1.5
Biotin (μg)	17.0	15.0	0.8	17.6	15.8	0.5
Pantothenic acid (mg)	2.81	2.57	0.09	2.77	2.59	0.03
Vitamin C (mg)	35.4	27.4	2.5	38.4	32.6	0.8
Vitamin D (μg)	1.39	1.15	0.11	1.55	1.30	0.04
Vitamin E (mg)	4.01	3.65	0.15	4.31	4.02	0.05
Base	*106*			*1004*		

Table 10.28   Average daily intake of vitamins from all sources by sex and region

Vitamin (units)	Region											
	Scotland			Northern			Central, South West and Wales			London and South East		
	Mean	Median	SE	Mean	Median	SE	Mean	Median	SE	Mean	Median	SE
Men												
Retinol (μg)	945	510	143	1300	585	105	1243	646	87	1385	633	108
Carotene (μg)	2146	1578	220	2431	1936	112	2464	2040	98	2422	1819	113
Retinol equivalents (μg)	1303	851	149	1705	1027	110	1653	1081	91	1789	1039	113
Thiamin (mg)	1.6	1.6	0.08	2.2	1.7	0.29	1.8	1.8	0.04	2.1	1.7	0.41
Riboflavin (mg)	2.0	1.8	0.09	2.4	2.0	0.22	2.2	2.1	0.05	2.4	2.1	0.21
Niacin equivalents (mg)	38.1	37.8	1.25	42.0	39.2	1.26	40.5	39.8	0.59	41.0	39.8	0.63
Vitamin B6 (mg)	2.6	2.2	0.25	2.9	2.5	0.19	2.6	2.4	0.05	2.7	2.3	0.21
Vitamin B12 (μg)	6.4	5.4	0.48	7.6	5.6	0.40	7.2	5.7	0.28	7.6	5.9	0.31
Folate (μg)	278	268	9.2	324	318	7.2	319	306	5.4	305	290	5.1
Biotin (μg)	35.7	36.1	1.39	39.3	37.7	0.92	39.5	37.5	0.83	39.4	38.3	0.81
Pantothenic acid (mg)	5.7	5.4	0.27	6.7	6.3	0.24	6.7	6.3	0.16	6.6	5.9	0.33
Vitamin C (mg)	64.9	48.7	5.0	73.2	54.2	5.2	71.9	61.0	2.5	81.2	59.8	5.7
Vitamin D (μg)	3.7	2.3	0.48	4.1	3.2	0.21	3.7	3.0	0.15	3.6	2.9	0.16
Vitamin E (mg)	10.0	8.4	1.15	11.5	9.3	0.94	11.9	9.4	1.68	12.0	9.4	1.22
Base		96			274			364			353	
Women												
Retinol (μg)	1018	454	148	1266	489	108	1145	499	78	1043	493	84
Carotene (μg)	1971	1745	147	2105	1668	107	2073	1575	100	2249	1867	98
Retinol equivalents (μg)	1347	833	154	1616	822	111	1490	875	80	1418	849	88
Thiamin (mg)	3.0	1.2	1.58	1.6	1.3	0.17	1.4	1.2	0.06	1.5	1.3	0.05
Riboflavin (mg)	1.8	1.5	0.20	1.9	1.5	0.18	1.7	1.6	0.05	1.9	1.6	0.10
Niacin equivalents (mg)	35.2	28.5	6.48	30.4	28.6	0.71	29.1	28.0	0.47	30.2	29.1	0.56
Vitamin B6 (mg)	1.9	1.5	0.24	2.0	1.6	0.23	2.3	1.5	0.35	4.3	1.6	0.76
Vitamin B12 (μg)	5.0	3.8	0.41	5.9	4.0	0.35	5.3	3.9	0.23	5.1	3.9	0.22
Folate (μg)	209	206	7.2	211	206	4.1	228	210	9.3	218	210	4.1
Biotin (μg)	28.6	25.8	1.90	27.8	26.1	0.70	28.9	27.1	0.74	29.3	27.2	0.88
Pantothenic acid (mg)	4.7	4.2	0.30	4.8	4.5	0.20	4.8	4.4	0.18	5.6	4.6	0.57
Vitamin C (mg)	75.2	50.9	11.1	66.9	48.2	4.8	74.0	53.4	5.3	76.7	59.7	5.3
Vitamin D (μg)	2.8	2.0	0.29	3.3	2.3	0.19	2.9	2.3	0.13	3.3	2.3	0.17
Vitamin E (mg)	7.7	6.3	0.61	7.7	6.3	0.38	8.5	6.8	0.65	9.7	7.1	0.83
Base		95			290			368			357	

Table 10.29 Vitamin intake (excluding supplements) per 1000kcal total energy by sex and region

Vitamin (units) per 1000kcals total energy	Region											
	Scotland			Northern			Central, South West and Wales			London and South East		
	Mean	Median	SE	Mean	Median	SE	Mean	Median	SE	Mean	Median	SE
Men												
Retinol (μg)	405	221	68	513	234	43	488	251	34	567	254	53
Carotene (μg)	962	697	88	1045	820	57	1022	815	43	1017	764	53
Retinol equivalents (μg)	565	382	70	688	402	45	658	417	36	737	413	57
Thiamin (mg)	0.71	0.69	0.02	0.69	0.67	0.01	0.73	0.70	0.02	0.69	0.66	0.01
Riboflavin (mg)	0.85	0.79	0.03	0.83	0.78	0.02	0.87	0.82	0.02	0.88	0.84	0.01
Niacin equivalents (mg)	17.0	16.6	0.31	16.5	15.9	0.30	16.5	15.9	0.23	16.7	16.1	0.18
Vitamin B6 (mg)	1.06	1.02	0.03	1.05	1.04	0.02	1.01	0.97	0.01	0.99	0.96	0.01
Vitamin B12 (μg)	2.86	2.26	0.21	3.06	2.34	0.14	2.91	2.32	0.11	3.15	2.35	0.15
Folate (μg)	126	121	3.4	131	126	2.2	132	125	3.5	125	121	1.6
Biotin (μg)	16.0	16.1	0.48	16.0	15.4	0.32	17.5	15.3	1.68	16.0	15.4	0.25
Pantothenic acid (mg)	2.48	2.42	0.07	2.66	2.53	0.05	2.67	2.51	0.06	2.55	2.46	0.03
Vitamin C (mg)	27.5	23.7	1.6	26.2	21.1	1.0	29.1	23.6	1.0	28.0	24.6	0.8
Vitamin D (μg)	1.42	1.01	0.14	1.46	1.25	0.07	1.47	1.17	0.09	1.35	1.15	0.05
Vitamin E (mg)	3.86	3.70	0.15	3.95	3.76	0.09	4.15	3.86	0.11	4.16	3.94	0.09
Base		96			274			364			353	
Women												
Retinol (μg)	624	253	104	747	268	80	666	285	50	573	264	51
Carotene (μg)	1212	989	87	1298	1008	68	1221	965	54	1388	1088	66
Retinol equivalents (μg)	826	467	107	964	493	83	870	499	50	804	479	53
Thiamin (mg)	0.75	0.71	0.03	0.76	0.74	0.01	0.75	0.71	0.01	0.75	0.72	0.01
Riboflavin (mg)	0.93	0.83	0.05	0.97	0.89	0.02	0.97	0.91	0.02	0.95	0.87	0.02
Niacin equivalents (mg)	17.6	15.8	0.57	17.7	16.6	0.28	17.2	16.2	0.26	17.5	16.6	0.25
Vitamin B6 (mg)	0.96	0.92	0.03	0.97	0.92	0.02	0.95	0.91	0.02	0.95	0.89	0.01
Vitamin B12 (μg)	3.18	2.14	0.29	3.58	2.32	0.25	3.18	2.24	0.14	3.00	2.22	0.13
Folate (μg)	134	119	8.9	128	123	2.4	130	121	2.3	131	122	2.4
Biotin (μg)	20.7	14.8	4.2	16.7	15.7	0.37	17.1	15.9	0.40	17.9	15.9	0.68
Pantothenic acid (mg)	2.78	2.54	0.12	2.78	2.60	0.05	2.74	2.54	0.05	2.81	2.63	0.05
Vitamin C (mg)	38.6	30.8	3.0	36.1	28.6	1.7	37.8	31.2	1.2	40.1	35.2	1.3
Vitamin D (μg)	1.59	1.18	0.23	1.62	1.35	0.08	1.48	1.31	0.05	1.52	1.25	0.06
Vitamin E (mg)	4.30	3.98	0.24	4.11	3.88	0.09	4.25	3.94	0.08	4.46	4.15	0.09
Base		95			290			368			357	

Table 10.30 Average daily intake of vitamins from all sources by sex and employment status of informant

Vitamin (units)	Employment status of informant								
	Working			Unemployed			Economically inactive		
	Mean	Median	SE	Mean	Median	SE	Mean	Median	SE
Men									
Retinol (µg)	1283	640	61	1330	442	196	1201	535	157
Carotene (µg)	2491	1987	66.7	1639	1130	162	2519	1882	206
Retinol equivalents (µg)	1698	1071	63	1603	665	206	1621	934	171
Thiamin (mg)	2.1	1.7	0.19	1.4	1.4	0.05	1.7	1.6	0.09
Riboflavin (mg)	2.4	2.1	0.11	1.7	1.6	0.08	2.1	1.9	0.09
Niacin equivalents (mg)	42.2	40.7	0.50	33.1	31.3	1.00	37.2	37.0	1.09
Vitamin B6 (mg)	2.8	2.5	0.11	2.4	2.1	0.25	2.4	2.2	0.11
Vitamin B12 (µg)	7.4	5.9	0.19	7.0	5.1	0.62	6.9	5.0	0.58
Folate (µg)	321	309	3.4	280	270	10.7	277	270	11.1
Biotin (µg)	40.5	39.2	0.51	31.8	31.3	1.45	34.7	34.0	1.44
Pantothenic acid (mg)	6.8	6.2	0.16	5.6	5.5	0.21	5.8	5.5	0.19
Vitamin C (mg)	79.1	61.1	2.9	47.7	41.5	3.3	64.3	54.1	4.5
Vitamin D (µg)	3.9	3.1	0.11	2.7	1.9	0.28	3.5	2.9	0.34
Vitamin E (mg)	12.5	9.7	0.90	7.1	6.6	0.32	9.7	8.1	0.99
Base	*875*			*99*			*111*		
Women									
Retinol (µg)	1156	501	61	698	359	104	1177	488	92
Carotene (µg)	2117	1705	66	1832	1228	230	2190	1732	105
Retinol equivalents (µg)	1508	864	63	1003	620	125	1542	866	94
Thiamin (mg)	1.8	1.3	0.24	1.2	1.1	0.06	1.4	1.3	0.06
Riboflavin (mg)	2.0	1.6	0.10	1.4	1.2	0.09	1.7	1.6	0.05
Niacin equivalents (mg)	31.5	29.0	0.99	26.4	25.0	1.20	28.9	28.3	0.53
Vitamin B6 (mg)	3.2	1.6	0.40	1.5	1.5	0.07	2.4	1.6	0.42
Vitamin B12 (µg)	5.5	4.0	0.18	3.9	3.3	0.33	5.4	3.8	0.26
Folate (µg)	219	213	2.7	190	177	8.8	222	205	9.3
Biotin (µg)	30.5	27.7	0.65	24.1	22.6	1.34	26.2	25.1	0.56
Pantothenic acid (mg)	5.3	4.5	0.32	4.1	4.0	0.19	4.8	4.6	0.16
Vitamin C (mg)	74.0	55.5	3.4	72.1	48.9	16.9	71.8	51.4	5.7
Vitamin D (µg)	3.1	2.3	0.11	3.1	1.6	0.52	3.1	2.2	0.15
Vitamin E (mg)	8.9	7.1	0.45	7.1	5.4	0.63	8.4	6.5	0.69
Base	*670*			*57*			*373*		

Table 10.31 Vitamin intake (excluding supplements) per 1000kcal total energy by sex and employment status of informant

Vitamin (units) per 1000kcal total energy	Employment status of informant								
	Working			Unemployed			Economically inactive		
	Mean	Median	SE	Mean	Median	SE	Mean	Median	SE
Men									
Retinol (μg)	505	250	27	594	212	83	503	233	67
Carotene (μg)	1026	813	30	797	552	74	1184	826	114
Retinol equivalents (μg)	677	413	29	727	341	87	700	430	73
Thiamin (mg)	0.70	0.68	0.01	0.69	0.66	0.02	0.73	0.70	0.02
Riboflavin (mg)	0.86	0.82	0.01	0.83	0.79	0.03	0.88	0.81	0.03
Niacin equivalents (mg)	16.6	16.0	0.14	16.2	16.0	0.37	16.6	16.1	0.36
Vitamin B6 (mg)	1.01	0.98	0.01	1.07	1.08	0.03	1.03	1.00	0.03
Vitamin B12 (μg)	2.99	2.32	0.08	3.29	2.52	0.25	3.03	2.26	0.23
Folate (μg)	129	123	1.7	136	137	3.8	124	115	3.5
Biotin (μg)	16.8	15.6	0.7	15.3	14.8	0.5	15.2	14.4	0.5
Pantothenic acid (mg)	2.60	2.47	0.03	2.72	2.72	0.08	2.60	2.46	0.06
Vitamin C (mg)	28.4	23.8	0.6	23.1	19.3	1.5	27.9	24.8	1.6
Vitamin D (μg)	1.45	1.20	0.05	1.21	0.89	0.10	1.41	1.21	0.10
Vitamin E (mg)	4.17	3.96	0.06	3.43	3.19	0.14	3.92	3.66	0.15
Base		*875*			*99*			*111*	
Women									
Retinol (μg)	660	265	41	355	238	56	699	277	62
Carotene (μg)	1298	1025	43	1103	760	121	1316	1043	60
Retinol equivalents (μg)	876	495	42	539	379	65	918	500	64
Thiamin (mg)	0.75	0.71	0.01	0.71	0.65	0.03	0.77	0.74	0.01
Riboflavin (mg)	0.96	0.88	0.02	0.80	0.73	0.04	0.98	0.91	0.02
Niacin equivalents (mg)	17.7	16.5	0.20	16.0	15.2	0.56	17.3	16.4	0.23
Vitamin B6 (mg)	0.96	0.90	0.01	0.89	0.85	0.03	0.97	0.92	0.01
Vitamin B12 (μg)	3.23	2.27	0.12	2.33	1.95	0.20	3.38	2.28	0.18
Folate (μg)	133	124	2.1	117	113	4.3	129	121	2.0
Biotin (μg)	18.7	16.1	0.7	15.1	13.5	0.8	16.0	15.2	0.3
Pantothenic acid (mg)	2.80	2.60	0.04	2.50	2.40	0.09	2.79	2.60	0.04
Vitamin C (mg)	39.2	32.8	1.1	36.4	27.8	3.9	36.5	30.0	1.2
Vitamin D (μg)	1.54	1.29	0.05	1.32	1.08	0.14	1.57	1.32	0.07
Vitamin E (mg)	4.39	4.12	0.07	3.91	3.51	0.22	4.16	3.89	0.08
Base		*670*			*57*			*373*	

Table 10.32 Average daily intake of vitamins from all sources by sex of informant and whether benefits received

Vitamin (units)	Whether benefits received					
	Received			Not received		
	Mean	Median	SE	Mean	Median	SE
Men						
Retinol (µg)	1355	493	180	1263	626	57
Carotene (µg)	2033	1474	185	2463	1957	63
Retinol equivalents (µg)	1694	770	192	1673	1055	59
Thiamin (mg)	1.5	1.5	0.05	2.1	1.7	0.17
Riboflavin (mg)	1.8	1.7	0.07	2.4	2.1	0.10
Niacin equivalents (mg)	34.8	34.4	0.99	41.6	40.1	0.48
Vitamin B6 (mg)	2.5	2.2	0.21	2.7	2.4	0.10
Vitamin B12 (µg)	7.1	5.1	0.57	7.4	5.8	0.18
Folate (µg)	285	276	9.5	315	303	3.4
Biotin (µg)	32.7	31.9	1.27	39.9	38.4	0.49
Pantothenic acid (mg)	5.8	5.7	0.18	6.7	6.1	0.15
Vitamin C (mg)	47.2	43.3	2.2	78.1	60.5	2.7
Vitamin D (µg)	3.0	2.3	0.25	3.9	3.1	0.11
Vitamin E (mg)	7.7	7.4	0.33	12.2	9.6	0.83
Base		*119*			*963*	
Women						
Retinol (µg)	1055	362	142	1144	508	52
Carotene (µg)	1633	1090	128	2208	1759	60
Retinol equivalents (µg)	1328	633	146	1512	884	53
Thiamin (mg)	1.4	1.1	0.12	1.7	1.3	0.17
Riboflavin (mg)	1.5	1.2	0.09	1.9	1.6	0.07
Niacin equivalents (mg)	25.5	26.1	0.71	31.1	28.9	0.72
Vitamin B6 (mg)	1.9	1.4	0.42	3.0	1.6	0.32
Vitamin B12 (µg)	5.4	3.4	0.47	5.3	4.0	0.15
Folate (µg)	192	180	6.6	223	212	4.0
Biotin (µg)	22.4	20.9	0.83	29.7	27.6	0.49
Pantothenic acid (mg)	4.2	3.9	0.21	5.2	4.6	0.23
Vitamin C (mg)	55.4	39.5	6.9	75.8	56.8	3.2
Vitamin D (µg)	2.4	1.8	0.19	3.2	2.4	0.10
Vitamin E (mg)	7.5	5.6	0.94	8.8	7.0	0.39
Base		*153*			*955*	

Table 10.33 Vitamin intake (excluding supplements) per 1000kcal total energy by sex of informant and whether benefits received

Vitamin (units) per 1000kcal total energy	Whether benefits received						
	Received				Not received		
	Mean	Median	SE		Mean	Median	SE
Men							
Retinol (μg)	576	226	74		501	249	25
Carotene (μg)	963	644	96		1031	815	29
Retinol equivalents (μg)	732	370	79		673	413	27
Thiamin (mg)	0.68	0.66	0.02		0.71	0.68	0.01
Riboflavin (mg)	0.83	0.78	0.02		0.87	0.82	0.01
Niacin equivalents (mg)	15.9	15.6	0.34		16.7	16.1	0.14
Vitamin B6 (mg)	1.06	1.04	0.03		1.01	0.98	0.01
Vitamin B12 (μg)	3.19	2.35	0.23		2.99	2.32	0.08
Folate (μg)	131	124	3.6		129	123	1.6
Biotin (μg)	14.9	14.6	0.48		16.7	15.5	0.65
Pantothenic acid (mg)	2.64	2.61	0.07		2.61	2.47	0.03
Vitamin C (mg)	21.9	19.5	1.0		28.6	24.1	0.6
Vitamin D (μg)	1.20	1.04	0.07		1.45	1.19	0.05
Vitamin E (mg)	3.48	3.19	0.13		4.15	3.93	0.06
Base		*119*				*963*	
Women							
Retinol (μg)	661	243	95		652	271	35
Carotene (μg)	1030	684	77		1336	1072	37
Retinol equivalents (μg)	833	379	97		875	503	36
Thiamin (mg)	0.75	0.71	0.02		0.76	0.72	0.01
Riboflavin (mg)	0.89	0.82	0.03		0.97	0.89	0.01
Niacin equivalents (mg)	16.4	15.8	0.33		17.6	16.5	0.16
Vitamin B6 (mg)	0.93	0.90	0.02		0.96	0.91	0.01
Vitamin B12 (μg)	3.36	2.08	0.29		3.21	2.27	0.10
Folate (μg)	120	113	3.0		132	123	1.6
Biotin (μg)	14.4	13.7	0.39		18.1	16.1	0.52
Pantothenic acid (mg)	2.64	2.39	0.07		2.80	2.61	0.03
Vitamin C (mg)	30.1	25.1	1.5		39.3	33.4	0.9
Vitamin D (μg)	1.39	1.11	0.09		1.56	1.32	0.04
Vitamin E (mg)	3.79	3.57	0.11		4.37	4.08	0.05
Base		*153*				*955*	

Table 10.34 Average daily intake of vitamins from all sources by sex of informant and social class of head of household

Vitamin (units)	Social class of head of household											
	I and II			III non-manual			III manual			IV and V		
	Mean	Median	SE	Mean	Median	SE	Mean	Median	SE	Mean	Median	SE
Men												
Retinol (µg)	1280	694	84	1475	574	206	1220	593	87	1217	564	128
Carotene (µg)	2731	2334	96	2315	1786	167	2362	1638	113	2040	1698	127
Retinol equivalents (µg)	1735	1169	87	1860	925	218	1613	992	92	1557	897	132
Thiamin (mg)	2.5	1.7	0.43	1.7	1.7	0.06	1.8	1.7	0.03	1.7	1.6	0.06
Riboflavin (mg)	2.7	2.2	0.25	2.2	2.0	0.07	2.1	2.0	0.04	2.0	1.9	0.06
Niacin equivalents (mg)	43.0	40.8	0.93	39.5	38.8	0.96	40.5	38.9	0.62	38.2	37.7	0.96
Vitamin B6 (mg)	3.0	2.4	0.24	2.4	2.4	0.07	2.6	2.4	0.06	2.5	2.4	0.15
Vitamin B12 (µg)	7.4	6.0	0.27	7.5	5.3	0.63	7.3	5.7	0.28	7.2	5.5	0.46
Folate (µg)	321	306	5.1	298	279	8.2	317	304	5.9	294	289	7.8
Biotin (µg)	42.6	41.0	0.75	36.6	35.2	1.04	38.4	36.8	0.84	35.3	35.3	1.13
Pantothenic acid (mg)	7.1	6.3	0.34	6.2	5.7	0.20	6.4	6.0	0.15	6.0	5.7	0.17
Vitamin C (mg)	96.8	70.5	5.7	73.2	58.5	8.0	63.8	54.5	2.2	53.8	46.7	2.4
Vitamin D (µg)	4.2	3.2	0.19	3.5	2.7	0.25	3.6	2.8	0.15	3.5	2.7	0.24
Vitamin E (mg)	12.4	10.2	0.71	13.9	9.1	3.04	9.7	9.2	0.23	12.7	8.5	3.5
Base		*377*			*138*			*378*			*177*	
Women												
Retinol (µg)	1300	553	91	1087	487	123	1068	478	84	948	423	93
Carotene (µg)	2533	2159	94	2376	1928	145	1903	1471	103	1613	1042	105
Retinol equivalents (µg)	1722	1019	93	1483	901	125	1385	771	88	1217	651	97
Thiamin (mg)	1.6	1.4	0.10	1.5	1.3	0.10	1.8	1.3	0.45	1.4	1.2	0.07
Riboflavin (mg)	2.0	1.7	0.06	1.9	1.6	0.17	1.8	1.5	0.17	1.6	1.4	0.07
Niacin equivalents (mg)	32.6	31.3	0.64	30.5	30.0	0.72	29.9	27.4	1.82	26.8	26.6	0.57
Vitamin B6 (mg)	3.3	1.7	0.54	3.5	1.6	0.95	2.8	1.5	0.50	1.9	1.4	0.29
Vitamin B12 (µg)	6.0	4.2	0.27	5.4	4.1	0.35	5.0	3.7	0.25	4.7	3.6	0.26
Folate (µg)	235	229	3.8	221	209	5.8	215	198	9.7	196	186	4.9
Biotin (µg)	32.3	29.5	0.85	30.3	28.0	1.43	26.6	25.5	0.62	24.7	22.6	0.85
Pantothenic acid (mg)	5.5	4.8	0.27	4.8	4.6	0.13	4.6	4.3	0.16	5.3	4.1	0.85
Vitamin C (mg)	96.2	70.4	7.1	74.6	57.2	5.3	55.2	45.4	2.1	55.8	44.1	3.1
Vitamin D (µg)	3.3	2.5	0.14	3.1	2.5	0.21	3.0	2.2	0.15	2.9	1.9	0.24
Vitamin E (mg)	8.7	7.5	0.31	9.6	7.1	1.48	8.2	6.4	0.58	8.2	5.7	1.10
Base		*386*			*141*			*347*			*222*	

Table 10.35 Vitamin intake (excluding supplements) per 1000kcal total energy by sex of informant and social class of head of household

Vitamin (units) per 1000kcal total energy	Social class of head of household											
	I and II			III non-manual			III manual			IV and V		
	Mean	Median	SE	Mean	Median	SE	Mean	Median	SE	Mean	Median	SE
Men												
Retinol (μg)	509	267	37	633	247	110	480	230	35	496	233	53
Carotene (μg)	1141	956	43	1033	800	88	994	672	53	870	660	54
Retinol equivalents (μg)	699	458	38	805	390	120	646	377	37	641	387	54
Thiamin (mg)	0.72	0.70	0.01	0.73	0.69	0.02	0.69	0.66	0.01	0.68	0.66	0.02
Riboflavin (mg)	0.91	0.86	0.01	0.92	0.88	0.03	0.83	0.78	0.02	0.80	0.77	0.02
Niacin equivalents (mg)	17.0	16.3	0.19	17.1	16.7	0.29	16.4	15.8	0.26	15.9	15.5	0.26
Vitamin B6 (mg)	1.03	1.01	0.01	1.03	0.98	0.02	1.02	0.97	0.02	0.99	0.96	0.02
Vitamin B12 (μg)	2.98	2.42	0.10	3.33	2.36	0.33	2.97	2.27	0.11	3.01	2.20	0.18
Folate (μg)	131	126	1.8	130	122	3.1	130	122	3.4	123	120	2.3
Biotin (μg)	17.2	16.6	0.3	15.8	15.3	0.4	17.0	14.8	1.6	14.6	14.2	0.4
Pantothenic acid (mg)	2.69	2.54	0.05	2.65	2.48	0.07	2.57	2.45	0.05	2.50	2.43	0.05
Vitamin C (mg)	33.2	27.6	1.0	28.6	25.9	1.3	25.3	21.2	0.9	22.3	19.3	0.8
Vitamin D (μg)	1.54	1.28	0.06	1.36	1.16	0.07	1.38	1.13	0.09	1.32	1.13	0.08
Vitamin E (mg)	4.36	4.16	0.08	4.32	4.04	0.18	3.94	3.61	0.10	3.58	3.24	0.11
Base		*377*			*138*			*378*			*177*	
Women												
Retinol (μg)	730	284	60	644	268	80	620	265	58	567	253	65
Carotene (μg)	1477	1226	53	1445	1212	94	1174	871	64	1057	688	74
Retinol equivalents (μg)	976	543	61	885	518	81	816	464	61	743	399	68
Thiamin (mg)	0.75	0.72	0.01	0.78	0.74	0.02	0.75	0.71	0.01	0.77	0.74	0.01
Riboflavin (mg)	1.01	0.94	0.02	0.97	0.85	0.04	0.92	0.84	0.02	0.93	0.84	0.03
Niacin equivalents (mg)	18.0	17.1	0.24	18.2	16.7	0.52	17.0	16.1	0.24	16.9	15.7	0.31
Vitamin B6 (mg)	0.98	0.94	0.01	0.97	0.89	0.02	0.94	0.89	0.02	0.94	0.89	0.02
Vitamin B12 (μg)	3.53	2.37	0.18	3.16	2.21	0.22	3.02	2.10	0.16	3.07	2.24	0.20
Folate (μg)	137	129	2.3	137	124	6.4	125	116	2.3	123	118	2.5
Biotin (μg)	18.9	16.9	0.6	20.1	15.7	2.9	16.2	15.1	0.4	15.5	14.4	0.4
Pantothenic acid (mg)	2.85	2.67	0.04	2.86	2.65	0.10	2.70	2.51	0.05	2.72	2.53	0.06
Vitamin C (mg)	45.2	39.0	1.5	41.4	32.7	2.3	32.5	26.8	1.2	32.7	26.5	1.4
Vitamin D (μg)	1.58	1.36	0.06	1.82	1.39	0.18	1.48	1.30	0.06	1.37	1.13	0.07
Vitamin E (mg)	4.59	4.28	0.08	4.61	4.17	0.18	4.14	3.90	0.08	3.72	3.54	0.09
Base		*386*			*141*			*347*			*222*	

Table 10.36 Average daily intake of vitamins from all sources by sex and household composition

Vitamin (units)	Household composition											
	Informant alone			With others, no dependent children						With dependent child		
				With spouse			No spouse					
	Mean	Median	SE	Mean	Median	SE	Mean	Median	SE	Mean	Median	SE
Men												
Retinol (μg)	1205	573	243	1488	659	109	989	526	81	1296	640	87
Carotene (μg)	2567	1748	347	2693	2233	102	1978	1439	103	2432	1884	99
Retinol equivalents (μg)	1632	912	249	1937	1140	115	1319	877	85	1701	1079	91
Thiamin (mg)	1.6	1.6	0.07	1.9	1.7	0.11	2.1	1.6	0.25	2.2	1.7	0.37
Riboflavin (mg)	2.1	2.0	0.10	2.3	2.1	0.15	2.2	2.0	0.12	2.3	2.0	0.19
Niacin equivalents (mg)	40.0	36.7	1.46	41.0	39.5	0.60	41.2	39.6	1.28	40.6	39.9	0.59
Vitamin B6 (mg)	2.9	2.2	0.36	2.6	2.3	0.12	2.8	2.6	0.12	2.7	2.4	0.19
Vitamin B12 (μg)	7.3	5.5	0.73	8.0	6.0	0.38	6.7	5.3	0.27	7.2	5.8	0.25
Folate (μg)	313	287	18.0	313	298	5.5	310	305	6.8	313	304	4.6
Biotin (μg)	39.6	37.5	1.96	39.4	37.9	0.71	36.9	35.4	0.94	40.2	38.9	0.84
Pantothenic acid (mg)	6.1	5.8	0.23	6.4	6.0	0.18	6.6	6.1	0.21	6.8	6.2	0.31
Vitamin C (mg)	97.5	52.7	19.9	76.8	62.7	3.7	69.4	55.3	3.7	72.1	57.9	4.0
Vitamin D (μg)	3.2	2.7	0.30	4.2	3.3	0.19	3.3	2.5	0.20	3.8	3.1	0.15
Vitamin E (mg)	8.9	8.6	0.51	12.5	9.2	1.82	10.5	9.3	0.73	12.2	9.6	1.07
Base		71			360			271			385	

Vitamin (units)	Informant alone			With others, no dependent children						With dependent child					
				With spouse			No spouse			With spouse			Lone mother		
	Mean	Median	SE	Mean	Median	SE	Mean	Median	SE	Mean	Median	SE	Mean	Median	SE
Women															
Retinol (μg)	1181	518	159	1326	536	91	929	443	97	1066	492	81	936	365	188
Carotene (μg)	2141	1527	197	2439	1924	107	1862	1571	101	2046	1656	85	1620	1097	233
Retinol equivalents (μg)	1537	936	171	1733	969	93	1239	745	100	1407	810	84	1206	627	192
Thiamin (mg)	1.4	1.3	0.10	1.9	1.3	0.40	1.7	1.3	0.27	1.4	1.3	0.05	1.4	1.2	0.16
Riboflavin (mg)	1.8	1.7	0.10	2.0	1.6	0.09	1.9	1.4	0.28	1.7	1.6	0.07	1.5	1.4	0.13
Niacin equivalents (mg)	30.1	29.5	1.07	32.2	29.0	1.68	29.7	28.1	0.92	29.4	28.6	0.46	27.0	26.9	1.24
Vitamin B6 (mg)	3.5	1.6	1.15	3.0	1.6	0.47	1.9	1.6	0.23	3.1	1.6	0.56	2.4	1.5	0.83
Vitamin B12 (μg)	5.4	4.0	0.37	5.8	4.2	0.24	4.9	3.7	0.38	5.1	3.9	0.22	5.5	3.5	0.73
Folate (μg)	212	199	9.6	225	218	3.7	211	205	4.6	221	204	8.9	199	199	9.9
Biotin (μg)	28.5	27.7	1.55	30.4	27.9	0.84	26.0	24.5	0.76	29.3	27.3	0.79	24.3	23.6	1.42
Pantothenic acid (mg)	4.8	4.6	0.23	5.5	4.5	0.53	4.8	4.4	0.29	4.9	4.6	0.18	4.2	4.2	0.22
Vitamin C (mg)	63.3	49.2	5.0	81.1	62.8	5.2	76.1	54.2	6.8	69.4	50.4	5.5	55.8	39.2	8.4
Vitamin D (μg)	3.3	2.6	0.31	3.6	2.4	0.18	2.9	2.0	0.24	2.8	2.3	0.11	2.2	1.5	0.26
Vitamin E (mg)	11.1	6.8	2.64	9.1	7.0	0.66	8.0	6.7	0.41	8.1	7.0	0.46	7.3	5.2	1.41
Base		84			382			182			386			76	

11 Minerals: nutrient intake, urinary sodium and urinary potassium

Minerals are inorganic elements. The essential minerals are required for normal functions of the body and are therefore required in the diet. They include calcium, phosphorus, iron, potassium, sodium, chlorine and magnesium. Trace elements are essential minerals that are required in minute amounts and include zinc, copper and iodine.

Results are presented here on the dietary intakes of a number of minerals, including sodium and potassium, and on mineral intakes per 1000kcal total energy consumed. Results are also given for urinary sodium and urinary potassium based on the analysis of specimens provided by co-operating male and female subjects.[1] Subjects taking diuretics have been excluded from the results for urinary sodium and urinary potassium because of their effects on the analytes being measured.

11.1 Iron
Average daily intakes of iron from all sources for the sample were 14.0mg for men and 12.3mg for women. These figures compare with an RDA for iron of 10mg for men and for women aged 55 years or more, and 12mg for women under the age of 55. However intakes of iron were skewed, with median values of 13.2mg for men and 10.0mg for women; median intakes of iron for women under 50 were below the UK RDA.

Although food supplements generally provided a smaller proportion of individuals' mineral than vitamin intakes, iron was an exception to this pattern. Supplementary iron was of greater importance for women than for men, providing 15% of women's average intake from all sources compared to 2% of men's intake.

As shown in Table 11.1, there was little variation in total iron intake according to age. Men in the youngest age group (16 to 24) and women between the ages of 16 and 34 had significantly lower mean intakes of iron from food sources than did older people (p<0.05); for women this difference was not apparent once iron from supplements was included, but younger men continued to have a lower intake even after the inclusion of supplements. *(Table 11.1)*

Table 11.2 shows the average amount of iron derived from each of the main food types for men and women, and expresses these amounts as a percentage of the average total intake of iron. Cereal products provided the highest proportion of iron (42% of total intake); within this category white bread contributed 9% of total iron intake, wholemeal and other bread 10%, and high fibre breakfast cereals 10% of the total. Meat and meat products and vegetables were also important sources of iron, contributing 23% and 15% respectively of total intake. The importance of the main food types did not differ significantly between men and women, except in the case of high fibre breakfast cereals, which provided a significantly greater proportion of the average daily intake of iron for women than for men (p<0.01). *(Table 11.2)*

11.2 Calcium
Table 11.3 shows that average daily intakes of calcium from all sources were 940mg for men (median 919mg) and 730mg (median 717mg) for women. Calcium derived from supplements had only a marginal effect on average intakes; food sources alone provided an average 937mg for men and 726mg for women. The RDA for calcium is 500mg both for men and for women, and average intakes for all age groups were well above this level. For both sexes calcium intake increased with age, with those aged 16 to 24 recording significantly lower intakes than those aged 35 or over (men, p<0.05; women, p<0.01). *(Table 11.3)*

Milk and milk products provided about half of total calcium intake (46% for men and 50% for women). Cereal products were also important, contributing a quarter of total intake (26% for men and 25% for women); white bread provided 9% of the overall total of calcium consumed. A number of other food types made a small contribution to calcium intake; the largest of these was vegetables which provided 7% of total intake. *(Table 11.4)*

11.3 Dietary sodium and chloride
Sodium chloride (salt) is present in all body fluids. Sodium and chloride are essential elements within the body and concentrations are maintained by a variety of complex regulatory mechanisms. Small amounts are necessary in the diet. High salt intakes have been associated with hypertension, but the relationship between dietary salt and blood pressure is still a subject of controversy.

Sodium and chloride are not naturally found in high concentrations in foods, but are added to many foods during processing as well as by the addition of salt in the home. Although the average sodium and chloride content of the foods consumed by respondents was assessed, it was not possible to measure the amount of salt added at the time of cooking or on the plate; the intakes of sodium and chloride measured are therefore based on average values attributed to foods eaten and do not allow for additions in cooking and at table. These results should therefore be treated with caution.

Questions on habitual practice with regard to the use of salt in cooking and at the table were included in the questionnaire and addressed to all respondents. For this Report these responses have not been quantified and there has been no attempt to combine them with the results for the measured intake of sodium and chloride. The best estimate of total sodium intake is that derived from urinary sodium excretion, since the body is normally maintained in sodium balance.

Table 11.5 summarises for men and women separately the responses to the questions on habitual use of salt in cooking and at the table. More than three quarters of informants reported that salt was generally added to their food during cooking; no attempt was made to differentiate between practices for different types of food. Use of salt in cooking may not necessarily be the informant's decision, but reflects the practice of the person responsible for cooking. Use of salt at table is, however, at the discretion of the individual, and Table 11.5 indicates some difference in practice between men and women. Overall, men were more likely to 'generally add salt to food at table' whilst women were more likely to add salt either 'sometimes' or 'rarely/never'; these differences were evident regardless of whether salt was usually added during cooking (p<0.01).

(Table 11.5)

Information on the intake of sodium and chloride from food is shown in Tables 11.6 and 11.7. Men's average intake of both minerals was about 44% higher than that of women. Amongst men the top 2.5% of consumers of sodium had intakes in excess of 5600mg. There was little variation by age in sodium and chloride intake from foods. *(Tables 11.6 & 11.7)*

11.4 Urinary sodium
The mean urinary sodium excretion per 24 hours for men was 173mmol (3980mg/24h), 31% higher than the mean amount for women—132mmol (3040mg/24h).

(Table 11.8)

Williams and Bingham, in a validation study of 24-hour urine collections using the PABA marker (see Chapter 4) found a mean urinary sodium excretion of 172.4mmol for men and 128.1mmol for women aged 25 to 44. Both values are similar to the current sample where the age range was 16 to 64.[2]

11.5 Dietary potassium
Average daily intakes of potassium from all sources for men and women are shown in Table 11.9. Supplements made only a very small contribution to total intake, and the average daily intakes from all sources were 3187mg for men (median 3143mg) and 2434mg (median 2410mg) for women. Men and women aged

16 to 24 recorded significantly lower intakes of potassium than the overall averages (p<0.01). *(Table 11.9)*

11.6 Urinary potassium
The mean urinary potassium excretion per 24 hours by men in the sample was 77mmol (3000mg/24h), 24% higher than the mean excretion by women, 62mmol (2610mg/24h). *(Table 11.10)*

The Williams and Bingham study reported mean urinary potassium excretion of 74.3mmol for men and 61.5mmol for women from validated 24-hour complete collections, which was very similar to the current sample.[2]

11.7 Magnesium and phosphorus
Both magnesium and phosphorus are found widely in foods. Magnesium is found particularly in foods of vegetable origin.

Neither magnesium nor phosphorus are common constituents of dietary supplements so most of the intake recorded was from food sources. Average daily intakes of magnesium for the sample were 323mg for men (median 312mg) and 237mg for women (median 226mg). The distributions of intakes were not markedly skewed, which reflects the spread of sources of the mineral. Intakes were significantly lower among the youngest group of men and women compared with the overall means for the samples (p<0.01). *(Table 11.11)*

Average daily intakes of phosphorus from all sources are shown in Table 11.12; men had an average intake of 1452mg (median 1429mg) and women had an average intake of 1072mg (median 1054mg). As for magnesium, compared with the overall average, intakes of phosphorus were lowest both for men and women in the youngest age group identified (p<0.05). *(Table 11.12)*

11.8 Trace elements: copper, zinc and iodine
Of the trace elements known to be essential copper, zinc and iodine were included in the nutrient databank. Average daily intakes for men and women by age are shown in Tables 11.13 to 11.15.

Average daily intakes of copper from all sources were 1.63mg for men (median 1.49mg) and 1.23mg for women (median 1.13mg). Little copper was derived from food supplements. Average intakes were significantly lower for younger respondents, men under the age of 25 and women under the age of 35, than for other groups (p<0.01). *(Table 11.13)*

Average daily intakes of zinc from all sources were 11.4mg for men (median 10.9mg) and 8.4mg for women (median 8.2mg). As for copper, the intake of zinc recorded by the sample was markedly lower for the youngest group of respondents, aged 16 to 24 years, compared with other men and women (p<0.05).

(Table 11.14)

A small amount of the iodine intake of the sample, comprising about 3% of the total, was obtained from food supplements, such as kelp. Average daily intakes of iodine from all sources were 243µg for men (median 226µg) and 176µg for women (median 163µg). Women below the age of 35 had intakes which were lower than older women (p<0.05), but there was no significant difference in intake with age for men. (*Table 11.15*)

11.9 Variation in intake of minerals
Age of informant
Table 11.16 shows average values for mineral intake per 1000kcal total energy by age and sex of the sample. Overall, women had higher levels of all nutrients per 1000kcal (p<0.01), except for sodium and chloride where there was little difference in the values for men and women. The mineral content per 1000kcal tended to increase with age of informant, as did the absolute intake of most minerals. This trend was less clearly seen for intakes of sodium and chloride. The differences between men and women in intakes per 1000kcal were most marked over the age of 35 (p<0.01); with the exception of iron and calcium, younger women had intakes per 1000kcal which were generally similar to those of men in the same age groups. (*Table 11.16*)

Dieters and the unwell
Informants who were on a slimming diet during the recording period did not have lower intakes of most minerals in spite of their lower total energy intake. The only significant differences between the mineral intakes of slimmers and non-slimmers were that dieting women had lower intakes of sodium and chloride from foods (p<0.01), but it should be remembered that the measures of sodium and chloride do not make allowance for salt added by the individual either in cooking or at the table. (*Table 11.17*)

Since slimmers had substantially lower energy intakes than non-slimmers yet had comparable total mineral intakes, it follows that their mineral intake per 1000kcal was substantially higher than that of non-slimmers. This is seen to be the case for all minerals, including sodium and chloride (p<0.01, except for intakes of iron, calcium and magnesium by men, where p<0.05). (*Table 11.18*)

In contrast to informants who were on a slimming diet, those who had a reduced energy intake as a result of being unwell did have lower intakes of most minerals than other men and women in the sample (p<0.01, except for intakes of calcium, chloride and potassium by men, where p<0.05). The exception to this pattern was that women who had been unwell did not have a significantly lower intake of iron than other women, and unwell men had similar iodine intakes to other men. (*Table 11.19*)

It can be seen from Table 11.20, however, that the diets of the unwell did not differ qualitatively in terms of mineral intake from those of informants whose eating was not affected by illness; there were no significant differences in values for mineral intake per 1000kcal for the two groups. Variation in absolute intakes of minerals was, therefore, largely a reflection of the lower energy intakes of the unwell.
(*Table 11.20*)

Region
Compared with average intakes for all men, men in Scotland had lower intakes of magnesium, phosphorus, copper and zinc (p<0.01), and also of iron and potassium (p<0.05). The chloride intakes from food of men in London and the South East were lower than for men in the North and Central regions (p<0.05). For women the pattern was less clear; women in Scotland had lower intakes from food of calcium compared with women in the Central and South West regions and Wales, and also lower intakes of potassium as compared with women in London and the South East (p<0.05). Intakes of chloride from food sources were significantly higher in Scottish women compared with the intakes of women in London and the South East (p<0.01), and those in the Central and South West regions and Wales (p<0.05). (*Table 11.21*)

Table 11.22 presents comparable figures for mineral intake per 1000kcal energy consumed, and shows little variation in the average quality of the diets of either men or women by region. There is, notably, no indication that Scottish men had lower mineral intakes per 1000kcal energy, indicating that their lower total mineral intakes are related to their recorded lower energy intake. Intakes of sodium and chloride in food per 1000kcal energy were higher for both men and women in Scotland compared with other regions (p<0.01, except for men as compared with the Northern region, where p<0.05). (*Table 11.22*)

Socio-economic characteristics
Table 11.23 shows that unemployed men had the lowest average daily intakes of all minerals and that their intakes and those of economically inactive men were significantly lower than the intakes of working men (p<0.01, except for intakes of copper by economically inactive men, where p<0.05, and iodine where the difference was not significant). The small group of unemployed women also had intakes of some minerals which were markedly lower than those of working women, (phosphorus, copper, zinc and iodine, where p<0.01, and iron, calcium and magnesium, where p<0.05). There were very few differences in the mineral intakes of working and economically inactive women, only for magnesium and zinc were the intakes of the economically inactive group significantly lower (p<0.05). (*Table 11.23*)

These differences between groups were not as marked when considering mineral intake per 1000kcal energy. Unemployed men had a lower average value than working men for calcium (p<0.01), and phosphorus intakes (p<0.05), per 1000kcal energy, but other differences were not statistically significant. Unemployed women, on the other hand, had lower intakes per 1000kcal of a range of minerals compared to working women, but not for iron, sodium or chloride, (for phosphorus, copper and zinc, p < 0.01, for calcium, potassium and iodine, p < 0.05). (*Table 11.24*)

The recorded intakes of all minerals, except iron in women, were significantly lower for both male and female informants in households receiving state benefits than for others, (p < 0.01, except for intakes of chloride by women, where p < 0.05). (*Table 11.25*)

The differences were less marked when considering mineral intake per 1000kcal energy, particularly for men, where calcium (p < 0.01), magnesium and phosphorus (p < 0.05) were the only minerals where intakes per 1000kcal were significantly lower for men in households receiving benefits. Women in households receiving benefits also had lower intakes per 1000kcal of potassium, magnesium, iodine, calcium and phosphorus (p < 0.01), and of zinc (p < 0.05).
(*Table 11.26*)

Table 11.27 shows a clear difference in intakes of almost all minerals according to social class, with highest intakes for informants in Social Classes I and II. Moreover for women, all minerals except iron, showed a consistent trend through the social classes from highest to lowest. This was not the case for men; only intakes of zinc fell progressively through the social class range. However for both men and women intakes of all minerals except sodium and chloride, iodine for men, and iron for women, were significantly higher among those in Social Classes I and II compared with those in manual social classes (p < 0.01). (*Table 11.27*)

The mineral content of the diet per 1000kcal showed a similar pattern. Among men significantly higher intakes were recorded for potassium, magnesium, calcium and phosphorus per 1000kcal (p < 0.01) for those in Social Classes I and II as compared with those in manual social classes. Additionally men in Social Classes IV and V had lower intakes per 1000kcal of iron (p < 0.01), and copper (p < 0.05) than those in professional and managerial social classes. Compared with women in manual social classes women in Social Classes I and II had markedly higher intakes per 1000kcal of iron, potassium, magnesium, phosphorus and copper (p < 0.01) and also of calcium and iodine (p < 0.05).
(*Table 11.28*)

Household composition
Among men the most marked differences were between the intakes of married men, either with or without dependent children, and those of non-married men. Compared with the group of non-married men living with others but without a spouse, the married men had higher intakes of all minerals except sodium, chloride and iodine (p < 0.01, except for intakes of magnesium, where p < 0.05). The highest average daily intakes for women were generally recorded by those who were married, either with or without dependent children.

Compared with married women living with dependent children, lone mothers had lower intakes of calcium, magnesium, phosphorus, and zinc (p < 0.01), and also of potassium, copper and iodine (p < 0.05). The differences were also found when the intakes of lone mothers and married women without children were compared.
(*Table 11.29*)

For iron, potassium, magnesium, phosphorus, copper, zinc and iodine the lowest intakes per 1000kcal total energy were recorded by men living with other adults but not a spouse; highest intakes of all these minerals per 1000 kcal, except iodine were recorded by married men without dependent children. Except in the case of iodine the differences between the highest and lowest intakes were all statistically significant (p < 0.01). Men living with others but not a spouse also had the lowest recorded intakes of sodium and chloride, and the highest intakes per 1000kcal of these minerals were by men living alone. However for these minerals the differences in recorded intakes were not statistically significant. Per 1000kcal of total energy, lone mothers recorded the lowest intakes of all minerals except sodium, chloride, zinc and iodine. The highest intakes of iron, calcium, potassium, and phosphorus were recorded by married women without dependent children; for these minerals the differences between the highest and lowest recorded intakes were statistically significant (p < 0.01). (*Table 11.30*)

11.10 Variation in total urinary sodium and urinary potassium

Age of informant
Although for both men and women mean urinary sodium and potassium excretion tended to decrease with age, the differences between the age groups were generally not significant. However, women aged 50 to 64 did have lower mean excretion of sodium than other women (p < 0.01) and potassium excretion was also significantly lower in the oldest group of women (p < 0.05). (*Table 11.31*)

Dieters and the unwell
The mean urinary sodium excretion was found to be significantly higher in women who were on a slimming diet at the time they kept a dietary record than in those not slimming; 141.0mmol compared with 130.4mmol (p < 0.05). Although higher among female slimmers, their mean potassium excretion was not significantly different from that of non-slimmers. (*Table 11.32*)

Mean excretion of both urinary sodium and potassium was markedly lower among men whose eating had been affected during the seven-day dietary recording period as compared with men who were not unwell (p < 0.05 for sodium, p < 0.01 for potassium). There were no such associations for women. (*Table 11.33*)

Region
Table 11.34 shows that there was a quite marked regional difference in the mean urinary sodium excretion of men, but there were no such associations

for women. For male subjects means were higher for those living in Scotland than elsewhere in Great Britain, except the Northern region (p<0.05).

In contrast to the mean values for total excretion of sodium in 24 hours men living in Scotland had lower mean excretion of potassium than all other men (p<0.01). The mean excretion of potassium by women living in Scotland was lower than that of women living in the Central and South West regions and Wales (p<0.01). *(Table 11.34)*

Socio-economic characteristics
There were no significant differences in mean sodium excretion associated with employment status for either men or women. However, unemployed men excreted less potassium in 24 hours than working men (p<0.01). Among women employment status was not associated with potassium excretion. *(Table 11.35)*

Men in households receiving benefits had significantly lower mean excretion of potassium compared with other men (p<0.01), but similar differences were not found for women, nor were there any differences associated with sodium excretion. *(Table 11.36)*

In relation to social class mean excretion of sodium showed no marked differences for either men or women. Excretion of potassium was however more clearly associated with social class. Both men and women in Social Classes I and II had higher potassium excretion than those in Social Classes III non-manual and manual but not those in Social Classes IV and V (p<0.01, except for men in Social Class III manual, where p<0.05). *(Table 11.37)*

These findings are in contrast to the Williams and Bingham study which found higher mean excretion of sodium from men in manual social classes but little difference in sodium excretion between manual and non-manual social classes among women. Williams and Bingham also reported that excretion rates of potassium were similar across the social classes for both men and women.[2]

Household composition
There was no significant variation in urinary sodium excretion associated with household composition.

Mean excretion of potassium was higher among women who were living with a spouse and dependent children as compared to women living alone p<0.05. *(Table 11.38)*

Cigarette smoking and alcohol consumption
There was no systematic relationship between sodium excretion and cigarette smoking. Although mean sodium excretion tended to increase with increasing alcohol consumption, the differences were not statistically significant for either men or women.

For both men and women mean potassium excretion tended to decrease with increasing numbers of cigarettes smoked a day, but the differences were only significant for men (p<0.01). Potassium excretion by men increased with increasing alcohol consumption; thus men reporting consuming no alcohol had lower mean excretion than all other men (p<0.05). The difference was most marked between those reporting consuming no alcohol and those consuming less than 168g (p<0.01). Among women mean potassium excretion was also greater for those consuming alcohol than those who did not record any alcohol consumption (p<0.01, except for the heaviest women drinkers, where the difference was not statistically significant, probably due to the very small size of this group). *(Tables 11.39 & 11.40)*

11.10.1 Dietary and urinary sodium and potassium
Table 11.41 shows correlation coefficients between the urine analytes and dietary intakes. The correlations were generally quite weak, the strongest correlation between intake and excretion being for potassium in women. Weak correlations, particularly between sodium excretion and dietary sodium, were not unexpected since the estimates of dietary intakes were based on average values for the content in food and made no allowance for additions at the table or in cooking. Also, the urine collection was made over a 24 hour period and the dietary record kept over a (different) seven-day period and the completeness of the 24-hour urine collection was not validated. *(Table 11.41)*

11.11 Summary
Although the average intakes of iron from all sources for the sample either met or were above the RDA, the median intakes for women under 50 were below the RDA. Calcium intakes were well above the current UK RDA. There are currently no UK RDAs for other minerals.

The intake of most minerals tended to increase with age of informant although a decline in intake with age was seen for sodium and chloride. The mineral content of the diet per 1000kcal of energy consumed was generally higher for women than men, and showed a more marked increase with age than did absolute mineral intakes.

The total intake of most minerals by slimmers did not differ significantly from that of non-slimmers, and slimmers had higher mineral intakes per 1000kcal energy. In contrast, informants who were unwell had lower total intakes of most minerals but their mineral intake per 1000kcal was similar to that of other informants.

Smaller amounts of most minerals were recorded by the unemployed, those in households receiving benefits, and those in lower social classes. These trends were still evident but were less marked when mineral intake per 1000kcal energy was considered. Men in Scotland had lower total intakes of some minerals, but this was largely a reflection of their lower energy intake rather than of lower mineral intakes per 1000kcal.

In general the average iron intake of different groups of women showed less variation than other minerals. Average amounts of sodium and chloride did not differ between groups in the same way as other minerals. Sodium and chloride intake per 1000kcal was higher for informants in Scotland.

Potassium excretion was lower from unemployed men, men in households receiving benefits, those in the lower social classes and from men living in Scotland. Mean urinary potassium excretion was also markedly lower in men who smoked, but mean excretion for both men and women increased with reported increased consumption of alcohol.

The next chapter looks further at differences in nutrient intake and uses analysis of variance to show which characteristics of the sample are most important in explaining variation in intakes of a range of nutrients.

Reference and note

1. Chapter 4 gives a description of the purpose of the urine analyses, and the methods and equipment used to obtain a 24-hour collection of urine and specimens from this total collection. Chapter 4 also describes some of the methodological problems associated with obtaining a complete 24-hour collection, and the possible effects on the results. Chapter 8 gives details of the basis on which the results from the urine analysis have been calculated.
2. Williams D R R, Bingham S A. Sodium and potassium intakes in a representative population sample: estimation from 24h urine collections known to be complete in a Cambridgeshire village. *Br J Nutr* 1986; 55: 1; 13–22.

Table 11.1 Average daily iron intake (mg) by age and sex

| | Sex and age of informant | | | | | | | | | |
| | Men | | | | All ages 16–64 | Women | | | | All ages 16–64 |
	16–24	25–34	35–49	50–64		16–24	25–34	35–49	50–64	
a) Intake from all sources (mg)										
Mean (average) value	13.0	14.1	14.5	14.1	14.0	11.8	11.1	12.9	12.9	12.3
Median value	12.5	13.3	13.4	13.7	13.2	9.5	9.6	10.3	10.3	10.0
Lower 2.5 percentile	5.6	6.8	6.9	6.2	6.5	4.3	4.5	4.9	5.7	4.7
Upper 2.5 percentile	24.5	28.1	26.9	27.5	27.1	39.3	23.0	31.0	36.9	30.7
Standard error of the mean	0.35	0.37	0.32	0.30	0.17	0.95	0.42	0.69	0.78	0.36
Base	*214*	*254*	*346*	*273*	*1087*	*189*	*253*	*385*	*283*	*1110*
b) Intake from food sources (mg)										
Mean (average) value	12.6	13.8	14.2	13.9	13.7	9.8	10.2	11.0	10.6	10.5
Median value	12.4	13.2	13.3	13.7	13.2	9.1	9.4	10.2	10.1	9.8
Lower 2.5 percentile	5.4	6.8	6.9	6.2	6.5	4.3	4.5	4.9	5.6	4.6
Upper 2.5 percentile	23.0	25.9	25.7	26.3	25.7	17.5	19.1	25.6	21.1	21.1
Standard error of the mean	0.29	0.36	0.26	0.28	0.15	0.28	0.25	0.25	0.23	0.13
Base	*214*	*254*	*346*	*273*	*1087*	*189*	*253*	*385*	*283*	*1110*

Table 11.2 Average daily iron intake (mg) from main food types by sex of informant

Food type	Men		Women		Total	
	Amount	% of total	Amount	% of total	Amount	% of total
Cereal products	5.64	41	4.52	43	5.07	42
of which						
—white bread	*1.40*	*10*	*.79*	*8*	*1.09*	*9*
—wholemeal & other breads	*1.34*	*10*	*1.04*	*10*	*1.19*	*10*
—high fibre breakfast cereals	*1.14*	*8*	*1.26*	*12*	*1.20*	*10*
Milk and products	.24	2	.20	2	.22	2
Eggs and egg dishes	.52	4	.36	3	.44	4
Fat spreads	.05	0	.03	0	.04	0
Meat and products	3.35	24	2.18	21	2.76	23
of which						
—beef and veal	*.97*	*7*	*.66*	*6*	*.81*	*7*
—liver and products	*.37*	*3*	*.36*	*3*	*.37*	*3*
Fish and fish dishes	.35	3	.25	2	.30	2
Vegetables	2.10	15	1.53	15	1.81	15
Fruit and nuts	.28	2	.32	3	.30	2
Sugar, confectionery and preserves	.24	2	.24	2	.24	2
Beverages	.52	4	.50	5	.51	4
Miscellaneous	.42	3	.39	4	.41	3
TOTAL	13.70	100	10.50	100	12.10	100
Number of cases	*1087*		*1110*		*2197*	

Table 11.3 Average daily calcium intake (mg) by age and sex

	Sex and age of informant									
	Men				All ages 16–64	Women				All ages 16–64
	16–24	25–34	35–49	50–64		16–24	25–34	35–49	50–64	
a) Intake from all sources (mg)										
Mean (average) value	899	933	961	952	940	675	700	764	747	730
Median value	863	908	959	947	919	656	692	739	732	717
Lower 2.5 percentile	390	379	439	420	410	240	231	328	305	266
Upper 2.5 percentile	1597	1607	1686	1528	1607	1220	1300	1379	1167	1317
Standard error of the mean	22.9	20.4	16.5	16.4	9.4	19.4	17.4	13.9	13.5	7.9
Base	*214*	*254*	*346*	*273*	*1087*	*189*	*253*	*385*	*283*	*1110*
b) Intake from food sources (mg)										
Mean (average) value	894	931	960	949	937	675	699	760	739	726
Median value	858	908	956	947	917	656	689	737	731	716
Lower 2.5 percentile	352	379	439	420	409	240	231	328	305	266
Upper 2.5 percentile	1597	1607	1683	1528	1597	1220	1299	1379	1131	1299
Standard error of the mean	23.1	20.0	16.5	16.3	9.3	19.4	17.4	13.8	12.9	7.8
Base	*214*	*254*	*346*	*273*	*1087*	*189*	*253*	*385*	*283*	*1110*

Table 11.4 Average daily intake of calcium (mg) from main food types by sex of informant

Food type	Men		Women		Total	
	Amount	% of total	Amount	% of total	Amount	% of total
Cereal products	246	26	178	25	211	25
of which						
—*white bread*	*93*	*10*	*52*	*7*	*72*	*9*
Milk and products	432	46	365	50	398	48
of which						
—*full fat milk*	*208*	*22*	*166*	*23*	*187*	*23*
—*cheese*	*125*	*13*	*87*	*12*	*106*	*13*
Eggs and egg dishes	20	2	16	2	18	2
Fat spreads	2	0	1	0	2	0
Meat and products	52	6	31	4	42	5
Fish and fish dishes	24	3	17	2	20	2
Vegetables	66	7	51	7	58	7
Fruit and nuts	10	1	12	2	11	1
Sugar, confectionery and preserves	17	2	16	2	16	2
Beverages	50	5	20	3	35	4
Miscellaneous	19	2	20	3	19	2
TOTAL	937	100	726	100	831	100
Number of cases	*1087*		*1110*		*2197*	

Table 11.5 Use of salt in cooking and at table by sex of informant

Use of salt at table	Use of salt in cooking							
	Adds salt		No salt		Uses salt substitute		Total	
	Men	Women	Men	Women	Men	Women	Men	Women
	%	%	%	%	%	%	%	%
Generally adds salt	49	35	41	30	(20)	(22)	47	34
Sometimes adds salt	16	20	10	14	(20)	(17)	15	19
Rarely or never adds salt	35	45	49	56	(40)	(48)	38	47
Uses salt substitute	0	0	1	1	(20)	(13)	1	1
Base	*866*	*866*	*204*	*219*	*15*	*23*	*1085*	*1108*

( ) indicates percentage based on small number of cases

Table 11.6 Average daily sodium intake (mg) by age and sex

Intake from all sources (mg)	Age				All ages 16–64
	16–24	25–34	35–49	50–64	
Men					
Mean (average) value	3432	3327	3459	3272	3376
Median value	3430	3309	3406	3232	3320
Lower 2.5 percentile	1459	1529	1804	1686	1551
Upper 2.5 percentile	5807	5638	5600	5320	5600
Standard error of the mean	78.2	61.2	51.9	51.8	29.8
Base	*214*	*254*	*346*	*273*	*1087*
Women					
Mean (average) value	2334	2372	2389	2294	2351
Median value	2291	2345	2356	2259	2313
Lower 2.5 percentile	1095	1106	1138	1225	1131
Upper 2.5 percentile	3837	3797	3801	3481	3724
Standard error of the mean	49.1	43.4	33.8	42.4	20.5
Base	*189*	*253*	*385*	*283*	*1110*

Table 11.7 Average daily chloride intake (mg) by age and sex

Intake from all sources (mg)	Age				All ages 16–64
	16–24	25–34	35–49	50–64	
Men					
Mean (average) value	5245	5125	5296	5029	5179
Median value	5252	5052	5216	4991	5115
Lower 2.5 percentile	2264	2311	2744	2611	2464
Upper 2.5 percentile	8668	8635	8510	8120	8510
Standard error of the mean	115.4	91.1	78.8	78.0	44.6
Base	*214*	*254*	*346*	*273*	*1087*
Women					
Mean (average) value	3572	3601	3615	3490	3573
Median value	3497	3575	3552	3485	3536
Lower 2.5 percentile	1666	1659	1755	1850	1723
Upper 2.5 percentile	5705	5563	5741	5062	5598
Standard error of the mean	74.0	64.5	50.4	63.3	30.7
Base	*189*	*253*	*385*	*283*	*1110*

Table 11.8 Percentage distribution of total urinary sodium by age and sex

Total urinary sodium (mmol/24h)	Age 16–24	25–34	35–49	50–64	All ages 16–64
	cum %	cum %	cum %	cum %	cum %
Men					
Less than 90	15	10	11	12	12
Less than 120	27	25	24	24	25
Less than 150	43	44	39	40	41
Less than 180	54	58	57	60	58
All	100	100	100	100	100
Base	*144*	*193*	*280*	*225*	*842*
Mean (average) value	179	175	175	166	173
Median value	171	167	166	164	166
Lower 5.0 percentile	68	73	66	57	68
Upper 5.0 percentile	317	308	310	273	306
Standard error of the mean	7.30	5.48	4.47	4.29	2.58
	cum %	cum %	cum %	cum %	cum %
Women					
Less than 90	17	21	20	18	19
Less than 120	46	41	43	52	45
Less than 150	66	65	68	71	68
Less than 180	80	84	83	88	84
All	100	100	100	100	100
Base	*136*	*213*	*293*	*223*	*865*
Mean (average) value	136	131	135	124	132
Median value	126	129	131	119	126
Lower 5.0 percentile	61	49	57	61	57
Upper 5.0 percentile	266	214	234	206	226
Standard error of the mean	5.05	3.51	3.23	2.96	1.78

Table 11.9 Average daily potassium intake (mg) by age and sex

Intake from all sources (mg)	Age 16–24	25–34	35–49	50–64	All ages 16–64
Men					
Mean (average) value	3018	3237	3279	3155	3187
Median value	3006	3223	3197	3089	3143
Lower 2.5 percentile	1511	1758	1846	1774	1724
Upper 2.5 percentile	4618	4802	5099	4699	4816
Standard error of the mean	60	50	45	43	25
Base	*214*	*254*	*346*	*273*	*1087*
Women					
Mean (average) value	2259	2324	2562	2476	2434
Median value	2228	2297	2510	2418	2410
Lower 2.5 percentile	1107	1137	1390	1175	1200
Upper 2.5 percentile	3582	3831	4280	4009	4017
Standard error of the mean	45	43	37	43	21
Base	*189*	*253*	*385*	*283*	*1110*

Table 11.10 Percentage distribution of total urinary potassium by age and sex

Total urinary potassium (mmol/24h)	Age 16–24	25–34	35–49	50–64	All ages 16–64
	cum %	cum %	cum %	cum %	cum %
Men					
Less than 40	12	7	10	11	10
Less than 60	31	21	31	34	30
Less than 80	56	53	58	65	58
All	100	100	100	100	100
Base	*144*	*193*	*280*	*225*	*842*
Mean (average) value	79	79	79	73	77
Median value	75	78	74	71	74
Lower 5.0 percentile	28	36	32	33	32
Upper 5.0 percentile	135	128	143	111	129
Standard error of the mean	3.49	1.95	2.26	2.00	1.19
	cum %	cum %	cum %	cum %	cum %
Women					
Less than 40	15	17	12	16	15
Less than 60	51	52	44	55	50
Less than 80	85	82	76	88	80
All	100	100	100	100	100
Base	*136*	*213*	*293*	*223*	*865*
Mean (average) value	62	62	66	58	62
Median value	58	59	62	56	60
Lower 5.0 percentile	30	27	30	28	28
Upper 5.0 percentile	108	103	102	91	101
Standard error of the mean	2.14	1.77	1.50	1.26	0.82

Table 11.11 Average daily magnesium intake (mg) by age and sex

Intake from all sources (mg)	Age 16–24	25–34	35–49	50–64	All ages 16–64
Men					
Mean (average) value	304	325	336	317	323
Median value	298	317	321	308	312
Lower 2.5 percentile	148	157	165	170	156
Upper 2.5 percentile	516	527	576	540	548
Standard error of the mean	6.8	5.9	5.8	5.8	3.1
Base	*214*	*254*	*346*	*273*	*1087*
Women					
Mean (average) value	215	232	250	238	237
Median value	208	225	233	226	226
Lower 2.5 percentile	104	99	116	117	105
Upper 2.5 percentile	395	413	473	437	441
Standard error of the mean	5.2	5.0	4.5	4.7	2.5
Base	*189*	*253*	*385*	*283*	*1110*

Table 11.12 Average daily phosphorus intake (mg) by age and sex

Intake from all sources (mg)	Age				All ages
	16–24	25–34	35–49	50–64	16–64
Men					
Mean (average) value	1382	1454	1492	1456	1452
Median value	1360	1421	1473	1435	1429
Lower 2.5 percentile	674	795	821	841	782
Upper 2.5 percentile	2312	2239	2334	2250	2310
Standard error of the mean	28.2	24.3	20.8	20.9	11.6
Base	*214*	*254*	*346*	*273*	*1087*
Women					
Mean (average) value	986	1032	1121	1099	1072
Median value	943	1017	1114	1103	1054
Lower 2.5 percentile	431	486	540	511	511
Upper 2.5 percentile	1617	1712	1734	1637	1719
Standard error of the mean	21.5	19.7	15.5	16.7	9.1
Base	*189*	*253*	*385*	*283*	*1110*

Table 11.13 Average daily copper intake (mg) by age and sex

	Sex and age of informant									
	Men				All ages	Women				All ages
	16–24	25–34	35–49	50–64	16–64	16–24	25–34	35–49	50–64	16–64
a) Intake from all sources (mg)										
Mean (average) value	1.41	1.57	1.82	1.63	1.63	1.10	1.16	1.31	1.29	1.23
Median value	1.37	1.45	1.56	1.52	1.49	1.01	1.08	1.18	1.17	1.13
Lower 2.5 percentile	0.68	0.83	0.76	0.81	0.74	0.46	0.55	0.64	0.61	0.56
Upper 2.5 percentile	2.39	3.57	3.44	3.63	3.44	2.12	2.18	3.30	2.81	2.79
Standard error of the mean	0.03	0.05	0.17	0.04	0.06	0.04	0.03	0.03	0.03	0.02
Base	*214*	*254*	*346*	*273*	*1087*	*189*	*253*	*385*	*283*	*1110*
b) Intake from food sources (mg)										
Mean (average) value	1.40	1.56	1.68	1.63	1.59	1.09	1.15	1.31	1.28	1.23
Median value	1.37	1.45	1.55	1.52	1.48	1.01	1.08	1.17	1.17	1.12
Lower 2.5 percentile	0.68	0.83	0.76	0.81	0.74	0.46	0.55	0.58	0.61	0.56
Upper 2.5 percentile	2.28	3.57	3.44	3.63	3.44	2.12	2.09	3.30	2.82	2.79
Standard error of the mean	0.03	0.05	0.05	0.04	0.02	0.04	0.03	0.03	0.03	0.02
Base	*214*	*254*	*346*	*273*	*1087*	*189*	*253*	*385*	*283*	*1110*

Table 11.14 Average daily zinc intake (mg) by age and sex

Intake from all sources (mg)	Age 16–24	25–34	35–49	50–64	All ages 16–64
Men					
Mean (average) value	10.7	11.3	11.7	11.5	11.4
Median value	10.4	11.0	11.1	11.1	10.9
Lower 2.5 percentile	5.2	6.1	5.6	6.0	5.7
Upper 2.5 percentile	18.4	19.0	19.0	20.2	19.0
Standard error of the mean	0.24	0.21	0.24	0.21	0.11
Base	*214*	*254*	*346*	*273*	*1087*
Women					
Mean (average) value	7.6	8.2	8.7	8.6	8.4
Median value	7.5	7.8	8.5	8.3	8.2
Lower 2.5 percentile	3.3	3.4	4.0	4.5	3.6
Upper 2.5 percentile	12.5	14.4	14.0	13.7	13.6
Standard error of the mean	0.16	0.17	0.13	0.14	0.08
Base	*189*	*253*	*385*	*283*	*1110*

Table 11.15 Average daily iodine intake (μg) by age and sex

	Sex and age of informant									
	Men 16–24	25–34	35–49	50–64	All ages 16–64	Women 16–24	25–34	35–49	50–64	All ages 16–64
a) Intake from all sources (μg)										
Mean (average) value	233	240	251	243	243	161	168	184	181	176
Median value	218	235	236	217	226	146	158	172	171	163
Lower 2.5 percentile	95	103	93	102	99	61	53	75	67	63
Upper 2.5 percentile	419	449	453	418	434	330	398	401	356	359
Standard error of the mean	8.8	5.8	6.7	9.8	3.9	4.7	5.0	3.9	5.0	2.3
Base	*214*	*254*	*346*	*273*	*1087*	*189*	*253*	*385*	*283*	*1110*
b) Intake from food sources (μg)										
Mean (average) value	225	238	248	231	237	158	166	180	174	171
Median value	217	235	235	216	225	144	157	168	164	161
Lower 2.5 percentile	93	103	93	102	96	51	53	75	67	63
Upper 2.5 percentile	419	449	440	404	418	314	341	401	325	355
Standard error of the mean	6.6	5.7	6.4	5.2	3.1	4.6	4.8	3.8	4.4	2.2
Base	*214*	*254*	*346*	*273*	*1087*	*189*	*253*	*385*	*283*	*1110*

Table 11.16 Mineral intake (excluding supplements) per 1000kcals total energy by age and sex

Mineral (units per 1000kcals)	Age of informant														
	16–24			25–34			35–49			50–64			All ages 16–64		
	Mean	Median	SE	Mean	Median	SE	Mean	Median	SE	Mean	Median	SE	Mean	Median	SE
Men															
Iron (mg)	5.19	4.97	0.09	5.84	5.31	0.22	5.68	5.43	0.08	5.94	5.62	0.12	5.69	5.35	0.07
Calcium (mg)	364	355	6.8	387	381	10.2	385	378	5.0	402	388	5.7	386	376	3.5
Sodium (mg)	1399	1413	21	1379	1335	21	1394	1374	16	1395	1354	19	1391	1360	9
Chloride (mg)	2139	2148	30	2114	2045	27	2132	2107	23	2140	2107	27	2131	2106	13
Potassium (mg)	1247	1235	17	1357	1304	26	1325	1280	13	1343	1311	15	1322	1283	9
Magnesium (mg)	124	122	1.8	137	128	4.2	135	131	1.7	135	129	2.1	133	128	1.3
Phosphorus (mg)	568	543	7.9	607	582	9.8	600	588	5.4	619	606	6.9	600	581	3.7
Copper (mg)	0.58	0.56	0.01	0.67	0.59	0.03	0.68	0.60	0.02	0.69	0.63	0.02	0.66	0.60	0.01
Zinc (mg)	4.41	4.26	0.08	4.86	4.57	0.18	4.63	4.58	0.06	4.90	4.69	0.08	4.71	4.54	0.05
Iodine (μg)	92	90	1.9	98	94	2.3	99	96	1.9	97	93	1.8	97	94	1.0
Base		*214*			*254*			*346*			*273*			*1087*	
Women															
Iron (mg)	5.84	5.41	0.17	6.23	5.66	0.15	6.54	5.80	0.15	6.73	6.23	0.13	6.40	5.77	0.08
Calcium (mg)	397	380	9.0	417	407	8.2	449	423	8.9	465	452	7.0	437	421	4.4
Sodium (mg)	1387	1380	20	1450	1412	22	1416	1371	18	1445	1396	21	1426	1387	10
Chloride (mg)	2123	2113	29	2203	2144	33	2139	2058	24	2198	2105	31	2166	2104	15
Potassium (mg)	1352	1306	21	1423	1353	22	1534	1440	24	1563	1487	24	1485	1401	12
Magnesium (mg)	127	122	2.1	141	133	2.7	148	136	2.8	149	144	2.5	143	134	1.4
Phosphorus (mg)	586	574	9.0	626	601	8.6	666	635	9.1	692	682	8.5	650	620	4.7
Copper (mg)	0.65	0.59	0.02	0.70	0.64	0.02	0.78	0.67	0.02	0.80	0.73	0.02	0.74	0.67	0.01
Zinc (mg)	4.58	4.33	0.09	4.98	4.69	0.12	5.19	4.78	0.10	5.36	5.14	0.08	5.08	4.79	0.05
Iodine (μg)	93	87	2.2	99	92	2.6	107	98	2.1	108	102	2.2	103	96	1.2
Base		*189*			*253*			*385*			*283*			*1110*	

Table 11.17 Average daily intake of minerals from all sources by sex of informant and whether on a slimming diet

Minerals (units)	Whether on a slimming diet					
	Dieting			Not dieting		
	Mean	Median	SE	Mean	Median	SE
Men						
Iron (mg)	14.9	13.8	0.97	14.0	13.2	0.17
Calcium (mg)	924	906	42.0	941	920	9.6
Sodium (mg)	3167	3000	169	3385	3337	30
Chloride (mg)	4815	4741	253	5195	5116	45
Potassium (mg)	3233	3159	120	3185	3143	25
Magnesium (mg)	328	325	14.2	322	312	3.1
Phosphorus (mg)	1461	1448	55	1452	1427	12
Copper (mg)	1.73	1.54	0.13	1.63	1.48	0.06
Zinc (mg)	12.0	11.4	0.53	11.3	10.9	0.12
Iodine (μg)	268	219	42.5	242	226	3.6
Base		*46*			*1041*	
Women						
Iron (mg)	12.6	10.6	0.83	12.3	10.0	0.40
Calcium (mg)	712	692	22.9	732	718	8.4
Sodium (mg)	2203	2192	60	2372	2341	22
Chloride (mg)	3317	3326	89	3609	3565	33
Potassium (mg)	2479	2370	64	2428	2412	22
Magnesium (mg)	245	226	7.7	236	225	2.6
Phosphorus (mg)	1077	1060	26	1071	1054	10
Copper (mg)	1.21	1.11	0.04	1.24	1.13	0.02
Zinc (mg)	8.7	8.4	0.26	8.3	8.1	0.08
Iodine (μg)	176	159	6.8	176	163	2.5
Base		*138*			*972*	

Table 11.18 Mineral intake (excluding supplements) per 1000kcals total energy by sex of informant and whether on a slimming diet

| Minerals (units) per 1000kcals total energy | Whether on a slimming diet | | | | | |
| | Dieting | | | Not dieting | | |
	Mean	Median	SE	Mean	Median	SE
Men						
Iron (mg)	7.76	6.12	1.09	5.60	5.33	0.05
Calcium (mg)	485	414	47	381	374	3
Sodium (mg)	1619	1538	88	1381	1356	9
Chloride (mg)	2428	2311	107	2118	2095	13
Potassium (mg)	1749	1570	125	1303	1275	7
Magnesium (mg)	184	151	21.6	131	127	0.9
Phosphorus (mg)	773	695	47.3	592	577	3.1
Copper (mg)	0.97	0.71	0.13	0.65	0.60	0.01
Zinc (mg)	6.83	5.61	0.91	4.62	4.52	0.03
Iodine (μg)	119	113	8.4	96	93	1.0
Base		46			1041	
Women						
Iron (mg)	8.34	7.19	0.40	6.12	5.66	0.06
Calcium (mg)	530	467	23	424	413	4
Sodium (mg)	1610	1511	34	1400	1373	10
Chloride (mg)	2422	2289	49	2129	2080	15
Potassium (mg)	1870	1777	54	1431	1377	10
Magnesium (mg)	183	167	6.7	138	131	1.2
Phosphorus (mg)	803	753	21.0	628	610	4.0
Copper (mg)	0.90	0.77	0.04	0.72	0.66	0.01
Zinc (mg)	6.49	5.87	0.28	4.88	4.67	0.04
Iodine (μg)	127	111	5.2	100	94	1.1
Base		138			972	

Table 11.19 Average daily intake of minerals from all sources by sex of informant and whether eating affected by being unwell

| Minerals (units) | Whether eating affected by being unwell | | | | | |
| | Eating affected | | | Not unwell/eating not affected | | |
	Mean	Median	SE	Mean	Median	SE
Men						
Iron (mg)	12.3	11.4	0.70	14.1	13.3	0.18
Calcium (mg)	820	739	57.9	946	925	9.4
Sodium (mg)	2991	3008	153	3395	3338	30
Chloride (mg)	4627	4753	223	5206	5123	45
Potassium (mg)	2882	2806	125	3202	3160	25
Magnesium (mg)	274	270	13.5	325	313	3.1
Phosphorus (mg)	1283	1175	63	1461	1435	12
Copper (mg)	1.32	1.27	0.05	1.65	1.49	0.06
Zinc (mg)	10.2	10.2	0.43	11.4	11.0	0.12
Iodine (μg)	227	197	18.0	244	226	4.0
Base		51			1036	
Women						
Iron (mg)	13.5	8.8	1.92	12.2	10.2	0.35
Calcium (mg)	592	544	26.7	744	726	8.1
Sodium (mg)	2012	1987	66	2387	2341	21
Chloride (mg)	3059	3003	97	3627	3570	32
Potassium (mg)	2062	2027	88	2474	2436	21
Magnesium (mg)	203	185	9.8	240	228	2.5
Phosphorus (mg)	898	871	34	1090	1072	9
Copper (mg)	1.02	0.91	0.05	1.26	1.15	0.02
Zinc (mg)	6.9	6.8	0.26	8.5	8.3	0.08
Iodine (μg)	152	140	7.8	178	165	2.4
Base		106			1004	

Table 11.20 Mineral intake (excluding supplements) per 1000kcals total energy intake by sex of informant and whether eating affected by being unwell

Minerals (units) per 1000kcals total energy	Whether eating affected by being unwell					
	Eating affected			Not unwell/eating not affected		
	Mean	Median	SE	Mean	Median	SE
Men						
Iron (mg)	5.70	5.14	0.26	5.69	5.36	0.07
Calcium (mg)	371	366	15	386	376	4
Sodium (mg)	1411	1419	54	1390	1358	9
Chloride (mg)	2157	2153	78	2130	2102	13
Potassium (mg)	1349	1343	36	1320	1281	9.2
Magnesium (mg)	129	126	3.6	133	128	1.3
Phosphorus (mg)	602	584	14.6	600	580	3.8
Copper (mg)	0.64	0.63	0.03	0.66	0.60	0.01
Zinc (mg)	4.93	4.63	0.18	4.70	4.54	0.05
Iodine (μg)	102	94	5.8	97	94	1.0
Base		51			1036	
Women						
Iron (mg)	6.59	5.47	0.26	6.38	5.78	0.08
Calcium (mg)	416	403	12	439	424	5
Sodium (mg)	1487	1427	38	1420	1382	10
Chloride (mg)	2262	2176	57	2156	2095	15
Potassium (mg)	1478	1401	40	1486	1401	13
Magnesium (mg)	146	133	5.2	143	134	1.4
Phosphorus (mg)	648	627	17.2	650	620	4.9
Copper (mg)	0.75	0.67	0.03	0.74	0.67	0.01
Zinc (mg)	5.10	4.69	0.19	5.08	4.79	0.05
Iodine (μg)	105	102	4.8	103	96	1.2
Base		106			1004	

Table 11.21 Average daily intake of minerals from all sources by sex and region

Mineral (units)	Region											
	Scotland			Northern			Central, South West and Wales			London and South East		
	Mean	Median	SE	Mean	Median	SE	Mean	Median	SE	Mean	Median	SE
Men												
Iron (mg)	12.9	12.3	0.48	14.1	13.1	0.37	14.5	13.4	0.30	13.9	13.3	0.28
Calcium (mg)	881	837	35.7	888	869	17.2	968	969	15.8	967	964	16.8
Sodium (mg)	3292	3331	96	3451	3356	63	3417	3338	50	3298	3280	52
Chloride (mg)	5064	5075	135	5299	5155	95	5254	5136	75	5038	5046	78
Potassium (mg)	2966	3003	84	3167	3113	50	3255	3232	41	3191	3184	44
Magnesium (mg)	295	292	9.7	324	312	6.5	330	318	5.2	322	312	5.2
Phosphorus (mg)	1343	1327	40	1428	1390	24	1479	1463	20	1474	1474	20
Copper (mg)	1.34	1.27	0.05	1.55	1.47	0.04	1.62	1.53	0.03	1.79	1.51	0.17
Zinc (mg)	10.5	10.5	0.31	11.2	10.7	0.20	11.5	11.0	0.19	11.6	11.2	0.23
Iodine (μg)	226	222	8.5	255	235	8.6	238	231	4.7	243	218	8.4
Base		96			274			364			353	
Women												
Iron (mg)	13.0	9.7	1.70	12.2	10.0	0.64	12.5	10.2	0.66	12.0	10.1	0.59
Calcium (mg)	692	696	24.5	705	705	15.0	750	727	13.9	738	720	14.3
Sodium (mg)	2524	2436	73	2395	2376	38	2348	2317	40	2274	2245	32
Chloride (mg)	3832	3723	111	3631	3579	57	3579	3555	60	3449	3433	47
Potassium (mg)	2299	2256	70	2419	2417	42	2453	2402	38	2463	2447	37
Magnesium (mg)	228	213	8.3	233	223	4.7	240	225	4.5	239	230	4.2
Phosphorus (mg)	1021	1036	28	1071	1036	19	1079	1051	16	1080	1078	16
Copper (mg)	1.22	1.04	0.07	1.22	1.12	0.03	1.25	1.15	0.03	1.24	1.15	0.03
Zinc (mg)	8.30	8.12	0.23	8.31	8.04	0.16	8.26	8.07	0.13	8.50	8.28	0.14
Iodine (μg)	168	162	6.3	178	167	4.5	175	164	3.8	176	160	4.6
Base		95			290			368			357	

Table 11.22 Mineral intake (excluding supplements) per 1000kcals total energy by sex and region

Mineral (units) per 1000kcals total energy	Region											
	Scotland			Northern			Central, South West and Wales			London and South East		
	Mean	Median	SE	Mean	Median	SE	Mean	Median	SE	Mean	Median	SE
Men												
Iron (mg)	5.68	5.42	0.15	5.56	5.30	0.10	5.90	5.45	0.17	5.57	5.29	0.09
Calcium (mg)	392	379	11	362	352	6	395	382	7	393	391	5
Sodium (mg)	1494	1452	32	1412	1375	18	1395	1365	18	1344	1322	15
Chloride (mg)	2288	2247	45	2166	2111	26	2140	2120	24	2054	2045	21
Potassium (mg)	1327	1324	24	1308	1272	16	1340	1283	20	1312	1279	13
Magnesium (mg)	133	128	2.8	132	127	1.9	136	128	3.2	131	127	1.5
Phosphorus (mg)	604	606	10.3	587	566	7.5	605	580	7.8	604	591	5.0
Copper (mg)	0.60	0.59	0.02	0.64	0.59	0.01	0.67	0.60	0.02	0.69	0.60	0.02
Zinc (mg)	4.77	4.76	0.11	4.61	4.45	0.07	4.79	4.52	0.13	4.69	4.59	0.06
Iodine (μg)	101	100	2.9	98	97	1.6	96	92	1.8	96	92	1.9
Base		*96*			*274*			*364*			*353*	
Women												
Iron (mg)	6.87	5.95	0.41	6.36	5.74	0.16	6.35	5.74	0.12	6.35	5.81	0.13
Calcium (mg)	433	413	19	423	414	7	449	428	9	438	423	7
Sodium (mg)	1579	1473	44	1458	1415	17	1407	1365	18	1380	1366	16
Chloride (mg)	2388	2245	63	2211	2145	25	2147	2073	28	2090	2051	22
Potassium (mg)	1455	1331	53	1473	1404	21	1485	1385	22	1503	1440	20
Magnesium (mg)	145	124	8.1	141	132	2.3	144	133	2.3	145	137	2.2
Phosphorus (mg)	643	600	21.5	649	622	8.6	651	618	8.6	652	631	7.2
Copper (mg)	0.78	0.64	0.06	0.73	0.67	0.02	0.74	0.66	0.02	0.75	0.68	0.02
Zinc (mg)	5.36	4.78	0.32	5.01	4.78	0.08	5.00	4.72	0.09	5.15	4.89	0.08
Iodine (μg)	102	98	4.2	105	100	2.2	103	95	2.2	101	94	2.0
Base		*95*			*290*			*368*			*357*	

Table 11.23 Average daily intake of minerals from all sources by sex and employment status of informant

Mineral (units)	Employment status of informant								
	Working			Unemployed			Economically inactive		
	Mean	Median	SE	Mean	Median	SE	Mean	Median	SE
Men									
Iron (mg)	14.5	13.5	0.19	11.6	10.2	0.44	12.5	12.4	0.41
Calcium (mg)	971	964	10.2	738	711	28.2	881	861	30.4
Sodium (mg)	3471	3408	32	2965	2907	107	3020	3083	89
Chloride (mg)	5319	5227	49	4599	4484	152	4631	4711	132
Potassium (mg)	3275	3224	27	2727	2651	73	2926	2894	76
Magnesium (mg)	333	322	3.4	267	252	8.7	293	281	8.8
Phosphorus (mg)	1496	1474	13	1197	1104	37	1350	1328	36
Copper (mg)	1.69	1.52	0.07	1.33	1.18	0.06	1.47	1.34	0.06
Zinc (mg)	11.7	11.2	0.13	9.6	8.8	0.38	10.6	10.3	0.35
Iodine (μg)	250	236	4.1	196	190	7.4	229	199	19.4
Base		*875*			*99*			*111*	
Women									
Iron (mg)	12.2	10.2	0.45	10.4	8.7	0.77	12.7	9.9	0.70
Calcium (mg)	738	728	9.7	642	612	32.5	727	716	14.6
Sodium (mg)	2371	2354	24	2311	2195	104	2321	2287	39
Chloride (mg)	3597	3572	36	3523	3470	154	3533	3487	59
Potassium (mg)	2483	2437	26	2240	2188	86	2377	2369	38
Magnesium (mg)	243	229	3.0	218	209	9.7	229	217	4.5
Phosphorus (mg)	1089	1076	11	972	926	41	1058	1041	17
Copper (mg)	1.26	1.16	0.02	1.08	1.05	0.05	1.22	1.11	0.03
Zinc (mg)	8.5	8.3	0.10	7.5	7.1	0.34	8.2	8.1	0.13
Iodine (μg)	180	165	3.0	153	143	8.8	172	162	4.2
Base		*670*			*57*			*373*	

Table 11.24 Mineral intake (excluding supplements) per 1000kcals total energy by sex and employment status of informant

Mineral (units) per 1000kcals total energy	Employment status of informant								
	Working			Unemployed			Economically inactive		
	Mean	Median	SE	Mean	Median	SE	Mean	Median	SE
Men									
Iron (mg)	5.72	5.35	0.08	5.56	5.18	0.17	5.59	5.45	0.15
Calcium (mg)	389	380	4	354	343	9	392	373	10
Sodium (mg)	1391	1362	10	1438	1380	37	1359	1349	31
Chloride (mg)	2128	2104	14	2220	2152	52	2081	2081	44
Potassium (mg)	1323	1279	10	1320	1296	22	1319	1295	24
Magnesium (mg)	134	128	1.5	130	126	2.8	131	128	2.6
Phosphorus (mg)	602	580	4.3	580	571	9.6	606	606	10.8
Copper (mg)	0.66	0.60	0.01	0.64	0.61	0.02	0.66	0.61	0.03
Zinc (mg)	4.70	4.55	0.06	4.68	4.46	0.15	4.78	4.57	0.13
Iodine (μg)	97	94	1.1	95	92	2.8	95	90	3.0
Base		*875*			*99*			*111*	
Women									
Iron (mg)	6.39	5.79	0.10	6.27	5.49	0.48	6.44	5.85	0.12
Calcium (mg)	439	423	6	397	376	18	440	425	7
Sodium (mg)	1420	1386	12	1421	1399	43	1437	1381	19
Chloride (mg)	2153	2094	18	2166	2139	64	2187	2112	28
Potassium (mg)	1505	1412	17	1395	1353	44	1465	1401	18
Magnesium (mg)	146	136	2.0	135	124	4.9	139	132	2.0
Phosphorus (mg)	655	620	6.5	601	572	19.7	650	625	7.0
Copper (mg)	0.75	0.67	0.01	0.66	0.64	0.02	0.74	0.67	0.02
Zinc (mg)	5.12	4.77	0.07	4.62	4.46	0.16	5.10	4.86	0.08
Iodine (μg)	104	97	1.5	92	85	4.1	103	96	2.1
Base		*670*			*57*			*373*	

Table 11.25 Average daily intake of minerals from all sources by sex of informant and whether benefits received

Minerals (units)	Whether benefits received					
	Received			Not received		
	Mean	Median	SE	Mean	Median	SE
Men						
Iron (mg)	12.1	11.5	0.45	14.3	13.3	0.18
Calcium (mg)	798	775	25.3	958	945	9.9
Sodium (mg)	3083	3118	100	3415	3362	31
Chloride (mg)	4786	4771	147	5231	5159	47
Potassium (mg)	2804	2716	63	3237	3195	26
Magnesium (mg)	282	280	8.2	328	317	3.3
Phosphorus (mg)	1271	1228	34	1476	1456	12
Copper (mg)	1.38	1.28	0.06	1.66	1.50	0.06
Zinc (mg)	10.2	9.6	0.35	11.5	11.1	0.12
Iodine (μg)	208	196	6.7	245	230	3.8
Base		*119*			*963*	
Women						
Iron (mg)	11.8	9.0	1.15	12.4	10.2	0.38
Calcium (mg)	636	581	24.3	745	730	8.2
Sodium (mg)	2213	2177	57	2374	2340	22
Chloride (mg)	3381	3309	86	3604	3564	33
Potassium (mg)	2094	2043	57	2488	2442	22
Magnesium (mg)	202	193	6.7	242	229	2.6
Phosphorus (mg)	939	885	28	1094	1081	9
Copper (mg)	1.16	0.99	0.06	1.25	1.15	0.02
Zinc (mg)	7.4	7.1	0.22	8.5	8.3	0.08
Iodine (μg)	156	138	7.2	179	166	2.5
Base		*153*			*955*	

Table 11.26 Mineral intake (excluding supplements) per 1000kcal total energy by sex of informant and whether benefits received

Minerals (units) per 1000kcals total energy	Whether benefits received					
	Received			Not received		
	Mean	Median	SE	Mean	Median	SE
Men						
Iron (mg)	5.44	4.97	0.16	5.72	5.37	0.08
Calcium (mg)	361	348	8	389	380	4
Sodium (mg)	1392	1377	31	1392	1359	10
Chloride (mg)	2161	2143	44	2128	2098	14
Potassium (mg)	1287	1284	20	1327	1283	10
Magnesium (mg)	128	123	2.6	134	128	1.4
Phosphorus (mg)	579	563	9.5	603	584	4.0
Copper (mg)	0.63	0.58	0.02	0.66	0.60	0.01
Zinc (mg)	4.67	4.46	0.13	4.72	4.55	0.06
Iodine (μg)	95	90	2.5	97	94	1.1
Base		*119*			*963*	
Women						
Iron (mg)	6.13	5.54	0.23	6.43	5.79	0.08
Calcium (mg)	404	378	11	443	429	5
Sodium (mg)	1469	1397	33	1420	1386	10
Chloride (mg)	2241	2135	46	2154	2093	15
Potassium (mg)	1360	1294	25	1505	1422	13
Magnesium (mg)	130	121	2.7	146	136	1.5
Phosphorus (mg)	607	581	11.5	657	628	5.1
Copper (mg)	0.74	0.65	0.03	0.74	0.67	0.01
Zinc (mg)	4.83	4.60	0.12	5.12	4.81	0.06
Iodine (μg)	96	92	2.7	104	97	1.3
Base		*153*			*955*	

Table 11.27 Average daily intake of minerals from all sources by sex of informant and social class of head of household

Mineral (units)	Social class of head of household											
	I and II			III non-manual			III manual			IV and V		
	Mean	Median	SE	Mean	Median	SE	Mean	Median	SE	Mean	Median	SE
Men												
Iron (mg)	15.0	14.1	0.30	13.7	12.7	0.52	13.8	13.1	0.27	12.8	12.4	0.38
Calcium (mg)	1006	979	15.6	912	900	24.9	917	904	15.5	868	837	24.3
Sodium (mg)	3364	3277	45	3147	3197	76	3462	3441	53	3368	3388	85
Chloride (mg)	5143	5006	67	4828	4943	116	5326	5273	79	5166	5269	124
Potassium (mg)	3363	3313	40	3070	3054	67	3153	3111	41	2987	2850	64
Magnesium (mg)	342	329	5.0	315	303	9.4	316	309	5.1	299	290	7.6
Phosphorus (mg)	1529	1499	19	1413	1400	32	1431	1423	20	1364	1338	31
Copper (mg)	1.67	1.55	0.04	1.95	1.42	0.42	1.53	1.47	0.03	1.51	1.41	0.05
Zinc (mg)	11.8	11.3	0.17	11.5	10.9	0.47	11.2	10.8	0.17	10.8	10.7	0.28
Iodine (μg)	244	227	5.6	237	217	10.9	252	233	8.2	224	209	6.9
Base		*377*			*138*			*378*			*177*	
Women												
Iron (mg)	12.9	11.0	0.49	13.4	10.6	1.30	11.8	9.2	0.71	11.6	9.2	0.81
Calcium (mg)	790	773	13.3	747	764	21.4	702	684	13.5	660	650	17.2
Sodium (mg)	2385	2364	33	2378	2343	51	2377	2310	40	2253	2248	47
Chloride (mg)	3618	3561	49	3607	3547	76	3601	3527	60	3451	3476	69
Potassium (mg)	2633	2546	38	2542	2520	60	2313	2279	33	2219	2226	45
Magnesium (mg)	261	248	4.5	254	239	7.0	222	212	3.8	207	199	4.8
Phosphorus (mg)	1157	1132	15	1110	1124	23	1030	1020	15	968	941	20
Copper (mg)	1.35	1.22	0.03	1.28	1.18	0.04	1.16	1.06	0.03	1.12	1.04	0.04
Zinc (mg)	8.96	8.81	0.13	8.57	8.26	0.21	8.04	7.84	0.13	7.65	7.55	0.17
Iodine (μg)	190	178	4.2	174	163	5.1	172	157	4.4	159	148	4.7
Base		*386*			*141*			*347*			*222*	

Table 11.28 Mineral intake (excluding supplements) per 1000kcals total energy by sex of informant and social class of head of household

Mineral (units) per 1000kcals total energy	Social class of head of household											
	I and II			III non-manual			III manual			IV and V		
	Mean	Median	SE	Mean	Median	SE	Mean	Median	SE	Mean	Median	SE
Men												
Iron (mg)	5.98	5.67	0.09	5.69	5.36	0.13	5.60	5.20	0.16	5.31	5.06	0.12
Calcium (mg)	410	404	5	391	397	7	373	360	7	361	348	7
Sodium (mg)	1380	1353	14	1360	1357	24	1407	1385	17	1406	1363	25
Chloride (mg)	2109	2083	20	2083	2083	36	2158	2120	24	2158	2127	35
Potassium (mg)	1382	1350	13	1335	1279	21	1295	1252	19	1255	1239	15
Magnesium (mg)	140	136	1.7	136	129	2.7	130	123	3.0	124	120	1.9
Phosphorus (mg)	629	610	5.8	611	593	8.1	585	563	7.5	571	553	7.0
Copper (mg)	0.69	0.62	0.02	0.69	0.60	0.04	0.64	0.58	0.02	0.63	0.60	0.02
Zinc (mg)	4.81	4.68	0.06	4.85	4.64	0.09	4.66	4.43	0.13	4.52	4.34	0.09
Iodine (μg)	97	95	1.3	98	96	2.3	99	93	2.2	93	90	5.8
Base		*377*			*138*			*378*			*177*	
Women												
Iron (mg)	6.72	6.09	0.13	6.69	5.98	0.32	6.12	5.55	0.12	6.05	5.51	0.15
Calcium (mg)	455	445	6	447	429	15	422	409	6	426	394	12
Sodium (mg)	1388	1369	14	1428	1380	29	1453	1414	20	1457	1392	23
Chloride (mg)	2104	2062	20	2156	2084	39	2200	2139	30	2235	2135	34
Potassium (mg)	1546	1461	20	1545	1465	43	1421	1345	18	1444	1375	28
Magnesium (mg)	152	143	2.2	155	141	5.9	135	127	2.0	134	124	2.6
Phosphorus (mg)	675	656	7.1	672	634	17.1	627	602	7.1	629	593	11.6
Copper (mg)	0.78	0.69	0.02	0.78	0.70	0.04	0.71	0.63	0.02	0.71	0.65	0.02
Zinc (mg)	5.22	4.98	0.07	5.22	4.85	0.23	4.92	4.67	0.09	4.97	4.62	0.11
Iodine (μg)	107	98	2.1	103	96	3.3	101	96	2.0	99	92	2.6
Base		*386*			*141*			*347*			*222*	

Table 11.29   **Average daily intake of minerals from all sources by sex of informant and household composition**

Minerals (units)	Household composition											
	Informant alone			With others, no dependent children						With dependent child		
				With spouse			No spouse					
	Mean	Median	SE	Mean	Median	SE	Mean	Median	SE	Mean	Median	SE
Men												
Iron (mg)	13.2	12.7	0.54	14.4	13.7	0.28	13.3	12.5	0.34	14.4	13.5	0.31
Calcium (mg)	857	808	35.6	973	955	15.6	897	867	20.0	955	937	15.5
Sodium (mg)	3308	3230	120	3318	3254	47	3385	3417	68	3436	3388	48
Chloride (mg)	5078	5036	180	5093	4998	71	5201	5267	100	5262	5199	73
Potassium (mg)	3065	2943	106	3246	3206	41	3054	3023	52	3247	3223	39
Magnesium (mg)	318	310	12.9	326	313	5.3	310	305	6.0	329	317	5.2
Phosphorus (mg)	1409	1349	46	1486	1466	19	1396	1371	25	1469	1433	20
Copper (mg)	1.49	1.36	0.09	1.67	1.52	0.04	1.44	1.38	0.03	1.75	1.53	0.15
Zinc (mg)	10.9	10.5	0.46	11.7	11.1	0.18	10.7	10.4	0.22	11.6	11.2	0.21
Iodine (µg)	255	237	16.1	241	224	5.4	245	226	10.2	241	226	6.0
Base		*71*			*360*			*271*			*385*	

	Informant alone			With others, no dependent children						With dependent child					
				With spouse			No spouse			With spouse			Lone mother		
	Mean	Median	SE	Mean	Median	SE	Mean	Median	SE	Mean	Median	SE	Mean	Median	SE
Women															
Iron (mg)	12.0	10.2	0.94	12.3	10.3	0.57	11.6	9.9	0.64	12.8	10.0	0.74	11.5	9.1	1.61
Calcium (mg)	731	728	30.1	744	729	12.3	700	677	19.5	754	736	13.9	605	579	31.9
Sodium (mg)	2334	2245	78	2343	2296	36	2391	2379	47	2376	2352	34	2195	2243	85
Chloride (mg)	3538	3491	116	3552	3491	53	3651	3607	71	3604	3572	51	3370	3368	127
Potassium (mg)	2349	2378	78	2508	2459	36	2357	2332	46	2460	2417	37	2214	2149	92
Magnesium (mg)	235	228	9.6	242	229	4.0	229	219	5.2	241	228	4.3	211	202	11.1
Phosphorus (mg)	1074	1095	36	1104	1095	15	1029	1006	21	1086	1052	16	941	911	39
Copper (mg)	1.27	1.15	0.07	1.31	1.18	0.03	1.16	1.07	0.03	1.22	1.11	0.03	1.06	1.00	0.06
Zinc (mg)	8.4	8.2	0.30	8.6	8.5	0.12	8.0	7.9	0.17	8.4	8.1	0.13	7.5	7.5	0.31
Iodine (µg)	180	167	8.4	178	167	4.0	167	149	5.0	180	165	4.2	157	161	8.6
Base		*84*			*382*			*182*			*386*			*76*	

Table 11.30 Mineral intake (excluding supplements) per 1000kcal total energy by sex of informant and household composition

Minerals (units)	Household composition											
	Informant alone			With others, no dependent children						With dependent child		
				With spouse			No spouse					
	Mean	Median	SE	Mean	Median	SE	Mean	Median	SE	Mean	Median	SE
Men												
Iron (mg)	5.58	5.35	0.20	5.89	5.59	0.10	5.29	5.03	0.10	5.79	5.38	0.15
Calcium (mg)	362	364	10.1	404	393	5.13	364	356	5.96	388	378	7.10
Sodium (mg)	1427	1400	41	1387	1342	15	1378	1360	19	1398	1383	16
Chloride (mg)	2181	2115	57	2127	2077	22	2116	2130	28	2137	2120	22
Potassium (mg)	1310	1275	31	1368	1339	14	1248	1240	13	1333	1282	18
Magnesium (mg)	135	130	3.6	137	132	1.8	126	125	1.5	135	127	3.0
Phosphorus (mg)	603	600	12.0	624	606	6.4	570	548	6.1	598	575	7.0
Copper (mg)	0.67	0.57	0.06	0.70	0.63	0.02	0.59	0.56	0.01	0.67	0.60	0.02
Zinc (mg)	4.78	4.39	0.19	4.90	4.75	0.06	4.39	4.23	0.07	4.74	4.55	0.12
Iodine (μg)	103.7	95.2	4.7	98.0	95.3	1.4	94.2	92.4	1.8	96.5	93.0	2.0
Base		*71*			*360*			*271*			*385*	

	Informant alone			With others, no dependent children						With dependent child					
				With spouse			No spouse			With spouse			Lone mother		
	Mean	Median	SE	Mean	Median	SE	Mean	Median	SE	Mean	Median	SE	Mean	Median	SE
Women															
Iron (mg)	6.57	6.02	0.27	6.68	6.18	0.12	6.11	5.75	0.18	6.36	5.55	0.15	5.67	5.35	0.18
Calcium (mg)	447	442	14.2	450	435	6.0	411	389	9.9	446	431	9.0	380	372	13.7
Sodium (mg)	1456	1412	32	1432	1379	18	1417	1409	20	1417	1376	18	1432	1398	43
Chloride (mg)	2203	2144	44	2170	2090	26	2164	2139	30	2148	2078	26	2197	2120	64
Potassium (mg)	1480	1367	46	1539	1483	19	1411	1351	26	1483	1373	24	1404	1317	35
Magnesium (mg)	148	139	5.6	148	141	2.1	136	130	2.5	144	133	2.8	133	120	4.3
Phosphorus (mg)	670	661	18.1	675	659	7.1	612	593	10.6	649	618	8.9	600	571	14.3
Copper (mg)	0.80	0.68	0.04	0.80	0.72	0.02	0.68	0.63	0.02	0.73	0.65	0.02	0.66	0.63	0.02
Zinc (mg)	5.32	4.85	0.19	5.27	5.09	0.07	4.79	4.58	0.10	5.03	4.67	0.11	4.85	4.42	0.18
Iodine (μg)	106.7	105.9	4.1	105.0	98.8	1.8	94.5	87.4	2.2	105.6	96.0	2.4	96.1	93.0	3.8
Base		*84*			*382*			*182*			*386*			*76*	

Table 11.31 Urinary sodium and potassium by sex and age

Urine analytes (units)	Age											
	16–24			25–34			35–49			50–64		
	Mean	Median	SE	Mean	Median	SE	Mean	Median	SE	Mean	Median	SE
Men												
Urine volume (ml/24h)	1373	1275	47.1	1609	1500	50.0	1729	1625	46.0	1693	1600	48.0
Total urinary sodium (mmol/24h)	179	171	7.30	175	167	5.48	175	166	4.47	173	166	2.58
Total urinary potassium (mmol/24h)	79	75	3.49	79	78	1.95	78	74	2.26	73	71	2.00
Base		*144*			*193*			*280*			*225*	
Women												
Urine volume (ml/24h)	1119	1038	40.6	1345	1250	39.3	1552	1500	36.6	1537	1500	37.2
Total urinary sodium (mmol/24h)	136	126	5.05	131	129	3.51	135	131	3.23	124	126	1.78
Total urinary potassium (mmol/24h)	62	58	2.14	62	59	1.77	66	62	1.50	58	56	1.26
Base		*136*			*213*			*293*			*223*	

Table 11.32 Urinary sodium and potassium by sex of informant and whether on a slimming diet

Urine analytes (units)	Whether on a slimming diet							
	Dieting				Not dieting			
	Mean	Median	SE	*Base*	Mean	Median	SE	*Base*
Men								
Urine volume (ml/24h)	1650	1525	133.8	*36*	1630	1512	25.2	*806*
Total urinary sodium (mmol/24h)	173.7	164.6	12.06	*36*	173.0	166.5	2.64	*806*
Total urinary potassium (mmol/24h)	73.1	78.2	5.13	*36*	73.1	74.0	1.22	*806*
Women								
Urine volume (ml/24h)	1525	1500	60.3	*106*	1416	1350	21.4	*759*
Urinary sodium (mmol/24h)	141.0	135.7	5.69	*106*	130.4	125.0	1.86	*759*
Urinary potassium (mmol/24h)	66.5	64.5	2.68	*106*	61.6	59.0	0.86	*759*

Table 11.33 Urinary sodium and potassium by sex of informant and whether unwell during seven-day dietary recording period

Urine analytes (units)	Whether unwell during seven-day dietary recording period											
	Completed food diary									No food diary		
	Not unwell			Unwell								
				Eating affected			Eating not affected					
	Mean	Median	SE	Mean	Median	SE	Mean	Median	SE	Mean	Median	SE
Men												
Urine volume (ml/24h)	1650	1525	27.6	1388	1267	107.0	1622	1500	88.6	1535	1425	89.6
Total urinary sodium (mmol/24h)	174.9	168.0	2.85	145.0	125.0	11.48	168.6	155.0	9.65	171.5	170.0	10.28
Total urinary potassium (mmol/24h)	78.4	75.3	1.33	64.7	61.8	4.46	74.2	70.0	2.96	71.9	61.9	5.91
Base		695			32			67			48	
Women												
Urine volume (ml/24h)	1425	1350	23.2	1390	1260	65.3	1564	1463	60.7	1218	950	95.6
Total urinary sodium (mmol/24h)	132.1	126.0	2.06	128.7	121.0	5.75	133.7	133.5	4.79	125.6	108.0	10.73
Total urinary potassium (mmol/24h)	63.0	60.0	0.97	59.2	58.0	2.52	61.2	59.8	2.10	56.9	52.4	4.05
Base		657			81			96			31	

Table 11.34 Urinary sodium and potassium by sex of informant and region

Urine analytes (units)	Region											
	Scotland			Northern			Central, South West and Wales			London and South East		
	Mean	Median	SE	Mean	Median	SE	Mean	Median	SE	Mean	Median	SE
Men												
Urine volume (ml/24h)	1480	1400	68.4	1604	1550	44.5	1651	1525	44.4	1674	1525	46.5
Total urinary sodium (mmol/24h)	191.1	173.7	8.48	175.6	169.5	5.55	168.2	164.0	4.33	170.9	161.0	4.37
Total urinary potassium (mmol/24h)	66.0	66.0	2.89	76.9	72.0	2.67	78.3	76.0	2.19	79.2	75.3	1.83
Base		77			212			276			277	
Women												
Urine volume (ml/24h)	1351	1225	74.4	1388	1313	40.8	1507	1400	34.5	1398	1375	34.4
Total urinary sodium (mmol/24h)	134.4	130.0	6.17	133.9	126.0	3.75	133.6	126.4	2.95	127.3	121.2	3.10
Total urinary potassium (mmol/24h)	56.4	54.0	2.63	61.6	60.5	1.61	64.4	60.0	1.54	61.9	60.5	1.32
Base		71			210			302			282	

Table 11.35 Urinary sodium and potassium by sex and employment status of informant

Urine analytes (units)	Employment status of informant								
	Working			Unemployed			Economically inactive		
	Mean	Median	SE	Mean	Median	SE	Mean	Median	SE
Men									
Urine volume (ml/24h)	1643	1525	27.1	1638	1500	100.3	1539	1400	73.4
Total urinary sodium (mmol/24h)	174.1	167.0	2.73	162.3	161.0	10.64	173.7	164.2	9.70
Total urinary potassium (mmol/24h)	78.8	75.4	1.34	66.9	61.0	3.42	72.1	70.0	3.34
Base		*688*			*68*			*85*	
Women									
Urine volume (ml/24h)	1427	1375	24.8	1242	1152	86.6	1461	1350	37.9
Total urinary sodium (mmol/24h)	133.4	131.0	2.29	133.1	129.5	7.77	127.9	117.9	3.03
Total urinary potassium (mmol/24h)	62.9	60.5	1.02	57.5	56.0	2.78	61.2	58.4	1.50
Base		*527*			*40*			*289*	

Table 11.36 Urinary sodium and potassium by sex of informant and whether benefits received

Urine analytes (units)	Whether benefits received							
	Received				Not received			
	Mean	Median	SE	*Base*	Mean	Median	SE	*Base*
Men								
Urine volume (ml/24h)	1632	1500	89.5	*85*	1626	1513	25.5	*754*
Total urinary sodium (mmol/24h)	166.3	179.0	9.48	*85*	173.7	165.8	2.68	*754*
Total urinary potassium (mmol/24h)	66.9	62.0	2.78	*85*	78.3	75.1	1.28	*754*
Women								
Urine volume (ml/24h)	1335	1250	53.7	*121*	1445	1375	21.8	*743*
Total urinary sodium (mmol/24h)	128.8	125.0	5.58	*121*	132.1	126.0	1.86	*743*
Total urinary potassium (mmol/24h)	58.5	55.1	2.63	*121*	62.8	60.5	0.85	*743*

Table 11.37 Urinary sodium and potassium by sex of informant and social class of head of household

Urine analytes (units)	Social class of head of household											
	I and II			III non-manual			III manual			IV and V		
	Mean	Median	SE	Mean	Median	SE	Mean	Median	SE	Mean	Median	SE
Men												
Urine volume (ml/24h)	1709	1580	42.1	1632	1463	73.9	1606	1475	42.6	1487	1500	48.7
Total urinary sodium (mmol/24h)	170.2	167.0	3.58	173.1	160.5	7.56	177.1	170.0	4.86	174.0	158.6	7.43
Total urinary potassium (mmol/24h)	82.7	79.0	1.90	74.4	72.0	2.89	72.7	70.0	1.92	76.2	69.0	3.86
Base		*314*			*114*			*273*			*128*	
Women												
Urine volume (ml/24h)	1520	1450	33.7	1365	1275	56.6	1356	1300	35.2	1419	1325	45.7
Total urinary sodium (mmol/24h)	131.7	122.0	2.98	125.0	120.0	4.15	133.2	129.0	3.17	134.1	129.7	4.32
Total urinary potassium (mmol/24h)	66.2	63.3	1.49	59.0	58.4	1.68	58.7	57.0	1.23	62.6	59.5	2.11
Base		*311*			*101*			*271*			*174*	

Table 11.38 Urinary sodium and potassium by sex of informant and household composition

Urine analytes (units)	Household composition										
	Informant alone			With others, no dependent children						With dependent child		
				With spouse			No spouse					
	Mean	Median	SE	Mean	Median	SE	Mean	Median	SE	Mean	Median	SE
Men												
Urine volume (ml/24h)	1562	1525	86.5	1731	1625	42.8	1462	1375	46.6	1654	1500	42.5
Total urinary sodium (mmol/24h)	168.5	166.0	9.36	172.8	164.5	4.20	170.4	156.3	6.35	175.6	173.0	4.01
Total urinary potassium (mmol/24h)	70.7	63.7	4.51	76.4	74.0	1.87	76.6	71.5	3.05	79.3	76.4	1.81
Base	*51*			*290*			*192*			*309*		

Urine analytes (units)	Informant alone			With others, no dependent children						With dependent child					
				With spouse			No spouse			With spouse			Lone mother		
	Mean	Median	SE	Mean	Median	SE	Mean	Median	SE	Mean	Median	SE	Mean	Median	SE
Women															
Urine volume (ml/24h)	1504	1500	75.0	1561	1500	35.1	1158	1050	44.6	1414	1350	31.7	1347	1175	88.9
Total urinary sodium (mmol/24h)	130.7	112.6	7.72	130.3	124.0	2.71	130.6	127.0	4.65	134.0	130.9	2.95	129.7	125.2	8.97
Total urinary potassium (mmol/24h)	57.0	59.2	2.47	61.9	60.0	1.19	62.4	62.0	2.40	63.1	59.0	1.42	64.0	57.6	4.20
Base	*62*			*298*			*126*			*326*			*53*		

Table 11.39 Urinary sodium and potassium by sex of informant and smoking behaviour

Urine analytes (units)	Smoking behaviour											
	None				Fewer than 20 cigarettes a day				20 or more cigarettes a day			
	Mean	Median	SE	*Base*	Mean	Median	SE	*Base*	Mean	Median	SE	*Base*
Men												
Urine volume (ml/24h)	1618	1500	29.0	*579*	1553	1462	56.9	*137*	1771	1563	75.1	*126*
Total urinary sodium (mmol/24h)	176.5	173.0	2.93	*579*	167.3	153.0	7.10	*137*	163.5	149.6	7.51	*126*
Total urinary potassium (mmol/24h)	80.3	77.0	1.47	*579*	69.7	65.7	2.62	*137*	70.6	65.7	2.88	*126*
Women												
Urine volume (ml/24h)	1410	1350	24.6	*562*	1435	1350	45.5	*194*	1527	1500	54.8	*109*
Total urinary sodium (mmol/24h)	131.3	126.0	2.05	*562*	131.9	124.1	4.24	*194*	133.4	130.0	5.57	*109*
Total urinary potassium (mmol/24h)	63.3	60.0	1.02	*562*	60.6	59.0	1.76	*194*	59.4	58.0	2.22	*109*

175

Urine analytes (units)	Alcohol consumption during seven-day dietary recording period (g/week)											
	Nil			Less than 168g			168g—less than 400g			400g or more		
	Mean	Median	SE	Mean	Median	SE	Mean	Median	SE	Mean	Median	SE
Men												
Urine volume (ml/24h)	1455	1338	46.6	1564	1500	34.3	1705	1588	51.8	2114	1875	106.3
Total urinary sodium (mmol/24h)	167.6	133.8	6.08	173.2	168.0	3.69	171.6	166.0	5.23	187.0	179.4	10.3
Total urinary potassium (mmol/24h)	70.6	63.8	2.91	79.9	76.8	1.85	77.8	76.0	2.14	79.8	79.0	3.68
Base		*162*			*344*			*202*			*86*	
	Nil			Less than 112g			112g—less than 280g			280g or more		
	Mean	Median	SE	Mean	Median	SE	Mean	Median	SE	Mean	Median	SE
Women												
Urine volume (ml/24h)	1328	1250	35.0	1470	1390	28.4	1559	1500	58.1	1700	1600	146.1
Total urinary sodium (mmol/24h)	128.9	121.6	3.13	133.4	129.1	2.45	133.4	132.3	5.28	134.7	122.2	15.87
Total urinary potassium (mmol/24h)	57.5	54.4	1.28	64.5	62.6	1.17	67.0	62.1	2.76	61.9	57.2	5.86
Base		*280*			*432*			*108*			*14*	

Table 11.41 Correlation coefficients between urine analytes and dietary intakes—total urinary potassium and sodium

Dietary intake	Urine analyte	
	Total potassium	Total sodium
Men		
Total dietary potassium (inc. supplements)	0.26 (*p < 0.01*)	–
Total dietary sodium (inc. supplements)	–	0.25 (*p < 0.01*)
Base	*794*	*794*
Women		
Total dietary potassium (inc. supplements)	0.36 (*p < 0.01*)	–
Total dietary sodium (inc. supplements)	–	0.26 (*p < 0.01*)
Base	*834*	*834*

12 Variations in nutrient intake

12.1 Introduction

The previous chapters describe in detail the nutrient intakes of the sample, considering men and women separately and looking in turn at a number of important characteristics of informants. This chapter develops the analysis by considering the combined effects on nutrient intakes of a number of characteristics of the sample, allowing the identification of those characteristics of most importance in explaining variation in nutrient intake.

Social and demographic characteristics, for example age, region, social class, and measures of income can be considered as 'background' factors which may in some way influence dietary behaviour but are not likely to be influenced by it.

A range of 'behavioural' variables, which are measures of various health-related habits and attitudes, for example smoking and drinking behaviour, slimming, taking food supplements, and the type of diet which is eaten, can be considered as an intermediate stage in the explanatory model, since they may be influenced by the background variables as well as themselves influencing nutrient intakes. The background variables may, however, continue to exert an influence on nutrient intake in their own right as well as through their effects on behavioural variables.

A two-stage approach was taken to the explanation of variation in nutrient intake, looking first at the effects of background factors and then of behavioural factors. The approach may also indicate the relationship between background and behavioural variables and the relative importance of these two types of factors in explaining variation in nutrient intake. The approach can be summarised as follows:

from: background factors (for example, region, social class),

via: behavioural variables (for example, smoking, dieting),

to: outcome variables (nutrient intake).

The model can be developed further to consider measurements related to health status, such as blood pressure and blood analytes, as outcome variables; nutrient intakes then serve as intermediate variables which may directly affect measures of health status. At this stage the model becomes increasingly complex since background and behavioural variables may directly affect the measures of health status as well as influencing and acting through nutrient intake.

12.2 Characteristics used in the analyses

Background factors

The tabulations in Chapters 7 to 11 make it possible to identify those of the characteristics described in Chapter 5 which were associated with differences in nutrient intake. In order to allow a standardised and relatively simple approach to the analysis of variance in nutrient intakes, a subset of the possible background variables for inclusion in the models was selected; these were age group, region, social class of head of household, a composite variable for economic status, and whether the informant's eating was affected by their having been unwell. The analysis was always undertaken separately for men and women.

The economic status variable was derived by combining the variables on receipt of benefits and informant's employment status; there was a high degree of overlap, particularly for men, between the unemployed and those receiving benefits. Both receipt of benefits and employment status are related to income level, but the more consistent indicator of relative deprivation is given by whether anyone in the household is receiving benefits; the definition of benefit households is given in Chapter 5. Informants who were living in households receiving benefits were identified as the first category. Others were classified on the basis of their own employment status as either working or not working, which included both economically inactive and unemployed informants.

A number of possible characteristics were not explicitly introduced as background variables. Household type was not included both because there was little consistent variation in nutrient intakes according to household type and because of its overlap with other characteristics, particularly age group. The season in which the informant kept the dietary record could also have been included in the analysis as a proxy for seasonal variation in the supply of certain foods. In practice, however, there was little variation in intake according to season for those nutrients included in these analyses except in the specific case of vitamin C (Section 12.8).

Behavioural variables

A number of behavioural variables, either based on dietary practices or reflecting health-related habits and attitudes were included at the second stage of analysis. The main characteristics relating to dietary practices were whether the informant was on a slimming diet or had taken any food supplements during the recording week. Broader health-related habits were indicated by smoking behaviour and a variable based on alcohol consumption during the recording week which classified informants as non-drinkers, lighter drinkers (alcohol intake of less than 168g for men or 112g for women), or heavier drinkers (see Chapter 5).

Although the behavioural variables listed covered a range of topics related to attitudes to health, a variable which indicated health-related dietary behaviour might also be important in explaining variation in nutrient intake. The variable created was based on recorded intakes of specific foods which had a 'healthy image' and were particularly associated with recent advice on diet through health education.

Three groups of foods were included in the measure: wholemeal bread; skimmed or semi-skimmed milk; and polyunsaturated margarine or low fat spreads. Informants were divided into three sets according to whether they had eaten foods from each of these three groups, from only one or two of the groups, or none of these foods during the seven-day dietary recording period. Each set of informants was then sub-divided according to whether the informant reported that he or she generally added salt to food at table, or added salt only occasionally or rarely.

The distribution by sex of informant of the indicator of a health-related diet is given in Table 12.1. The sample is concentrated particularly in the middle of the range of values; relatively few informants (17%) had eaten foods from all three of the specified food groups and a quarter of informants (25%) had eaten none of the food types. Men were more likely than women to have eaten none of the specified food types (p<0.05). The distributions also differ because women were more likely than men to have reported that they only rarely or occasionally added salt to their food at table (p<0.01) (Table 11.5 refers). *(Table 12.1)*

Some care is needed in the use and interpretation of this indicator of a health-related diet since it is derived from the measures of food from which nutrient intake is also assessed. Variation in some nutrients and ratios, such as fibre intake and the ratio of polyunsaturated to saturated fatty acids, might be expected to be well explained by this variable. However, the indicator also appears to have predictive and explanatory power of a non-circular kind and comments on the likely source of particular effects have, where appropriate, been made in the text.

12.3 Methodology
Analysis of variance was used to explain variation in nutrient intake. This method allows the effect of a number of sample characteristics on the intake of a nutrient (the dependent variable) to be considered simultaneously. It operates by testing whether observed differences in mean nutrient intake between subgroups of the sample are greater than those which might be attributed to sampling variation alone, and so would be unlikely to have occurred by chance.

In order to test for significant differences in mean intakes, the observed variability in nutrient intake is divided into two components—within-group variability which measures variation about the group mean, and between-group variability which measures the variability of the group means. The ratio of these two measures is calculated for each characteristic considered, and this F ratio is then tested for significance. When a number of characteristics are included in the same analysis, the means are adjusted for the influence of other characteristics before testing for significance; the method therefore identifies those characteristics which explain a significant amount of the total variation in nutrient intake after allowing for the effects of all other variables considered.

The tables of results give those characteristics where there was a significant difference (p<0.01 or p<0.05) between the means for the sample subgroups after allowing for the effects of the other characteristics included in the analysis. The deviations of the means for the various groups within the sample from the overall (grand) mean are also given; the deviations shown are adjusted for the effects of other characteristics included in the analysis. Thus, for example in Table 12.2, the mean values shown for the energy intake of different age groups take account of differences due to the effects of region, social class, economic status and whether the informant was unwell during the recording period. Statistically this is akin to standardising for the effects of the other independent variables included in the analysis.

Analysis of variance tests for the effects not only of individual variables but also of interactions between independent variables in their effect on the dependent (outcome) variable. A significant interaction between, for example, age and region, might indicate that the direction of the difference in mean intakes by age differs according to region; for example, younger people in the north might have lower intakes than older people, but young people in the south have greater intakes than older people. In general, however, it was found that two-way interactions between characteristics were not significant and these results have not been tabulated.

Dependent variables
The analysis of variance was primarily performed to account for variation in intakes of the major nutrients inclusive of supplements. Where appropriate, the analysis included as a behavioural characteristic whether the informant had been taking any food supplements during the recording period.

Since the amount of food eaten may affect the intake of any nutrient, total energy intake was included as a covariate in the analysis. Values for correlation coefficients between nutrient intake and total energy intake are shown in the tables as an indication of the strength of the relationships. Inclusion of a variable as 'covariate' controls for its effect on the outcome variable. Thus differences in average nutrient intakes have been tested for significance after taking into account any variation in total energy intake between groups. The characteristics identified as significant are the same as those which would be identified by analysis of variance using the dependent variable total nutrient intake (including supplements) per 1000kcal of total energy consumed. The percentage of total variance explained would, however, be lower for the analysis using nutrient intake per 1000kcal energy.

Analysis of variance has also been carried out using as the dependent variable per individual the proportions and ratio which are commonly used as markers of fat intake; fat and saturated fatty acids as percentages of food energy, and the ratio of polyunsaturated to saturated fatty acids.

The distribution of many nutrient intakes was positively skewed, that is, most individuals consumed at, or above, the mean intake and those who consumed substantially less form a long, thin 'tail' of the distribution: this was particularly the case for vitamin intakes. Since analysis of variance requires that values of the dependent variable for each subgroup be normally distributed, appropriate transformations were used for dependent variables; in most cases this was a logarithmic transformation. Where a transformation was used this is stated on the table. In these cases the significance levels and correlation coefficients shown relate to the analysis of variance on the transformed variable. Adjusted deviations from the grand mean are, however, based on the analysis of variance for the untransformed variable in order to give an indication of the relative size of differences in mean nutrient intake in the same units as used elsewhere in the Report.

12.4 Energy and alcohol
Results of the analysis of variance for total energy and alcohol intakes of men and women are shown in Tables 12.2 to 12.7. The analysis of variance was carried out first using the background characteristics identified above. The second stage eliminated some of the background characteristics for which there was no significant difference in intake but included the behavioural characteristics which were appropriate for the analysis; thus the drinking variable was not included in the analysis of variance for alcohol since it was derived directly from alcohol intake.

For men, energy intake varied significantly with region, social class (p < 0.05), economic status, and whether the informant's eating was affected by their being unwell during the recording period (p < 0.01); it did not vary significantly with the informant's age once these other characteristics had been taken into account. Lower energy intakes were recorded by men in Scotland, those in Social Class III non-manual, men in households receiving benefits and others who were not themselves working, and by those whose eating was affected by their having been unwell. These characteristics only accounted, however, for 8% of the variance in energy intakes recorded. *(Table 12.2)*

Table 12.3 develops the analysis of variance for energy intake by the addition of the four behavioural variables. Average energy intakes still differed significantly according to the background characteristics identified, but slimming and drinking behaviour also had a significant effect on average energy intake (p < 0.01). Slimmers had substantially lower energy intakes on average than did non-slimmers, and heavier drinkers had higher total energy intakes than others. *(Table 12.3)*

The background characteristics explained only 4% of the variation in men's alcohol intake and in the percentage of energy derived from alcohol. Men in Social Class III manual had higher absolute intakes of alcohol than men in other social classes (p < 0.05), while men who were not working (mainly the economically inactive) had lower intakes than both working men and those in households receiving benefits (p < 0.01). There was a similar relationship between social class and alcohol intake as a percentage of total energy (p < 0.05) and the average percentage also varied significantly according to age (p < 0.05); men in both the youngest and the oldest age groups derived lower percentages of energy from alcohol than did men in the middle of the age range covered. *(Table 12.2)*

Table 12.4 shows variation in the alcohol intake of men by both background and behavioural characteristics of the sample. Alcohol consumption varied significantly with the health-related diet indicator (p < 0.01) and alcohol intake expressed as a percentage of total energy intake also varied significantly with smoking behaviour (p < 0.05). Informants who were lower on the health-related diet scale had alcohol intakes which were well above average, but the average alcohol intake and percentage of energy from alcohol were highest for the small group who had eaten foods from each of the three specified food types and also generally added salt to their food at table. Smokers also derived a higher percentage of their energy from alcohol than did non-smokers. *(Table 12.4)*

The energy intake of women varied by social class, whether the informant was unwell (p < 0.01), age and economic status (p < 0.05). As for men, the average energy intake was lower for the group whose eating had been affected by their having been unwell during the recording period, but otherwise the pattern for men and women differed. Women in benefit households had a significantly lower average energy intake than others, as did those in Social Classes III manual, IV and V, and older women. *(Table 12.5)*

Table 12.6 shows the results of analysis of variance for energy intake using both background and behavioural characteristics, and indicates that the latter were more powerful predictors of observed differences in intakes than were the background characteristics considered. Slimmers and smokers both had lower average energy intakes than did others (p < 0.01), and total energy intake increased with the amount of alcohol consumed (p < 0.01). The characteristics shown explained more of the total variability in energy intake than did the model for men (20% compared to 16%) (p < 0.05).

(*Table 12.6*)

The alcohol intake of women and the proportion of energy derived from alcohol varied according to age, social class and economic status (p < 0.01). As for men, intakes were lower amongst women in the youngest and oldest age groups considered. However, women in non-manual social classes had higher alcohol intakes than did others, and intakes were higher for working women than for those in households receiving benefits and for those not working.

(*Table 12.5*)

The alcohol intake of women still varied significantly by these characteristics after the inclusion in the model of smoking, slimming and dietary characteristics. Only smoking was significantly associated with alcohol intake (p < 0.01); smokers had higher average daily alcohol intakes and derived a greater percentage of their energy from alcohol than did non-smokers.

(*Table 12.7*)

12.5 Protein, sugars and fibre

The intakes of protein, sugars and fibre all showed strong correlations with total energy intake for both men and women (p < 0.01) and, as for most nutrients considered, differences in total energy intake accounted for the major part of the variance explained in the analyses of variance.

(*Tables 12.8 to 12.11*)

After allowing for differences in total energy intake among men, protein intake showed significant variation only according to the age of the informant (p < 0.01) and average intake increased with age. Intake of sugars varied significantly by region (p < 0.05) and social class (p < 0.01), as did the intake of fibre (p < 0.01 by region and p < 0.05 by social class). The direction of the variation in average intakes differed between the two nutrients. The intake of sugars, after allowing for variation in total energy intake, was lowest for men in Scotland and also below average for men in Northern England and those in manual social classes. Fibre intakes per unit energy were again lower among Scottish men but also for men in London and the South East, and were higher for men in Social Classes I and II.

(*Table 12.8*)

All of the behavioural variables considered were significantly associated with men's protein intake (p < 0.01), and differences in average intake according to age of informant were still significant (p < 0.01). Slimmers, non-smokers and non-drinkers had higher intakes of protein per unit of energy, and the protein content of the diet also increased through the scale for the indicator of a health-related diet.

(*Table 12.9*)

Intake of sugars was greater both for smokers (p < 0.05) and for non-drinkers (p < 0.01) than other men. These two effects reduced the variation by region in intake of sugars so that the effect was no longer significant. Fibre intake varied significantly by smoking, drinking

behaviour, and by the indicator of a health-related diet (p < 0.01). Non-smokers and non-drinkers had a higher fibre content to their diet. Fibre intake also increased through the scale for the indicator of a health-related diet; this effect could, in part, be related to the inclusion of wholemeal bread as one of the specified foods for defining dietary types, although other high fibre products were not included in the definition.

(*Table 12.9*)

The protein content of women's diets varied with more of the background variables considered than did that of men. Protein intakes per unit energy were higher for older women (p < 0.01) and those in higher social classes (p < 0.01), and were lower among women who were unwell (p < 0.05) and those in households receiving benefits (p < 0.01). The fibre content of women's diets showed a similar pattern, being higher for older women (p < 0.01) and those in Social Classes I, II and III non-manual (p < 0.01). On the other hand, younger women and those whose eating was affected by being unwell had a relatively high intake of sugars (p < 0.05).

(*Table 12.10*)

After the inclusion of behavioural variables in the analysis, Table 12.11 shows that the protein intake of women varied significantly with all of the variables except smoking behaviour, but the relationships between protein intake and economic status and whether the informant had been unwell were no longer significant. As for men, protein intake per unit energy was higher among slimmers (p < 0.01) and non-drinkers (p < 0.05), and increased through the scale for a health-related diet (p < 0.01). Among the behavioural variables only drinking behaviour showed a significant relationship with intake of sugars; heavier drinkers had the lowest average intakes of sugars per unit energy (p < 0.01). Fibre intake followed the same pattern as for men with non-drinkers, non-smokers, and those high on the health-related diet scale having higher intakes (p < 0.01).

(*Table 12.11*)

12.6 Fat and fatty acids

Fat intake showed a strong positive correlation with total energy intake, with correlation coefficients of 0.87 for men and 0.91 for women. A number of background characteristics were significantly related to the fat intake of men but not of women, but the amount of variance explained by these variables was relatively small. This is illustrated by the small amount of total variance (4% for men) explained by the analysis of variance for fat as a percentage of food energy; this contrasts with the much higher figure of 76% of variance in fat intake explained by the model which includes total energy intake as a covariate in the analysis. Differences between the two models also result since the first uses *total* energy, including energy derived from alcohol, as a covariate for absolute fat intake while the second uses fat as a percentage of *food* energy as the dependent variable.

(*Table 12.12*)

The fat intake of men in the sample showed significant variation by economic status ($p < 0.01$), region, and whether the informant was unwell ($p < 0.05$); men who were unwell and those living in London and the South East had relatively high fat intakes, while men in households receiving benefits and those who were not working had relatively low intakes.

Variation in the percentage of food energy derived from saturated fatty acids followed the same pattern as for the percentage of energy from fat, with higher levels in Scotland and in London and the South East ($p < 0.05$ for total fat, $p < 0.01$ for saturated fatty acids) and for working men ($p < 0.01$). Informants who were unwell also derived a higher percentage of their food energy from fat ($p < 0.05$), and older men derived a higher percentage of food energy from saturated fatty acids ($p < 0.01$). The ratio of polyunsaturated to saturated fatty acids varied significantly only by age ($p < 0.01$) and social class ($p < 0.05$); older men and those in Social Classes IV and V had a lower average ratio than did others. *(Table 12.12)*

Table 12.13 shows the results of analysis of variance for fat intake using behavioural as well as background characteristics. Fat intake as a percentage of food energy was lower for slimmers ($p < 0.05$) and for those who were higher on the scale of the health-related diet variable ($p < 0.01$). Drinking behaviour was a significant factor but the nature of the relationship between fat intake and drinking depended on whether intakes were adjusted for total or food energy intake; heavier drinkers had higher values for fat as a percentage of their food energy intake ($p < 0.01$), but had lower than average fat intakes when allowance was made for total energy intake ($p < 0.01$). *(Table 12.13)*

All of the behavioural variables included showed significant relationships with the percentage of food energy which men derived from saturated fatty acids; slimmers, non-smokers ($p < 0.05$), non-drinkers and those higher on the indicator of a health-related diet ($p < 0.01$) had lower values for saturated fatty acids as a percentage of food energy. The average P:S ratio was higher for non-smokers and those following a health-related diet ($p < 0.01$), but drinking behaviour and slimming were not significantly related to the P:S ratio. *(Table 12.14)*

The fat intake of women, in contrast to that of men, showed no significant variation with any of the background variables considered, after allowing for differences in total energy intake. There was, however, a strong correlation between fat intake and total energy intake and the model explained as much as 83% of the variance in fat intake. When fat intake was considered as a percentage of food energy, the only significant effect was whether the woman was unwell ($p < 0.05$). Older women had higher values for the percentage of food energy from saturated fatty acids ($p < 0.05$), and their average P:S ratio was lower than for younger women ($p < 0.01$). The P:S ratio was also lower for women in manual social classes ($p < 0.01$).
(Table 12.15)

Behavioural factors added little to the explanation of variation in fat intake, although drinking behaviour and the health-related diet variable had significant effects. Women higher on the indicator of a health-related diet had lower fat intakes and lower values for fat as a percentage of food energy ($p < 0.01$). As for men, the direction of the relationship with drinking behaviour ($p < 0.01$) varied depending on whether fat intake was considered after making allowance for total energy intake (including alcohol) or as a percentage of food energy only. *(Table 12.16)*

Average values for saturated fatty acids as a percentage of food energy and the P:S ratio varied significantly with women's age ($p < 0.01$) but not with social class after the inclusion of the behavioural variables. The indicator of a health-related diet had the most consistent effect of the behavioural variables considered, with the percentage of food energy from saturated fatty acids decreasing ($p < 0.01$) and the P:S ratio increasing ($p < 0.01$) through the range. In addition, slimmers and non-drinkers derived a lower percentage of their food energy ($p < 0.01$) from saturated fatty acids than did other women. *(Table 12.17)*

12.7 Intake of minerals

Tables 12.18 to 12.22 show results for the analysis of variance for intakes of a number of minerals, with total energy intake as a covariate in the analyses. Again there were strong correlations between intake of minerals and total energy intake, although the correlation coefficients were somewhat lower for those minerals which are commonly derived from food supplements, such as iron and calcium. Since food supplements may contribute significantly to the intakes of some minerals, the analysis included whether the informant had taken a food supplement during the recording week.

Among the men there was a similar pattern for intakes of all minerals except sodium, with significant variation in average intakes according to age and social class ($p < 0.01$), after allowing for differences in total energy intake. Younger men (aged 16 to 24) and those in lower social classes had lower mineral intakes per unit energy than other men. There were no significant relationships between mineral intakes and either economic status or whether the informant was unwell. Calcium intakes were, however, lower among men in Northern England ($p < 0.01$) in addition to the effects of age and social class. The pattern for intake of sodium from foods (excluding sodium from salt in cooking and added at table) differed from that of other minerals. Only region showed a significant effect on sodium intake, with higher intakes per unit energy for men in Scotland and the North of England compared with men in the Central and South West regions and Wales, and Southern England ($p < 0.01$). *(Table 12.18)*

The background variables identified as being related to mineral intake were still significant after inclusion of the behavioural variables. Slimming, supplement taking and the health-related diet variable were significantly related (p<0.01) to the intakes of all of the minerals considered except sodium. Intakes per unit energy were higher among slimmers, supplement takers, and those higher on the indicator of a health-related diet. In addition, smokers and drinkers had significantly lower intakes per unit of energy of most minerals other than sodium (smoking: p<0.01 for iron, phosphorus, magnesium and potassium; drinking: p<0.01 for calcium, iron and magnesium). (*Table 12.19*)

The model for sodium intake differed from those for other minerals in that supplement taking was not significant. However, as for the other minerals, slimmers (p<0.05), non-drinkers (p<0.01) and those high on the indicator of a health-related diet (p<0.01) had relatively high average sodium intakes per unit of energy. (*Table 12.19*)

For women, as for men, the analysis of variance for sodium differed substantially from that for other minerals. Intakes of most minerals, after adjusting for total energy intake, were lower among younger women (p<0.01), those in lower social classes (p<0.01), and women in households receiving benefits (p<0.01 for phosphorus, magnesium and potassium, p<0.05 for calcium). There was no marked regional effect for mineral intakes except in the case of sodium, with women in Scotland having a relatively high sodium intake from foods (p<0.01). (*Table 12.20*)

Apart from sodium the inclusion of behavioural variables added considerably to the explanatory power of the analyses of variance, with each of the characteristics having a significant effect on women's intake of some minerals. Slimmers (p<0.01) and non-smokers (p<0.01 except for potassium, where p<0.05) had higher mineral intakes per unit of energy, as did women who were higher on the indicator of a health-related diet (p<0.01). Supplement taking was significantly related only to intakes of calcium, iron (p<0.01) and magnesium (p<0.05). Drinking behaviour was a significant factor for few minerals; heavier drinkers had a lower average intake of calcium (p<0.01) and a higher average intake of magnesium (p<0.05). After inclusion of the behavioural variables in the analyses of variance economic status was not significantly related to mineral intake (except for potassium, p<0.05), and the relationship between social class and mineral intake was also less strong (p<0.01 for magnesium and potassium, p<0.05 for phosphorus). There was still a strong relationship between age and intake of minerals (p<0.01 for minerals other than iron). (*Table 12.21*)

Of the behavioural variables only slimming accounted for a significant amount of variance in sodium intake (p<0.01) in addition to the effects of region; slimmers had a higher average intake of sodium from food after allowing for their lower energy intake. (*Table 12.22*)

12.8 Intake of vitamins
Intakes of vitamins again showed strong positive correlations with total energy intake, although the relation-

ships were less strong for women than for men because of the greater contribution of food supplements to women's vitamin intakes. The vitamins are presented in two groups, and vitamin C is considered separately because of the seasonal effect on intakes.

Table 12.23 shows that, for men, intakes of retinol equivalents, thiamin, riboflavin and niacin equivalents varied consistently with social class (p<0.01 except for retinol equivalents, where p<0.05); the vitamin content of the diet was greater for men in Social Classes I and II than for others. There were also some differences in vitamin intake by age of informant and economic status. Older men had higher intakes of vitamin A (as retinol equivalents) (p<0.01) and riboflavin (p<0.05), while men in households receiving benefits had lower intakes of niacin equivalents per unit energy. (*Table 12.23*)

Inclusion of the behavioural variables in the analyses for men tended to reduce the relationship between vitamin intakes and both social class and economic status. Variation in intake of retinol equivalents was less well explained by the behavioural characteristics than were intakes of other vitamins; intakes were significantly higher only among supplement takers (p<0.01) and older informants (p<0.01). Supplement takers had consistently higher intakes of vitamins from all sources than informants who were not taking supplements (p<0.01). The average vitamin intakes of supplement takers were higher than for any other group identified. Slimmers and non-smokers also had higher intakes of most vitamins after allowing for differences in total energy intake (slimming: p<0.01 for riboflavin and niacin equivalents, p<0.05 for thiamin; smoking: p<0.01 for thiamin and niacin equivalents). Drinking behaviour was significantly related only to men's intake of thiamin (p<0.01) with lighter drinkers having above-average intakes. Intakes of thiamin, riboflavin and niacin equivalents were lower among men who were lower on the indicator of a health-related diet (p<0.01). (*Table 12.24*)

The analysis of variance for vitamin C includes the season in which the dietary record was made, since the vitamin is particularly concentrated in fruit and vegetables which vary in availability throughout the year. Table 12.25 shows that men's intakes of vitamin C did differ significantly according to season (p<0.01), with the highest intakes per unit energy in summer. In addition there was a strong social class effect, with higher intakes for men in Social Classes I and II (p<0.01) and an effect of economic status with lower intakes among men in households receiving benefits (p<0.01). (*Table 12.25*)

In the second model for men's intakes of vitamin C, season and social class effects remained significant after inclusion of the behavioural variables considered, although economic status was no longer significant. Intakes were markedly higher for supplement takers, slimmers, non-smokers, and those higher on the indicator of a health-related diet (p<0.01). The effect of drinking behaviour was also significant (p<0.01) but the pattern was less easy to interpret; vitamin C intakes were higher among light drinkers compared with both heavier and non-drinkers. (*Table 12.26*)

Variation in men's intakes of vitamins B6, B12 and folate did not conform closely to the pattern for the other vitamins considered above. Intake of vitamin B12 was significantly related only to age of informant, with higher intakes among older men. Intakes of vitamin B6 and folate were again higher for men in Social Classes I and II (p<0.01), and there were also significant, although not consistent, differences in intake between regions (p<0.05). Men who were unwell also had significantly lower intakes of vitamin B6 (p<0.05) and men in the middle of the age range of the sample had higher intakes of folate (p<0.05) than both younger and older men. (*Table 12.27*)

Tables 12.28 and 12.29 show that behavioural factors tended to overshadow the effects of background factors, and especially social class, on men's vitamin intakes. Region continued to have a significant effect on intakes of vitamin B6 and folate (p<0.05) and age on intake of vitamin B12 (p<0.01). Consistently higher vitamin intakes per unit of total energy consumed were recorded by slimmers (p<0.01 for vitamin B12 and folate, p<0.05 for vitamin B6), supplement takers (p<0.01) and heavier drinkers (p<0.01). There was no significant relationship between intakes of vitamins B6 and B12 and either smoking behaviour or the indicator of a health-related diet, but intake of folate increased through the scale for the health-related diet (p<0.01) and was higher for non-smokers (p<0.01). (*Tables 12.28 & 12.29*)

Tables 12.30 to 12.36 show results of the analyses of variance for the vitamin intakes of women. Of the background variables only age was related to thiamin intake (p<0.05). Average intakes of retinol equivalents, riboflavin and niacin equivalents varied significantly with age (p<0.01), social class (p<0.01), and economic status (p<0.01 for riboflavin and niacin, p<0.05 for retinol equivalents). Intakes were higher for older informants and those in Social Classes I and II, while women in households receiving benefits or those who were not themselves working had lower average intakes. (*Table 12.30*)

After inclusion of behavioural variables in the analyses, economic status and social class were less strongly related to vitamin intakes, although age still had a significant effect. Supplement takers had consistently higher intakes of the vitamins shown (p<0.01), and slimmers also had above-average intakes of riboflavin and niacin equivalents (p<0.01). Intakes of riboflavin increased through the scale for the indicator of a health-related diet (p<0.01) but the pattern was less clear for thiamin (p<0.05) and niacin equivalents (p<0.01). The other variables included in the analyses did not have a consistent effect on intakes of these vitamins; non-

drinkers had higher intakes of thiamin (p<0.01) and non-smokers had higher intakes of riboflavin (p<0.01). (*Table 12.31*)

As for men, the vitamin C intake of women varied according to season (p<0.05), social class and economic status (p<0.01), but age was also a significant effect (p<0.01). Older women and those in Social Classes I and II had higher average intakes of vitamin C than others, and intakes were lower among women in households receiving benefits. Other than economic status, these effects continued to be significant after the inclusion of behavioural variables into the analysis. Vitamin C intakes were markedly higher for those taking food supplements (p<0.01), and also higher for slimmers, non-smokers, drinkers, and women higher on the scale for a health-related diet (p<0.01). (*Tables 12.32 & 12.33*)

Social class and age showed the strongest relationship with women's intakes of vitamins B6, B12 and folate; older women and those in Social Classes I and II had higher vitamin intakes after allowing for differences in energy intake (age: p<0.01 for vitamin B12 and folate; social class: p<0.01 for vitamin B12 and folate, p<0.05 for vitamin B6). In addition, average folate intake was also lower for women in households receiving benefits (p<0.01) and for women who were unwell (p<0.01), while intake of vitamin B6 was higher for women in London and the South East (p<0.05). (*Table 12.34*)

After inclusion of behavioural variables in the analyses, vitamin B6 intake was seen to be significantly higher only among supplement takers (p<0.01) and women in London and the South East (p<0.05). Slimmers (p<0.05) and supplement takers (p<0.01) had higher intakes of vitamin B12, and the effects of age and social class were still significant (p<0.05). As for men, intake of folate was related to all of the behavioural variables considered (p<0.01 for all except smoking, where p<0.05) as well as to age and whether women had been unwell during the dietary recording period (p<0.01). (*Tables 12.35 & 12.36*)

12.9 Summary

While the characteristics which explain a significant amount of variation in nutrient intake were not consistent for all nutrients, a number of trends can be identified. For both men and women, intakes of all nutrients showed strong positive correlation with total energy intake, although correlation coefficients were smaller for vitamins and minerals which are commonly found in food supplements.

Among men, age and social class were the background factors which were most commonly related to nutrient intake. Older men and those in higher social classes tended to have higher adjusted intakes of minerals and vitamins, and those in non-manual social classes also had higher intakes of both sugars and fibre. Economic status was, however, a significant factor in explaining variation in the percentages of food energy from fat, with men in benefit households having lower percentages of energy from fat.

For women, age and social class were again the characteristics which were most frequently significant in explaining variation in nutrient intake, but economic status was also important. Older women and those in Social Classes I and II had higher intakes of protein and fibre and greater intakes of most minerals and vitamins per unit of total energy consumed; however, their diets also contained more fat. Women in households receiving benefits had diets which were lower in minerals and vitamins, but which were also lower in total fat.

The effects of these background characteristics were frequently reduced by the inclusion in the models of behavioural factors. Supplement takers had significantly greater intakes of vitamins and minerals, and the diets of slimmers also contained greater amounts per unit of total energy of most vitamins and minerals. There were also significant relationships between nutrient intakes and both smoking behaviour and the indicator of a health-related diet, which was able to identify differences in intake for nutrients other than those closely related to the foods from which the scale was derived. Both non-smokers and those who followed a health-related diet had higher vitamin and mineral intakes as well as having diets which were higher in fibre and lower in fat. Drinking behaviour was a significant effect for fewer nutrients than were the other behavioural variables, and the explanation of the effects was complicated because of the contribution of alcohol to total energy intake which was used as a covariate in the analyses.

Table 12.1 Indicator of health related diet by sex of informant
Diary sample

Characteristics of diet	Men	Women	Total
	%	%	%
None of specified foods, generally adds salt at table	14	9	12
None of specified foods, rarely adds salt at table	13	12	13
Some of specified foods, generally adds salt at table	27	20	24
Some of specified foods, rarely adds salt at table	30	40	35
All of specified foods, generally adds salt at table	5	4	5
All of specified foods, rarely adds salt at table	10	14	12
Base = 100%	*1085*	*1108*	*2193*

Table 12.2 Men—analysis of variance for total energy and alcohol intakes: background factors

Characteristic	No. of cases	Adjusted deviations from grand mean and significance of F ratios for:		
		Energy (kcals)	Alcohol (g)	Alcohol (% energy)
Grand mean	*1064*	2451	25.0	6.90
Age		NS	NS	*
16–24	*204*	65	−2.8	−1.12
25–34	*249*	−27	0.5	0.30
35–49	*343*	13	2.8	0.72
50–64	*268*	−41	−1.9	−0.35
Region		*	NS	NS
Scotland	*92*	−159	1.3	0.75
Northern	*266*	22	4.3	0.94
Central, South West & Wales	*359*	39	−2.1	−0.69
London & South East	*347*	−16	−1.5	−0.21
Social class of HOH		*	*	*
I and II	*377*	−6	−0.8	−0.12
IIINM	*138*	−126	−4.3	−0.71
IIIM	*375*	37	3.3	0.69
IV and V	*174*	35	−2.0	−0.66
Economic status		**	**	NS
Receiving benefits	*112*	−245	0.5	1.18
Working	*847*	67	0.5	−0.08
Not working	*105*	−283	−4.3	−0.62
Unwell and eating affected		**	NS	NS
Unwell and eating affected	*51*	−281	−6.4	−1.67
Not unwell/eating not affected	*1013*	14	0.3	0.08
% of variance explained		*8%*	*4%*	*4%*

*** F ratio $p < 0.01$ NS F ratio $p > 0.05$
* F ratio $p < 0.05$

Table 12.3 Men—analysis of variance for total energy intake: including behavioural variables

Characteristic	No. of cases	Adjusted deviations from grand mean and significance of F ratios for: Energy (kcals)
Grand mean	1060	2452
Region		*
Scotland	91	−149
Northern	266	10
Central, South West & Wales	358	50
London & South East	345	−20
Social class of HOH		*
I and II	377	−14
IIINM	136	−109
IIIM	373	30
IV and V	174	51
Economic status		**
Receiving benefits	112	−234
Working	843	63
Not working	105	−253
Unwell and eating affected		**
Unwell and eating affected	51	−214
Not unwell/eating not affected	1009	11
Slimming		**
On a slimming diet	44	−417
Not on a slimming diet	1016	18
Cigarette smoking		NS
Smoker	351	−49
Non-smoker	709	24
Drinking behaviour		**
Non-drinker	216	−161
Light drinker	430	−72
Heavier drinker	414	159
Health related diet		NS
None of foods, high salt	153	44
None of foods, low salt	135	−79
Some of foods, high salt	290	−8
Some of foods, low salt	316	25
All foods, high salt	58	−2
All foods, low salt	108	−12
% of variance explained		*16%*

** F ratio $p < 0.01$ NS F ratio $p > 0.05$
* F ratio $p < 0.05$

Table 12.4 Men—analysis of variance for alcohol intake: background factors

Characteristic	No. of cases	Alcohol (g)	Alcohol (% energy)
Grand mean	1060	25.0	6.90
Age		*	*
16–24	204	−2.9	−1.11
25–34	248	0.8	0.37
35–49	341	2.6	0.69
50–64	267	−1.9	−0.37
Social class of HOH		*	*
I and II	377	−0.1	0.05
IIINM	136	−3.9	−0.58
IIIM	373	2.7	0.51
IV and V	174	−2.4	−0.76
Economic status		**	NS
Receiving benefits	112	−0.4	0.99
Working	843	0.5	−0.07
Not working	105	−3.9	−0.52
Slimming		NS	NS
On a slimming diet	44	−3.9	−0.49
Not on a slimming diet	1016	0.2	0.02
Cigarette smoking		NS	*
Smoker	351	4.3	1.25
Non-smoker	709	−2.1	−0.62
Health related diet		**	**
None of foods, high salt	153	6.3	1.44
None of foods, low salt	135	−4.0	−1.01
Some of foods, high salt	290	−0.9	−0.30
Some of foods, low salt	316	−0.7	−0.17
All foods, high salt	58	8.7	2.47
All foods, low salt	108	−4.1	−0.81
% of variance explained		*6%*	*5%*

** F ratio $p < 0.01$ NS F ratio $p > 0.05$
* F ratio $p < 0.05$

Table 12.5 Women—analysis of variance for total energy and alcohol intakes: background factors

Characteristic	No. of cases	Adjusted deviations from grand mean and significance of F ratios for:		
		Energy (kcals)	Alcohol (g)	Alcohol (% energy)
Grand mean	1084	1682	6.84	2.77
Age		*	**	**
16–24	184	25	−0.42	−0.22
25–34	248	21	0.99	0.34
35–49	378	30	0.36	0.18
50–64	274	−77	−1.12	−0.41
Region		NS	NS	NS
Scotland	95	−17	−0.53	−0.28
Northern	283	−14	0.35	0.17
Central, South West & Wales	361	31	0.13	0.07
London & South East	345	−17	−0.27	−0.13
Social class of HOH		**	**	**
I and II	382	49	1.43	0.58
IIINM	140	51	0.18	−0.09
IIIM	345	−30	−0.78	−0.25
IV and V	217	−72	−1.40	−0.57
Economic status		*	**	**
Receiving benefits	145	−91	−1.68	−0.67
Working	619	15	1.12	0.46
Not working	320	12	−1.40	−0.57
Unwell and eating affected		**	NS	NS
Unwell and eating affected	102	−274	−1.10	−0.24
Not unwell/eating not affected	982	28	0.11	0.02
% of variance explained		*8%*	*8%*	*7%*

** F ratio p<0.01   NS F ratio p>0.05
* F ratio p<0.05

Table 12.6 Women—analysis of variance for total energy intake: including behavioural variables

Characteristic	No. of cases	Adjusted deviations from grand mean and significance of F ratios for:
		Energy (kcals)
Grand mean	1081	1680
Age		**
16–24	184	39
25–34	248	2
35–49	376	33
50–64	273	−74
Social class of HOH		NS
I and II	380	12
IIINM	139	47
IIIM	345	−8
IV and V	217	−38
Economic status		NS
Receiving benefits	145	−55
Working	616	4
Not working	320	17
Unwell and eating affected		**
Unwell and eating affected	102	−251
Not unwell/eating not affected	979	26
Slimming		**
On a slimming diet	134	−292
Not on a slimming diet	947	41
Cigarette smoking		**
Smoker	374	−68
Non-smoker	707	36
Drinking behaviour		**
Non-drinker	378	−119
Light drinker	546	29
Heavier drinker	157	188
Health related diet		NS
None of foods, high salt	97	25
None of foods, low salt	135	−61
Some of foods, high salt	218	13
Some of foods, low salt	427	−4
All foods, high salt	47	−6
All foods, low salt	157	32
% of variance explained		*20%*

** F ratio p<0.01   NS F ratio p>0.05
* F ratio p<0.05

Table 12.7 Women—analysis of variance for alcohol intake: including behavioural variables

Characteristic	No. of cases	Adjusted deviations from grand mean and significance of F ratios for:	
		Alcohol (g)	Alcohol (% energy)
Grand mean	1081	6.83	2.77
Age		*	*
16–24	184	−0.17	−0.13
25–34	248	0.72	0.24
35–49	376	0.28	0.14
50–64	273	−0.93	−0.33
Social class of HOH		**	**
I and II	380	1.64	0.69
IIINM	139	0.12	−0.10
IIIM	345	−0.83	−0.29
IV and V	217	−1.63	−0.67
Economic status		**	**
Receiving benefits	145	−1.84	−0.73
Working	616	1.07	0.43
Not working	320	−1.23	−0.50
Slimming		NS	NS
On a slimming diet	134	0.36	0.44
Not on a slimming diet	947	−0.05	−0.06
Cigarette smoking		**	**
Smoker	374	1.89	0.83
Non-smoker	707	−1.00	−0.44
Health related diet		NS	NS
None of foods, high salt	97	−0.85	−0.39
None of foods, low salt	135	−0.82	−0.26
Some of foods, high salt	218	−0.27	−0.02
Some of foods, low salt	427	0.21	0.06
All foods, high salt	47	2.93	0.97
All foods, low salt	157	0.14	0.04
% of variance explained		9%	9%

** F ratio p<0.01 NS F ratio p>0.05
* F ratio p<0.05

Table 12.8 Men—analysis of variance for protein, sugars and fibre: background factors

Characteristic	No. of cases	Adjusted deviations from grand mean and significance of F ratios for:		
		Protein (g)	Sugars (g)	Fibre (g)
Grand mean	1064	84.8	114.6	24.9
Covariate—Total energy		**	**	**
Correlation coefficient		0.72	0.66	0.55
Age		**	NS	NS
16–24	204	−3.2	0.1	−0.8
25–34	249	−0.4	−0.8	−0.2
35–49	343	−0.4	−1.3	0.4
50–64	268	3.3	2.4	0.3
Region		NS	*	**
Scotland	92	0.4	−7.7	−1.6
Northern	266	−0.2	−2.8	0.0
Central, South West & Wales	359	−0.2	1.9	1.1
London & South East	347	0.3	2.2	−0.7
Social class of HOH		NS	**	*
I and II	377	1.4	4.7	0.9
IIINM	138	−0.1	5.4	−0.1
IIIM	375	−0.7	−6.2	−0.7
IV and V	174	−1.5	−1.1	−0.5
Economic status		NS	NS	NS
Receiving benefits	112	−2.9	−2.0	0.6
Working	847	0.4	0.0	0.1
Not working	105	0.1	2.4	−0.1
Unwell and eating affected		NS	NS	NS
Unwell and eating affected	51	2.0	−9.6	−0.8
Not unwell/eating not affected	1013	−0.1	0.5	0.0
% of variance explained		53%	46%	32%

** F ratio p<0.01 NS F ratio p>0.05
* F ratio p<0.05

Table 12.9 Men—analysis of variance for protein, sugars and fibre: including behavioural variables

Characteristic	No. of cases	Adjusted deviations from grand mean and significance of F ratios for:		
		Protein (g)	Sugars (g)	Fibre (g)
Grand mean	1066	84.8	114.7	24.9
Covariate—Total energy		**	**	**
Correlation coefficient		0.72	0.66	0.55
Age		**	NS	NS
16–24	206	−3.3	−2.2	−0.6
25–34	248	−0.2	−0.9	−0.4
35–49	342	−0.3	−0.3	0.5
50–64	270	3.0	2.9	0.2
Region		NS	NS	**
Scotland	92	0.1	−6.9	−1.6
Northern	268	−0.1	−1.3	0.3
Central, South West & Wales	359	−0.6	1.5	0.8
London & South East	347	0.7	1.3	−0.6
Social class of HOH		NS	**	NS
I and II	377	0.4	5.5	−0.4
IIINM	136	−0.4	5.0	−0.6
IIIM	376	0.4	−5.7	0.4
IV and V	177	−1.3	−3.3	0.4
Slimming		**	NS	NS
On a slimming diet	45	8.9	−3.0	0.9
Not on a slimming diet	1021	−0.4	0.1	−0.5
Cigarette smoking		**	*	**
Smoker	354	−2.4	3.2	−1.6
Non-smoker	712	1.2	−1.6	0.8
Drinking behaviour		**	**	**
Non-drinker	221	3.9	11.7	1.8
Light drinker	430	1.7	6.6	1.4
Heavier drinker	415	−3.8	−13.1	−2.4
Health related diet		**	NS	**
None of foods, high salt	155	−4.7	2.4	−4.0
None of foods, low salt	136	−0.0	−2.6	−2.3
Some of foods, high salt	291	−0.4	−1.2	−0.6
Some of foods, low salt	318	0.2	2.9	0.7
All foods, high salt	58	2.2	−0.2	1.6
All foods, low salt	108	6.0	−5.4	7.4
% of variance explained		*59%*	*50%*	*51%*

** F ratio p < 0.01   NS F ratio p > 0.05
* F ratio p < 0.05

Table 12.10 Women—analysis of variance for protein, sugars and fibre: background factors

Characteristic	No. of cases	Adjusted deviations from grand mean and significance of F ratios for:		
		Protein (g)	Sugars (g)	Fibre (g)
Grand mean	1084	62.0	86.0	18.6
Covariate—Total energy		**	**	**
Correlation coefficient		0.71	0.72	0.59
Age		**	*	**
16–24	184	−3.8	4.5	−1.3
25–34	248	−1.9	−0.4	−0.1
35–49	378	0.7	0.0	−0.1
50–64	274	3.3	−2.6	1.2
Region		NS	NS	*
Scotland	95	0.7	−3.3	−0.9
Northern	283	1.0	−1.1	−0.3
Central, South West & Wales	361	−1.0	0.1	0.6
London & South East	345	0.1	1.7	−0.2
Social class of HOH		**	NS	**
I and II	382	2.0	1.0	0.7
IIINM	140	0.4	3.1	1.0
IIIM	345	−1.1	−1.5	−0.6
IV and V	217	−2.0	−1.4	−0.9
Economic status		**	NS	NS
Receiving benefits	145	−2.3	−1.3	−0.4
Working	619	0.7	0.1	−0.2
Not working	320	−0.2	0.4	0.6
Unwell and eating affected		*	*	NS
Unwell and eating affected	102	−2.0	5.7	−0.4
Not unwell/eating not affected	982	0.2	−0.6	0.0
% of variance explained		*56%*	*53%*	*39%*

** F ratio p < 0.01   NS F ratio p > 0.05
* F ratio p < 0.05

188

Table 12.11 Women—analysis of variance for protein, sugars and fibre: including behavioural variables

Characteristic	No. of cases (Protein)	No. of cases (Sugars, Fibre)	Adjusted deviations from grand mean and significance of F ratios for:		
			Protein (g)	Sugars (g)	Fibre (g)
Grand mean	1081	1093	61.9	86.1	18.6
Covariate—Total energy			**	**	**
Correlation coefficient			0.71	0.72	0.59
Age			**	**	**
16–24	184	186	−3.4	4.5	−1.0
25–34	248	250	−1.7	0.2	−0.1
35–49	376	378	0.6	0.4	−0.2
50–64	273	279	3.0	−3.7	1.0
Social class of HOH			**	NS	NS
I and II	380	384	1.6	1.1	0.0
IIINM	139	140	0.2	3.0	0.7
IIIM	345	347	−1.0	−1.5	−0.2
IV and V	217	222	−1.3	−1.5	−0.1
Economic status			NS		
Receiving benefits	145		−1.6	—	—
Working	616		0.4	—	—
Not working	320		0.1	—	—
Unwell and eating affected			NS	*	
Unwell and eating affected	102	105	−1.8	5.4	—
Not unwell/eating not affected	979	988	0.2	−0.6	—
Slimming			**	NS	**
On a slimming diet	134	135	5.5	1.3	1.4
Not on a slimming diet	947	958	−0.8	−0.2	−0.2
Cigarette smoking			NS	NS	**
Smoker	374	380	−0.5	−1.7	−0.9
Non-smoker	707	713	0.3	0.9	0.5
Drinking behaviour			*	**	**
Non-drinker	378	383	0.5	4.6	0.4
Light drinker	546	552	0.3	0.1	0.2
Heavier drinker	157	158	−2.3	−11.4	−1.5
Health related diet			**	NS	**
None of foods, high salt	97	98	−1.4	−0.5	−2.5
None of foods, low salt	135	135	−2.3	−2.5	−2.5
Some of foods, high salt	218	221	−0.1	−2.0	−0.6
Some of foods, low salt	427	434	−0.2	0.3	0.2
All foods, high salt	47	47	3.4	0.8	2.2
All foods, low salt	157	158	2.5	4.1	3.3
% of variance explained			59%	56%	50%

** *F ratio p < 0.01*   NS *F ratio p > 0.05*
* *F ratio p < 0.05*

Table 12.12   Men—analysis of variance for fat intake: background factors

Characteristic	No. of cases	Adjusted deviations from grand mean and significance of F ratios for:			
		Total fat (g)	Total fat (% food energy)	Saturated fatty acids (% food energy)	P:S ratio (Log)
Grand mean	1064	102.4	40.40	16.55	0.40
Covariate—Total energy		**	—	—	—
Correlation coefficient		0.87			
Age		NS	NS	**	**
16–24	204	1.4	0.04	−0.31	0.01
25–34	249	0.6	0.36	−0.14	0.02
35–49	343	−1.7	−0.33	−0.33	0.02
50–64	268	0.5	0.06	0.79	−0.05
Region		*	*	**	NS
Scotland	92	0.0	0.47	0.36	−0.03
Northern	266	−2.1	−0.29	−0.36	0.00
Central, South West & Wales	359	−0.1	−0.42	−0.21	0.01
London & South East	347	1.7	0.53	0.40	−0.01
Social class of HOH		NS	NS	NS	*
I and II	377	0.2	0.02	−0.03	0.01
IIINM	138	0.4	−0.09	−0.11	0.02
IIIM	375	−0.5	0.09	0.03	0.00
IV and V	174	0.5	−0.17	0.08	−0.03
Economic status		**	**	**	NS
Receiving benefits	112	−4.5	−1.28	−0.83	−0.01
Working	847	0.9	0.34	0.17	0.00
Not working	105	−2.2	−1.37	−0.50	0.00
Unwell and eating affected		*	*	NS	NS
Unwell and eating affected	51	4.4	1.51	0.35	0.03
Not unwell/eating not affected	1013	−0.2	−0.08	−0.02	0.00
% of variance explained		*76%*	*4%*	*5%*	*5%*

** *F ratio $p < 0.01$*   NS *F ratio $p > 0.05$*
*   *F ratio $p < 0.05$*

Table 12.13 Men—analysis of variance for fat intake: including behavioural variables

Characteristic	No. of cases	Adjusted deviations from grand mean and significance of F ratios for:	
		Total fat (g)	Total fat (% food energy)
Grand mean	1076	102.5	40.4
Covariate—Total energy		**	—
Correlation coefficient		0.87	
Region		*	*
Scotland	94	0.8	0.64
Northern	272	−1.4	−0.35
Central, South West & Wales	361	−0.6	−0.36
London & South East	349	1.4	0.48
Economic status		**	**
Receiving benefits	118	−4.3	−1.38
Working	848	0.9	0.33
Not working	110	−2.0	−1.07
Unwell and eating affected		*	**
Unwell & eating affected	51	4.1	1.76
Not unwell/eating not affected	1025	−0.2	−0.09
Slimming		NS	*
On a slimming diet	45	−2.0	−1.40
Not on a slimming diet	1031	0.1	0.06
Cigarette smoking		NS	NS
Smoker	357	−0.1	0.35
Non-smoker	719	0.0	−0.17
Drinking behaviour		**	**
Non-drinker	222	4.2	−1.50
Light drinker	434	4.3	0.04
Heavier drinker	420	−6.7	0.75
Health related diet		*	**
None of foods, high salt	153	0.0	0.34
None of foods, low salt	140	1.1	0.29
Some of foods, high salt	293	1.4	0.43
Some of foods, low salt	324	−0.2	−0.03
All foods, high salt	58	−1.7	−0.49
All foods, low salt	108	−3.7	−1.69
% of variance explained		80%	9%

** F ratio p<0.01   NS F ratio p>0.05
* F ratio p<0.05

Table 12.14 Men—analysis of variance for fat intake: including behavioural variables

Characteristic	No. of cases	Adjusted deviations from grand mean and significance of F ratios for:	
		Saturated fatty acids (% food energy)	P:S ratio (Log)
Grand mean	1060	16.55	0.40
Age		**	**
16–24	204	−0.37	0.02
25–34	248	−0.12	0.02
35–49	341	−0.33	0.01
50–64	267	0.81	−0.05
Region		**	NS
Scotland	91	0.50	−0.04
Northern	266	−0.40	0.00
Central, South West & Wales	358	−0.16	0.01
London & South East	345	0.34	0.00
Social class		NS	NS
I and II	377	0.28	−0.01
IIINM	136	−0.04	0.01
IIIM	375	−0.22	0.02
IV and V	174	−0.10	−0.01
Economic status		**	NS
Receiving benefits	112	−1.10	0.02
Working	843	0.19	0.00
Not working	105	−0.35	−0.01
Slimming		*	NS
On a slimming diet	44	−0.96	0.09
Not on a slimming diet	1016	0.04	0.00
Cigarette smoking		*	**
Smoker	351	0.31	−0.02
Non-smoker	709	−0.15	0.01
Drinking behaviour		**	NS
Non-drinker	216	−0.71	0.03
Light drinker	430	0.06	−0.01
Heavier drinker	414	0.31	−0.01
Heath related diet		**	**
None of foods, high salt	153	0.91	−0.09
None of foods, low salt	135	0.77	−0.04
Some of foods, high salt	290	0.37	−0.02
Some of foods, low salt	316	−0.12	0.00
All foods, high salt	58	−1.05	0.08
All foods, low salt	108	−2.32	0.18
% of variance explained		17%	21%

** F ratio p<0.01   NS F ratio p>0.05
* F ratio p<0.05

Table 12.15 Women—analysis of variance for fat intake: background factors

Characteristic	No. of cases	Adjusted deviations from grand mean and significance of F ratios for:			
		Total fat (g)	Total fat (% food energy)	Saturated fatty acids (% food energy)	P:S ratio (Log)
Grand mean	1084	73.6	40.33	16.99	0.38
Covariate—Total energy		**	—	—	—
Correlation coefficient		0.91			
Age		NS	NS	*	**
16–24	184	−1.0	−0.59	−0.55	0.01
25–34	248	0.3	0.29	−0.08	0.02
35–49	378	−0.1	0.04	−0.04	0.00
50–64	274	0.6	0.09	0.49	−0.03
Region		NS	NS	NS	NS
Scotland	95	0.7	0.09	−0.04	−0.01
Northern	283	−0.6	−0.18	−0.12	0.00
Central, South West & Wales	361	−0.4	−0.23	−0.10	0.00
London & South East	345	0.7	0.36	0.22	0.00
Social class of HOH		NS	NS	NS	**
I and II	382	−0.8	−0.11	−0.15	0.02
IIINM	140	−1.0	−0.63	−0.31	0.02
IIIM	345	0.8	0.47	0.24	−0.01
IV and V	217	0.6	−0.14	0.09	−0.03
Economic status		NS	NS	NS	NS
Receiving benefits	145	0.0	−0.10	−0.05	−0.01
Working	619	−0.7	0.12	−0.04	0.00
Not working	320	0.1	−0.18	0.11	0.00
Unwell and eating affected		NS	*	NS	NS
Unwell & eating affected	102	−0.8	−1.27	−0.36	0.00
Not unwell/eating not affected	982	0.1	0.13	0.04	0.00
% of variance explained		*83%*	*2%*	*2%*	*3%*

** F ratio $p < 0.01$ NS F ratio $p > 0.05$
* F ratio $p < 0.05$

Table 12.16	Women—analysis of variance for fat intake: including behavioural variables		

Characteristic	No. of cases	Total fat (g)	Total fat (% food energy)
Grand mean	1107	73.4	40.30
Covariate—Total energy		**	—
Correlation coefficient		0.91	
Age		NS	NS
16–24	189	−1.5	−0.69
25–34	253	0.6	0.22
35–49	383	−0.1	0.05
50–64	282	0.6	0.20
Unwell and eating affected		NS	*
Unwell & eating affected	106	−1.2	−1.19
Not unwell/eating not affected	1001	0.1	0.13
Slimming		NS	**
On a slimming diet	138	−1.5	−1.97
Not on a slimming diet	969	0.2	0.28
Cigarette smoking		NS	NS
Smoker	382	0.7	0.29
Non-smoker	725	−0.4	−0.15
Drinking behaviour		**	**
Non-drinker	390	1.0	−0.72
Light drinker	555	0.5	0.03
Heavier drinker	162	−4.0	1.64
Health related diet		**	**
None of foods, high salt	101	0.1	0.25
None of foods, low salt	135	2.2	1.09
Some of foods, high salt	224	1.6	0.88
Some of foods, low salt	440	0.0	−0.01
All foods, high salt	47	−2.3	−1.44
All foods, low salt	160	−3.5	−1.85
% of variance explained		84%	8%

** F ratio p<0.01   NS F ratio p>0.05
* F ratio p<0.05

Table 12.17	Women—analysis of variance for fat intake: including behavioural variables		

Characteristic	No. of cases	Saturated fatty acids (% food energy)	P:S ratio (Log)
Grand mean	1093	16.98	0.38
Age		**	**
16–24	186	−0.76	0.02
25–34	250	−0.14	0.02
35–49	378	−0.02	0.00
50–64	279	0.66	−0.03
Social class of HOH		NS	NS
I and II	384	0.11	0.00
IIINM	140	−0.33	0.02
IIIM	347	0.14	0.00
IV and V	222	−0.20	−0.02
Slimming		**	NS
On a slimming diet	135	−1.20	0.01
Not on a slimming diet	958	0.17	0.00
Cigarette smoking		NS	NS
Smoker	380	0.14	−0.01
Non-smoker	713	−0.07	0.00
Drinking behaviour		**	NS
Non-drinker	383	−0.36	0.01
Light drinker	552	0.10	−0.01
Heavier drinker	158	0.51	0.01
Heath related diet		**	**
None of foods, high salt	98	0.90	−0.08
None of foods, low salt	135	1.09	−0.07
Some of foods, high salt	221	0.38	−0.01
Some of foods, low salt	434	0.08	−0.01
All foods, high salt	47	−1.18	0.06
All foods, low salt	158	−1.90	0.12
% of variance explained		12%	14%

** F ratio p<0.01   NS F ratio p>0.05
* F ratio p<0.05

Table 12.18 Men—analysis of variance for minerals: background factors

Characteristic	No. of cases	Adjusted deviations from grand mean and significance of F ratios for:					
		Calcium (mg)	Iron (mg) (Log)	Phosphorus (mg)	Magnesium (mg) (Log)	Potassium (mg)	Sodium (mg)
Grand mean	1064	941	14.1	1455	323	3194	3377
Covariate—Total energy		**	**	**	**	**	**
Correlation coefficient		0.66	0.57	0.77	0.73	0.74	0.72
Age		**	**	**	**	**	NS
16–24	204	−36	−1.0	−67	−18	−170	35
25–34	249	−4	0.1	5	4	58	−38
35–49	343	−5	0.2	5	5	27	17
50–64	268	38	0.4	40	3	41	−13
Region		**	NS	NS	NS	NS	**
Scotland	92	21	0	7	0	14	188
Northern	266	−46	0.2	−16	4	1	72
Central, South West & Wales	359	12	0.2	1	1	16	−8
London & South East	347	17	−0.4	9	−4	−20	−97
Social class of HOH		**	**	**	**	**	NS
I and II	377	54	0.8	62	17	145	−28
IIINM	138	10	0.1	17	7	−3	−92
IIIM	375	−36	−0.4	−40	−11	−74	41
IV and V	174	−49	−1.0	−62	−18	−152	46
Economic status		NS	NS	NS	NS	NS	NS
Receiving benefits	112	−29	−0.3	−24	−1	−49	−72
Working	847	2	0.1	1	0	−2	15
Not working	105	10	−0.2	19	2	69	−44
Unwell and eating affected		NS	NS	NS	NS	NS	NS
Unwell & eating affected	51	7	0	10	−7	52	−5
Not unwell/eating not affected	1013	0	0	0	0	−3	0
% of variance explained		*48%*	*36%*	*62%*	*56%*	*58%*	*53%*

** F ratio $p < 0.01$ NS F ratio $p > 0.05$
*   F ratio $p < 0.05$

Table 12.19 Men—analysis of variance for minerals: including behavioural variables

Characteristic	No. of cases	Adjusted deviations from grand mean and significance of F ratios for:					
		Calcium (mg)	Iron (mg) (Log)	Phosphorus (mg)	Magnesium (mg) (Log)	Potassium (mg)	Sodium (mg)
Grand mean	1066	940	14.1	1453	323	3191	3372
Covariate—Total energy		**	**	**	**	**	**
Correlation coefficient		0.66	0.57	0.77	0.73	0.74	0.72
Age		**	**	**	*	**	NS
16–24	206	−33	−0.9	−50	−9	−116	25
25–34	248	−3	−0.1	0	1	47	−33
35–49	342	−6	0.3	0	3	7	29
50–64	270	35	0.4	38	2	36	−25
Region		**	NS	NS	NS	NS	**
Scotland	92	14	0.1	−1	−3	−8	198
Northern	268	−46	0.2	−21	2	−11	74
Central, South West & Wales	359	8	0.1	−2	1	10	−18
London & South East	347	24	−0.3	18	−1	0	−91
Social class of HOH		**	**	**	**	**	**
I and II	377	40	0.2	26	4	79	−61
IIINM	136	4	0.1	14	7	0	−106
IIIM	376	−22	0.0	−16	−4	−35	71
IV and V	177	−42	−0.6	−34	−6	−95	60
Slimming		**	**	**	**	**	*
On a slimming diet	45	91	1.7	149	36	349	243
Not on a slimming diet	1021	−4	−0.1	−7	−2	−15	−11
Cigarette smoking		NS	**	**	**	**	NS
Smoker	354	−9	−0.8	−31	−10	−59	−46
Non-smoker	712	4	0.4	16	5	29	23
Food supplements		**	**	**	**	**	NS
Taking food supplements	973	80	4.9	109	27	247	1
Not taking supplements	93	−8	−0.5	−10	−3	−24	0
Drinking behaviour		**	**	NS	**	NS	**
Non-drinker	221	48	1.0	15	−17	−50	86
Light drinker	430	18	0.7	−3	−7	−7	76
Heavier drinker	415	−45	−1.3	−5	17	34	−124
Health related diet		**	**	**	**	**	**
None of foods, high salt	155	−57	−1.7	−108	−35	−159	−126
None of foods, low salt	136	−33	−0.6	−79	−23	−68	−137
Some of foods, high salt	291	−2	−0.4	−16	−10	−51	43
Some of foods, low salt	318	2	0.8	17	9	−4	7
All foods, high salt	58	87	0.7	101	30	167	69
All foods, low salt	108	77	1.8	193	65	374	179
% of variance explained		52%	52%	69%	68%	64%	56%

** F ratio $p < 0.01$ NS F ratio $p > 0.05$
* F ratio $p < 0.05$

Table 12.20 Women—analysis of variance for intake of minerals: background factors

Characteristic	No. of cases	Adjusted deviations from grand mean and significance of F ratios for:					
		Calcium (mg)	Iron (mg) (Log)	Phosphorus (mg)	Magnesium (mg) (Log)	Potassium (mg)	Sodium (mg)
Grand mean	1084	730	12.3	1073	237	2436	2354
Covariate—Total energy		**	**	**	**	**	**
Correlation coefficient		0.65	0.42	0.71	0.66	0.63	0.69
Age		**	**	**	**	**	NS
16–24	184	−55	−0.6	−91	−23	−180	−43
25–34	248	−23	−1.3	−27	−1	−78	28
35–49	378	9	0.3	14	4	55	−6
50–64	274	46	1.0	66	11	114	13
Region		NS	NS	NS	NS	NS	**
Scotland	95	−18	0.8	−27	−3	−78	203
Northern	283	−21	0	6	−1	7	57
Central, South West & Wales	361	12	0.1	−3	2	4	−26
London & South East	345	10	−0.3	5	0	11	−76
Social class of HOH		**	**	**	**	**	NS
I and II	382	32	0.3	47	16	113	−35
IIINM	140	4	0.6	21	14	72	−3
IIIM	345	−19	−0.3	−29	−13	−97	34
IV and V	217	−29	−0.4	−51	−17	−90	9
Economic status		*	NS	**	**	**	NS
Receiving benefits	145	−39	0.3	−54	−15	−169	−34
Working	619	7	0.0	13	5	36	2
Not working	320	5	−0.2	0	−2	7	12
Unwell and eating affected		NS	NS	NS	NS	NS	NS
Unwell & eating affected	102	−24	2.9	−23	−1	−65	−31
Not unwell/eating not affected	982	3	−0.3	2	0	7	3
% of variance explained		46%	20%	57%	50%	45%	49%

** F ratio $p < 0.01$ NS F ratio $p > 0.05$
*   F ratio $p < 0.05$

Table 12.21   Women—analysis of variance for intake of minerals: including behavioural variables

Characteristic	No. of cases	Adjusted deviations from grand mean and significance of F ratios for:				
		Calcium (mg)	Iron (mg) (Log)	Phosphorus (mg)	Magnesium (mg) (Log)	Potassium (mg)
Grand mean	1081	729	12.3	1072	237	2435
Covariate—Total energy		**	**	**	**	**
Correlation coefficient		0.65	0.42	0.71	0.66	0.63
Age		**	NS	**	**	**
16–24	184	−46	0.1	−73	−16	−137
25–34	248	−18	−0.9	−25	−1	−87
35–49	376	9	0.3	13	4	51
50–64	273	35	0.3	54	7	102
Social class of HOH		NS	NS	*	**	**
I and II	380	15	−0.3	22	7	58
IIINM	139	−4	0.9	12	12	52
IIIM	345	−9	0.0	−15	−7	−68
IV and V	217	−9	0.0	−22	−7	−28
Economic status		NS	NS	NS	NS	*
Receiving benefits	145	−23	1.1	−25	−4	−101
Working	616	2	−0.3	3	0	9
Not working	320	6	0.0	6	1	28
Slimming		**	**	**	**	**
On a slimming diet	134	76	0.6	120	31	268
Not on a slimming diet	947	−11	−0.1	−17	−4	−38
Cigarette smoking		**	**	**	**	*
Smoker	374	−29	−1.4	−35	−9	−48
Non-smoker	707	16	0.7	19	5	25
Food supplements		**	**	NS	*	NS
Taking food supplements	190	33	6.8	20	9	−2
Not taking supplements	891	−7	−1.5	−4	−2	0
Drinking behaviour		**	NS	NS	*	NS
Non-drinker	378	18	0.2	6	−4	−34
Light drinker	546	3	−0.3	1	1	8
Heavier drinker	157	−53	0.5	−20	7	56
Health related diet		**	**	**	**	**
None of foods, high salt	97	−68	2.3	−84	−32	−234
None of foods, low salt	135	−46	−2.2	86	−30	−178
Some of foods, high salt	218	−19	0.1	−22	−7	−26
Some of foods, low salt	427	5	−0.7	4	1	−2
All foods, high salt	47	50	2.9	93	38	329
All foods, low salt	157	79	1.4	119	42	240
% of variance explained		*51%*	*32%*	*65%*	*62%*	*52%*

** F ratio p<0.01   NS F ratio p>0.05
* F ratio p<0.05

Table 12.22 Women—analysis of variance for intake of minerals: including behavioural variables

Characteristic	No. of cases	Adjusted deviations from grand mean and significance of F ratios for:
		Sodium (mg)
Grand mean	1093	2353
Covariate—Total energy		**
Correlation coefficient		0.69
Age		NS
16–24	186	−41
25–34	250	29
35–49	378	−12
50–64	279	17
Region		**
Scotland	95	211
Northern	286	50
Central, South West & Wales	365	−34
London & South East	347	−63
Social class of HOH		NS
I and II	384	−45
IIINM	140	−10
IIIM	347	41
IV and V	222	19
Slimming		**
On a slimming diet	135	162
Not on a slimming diet	958	−23
Cigarette smoking		NS
Smoker	380	−22
Non-smoker	713	12
Food supplements		NS
Taking food supplements	190	−12
Not taking supplements	903	3
Drinking behaviour		NS
Non-drinker	383	31
Light drinker	552	2
Heavier drinker	158	−81
Health related diet		NS
None of foods, high salt	98	−2
None of foods, low salt	135	−57
Some of foods, high salt	221	12
Some of foods, low salt	434	−25
All foods, high salt	47	118
All foods, low salt	158	66
% of variance explained		*51%*

** F ratio $p < 0.01$ NS F ratio $p > 0.05$
* F ratio $p < 0.05$

Table 12.23 Men—analysis of variance for vitamins: background factors

Characteristic	No. of cases	Retinol equivs (μg) (Log)	Thiamin (mg) (Log)	Riboflavin (mg) (Log)	Niacin equivs (mg) (Log)
		Adjusted deviations from grand mean and significance of F ratios for:			
Grand mean	1064	1677	2.02	2.30	40.9
Covariate—Total energy		**	**	**	**
Correlation coefficient		0.26	0.49	0.51	0.65
Age		**	NS	*	NS
16–24	204	−501	−0.02	−0.07	−0.8
25–34	249	−70	0.30	0.15	0.2
35–49	343	109	−0.14	−0.15	0.2
50–64	268	308	−0.09	0.10	0.2
Region		NS	NS	NS	NS
Scotland	92	−260	−0.22	−0.16	0.6
Northern	266	82	0.29	0.18	1.6
Central, South West & Wales	359	−51	−0.22	−0.13	−1.0
London & South East	347	60	0.06	0.05	0.3
Social class of HOH		*	**	**	**
I and II	377	55	0.51	0.39	1.8
IIINM	138	244	−0.21	−0.06	0.0
IIIM	375	−74	−0.30	−0.23	−0.9
IV and V	174	−154	−0.30	−0.30	−1.8
Economic status		NS	NS	NS	**
Receiving benefits	112	290	−0.12	−0.10	−2.3
Working	847	−30	0.02	0.02	0.4
Not working	105	−69	−0.06	−0.09	−0.6
Unwell and eating affected		NS	NS	NS	NS
Unwell & eating affected	51	244	−0.35	−0.19	−0.2
Not unwell/eating not affected	1013	−12	0.02	0.01	0.0
% of variance explained		*13%*	*26%*	*30%*	*44%*

** *F ratio p < 0.01*
* *F ratio p < 0.05*
NS *F ratio p > 0.05*

199

Table 12.24 Men—analysis of variance for vitamins: including behavioural variables

Characteristic	No. of cases	Retinol equivs (µg) (Log)	Thiamin (mg) (Log)	Riboflavin (mg) (Log)	Niacin equivs (mg) (Log)
		Adjusted deviations from grand mean and significance of F ratios for:			
Grand mean	1060	1679	2.02	2.31	40.9
Covariate—Total energy		**	**	**	**
Correlation coefficient		0.26	0.49	0.51	0.65
Age		**	NS	*	NS
16–24	204	−470	0.07	0.00	0.1
25–34	248	−98	0.20	0.06	−0.1
35–49	341	118	−0.10	−0.12	0.0
50–64	267	300	−0.11	0.09	0.0
Social class of HOH		NS	NS	**	NS
I and II	377	3	0.32	0.25	0.3
IIINM	136	246	−0.16	0.00	0.3
IIIM	373	−41	−0.21	−0.17	−0.2
IV and V	174	−112	−0.13	−0.18	−0.6
Economic status		NS	NS	NS	NS
Receiving benefits	112	324	0.09	0.05	−0.6
Working	843	−31	0.01	0.01	0.2
Not working	105	−97	−0.13	−0.13	−0.8
Slimming		NS	*	**	**
On a slimming diet	44	131	0.09	0.36	6.3
Not on a slimming diet	1016	−6	0.00	−0.02	−0.3
Cigarette smoking		NS	**	NS	**
Smoker	351	−32	−0.18	−0.08	−1.4
Non-smoker	709	16	0.09	0.04	0.7
Food supplements		**	**	**	**
Taking food supplements	92	965	3.39	2.41	13.5
Not taking supplements	968	−92	−0.32	−0.23	−1.3
Drinking behaviour		NS	**	NS	NS
Non-drinker	216	149	0.05	−0.07	−0.2
Light drinker	430	−17	0.28	0.17	−0.1
Heavier drinker	414	−60	−0.31	−0.14	0.2
Health related diet		NS	**	**	**
None of foods, high salt	153	−190	−0.13	−0.13	−2.7
None of foods, low salt	135	−97	−0.23	−0.18	−1.9
Some of foods, high salt	290	64	−0.12	−0.06	−0.6
Some of foods, low salt	316	14	0.27	0.25	0.7
All foods, high salt	58	189	0.85	0.12	4.8
All foods, low salt	108	76	−0.44	−0.22	3.1
% of variance explained		*83%*	*2%*	*2%*	*3%*

** F ratio $p < 0.01$ NS F ratio $p > 0.05$
* F ratio $p < 0.05$

Table 12.25	Men—analysis of variance for vitamin C: background factors		
Characteristic	No. of cases	Adjusted deviations from grand mean and significance of F ratios for:	
		Vitamin C (mg) (Log)	
Grand mean	1064	75.2	
Covariate—Total energy		**	
Correlation coefficient		0.26	
Season		**	
Autumn	272	1.9	
Winter	262	−4.8	
Spring	280	−2.6	
Summer	250	5.9	
Age		NS	
16–24	204	0.1	
25–34	249	5.8	
35–49	343	−0.3	
50–64	268	−5.1	
Region		NS	
Scotland	92	−3.7	
Northern	266	1.9	
Central, South West & Wales	359	−4.4	
London & South East	347	4.0	
Social class of HOH		**	
I and II	377	20.3	
IIINM	138	−0.8	
IIIM	375	−11.7	
IV and V	174	−18.1	
Economic status		**	
Receiving benefits	112	−12.4	
Working	847	1.8	
Not working	105	−1.2	
Unwell and eating affected		NS	
Unwell & eating affected	51	−15.0	
Not unwell/eating not affected	1013	0.8	
% of variance explained		*19%*	

** F ratio p < 0.01   NS F ratio p > 0.05
* F ratio p < 0.05

Table 12.26	Men—analysis of variance for vitamin C: including behavioural variables		
Characteristic	No. of cases	Adjusted deviations from grand mean and significance of F ratios for:	
		Vitamin C (mg) (Log)	
Grand mean	1060	75.2	
Covariate—Total energy		**	
Correlation coefficient		0.26	
Season		**	
Autumn	271	−1.1	
Winter	260	−4.2	
Spring	279	−2.8	
Summer	250	8.8	
Social class of HOH		**	
I and II	377	13.4	
IIINM	136	0.6	
IIIM	373	−7.9	
IV and V	174	−12.6	
Economic status		NS	
Receiving benefits	112	−5.6	
Working	843	1.2	
Not working	105	−3.8	
Slimming		**	
On a slimming diet	44	10.7	
Not on a slimming diet	1016	−0.5	
Cigarette smoking		**	
Smoker	351	−0.3	
Non-smoker	709	0.2	
Food supplements		**	
Taking food supplements	92	100.0	
Not taking supplements	968	−9.5	
Drinking behaviour		**	
Non-drinker	216	−5.2	
Light drinker	430	6.8	
Heavier drinker	414	−4.4	
Health related diet		**	
None of foods, high salt	153	−13.4	
None of foods, low salt	135	−3.9	
Some of foods, high salt	290	−3.8	
Some of foods, low salt	316	3.4	
All foods, high salt	58	3.2	
All foods, low salt	108	22.6	
% of variance explained		*36%*	

** F ratio p < 0.01   NS F ratio p > 0.05
* F ratio p < 0.05

Table 12.27 Men—analysis of variance for vitamins B6, B12 and folate: background factors

Characteristic	No. of cases	Adjusted deviations from grand mean and significance of F ratios for:		
		Vitamin B6 (mg) (Log)	Vitamin B12 (µg) (Log)	Folate (µg) (Log)
Grand mean	1064	2.69	7.33	312.6
Covariate—Total energy		**	**	**
Correlation coefficient		0.58	0.36	0.64
Age		NS	**	*
16–24	204	0.08	−1.16	−10.7
25–34	249	0.25	−0.17	7.9
35–49	343	−0.17	0.18	3.6
50–64	268	−0.08	0.82	−3.7
Region		*	NS	*
Scotland	92	0.11	−0.44	−9.4
Northern	266	0.25	0.36	13.1
Central, South West & Wales	359	−0.18	−0.28	1.5
London & South East	347	−0.03	0.13	−9.1
Social class of HOH		**	NS	**
I and II	377	0.29	0.01	7.5
IIINM	138	−0.16	0.45	0.3
IIIM	375	−0.16	−0.12	−0.3
IV and V	174	−0.16	−0.12	−15.8
Economic status		NS	NS	NS
Receiving benefits	112	0.16	0.52	6.8
Working	847	−0.01	−0.05	−0.7
Not working	105	−0.07	−0.11	−1.5
Unwell and eating affected		*	NS	NS
Unwell & eating affected	51	−0.39	0.67	−12.5
Not unwell/eating not affected	1013	0.02	−0.03	0.6
% of variance explained		*34%*	*15%*	*42%*

** F ratio p<0.01   NS F ratio p>0.05
* F ratio p<0.05

Table 12.28 Men—analysis of variance for vitamin B6: including behavioural variables

Characteristic	No. of cases	Adjusted deviations from grand mean and significance of F ratios for:
		Vitamin B6 (mg) (Log)
Grand mean	1066	2.69
Covariate—Total energy		**
Correlation coefficient		0.58
Region		*
Scotland	92	0.19
Northern	268	0.18
Central, South West & Wales	359	−0.15
London & South East	347	−0.04
Social class of HOH		NS
I and II	377	0.16
IIINM	136	−0.08
IIIM	376	−0.13
IV and V	177	−0.01
Unwell & eating affected		NS
Unwell & eating affected	51	−0.31
Not unwell/eating not affected	1015	0.02
Slimming		*
On a slimming diet	45	0.19
Not on a slimming diet	1015	−0.01
Cigarette smoking		NS
Smoker	45	−0.05
Non-smoker	1021	0.02
Food supplements		**
Taking food supplements	93	2.25
Not taking supplements	973	−0.21
Drinking behaviour		**
Non-drinker	221	−0.40
Light drinker	430	−0.02
Heavier drinker	415	0.23
Health related diet		NS
None of foods, high salt	155	0.10
None of foods, low salt	136	−0.11
Some of foods, high salt	291	−0.09
Some of foods, low salt	318	0.17
All foods, high salt	58	−0.08
All foods, low salt	108	−0.21
% of variance explained		*47%*

** F ratio p<0.01   NS F ratio p>0.05
* F ratio p<0.05

Table 12.29   Men—analysis of variance for vitamin B12 and folate: including behavioural variables

Characteristic	No. of cases	Adjusted deviations from grand mean and significance of F ratios for:	
		Vitamin B12 (μg) (Log)	Folate (μg) (Log)
Grand mean	1066	7.34	312.5
Covariate—Total energy		**	**
Correlation coefficient		0.36	0.64
Age		**	NS
16–24	206	−1.04	−0.1
25–34	248	−0.21	4.7
35–49	342	0.15	−0.9
50–64	270	0.80	−3.1
Region		NS	*
Scotland	92	−0.40	−12.8
Northern	268	0.20	8.1
Central, South West & Wales	359	−0.25	3.3
London & South East	347	0.21	−6.3
Social class of HOH		NS	NS
I and II	377	−0.13	−1.3
IIINM	136	0.53	3.2
IIIM	376	−0.10	1.8
IV and V	177	0.09	−3.5
Slimming		**	**
On a slimming diet	45	2.12	54.5
Not on a slimming diet	1021	−0.09	−2.4
Cigarette smoking		NS	**
Smoker	354	0.13	−5.5
Non-smoker	712	−0.06	2.7
Food supplements		**	**
Taking food supplements	93	1.98	37.6
Not taking supplements	973	−0.19	−3.6
Drinking behaviour		**	**
Non-drinker	221	−0.10	−41.4
Light drinker	430	−0.24	−18.8
Heavier drinker	415	0.31	41.5
Health related diet		NS	**
None of foods, high salt	155	−0.14	−12.7
None of foods, low salt	136	−0.28	−7.0
Some of foods, high salt	291	0.10	−6.9
Some of foods, low salt	318	0.11	−1.6
All foods, high salt	58	0.42	15.1
All foods, low salt	108	−0.28	42.0
		18%	58%

** F ratio $p < 0.01$ NS F ratio $p > 0.05$
* F ratio $p < 0.05$

Table 12.30 Women—analysis of variance for intake of vitamins: background factors

Characteristic	No. of cases	Adjusted deviations from grand mean and significance of F ratios for:			
		Retinol equivs (μg) (Log)	Thiamin (mg) (Log)	Riboflavin (mg) (Log)	Niacin equivs (mg) (Log)
Grand mean	1084	1488	1.62	1.84	30.4
Covariate—Total energy		**	**	**	**
Correlation coefficient		0.30	0.45	0.42	0.56
Age		**	*	**	**
16–24	184	−434	−0.20	−0.33	−2.1
25–34	248	−179	−0.33	−0.14	−1.7
35–49	378	71	−0.11	0.08	−0.4
50–64	274	355	0.59	0.24	3.5
Region		NS	NS	NS	NS
Scotland	95	−87	1.47	0.05	5.8
Northern	283	158	−0.01	0.07	0.3
Central, South West & Wales	361	−28	−0.22	−0.12	−1.5
London & South East	345	−77	−0.17	0.06	−0.3
Social class of HOH		**	NS	**	**
I and II	382	196	−0.02	0.06	1.4
IIINM	140	−26	−0.21	−0.02	0.5
IIIM	345	−51	0.26	0.05	0.0
IV and V	217	−248	−0.24	−0.17	−2.1
Economic status		*	NS	**	**
Receiving benefits	145	11	−0.13	−0.15	−2.6
Working	619	12	0.21	0.12	1.4
Not working	320	−28	−0.35	−0.15	−1.6
Unwell and eating affected		NS	NS	NS	NS
Unwell & eating affected	102	−123	−0.19	−0.16	−1.5
Not unwell/eating not affected	982	13	0.02	0.02	0.2
% of variance explained		18%	22%	23%	36%

** F ratio p<0.01   NS F ratio p>0.05
* F ratio p<0.05

Table 12.31 Women—analysis of variance for intake of vitamins: including behavioural variables

Characteristic	No. of cases	Adjusted deviations from grand mean and significance of F ratios for:			
		Retinol equivs (µg) (Log)	Thiamin (mg) (Log)	Riboflavin (mg) (Log)	Niacin equivs (mg) (Log)
Grand mean	1081	1486	1.62	1.84	30.33
Covariate—Total energy		**	**	**	**
Correlation coefficient		0.30	0.45	0.42	0.56
Age		**	NS	**	*
16–24	184	−416	−0.13	−0.17	−1.3
25–34	248	−181	−0.19	−0.09	−1.2
35–49	376	66	−0.15	0.07	−0.6
50–64	273	354	0.47	0.10	2.8
Social class of HOH		**	NS	NS	*
I and II	380	202	0.02	−0.04	1.2
IIINM	139	−61	−0.13	−0.05	−0.3
IIIM	345	−38	0.27	0.12	0.2
IV and V	217	−255	−0.37	−0.08	−2.3
Economic status		NS	NS	NS	**
Receiving benefits	145	39	−0.21	−0.06	−2.4
Working	616	3	0.22	0.07	1.2
Not working	320	−23	−0.33	−0.11	−1.2
Slimming		NS	NS	**	**
On a slimming diet	134	192	−0.21	0.21	2.0
Not on a slimming diet	947	−27	0.03	−0.03	−0.3
Cigarette smoking		NS	NS	**	NS
Smoker	374	−17	0.16	−0.14	0.5
Non-smoker	707	9	−0.08	0.07	−0.2
Food supplements		**	**	**	**
Taking food supplements	190	358	1.80	1.21	8.7
Not taking supplements	891	−76	−0.38	−0.26	−1.9
Drinking behaviour		NS	**	NS	NS
Non-drinker	378	85	0.42	0.02	1.1
Light drinker	546	−97	−0.19	0.00	−0.9
Heavier drinker	157	133	−0.33	−0.03	0.4
Health related diet		NS	*	**	**
None of foods, high salt	97	−83	1.29	−0.04	4.0
None of foods, low salt	135	−13	−0.29	−0.21	−2.3
Some of foods, high salt	218	−10	−0.24	−0.16	−0.9
Some of foods, low salt	427	93	−0.07	0.01	−0.5
All foods, high salt	47	−100	0.04	0.01	2.9
All foods, low salt	157	−147	−0.02	0.40	1.2
% of variance explained		*21%*	*38%*	*38%*	*44%*

** F ratio $p < 0.01$ NS F ratio $p > 0.05$
* F ratio $p < 0.05$

Table 12.32 Women—analysis of variance for intake of vitamin C: background factors

Characteristic	No. of cases	Adjusted deviations from grand mean and significance of F ratios for:
		Vitamin C (mg) (Log)
Grand mean	1084	72.1
Covariate—Total energy		**
Correlation coefficient		0.31
Season		*
Autumn	270	−0.8
Winter	275	−2.4
Spring	274	−0.2
Summer	265	3.5
Age		**
16–24	184	−7.9
25–34	248	−4.0
35–49	378	3.1
50–64	274	4.6
Region		NS
Scotland	95	6.4
Northern	283	−7.6
Central, South West & Wales	361	2.7
London & South East	345	1.7
Social class of HOH		**
I and II	382	20.2
IIINM	140	1.2
IIIM	345	−16.1
IV and V	217	−10.7
Economic status		**
Receiving benefits	145	−10.3
Working	619	1.0
Not working	320	2.7
Unwell and eating affected		*
Unwell & eating affected	102	−4.2
Not unwell/eating not affected	982	0.4
% of variance explained		*21%*

** F ratio p<0.01   NS F ratio p>0.05
* F ratio p<0.05

Table 12.33 Women—analysis of variance for intake of vitamin C: including behavioural variables

Characteristic	No. of cases	Adjusted deviations from grand mean and significance of F ratios for:
		Vitamin C (mg) (Log)
Grand mean	1081	72.1
Covariate—Total energy		**
Correlation coefficient		0.31
Season		*
Autumn	269	−0.4
Winter	273	−1.3
Spring	274	−1.9
Summer	265	3.7
Age		**
16–24	184	−2.7
25–34	248	−2.2
35–49	376	3.4
50–64	273	−0.8
Social class of HOH		**
I and II	380	14.9
IIINM	139	−1.5
IIIM	345	−12.0
IV and V	217	−6.0
Economic status		NS
Receiving benefits	145	−4.0
Working	616	−1.4
Not working	320	4.5
Slimming		**
On a slimming diet	134	10.1
Not on a slimming diet	947	−1.4
Cigarette smoking		**
Smoker	374	−10.1
Non-smoker	707	5.4
Food supplements		**
Taking food supplements	190	55.0
Not taking supplements	891	−11.7
Drinking behaviour		**
Non-drinker	378	−2.6
Light drinker	546	−1.3
Heavier drinker	157	10.8
Health related diet		**
None of foods, high salt	97	−14.2
None of foods, low salt	135	−9.2
Some of foods, high salt	218	2.6
Some of foods, low salt	427	2.9
All foods, high salt	47	−6.0
All foods, low salt	157	7.1
% of variance explained		*36%*

** F ratio p<0.01   NS F ratio p>0.05
* F ratio p<0.05

Table 12.34 Women—analysis of variance for intake of vitamins B6, B12 and folate: background factors

Characteristic	No. of cases	Vitamin B6 (mg) (Log)	Vitamin B12 (µg) (Log)	Folate (µg) (Log)
Grand mean	1084	2.87	5.35	219
Covariate—Total energy		**	**	**
Correlation coefficient		0.31	0.31	0.53
Age		NS	**	**
16–24	184	−1.16	−1.02	−1.2
25–34	248	0.04	−0.69	−8.4
35–49	378	0.48	0.39	0.8
50–64	274	0.09	0.78	7.3
Region		*	NS	NS
Scotland	95	−0.87	−0.23	−5.9
Northern	283	−0.80	0.63	−6.9
Central, South West & Wales	361	−0.54	−0.18	8.4
London & South East	345	1.46	−0.27	−1.5
Social class of HOH		*	**	**
I and II	382	0.29	0.62	9.9
IIINM	140	0.55	−0.09	1.3
IIIM	345	0.00	−0.19	−3.6
IV and V	217	−0.86	−0.73	−12.6
Economic status		NS	NS	**
Receiving benefits	145	−0.23	0.54	−11.4
Working	619	0.31	0.02	−0.8
Not working	320	−0.50	−0.28	6.6
Unwell and eating affected		NS	NS	**
Unwell & eating affected	102	−0.51	−0.25	−20.0
Not unwell/eating not affected	982	0.05	0.03	2.1
% of variance explained		12%	15%	33%

** F ratio p<0.01 NS F ratio p>0.05
* F ratio p<0.05

Table 12.35 Women—analysis of variance for intake of vitamin B6: including behavioural variables

Characteristic	No. of cases	Vitamin B6 (mg) (Log)
Grand mean	1093	2.86
Covariate—Total energy		**
Correlation coefficient		0.31
Region		*
Scotland	95	−0.98
Northern	286	−0.68
Central, South West & Wales	365	−0.37
London & South East	347	1.22
Social class of HOH		NS
I and II	384	0.25
IIINM	140	0.59
IIIM	347	0.10
IV and V	222	−0.96
Slimming		NS
On a slimming diet	135	0.19
Not on a slimming diet	958	−0.03
Cigarette smoking		NS
Smoker	380	0.08
Non-smoker	713	−0.04
Food supplements		**
Taking food supplements	190	5.53
Not taking supplements	903	−1.16
Drinking behaviour		NS
Non-drinker	383	0.62
Light drinker	552	−0.38
Heavier drinker	158	−0.17
Health related diet		NS
None of foods, high salt	98	0.42
None of foods, low salt	135	−0.77
Some of foods, high salt	221	0.78
Some of foods, low salt	434	−0.35
All foods, high salt	47	−0.95
All foods, low salt	158	0.56
% of variance explained		26%

** F ratio p<0.01 NS F ratio p>0.05
* F ratio p<0.05

Table 12.36 Women—analysis of variance for intake of vitamin B12 and folate: including behavioural variables

Characteristic	No. of cases	Vitamin B12 (μg) (Log)	Folate (μg) (Log)
		Adjusted deviations from grand mean and significance of F ratios for:	
Grand mean	1081	5.34	219.0
Covariate—Total energy		**	**
Correlation coefficient		0.31	0.53
Age		*	**
16–24	184	−0.99	3.3
25–34	248	−0.65	−7.7
35–49	376	0.36	−0.3
50–64	273	0.76	5.2
Social class of HOH		*	NS
I and II	380	0.62	4.2
IIINM	139	−0.14	0.7
IIIM	345	−0.16	−0.2
IV and V	217	−0.75	−7.6
Economic status		NS	NS
Receiving benefits	145	0.60	−5.5
Working	616	0.00	−3.4
Not working	320	−0.27	9.0
Unwell and eating affected		–	**
Unwell & eating affected	102	–	−16.9
Not unwell/eating not affected	979	–	1.8
Slimming		*	**
On a slimming diet	134	0.53	22.6
Not on a slimming diet	947	−0.07	−3.2
Cigarette smoking		NS	*
Smoker	374	−0.14	−3.0
Non-smoker	707	0.07	1.6
Food supplements		**	**
Taking food supplements	190	0.72	22.8
Not taking supplements	891	−0.15	−4.9
Drinking behaviour		NS	**
Non-drinker	378	0.36	−2.2
Light drinker	546	−0.34	−3.1
Heavier drinker	157	0.33	16.0
Health related diet		NS	**
None of foods, high salt	97	0.12	6.5
None of foods, low salt	135	−0.01	−24.0
Some of foods, high salt	218	−0.12	−7.8
Some of foods, low salt	427	0.09	−2.6
All foods, high salt	47	−0.53	20.7
All foods, low salt	157	0.01	28.4
% of variance explained		*16%*	*41%*

** F ratio $p < 0.01$ NS F ratio $p > 0.05$
* F ratio $p < 0.05$

13 Classification of types of diet

13.1 Methodology

Chapter 6 showed that there was some variation by sex, age, social class and region in the types of food eaten and in the amount consumed by members of the sample. In this chapter the method of principal components analysis is used to summarise the mass of information on average consumption of different foods and attempts to identify the main types of dietary behaviour. These types of dietary behaviour are then related to the main characteristics of the sample, using analysis of variance, in order to identify those characteristics which are statistically significant in explaining variation in behaviour.

The technique of principal components analysis was used by Gex-Fabry et al[1] to identify three distinct eating patterns using dietary information from Swiss adults. The technique has, however, not been used to identify eating patterns in Great Britain.

Principal components analysis is a technique used to identify a relatively small number of components, or factors, that represent the relationships among a set of interrelated variables. The aim is to summarise patterns of intercorrelations among variables and to identify subgroups of variables that are closely related to each other but relatively independent of other subgroups. The technique therefore attempts to explain complex phenomena by identifying underlying dimensions or components; in this case, data on the amount of different types of food consumed are summarised by identifying different aspects of dietary behaviour.

In its operation, the principal components analysis identifies as the first component that combination of the observed variables which accounts for the largest amount of variation in the sample; subsequent components account for progressively smaller amounts of the variation and are uncorrelated with each other. The components that have been identified in this process can then be interpreted by means of their correlations, or factor loadings, with the original variables in the analysis (quantities of foods). Foods which have large loadings on a component are closely related to that component, so greater attention is given to these variables when attempting to describe the components.

Each individual in the sample can be attributed a score on each of the components, or dietary types, identified; these scores are equivalent to the values subjects would have recorded if the components could have been measured directly. The mean value across the total sample for each component is zero. Each individual within the sample has a score on each component, and it is possible for an individual to have high scores on a number of different components. The scores can be used in subsequent analysis to identify those characteristics of informants which were more likely to be identified with each type of dietary behaviour.

The average intake of food from each of the defined groups provided a suitable, albeit large, set of variables from which to identify types of dietary behaviour. A number of the food types were identified as having a relatively low correlation with other foods (by having small values for the measure of sampling adequacy) and so were less likely to be helpful in identifying components; these food types were combined with others in the same main group. This provided a set of variables which was more suitable for a principal components analysis and which was also more manageable in size. A total of 54 food types were used in the analysis and Table 13.1 shows for each of these foods the average intake and standard deviation (grams per week) for the total sample. *(Table 13.1)*

The first five components of the principal components analysis accounted for a total of 22.6% of the total variation in food intake between individuals in the sample. Since the next component identified by the analysis added less than 3% to the total variance explained, subsequent analysis used only the first five components.

In order to obtain factors which could more readily be interpreted, the first five components identified were rotated to achieve a simpler structure. The varimax method of rotation was used, which attempts to minimise the number of variables which have high loadings on each component and hence enables the factors to be more easily differentiated from each other. Use of rotation does not affect the total percentage of variance explained although it does redistribute the explained variance across the components.

13.2 Results of the principal components analysis

Table 13.2 shows the factor loadings or correlations of the various food groups on each of the five rotated components. The loadings indicate the strength of the relationship between the individual food types and the principal components identified; small loadings of less than 0.20 have been omitted in order to highlight the stronger associations. *(Table 13.2)*

In attempting to describe the characteristics of the dietary types represented by the components it is also helpful to consider the correlation between individuals' scores on each of the five factors and their recorded intake of a number of major nutrients. Table 13.3 shows those correlation coefficients which were significantly different from zero (p<0.01 or p<0.05).

(*Table 13.3*)

Component 1
For the first component the strongest positive loadings were for wholemeal bread, high-fibre breakfast cereals, reduced fat milks, polyunsaturated margarine and low fat spreads, salad vegetables and fresh fruit. Foods with negative loadings were white bread, whole milk and cream, butter and sugar. The positive loadings are associated mainly with high fibre and reduced fat products, and other foods with a healthy image such as fruit and salad vegetables. The first component therefore appears to be related to a more 'health-conscious' diet.

The first component had a strong positive correlation with intakes of dietary vitamin C, dietary iron, fibre and the P:S ratio, and a strong negative correlation with saturated fatty acids as a percentage of food energy. Component 1 was also the only component identified which showed a negative association with intake of fat, sugars and of fat as a percentage of food energy, although the correlation coefficients were relatively small. The correlations with intakes of sodium, alcohol, protein and calcium were also less strong for component 1 than for other components.

Component 2
Table 13.2 shows that a greater number of foods had strong loadings (> +0.2) with the second component of the diet, and these covered a range of foods. Those with the largest positive loadings were white bread, bacon and ham, sausages, meat pies, peas, beans and carrots, leafy green vegetables, potatoes in all forms, and beer and cider. The only food group with a negative loading in excess of −0.2 was yoghurt and cottage cheese.

This second component showed strong positive correlations with total energy intake and intake of alcohol, fat, protein, fibre and sodium. It was also positively related to intakes of calcium, iron and sugars, and showed a weak negative correlation with the P:S ratio. Component 2 appears, therefore, to represent a higher energy diet with high alcohol intake. The foods loading most strongly on the component might be considered to be a traditional British range, with meat, vegetables, white bread and potatoes being of particular importance.

Component 3
The third component was similar to the second in having a strong association with total energy intake, but was more strongly positively correlated with intake of sugars and was negatively associated with alcohol intake. This component was positively associated with intakes of fat, fibre, protein, sodium, calcium and iron, but negatively associated with fat as a percentage of food energy and the P:S ratio.

Foods which had strong loadings on component 3 were puddings, buns, cakes and pastries, biscuits and breakfast cereals, as well as preserves, confectionery and canned fruit. The component therefore represents a diet with high total energy and sugars intakes, particularly derived from puddings and sweet items. It can be characterised as a traditional British diet which emphasises puddings and cakes.

Component 4
All alcoholic drinks except beer and cider showed strong loadings on the fourth component. Foods with large positive loadings were pasta, rice and cereals, cheeses, non-fried fish, salad and other vegetables, fruit juice and coffee. Chips and tea showed negative loadings. The range of foods mentioned suggests that this component represents a varied, less traditional diet, with wines and spirits being of importance in the diet.

Component 4 was less strongly correlated with total energy intake than components 2 and 3, but was strongly associated with alcohol intake. The correlations with intakes of fat, sugars, fibre, sodium, calcium and iron were also weaker than for components 2 and 3. This component also had a strong positive association with intakes of protein and vitamin C.

Component 5
Foods which had strong positive loadings on component 5 were burgers and kebabs, meat pies, chips, baked beans, savoury snacks, confectionery and soft drinks. Only tea and leafy green vegetables had negative loadings greater than −0.2. The factor appears, therefore, to represent a diet in which 'fast foods' and snack foods were important. Component 5 was similar to component 4 in its positive correlation with intakes of energy, fat and sodium, but was not so strongly associated with intakes of alcohol, iron, calcium and vitamin C.

13.3 Characteristics of the sample associated with these dietary components
As part of the principal components analysis, members of the sample were attributed a score on each of the five components identified; these scores represented the values which subjects would have recorded if the components could have been measured directly. In order to explore the main characteristics of informants which were associated with the five components of diet, analysis of variance was carried out for the factor scores of individuals on each of the components. In interpreting the following analysis it should, however, be emphasised that the components represent types of dietary behaviour rather than people. Any individual could score highly on a number of the components, or indeed on none of them.

As in Chapter 12, the analysis of variance was performed in two stages. At the first stage a number of variables representing background characteristics of the sample were used; these were age, social class, region, and a variable combining receipt of benefits by the household and the informant's employment status. At the second stage a small number of behavioural variables were also included in the analysis considered; these were smoking behaviour, and whether the informant was either on a slimming diet or taking food supplements. At both stages total energy intake was included in the analysis as a covariate.

Scores on all of the components other than that associated with a 'health-conscious' diet showed significant differences between men and women; men had a higher average factor score on each of components 2 to 5. Since the characteristics explaining nutrient intake differ for men and women, their analyses of variance for component scores were undertaken separately.

Tables 13.4 and 13.5 show the results of the analysis of variance, for men and women respectively, using the background social and demographic characteristics. Tables 13.6 and 13.7 show the results after inclusion of behavioural variables.

Component 1
Component 1 was related to relatively few of the background characteristics. This dietary pattern was more likely to be found among men and women in higher social classes and among older women (aged 50 or more), and less likely to be followed by women in households receiving benefits. However, these characteristics explained relatively little of the total variance in factor scores (6% for men and 9% for women).

Inclusion of behavioural variables approximately doubled the percentage of variance explained, to 14% for men and 17% for women. All three of the behavioural variables were significant both for men and women, and the pattern was similar; this type of diet was more likely to be followed by slimmers, non-smokers and those taking food supplements.

Component 2
The second component, representing a traditional meat and vegetable diet, was well explained by the initial model, especially for men. The explanatory power of the model mainly reflected, however, the strong correlation between this component and total energy intake. This type of diet was likely to be found among men and women in manual social classes and those aged 35 or over. The dietary behaviour associated with component 2 was also more likely to be found among men in Northern or Central and South West England and Wales, and men living in households receiving benefits.

The variance explained was little affected by the inclusion of behavioural variables, although this type of dietary behaviour was also more likely to be followed by smokers and less likely to be found among women taking food supplements. Men on a slimming diet also had higher scores on this component.

Component 3
The model based on background variables again explained a substantial percentage of the total variance in scores on the component representing a 'traditional puddings and cakes' diet; the amount of variance explained was, however, again due largely to the inclusion of total energy intake as a covariate in the analysis. This type of diet was associated with older men and women (aged 50 or more), and those living in the Central and South West regions and Wales and in London and the South East. It was also more likely to be found among men in higher social classes, and women who were neither working nor in households receiving benefits.

The explanatory power of the model was improved little by the addition of the behavioural variables although this dietary behaviour was more likely to be found among non-smokers than smokers.

Component 4
The fourth component was characterised as a diet with high consumption of wines and spirits and a variety of non-traditional foods. This diet was more likely to be followed by men and women in Social Classes I and II, and by those in Scotland and South East England. Older men and working women were also more likely to have a higher score on this component.

Again the behavioural variables added little to the explanatory power of the model. Both men and women on slimming diets were, however, more likely than non-slimmers to follow this type of dietary pattern.

Component 5
Variation in scores on the fifth component was strongly associated with the age of informant; it was more likely to be found among informants aged under 25 years. Men in Scotland, working women, and women in lower social classes were also more likely to follow this type of dietary behaviour. None of the behavioural variables used was significant in explaining variation in this component.

13.4 Summary
Principal components analysis identified five main components of diet which explained 22.6% of the total variance in amounts of different food groups eaten.

The first component related to a 'health-conscious' diet and was more likely to be associated with those in higher social classes, slimmers, non-smokers, and those taking food supplements. The second component had a strong positive correlation with energy and alcohol intakes, and was characterised as a traditional meat and vegetable diet. This type of diet was more likely to be found among those in manual social classes, informants aged 35 or over, and among smokers.

The third component was, like the second, associated with high total energy intake but not with high alcohol intakes. Sweet items such as cakes, puddings and bisits were of particular importance within this type of dietary behaviour. It tended to be associated with older informants (aged 50 or more), non-smokers, and those living in the Central and South West regions, Wales, London and the South East.

The diet represented by the fourth component was strongly correlated with alcohol intakes; it was associated with wines and spirits and with a range of non traditional foods. This type of dietary behaviour was more likely to be found among those in Social Classes I and II, those on a slimming diet and informants

living in South East England. The final component identified was associated with fast foods and snacks, and was more likely to be followed by informants under the age of 25.

Reference

1 Gex-Fabry M, Raymond L, and Jeanneret O. Multivariate analysis of dietary patterns in 939 Swiss adults. Socio-demographic parameters and alcohol consumption profiles. *Int J Epidemiol* 1988; 17(3): 548–555.

Table 13.1   Mean intake and standard deviation (grams per week) for food types
Diary sample

Food	Mean (g/wk)	Standard deviation	Food	Mean (g/wk)	Standard deviation
Pasta, rice and cereals	235.2	329.6	Salad vegetables	238.5	272.1
White bread	458.0	429.2	Peas, beans and carrots	206.9	188.3
Wholemeal and other bread	304.7	375.8	Baked beans	101.2	156.3
High fibre breakfast cereals	102.3	218.8	Leafy green vegetables	110.2	140.8
Other breakfast cereals	40.8	94.1	Other vegetables	294.2	304.9
Biscuits	100.4	126.0	Potato chips	290.7	316.7
Buns, cakes and pastries	225.8	242.8	Other fried/roast potatoes/potato products	106.5	153.4
Ice cream	45.1	87.3	Other potatoes	486.4	388.6
Puddings	181.9	268.0	Savoury snacks	40.9	65.5
Whole milk and cream	1204.4	1107.6			
Reduced fat milks	435.0	829.6	Apples, oranges and bananas	329.4	425.8
Yoghurt and cottage cheese	89.9	199.5	Canned fruit	42.2	114.8
Other cheeses	110.7	113.5	Unsalted nuts and mixes	7.8	39.9
Eggs	159.9	155.8	Other fruit and nuts	131.5	262.4
Butter	46.8	67.9			
Polyunsaturated margarine and low fat spreads	42.9	70.8	Sugar	125.8	181.0
Other margarine and spreads	39.8	68.7	Preserves	38.2	66.6
			Confectionery	74.1	115.7
Bacon and ham	111.2	120.7			
Beef and veal	258.1	274.5	Fruit juice	266.7	473.7
Lamb and pork	130.5	198.1	Soft drinks	800.2	1301.4
Coated chicken	13.6	55.6	Spirits and liqueurs	35.8	124.5
Chicken and turkey	164.0	211.8	Wine	172.2	381.5
Liver and products	28.7	68.9	Fortified wine	31.1	124.5
Burgers and kebabs	48.3	116.3	Beer and cider	1876.6	3882.5
Sausages	74.5	108.9	Coffee	2725.4	4677.2
Meat pies	134.5	192.5	Tea	3651.0	3012.5
Other meat products	90.9	173.6			
Fried white fish	81.8	119.9			
Other white and oily fish	104.8	159.4	Miscellaneous	409.3	406.1

Table 13.2 Factor loadings (>0.2) of food groups for each rotated component
Diary sample

Food	Component 1	2	3	4	5
Pasta, rice and cereals				0.25	
White bread	−0.44	0.47			
Wholemeal and other bread	0.58				
High fibre breakfast cereals	0.31		0.27		
Other breakfast cereals			0.39		
Biscuits			0.42		
Buns, cakes and pastries			0.60		
Ice cream			0.38		
Puddings			0.53		
Whole milk and cream	−0.48		0.39		
Reduced fat milks	0.56				
Yoghurt and cottage cheese	0.24	−0.23			
Other cheeses				0.28	
Eggs		0.29			
Butter	−0.38				
Polyunsaturated margarine and low fat spreads	0.55				
Other margarine and spreads		0.27			
Bacon and ham		0.40			
Beef and veal		0.26			
Lamb and pork		0.22			
Coated chicken					
Chicken and turkey					
Liver and products					
Burgers and kebabs					0.41
Sausages		0.40			
Meat pies		0.31			0.28
Other meat products					
Fried white fish					
Other white and oily fish				0.41	
Salad vegetables	0.37			0.34	
Peas, beans and carrots		0.46			
Baked beans		0.29			0.30
Leafy green vegetables		0.33			−0.33
Other vegetables	0.26			0.36	
Potato chips	−0.22	0.32		−0.28	0.42
Other fried/roast potatoes/potato products		0.31			
Other potatoes		0.52			
Savoury snacks					0.55
Apples, oranges and bananas	0.46				
Canned fruit			0.31		
Unsalted nuts and mixes					
Other fruit and nuts	0.29			0.33	
Sugar	−0.44	0.27			
Preserves			0.46		
Confectionery			0.30		0.49
Fruit juice	0.25			0.32	
Soft drinks					0.57
Spirits and liqueurs				0.49	
Wine				0.67	
Fortified wine				0.40	
Beer and cider		0.45	−0.29		
Coffee				0.25	
Tea			0.23	−0.23	−0.41
Miscellaneous		0.22			

Table 13.3 Correlation between component scores and nutrient intakes for diary sample

Nutrient	Pearson correlation coefficients and significance level for:				
	Component 1	Component 2	Component 3	Component 4	Component 5
Total energy	NS	0.69**	0.42**	0.23**	0.28**
Alcohol	−0.04*	0.41**	−0.29**	0.36**	0.15**
Total fat	−0.07**	0.61**	0.44**	0.20**	0.25**
Fat as % of food energy	−0.19**	0.11**	−0.12**	0.17**	0.04*
Saturated fatty acids as % food energy	−0.45**	NS	0.13**	0.18**	−0.10**
Polyunsaturated:saturated fatty acids	0.46**	−0.04*	−0.16**	NS	0.11**
Sugars	−0.05**	0.28**	0.64**	0.10**	0.22**
Fibre	0.49**	0.47**	0.44**	0.11**	0.06**
Protein	0.19**	0.67**	0.30**	0.30**	0.06**
Dietary sodium	0.08**	0.68**	0.32**	0.15**	0.21**
Dietary calcium[a]	0.15**	0.33**	0.57**	0.22**	0.07**
Dietary iron[a]	0.29**	0.38**	0.38**	0.26**	NS
Dietary vitamin C[a]	0.42**	0.07**	0.19**	0.41**	0.04*

** $p < 0.01$ NS $p > 0.05$
* $p < 0.05$
a *Intake excluding supplements*

Table 13.4 Men—analysis of variance for component scores: background factors

Characteristic	No. of cases	Adjusted deviations from grand mean and significance of F ratios for:				
		Component 1	Component 2	Component 3	Component 4	Component 5
Grand mean		0.02	0.58	0.07	0.07	0.14
Covariate—Total energy		NS	**	**	**	**
Age		NS	**	**	**	**
16–24	204	−0.11	−0.09	−0.20	−0.31	0.98
25–34	249	0.07	−0.10	−0.18	−0.04	0.36
35–49	343	0.06	0.10	0.00	0.02	−0.29
50–64	268	−0.05	0.04	0.32	0.25	−0.71
Region		NS	**	**	**	**
Scotland	92	−0.01	−0.17	−0.06	0.28	0.34
Northern	266	0.12	0.06	−0.20	−0.16	0.04
Central, South West & Wales	359	0.03	0.08	0.09	−0.14	−0.12
London & South East	347	−0.12	−0.08	0.08	0.20	0.00
Social class of HOH		**	**	**	**	NS
I and II	377	0.26	−0.20	0.19	0.35	−0.02
IIINM	138	0.05	−0.17	0.15	0.04	0.05
IIIM	375	−0.17	0.20	−0.19	−0.22	−0.01
IV and V	174	−0.25	0.13	−0.13	−0.33	0.02
Economic status		NS	**	NS	NS	NS
Receiving benefits	112	−0.22	0.22	−0.19	−0.22	−0.15
Working	847	0.02	−0.02	0.02	0.02	0.01
Not working	105	0.04	−0.05	0.07	0.05	0.05
% of variance explained		*6%*	*40%*	*24%*	*18%*	*37%*

** F ratio $p < 0.01$ NS F ratio $p > 0.05$
* F ratio $p < 0.05$

Table 13.5   Women—analysis of variance for component scores: background factors

Characteristic	No. of cases	Adjusted deviations from grand mean and significance of F ratios for:				
		Component 1	Component 2	Component 3	Component 4	Component 5
Grand mean		−0.01	−0.56	−0.06	−0.07	−0.14
Covariate—Total energy		NS	**	**	**	**
Age		**	**	**	NS	**
16–24	184	−0.20	−0.15	−0.13	−0.12	0.72
25–34	248	−0.03	−0.03	−0.12	0.01	0.20
35–49	378	0.00	0.04	0.02	0.03	−0.14
50–64	274	0.17	0.08	0.18	0.04	−0.47
Region		NS	NS	*	**	NS
Scotland	95	−0.11	−0.05	0.02	0.04	0.15
Northern	283	−0.05	0.04	−0.09	−0.08	−0.01
Central, South West & Wales	361	0.08	0.00	0.07	−0.06	0.02
London & South East	345	−0.02	−0.02	−0.01	0.12	−0.05
Social class of HOH		**	**	NS	**	**
I and II	382	0.23	−0.09	0.02	0.29	−0.10
IIINM	140	0.11	−0.12	0.02	0.15	−0.02
IIIM	345	−0.15	0.08	0.03	−0.21	0.05
IV and V	217	−0.24	0.11	−0.09	−0.28	0.11
Economic status		*	NS	**	**	**
Receiving benefits	145	−0.20	0.04	−0.08	−0.22	−0.07
Working	619	0.05	−0.03	−0.03	0.11	0.06
Not working	320	0.00	0.04	0.10	−0.12	−0.09
% of variance explained		9%	24%	45%	22%	33%

** F ratio $p < 0.01$ NS F ratio $p > 0.05$
* F ratio $p < 0.05$

Table 13.6   Men—analysis of variance for component scores: including behavioural variables

Characteristic	No. of cases	Adjusted deviations from grand mean and significance of F ratios for:				
		Component 1	Component 2	Component 3	Component 4	Component 5
Grand mean		0.02	0.58	0.07	0.07	0.14
Covariate—Total energy		NS	**	**	**	**
Age		NS	**	**	**	**
16–24	204	−0.08	−0.09	−0.20	−0.30	0.97
25–34	248	0.06	−0.10	−0.18	−0.04	0.36
35–49	342	0.05	0.09	−0.01	0.02	−0.28
50–64	268	−0.05	0.04	0.32	0.25	−0.71
Region		NS	**	**	**	**
Scotland	91	0.03	−0.17	−0.05	0.29	0.35
Northern	266	0.07	0.06	−0.21	−0.17	0.04
Central, South West & Wales	359	0.03	0.08	0.09	−0.14	−0.12
London & South East	346	−0.10	−0.08	0.08	0.21	0.00
Social class of HOH		**	**	**	**	NS
I and II	377	0.18	−0.19	0.15	0.34	−0.03
IIINM	137	0.05	−0.16	0.13	0.04	0.04
IIIM	374	−0.12	0.19	−0.16	−0.21	0.00
IV and V	174	−0.17	0.13	−0.09	−0.32	0.03
Economic status		NS	**	NS	NS	NS
Receiving benefits	112	−0.11	0.22	−0.15	−0.20	−0.15
Working	845	0.01	−0.02	0.01	0.02	0.01
Not working	105	0.02	−0.03	0.06	0.05	0.04
Slimming		**	*	NS	*	NS
On a slimming diet	44	0.58	0.28	−0.13	0.32	−0.09
Not on a slimming diet	1018	−0.03	−0.01	0.01	−0.01	0.00
Smoking behaviour		**	*	**	NS	NS
Smoker	351	−0.37	0.08	−0.23	−0.01	−0.06
Non-smoker	711	0.18	−0.04	0.11	0.00	0.03
Food supplements		**	NS	NS	NS	NS
Taking food supplements	92	0.42	0.00	0.01	0.19	−0.11
Not taking supplements	970	−0.04	0.00	0.00	−0.02	0.01
% of variance explained		*14%*	*41%*	*25%*	*19%*	*37%*

** F ratio p < 0.01   NS F ratio p > 0.05
*   F ratio p < 0.05

Table 13.7 Women—analysis of variance for component scores: including behavioural variables

Characteristic	No. of cases	Adjusted deviations from grand mean and significance of F ratios for:				
		Component 1	Component 2	Component 3	Component 4	Component 5
Grand mean		−0.01	−0.56	−0.06	−0.07	−0.14
Covariate—Total energy		NS	**	**	**	**
Age		**	**	**	NS	**
16–24	184	−0.20	−0.16	−0.13	−0.11	0.72
25–34	248	−0.01	−0.04	−0.12	0.01	0.21
35–49	377	0.01	0.03	0.03	0.02	−0.15
50–64	274	0.13	0.10	0.16	0.03	−0.47
Region		NS	NS	*	**	NS
Scotland	95	−0.06	−0.07	0.05	0.05	0.15
Northern	283	−0.04	0.03	−0.08	−0.08	−0.01
Central, South West & Wales	361	0.06	0.00	0.06	−0.06	0.02
London & South East	344	−0.01	−0.01	−0.01	0.12	−0.06
Social class of HOH		**	**	NS	**	**
I and II	381	0.17	−0.06	−0.01	0.28	−0.10
IIINM	140	0.08	−0.12	0.02	0.14	−0.02
IIIM	345	−0.12	0.06	0.04	−0.20	0.05
IV and V	217	−0.17	0.08	−0.06	−0.27	0.11
Economic status		NS	NS	**	**	**
Receiving benefits	145	−0.13	0.01	−0.06	−0.20	−0.07
Working	618	0.03	−0.03	−0.03	0.10	0.06
Not working	320	0.00	0.05	0.09	−0.11	−0.09
Slimming		**	NS	NS	**	NS
On a slimming diet	134	0.31	0.01	−0.09	0.25	0.02
Not on a slimming diet	949	−0.04	0.00	0.01	−0.04	0.00
Smoking behaviour		**	**	**	NS	NS
Smoker	374	−0.27	0.13	−0.17	−0.02	0.00
Non-smoker	709	0.14	−0.07	0.09	0.01	0.00
Food supplements		**	**	NS	NS	NS
Taking food supplements	190	0.17	−0.17	0.07	0.10	0.02
Not taking supplements	893	−0.04	0.04	−0.02	−0.02	0.00
% of variance explained		*17%*	*28%*	*47%*	*24%*	*33%*

** F ratio $p < 0.01$ NS F ratio $p > 0.05$
* F ratio $p < 0.05$

14 Nutrients from foods eaten out of the home

There is interest in the contribution to nutrient intake made by foods eaten outside the home both because eating out is thought to be increasingly prevalent and since foods which are commonly eaten out may differ nutritionally from those eaten at home. Little information is, however, available at a national level on eating out. The National Food Survey,[1] for example, although a major source of information on food entering the home, currently provides no information on the type and quantity of foods eaten outside the home, although a record is kept of the number and nature of meals obtained outside the home during the survey period by each member of the household.

The precise definition of eating out may vary between different studies. For this survey eating out was taken to include all items which were consumed out of the home, regardless of where they were prepared. The definition therefore includes packed lunches and drinks made up at home but eaten at work or elsewhere, and meals or drinks taken at the homes of friends and relatives. Under the definition, take-away meals are included as food eaten out if they were consumed out of the home, but not if they were eaten at home.

As outlined in Chapter 2 and Appendix D, weight information for items eaten outside the home was either obtained from the purchase of a duplicate or was estimated on the basis of the description of the portion size. Where foods had been prepared at home before being eaten elsewhere a full description of each food item and precise weight information was available from the seven-day dietary record. Alcoholic drinks consumed outside the home were recorded in the same way as foods, so the contribution of these drinks to total consumption of alcohol could be assessed.

Most of the analyses in this chapter show nutrient intake from eating out either as a percentage of energy intake excluding alcohol, or as a value per 1000kcal of food energy (excluding alcohol) consumed out of the home. Most of the tables refer to 'consumers only', that is those who obtained some *food* energy from eating out.

14.1 Nutrient intakes from eating out as a percentage of total intakes

Tables 14.1 and 14.2 show nutrient intakes from food and drink consumed out of the home as a percentage of total intake of those nutrients from dietary sources (excluding supplements). The data are presented first for all men and women, and then for those who consumed some food energy out of the home.

On average, men consumed a greater proportion of their total energy out of the home than did women (34.0% compared to 24.0%, p<0.01). This total includes energy from alcohol consumed out of the home, which was more important for men than for women; more than half (54.6%) of men's alcohol intake was consumed out of the home compared with just over one third (35.8%) for women. When energy from alcohol was excluded there was still a difference between men and women in the percentage of food energy (excluding alcohol) obtained from eating out; men obtained 31.0% of their food energy out of the home compared to 23.1% for women (p<0.01).

(Table 14.1)

Men derived a greater proportion of all nutrients from eating out than did women (p<0.01 for all nutrients except carotene, where p<0.05). The nutrient composition of foods eaten out of the home can be assessed by comparing the proportion of each nutrient obtained from eating out with the overall proportion of food energy from eating out. From Table 14.1 it can be seen, for example, that foods eaten away from home provided 31.0%, on average, of the food energy intake of men in the sample. If the nutrient content of foods eaten away from home was similar to that of foods eaten at home it would be expected that the percentage of any nutrient derived from eating out would not differ significantly from 31%.

Comparison for men of the percentage of individual nutrients derived from eating out with the percentage of food energy obtained out of the home suggests that foods eaten out provided less protein, fibre and iron per unit energy than in the total diet (p<0.01). This was also the case for some vitamins, for example carotene, thiamin and vitamin C (p<0.01). Although men derived larger proportions of all nutrients from eating out than did women, there was a similar pattern for both sexes in the contribution that food eaten out of the home made to intakes of various nutrients. Women also derived lower percentages of fibre, protein, iron and all vitamins than of food energy (p<0.01) from foods consumed outside the home.

On average, men obtained a greater percentage of their intake of sugars than of food energy out of the home (p<0.01), but there was no significant difference for women. There was no significant difference in the percentage of fat, saturated fatty acids or polyunsaturated fatty acids from eating out and the percentage of food energy from eating out, but the percentage of trans fatty acids obtained from foods eaten out of the home was significantly greater than the proportion of food energy from eating out (p<0.01).

Ninety-four per cent of men and 90% of women derived some food energy out of the home during the seven-day recording period. Table 14.2 shows that, as for the total sample, men who consumed some food out of the home obtained greater proportions of food energy (excluding alcohol) than women, 32.9% compared to 25.7% (p<0.01). The proportion of alcohol consumed out of the home by this group was again much higher for men than for women (57.4% compared to 39.7% (p<0.01)). (*Table 14.2*)

The pattern of the percentages of individual nutrients obtained from eating out compared to the percentage of food energy obtained was similar to that described for the total sample (Table 14.1). Men who consumed some food energy out of the home obtained a higher proportion of their intake of sugars from eating out (p<0.01) and, for both sexes, food and drink consumed out of the home provided lower proportions of fibre, iron and vitamin C (p<0.01).

14.2 Major nutrients as a proportion of energy intake and nutrient intakes per 1000kcal food energy from eating out

In order to make comparisons between subgroups of the sample and to compare the nutrient content of foods eaten out with that of the total diet, nutrients derived from eating out were standardised as intakes per 1000kcal. The main components of the diet were then calculated as proportions of food energy intake out of the home. Table 14.3 shows the calculated values for those men and women who consumed some food energy out of the home, and Table 14.4 presents comparable data based on the total diet, consumed both inside and outside the home, of all men and women in the sample.

Alcohol provided a greater percentage of total energy intake from eating out for men than for women (15.8% compared with 7.1%) (p<0.01). The contribution to the diet of other nutrients was therefore calculated using energy from food excluding alcohol.
(*Table 14.3*)

The foods consumed out of the home by women contained more protein (p<0.05) and total fat, and saturated, trans and monounsaturated fatty acids (p<0.01), and a lower percentage of carbohydrate (p<0.01) than did foods eaten by men. In particular women had higher percentages of saturated fatty acids (p<0.01) than men. Comparison with Table 14.4 shows that, for both men and women, foods eaten out of the home contained a lower percentage of protein (p<0.01) than did their diet as a whole. Men obtained more carbohydrate from foods eaten outside of the home than from all foods (p<0.01), and women obtained more fat from foods eaten out of the home than the average for their diet as a whole (p<0.01).
(*Table 14.4*)

The only significant differences between men and women in the importance of individual nutrients were that women obtained more iron, carotene and vitamin C per 1000kcal food eaten out than did men (p<0.01). Comparison between Tables 14.3 and 14.4 shows that foods eaten out of the home contained more sugars than the diet of men and women as a whole, but foods eaten out of the home contained less fibre (p<0.01), iron (p<0.01) and some vitamins per unit energy (retinol, carotene, thiamin and vitamin D: p<0.01).

14.3 Variation in the nutrient content of foods eaten out of the home by the proportion of energy obtained from eating out

The nutrient content of food eaten outside the home by an individual may vary according to the proportion of the individual's energy which is derived from eating out. Those who consume a relatively large amount of their food energy intake outside the home might, for example, consume a more balanced range of nutrients than those who eat only a few items out of the home.

Those who consumed some food energy outside the home were divided into three groups according to whether they obtained less than 20% of food energy, 20% to 40%, or 40% or more of their food energy from eating out. Table 14.5 shows the proportions of all food energy and alcohol obtained out of the home for men and women in these groups, and data on selected nutrients.

The percentage of total alcohol intake which was obtained out of the home was lowest for men and women who derived less than 20% of their food energy from eating out; the percentage increased as more food energy was obtained out of the home (p<0.01). Those who derived less than 20% of their food energy from eating out obtained a smaller proportion of energy from protein and fat, and more from carbohydrate, than did those deriving more of their food energy out of the home (p<0.01). Those who obtained less than 20% of their food energy intake out of the home had a lower fibre intake per unit energy (p<0.05), but there was no significant difference in the iron and vitamin C content of the food eaten out. (*Table 14.5*)

14.4 Variation in the nutrient content of foods eaten out of the home

It is possible that the incidence of eating out and the nutrient content of foods eaten out might vary according to the informant's age and socio-economic characteristics. Tables 14.6 to 14.8 show the proportion of total food energy and alcohol intake derived from eating out, and selected data on the nutrient content of foods eaten out, by age, social class and the employment status of informants.

Age group
The oldest group of people in the survey (aged 50 to 64) were less likely than others to have eaten out at all

during the week (men p<0.05; women p<0.01); 82% of women and 90% men in this age group derived some food energy out of the home. The lesser importance of eating out for older groups can also be seen in that the proportion of the total food energy intake of consumers obtained from eating out decreased through the age range. The percentage of food energy derived from eating out was lower for men above the age of 35 (p<0.01) than for younger men, and decreased again for those aged 50 or over (p<0.01). For women the proportion of food energy from eating out declined most markedly between the 16 to 24 and 25 to 34 age groups (from 36.1% to 27.9% (p<0.01)), and then again between the two older age groups, from 24.0% to 18.1%, (p<0.01). In all age groups men derived a greater proportion of their food energy from eating out than did women (p<0.01).   (*Table 14.6*)

The proportion of total alcohol intake consumed out of the home was higher in all age groups for men than women (p<0.01). Among men the proportion was lower for those aged 50 or over than for men aged 35 to 49 (p<0.01). Among women the proportion was similar for the two younger age groups but was lower for women aged 35 or more than for those aged 25 to 34 (p<0.01).

Both men and women in the 16 to 24 age group derived less protein from food eaten out than older informants (men p<0.01; women p<0.05 compared with age 25 to 34, p<0.01 compared with other age groups), and women aged 16 to 24 obtained more carbohydrate than others (p<0.05). Foods eaten out of the home by those in the youngest age group contained less iron than foods eaten by men and women in the middle of the age range (men p<0.01; women p<0.01 for age 25 to 34, p<0.05 for age 35 to 49). Intakes per 1000kcal of fibre and vitamin C did not show a consistent trend with age of informant and differences in intake were not statistically significant.

Social class
The percentages of men and women who consumed some food out of the home were similar for most social classes, although a smaller proportion of men and women in Social Classes IV and V had eaten out during the recording period (p<0.05). The proportions of alcohol and of food energy derived from eating out varied little according to social class.   (*Table 14.7*)

There were some differences between social classes in the nutrient content of the foods eaten out of the home. Foods eaten out by men in Social Classes I and II had a higher protein content than foods eaten by other men (p<0.01). Foods eaten out by women in Social Classes I and II had a higher protein content than foods eaten by women in Social Classes III non-manual and manual (p<0.01) or by women in Social Classes IV and V (p<0.05). The proportion of food energy provided by carbohydrate was lower for men in Social Classes I and II than for men in manual occupations (p<0.01). Men and women in Social Classes I

and II obtained more iron per unit energy eaten out of the home than did those in Social Classes IV and V (p<0.01) and men in the higher social classes also obtained more fibre than others (p<0.05).

Employment status
The relationship between eating out and economic activity was different for men and women. Unemployed and economically inactive men derived smaller percentages of their food energy from eating out than did working men, 18.2% and 20.3% compared to 35.6%, (p<0.01). Unemployed women also obtained a smaller percentage of their food energy from eating out than did working women, 22.9% compared with 30.8%, (p<0.01), but economically inactive women derived the smallest percentage of energy from eating out (14.9%). Economically inactive women were also less likely than the other groups to have obtained some food energy out of the home during the recording week (p<0.01).
    (*Table 14.8*)

The proportion of alcohol obtained out of the home did not vary according to employment status for men, although economically inactive women obtained a smaller percentage of their alcohol intake out of the home than did other women (p<0.05).

Working men obtained more of their energy out of the home from protein than the economically inactive (p<0.05) or the unemployed (p<0.01). Working men also obtained more energy out of the home from fat and more fibre and iron per 1000 kcal (p<0.01) and less energy from carbohydrate (p<0.01) than other groups. There were no significant differences by employment status in the nutrient content of foods eaten by women.

14.5 Summary
An average of 27.0% of food energy and 45.1% of alcohol intake was consumed out of the home. Men obtained higher percentages than women both of their food energy and of their total alcohol intake from eating out.

Foods eaten out of the home contained a lower proportion of protein than the diet as a whole, and they contained more sugars and less fibre, iron and vitamins per unit energy than all foods consumed by the sample. The foods eaten out of the home by women contained more protein and fat and less carbohydrate than the foods eaten out by men. Women obtained more iron, carotene and vitamin C per 1000kcal food energy eaten out than men.

The nutrient content of foods eaten out of the home varied little according to the proportion of an individual's total food intake which was provided by foods eaten out of the home. Those obtaining less of their food out of the home obtained a lower proportion of their food energy from protein and fat and more from carbohydrate.

Older informants, those in Social Classes IV and V, and the economically inactive obtained smaller percentages of their food energy and of their alcohol intake from eating out than did other informants. The unemployed obtained a smaller percentage of their food energy from eating out than did informants who were working, but the percentage of alcohol they derived out of the home was not significantly different.

The foods eaten out of the home by working men and by informants in Social Classes I and II had a higher protein content and contained more iron and fibre per unit of energy than the foods eaten out by non-working men and informants in other social classes. Younger informants, on the other hand, obtained less iron and lower percentages of energy from protein in foods eaten out of the home than older groups.

Reference

1. Ministry of Agriculture, Fisheries and Food. *Household food consumption and expenditure, 1988. Annual Report of the National Food Survey Committee.* HMSO (London, 1989).

Table 14.1 Percentage of intake of selected nutrients derived from eating out by sex of informant
Total sample

Nutrient	Men			Women			Total		
	Mean	Median	SE	Mean	Median	SE	Mean	Median	SE
Total energy	34.0	33.8	0.61	24.0	20.5	0.59	28.9	27.3	0.44
Food energy	31.0	30.8	0.60	23.1	19.4	0.58	27.0	25.1	0.43
Alcohol	54.6	67.3	1.32	35.8	0.00	1.29	45.1	40.2	0.95
Protein	28.0	27.4	0.58	21.0	17.1	0.56	24.4	22.5	0.41
Total fat	31.8	31.0	0.64	24.7	20.8	0.63	28.2	26.3	0.45
Carbohydrate	31.5	30.7	0.60	22.8	18.3	0.58	27.1	25.0	0.43
Sugars	34.6	33.1	0.66	24.4	19.0	0.63	29.5	26.6	0.47
Fibre	26.7	25.2	0.58	20.0	15.1	0.56	23.3	20.5	0.41
Calcium	31.3	30.2	0.62	21.5	17.0	0.57	26.4	23.6	0.43
Iron	27.2	25.4	0.59	20.3	15.6	0.56	23.7	20.7	0.41
Retinol	28.7	24.8	0.75	20.1	11.6	0.67	24.4	17.3	0.51
Carotene	22.0	12.2	0.75	19.7	8.6	0.74	20.8	10.9	0.53
Thiamin	25.6	23.5	0.57	19.4	15.0	0.54	22.5	19.7	0.40
Riboflavin	29.2	27.6	0.59	18.9	14.3	0.52	24.0	20.8	0.41
Niacin equivalents	30.3	29.6	0.59	21.1	16.5	0.56	25.7	23.7	0.42
Vitamin C	24.3	19.6	0.66	20.8	13.7	0.67	22.5	16.3	0.47
Vitamin D	29.5	25.0	0.77	21.2	12.7	0.70	25.3	17.8	0.53
Saturated fatty acids	32.0	31.8	0.64	25.0	20.9	0.63	28.5	26.6	0.46
Trans fatty acids	35.5	34.6	0.74	27.2	22.3	0.71	31.3	28.4	0.52
Monounsaturated fatty acids	31.4	30.0	0.64	24.5	20.8	0.63	27.9	26.0	0.64
n-3 polyunsaturated fatty acids	32.5	30.0	0.71	24.7	19.1	0.69	28.6	24.8	0.50
n-6 polyunsaturated fatty acids	31.9	30.0	0.69	24.6	19.0	0.68	28.2	24.6	0.49
Base		*1087*			*1110*			*2197*	

Table 14.2   Percentage of intake of selected nutrients derived from eating out by sex of informant for consumers of some food energy out of the home

Consumers of food energy out of the home

Nutrient	Men			Women			Total		
	Mean	Median	SE	Mean	Median	SE	Mean	Median	SE
Total energy	35.9	35.6	0.59	26.7	24.1	0.60	31.4	29.5	0.43
Food energy	32.9	31.7	0.59	25.7	22.5	0.60	29.3	27.4	0.42
Alcohol	57.4	72.4	1.34	39.7	16.4	1.38	48.6	51.8	0.98
Protein	29.6	28.5	0.57	23.3	19.5	0.57	26.5	25.0	0.41
Total fat	33.7	32.7	0.63	27.4	23.9	0.64	30.6	28.5	0.45
Carbohydrate	33.3	32.2	0.59	25.3	21.7	0.60	29.4	27.3	0.43
Sugars	36.7	34.9	0.65	27.1	22.2	0.65	32.0	29.3	0.47
Fibre	28.3	26.7	0.58	22.2	17.9	0.59	25.3	22.9	0.42
Calcium	33.1	31.7	0.61	23.9	19.4	0.59	28.6	26.1	0.43
Iron	28.8	26.8	0.59	22.6	18.7	0.58	25.8	22.9	0.42
Retinol	30.4	26.7	0.77	22.3	14.7	0.70	26.4	20.0	0.53
Carotene	23.2	13.6	0.78	21.9	11.9	0.79	22.6	12.7	0.55
Thiamin	27.1	24.7	0.57	21.6	17.8	0.56	24.4	21.6	0.41
Riboflavin	30.8	28.9	0.58	21.0	16.6	0.54	26.0	23.0	0.41
Niacin equivalents	32.0	30.9	0.58	23.5	19.9	0.58	27.8	25.8	0.42
Vitamin C	25.7	21.2	0.67	23.1	16.3	0.70	24.4	18.9	0.49
Vitamin D	31.3	27.0	0.78	23.6	15.7	0.75	27.5	20.8	0.55
Saturated fatty acids	33.9	33.9	0.63	27.7	24.6	0.65	30.9	28.7	0.46
Trans fatty acids	37.6	37.0	0.73	30.2	26.0	0.73	33.9	31.7	0.52
Monounsaturated fatty acids	33.2	31.7	0.63	27.3	24.0	0.65	30.3	28.3	0.46
n-3 polyunsaturated fatty acids	34.4	31.3	0.71	27.5	22.4	0.71	31.0	27.7	0.51
n-6 polyunsaturated fatty acids	33.8	31.8	0.68	27.4	23.0	0.70	30.6	27.7	0.49
Base		*1026*			*999*			*2025*	

Table 14.3   Eating out: proportion of energy from main nutrients and nutrient intake per 1000kcals food energy eaten out of the home by sex of informant

Consumers of food energy out of the home

Nutrient	Men			Women			Total		
	Mean	Median	SE	Mean	Median	SE	Mean	Median	SE
i. Proportion of total energy eaten out from:									
Alcohol	15.8	8.5	0.62	7.1	0.5	0.40	11.5	4.4	0.38
ii. Proportion of food energy eaten out from:									
Protein	13.2	12.9	0.16	13.7	13.0	0.18	13.4	12.9	0.12
Carbohydrate	47.7	45.0	0.52	44.8	43.7	0.38	46.3	44.4	0.33
Total fat	39.9	41.9	0.33	41.9	42.6	0.32	40.9	42.3	0.23
Saturated fatty acids	16.5	16.9	0.17	18.2	18.1	0.19	17.4	17.5	0.13
Trans fatty acids	2.43	2.28	0.04	2.49	2.23	0.05	2.46	2.26	0.03
Monounsaturated fatty acids	12.0	12.4	0.12	12.4	12.6	0.12	12.2	12.5	0.08
n-3 polyunsaturated fatty acids	0.78	0.70	0.02	0.76	0.62	0.02	0.77	0.66	0.01
n-6 polyunsaturated fatty acids	5.29	5.00	0.09	5.10	4.72	0.09	5.19	4.86	0.06
iii. Nutrient intake (units) per 1000kcals of food energy from eating out:									
Sugars (g)	66.1	54.8	1.72	62.1	54.4	1.29	64.1	54.5	1.08
Fibre (g)	8.87	8.38	0.14	8.88	8.55	0.14	8.88	8.48	0.10
Calcium (mg)	501	403	48.9	443	386	8.6	472	393	25.2
Iron (mg)	5.07	4.80	0.08	5.41	4.89	0.10	5.24	4.84	0.06
Retinol (μg)	326	231	17.9	301	235	13.6	314	234	11.3
Carotene (μg)	626	283	30.7	885	379	43.6	754	330	26.7
Thiamin (mg)	0.60	0.56	0.01	0.61	0.57	0.01	0.60	0.57	0.01
Riboflavin (mg)	1.45	0.78	0.39	0.87	0.70	0.06	1.16	0.74	0.20
Niacin equivalents (mg)	26.3	16.2	6.54	16.9	14.8	0.42	21.6	15.5	3.32
Vitamin C (mg)	26.0	17.0	2.08	35.2	22.4	2.00	30.5	19.1	1.45
Vitamin D (μg)	1.32	0.94	0.05	1.25	0.87	0.06	1.29	0.91	0.04
Base		*1026*			*999*			*2025*	

Table 14.4 Total intake both inside and outside the home: proportion of energy from main nutrients and nutrient intake per 1000kcals food energy by sex of informant

Total sample

Nutrient	Men			Women			Total		
	Mean	Median	SE	Mean	Median	SE	Mean	Median	SE
i. Proportion of total energy from:									
Alcohol	6.9	4.2	0.24	2.8	1.0	0.12	4.8	2.0	0.14
ii. Proportion of food energy from:									
Protein	15.2	14.8	0.09	15.6	14.9	0.11	15.4	14.9	0.07
Carbohydrate	44.7	44.7	0.17	44.2	44.2	0.18	44.4	44.4	0.12
Total fat	40.4	40.5	0.14	40.3	40.5	0.16	40.4	40.5	0.11
Saturated fatty acids	18.7	18.9	0.10	19.1	19.2	0.11	18.9	19.0	0.07
Trans fatty acids	2.19	2.09	0.02	2.16	2.07	0.02	2.17	2.08	0.02
Monounsaturated fatty acids	12.4	12.3	0.06	12.2	12.2	0.06	12.3	12.3	0.04
n-3 polyunsaturated fatty acids	0.78	0.73	0.01	0.75	0.69	0.01	0.77	0.71	0.01
n-6 polyunsaturated fatty acids	5.44	5.03	0.06	5.27	4.88	0.06	5.36	4.96	0.04
iii. Nutrient intake (units) per 1000kcals food energy:									
Sugars (g)	49.7	49.4	0.47	51.9	50.8	0.47	50.8	50.1	0.33
Fibre (g)	11.0	10.5	0.09	11.6	11.0	0.10	11.3	10.7	0.07
Calcium (mg)	417	404	3.76	452	437	4.53	435	419	2.97
Iron (mg)	6.29	5.75	0.10	7.91	6.08	0.30	7.1	5.9	0.16
Retinol (μg)	552	263	25.8	674	276	33.8	614	269	21.4
Carotene (μg)	1097	854	29.1	1332	1066	34.4	1216	946	22.7
Thiamin (mg)	0.75	0.73	0.01	0.78	0.74	0.01	0.77	0.74	0.00
Riboflavin (mg)	0.93	0.88	0.01	0.99	0.91	0.01	0.96	0.90	0.01
Niacin equivalents (mg)	17.9	17.2	0.14	18.0	16.9	0.15	18.0	17.1	0.10
Vitamin C (mg)	29.9	25.2	0.55	39.4	33.2	0.80	34.7	28.4	0.50
Vitamin D (μg)	1.52	1.27	0.04	1.58	1.33	0.04	1.55	1.30	0.03
Base		*1087*			*1110*			*2197*	

Table 14.5 Eating out: proportion of energy from main nutrients and nutrient intake per 1000kcals food energy by sex and percentage of food energy from eating out
Consumers of food energy out of the home

Nutrient	Percentage of food energy from eating out											
	Less than 20%			20% to 40%			40% or more			All consumers		
	Mean	Median	SE	Mean	Median	SE	Mean	Median	SE	Mean	Median	SE
Men												
i. Percentage of total intake derived from eating out:												
Food energy	10.1	9.9	0.34	29.9	30.3	0.29	53.1	50.1	0.59	32.9	31.7	0.59
Alcohol	44.1	37.0	2.63	54.1	63.2	2.16	70.9	92.6	2.05	57.4	72.4	1.34
ii. Proportion of food energy eaten out from:												
Protein	11.9	11.1	0.47	13.7	13.2	0.22	13.6	13.1	0.17	13.2	12.9	0.16
Carbohydrate	56.1	49.5	1.71	45.8	44.9	0.44	43.5	43.3	0.35	47.7	45.0	0.52
Total fat	33.8	38.1	0.95	41.0	41.9	0.38	43.2	43.5	0.28	39.9	42.0	0.33
iii. Nutrient intake (units) per 1000kcals of food energy from eating out												
Fibre (g)	8.11	7.24	0.39	9.33	8.77	0.17	8.94	8.47	0.15	8.87	8.38	0.14
Iron (mg)	4.78	4.24	0.21	5.20	4.85	0.14	5.13	4.86	0.08	5.07	4.80	0.08
Vitamin C (mg)	36.0	15.3	7.59	21.9	16.5	1.11	22.9	18.7	0.93	26.0	17.0	2.08
Base	271			393			362			1026		
Women												
i. Percentage of total intake derived from eating out:												
Food energy	9.5	9.6	0.26	29.0	28.3	0.32	53.0	49.4	0.76	25.7	22.5	0.60
Alcohol	25.7	0.0	1.81	44.1	40.2	2.45	61.0	82.3	2.85	39.7	16.4	1.38
ii. Proportion of food energy eaten out from:												
Protein	13.2	12.2	0.32	14.2	13.4	0.25	13.9	13.5	0.23	13.7	13.0	0.18
Carbohydrate	46.8	44.7	0.73	43.2	43.0	0.49	43.0	43.4	0.43	44.8	43.7	0.38
Total fat	40.5	42.1	0.62	42.9	42.8	0.43	43.3	43.2	0.32	41.9	42.6	0.32
iii. Nutrient intake (units) per 1000kcals of food energy from eating out												
Fibre (g)	8.21	7.64	0.27	9.42	8.82	0.20	9.49	9.09	0.17	8.88	8.55	0.14
Iron (mg)	5.39	4.62	0.19	5.42	5.12	0.11	5.44	5.11	0.11	5.41	4.89	0.10
Vitamin C (mg)	35.8	18.3	4.03	33.6	22.6	2.11	36.1	29.9	1.77	35.2	22.4	2.00
Base	456			309			234			999		

Table 14.6 Eating out: proportion of energy from main nutrients and nutrient intake per 1000kcals food energy by sex and age of informant
Consumers of food energy out of the home

Nutrient	Age of informant											
	16–24			25–34			35–49			50–64		
	Mean	Median	SE	Mean	Median	SE	Mean	Median	SE	Mean	Median	SE
Men												
i. Percentage of total intake derived from eating out:												
Food energy	41.4	41.3	1.42	37.7	38.5	1.19	30.0	30.3	0.89	24.8	22.0	1.05
Alcohol	57.0	79.3	3.24	58.8	78.5	2.77	60.2	74.4	2.23	52.4	59.9	2.72
ii. Proportion of food energy eaten out from:												
Protein	12.1	12.1	0.32	13.5	13.1	0.30	13.2	13.1	0.25	13.7	13.4	0.42
Carbohydrate	47.6	46.1	0.74	45.6	43.7	0.71	49.2	45.2	1.25	47.8	45.1	1.04
Total fat	40.8	42.6	0.60	41.2	42.6	0.59	39.1	41.0	0.59	38.8	41.6	0.79
iii. Nutrient intake (units) per 1000kcals of food energy from eating out												
Fibre (g)	8.70	8.50	0.22	8.70	8.38	0.23	9.29	8.35	0.27	8.60	8.21	0.31
Iron (mg)	4.50	4.39	0.09	5.35	4.85	0.25	5.23	4.92	0.12	5.04	4.92	0.16
Vitamin C (mg)	26.2	17.7	2.80	23.6	18.7	1.64	23.8	16.1	1.89	31.2	16.2	7.84
Base		203			248			330			245	
Percentage of all men deriving some food energy out of the home (base):												
	95%	(214)		98%	(254)		95%	(346)		90%	(273)	
Women												
i. Percentage of total intake derived from eating out:												
Food energy	36.1	33.3	1.49	27.9	24.5	1.28	24.0	21.4	0.92	18.1	13.9	0.98
Alcohol	43.0	0.0	3.46	48.1	50.5	2.90	37.4	11.7	2.24	32.2	0.0	2.70
ii. Proportion of food energy eaten out from:												
Protein	12.5	12.0	0.30	13.5	13.2	0.35	14.2	13.2	0.32	13.9	13.3	0.38
Carbohydrate	47.2	46.1	0.79	44.6	43.7	0.72	44.4	43.6	0.67	43.6	42.3	0.88
Total fat	40.5	41.6	0.65	42.0	42.9	0.61	41.7	42.6	0.57	43.2	43.6	0.74
iii. Nutrient intake (units) per 1000kcals of food energy from eating out												
Fibre (g)	9.02	8.59	0.27	8.92	8.66	0.28	8.92	8.47	0.25	8.69	8.38	0.33
Iron (mg)	5.01	4.59	0.15	5.75	5.13	0.24	5.51	5.00	0.17	5.23	4.92	0.18
Vitamin C (mg)	46.8	24.6	6.37	31.1	22.5	2.29	33.5	22.2	3.02	32.9	20.9	4.74
Base		180			232			354			233	
Percentage of all women deriving some food energy out of the home (base):												
	95%	(189)		92%	(253)		92%	(385)		82%	(283)	

Table 14.7 **Eating out: proportion of energy from main nutrients and nutrient intake per 1000kcals food energy by sex and age of informant and social class of head of household**
Consumers of food energy out of the home

Nutrient	Social class of head of household											
	I and II			III non-manual			III manual			IV and V		
	Mean	Median	SE	Mean	Median	SE	Mean	Median	SE	Mean	Median	SE
Men												
i. Percentage of total intake derived from eating out:												
Food energy	32.1	31.1	0.97	32.6	31.3	1.55	34.9	34.7	1.00	29.5	28.1	1.49
Alcohol	54.8	66.3	2.16	53.9	63.5	3.81	61.2	81.0	2.26	57.3	80.8	3.66
ii. Proportion of food energy eaten out from:												
Protein	14.2	13.4	0.29	13.4	13.5	0.33	12.9	12.5	0.27	11.6	12.1	0.40
Carbohydrate	44.9	43.0	0.59	46.0	43.4	1.06	49.0	46.4	1.13	52.8	48.0	1.42
Total fat	41.3	42.9	0.46	41.1	43.0	0.86	39.4	41.5	0.55	36.3	39.6	1.10
iii. Nutrient intake (units) per 1000kcals of food energy from eating out												
Fibre (g)	9.31	8.89	0.23	9.30	8.36	0.36	8.58	8.22	0.22	8.19	8.00	0.38
Iron (mg)	5.47	5.18	0.12	5.13	4.92	0.16	4.94	4.52	0.18	4.40	4.39	0.17
Vitamin C (mg)	29.2	21.1	1.86	41.9	20.8	14.3	19.6	14.8	1.30	21.2	15.8	3.27
Base		*363*			*132*			*360*			*158*	
Percentage of all men deriving some food energy out of the home (base):												
	96%	(377)		96%	(138)		96%	(378)		89%	(177)	
Women												
i. Percentage of total intake derived from eating out:												
Food energy	25.8	23.0	1.00	27.2	26.0	1.76	24.5	20.1	1.04	25.5	22.6	1.23
Alcohol	39.5	25.5	2.21	43.6	28.0	3.92	40.8	18.8	2.47	34.5	0.0	3.29
ii. Proportion of food energy eaten out from:												
Protein	14.4	13.8	0.32	13.6	12.7	0.48	13.0	12.4	0.30	13.4	12.9	0.35
Carbohydrate	43.6	42.3	0.67	45.7	43.9	1.19	45.7	44.3	0.68	45.0	44.7	0.74
Total fat	42.1	43.1	0.58	41.8	43.3	0.99	41.5	42.5	0.56	41.9	41.6	0.65
iii. Nutrient intake (units) per 1000kcals of food energy from eating out												
Fibre (g)	9.15	8.91	0.24	8.95	8.72	0.42	8.48	7.92	0.23	8.99	8.34	0.36
Iron (mg)	5.96	5.49	0.19	5.42	4.94	0.25	5.12	4.70	0.17	4.86	4.57	0.15
Vitamin C (mg)	41.4	24.6	4.15	33.4	22.2	3.37	30.4	21.5	2.18	33.4	17.5	5.78
Base		*350*			*130*			*322*			*187*	
Percentage of all women deriving some food energy out of the home (base):												
	91%	(386)		92%	(141)		93%	(347)		84%	(222)	

Table 14.8 Eating out: proportion of energy from main nutrients and nutrient intake per 1000kcals food energy by sex and employment status of informant

Consumers of food energy out of the home

Nutrient	Employment status of informant								
	Working			Unemployed			Economically inactive		
	Mean	Median	SE	Mean	Median	SE	Mean	Median	SE
Men									
i. Percentage of total intake derived from eating out:									
Food energy	35.6	34.7	0.62	18.2	15.3	1.77	20.3	15.5	1.70
Alcohol	58.2	73.0	1.45	55.1	68.6	5.07	51.8	57.7	4.76
ii. Proportion of food energy eaten out from:									
Protein	13.6	13.1	0.16	10.9	10.8	0.69	11.8	11.7	0.79
Carbohydrate	46.2	44.5	0.53	59.1	52.4	2.32	52.1	46.7	2.06
Total fat	41.0	42.3	0.30	30.9	34.6	1.74	36.8	40.7	1.55
iii. Nutrient intake (units) per 1000kcals of food energy from eating out									
Fibre (g)	9.15	8.52	0.14	7.39	7.27	0.65	7.55	7.77	0.48
Iron (mg)	5.25	4.85	0.09	4.03	4.04	0.24	4.26	4.12	0.28
Vitamin C (mg)	24.0	17.1	1.00	32.5	16.9	9.46	38.9	15.9	19.9
Base		853			81			91	
Percentage of all men deriving some food energy out of the home (base):									
	98%	(875)		82%	(99)		82%	(373)	
Women									
i. Percentage of total intake derived from eating out:									
Food energy	30.8	28.9	0.76	22.9	18.8	2.24	14.9	12.2	0.73
Alcohol	44.5	35.2	1.72	44.0	0.0	6.86	28.6	0.0	2.32
ii. Proportion of food energy eaten out from:									
Protein	13.7	13.0	0.19	14.1	13.7	0.72	13.5	12.6	0.41
Carbohydrate	44.5	43.9	0.42	43.0	42.0	1.43	45.5	43.8	0.87
Total fat	42.0	42.6	0.35	43.1	42.8	1.16	41.5	42.9	0.76
iii. Nutrient intake (units) per 1000kcals of food energy from eating out									
Fibre (g)	9.08	8.65	0.16	8.06	7.94	0.55	8.58	8.38	0.30
Iron (mg)	5.43	5.04	0.09	5.45	4.64	0.41	5.38	4.72	0.25
Vitamin C (mg)	34.5	23.6	1.94	32.4	17.3	6.91	33.8	21.4	3.89
Base		650			50			291	
Percentage of all women deriving some food energy out of the home (base):									
	97%	(670)		88%	(57)		78%	(373)	

15 Anthropometric measurements and urinary creatinine: results

Chapter 3 described the purpose of making the various anthropometric measurements and taking blood pressure, and the equipment and methodologies used. This chapter gives results from the anthropometric measurements, presenting descriptive statistics for various subgroups within the population.

Data on urinary creatinine excretion obtained from the analysis of the specimens of urine are also presented.[1] Creatinine in the urine is mainly an end product of muscle catabolism, but other factors such as meat consumption can affect it.

The anthropometric variables measured and urinary creatinine excretion tables are tabulated according to a number of social and behavioural variables; not all the tables are commented on. The variables show whether the subject was on a slimming diet, or was unwell at the time of the dietary recording period; area of residence; employment status; whether the household was in receipt of certain state benefits; social class; household composition; smoking behaviour; and reported quantity of alcohol consumed.

(Tables 15.9 to 15.17, and 15.22 to 15.30)

15.1 Height
In its own right present height may be regarded as a useful single index which reflects the effects of previous nutrition and other influences on growth. Many studies have shown an inverse relationship between achieved height and mortality.[2]

The results presented here are based on measurements taken from 1160 male and 1163 female subjects; excluded from the analyses are the small number of cases where the measurement was known to be inaccurate because, for example, the subject had a disability affecting his or her posture, was chairfast, or was wearing a hairstyle or turban which prevented an accurate measurement being made.

In general men were taller than women, and older groups were shorter than younger subjects. However, among men, those aged 16 to 24 were, on average, slightly shorter than those aged 25 to 34, possibly because a proportion of the younger group had not yet reached their maximum height. Indeed, results from the analysis of the blood samples for alkaline phosphatase are consistent with continuing growth in this age group (see Table 17.50). However, these differences were not found for women. *(Table 15.1)*

The smaller height in the oldest group may reflect a true loss of height with age, although this might not be expected to occur until after the age of 64, or it may reflect a secular trend to an increase in height only apparent in younger ages—a cohort effect. Although the relative differences identified in this study between men and women and the decline in mean height with age are similar to the findings of, for example, Knight's study carried out in 1980, overall the mean height of both men and women in this study is significantly greater than in the earlier study (by 0.6cm for men (p<0.01), and 0.8cm for women (p<0.05));[3] this suggests a secular trend. In a more recent study carried out in 1986 and 1987 in Northern Ireland the mean height of men was 174cm and of women, 160cm.[4]

The data show for both male and female informants an association between mean height and area of residence; those informants living in Scotland were shortest and those in London and the South East of England the tallest. For men there was a difference in mean height of 1.3cm between those living in Scotland and those living in London and the South East (p<0.01); for women the difference was 1.4cm (p<0.05).

(Table 15.11)

There was a difference between the mean height of economically inactive men and working men of 2.1cm, (p<0.01), working men being, on average, taller, but unlike other studies no difference was found in this sample between those men who were working and the unemployed. Economically inactive women were also shorter than working women (p<0.05). It is likely that these differences are at least partly associated with differences observed between different age groups, since the economically inactive includes disproportionately larger numbers of the youngest and oldest age groups (students and, particularly for men, retired persons).[5]

(Table 15.12)

In common with other studies there was an association between height and social class; men in households where the head was in Social Classes I or II were on average about 1.8cm taller than men in households where the head was in Social Classes IV or V (p<0.01); for women the comparable difference was even larger— 2.8cm (p<0.01). *(Table 15.14)*

Knight reported a difference of 1.82% in the mean height of men from households with a head in Social Classes I and II compared with those from households with a head in Social Classes IV or V. For women he reported that the comparable difference was 1.78%.[3]

The differences between these social classes in mean height in this study were 1.03% for men and 1.72% for women.

15.2 Weight

Weight alone is not a measure of fat, since total body weight includes the weights of bone, non-fat tissues and fluid, and is highly correlated with height. This drawback can however partly be overcome by standardising weight for height. However, as noted earlier there are also difficulties with the measurement of weight, in that it can vary in an individual from day to day and with the time of day. It does nevertheless provide a useful measure for intergroup comparisons.

The results presented below are based on measurements taken from 1194 males and 1189 female subjects. Subjects who could not be weighed accurately, for example, because of some disability, have been excluded from these analyses. The weights shown have not been adjusted to take account of the weight of clothing.

The mean weight of men was 75.9kg; women were, on average, about 15% lighter than men, with a mean weight of 64.3kg (p<0.01). The weight distributions for both men and women were skewed, with more subjects being below the mean weight than above. The median weight for men was 74.9kg and for women 62.0kg.

Among both men and women those aged 35 and over were significantly heavier than subjects aged between 16 and 24 (p<0.01). In the Northern Ireland study men aged 50 to 64 ($n = 41$) were 2.8kg lighter than men aged 40 to 49 ($n = 52$). Among women, those in the oldest age group were, on average, 0.6kg heavier than women aged 40 to 49.[4] Knight found that beyond age 50 average weight was less for men, but for women mean weight increased with age up to 60.[3]

(Table 15.2)

Men who were on a slimming diet at the time they kept their seven-day dietary record weighed, on average, 8.8kg more than men who were not slimming and were 8.4kg heavier than the mean weight for all male subjects in the survey (p<0.01). Female 'slimmers' were 8.9kg heavier on average than non-slimming women, and 7.8kg heavier than the overall mean for women (p<0.01). *(Table 15.9)*

Working men were found to be on average 3.2kg and 4.4% heavier than economically inactive men (p<0.01). For women there was no significant association between mean weight and working status at the time of the interview. *(Table 15.12)*

Women in the manual social classes were heavier than those in Social Classes I and II (p<0.05), in spite of the fact that they were generally shorter. Although the data showed that men in households assigned to Social Classes IV or V were, on average, lighter than men in other groups, these differences were not statistically significant. *(Table 15.14)*

Knight found that for men under age 50, those in Social Class III manual tended to be the heaviest, but in common with the results from the Northern Ireland study, he found that men in the non-manual groups were on average heavier than those in the manual group. Among women, Knight found the mean weight was greatest in the lowest social classes only for those aged 30 to 49 and 60 to 64. Otherwise there was no clear association between weight and social class for women. In Northern Ireland female subjects in the manual group were reported as being 4.8% heavier than women in non-manual group.[3,4]

Both men and women without spouses were lighter on average than other men and women, and this was true for subjects living alone, with others (but no husband or wife), and for lone mothers (p<0.05). At least part of these differences between household types are likely to be related to differences in age.[6] *(Table 15.15)*

Men who were non-smokers were, on average, heavier than smokers. Male non-smokers were an average of 2.7kg heavier than those who smoked fewer than 20 cigarettes a day (p<0.01), and 1.8kg heavier than those smoking at least 20 cigarettes a day (p<0.05). Among women however there were no significant differences in mean weight between non-smokers, light and heavy smokers. *(Table 15.16)*

Similarly, reported alcohol consumption was related to mean weight for men but not women. Men who reported consuming no alcohol during the seven-day dietary recording period were significantly lighter than other men (p<0.01). *(Table 15.17)*

15.3 Body mass index (BMI)

Weight alone is not a very useful indicator of obesity or predictor of morbidity or mortality as it is correlated with height.

Of the various indices which standardise weight for height the most widely used is the Quetelet (Body Mass) Index, which has the advantage over other indices of having a relatively low correlation itself with height in adults, but being correlated with the percentage of body weight that is fat. (See Knight for a review and evaluation of the various indices).[3]

BMI does however have the disadvantage, because it is based solely on measurements of height and weight, of giving a misleading measure of fatness in lean individuals with muscular physiques, and for the elderly.

Body mass index, BMI, is calculated as weight (kg)/height $(m)^2$. The index is a continuous variable, but for convenience of interpretation can be divided into categories, to represent degrees of fatness. The categories used for this study are those used in the Knight study and are as follows:

Descriptor	Index
'Underweight'	20 or less
'Average'	over 20 to 25
'Overweight'	over 25 to 30
'Obese'	over 30

The data below are based on the BMI calculations for the survey population; those cases excluded from the analyses of height and weight measurements, as described in the previous sections, are also excluded from the analyses based on BMI calculations.

Mean BMI for men was 24.9 and for women 24.6. The data show that 45% of male informants and 36% of female informants would be classified as overweight, that is having a BMI of over 25 (p<0.01). About one in 12 men, and one in eight women had a BMI of over 30 (p<0.01). (*Table 15.3 & Figure 15.1*)

In 1980 Knight[3] reported a mean BMI for men aged 16 to 64 of 24.3, and for women of 23.9, significantly lower than in the present study (p<0.01). In the earlier study it was also reported that 39% of men and 32% of women had a BMI of over 25, (p<0.01 compared with this present study) and only 6% of men (p<0.05 compared with this study) and 8% of women had a BMI of over 30 (p<0.01). Thus the proportion of men who would be classified as overweight or obese has increased by about 15% and the increase in the proportion of overweight women is about 12%.

BMI increased with age for both men and women; for men the proportion with a BMI above 25 was greatest in the oldest age group (62%), but the largest proportion of those with a BMI above 30 was among the middle-aged, 35 to 49 (11%). Among women the oldest age group was most likely to be both overweight (46%), and to be obese (18%). (*Table 15.3*)

In the recent Northern Ireland study the mean values for BMI for men and women were identical with the values found in this study. However, in Northern Ireland the highest proportion of obese men was among those aged 40 to 49 (15.4%) and for women among those aged 50 to 64 (25%). (In the Northern Ireland study women with a BMI greater than 28.6 were classified as obese.)[4]

Men on a slimming diet during the dietary recording period had a mean BMI 3.2 points above that for non-slimmers and for women the difference was 3.6 points (p<0.01). (*Table 15.9*)

Social class showed a somewhat stronger relationship to BMI for women than for men; for men, mean BMI was highest (25.2) for those in households whose head was in Social Class III manual, and lowest (24.7) in the professional and managerial social classes (I and II), (p<0.05). For women, mean BMI was highest for those in Social Classes IV and V, 25.8; for women in Social Classes I and II mean BMI was 23.8 (p<0.01). (*Table 15.14*)

There was no difference for women in mean BMI according to the number of cigarettes smoked, but for men mean BMI was higher for non-smokers than smokers (p<0.01). (*Table 15.16*)

For men, mean BMI increased with the reported alcohol consumption, from 24.0 for non-drinkers, to 25.5 for those drinking the greatest amounts (p<0.01). For women the trend was in the reverse direction, with women who reported drinking no alcohol having a

Figure 15.1 Percentage distribution of body mass index by sex

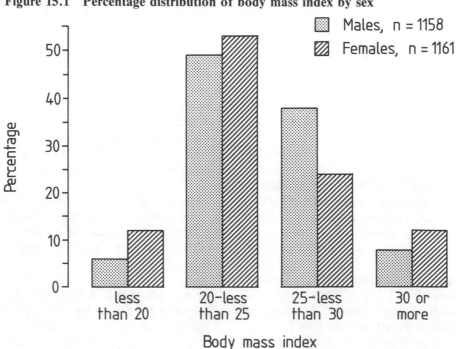

higher BMI, 24.8, than those drinking between 112g and 280g of alcohol, 23.7, (p<0.05). *(Table 15.17)*

Generally the other social and demographic variables examined showed relatively weak associations with BMI, mean values showing somewhat greater variation for women than for men.

15.4 Fat free mass, body fat and body fat as a percentage of body weight

It was explained in Chapter 3 that by making measurements of a number of different sites on the body it is possible to calculate the weight of fat free mass (FFM); the equations used in the calculation for men and women of different ages are given in Appendix F.

Tables 15.4 to 15.17 show the distributions, means and percentiles of the anthropometric measurements for the survey population, analysed by social, demographic and behavioural variables. The data are based on measurements from the survey population excluding those cases where, as explained previously, the measurements were judged to be invalid.

The commentary is confined to the results obtained by using these measurements to calculate FFM. Data on two further variables calculated from FFM are also presented: weight of body fat (total body weight minus FFM), and weight of body fat as a percentage of total body weight.

15.4.1 Fat free mass (kg)

Fat free mass is a measure of lean body tissue (muscle) and bone mass. As a measure it is especially helpful in that it allows the calculation of the weight of body fat as a proportion of total body weight, a specific measure of body fatness.

Table 15.5 shows that, on average, men had FFM 36.2% greater than women (p<0.01). For men the average value was 60.2kg and for women 44.2kg. The oldest age group of men had a significantly higher FFM compared with the overall average figure, (p<0.01), but for women there was no systematic relationship between FFM and age.

Men who reported being on a slimming diet had, on average, FFM about 6% greater than men who were not slimming during the dietary recording period; women who were slimming had FFM 8.5% greater than other women (p<0.01). *(Table 15.9)*

Men not living with a spouse had a lower FFM than married men without dependent children, (p<0.01), but there were no significant differences associated with household composition for women. *(Table 15.15)*

The average value for mean FFM for men who reported consuming no alcohol during the dietary recording period was 3.2kg (5.5%) greater than for the heaviest male drinkers, (p<0.01), but again there were no differences in FFM for women associated with alcohol consumption. *(Table 15.17)*

There was no systematic relationship between FFM and any of the other variables examined.

15.4.2 Weight of body fat (kg)

The mean weight of body fat for male subjects in this study was calculated as 15.7kg; women had an average of 29.3% more body fat, with a mean weight of 20.3kg (p<0.01).

The mean weight of body fat was associated with age for both men and women. For women body fat weight increased significantly across each age group, from 17.2kg for the group aged 16 to 24, to 22.0kg for women aged 50 to 64, (p<0.05, except between ages 16 to 24 and 25 to 34, where p<0.01). For men the mean weight of body fat also increased significantly across each age group up to age 49, but then dropped markedly in the oldest age group, (p<0.01).

Table 15.6 shows that only 1% of men aged 16 to 24 had more than 24kg of body fat, compared with 16% of men aged 35 to 49, and 5% of the other age groups (p<0.05). Among women 29% of those aged 50 to 64 had more than 24kg of body fat, but in the youngest group only 12% had this amount of fat (p<0.05).

The proportionate difference in mean weight of body fat between men and women in different age groups was highest in the youngest and oldest age groups. Women aged 16 to 24 had a mean weight of body fat 38.7% greater than men of similar ages, and the 50 to 64 year old women, on average, had nearly 50% more body fat than men (p<0.01). *(Table 15.6)*

Analysis of mean weights of body fat by sex and other social, demographic and behavioural variables showed the same patterns as for analyses of the weight of body fat as a percentage of total body weight. Since this index controls for body weight those data have been commented on more fully, although tables are given for all analyses of weight of body fat.

Men who were slimming at the time they kept the dietary record had, on average, 33% more body fat than those who were not slimming (p<0.01). Similar differences were observed for women, (p<0.01), although the proportionate difference in mean weight of body fat between slimmers and non-slimmers was somewhat smaller than for men—26.5%. *(Table 15.9)*

For men, the mean weight of body fat increased with the increase in the reported consumption of alcohol during the dietary recording period. Thus for non-drinkers the mean weight was 13.9kg; this rose to 17.0kg for those reporting consuming 400g or more of alcohol during the seven-day period (p<0.01). For women there was no association between reported alcohol consumption and weight of body fat.

(Table 15.17)

15.4.3 Body fat as a percentage of total body weight

For male subjects in this survey the mean percentage of body fat was 20.1% and for female subjects 30.6% (p<0.01).

For men, the percentage of body fat increased significantly across each age group up to, but not beyond, age 49, when it dropped markedly (p<0.01). A significant increase in the percentage of body fat across all the age groups was observed for women (p<0.01).

At the youngest age group the percentage of body fat was 58% greater for women than men (p<0.01). The proportionate difference between the sexes then decreased slightly to 52% at ages 25 to 34, and to 35% at ages 35 to 49. However, in the oldest age group the proportionate difference between men and women was at its highest, 71%. *(Table 15.7)*

In their study to design a method of assessing fatness and desirable weight from measurements of a number of body sites, Durnin *et al* reported on measurements taken from 6495 men and 2304 women in the United Kingdom aged 16 to 64. About two thirds of the survey population were members of the Armed Forces. For men they found that mean percentage body fat rose gradually with age from about 15% in the under 20s, to about 27% for men over age 50—much higher than for men aged 50 to 64 in the present study (p<0.01). In the population of civilian women they also found an increase in mean percentage of body fat to body weight, rising to about 36% in women aged over 50; most of the increase appeared to occur after the age of 30.[7]

On the basis of their data and taking account of other published material Durnin *et al* suggest what might be regarded as an acceptable percentage body fat for adult men and women.

They suggest that for men aged between 16 and 40 the maximum acceptable percentage body fat should be 20%, and that 15% would be a more desirable level. For men aged 40 and over they allow a further 5% on the maximum and desirable percentages quoted.[7]

Data from this survey showed that 36% of men aged 16 to 24 were below the desirable level, having less than 15% body fat, and 23% were at or above the suggested maximum of 20% body fat. Of men aged 25 to 34 only 11% were below the desirable level and 42% had more than the maximum acceptable percentage of body fat. Of men aged 35 to 49 only 2% had less than 15% body fat and only 25% less than 20% body fat (the suggested desirable figure for older men); about one third were at or above the maximum of 25%. In the oldest age group just over half the men were below the desirable level and only 1% were at or above the suggested maximum percentage.

For women between 16 and 39, Durnin *et al* suggest a maximum acceptable percentage of body fat of 30%, and for those aged 40 and over a maximum of 35%. Again the desirable percentages in each case would be 5% lower.[7]

Among women aged 16 to 24 37% were below the desirable level and 29% were at or above the maximum

percentage; for women aged 25 to 34 these proportions were 16% and 42% respectively. Among women aged 35 to 49, 38% had less than 30% body fat and 17% had 35% or more body fat. In the oldest age group 31% of women were below the desirable level and 23% at or above the suggested maximum.

The percentage of body weight as fat was higher in slimming men and women than in non-slimmers (p<0.01). *(Table 15.9)*

Men living in Scotland had the lowest mean percentage of body fat, 18.5%; for men living in London and the South East the figure was about two percentage points higher (p<0.01). Among women also, those living in Scotland had the lowest mean percentage of body fat, 29.8%, but women living in the Central and South West regions and Wales were much higher, at 31.1% (p<0.01). *(Table 15.11)*

This study showed that working men had a higher percentage of body fat than economically inactive men, 20.4% compared with 18.0%, (p<0.01), but there was no obvious relationship with employment status for women. *(Table 15.12)*

There were only minimal differences in percentage of body fat in relation to social class among men, but women in Social Classes IV and V had a higher percentage of body fat than women in Social Classes I and II (p<0.01). *(Table 15.14)*

It has already been noted that men and women living in households without a spouse tended to be lighter and have a lower BMI than those living with a spouse. Among women, those who were married and without dependent children in their household had a higher mean percentage of body fat than all other women (p<0.01). Among men, those who were married and had dependent children had a higher percentage of body fat than other married men, (p<0.01), and men living alone or with other adults but no spouse had a significantly lower percentage of body fat than all other men (p<0.01). *(Table 15.15)*

For men, but not women, drinking behaviour showed an association with percentage of body fat. The mean percentage of body fat increased with increasing alcohol consumption from 18.7% for men who had not consumed alcohol during the recording period to 21.1% for the heaviest drinkers (p<0.01). *(Table 15.17)*

15.5 Variation in body mass index

Tables 15.18 and 15.19 show the combined effects of a number of characteristics of the sample on body mass index; this identifies those characteristics which are of most importance in explaining variation in BMI. The method used was analysis of variance, as described in Chapter 12 (see 12.3). This analysis was carried out as a single stage; thus all the independent variables included in the analysis are shown in the tables.[8]

For both men and women BMI varied significantly with age, social class and whether the subject reported being on a slimming diet at the time of the seven-day dietary recording period ($p < 0.01$, except for social class for men, where $p < 0.05$). Additionally, for men, but not women, BMI showed a strong association with drinking ($p < 0.01$) and smoking behaviour, ($p < 0.05$). However for both men and women the independent variables used in the model accounted for a relatively small proportion of the variation in BMI (16% for men and 14% for women).

Men in Social Classes I and II, and women in all the non-manual social classes had a lower BMI ($p < 0.05$ for men; $p < 0.01$ for women), as did male and female subjects who were not slimming during the dietary recording period ($p < 0.01$). Among men, non-smokers and those reporting medium and highest intakes of alcohol had a higher BMI than others ($p < 0.05$ for smoking behaviour; $p < 0.01$ for drinking behaviour).

(Tables 15.18 & 15.19)

Tables 15.20 and 15.21 give standard regression coefficients for a number of independent variables found to be significantly associated ($p < 0.05$) with variation in BMI. The technique used was backwards stepwise regression and all the independent variables included in the model are shown in the tables. In this analysis, as well as age and drinking and smoking behaviour which were found to be associated with variation in BMI in the analysis of variance model, variables for urinary sodium excretion (total excretion in 24 hours), and the average daily intake of saturated fatty acids are also included. For this analysis social class was approximated by a dichotomous variable indicating whether or not the head of household was in a manual occupation, and because the distribution of reported alcohol intake was skewed this was logarithmically transformed.

For men, age, drinking and smoking behaviour were again found to be significantly associated with BMI ($p < 0.01$), but the manual/non-manual occupation dichotomy was not. Of the two additional independent variables in the model only total urinary sodium was found to be correlated with BMI ($p < 0.01$), BMI increasing with increasing urinary sodium output.

(Table 15.20)

Among women, age and whether the head of household was in a manual or non-manual occupation were, as expected, again significantly associated with BMI ($p < 0.01$). Unlike men, among women there was no significant association between BMI and reported alcohol intake or smoking behaviour. However, for women both total sodium excretion and average daily intake of saturated fatty acids were significantly associated with variation in BMI, BMI increasing as average saturated fatty acid intake decreased. *(Table 15.21)*

15.6 Urinary creatinine

Although the amount of creatinine excreted daily by an individual is often assumed to be constant per unit of lean body mass, regardless of diet, a number of published reports indicate that this may not be so. Moreover estimates of urinary creatinine made from a 24-hour urine collection may be inaccurate if the collection is not complete. Although it has been suggested that population estimates made on incomplete collections might be unbiased (undercollection of urine being cancelled by overcollection), research suggests this is unlikely.[9]

Although creatinine excretion is related to lean body mass, in the tables and discussion that follow absolute values are given, unadjusted for body weight.

Mean values for creatinine excretion were 14.4mmol/ 24h for men and 9.72mmol/24h for women ($p < 0.01$).

For both male and female subjects, mean creatinine excretion was lower in the oldest age group compared with samples from those aged 16 to 24 ($p < 0.01$).

(Table 15.22)

Mean creatinine excretion was found to be higher from men who were on a slimming diet at the time of the dietary recording period than from other men, ($p < 0.05$), but this was not true for women.

(Table 15.23)

There were no significant differences in the mean creatinine excretion of men and women associated with their area of residence. *(Table 15.25)*

Table 15.26 shows an association with employment status. Among male subjects mean excretion was lower for both the unemployed, ($p < 0.01$), and the economically inactive, ($p < 0.05$) compared with working men. Mean excretion of the analyte was also higher among working women than among economically inactive women ($p < 0.01$). *(Table 15.26)*

Mean excretion decreased with decreasing social class, particularly for men. Among male subjects the mean values for creatinine excretion ranged from 14.9mmol for those in Social Class I and II type households to 13.7mmol for men in Social Class IV and V type households ($p < 0.05$). *(Table 15.28)*

There was no systematic association with household type for men, but women living alone had a lower mean creatinine excretion than lone mothers, women living with other adults, ($p < 0.05$), and married women with dependent children ($p < 0.01$). *(Table 15.29)*

Male non-smokers had higher mean creatinine excretion than males who smoked cigarettes, ($p < 0.01$), but there was no association with the number of cigarettes smoked a day. For female subjects creatinine excretion was significantly lower among the heaviest smokers compared with non-smokers ($p < 0.01$). *(Table 15.30)*

15.7 Summary

In this chapter results are presented for the various anthropometric measurements and for total urinary creatinine excretion.

This study showed that the mean height of both men and women had increased in comparison with the results from a study carried out in 1980, suggesting in part a secular trend associated with height. However like the earlier study this study also found that older groups were on average shorter than younger men and women which might reflect a true loss of height with increasing age.

The data showed that just under half of male inform-ants and about one third of females had a BMI of over 25, and would therefore generally be classified as overweight. About one in 12 men and one in eight women would be classified as obese having a BMI of over 30. Moreover, compared with a study carried out in 1980, this study found that the proportion of men who would be classified as overweight or obese had increased by about 15%; the relative increase for women was about 12%.

Analysis of variance showed that the most significant factors associated with BMI were age, social class and whether or not the subject reported being on a slimming diet. Additionally for men, but not for women, BMI was strongly associated with drinking and smoking behaviour. However these variables all accounted for a relatively small proportion of the total variation in BMI. A multiple regression analysis confirmed the association of age, drinking and smoking behaviour with BMI for men, and age and social class for women. Additionally, BMI was correlated with total sodium excretion for both men and women, and for women BMI increased as average daily intake of saturated fatty acids decreased.

Of the other anthropometric variables considered for both men and women weight, body fat and fat as a proportion of body weight generally increased with age. Slimmers were, on average, heavier than non-slimmers; they also had a higher FFM, weight of body fat, and percentage of body fat. This was true for both men and women. The data showed that working men and women were taller than those who were economically inactive; working men also had a greater percentage of body fat than economically inactive men. There were marked differences between men and women in the association between smoking and drinking behaviour and some of the measurements. For example, men who reported consuming no alcohol during the seven-day dietary recording period had a lower average weight of body fat and lower percentage of body fat than other men; male non-smokers were heavier than smokers. These differences were not found for women.

Total creatinine excretion was higher for younger men and women, and was also, on average, higher for those who were working and non-smokers.

References and notes

1. Chapter 4 gives a description of the purpose of the urine analyses, and the methods and equipment used to obtain a 24-hour collection of urine and specimens from this total collection. Chapter 8 also describes some of the methodological problems associated with obtaining a complete 24-hour collection, and the possible effects on the results. Chapter 8 gives details of the basis on which the results from the urine analysis have been calculated.
2. Marmot M G, Shipley M, Rose G. Inequalities in death—specific explanations of a general pattern? *Lancet* 1984; i: 1003–1006.
3. Knight I. *The heights and weights of adults in Great Britain.* HMSO (London, 1984).
4. Barker M E, McClean S I, McKenna P G *et al. Diet, Lifestyle and Health in Northern Ireland.* Centre for Applied Health Studies, University of Ulster, Coleraine, NI. (1988).
5. Among men 91% of the economically inactive were aged between 16 and 24 or 50 and 64; for working and unemployed men the proportions in these age groups were 38% and 52% respectively (p<0.01). Among women 51% of the economically inactive were aged between 16 and 24 or 50 and 64; for working and unemployed women the proportions in these age groups were 36% (p<0.01) and 53% (p<0.05) respectively.
6. Among men living alone or with others but no spouse, 54% were aged between 16 and 24, compared with 4% in this age group among all other men (p<0.01). Among lone mothers, women living alone or women living with others but no spouse, 43% were aged between 16 and 24, compared with 6% in this age group among all other women (p<0.01).
7. Durnin J V G A, McKay F C, Webster C I. *A new method of assessing fatness and desirable weight, for use in the armed services.* University of Glasgow (1985) Unpublished paper.
8. For definitions of the economic status and drinking behaviour variables used in the analysis of variance see Chapter 12 (12.2).
9. Bingham S A, Cummings J H. The use of creatinine output as a check on the completeness of 24-hour urine collections. *Hum Nutr: Appl Nutr* 1985; 39C: 343–353.

| Table 15.1 | Percentage distribution of height by age and sex |

Height (cm)	Age				All ages
	16–24	25–34	35–49	50–64	16–64
	cum %	cum %	cum %	cum %	cum %
Men					
Less than 165	6	6	9	10	8
Less than 170	22	20	24	29	24
Less than 175	50	44	54	64	54
Less than 180	74	71	82	85	79
All	100	100	100	100	100
Base	*223*	*269*	*370*	*298*	*1160*
Mean (average) value	175.2	175.9	174.2	173.1	174.5
Median value	175.0	175.6	174.3	172.5	174.3
Lower 5.0 percentile	164.1	164.5	162.8	161.5	163.0
Upper 5.0 percentile	185.9	188.4	184.6	183.9	185.8
Standard error of the mean	0.47	0.44	0.34	0.39	0.20
	cum %	cum %	cum %	cum %	cum %
Women					
Less than 160	28	33	36	53	39
Less than 165	60	64	70	84	71
Less than 170	86	89	92	95	91
Less than 175	97	97	99	100	98
All	100	100	100	100	100
Base	*194*	*261*	*402*	*306*	*1163*
Mean (average) value	163.2	162.6	161.9	159.5	161.7
Median value	163.4	162.7	161.9	159.2	161.6
Lower 5.0 percentile	152.2	152.8	152.5	149.9	151.8
Upper 5.0 percentile	173.7	173.0	171.8	170.3	172.1
Standard error of the mean	0.45	0.39	0.30	0.34	0.18

| Table 15.2 | Percentage distribution of weight by age and sex |

Weight (kg)	Age				All ages
	16–24	25–34	35–49	50–64	16–64
	cum %	cum %	cum %	cum %	cum %
Men					
Less than 60	15	5	4	5	7
Less than 70	53	31	24	21	30
Less than 80	82	72	64	61	69
All	100	100	100	100	100
Base	*225*	*279*	*379*	*311*	*1194*
Mean (average) value	70.4	76.3	77.5	77.6	75.9
Median value	69.6	75.0	76.6	77.0	74.9
Lower 5.0 percentile	53.8	59.6	60.6	60.0	58.2
Upper 5.0 percentile	88.8	98.0	97.0	96.2	96.2
Standard error of the mean	0.71	0.70	0.60	0.63	0.34
	cum %	cum %	cum %	cum %	cum %
Women					
Less than 50	14	10	5	4	8
Less than 60	58	49	37	34	42
Less than 70	88	80	72	70	75
Less than 80	92	91	90	88	90
All	100	100	100	100	100
Base	*196*	*267*	*411*	*315*	*1189*
Mean (average) value	60.9	63.2	65.0	66.4	64.3
Median value	58.2	60.2	62.8	63.2	62.0
Lower 5.0 percentile	46.0	47.8	49.6	51.0	48.6
Upper 5.0 percentile	82.2	92.4	96.6	91.4	89.0
Standard error of the mean	0.95	0.87	0.61	0.77	0.39

Table 15.3	Percentage distribution of body mass index by age and sex

Body mass index	Age				All ages
	16–24	25–34	35–49	50–64	16–64
	cum %	*cum %*	*cum %*	*cum %*	*cum %*
Men					
20 or less	15	4	4	5	6
25 or less	79	64	48	38	55
30 or less	97	94	89	91	92
All	100	100	100	100	100
Base	*222*	*269*	*369*	*298*	*1158*
Mean (average) value	22.9	24.6	25.6	25.9	24.9
Median value	22.4	24.4	25.1	25.8	24.6
Lower 5.0 percentile	18.6	20.0	20.4	20.0	19.7
Upper 5.0 percentile	28.4	31.3	32.3	31.6	31.5
Standard error of the mean	0.22	0.20	0.19	0.19	0.11
	cum %	*cum %*	*cum %*	*cum %*	*cum %*
Women					
20 or less	25	17	8	5	12
25 or less	77	73	60	54	64
30 or less	94	89	90	82	88
All	100	100	100	100	100
Base	*193*	*261*	*402*	*305*	*1161*
Mean (average) value	22.9	23.9	24.8	26.2	24.6
Median value	21.9	22.5	24.1	24.7	23.6
Lower 5.0 percentile	17.7	18.7	19.5	20.0	18.9
Upper 5.0 percentile	31.7	33.8	32.4	36.1	34.2
Standard error of the mean	0.35	0.33	0.21	0.33	0.15

Table 15.4	Percentage distribution of mid-upper arm circumference by age and sex

Mid-upper arm circumference (cm)	Age				All ages
	16–24	25–34	35–49	50–64	16–64
	cum %	*cum %*	*cum %*	*cum %*	*cum %*
Men					
Less than 25.0	8	1	2	3	3
Less than 27.5	36	15	12	13	17
Less than 30.0	68	44	38	37	45
Less than 32.5	88	77	70	75	76
All	100	100	100	100	100
Base	*226*	*278*	*376*	*310*	*1190*
Mean (average) value	28.8	30.5	31.1	30.7	30.4
Median value	28.6	30.4	31.0	30.9	30.4
Lower 5.0 percentile	24.0	26.0	26.4	25.6	25.6
Upper 5.0 percentile	34.4	35.8	36.6	35.2	35.8
Standard error of the mean	0.21	0.17	0.16	0.17	0.09
	cum %	*cum %*	*cum %*	*cum %*	*cum %*
Women					
Less than 25.0	32	19	8	6	14
Less than 27.5	62	50	36	26	41
Less than 30.0	84	76	63	58	68
Less than 32.5	95	89	83	80	85
All	100	100	100	100	100
Base	*197*	*267*	*409*	*315*	*1188*
Mean (average) value	26.8	28.1	29.1	29.8	28.7
Median value	29.0	29.8	31.0	31.8	30.6
Lower 5.0 percentile	21.8	23.6	24.4	24.6	23.4
Upper 5.0 percentile	33.4	36.2	35.2	36.6	35.8
Standard error of the mean	0.25	0.23	0.17	0.22	0.11

Table 15.5 Percentage distribution of fat free mass by age and sex

Fat free mass (kg)	Age				All ages
	16–24	25–34	35–49	50–64	16–64
	cum %	cum %	cum %	cum %	cum %
Men					
Less than 45	1	0	1	1	1
Less than 50	10	5	7	3	6
Less than 55	29	17	26	9	20
Less than 60	64	49	58	33	51
Less than 65	86	77	87	68	79
All	100	100	100	100	100
Base	*218*	*264*	*366*	*295*	*1143*
Mean (average) value	58.1	61.1	59.1	62.5	60.2
Median value	57.8	60.1	59.1	62.3	59.9
Lower 5.0 percentile	47.2	50.1	49.1	51.9	49.5
Upper 5.0 percentile	68.4	74.9	70.1	72.3	72.6
Standard error of the mean	0.43	0.44	0.34	0.37	0.20
	cum %	cum %	cum %	cum %	cum %
Women					
Less than 40	23	26	22	23	23
Less than 45	63	67	63	65	65
Less than 50	90	87	89	88	88
Less than 55	96	93	96	94	95
Less than 60	98	98	99	97	98
Less than 65	99	98	99	99	99
All	100	100	100	100	100
Base	*172*	*262*	*399*	*302*	*1134*
Mean (average) value	42.2	44.0	44.1	44.3	44.2
Median value	43.0	42.9	43.4	43.2	43.2
Lower 5.0 percentile	37.3	36.5	36.6	37.4	36.9
Upper 5.0 percentile	54.0	57.8	54.1	55.5	55.2
Standard error of the mean	0.51	0.40	0.28	0.34	0.18

Table 15.6 Percentage distribution of body fat by age and sex

Body fat (kg)	Age				All ages
	16–24	25–34	35–49	50–64	16–64
	cum %	cum %	cum %	cum %	cum %
Men					
Less than 12	52	28	10	29	27
Less than 16	79	65	38	59	58
Less than 20	94	85	65	81	80
Less than 24	99	95	84	94	92
All	100	100	100	100	100
Base	*218*	*264*	*366*	*295*	*1143*
Mean (average) value	12.4	15.2	18.5	15.1	15.7
Median value	11.8	14.4	17.7	14.8	14.9
Lower 5.0 percentile	6.1	8.5	10.7	5.4	7.3
Upper 5.0 percentile	21.0	24.4	29.1	24.7	25.9
Standard error of the mean	0.33	0.32	0.31	0.34	0.18
	cum %	cum %	cum %	cum %	cum %
Women					
Less than 12	22	11	3	2	7
Less than 16	52	40	22	17	29
Less than 20	73	66	51	49	57
Less than 24	88	84	76	71	78
All	100	100	100	100	100
Base	*172*	*261*	*399*	*302*	*1134*
Mean (average) value	17.2	19.3	20.9	22.0	20.3
Median value	15.6	17.3	19.7	20.1	18.9
Lower 5.0 percentile	8.7	10.5	12.8	13.9	11.3
Upper 5.0 percentile	28.9	35.1	33.5	36.5	34.9
Standard error of the mean	0.54	0.50	0.34	0.45	0.23

Table 15.7 Percentage distribution of body fat as percentage of body weight by age and sex

Fat as % of body weight	Age				All ages
	16–24	25–34	35–49	50–64	16–64
	cum %	cum %	cum %	cum %	cum %
Men					
Less than 15	36	11	2	22	16
Less than 20	77	58	25	56	50
Less than 25	97	93	64	90	84
Less than 30	99	99	92	99	97
All	100	100	100	100	100
Base	*218*	*264*	*366*	*295*	*1143*
Mean (average) value	17.1	19.4	23.4	18.9	20.1
Median value	17.0	19.4	23.2	19.3	20.0
Lower 5.0 percentile	10.4	13.6	16.4	8.2	12.2
Upper 5.0 percentile	23.8	26.0	30.7	26.5	28.5
Standard error of the mean	0.29	0.24	0.23	0.31	0.15
	cum %	cum %	cum %	cum %	cum %
Women					
Less than 20	8	1	0	1	2
Less than 25	37	16	4	2	11
Less than 30	71	58	38	31	46
Less than 35	93	87	83	77	84
All	100	100	100	100	100
Base	*172*	*261*	*399*	*302*	*1134*
Mean (average) value	27.1	29.5	31.5	32.3	30.6
Median value	26.7	29.0	31.3	31.9	30.6
Lower 5.0 percentile	17.9	21.9	25.7	26.7	22.6
Upper 5.0 percentile	35.6	38.6	38.1	39.5	38.6
Standard error of the mean	0.40	0.31	0.19	0.24	0.14

Table 15.8 Percentage distribution of wrist diameter by age and sex

Wrist diameter (cm)	Age				All ages
	16–24	25–34	35–49	50–64	16–64
	cum %	cum %	cum %	cum %	cum %
Men					
Less than 5.4	13	13	11	6	11
Less than 5.6	38	37	30	20	30
Less than 5.8	50	50	43	31	43
Less than 6.0	73	77	64	56	66
All	100	100	100	100	100
Base	*225*	*277*	*375*	*310*	*1187*
Mean (average) value	5.7	5.7	5.8	5.9	5.8
Median value	5.8	5.8	5.8	5.9	5.8
Lower 5.0 percentile	5.1	5.1	5.1	5.3	5.1
Upper 5.0 percentile	6.3	6.4	6.4	6.5	6.4
Standard error of the mean	0.03	0.02	0.02	0.02	0.01
	cum %	cum %	cum %	cum %	cum %
Women					
Less than 4.8	14	16	12	9	13
Less than 5.0	36	36	29	26	31
Less than 5.2	82	74	70	66	72
Less than 5.4	88	84	81	78	82
Less than 5.6	98	96	96	94	96
All	100	100	100	100	100
Base	*197*	*267*	*410*	*316*	*1187*
Mean (average) value	5.0	5.0	5.0	5.1	5.1
Median value	5.0	5.1	5.1	5.1	5.1
Lower 5.0 percentile	4.3	4.6	4.6	4.7	4.6
Upper 5.0 percentile	5.5	5.6	5.6	5.7	5.6
Standard error of the mean	0.03	0.03	0.02	0.02	0.01

Table 15.9 Anthropometric measurements by sex of informant and whether on a slimming diet

Measurements (units)	Whether on a slimming diet							
	Dieting				Not dieting			
	Mean	Median	SE	*Base*	Mean	Median	SE	*Base*
Men								
Height (cm)	173.5	174.4	0.85	*50*	174.5	174.3	0.21	*1110*
Weight (kg)	84.3	83.0	1.52	*50*	75.5	74.6	0.34	*1144*
Mid-upper arm circumference (cm)	32.7	32.8	0.39	*49*	30.3	30.2	0.09	*1140*
Wrist diameter (cm)	5.9	5.9	0.04	*50*	5.8	5.8	0.01	*1137*
Body mass index	28.0	26.9	0.48	*49*	24.8	24.5	0.11	*1109*
Fat free mass (kg)	63.7	62.9	0.91	*49*	60.1	59.8	0.20	*1094*
Body fat (kg)	20.6	20.6	0.78	*49*	15.5	14.7	0.18	*1094*
Body fat as % of total weight	24.1	24.6	0.54	*49*	19.9	19.7	0.15	*1094*
Women								
Height (cm)	161.1	161.8	0.51	*144*	161.7	161.6	0.20	*1019*
Weight (kg)	72.1	68.6	1.27	*147*	63.2	61.0	0.39	*1042*
Mid-upper arm circumference (cm)	30.9	30.2	0.32	*147*	28.4	28.0	0.12	*1039*
Wrist diameter (cm)	5.1	5.1	0.03	*146*	5.1	5.1	0.01	*1041*
Body mass index	27.8	26.4	0.50	*144*	24.2	23.2	0.15	*1017*
Fat free mass (kg)	47.4	46.5	0.57	*143*	43.7	42.8	0.18	*991*
Body fat (kg)	24.8	22.8	0.74	*143*	19.6	18.3	0.23	*991*
Body fat as % of total weight	33.5	33.1	0.36	*143*	30.2	30.1	0.15	*991*

Table 15.10 Anthropometric measurements by sex of informant and whether unwell during seven-day dietary recording period

Measurements (units)	Whether unwell during seven-day dietary recording period											
	Completed food diary									No food diary		
	Not unwell			Unwell								
				Eating affected			Eating not affected					
	Mean	Median	SE	Mean	Median	SE	Mean	Median	SE	Mean	Median	SE
Men												
Height (cm)	174.4	174.2	0.23	176.0	176.4	1.01	174.7	173.9	0.70	174.4	174.2	0.69
Weight (kg)	75.7	74.8	0.38	75.1	73.6	1.85	77.4	75.2	1.41	76.9	75.4	1.04
Mid-upper arm circumference (cm)	30.3	30.4	0.10	30.2	29.6	0.48	31.1	31.1	0.37	30.7	31.0	0.28
Wrist diameter (cm)	5.8	5.8	0.01	5.8	5.8	0.07	5.8	5.8	0.05	5.8	5.8	0.03
Body mass index	24.9	24.5	0.12	24.3	24.4	0.61	25.4	24.9	0.43	25.3	25.2	0.33
Fat free mass (kg)	60.1	59.9	0.22	60.2	59.9	1.08	60.6	60.0	0.80	60.8	59.8	0.64
Body fat (kg)	15.6	14.9	0.20	14.8	14.4	0.89	16.2	15.9	0.68	16.2	15.7	0.61
Body fat as % of total weight	20.1	19.9	0.17	19.0	19.5	0.73	20.6	20.5	0.51	20.4	20.4	0.54
Women												
Height (cm)	161.8	161.9	0.21	161.1	160.9	0.66	162.0	161.6	0.60	160.5	160.6	0.67
Weight (kg)	64.3	62.0	0.45	64.7	63.3	1.35	62.9	60.3	1.18	65.3	62.9	1.54
Mid-upper arm circumference (cm)	28.7	28.4	0.13	29.1	28.6	0.40	28.3	27.8	0.34	28.8	28.8	0.38
Wrist diameter (cm)	5.1	5.1	0.01	5.1	5.1	0.03	5.1	5.1	0.04	5.0	5.1	0.05
Body mass index	24.6	23.5	0.17	25.0	24.4	0.51	24.0	23.3	0.47	25.5	24.5	0.66
Fat free mass (kg)	44.2	43.3	0.21	44.3	43.1	0.61	43.7	42.5	0.62	44.4	43.6	0.68
Body fat (kg)	20.2	18.8	0.26	20.5	19.6	0.76	19.7	18.0	0.67	21.1	20.2	0.95
Body fat as % of total weight	30.5	30.5	0.17	30.7	31.2	0.51	30.4	30.3	0.39	31.2	31.5	0.55

Base numbers	Men	Women		Men	Women		Men	Women		Men	Women	
Height	915	865		49	103		83	108		113	87	
Weight	940	883		50	104		85	114		119	88	
Mid-upper arm circumference	936	881		51	104		84	114		118	87	
Wrist diameter	937	880		51	104		82	115		117	88	
Body mass index	915	864		49	103		83	108		111	86	
Fat free mass	907	846		49	103		80	102		107	83	
Body fat	907	846		49	103		80	102		107	83	
Body fat as % of total weight	907	846		49	103		80	102		107	83	

Table 15.11 Anthropometric measurements by sex of informant and region

Measurements (units)	Region											
	Scotland			Northern			Central, South West and Wales			London and South East		
	Mean	Median	SE	Mean	Median	SE	Mean	Median	SE	Mean	Median	SE
Men												
Height (cm)	173.7	173.6	0.62	174.1	174.0	0.37	174.6	174.5	0.38	175.0	175.0	0.36
Weight (kg)	73.7	71.9	1.24	75.8	74.5	0.64	76.4	75.8	0.58	76.2	75.3	0.61
Mid-upper arm circumference (cm)	30.4	30.5	0.36	30.6	30.6	0.16	30.6	30.8	0.16	30.2	29.9	0.16
Wrist diameter (cm)	5.9	5.8	0.04	5.8	5.8	0.02	5.9	5.8	0.02	5.7	5.8	0.02
Body mass index	24.4	23.8	0.39	25.0	24.6	0.20	25.0	24.9	0.18	24.9	24.4	0.19
Fat free mass (kg)	59.5	59.5	0.69	60.3	60.0	0.37	60.5	60.1	0.35	60.2	59.9	0.37
Body fat (kg)	14.3	12.6	0.68	15.7	15.0	0.33	15.6	15.1	0.29	16.2	15.3	0.32
Body fat as % of total weight	18.5	18.1	0.58	20.1	20.2	0.28	20.0	20.1	0.26	20.6	20.2	0.26
Women												
Height (cm)	160.9	161.1	0.61	161.5	161.5	0.35	161.3	161.5	0.31	162.3	161.9	0.33
Weight (kg)	61.7	59.4	1.04	64.4	62.2	0.74	65.4	62.5	0.76	63.7	62.2	0.64
Mid-upper arm circumference (cm)	28.6	28.0	0.37	28.9	28.6	0.21	28.9	28.5	0.20	28.3	28.0	0.19
Wrist diameter (cm)	5.1	5.1	0.03	5.0	5.1	0.02	5.1	5.1	0.02	5.0	5.1	0.02
Body mass index	23.9	22.9	0.41	24.7	23.6	0.26	25.2	23.6	0.32	24.2	23.7	0.24
Fat free mass (kg)	43.1	42.3	0.48	44.2	43.1	0.34	44.5	43.3	0.35	44.1	43.4	0.30
Body fat (kg)	18.9	17.5	0.61	20.3	19.2	0.42	21.0	19.0	0.45	19.9	18.9	0.37
Body fat as % of total weight	29.8	29.8	0.45	30.6	30.6	0.27	31.1	30.6	0.26	30.3	30.7	0.25
Base numbers	*Men*	*Women*		*Men*	*Women*		*Men*	*Women*		*Men*	*Women*	
Height	*110*	*105*		*307*	*308*		*376*	*377*		*367*	*373*	
Weight	*112*	*106*		*310*	*310*		*390*	*390*		*382*	*383*	
Mid-upper arm circumference	*112*	*107*		*312*	*308*		*386*	*390*		*379*	*381*	
Wrist diameter	*112*	*107*		*311*	*305*		*385*	*392*		*379*	*383*	
Body mass index	*110*	*105*		*306*	*308*		*375*	*375*		*367*	*373*	
Fat free mass	*109*	*103*		*304*	*302*		*370*	*365*		*360*	*364*	
Body fat	*109*	*103*		*304*	*302*		*370*	*365*		*360*	*364*	
Body fat as % of total weight	*109*	*103*		*304*	*302*		*370*	*365*		*360*	*364*	

Table 15.12 Anthropometric measurements by sex and employment status of informant

Measurements (units)	Employment status of informant											
	Working				Unemployed				Economically inactive			
	Mean	Median	SE	Base	Mean	Median	SE	Base	Mean	Median	SE	Base
Men												
Height (cm)	174.8	174.6	0.22	931	174.2	174.0	0.72	101	172.7	172.6	0.72	125
Weight (kg)	76.4	75.4	0.37	953	75.2	74.1	1.20	104	73.2	73.4	1.15	134
Mid-upper arm circumference (cm)	30.6	30.4	0.10	949	30.6	30.3	0.33	104	29.5	29.6	0.32	103
Wrist diameter (cm)	5.8	5.8	0.01	947	5.8	5.8	0.04	105	5.8	5.8	0.04	132
Body mass index	25.0	24.6	0.11	929	24.8	24.4	0.42	101	24.7	24.8	0.38	125
Fat free mass (kg)	60.4	60.1	0.22	917	59.7	59.4	0.69	100	59.5	59.4	0.68	123
Body fat (kg)	16.0	15.2	0.19	917	15.4	14.0	0.62	100	13.9	3.8	0.62	123
Body fat as % of total weight	20.4	20.3	0.16	907	19.9	19.6	0.51	100	18.0	18.2	0.54	123
Women												
Height (cm)	162.1	162.1	0.23	706	162.1	162.5	0.88	61	160.8	160.7	0.33	386
Weight (kg)	64.4	62.2	0.49	720	63.4	60.1	1.83	62	64.1	62.0	0.68	397
Mid-upper arm circumference (cm)	28.7	28.4	0.14	716	28.4	28.0	0.55	61	28.7	28.4	0.19	399
Wrist diameter (cm)	5.1	5.1	0.01	719	4.9	5.0	0.06	61	5.1	5.1	0.02	397
Body mass index	24.5	23.6	0.19	705	24.1	22.9	0.64	61	24.8	23.6	0.27	385
Fat free mass (kg)	44.3	43.4	0.23	692	44.3	43.2	0.89	59	43.8	43.0	0.31	375
Body fat (kg)	20.3	18.9	0.29	692	19.4	18.1	1.06	59	20.3	19.0	0.39	375
Body fat as % of total weight	30.6	30.6	0.18	692	29.4	29.4	0.73	59	30.8	30.7	0.25	375

Table 15.13 Anthropometric measurements by sex of informant and whether benefits received

Measurements (units)	Whether benefits received							
	Received				Not received			
	Mean	Median	SE	Base	Mean	Median	SE	Base
Men								
Height (cm)	173.5	173.6	0.64	127	174.6	174.4	0.22	1027
Weight (kg)	73.8	73.8	1.05	133	76.2	75.4	0.36	1055
Mid-upper arm circumference (cm)	30.3	29.9	0.28	132	30.5	30.4	0.10	1051
Wrist diameter (cm)	5.8	5.7	0.04	133	5.8	5.8	0.01	1048
Body mass index	24.6	24.4	0.36	127	25.0	24.6	0.11	1025
Fat free mass (kg)	59.4	59.8	0.60	124	60.4	60.0	0.21	1013
Body fat (kg)	14.5	13.9	0.56	124	15.8	15.0	0.19	1013
Body fat as % of total weight	18.9	19.4	0.52	124	20.3	20.1	0.16	1013
Women								
Height (cm)	161.0	160.8	0.56	165	161.8	161.8	0.19	995
Weight (kg)	62.7	60.0	1.02	170	64.6	62.2	0.42	1016
Mid-upper arm circumference (cm)	28.3	27.6	0.31	167	28.8	28.5	0.12	1016
Wrist diameter (cm)	5.0	5.1	0.03	166	5.1	5.1	0.01	1018
Body mass index	24.1	22.9	0.39	165	24.7	23.7	0.16	993
Fat free mass (kg)	43.1	42.5	0.47	159	44.3	43.4	0.20	972
Body fat (kg)	19.2	17.7	0.59	159	20.4	19.0	0.24	972
Body fat as % of total weight	29.8	29.8	0.40	159	30.7	30.7	0.15	972

Table 15.14 Anthropometric measurements by sex of informant and social class of head of household

Measurements (units)	Social class of head of household											
	I and II			III non-manual			III manual			IV and V		
	Mean	Median	SE	Mean	Median	SE	Mean	Median	SE	Mean	Median	SE
Men												
Height (cm)	175.6	175.5	0.33	174.9	174.6	0.53	173.6	173.6	0.34	173.8	173.4	0.57
Weight (kg)	76.2	75.2	0.55	76.7	75.7	0.98	76.1	75.4	0.56	74.9	73.2	0.91
Mid-upper arm circumference (cm)	30.3	30.2	0.15	30.3	30.2	0.26	30.8	30.6	0.15	30.3	30.4	0.23
Wrist diameter (cm)	5.8	5.8	0.02	5.8	5.8	0.04	5.8	5.8	0.02	5.8	5.8	0.03
Body mass index	24.7	24.4	0.17	25.1	24.9	0.29	25.2	24.9	0.19	24.8	24.4	0.27
Fat free mass (kg)	60.5	59.9	0.34	60.6	60.9	0.56	60.1	59.9	0.32	59.9	59.4	0.57
Body fat (kg)	15.7	15.0	0.28	16.0	15.0	0.53	15.8	15.1	0.30	15.3	14.8	0.48
Body fat as % of total weight	20.1	20.0	0.24	20.3	20.1	0.43	20.3	20.1	0.25	19.6	19.6	0.43
Women												
Height (cm)	162.6	166.8	0.30	162.1	162.6	0.50	161.5	161.7	0.31	159.8	159.5	0.43
Weight (kg)	62.7	60.7	0.57	64.3	62.2	1.07	65.0	62.8	0.71	65.9	62.9	0.98
Mid-upper arm circumference (cm)	28.1	28.0	0.16	28.8	28.6	0.34	28.9	28.8	0.20	29.5	28.7	0.28
Wrist diameter (cm)	5.1	5.1	0.02	5.1	5.1	0.03	5.1	5.1	0.02	5.1	5.1	0.02
Body mass index	23.8	22.9	0.23	24.5	23.3	0.39	24.9	23.8	0.27	25.8	24.6	0.38
Fat free mass (kg)	43.5	42.7	0.26	44.4	43.2	0.50	44.5	43.5	0.32	44.6	43.7	0.47
Body fat (kg)	19.3	18.1	0.34	20.4	19.0	0.61	20.6	19.2	0.41	21.2	19.9	0.55
Body fat as % of total weight	30.1	30.0	0.22	30.6	30.6	0.39	30.7	30.8	0.27	31.3	31.2	0.33

Base numbers	Men	Women		Men	Women		Men	Women		Men	Women	
Height	405	401		146	152		398	358		189	236	
Weight	414	414		146	155		409	366		203	238	
Mid-upper arm circumference	411	412		145	155		410	365		201	238	
Wrist diameter	412	413		145	155		408	365		200	238	
Body mass index	405	401		145	152		397	357		189	235	
Fat free mass	402	387		144	149		389	351		186	231	
Body fat	402	387		144	149		389	351		186	231	
Body fat as % of total weight	402	387		144	149		389	351		186	231	

Table 15.15 Anthropometric measurements by sex of informant and household composition

Measurements (units)	Household composition											
	Informant alone			With others, no dependent children						With dependent child		
				With spouse			No spouse					
	Mean	Median	SE	Mean	Median	SE	Mean	Median	SE	Mean	Median	SE
Men												
Height (cm)	174.3	174.3	0.78	174.1	173.6	0.35	174.6	174.8	0.43	174.8	175.0	0.33
Weight (kg)	73.5	72.0	1.45	78.2	77.2	0.55	72.0	70.9	0.70	77.0	76.2	0.54
Mid-upper arm circumference (cm)	29.7	29.8	0.37	30.9	30.8	0.15	29.3	29.0	0.20	30.9	30.8	0.14
Wrist diameter (cm)	5.7	5.7	0.04	5.9	5.9	0.02	5.7	5.7	0.02	5.8	5.8	0.02
Body mass index	24.1	24.0	0.43	25.8	25.6	0.17	23.6	23.0	0.23	25.2	24.9	0.16
Fat free mass (kg)	59.1	59.1	0.87	61.9	61.7	0.33	58.4	58.1	0.40	60.1	59.7	0.34
Body fat (kg)	14.6	14.2	0.75	16.4	15.9	0.31	13.4	12.5	0.35	16.8	15.9	0.27
Body fat as % of total weight	18.9	19.4	0.70	20.5	20.3	0.26	18.0	17.8	0.30	21.5	21.0	0.22

Measurements (units)	Informant alone			With others, no dependent children						With dependent child					
				With spouse			No spouse			With spouse			Lone mother		
	Mean	Median	SE	Mean	Median	SE	Mean	Median	SE	Mean	Median	SE	Mean	Median	SE
Women															
Height (cm)	161.4	161.0	0.67	160.1	161.0	0.30	162.5	162.9	0.46	162.1	162.1	0.30	162.1	162.2	0.81
Weight (kg)	63.8	59.4	1.52	66.0	63.3	0.64	62.1	59.0	0.95	64.1	62.0	0.67	62.1	58.0	1.34
Mid-upper arm circumference (cm)	28.2	27.6	0.37	29.6	29.2	0.18	27.5	27.2	0.28	28.6	28.0	0.19	27.9	27.4	0.40
Wrist diameter (cm)	5.1	5.1	0.04	5.1	5.1	0.02	5.0	5.0	0.03	5.1	5.1	0.02	5.1	5.1	0.05
Body mass index	24.6	22.9	0.57	25.6	24.5	0.27	23.5	22.9	0.33	24.4	23.3	0.25	23.6	21.9	0.52
Fat free mass (kg)	44.0	42.8	0.80	44.6	43.6	0.29	44.1	43.0	0.46	44.0	42.9	0.31	43.4	42.7	0.63
Body fat (kg)	20.0	17.9	0.81	21.5	20.1	0.38	18.6	17.5	0.58	20.1	18.7	0.38	18.7	16.1	0.79
Body fat as % of total weight	30.5	29.7	0.46	31.6	31.6	0.22	28.6	29.3	0.42	30.5	30.4	0.24	29.3	28.4	0.55

Base numbers	Men	Women	Men	Women	Men	Women	Men	Women	Women
Height	79	93	386	400	291	192	404	396	82
Weight	81	97	402	412	296	194	415	403	83
Mid-upper arm circumference	79	95	402	412	296	194	412	402	83
Wrist diameter	79	94	401	413	294	194	413	403	83
Body mass index	79	93	386	399	290	191	403	396	82
Fat free mass	77	92	383	396	285	171	398	395	80
Body fat	77	92	383	396	285	171	398	395	80
Body fat as % of total weight	77	92	383	396	285	171	398	395	80

Table 15.16 Anthropometric measurements by sex of informant and smoking behaviour

Mearurements (units)	Smoking behaviour											
	None				Fewer than 20 cigarettes a day				20 or more cigarettes a day			
	Mean	Median	SE	*Base*	Mean	Median	SE	*Base*	Mean	Median	SE	*Base*
Men												
Height (cm)	174.5	174.2	0.25	*769*	174.5	174.5	0.53	*198*	174.5	174.5	0.45	*193*
Weight (kg)	76.7	75.8	0.41	*791*	74.0	72.9	0.91	*204*	74.9	73.8	0.77	*199*
Mid-upper arm circumference (cm)	30.6	30.6	0.11	*786*	30.0	29.7	0.24	*204*	30.3	30.2	0.22	*199*
Wrist diameter (cm)	5.8	5.8	0.01	*783*	5.8	5.8	0.03	*204*	5.8	5.8	0.03	*200*
Body mass index	25.2	24.9	0.13	*768*	24.2	23.9	0.28	*197*	24.6	24.4	0.24	*193*
Fat free mass (kg)	60.6	60.2	0.24	*758*	59.4	58.6	0.53	*196*	59.8	59.5	0.47	*189*
Body fat (kg)	16.1	15.4	0.21	*758*	14.6	13.6	0.48	*196*	15.3	14.5	0.41	*189*
Body fat as % of total weight	20.4	20.3	0.18	*758*	18.9	18.8	0.41	*196*	19.9	20.0	0.37	*189*
Women												
Height (cm)	161.6	161.4	0.23	*758*	161.9	162.5	0.41	*259*	161.3	161.3	0.44	*146*
Weight (kg)	64.2	62.4	0.46	*779*	64.0	61.2	0.89	*260*	64.9	61.8	1.15	*150*
Mid-upper arm circumference (cm)	28.7	28.4	0.13	*778*	28.5	28.0	0.25	*258*	29.3	28.6	0.36	*150*
Wrist diameter (cm)	5.1	5.1	0.01	*779*	5.1	5.1	0.03	*258*	5.1	5.1	0.03	*150*
Body mass index	24.6	23.7	0.18	*757*	24.5	22.9	0.35	*258*	24.9	23.8	0.43	*146*
Fat free mass (kg)	44.2	43.4	0.22	*736*	44.1	42.8	0.40	*252*	44.2	43.1	0.52	*146*
Body fat (kg)	20.2	19.0	0.27	*736*	20.1	18.3	0.53	*252*	20.7	19.1	0.65	*146*
Body fat as % of total weight	30.6	30.7	0.17	*736*	30.3	30.0	0.33	*252*	30.9	30.7	0.41	*146*

Table 15.17 Anthropometric measurements by sex of informant and alcohol consumption during seven-day dietary recording period

Measurements (units)	Alcohol consumption during seven-day dietary recording period (g/week)											
	Nil			Less than 168g			168g—less than 400g			400g or more		
	Mean	Median	SE	Mean	Median	SE	Mean	Median	SE	Mean	Median	SE
Men												
Height (cm)	173.1	172.9	0.49	174.8	174.3	0.34	174.8	175.0	0.41	175.3	176.0	0.55
Weight (kg)	71.9	70.6	0.79	75.9	75.2	0.53	77.7	76.4	0.69	78.0	76.9	1.03
Mid-upper arm circumference (cm)	29.6	29.6	0.21	30.4	30.4	0.15	30.7	30.7	0.18	31.1	30.8	0.30
Wrist diameter (cm)	5.73	5.70	0.03	5.83	5.80	0.02	5.79	5.80	0.03	5.81	5.90	0.03
Body mass index	24.0	23.6	0.25	24.9	24.6	0.17	25.4	24.9	0.21	25.5	25.1	0.34
Fat free mass (kg)	58.1	57.8	0.48	60.4	60.0	0.32	61.0	60.5	0.41	61.3	61.2	0.57
Body fat (kg)	13.9	13.1	0.40	15.4	14.9	0.27	16.6	15.6	0.37	17.0	16.1	0.57
Body fat as % of total weight	18.7	18.5	0.37	19.9	19.8	0.24	20.9	20.4	0.29	21.1	20.8	0.45
	Nil			Less than 112g			112g—less than 280g			280g or more		
	Mean	Median	SE	Mean	Median	SE	Mean	Median	SE	Mean	Median	SE
Women												
Height (cm)	161.0	160.8	0.35	162.0	162.2	0.25	162.6	162.5	0.45	162.0	161.4	2.15
Weight (kg)	64.3	61.8	0.74	64.5	62.4	0.55	62.7	61.2	0.95	62.3	60.6	3.14
Mid-upper arm circumference (cm)	28.8	28.4	0.23	28.7	28.4	0.15	28.3	28.2	0.25	28.0	28.6	0.80
Wrist diameter (cm)	5.06	5.10	0.02	5.08	5.10	0.02	5.06	5.10	0.03	5.25	5.20	0.07
Body mass index	24.8	23.6	0.29	24.6	23.7	0.21	23.7	22.7	0.34	23.6	23.7	1.06
Fat free mass (kg)	44.2	43.1	0.36	44.3	43.4	0.25	43.6	42.8	0.43	43.2	42.3	1.60
Body fat (kg)	20.4	19.0	0.43	20.3	18.9	0.32	19.3	18.1	0.56	18.9	18.8	1.82
Body fat as % of total weight	30.6	30.6	0.28	30.7	30.6	0.20	30.0	29.8	0.34	29.4	30.7	1.42

Base numbers	Men				Women			
	Nil	Less than 168g	168g—less than 400g	400g or more	Nil	Less than 112g	112g—less than 280g	280g or more
Height	218	423	272	134	371	546	143	16
Weight	224	433	282	136	386	553	145	17
Mid-upper arm circumference	224	430	282	135	385	552	145	17
Wrist diameter	221	431	282	136	386	551	145	17
Body mass index	218	423	272	134	370	546	143	16
Fat free mass	215	420	269	132	355	539	141	16
Body fat	215	420	269	132	355	539	141	16
Body fat as % of total weight	215	420	269	132	355	539	141	16

245

Table 15.18 Men—analysis of variance for body mass index

Characteristic	No. of cases	Adjusted deviations from grand mean and significance of F ratios for body mass index
Grand mean		24.93
Covariate—Age		**
Correlation coefficient		0.29
Region		NS
Scotland	89	−0.02
Northern	261	0.06
Central, South West & Wales	339	−0.01
London & South East	333	−0.03
Social class of HOH		*
I and II	369	−0.45
IIINM	135	0.10
IIIM	355	0.37
IV and V	163	0.13
Economic status		NS
Receiving benefits	105	0.14
Working	817	0.03
Not working	100	−0.36
Household type		NS
Informant alone	64	−0.66
Informant, spouse, no dep. children	341	0.16
Informant, adults, no dep. children	246	−0.43
Informant, spouse, dep. children	371	0.25
Smoking behaviour		*
Non-smoker	685	0.21
Less than 20 per day	171	−0.25
20 or more per day	166	−0.60
Whether on a slimming diet		**
Slimming	43	3.00
Not slimming	979	−0.13
Unwell and eating affected		NS
Unwell & eating affected	49	0.15
Eating not affected	82	0.20
Not unwell	891	−0.03
Drinking behaviour		**
Non-drinker	207	−0.74
Lowest intakes	417	−0.17
Medium intakes	268	0.44
Highest intakes	130	0.80
% of variance explained		16.3%

** F ratio P<0.01   NS F ratio P>0.05
* F ratio P<0.05

Table 15.19 Women—analysis of variance for body mass index

Characteristic	No. of cases	Adjusted deviations from grand mean and significance of F ratios for body mass index
Grand mean		24.54
Covariate—Age		**
Correlation coefficient		0.22
Region		NS
Scotland	93	−0.75
Northern	278	−0.02
Central, South West & Wales	345	0.35
London & South East	332	−0.13
Social class of HOH		**
I and II	366	−0.98
IIINM	136	−0.28
IIIM	336	0.43
IV and V	210	1.21
Economic status		NS
Receiving benefits	138	−0.83
Working	602	0.16
Not working	308	0.06
Household type		NS
Informant alone	76	−0.07
Informant, spouse, no dep. children	357	0.16
Informant, adults, no dep. children	170	−0.29
Informant, spouse, dep. children	375	0.09
Lone mother	70	−0.52
Smoking behaviour		NS
Non-smoker	681	−0.04
Less than 20 per day	235	−0.04
20 or more per day	132	0.26
Whether on a slimming diet		**
Slimming	130	3.23
Not slimming	918	−0.46
Unwell and eating affected		NS
Unwell & eating affected	99	0.57
Eating not affected	107	−0.41
Not unwell	842	−0.01
Drinking behaviour		NS
Non-drinker	358	0.14
Lowest intakes	536	0.08
Medium intakes	139	−0.56
Highest intakes	15	−1.10
% of variance explained		13.9%

** F ratio p<0.01   NS F ratio p>0.05
* F ratio p<0.05 (p<0.01)

Table 15.20 Men—multiple regression analysis for body mass index

Variables in regression	Body mass index		
	Standard regression coefficient*	T-value	Significance of T-value
Alcohol intake (*log value*)	0.1311	3.911	(p<0.01)
Age	0.3114	9.309	(p<0.01)
Sodium excretion (adjusted total)	0.1779	5.292	(p<0.01)
If smokes: *yes = 1; no = 0*	−0.0984	−2.936	(p<0.01)
If head of household in manual occupation: *yes = 1; no = 0*		1.088	NS
Average daily intake of saturated fatty acids		−0.167	NS
% *of variance explained*	15.3%		

* *the standard regression coefficient is given only for those variables with a significant T-value of <0.05*

Table 15.21 Women—multiple regression analysis for body mass index

Variables in regression	Body mass index		
	Standard regression coefficient*	T-value	Significance of T-value
Alcohol intake (*log value*)		−0.772	NS
Age	0.2089	6.221	(p<0.01)
Sodium excretion (adjusted total)	0.1840	5.405	(p<0.01)
If smokes: *yes = 1; no = 0*		0.124	NS
If head of household in manual occupation: *yes = 1; no = 0*	0.1452	4.318	(p<0.01)
Average daily intake of saturated fatty acids	−0.1068	−3.139	(p<0.01)
% *of variance explained*	9.67%		

* *the standard regression coefficient is given only for those variables with a significant T-value of p<0.05.*

Table 15.22 Percentage distribution of total urinary creatinine by age and sex

Total urinary creatinine (mmol/24h)	Age				All ages
	16–24	25–34	35–49	50–64	16–64
	cum %	*cum %*	*cum %*	*cum %*	*cum %*
Men					
Less than 8	6	8	7	10	8
Less than 12	24	23	25	29	26
Less than 16	63	64	63	78	67
Less than 20	90	86	92	97	92
All	100	100	100	100	100
Base	*144*	*193*	*279*	*225*	*841*
Mean (average) value	15.0	14.8	14.6	13.6	14.4
Median value	14.6	15.1	14.7	14.0	14.5
Lower 5.0 percentile	8.28	6.57	6.89	6.21	6.62
Upper 5.0 percentile	24.3	22.3	21.3	19.1	21.4
Standard error of the mean	0.41	0.33	0.27	0.27	0.16
	cum %	*cum %*	*cum %*	*cum %*	*cum %*
Women					
Less than 8	25	19	17	35	22
Less than 12	83	79	81	94	84
Less than 16	96	99	97	99	98
Less than 20	97	100	99	100	99
All	100		100		100
Base	*136*	*213*	*293*	*223*	*865*
Mean (average) value	10.26	10.00	10.00	8.76	9.72
Median value	9.92	10.11	10.18	8.82	9.71
Lower 5.0 percentile	5.34	4.39	5.17	4.55	5.02
Upper 5.0 percentile	15.5	14.5	13.7	12.3	13.9
Standard error of the mean	0.29	0.19	0.16	0.16	0.10

Table 15.23 Urinary creatinine by sex and whether informant was on a slimming diet during the seven-day dietary recording period

Urine analytes (units)	Whether on a slimming diet					
	Dieting			Not dieting		
	Mean	Median	SE	Mean	Median	SE
Men						
Urine volume (ml/24h)	1650	1525	133.8	1630	1513	25.2
Total urinary creatinine (mmol/24h)	15.6	15.6	1.01	14.4	14.5	0.16
Base		*36*			*805*	
Women						
Urine volume (ml/24h)	1525	1500	60.3	1416	1350	21.4
Total urinary creatinine (mmol/24h)	9.87	9.94	0.28	9.70	9.68	0.10
Base		*106*			*759*	

Table 15.24 Urinary creatinine by sex of informant and whether unwell during seven-day dietary recording period

Unine analytes (units)	Whether unwell during seven-day dietary recording period											
	Completed food diary									No food diary		
	Not unwell			Unwell								
				Eating affected			Eating not affected					
	Mean	Median	SE	Mean	Median	SE	Mean	Median	SE	Mean	Median	SE
Men												
Urine volume (ml/24h)	1650	1525	27.6	1389	1267	107.0	1622	1500	88.6	1535	1425	89.6
Total urinary creatinine (mmol/24h)	14.6	14.6	0.17	13.9	14.0	0.60	13.8	14.2	0.50	13.4	14.6	0.65
Base		695			32			67			48	
Women												
Urine volume (ml/24h)	1425	1350	23.2	1390	1260	65.3	1564	1463	60.7	1218	950	95.6
Total urinary creatinine (mmol/24h)	9.75	9.74	0.11	9.86	9.61	0.34	9.62	9.81	0.27	8.93	8.92	0.56
Base		657			81			96			31	

Table 15.25 Urine analytes by sex of informant and region

Urine analytes (units)	Region											
	Scotland			Northern			Central, South West and Wales			London and South East		
	Mean	Median	SE	Mean	Median	SE	Mean	Median	SE	Mean	Median	SE
Men												
Urine volume (ml/24h)	1480	1400	68.4	1604	1550	44.5	1651	1525	44.4	1674	1525	46.5
Total urinary creatinine (mmol/24h)	14.3	14.0	0.63	14.3	14.4	0.32	14.4	14.7	0.26	14.6	14.5	0.26
Base		77			212			276			277	
Women												
Urine volume (ml/24h)	1351	1225	74.4	1388	1312	40.8	1507	1400	34.5	1398	1375	34.3
Total urinary creatinine (mmol/24h)	9.42	9.95	0.33	9.75	9.76	0.19	9.80	9.72	0.16	9.68	9.44	0.17
Base		71			210			302			282	

Table 15.26 Urinary creatinine by sex and employment status of informant

Urine analytes (units)	Employment status of informant								
	Working			Unemployed			Economically inactive		
	Mean	Median	SE	Mean	Median	SE	Mean	Median	SE
Men									
Urine volume (ml/24h)	1643	1525	27.1	1638	1500	100.3	1539	1400	73.4
Total urinary creatinine (mmol/24h)	14.7	14.8	0.17	12.5	12.7	0.50	13.6	13.7	0.52
Base		688			68			85	
Women									
Urine volume (ml/24h)	1427	1375	24.8	1242	1152	86.6	1461	1350	37.9
Total urinary creatinine (mmol/24h)	9.91	9.98	0.12	9.55	9.75	0.38	9.36	9.23	0.18
Base		527			40			289	

Table 15.27 Urinary creatinine by sex of informant and whether benefits received

Urine analytes (units)	Whether benefits received					
	Received			Not received		
	Mean	Median	SE	Mean	Median	SE
Men						
Urine volume (ml/24h)	1632	1500	89.5	1627	1513	25.5
Total urinary creatinine (mmol/24h)	12.6	13.3	0.46	14.7	14.7	0.16
Base		*85*			*753*	
Women						
Urine volume (ml/24h)	1335	1250	53.7	1445	1375	21.8
Total urinary creatinine (mmol/24h)	9.45	9.38	0.34	9.76	9.72	0.10
Base		*121*			*743*	

Table 15.28 Urinary creatinine by sex of informant and social class of head of household

Urine analytes (units)	Social class of head of household											
	I and II			III non-manual			III manual			IV and V		
	Mean	Median	SE	Mean	Median	SE	Mean	Median	SE	Mean	Median	SE
Men												
Urine volume (ml/24h)	1709	1580	42.1	1632	1462	73.9	1606	1475	42.6	1486	1500	48.7
Total urinary creatinine (mmol/24h)	14.9	14.9	0.20	14.7	14.6	0.44	14.2	14.2	0.31	13.7	13.8	0.43
Base		*314*			*114*			*273*			*128*	
Women												
Urine volume (ml/24h)	1520	1450	33.7	1365	1275	56.6	1356	1300	35.2	1419	1325	45.7
Total urinary creatinine (mmol/24h)	10.01	9.98	0.16	9.80	9.52	0.23	9.46	9.60	0.16	9.57	9.27	0.24
Base		*311*			*101*			*271*			*174*	

Table 15.29 Urinary creatinine by sex of informant and household composition

Urine analytes (units)	Household composition											
	Informant alone			With others, no dependent children						With dependent child		
				With spouse			No spouse					
	Mean	Median	SE	Mean	Median	SE	Mean	Median	SE	Mean	Median	SE
Men												
Urine volume (ml/24h)	1562	1525	86.5	1731	1625	42.8	1462	1375	46.6	1654	1500	42.5
Total urinary creatinine (mmol/24h)	13.6	13.3	0.69	14.4	14.4	0.25	14.2	14.0	0.35	14.8	14.9	0.26
Base		*50*			*290*			*192*			*309*	

Urine analytes (units)	Informant alone			With others, no dependent children						With dependent child					
				With spouse			No spouse			With spouse			Lone mother		
	Mean	Median	SE	Mean	Median	SE	Mean	Median	SE	Mean	Median	SE	Mean	Median	SE
Women															
Urine volume (ml/24h)	1504	1500	76.0	1561	1500	35.1	1158	1050	44.6	1414	1350	31.7	1347	1175	88.9
Total urinary creatinine (mmol/24h)	8.83	9.20	0.42	9.44	9.31	0.15	9.88	10.11	0.25	9.99	10.05	0.15	10.30	9.72	0.50
Base		*62*			*298*			*126*			*326*			*53*	

Table 15.30 Urinary creatinine by sex of informant and smoking behaviour

Urine analytes (units)	Smoking behaviour								
	None			Fewer than 20 cigarettes a day			20 or more cigarettes a day		
	Mean	Median	SE	Mean	Median	SE	Mean	Median	SE
Men									
Urine volume (ml/24h)	1618	1500	29.0	1554	1463	56.9	1771	1563	75.1
Total urinary creatinine (mmol/24h)	14.8	14.9	0.17	13.5	13.1	0.47	13.6	13.6	0.40
Base		578			137			126	
Women									
Urine volume (ml/24h)	1410	1350	24.6	1435	1350	45.5	1527	1500	54.8
Total urinary creatinine (mmol/24h)	9.87	9.76	0.12	9.64	9.82	0.22	9.08	9.16	0.26
Base		562			194			109	

Table 15.31 Urinary creatinine by sex of informant and alcohol consumption during seven-day dietary recording period

Urine analytes (units)	Alcohol consumption during seven-day dietary recording period (g/week)											
	Nil			Less than 168g			168g—less than 400g			400g or more		
	Mean	Median	SE	Mean	Median	SE	Mean	Median	SE	Mean	Median	SE
Men												
Urine volume (ml/24h)	1455	1338	46.6	1564	1500	34.3	1705	1588	51.8	2114	1875	106.3
Total urinary creatinine (mmol/24h)	14.5	14.0	0.41	14.7	14.6	0.23	14.2	14.7	0.29	14.3	14.3	0.51
Base		162			344			202			86	
	Nil			Less than 112g			112g—less than 280g			280g or more		
	Mean	Median	SE	Mean	Median	SE	Mean	Median	SE	Mean	Median	SE
Women												
Urine volume (ml/24h)	1328	1250	35.0	1470	1390	28.4	1559	1500	58.1	1700	1600	146.1
Total urinary creatinine (mmol/24h)	9.42	9.35	0.19	9.95	9.99	0.13	9.86	9.98	0.24	9.38	8.98	0.93
Base		280			432			108			14	

16 Blood pressure measurements: results

In Chapter 3 the purpose of making the blood pressure measurements is explained, and in that chapter and in Appendix G the equipment and methodology used are described in detail. This chapter gives the basic descriptive data on blood pressure for the various subgroups in the survey population.

16.1 Basis for the analyses of blood pressure results

For each co-operating subject three measurements of blood pressure and heart rate were taken at pre-set intervals of one minute (see Chapter 3, section 3.3). In a paper prepared by a working group for the British Hypertension Society which sets out recommendations on procedures for taking blood pressure it is reported that there is a 'defence reaction (to the measurement being made), causing an increase in blood pressure, (which) tends to subside once the patient has become accustomed to the procedure and the observer'.[1] This defence reaction is most likely to result in the first measurement being higher than any subsequent measurement. In an attempt to reduce this effect and thus obtain a better measure of the subject's 'usual' blood pressure the results from the first measurement cycle for each subject have been excluded and the analyses based on the mean (average) of the two subsequent measurements.

Any subject taking an anti-hypertensive drug, a diuretic or corticosteroid has been excluded from the analysis.

16.2 The interpretation of blood pressure and comparison with other studies; *caveat*

Comparisons with data on blood pressure from other studies are particularly complex; differences in, for example, techniques of measurement, the type of instrument used, observer variation, and the population being studied (including whether or not those receiving treatment for hypertension were excluded) make comparisons difficult.

At pressures above about 140/90mm Hg there is a graded increase in mortality.[2] There is however some disagreement as to whether systolic or diastolic pressure is the best predictor of deaths from cardiovascular and cerebrovascular disease, and they are highly correlated. For example, the Whitehall study of about 18,000 male civil servants aged 40 to 64, found systolic pressure a better predictor for men except for those aged between 40 and 44 at the time of recruitment to the study.[3] The Framingham study of men and women aged 30 to 69 who had no symptoms of coronary heart disease at the time of the study, found diastolic pressure a better predictor for men aged under 45, systolic for those aged 60 and over, but regarded either as equally powerful for men between these ages.[4] A large scale survey in Norway concluded that as a predictor of death from coronary heart disease, between the ages of 35 and 50, diastolic pressure was probably the better for men, especially for the age group 35 to 39. At ages 45 to 49 the predictive powers of systolic and diastolic pressures were about equal. The latter study also noted that the relationship between blood pressure and death from coronary heart disease for obese men was generally weaker.[5] Others have noted a higher mortality for given levels of blood pressure in lean individuals, but this has not been confirmed by all authors.[6, 7]

16.3 Results

The measurements from 1110 male and 1090 female subjects are presented. Results are the average readings of the second and third measurements for systolic pressure and diastolic pressure.

Mean systolic pressure was 125mm Hg for men and 118mm Hg for women (p < 0.01). For both sexes there was a significant increase in mean systolic pressure with increasing age. Table 16.1 shows that 13% of men aged between 16 and 64 and not being treated for hypertension had a systolic pressure above 140mm Hg, and 3% were above 160mm Hg. In the oldest age group one in four male subjects had a systolic blood pressure above 140mm Hg (p < 0.01), and 6% above 160mm Hg (p < 0.05). Among female subjects aged between 16 and 64, 8% had a systolic pressure above 140mm Hg, and 2% were above 160mm Hg. In the oldest age group 23% were above 140mm Hg, but 8% of women had a systolic pressure above 160mm Hg (p < 0.01).

(Table 16.1 & Fig. 16.1)

The mean diastolic pressure for men was 77mm Hg, and for women 73mm Hg (p < 0.01), pressures tending to rise with age.

Six per cent of all men and 3% of all women had a diastolic blood pressure above 95mm Hg (p < 0.01). In the oldest age group, in 9% of men and 6% of women pressures above this level were recorded (not significant, p > 0.05).

(Table 16.2 & Fig. 16.2)

Mean blood pressure was calculated as:

$$\text{mean} = \text{diastolic} + \frac{(\text{systolic} - \text{diastolic})}{3}$$

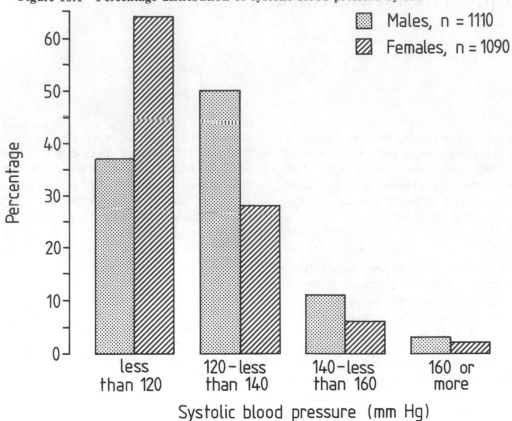

Figure 16.1   **Percentage distribution of systolic blood pressure by sex**

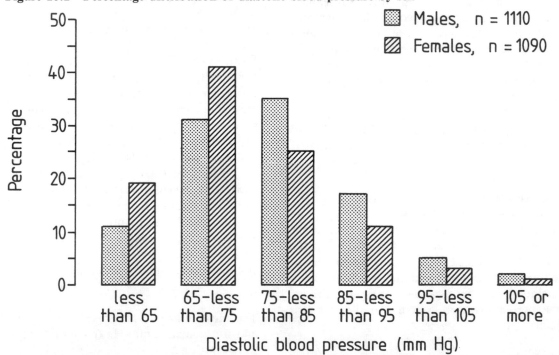

Figure 16.2   **Percentage distribution of diastolic blood pressure by sex**

Average values for mean blood pressure were 93mm Hg for men and 88mm Hg for women (p < 0.01).

(Table 16.3)

These results for systolic and diastolic pressures are consistent with data from other reported studies in Great Britain.[8, 9]

In a recent study carried out in Northern Ireland using the Copal UA–231 sphygmomanometer the mean

systolic pressures of men and women were somewhat higher than those observed in this survey (an average of 5mm Hg higher for men and 4mm Hg for women, p < 0.01). However the variation between the age groups was somewhat smaller for men in the Northern Ireland study (6% over the age range), but markedly larger for women (nearly 22% over the age range).

Mean diastolic pressures among men in Northern Ireland were only marginally higher than in this study

(78.3mm Hg, not significant, p>0.05) but about 5mm Hg higher for women (p<0.01). There was also a greater proportionate increase in average diastolic pressures observed with age for both men and women in the Northern Ireland study, (13.8% for men, and 27.8% for women).[10]

The relationships of various other characteristics of the sample to average blood pressures are shown in Tables 16.4 to 16.12.

Blood pressure was not significantly associated with being on a slimming diet during the dietary recording period.   (*Table 16.4*)

The average values for systolic pressure were lower for men living in Scotland, and in London and the South East than elsewhere (p<0.05). Diastolic pressure was also lower for Scottish men than for all others except those living in London and the South East (p<0.05).

This is somewhat at variance with the findings from the British Regional Heart Study. In the British Regional Heart Study, which is confined to middle-aged men, high mean systolic values were found in the North of England, but also for men in Scotland; low values were obtained for men living in the South and South East regions of England.[11]

The data presented here exclude those on antihypertensive medication, and different prescribing patterns may have affected the results. Five per cent of men in London and the South East, and in Scotland, were taking antihypertensive treatment, as were 7% in the North and 8% in the Central and South West regions and Wales (not significant, p>0.05).

Women living in London and the South East had a lower average systolic blood pressure than women in the Central and South West regions and Wales (p<0.05), but there were no significant differences by area of residence in average diastolic values.
                                        (*Table 16.6*)

There was no significant difference in blood pressure associated with employment status for men. Economically inactive women had a higher average systolic blood pressure than either unemployed women (p<0.05), or those who were working (p<0.01). Economically inactive women also had an average diastolic blood pressure higher than working women (p<0.05), but these differences are, at least in part, related to differences in the age structures of the different groups.[12]   (*Table 16.7*)

Men and women in the lowest social class households had significantly higher average systolic and diastolic blood pressures than those in Social Classes I and II (p<0.01, except for diastolic pressure for men, where p<0.05). Other studies have also found a trend of increasing mean blood pressure with decreasing social class.[13]   (*Table 16.9*)

For both male and female subjects mean systolic and diastolic pressures were higher for those living alone and with a spouse but no children than for those in other types of household (p<0.01); these associations may, at least in part, be accounted for by differences in the age structure of the groups.[14] The mean systolic pressure for men living alone was 130mm Hg compared with 123mm Hg for men with a wife and dependent children. Mean diastolic blood pressures for these two groups of men were 82mm Hg and 77mm Hg. For women, the mean systolic and diastolic pressures for those living alone were 121mm Hg and 75mm Hg, compared with mean values of 114mm Hg and 71mm Hg for women living with a husband and dependent children.   (*Table 16.10*)

Mean systolic pressure for men was significantly higher for the heaviest smokers—those smoking 20 or more cigarettes a day compared with non-smokers (p<0.01)—but the differences in mean values between non-smokers and light smokers were very small, and there were no significant differences for women.

Smoking behaviour had no significant association with average diastolic blood pressure for men. Among women, however, those smoking 20 or more cigarettes a day had a mean diastolic pressure of 75mm Hg, compared with 73mm Hg for female non-smokers and 72mm Hg for light smokers (p<0.05).   (*Table 16.11*)

A relationship between mean systolic and diastolic blood pressures and the amount of alcohol consumed during the seven-day dietary recording period was observed only for men; both systolic and diastolic pressures were significantly higher for men reporting the heaviest consumption of alcohol compared with those drinking no alcohol (p<0.01).   (*Table 16.12*)

16.4 Variation in blood pressure

Tables 16.13 and 16.14 show the combined effects of a number of characteristics of the sample on average systolic and diastolic blood pressure; this allows the identification of those characteristics which are of most importance in explaining variation in blood pressure. The method used was analysis of variance (see Chapter 12, section 12.3), and the analysis was carried out as a single stage; thus all the independent variables used in the analysis are shown in the tables.[15]

For both men and women average systolic and diastolic pressures varied significantly with age (p<0.01), and to a lesser extent with household composition (p<0.05, except for systolic pressure among women, where p<0.01). Among men both systolic and diastolic blood pressure rose with the reported consumption of alcohol during the dietary recording week (p<0.01), but there was no such association for women. Smoking behaviour was significantly associated only with diastolic blood pressure for women (p<0.05).

The model accounted for about one fifth of the total variation in diastolic blood pressure among men and systolic pressure among women, and a slightly smaller proportion of the total variance in systolic blood pressure in men and diastolic pressure among women.

Although the variation in blood pressure with household composition might partly be accounted for by differences in the age structures of the different household types, the analysis of variance shows that, independently of age, informants who were living alone had higher average systolic and diastolic blood pressures than other groups. This analysis also confirms that among men, average blood pressure increased with increasing reported consumption of alcohol, and that among women the heaviest smokers had a higher than average diastolic blood pressure.

(Tables 16.13 & 16.14)

Tables 16.15 and 16.16 give standard regression coefficients for a number of independent variables found to be significantly associated ($p < 0.05$) with variation in diastolic blood pressure. The technique used was backwards stepwise regression. In this analysis, as well as age and drinking and smoking behaviour which were found to be associated with variation in blood pressure in the analysis of variance model, variables for body mass index, dietary calcium intake and dietary fibre intake were included for both men and women. Variables with a skewed intake (reported alcohol consumption and dietary fibre intake) were logarithmically transformed.

For both men and women, body mass index and age were significantly correlated with diastolic blood pressure ($p < 0.01$), diastolic blood pressure increasing with age and with increasing BMI. Additionally for men, but not for women, average diastolic blood pressure increased with increasing alcohol consumption ($p < 0.05$). *(Tables 16.15 & 16.16)*

16.5 Summary

This chapter presents results of systolic and diastolic blood pressure made in co-operating male and female subjects, measured using the Accutorr automatic sphygmomanometer.

For subjects aged between 16 and 64 and not taking anti-hypertensive drugs the average systolic blood pressure (calculated as the mean of the second and third readings taken) was 125mm Hg for men and 118mm Hg for women. The average diastolic pressure for men was 77mm Hg and for women 73mm Hg.

Thirteen per cent of men had a systolic blood pressure above 140mm Hg and 3% were above 160mm Hg. Among women, the proportions were 8% and 2% respectively. Average diastolic pressures above 95mm Hg were recorded for 6% of all men and 3% of all women.

For both men and women average systolic and diastolic pressures increased significantly with age and varied to a lesser extent with household composition, independent of the effect of age. Among men blood pressure showed a marked association with the reported amount of alcohol consumed, but this association was not found for women. However, women who were relatively heavy smokers did have a higher average diastolic blood pressure than women who did not smoke.

Diastolic blood pressure was also found to increase in both men and women with increasing BMI and in men with increasing alcohol consumption.

References and notes

1. Petrie J C, O'Brien E T, Littler W A, de Swiet M. Recommendations on blood pressure measurement. *Br Med J* 1986; 293: 611–615.
2. Lew E. High blood pressure, other risk factors and longevity: the insurance viewpoint. *Am J Med* 1973; 55: 281–294.
3. Lichtenstein M J, Shipley M J, Rose G. Systolic and diastolic blood pressures as predictors of coronary heart disease in the Whitehall study. *Br Med J* 1985; 3: 243–245.
4. Kannell W B, Gordon T, Schwartz M J. Systolic versus diastolic blood pressure and risk of coronary heart disease in Framingham. *Am J Cardiol* 1971; 27: 335–346.
5. Tverdal A. Systolic and diastolic blood pressures as predictors of coronary heart disease in middle aged Norwegian men. *Br Med J* 1987; 294: 671–673.
6. Barrett-Connor E, Khaw K. Is hypertension more benign when associated with obesity? *Circulation* 1985; 72: 53–60.
7. Phillips A, Shaper A G. Relative weight and major ischaemic heart disease events in hypertensive men. *Lancet* 1989; i: 1005–1008.
8. Cox B D, Blaxter M, Buckle A L J *et al. The health and lifestyle survey: preliminary report of a nationwide survey of the physical and mental health, attitudes and lifestyle of a random sample of 9,003 British adults.* Health Promotion Research Trust (London, 1987).
9. Hawthorne V M, Greaves D A, Beevers D G. Blood pressure in a Scottish town. *Br Med J* 1974; iii: 600–603.
10. Barker M E, McClean S I, McKenna P G *et al. Diet, Lifestyle and Health in Northern Ireland.* Centre for Applied Health Studies, University of Ulster, Coleraine, NI. (1988).
11. Shaper A G, Pocock S J, Walker M, Cohen N M, Wale C J, Thomson A G. British Regional Heart Study: cardiovascular risk factors in middle aged men in 24 towns. *Br Med J* 1981; 3: 179–186.
12. Among men 56% of the economically inactive were aged between 50 and 64; for working and unemployed men the proportions in this age group were 21% and 24% respectively ($p < 0.01$). Among women 38% of the economically inactive were aged between 50 and 60; for working and unemployed women the proportions in this age group were 19% and 16% respectively ($p < 0.01$).

13. Rose G, Marmot M G. Social class and coronary heart disease. *Br Heart J* 1981; 45: 13–19.
14. Of men living alone 30% were aged between 50 and 64, and of those with a spouse but no dependent children in their household 58% were in this age group. Among all other men, only 7% were aged between 50 and 64 (p<0.01). Of women living alone 45% were aged between 50 and 64, and of those with a spouse but no dependent children in their household 57% were in this age group. Among all other women only 4% were aged between 50 and 64 (p<0.01).
15. For definitions of the economic status and drinking behaviour variables used in the analysis of variance see Chapter 12 (12.2).

Table 16.1   Percentage distribution of systolic blood pressure by age and sex

Systolic blood pressure (mm Hg)	Men				All ages	Women				All ages
	16–24	25–34	35–49	50–64	16–64	16–24	25–34	35–49	50–64	16–64
	cum %	cum %	cum %	cum %	cum %	cum %	cum %	cum %	cum %	cum %
Less than 120	58	40	35	19	37	84	82	60	35	63
Less than 140	99	93	83	75	87	100	99	92	77	92
Less than 160	100	99	97	94	97		100	99	92	98
All		100	100	100	100			100	100	100
Base	*224*	*278*	*356*	*252*	*1110*	*194*	*259*	*380*	*257*	*1090*
Mean (average) value	118	123	126	132	125	111	111	118	128	118
Median value	117	122	125	131	124	111	111	116	125	115
Lower 5.0 percentile	101	106	105	107	104	96	96	100	103	98
Upper 5.0 percentile	135	142	152	161	152	128	133	144	162	147
Standard error of the mean	0.7	0.7	0.8	1.1	0.4	0.7	0.7	0.7	1.2	0.5

Table 16.2   Percentage distribution of diastolic blood pressure by age and sex

Diastolic blood pressure (mm Hg)	Men				All ages	Women				All ages
	16–24	25–34	35–49	50–64	16–64	16–24	25–34	35–49	50–64	16–64
	cum %	cum %	cum %	cum %	cum %	cum %	cum %	cum %	cum %	cum %
Less than 65	24	11	7	4	11	30	31	14	7	19
Less than 75	71	48	35	20	42	82	74	57	37	61
Less than 85	93	84	70	62	77	97	95	84	72	86
Less than 95	100	97	90	91	94	99	98	96	94	97
Less than 105		99	98	97	98	100	100	99	98	99
All		100	100	100	100			100	100	100
Base	*224*	*278*	*356*	*252*	*1110*	*194*	*259*	*380*	*257*	*1090*
Mean (average) value	70	76	80	82	77	68	69	74	79	73
Median value	70	75	79	82	77	68	69	73	78	72
Lower 5.0 percentile	57	62	63	67	61	55	55	60	62	57
Upper 5.0 percentile	85	91	99	98	96	80	84	94	98	93
Standard error of the mean	0.6	0.6	0.6	0.6	0.3	0.6	0.6	0.5	0.7	0.3

Table 16.3 Percentage distribution of mean blood pressure by age and sex

Mean blood pressure (mm Hg)	Men				All ages	Women				All ages
	16–24	25–34	35–49	50–64	16–64	16–24	25–34	35–49	50–64	16–64
	cum %	cum %	cum %	cum %	cum %	cum %	cum %	cum %	cum %	cum %
Less than 80	24	11	8	4	11	38	37	20	8	24
Less than 90	67	47	35	20	41	86	78	58	37	63
Less than 100	92	82	68	57	74	98	96	86	66	86
Less than 110	99	96	88	85	91	99	99	95	88	95
All	100	100	100	100	100	100	100	100	100	100
Base	*224*	*278*	*356*	*252*	*1110*	*194*	*259*	*380*	*257*	*1090*
Mean (average) value	86	91	95	99	93	82	83	89	95	88
Median value	85	91	94	98	93	82	83	87	94	86
Lower 5.0 percentile	72	77	77	81	77	69	69	75	77	71
Upper 5.0 percentile	101	107	117	120	114	98	99	110	119	110
Standard error of the mean	0.6	0.6	0.6	0.7	0.4	0.6	0.6	0.6	0.8	0.4

Table 16.4 Blood pressure by sex of informant and whether on a slimming diet

Measurements (units)	Whether on a slimming diet					
	Dieting			Not dieting		
	Mean	Median	SE	Mean	Median	SE
Men						
Systolic pressure (mm Hg)	124.0	123.0	2.14	125.2	124.0	0.45
Diastolic pressure (mm Hg)	76.5	76.0	1.49	77.4	77.0	0.33
Mean blood pressure (mm Hg)	92.3	91.3	1.66	93.3	92.7	0.36
Base	*43*			*1067*		
Women						
Systolic pressure (mm Hg)	117.1	114.0	1.30	117.7	115.0	0.49
Diastolic pressure (mm Hg)	73.0	72.0	0.90	73.0	72.0	0.34
Mean blood pressure (mm Hg)	87.7	86.0	1.01	87.9	86.3	0.38
Base	*133*			*957*		

Table 16.5 Blood pressure by sex of informant and whether unwell during seven-day dietary recording period

Measurements (units)	Whether unwell during seven-day dietary recording period											
	Completed food diary									No food diary		
	Not unwell			Unwell								
				Eating affected			Eating not affected					
	Mean	Median	SE	Mean	Median	SE	Mean	Median	SE	Mean	Median	SE
Men												
Systolic pressure (mm Hg)	125.0	124.0	0.49	121.0	119.5	1.74	123.5	122.0	1.51	128.7	127.0	1.56
Diastolic pressure (mm Hg)	77.3	77.0	0.37	73.3	72.5	1.23	76.9	76.0	1.11	80.7	80.0	0.97
Mean blood pressure (mm Hg)	93.2	92.3	0.40	89.2	88.3	1.36	92.4	90.7	1.21	96.7	96.0	1.11
Base	*872*			*50*			*77*			*111*		
Women												
Systolic pressure (mm Hg)	117.4	115.0	0.52	114.7	112.0	1.53	117.8	113.0	1.38	122.8	118.0	2.08
Diastolic pressure (mm Hg)	73.0	72.0	0.38	70.8	69.0	1.06	73.3	72.0	0.91	75.4	75.0	1.25
Mean blood pressure (mm Hg)	87.8	86.3	0.41	85.5	83.7	1.18	88.1	86.0	1.02	91.2	89.0	1.49
Base	*815*			*94*			*100*			*81*		

Table 16.6 Blood pressure by sex of informant and region

Measurements (units)	Region											
	Scotland			Northern			Central, South West and Wales			London and South East		
	Mean	Median	SE	Mean	Median	SE	Mean	Median	SE	Mean	Median	SE
Men												
Systolic pressure (mm Hg)	122.7	121.0	1.27	126.6	124.0	0.91	126.0	126.0	0.77	123.8	122.0	0.74
Diastolic pressure (mm Hg)	75.4	74.0	1.04	78.3	78.0	0.65	77.8	77.0	0.59	76.9	76.0	0.54
Mean blood pressure (mm Hg)	91.1	88.8	1.07	94.4	94.0	0.72	93.8	93.3	0.63	92.5	91.7	0.59
Base		*106*			*289*			*355*			*360*	
Women												
Systolic pressure (mm Hg)	118.1	114.0	1.90	117.2	115.0	0.90	118.9	116.0	0.80	116.6	114.0	0.76
Diastolic pressure (mm Hg)	73.0	71.0	1.24	73.0	72.0	0.64	73.5	72.5	0.55	72.6	72.0	0.55
Mean blood pressure (mm Hg)	88.0	85.8	1.42	87.7	86.3	0.70	88.6	87.0	0.61	87.3	85.7	0.60
Base		*100*			*280*			*354*			*356*	

Table 16.7 Blood pressure by sex and employment status of informant

Measurements (units)	Employment status of informant								
	Working			Unemployed			Economically inactive		
	Mean	Median	SE	Mean	Median	SE	Mean	Median	SE
Men									
Systolic pressure (mm Hg)	125.0	124.0	0.47	126.0	125.5	1.34	125.1	122.0	1.86
Diastolic pressure (mm Hg)	77.5	77.0	0.36	78.1	77.0	1.05	75.8	72.0	1.21
Mean blood pressure (mm Hg)	93.3	92.7	0.38	94.1	93.0	1.10	92.2	88.3	1.39
Base		*908*			*94*			*105*	
Women									
Systolic pressure (mm Hg)	116.7	114.0	0.56	115.1	113.5	1.93	119.4	116.0	0.85
Diastolic pressure (mm Hg)	72.5	72.0	0.40	71.1	69.0	1.39	74.0	74.0	0.59
Mean blood pressure (mm Hg)	87.3	85.7	0.44	85.8	84.3	1.52	89.1	87.7	0.66
Base		*676*			*60*			*345*	

Table 16.8 Blood pressure by sex of informant and whether benefits received

Measurements (units)	Whether benefits received					
	Receiving			Not receiving		
	Mean	Median	SE	Mean	Median	SE
Men						
Systolic pressure (mm Hg)	125.4	124.0	1.38	125.0	124.0	0.46
Diastolic pressure (mm Hg)	77.1	77.0	0.99	77.4	77.0	0.34
Mean blood pressure (mm Hg)	93.2	93.2	1.08	93.3	92.3	0.37
Base		*122*			*983*	
Women						
Systolic pressure (mm Hg)	117.9	115.0	1.37	117.6	115.0	0.49
Diastolic pressure (mm Hg)	73.3	71.5	0.95	73.0	72.0	0.34
Mean blood pressure (mm Hg)	88.2	85.5	1.06	87.9	86.3	0.38
Base		*150*			*937*	

Table 16.9 Blood pressure by sex of informant and social class of head of household

Measurements (units)	Social class of head of household											
	I and II			III non-manual			III manual			IV and V		
	Mean	Median	SE	Mean	Median	SE	Mean	Median	SE	Mean	Median	SE
Men												
Systolic pressure (mm Hg)	123.5	122.0	0.72	125.3	123.0	1.31	125.4	124.0	0.70	127.8	127.0	1.18
Diastolic pressure (mm Hg)	76.5	76.0	0.54	77.5	77.0	0.95	77.6	77.0	0.55	78.8	79.0	0.81
Mean blood pressure (mm Hg)	92.2	91.2	0.58	93.4	92.7	1.04	93.5	93.0	0.58	95.1	95.0	0.90
Base		*390*			*134*			*386*			*178*	
Women												
Systolic pressure (mm Hg)	117.0	114.0	0.76	118.0	114.5	1.25	116.6	114.0	0.81	120.6	118.0	1.13
Diastolic pressure (mm Hg)	72.5	72.0	0.53	73.0	73.0	0.90	72.4	72.0	0.56	75.1	72.0	0.79
Mean blood pressure (mm Hg)	87.3	86.0	0.59	88.0	85.8	0.97	87.2	86.0	0.62	90.3	87.3	0.88
Base		*387*			*140*			*333*			*215*	

Table 16.10 Blood pressure by sex of informant and household composition

Measurements (units)	Household composition											
	Informant alone			With others, no dependent children						With dependent child		
				With spouse			No spouse					
	Mean	Median	SE	Mean	Median	SE	Mean	Median	SE	Mean	Median	SE
Men												
Systolic pressure (mm Hg)	130.1	129.0	1.60	129.1	127.0	0.83	121.4	120.0	0.80	123.4	122.0	0.67
Diastolic pressure (mm Hg)	82.0	81.0	1.18	80.2	80.0	0.54	73.4	72.0	0.65	77.0	76.0	0.53
Mean blood pressure (mm Hg)	98.0	97.2	1.26	96.5	96.0	0.61	89.4	87.3	0.68	92.5	91.3	0.56
Base		*72*			*349*			*288*			*401*	

	Informant alone			With others, no dependent children						With dependent child					
				With spouse			No spouse			With spouse			Lone mother		
	Mean	Median	SE	Mean	Median	SE	Mean	Median	SE	Mean	Median	SE	Mean	Median	SE
Women															
Systolic pressure (mm Hg)	121.4	120.0	1.49	123.3	120.0	0.91	114.3	112.0	0.99	113.8	112.0	0.63	114.7	114.0	1.68
Diastolic pressure (mm Hg)	75.3	74.0	0.93	76.6	76.0	0.58	70.6	69.0	0.77	70.6	70.0	0.48	71.7	70.0	1.30
Mean blood pressure (mm Hg)	90.7	88.8	1.06	92.2	91.0	0.67	85.2	83.3	0.82	85.0	84.0	0.51	86.0	84.3	1.40
Base		*84*			*358*			*184*			*385*			*79*	

Table 16.11 Blood pressure by sex of informant and smoking behaviour

Measurements (units)	Smoking behaviour								
	None			Fewer than 20 cigarettes a day			20 or more cigarettes a day		
	Mean	Median	SE	Mean	Median	SE	Mean	Median	SE
Men									
Systolic pressure (mm Hg)	124.5	123.0	0.54	124.9	124.0	1.07	127.7	126.0	1.05
Diastolic pressure (mm Hg)	77.2	77.0	0.41	77.7	77.0	0.81	78.0	78.0	0.72
Mean blood pressure (mm Hg)	92.9	92.3	0.44	93.5	92.5	0.87	94.5	93.7	0.80
Base		725			192			193	
Women									
Systolic pressure (mm Hg)	117.7	114.5	0.56	116.3	114.0	0.98	119.9	116.0	1.44
Diastolic pressure (mm Hg)	72.8	72.0	0.39	72.4	71.0	0.72	75.3	74.0	0.94
Mean blood pressure (mm Hg)	87.8	86.0	0.43	87.0	85.3	0.78	90.1	88.0	1.07
Base		714			243			133	

Table 16.12 Blood pressure by sex of informant and alcohol consumption during seven-day dietary recording period

Measurements (units)	Alcohol consumption during seven-day dietary recording period (g/week)											
	Nil			Less than 168g			168g–less than 400g			400g or more		
	Mean	Median	SE	Mean	Median	SE	Mean	Median	SE	Mean	Median	SE
Men												
Systolic pressure (mm Hg)	123.4	122.0	1.03	122.9	121.0	0.67	126.3	125.5	0.88	129.0	128.0	1.31
Diastolic pressure (mm Hg)	75.2	74.0	0.75	76.2	75.0	0.53	78.5	78.0	0.67	79.5	80.0	0.97
Mean blood pressure (mm Hg)	91.2	90.0	0.82	91.8	90.5	0.56	94.4	94.2	0.72	96.0	96.3	1.04
Base		207			396			368			128	
	Nil			Less than 112g			112g–less than 280g			280g or more		
	Mean	Median	SE	Mean	Median	SE	Mean	Median	SE	Mean	Median	SE
Women												
Systolic pressure (mm Hg)	117.9	115.0	0.85	117.0	114.0	0.65	116.6	114.0	1.14	114.1	111.0	2.28
Diastolic pressure (mm Hg)	73.0	72.0	0.59	72.7	72.0	0.46	72.8	73.0	0.90	72.1	71.5	1.64
Mean blood pressure (mm Hg)	88.0	86.0	0.66	87.5	86.0	0.51	87.4	86.7	0.95	86.1	85.2	1.69
Base		345			511			137			16	

Table 16.13 Men—analysis of variance for systolic and diastolic blood pressure			
Characteristic	No. of cases	Adjusted deviations from grand mean and significance of F ratios for:	
		Systolic blood pressure	Diastolic blood pressure
Grand mean		124.5	76.95
Covariate—Age		**	**
Correlation coefficient		0.35	0.39
Region		NS	NS
Scotland	85	−1.96	−1.61
Northern	245	1.13	0.86
Central, South West & Wales	318	0.68	0.19
London & South East	327	−1.01	−0.41
Social class of HOH		NS	NS
I and II	355	−1.05	−0.92
IIINM	122	0.96	0.20
IIIM	347	−0.11	0.17
IV and V	151	1.96	1.62
Economic status		NS	NS
Receiving benefits	100	−0.79	−0.88
Working	795	0.21	0.23
Not working	80	−1.07	−1.23
Household type		*	*
Informant alone	59	4.21	3.98
Informant, spouse, no dep. children	304	0.10	−0.26
Informant, adults, no dep. children	246	0.88	−0.27
Informant, spouse, dep. children	366	−1.35	−0.25
Smoking behaviour		NS	NS
Non-smoker	644	−0.50	−0.10
Less than 20 per day	167	0.44	0.74
20 or more per day	164	1.52	−0.35
Whether on a slimming diet		NS	NS
Slimming	37	−0.74	−0.55
Not slimming	938	0.03	0.02
Unwell and eating affected		NS	NS
Unwell and eating affected	50	−0.19	−0.54
Eating not affected	76	−1.51	−0.61
Not unwell	849	0.15	0.09
Drinking behaviour		**	**
Non-drinker	197	−1.36	−1.40
Lowest intakes	390	−1.79	−1.02
Medium intakes	264	1.53	1.25
Highest intakes	124	4.52	2.76
% of variance explained		17.4%	20.2%

** F ratio $p < 0.01$ NS F ratio $p > 0.05$
* F ratio $p < 0.05$

Table 16.14 Women—analysis of variance for systolic and diastolic blood pressure			
Characteristic	No. of cases	Adjusted deviations from grand mean and significance of F ratios for:	
		Systolic blood pressure	Diastolic blood pressure
Grand mean		117.1	72.76
Covariate—Age		**	**
Correlation coefficient		0.45	0.40
Region		NS	NS
Scotland	87	−0.25	−0.75
Northern	254	−0.41	−0.14
Central, South West & Wales	326	0.91	0.42
London & South East	317	−0.54	−0.11
Social class of HOH		NS	NS
I and II	352	−1.29	−0.80
IIINM	122	−0.69	−0.74
IIIM	318	0.79	0.53
IV and V	192	1.13	1.05
Economic status		NS	NS
Receiving benefits	128	0.39	0.33
Working	575	−0.44	−0.24
Not working	281	0.72	0.35
Household type		**	*
Informant alone	68	1.86	1.59
Informant, spouse, no dep. children	321	0.62	0.42
Informant, adults, no dep. children	164	2.81	1.51
Informant, spouse, dep. children	363	−2.15	−1.39
Lone mother	68	−0.11	0.22
Smoking behaviour		NS	*
Non-smoker	640	−0.07	−0.23
Less than 20 per day	222	−0.82	−0.50
20 or more per day	122	1.85	2.14
Whether on a slimming diet		NS	NS
Slimming	120	0.61	0.82
Not slimming	864	−0.08	−0.11
Unwell and eating affected		NS	NS
Unwell and eating affected	90	−1.51	−1.30
Eating not affected	99	0.68	0.44
Not unwell	795	0.09	0.09
Drinking behaviour		NS	NS
Non-drinker	335	0.75	0.20
Lowest intakes	501	−0.50	−0.27
Medium intakes	133	0.50	0.71
Highest intakes	15	−4.33	−1.68
% of variance explained		21.5%	18.1%

** F ratio $p < 0.01$ NS F ratio $p > 0.05$
* F ratio $p < 0.05$

Table 16.15   Men—multiple regression analysis for diastolic blood pressure*

Variables in regression	Diastolic blood pressure		
	Standard regression coefficient**	T-value	Significance of T-value
Body mass index	0.2662	8.891	(p<0.01)
Alcohol intake (*log value*)	0.0688	2.402	(p<0.05)
Age	0.3040	10.248	(p<0.01)
If smokes: *yes = 1; no = 0*		0.060	NS
Dietary fibre intake (*log value*)		0.241	NS
Dietary calcium intake		0.961	NS
% of variance explained		23.9%	

* *variables for sodium excretion* (adjusted total), *potassium excretion* (adjusted total) *and the ratio of urinary sodium to urinary potassium* (log value) *were included separately in the regression analysis, but none reached the level of significance.*

** *the standard regression coefficient is given only for those variables where p<0.05*

Table 16.16   Women—multiple regression analysis for diastolic blood pressure*

Variables in regression	Diastolic blood pressure		
	Standard regression coefficient**	T-value	Significance of T-value
Body mass index	0.2223	7.607	(p<0.01)
Age	0.3395	11.618	(p<0.01)
If smokes: *yes = 1; no = 0*		1.285	NS
Alcohol intake (*log value*)		0.248	NS
Dietary fibre intake (*log value*)		−0.656	NS
Dietary calcium intake		−0.671	NS
% of variance explained		19.4%	

* *variables for sodium excretion* (adjusted total), *potassium excretion* (adjusted total) *and the ratio of urinary sodium to urinary potassium* (log value) *were included separately in the regression analysis, but none reached the level of significance.*

** *the standard regression coefficient is given only for those variables where p<0.05*

17 Blood, serum and plasma analytes: results

This chapter presents the results from the analyses of the specimens of blood given by co-operating male and female subjects aged 18 and over.

Chapter 4 gives a description of the objectives of obtaining a specimen of venous blood, and the methods and equipment used to obtain the sample. In Chapter 5 response rates for obtaining the blood specimen are given.

17.1 Basis for the results

As explained in Chapter 4, it was not possible in all cases to obtain the 20ml of whole blood required to carry out the full range of analyses and the numbers on which the results for the various analytes are based therefore vary. In addition some samples which were sent to the laboratory were not analysed for technical reasons.

Subjects taking the following drugs have been excluded from the results presented here because of the potential effect on specific analytes of the drugs or diseases they are used to treat (see Chapter 8).

Analyte	Drug
vitamin B12	antibiotics; drugs for the treatment of anaemia; sex hormones*
calcium	corticosteroids; prescribed vitamin and mineral supplements; cytotoxics
carotenoids	laxatives; lipid-lowering drugs
serum cholesterol, HDL cholesterol, LDL cholesterol	lipid-lowering drugs; thyroid and anti-thyroid drugs; sex hormones*; anti-diabetic drugs
serum ferritin	antacids; anti-coagulants; analgesics; antibiotics; drugs for the treatment of anaemia; sex hormones*
red cell folate	antacids; anti-malarials; drugs for the treatment of anaemia; cytotoxics; sex hormones*; antibiotics
γ-glutamyl transpeptidase	anti-hypertensives; anti-malarials

* includes oral contraceptives

17.2 The haematological profile, serum ferritin, red cell folate and vitamin B12

Haemoglobin concentration (g/dl)
Haemoglobin is the oxygen-carrying, iron-containing molecule in red blood cells. Circulating levels are an indication of the oxygen-carrying capacity of the blood. Nutrients essential for its production include iron, folic acid, and vitamin B12. Low concentrations in the blood are termed anaemia. Women of childbearing age tend to have lower haemoglobin concentrations because of menstrual losses. Haemoglobin concentrations are usually between 12.0g/dl and 17.0g/dl in men, and 11.0g/dl and 16.0g/dl in women.

Mean corpuscular volume (MCV) (fl)
This is a measure of the average size of red blood cells, usually between about 79fl and 99fl. A low MCV (microcytosis) is usually an indication of iron deficiency. High MCV (macrocytosis) may be due to deficiency of vitamin B12 or folic acid, to a high alcohol intake, or to a number of less common conditions, such as hypothyroidism.

Haematocrit (packed cell volume—PCV)
This is the proportion of the blood volume taken up by the red cells, and is determined by both cell size and number. PCV in men usually lies between about 40% and 50%, and in women about 35% to 45%.

Mean corpuscular haemoglobin concentration (MCHC) (g/dl)
This is a measure of the mean haemoglobin concentration in each red blood cell. If this value is lower than about 30g/dl the red cells are termed hypochromic. Hypochromic anaemia is a feature of iron deficiency. MCHC usually lies between about 32g/dl and 36g/dl.

Serum ferritin
Ferritin is a circulating protein which provides a measure of iron stored. It may also increase with heavy alcohol intake, possibly due to enhanced iron absorption. A value below 25µg/l is generally considered to indicate low iron stores.

Red cell folate
The time between the specimen being taken and arriving at the laboratory was critical for the analysis of red cell folate levels. Samples arriving more than 48 hours after being taken would have been likely to have deteriorated as a result of oxidation.[1] Nevertheless red cell folate analysis was performed on all available samples. However the quality assurance data for the analysis were not satisfactory (see Appendix J) and therefore the data are presented without commentary. In Appendix K tables showing the age and sex distribution for red cell folate for samples arriving within 48 hours, and for all samples, are given. In this chapter tables which show data for red cell folate are for samples arriving within 48 hours.

Vitamin B12

Circulating levels of vitamin B12 are a good indicator of vitamin B12 status. Unfortunately the quality control data on the serum vitamin B12 analyses were not satisfactory (see Appendix J). Results of vitamin B12 analyses are therefore given without comment.

Tables 17.1 to 17.6 show distributions of these analytes for male and female subjects in different age groups.

The mean value for *haemoglobin concentration* for men was 14.8g/dl and 13.2g/dl for women (p<0.01). For men there was little variation with age. A smaller proportion of women aged 50 to 64 (the majority of whom were probably post-menopausal) than those in the younger age groups had haemoglobin concentrations below 12.5g/dl (p<0.01, except compared with the youngest age group, where p<0.05).

There were fewer than 1% of men with haemoglobin concentrations below 11.0g/dl, but 4% of all the women had haemoglobin concentrations this low (p<0.01). *(Table 17.1 & Fig 17.1)*

The average *mean corpuscular volume* for male and female subjects was very similar (91.8fl and 91.3fl respectively). Seven per cent of male subjects and 6% of females had an average mean corpuscular volume of 98fl or more, and among men aged between 50 and 60 this proportion rose to 10% (p<0.05). *(Table 17.2)*

Mean values for *haematocrit* were lower for women than men (mean 0.39 compared with 0.44, p<0.01) but for neither sex was there an association with age. *(Table 17.3)*

Mean corpuscular haemoglobin concentration was also lower for women than men, 33.6g/dl compared with 33.8g/dl (p<0.01), but there was no trend associated with age for either sex. *(Table 17.4)*

Age and sex distributions for *vitamin B12* are given in Table 17.5. *(Table 17.5)*

Mean levels of *serum ferritin* were more than twice as high for male subjects compared with females (106.9µg/l and 46.8µg/l, p<0.01), but for both sexes mean levels increased with increasing age. The mean values for serum ferritin ranged from 63.4µg/l for the specimens from the youngest men, to 129.8µg/l for those from men aged 50 to 64 (p<0.01). For women the range in mean values across the ages was from 31.3µg/l to 76.2µg/l (p<0.01).

One in three of all women in this study had serum ferritin levels below 25µg/l but in those aged 50 to 64 only about one in eight of the specimens gave values this low (p<0.01). *(Table 17.6 & Fig 17.2)*

Results for these analytes for male and female subjects were examined in relation to a number of social and demographic variables, and generally the associations were weak, not statistically significant, and showed no definable patterns.

There were no significant differences in haematology or serum ferritin for either men or women between those who were on a slimming diet at the time of the seven-day dietary recording period and non-dieters. *(Table 17.7)*

Both male and female subjects living in Scotland had higher than average mean corpuscular volumes (for men, p<0.05, except compared with those living in London and the South East, where p<0.05; for women, p<0.01, except compared with those living in the Northern region, where p<0.05). Mean values for haemoglobin concentration, haematocrit and mean corpuscular haemoglobin concentrations showed almost no variation across the regions of Great Britain.

For serum ferritin none of the differences observed between subjects living in different areas in Great Britain were statistically significant although for men mean levels were highest among those living in Scotland. *(Table 17.9)*

The value obtained for mean corpuscular volume from unemployed men, 93.1fl, was significantly higher than the value for working men, 91.5fl, (p<0.01).

There were no differences associated with the working status of women in respect of haematological analytes.

However, mean levels of serum ferritin were higher in the specimens obtained from economically inactive women compared with working women (p<0.01), and although the mean level was higher among unemployed men than working men this difference was not significant. *(Table 17.10)*

For both men and women mean values for haemoglobin concentration and mean corpuscular volume were significantly lower among non-smokers compared with those who smoked 20 or more cigarettes a day (p<0.01).

Serum ferritin was higher among male non-smokers than among the heaviest smokers (p<0.01), but there were no significant differences associated with smoking behaviour for women. *(Table 17.14)*

Mean corpuscular volume was associated with drinking behaviour for both men and women, increasing with increasing amounts of alcohol consumed during the dietary recording period and was significantly higher among men reporting consuming the largest amounts of alcohol and for women consuming between 112g and 280g of alcohol compared with non-drinkers (p<0.01). The same pattern was observed with respect to haemoglobin concentrations for men (p<0.05); among women haemoglobin concentrations were apparently not related to drinking behaviour.

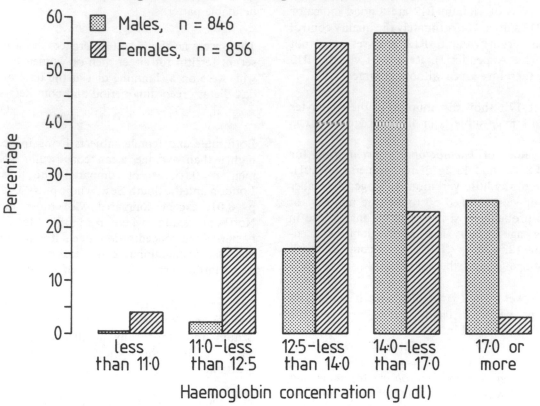

Figure 17.1 Percentage distribution of haemoglobin concentration by sex

Males, n = 846
Females, n = 856

Percentage

Haemoglobin concentration (g/dl)

less than 11·0   11·0–less than 12·5   12·5–less than 14·0   14·0–less than 17·0   17·0 or more

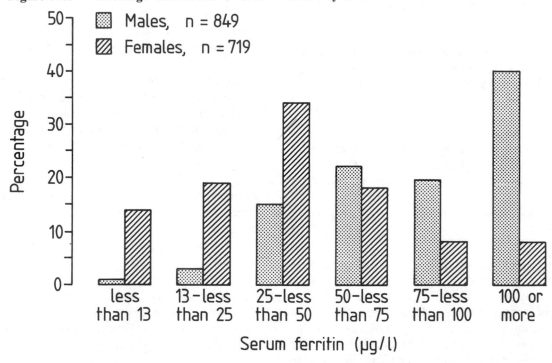

Figure 17.2 Percentage distribution of serum ferritin by sex

Males, n = 849
Females, n = 719

Percentage

Serum ferritin (µg/l)

less than 13   13–less than 25   25–less than 50   50–less than 75   75–less than 100   100 or more

In men, serum ferritin was positively associated with alcohol consumption, being significantly higher in the heaviest drinkers compared with those reporting consuming no alcohol (p<0.01). Among women there was not a clear trend with increasing alcohol consumption although again there was a difference between non-drinkers and the heaviest drinkers (p<0.05).

(*Table 17.15*)

17.2.1 Correlation with dietary intakes
Table 17.16 gives correlation coefficients for haemoglobin, serum ferritin and red cell folate with dietary intakes of iron, vitamin B12 (haemoglobin and ferritin only), and dietary folate.

Haemoglobin concentrations were negatively correlated with dietary intakes of total iron, (including iron from food supplements) for men (p<0.05), and positively correlated with intakes of vitamin B12 from food sources for women (p<0.05). All other correlations were not significant (p>0.05).

None of the dietary intakes showed any significant correlation with serum ferritin concentrations for women, but for men serum ferritin levels were positively correlated with dietary folate, from food and from all sources (p<0.01), and with intakes of vitamin B12, again from food, and from all sources (p<0.05).

For both men and women, red cell folate concentrations were positively correlated with intakes of folate (p<0.01). *(Table 17.16)*

Intakes of vitamin B12 were significantly correlated with serum vitamin B12 levels for both men and women (p<0.01, except for total intake, including vitamin B12 from food supplements for women, where p<0.05). *(Table 17.17)*

17.3 Serum cholesterol
Serum total cholesterol
High circulating levels of total cholesterol are a risk factor for cardiovascular disease. They vary with genetic and environmental influences, including dietary factors, notably the amount of saturated fatty acids in the diet.

Cholesterol circulates in the blood bound to a variety of different proteins—the lipoproteins. Cholesterol bound to low density lipoproteins (*LDL cholesterol*), is the major proportion of total circulating cholesterol. High circulating levels of LDL cholesterol are associated with increased risk of cardiovascular disease. Cholesterol bound to high density lipoproteins (*HDL cholesterol*) is a smaller proportion of the total, and may be inversely related to the development of cardiovascular disease.[2]

As the samples were not obtained from fasting subjects, triglycerides were not measured. An accurate calculation of LDL cholesterol cannot therefore be made, and total cholesterol minus HDL cholesterol has been taken as an approximation of LDL cholesterol, uncorrected for serum triglycerides. *For brevity in this Report the term 'LDL cholesterol' has been used for non-HDL cholesterol.*

Expert groups both in Europe and the USA have accepted conventional categories for serum cholesterol such that concentrations below 5.2mmol/l represent a desirable range, 5.2mmol/l to 6.4mmol/l mildly elevated, 6.5mmol/l to 7.8mmol/l moderately elevated, and above 7.8mmol/l severely elevated.[3,4]

The mean *serum total cholesterol concentration* for both men and women was 5.8mmol/l, and for both sexes mean concentrations increased with increasing age; this was particularly marked in the oldest women

(p<0.01, except between women aged 18 to 24 and 25 to 34, where the differences were not significant). At ages 25 to 49 the mean values for men were significantly higher than the values for women, but in the oldest age group the mean total cholesterol for women was significantly greater than for men (p<0.01).

Table 17.18 shows that the proportion of men with serum total cholesterol below 5.2mmol/l declined from 75% for the group aged 18 to 24, to only 13% for those aged 50 to 64 (p<0.01). Correspondingly only 4% of men aged 25 to 34 but 10% of men aged 50 to 64 had total cholesterol of 7.8mmol/l or above (p<0.01).

Women showed the same overall pattern. Thus 66% of the youngest group of women had a total cholesterol level below 5.2mmol/l, compared with only 10% of women aged between 50 and 64 (p<0.01). However there was a more marked effect between women under and over the age of 50. For example, up to age 24, only 6% of women had a total cholesterol of 6.5mmol/l or more; this increased to 21% among women aged 35 to 49, and to 59% for women aged between 50 and 64 (p<0.01). This effect was even more marked when the highest total cholesterol levels were considered; up to age 49 no more than 3% of women had a total cholesterol at or above 7.8mmol/l, but among those aged 50 to 64, one in five women had a total cholesterol this high (p<0.01). *(Table 17.18 & Fig 17.3)*

Mean *HDL cholesterol concentrations* were significantly lower overall in male subjects compared with females (1.2mmol/l and 1.4mmol/l, p<0.01), but there was no systematic variation with age.
(Table 17.19 & Fig 17.4)

Distributions by age and sex for *LDL cholesterol concentrations* are shown in Table 17.20 and Figure 17.5.
(Table 17.20 & Fig 17.5)

There were no significant differences associated with whether male or female subjects were on a slimming diet for total and LDL cholesterol. However both men and women who were dieting during the recording period had a significantly lower concentration of HDL cholesterol than other subjects (p<0.01).
(Table 17.21)

Total cholesterol concentrations were not higher among subjects living in the North of England and Scotland compared with those living in other parts of Great Britain. *(Table 17.23)*

Economically inactive men and women had a higher mean serum total cholesterol concentration than those who were working (p<0.01), or unemployed (for men, p<0.01, for women, p<0.05); however this, at least in part, may be an age-related effect, since there were higher proportions of older men and women in the economically inactive groups than in other economic status groups[5] (see also 17.4.1). *(Table 17.24)*

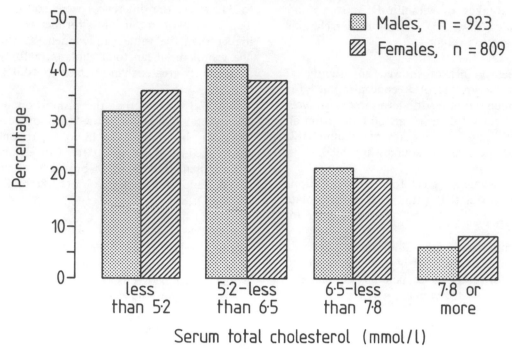

Figure 17.3   Percentage distribution of serum total cholesterol by sex

Percentage

Serum total cholesterol (mmol/l)

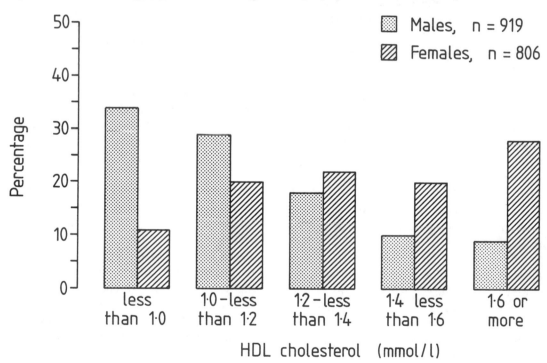

Figure 17.4   Percentage distribution of high density lipoprotein cholesterol by sex

Percentage

HDL cholesterol (mmol/l)

The mean total cholesterol concentration for men from households where the head was from Social Classes IV and V was lower than for men in the non-manual social classes (p < 0.05), but there was no apparent association with social class for HDL cholesterol. Among women HDL cholesterol concentration was lower in Social Classes IV and V than in the non-manual classes (p < 0.05), but there were no significant differences associated with total cholesterol and social class.

(*Table 17.26*)

Both married men and women without dependent children had total cholesterol concentrations significantly higher than all others except those living alone without children (p < 0.01). Married women without dependent children also had higher average concentrations of HDL cholesterol than either lone mothers (p < 0.01), or married women with dependent children (p < 0.05), but similar differences were not observed for men.

(*Table 17.27*)

Figure 17.5 Percentage distribution of LDL cholesterol by sex

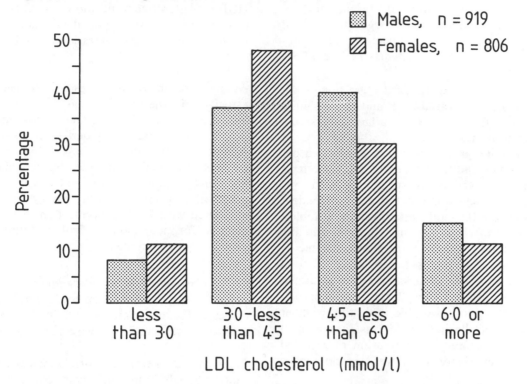

Mean concentrations of total and LDL cholesterol were lowest in men who were light smokers and highest in the heaviest smokers (p<0.01). HDL concentrations were highest in male non-smokers and lowest in those smoking the greatest number of cigarettes (p<0.05). The same pattern was observed for women; however the differences in total cholesterol were not significant (p<0.05); those for LDL cholesterol were less marked than for men (p<0.05), but for HDL the association was stronger (p<0.01). (*Table 17.28*)

For total and HDL cholesterol in men there was a trend to increasing concentrations with increasing reported amounts of alcohol consumed. For LDL cholesterol there was no such trend. Mean concentrations of total, LDL and HDL cholesterol were highest in the heaviest male drinkers; male non-drinkers had the lowest total and HDL cholesterol concentrations (p<0.05). Among women, total and LDL cholesterol concentrations were highest in non-drinkers and lowest among those reporting consuming moderate amounts of alcohol (between 112g and 280g) (p<0.01). HDL cholesterol concentrations were lowest in female non-drinkers and highest in those consuming moderate amounts of alcohol (p<0.01). (*Table 17.29*)

17.3.1 Variation in serum cholesterol concentrations

This section develops the analysis of serum total cholesterol and HDL cholesterol concentrations in relation to a number of demographic, social and behavioural variables by considering their combined effects. In this way those characteristics which are most important in explaining variation in the concentrations of these serum analytes can be identified. The method used to undertake this analysis was the technique of analysis of variance as described in Chapter 12 (see 12.3), except here the analysis was carried out as a single stage; thus all the independent variables used in the analysis are shown in the tables.[6]

The analysis was carried out for men and women and for total and HDL cholesterol concentrations separately.

Tables 17.30 and 17.31 show that serum total cholesterol concentration was significantly related to very few of the variables considered.

For both men and women serum total cholesterol concentration varied significantly with age (p<0.01). For women, there was no association with any of the other variables in the analysis independent of age. For men however, household composition and drinking behaviour were significantly related to total cholesterol concentration (p<0.01). The heaviest male drinkers and men living with a spouse had a higher total cholesterol concentration than those consuming no alcohol or only moderate amounts, and men living alone or with other adults. Overall for men 26% of the variation and for women 37% of the variation was explained by the variables in the model. (*Tables 17.30 & 17.31*)

Of the total variation in HDL cholesterol concentration only 8% for men and 12% for women was explained by the variables included in the analysis. There was no significant age effect in relation to HDL cholesterol (compared with total cholesterol where the age effect was marked), but a greater number of independent variables were significantly associated for both men and women. Higher HDL concentrations were found for

267

non-smokers (p<0.05), those not on a slimming diet (for men: p<0.01; for women: p<0.05), and for those reporting consuming moderate or large quantities of alcohol (for men: p<0.01; for women: p<0.05).

(*Tables 17.30 & 17.31*)

Tables 17.32 to 17.35 give standard regression coefficients for a number of variables found to be significantly associated (p<0.05) with variation in serum cholesterol concentrations. As with the analysis of variance model the regression analysis was carried out for men and women and for total and HDL cholesterol concentrations separately. The technique used was backwards stepwise regression and all the independent variables included in the model are shown in the tables. In this analysis, as well as age, smoking and drinking behaviour, variables for body mass index, total energy intake, total intake of fat as a percentage of food energy, and the ratio of polyunsaturated to saturated fatty acids were included. Social class was approximated by a dichotomous variable indicating whether or not the head of the household was in a manual occupation, and because the distribution of reported alcohol intake was skewed this was logarithmically transformed.

For men, age was again found to be significantly associated with serum total cholesterol concentration (p<0.01); alcohol intake, smoking behaviour and whether the head of household was in a manual or non-manual occupation showed no association in this analysis nor did energy intake, intake of fat as a percentage of energy nor the P:S ratio (p>0.05). However there was a marked relationship between total cholesterol concentration and body mass index (p<0.01), concentrations increasing with increasing body mass index. Table 17.32 shows that about one quarter of the total variance in serum total cholesterol concentration among men was explained by the variables in the regression analysis. (*Table 17.32*)

Among women serum total cholesterol concentration was significantly associated with age (p<0.01) and, to a lesser extent, with body mass index (p<0.05). Smoking and drinking behaviour, and whether the head of the woman's household was in a manual or non-manual occupation had no association. Of the variables related to dietary intake of fat and fatty acids, only the P:S ratio was significantly associated with total cholesterol concentration (p<0.05), the lower the ratio, the higher the total concentration. Just over one third of the variance was explained by the variables in the regression analysis. (*Table 17.33*)

Among men, in contrast to total cholesterol concentration, HDL cholesterol concentration was found to be associated with energy intake and intake of fat as a proportion of total food energy (p<0.05). HDL cholesterol concentration increased with increases in the proportion of food energy derived from fat, and decreased with decreases in total energy intake. A lower body mass index, higher intakes of alcohol and not smoking were also associated significantly with a higher HDL cholesterol concentration (p<0.01). Overall, for men, about 12% of the total variance was explained by the variables in the regression analysis.

(*Table 17.34*)

Among women HDL cholesterol concentration was associated in the same way as for men with alcohol intake, smoking behaviour, body mass index and the proportion of food energy derived from fat (p<0.01). Additionally the analysis showed that HDL concentrations were higher in older women and when the head of the subject's household was in a non-manual occupation (p<0.05). Total energy intake was not associated with HDL concentration in women, unlike men. As for men, about 12% of the total variance was explained by the model. (*Table 17.35*)

17.3.2 Correlation with dietary intakes

Table 17.36 gives correlation coefficients between serum cholesterol concentrations and intakes of fat, fatty acids and cholesterol for men and women separately.

For men, in general, the correlations were not significant, although serum total cholesterol and LDL cholesterol were positively correlated with intakes of cholesterol (p<0.01 and p<0.05 respectively). Serum total cholesterol also showed a significant positive correlation with the percentage of food energy derived from saturated fatty acids and HDL cholesterol with the percentage of food energy derived from fat in the diet (p<0.05).

For women, HDL cholesterol concentrations showed significant positive correlations with intakes of fatty acids and fat, with cholesterol, and with the proportion of food energy derived from fat (p<0.01). There were also less marked associations with the proportion of food energy obtained from saturated and saturated plus trans fatty acids (p<0.05). Serum total cholesterol and LDL cholesterol concentrations were also positively correlated with the proportion of food energy derived from saturated and saturated plus trans fatty acids (p<0.05 for total cholesterol; p<0.01 for LDL cholesterol). As for men serum total cholesterol concentrations for women were correlated with dietary intakes of cholesterol (p<0.05). (*Table 17.36*)

17.4 Serum albumin, serum globulin and serum total protein

The mean values of both *serum albumin* and *serum total protein* were higher in male subjects than females (p<0.01). Mean levels decreased as age increased, with those in the oldest age group having significantly lower mean values than all other age groups, except for serum total protein among women where the only significant difference was between the youngest and oldest age groups (p<0.01). (*Tables 17.37 & 17.38*)

Distributions by age and sex for *serum globulin* are shown in Table 17.39. (*Table 17.39*)

There were no differences in mean serum total protein or mean albumin concentrations between subjects who were on a slimming diet at the time of keeping the dietary record, and other subjects. *(Table 17.40)*

Levels of serum total protein also showed no significant association with area of residence for men; for women, serum total protein was highest for those living in London and the South East and lowest for women living in Scotland (p < 0.05). *(Table 17.42)*

There was no association for either men or women between serum total protein and economic status. However, working men and women had a higher average serum albumin than those who were economically inactive (p < 0.01); unemployed men also had a lower average serum albumin than working men (p < 0.01).
(Table 17.43)

Women in Social Classes IV and V had lower serum total protein than other women (p < 0.05), but this was not true for men. Mean serum albumin levels were higher for both men and women in non-manual social classes compared with those in manual groups (p < 0.05). *(Table 17.45)*

For both male and female subjects, those who were married with no dependent children had the lowest total serum protein; the highest values for men were for those married with children, and for women, for those living with other adults but no spouse (p < 0.01). *(Table 17.46)*

In relation to the composition of the household that the subject was living in, men living alone had, on average, the lowest serum albumin levels and those who were married with children, the highest (p < 0.01). Among women the lowest average values were for lone mothers; women living with other adults but no spouse had the highest values (p < 0.05). *(Table 17.46)*

Specimens from men and women who were heavy smokers (more than 20 cigarettes a day) contained the lowest mean levels of both protein and albumin, and those from non-smokers the highest mean levels of these analytes. For men the range in serum total protein was from a mean of 71.4g/l to 72.1g/l (p < 0.05), and for serum albumin, from 44.5g/l to 45.5g/l (p < 0.01). For women non-smokers the mean value for serum total protein was 71.8g/l falling to 69.7g/l for the heaviest women smokers (p < 0.05), and for serum albumin from 44.4g/l to 43.1g/l (p < 0.01).
(Table 17.47)

Average serum total protein levels increased with increasing alcohol consumption in men from 71.6g/l for non-drinkers to 72.7g/l for the heaviest drinkers (p < 0.05). These differences were not observed in the data for women. Mean values for serum albumin did not show the same steady increase with increasing amounts of alcohol for both men and women, but non-drinkers had significantly lower levels of this analyte than consumers of light or moderate amounts of alcohol (p < 0.01). *(Table 17.48)*

Table 17.49 shows that serum albumin levels were not significantly correlated with intakes of protein for either men or women (p > 0.05). *(Table 17.49)*

17.5 Alkaline phosphatase, γ-glutamyl transpeptidase, serum calcium and serum creatinine

Alkaline phosphatase
Alkaline phosphatase is an enzyme formed in the osteoblast cells in bone, and in cells lining the biliary tract. High levels are found during growth, or vitamin D deficiency, and may also be found in secondary bone cancer and obstruction of the biliary tract.

γ-glutamyl transpeptidase
This enzyme is found in the parenchymal cells of the liver, and is released in response to non-specific damage of the liver by a variety of causes. In the absence of an obvious cause, such as some drugs, alcohol should be considered.

Serum calcium and serum creatinine
These measures were obtained as part of a routine package of analyses carried out on the serum specimens. Although the results for these analytes are given in the tables, they are not discussed here.

Mean levels of *alkaline phosphatase* were about 16% higher in the serum specimens obtained from male subjects than for those obtained from female subjects; the overall mean for men was 176.2u/l and for women 152.0u/l (p < 0.01). The highest mean values were from specimens provided by young men aged 18 to 24, 204.0u/l (p < 0.01), and are likely to be due to continuing growth in a number of these individuals. Table 17.50 shows that for 45% of the youngest men alkaline phosphatase exceeded 200u/l, compared with 26% overall (p < 0.01). *(Table 17.50)*

The highest mean values for γ-*glutamyl transpeptidase*, 44.8u/l, were found for men aged between 35 and 49, (p < 0.01 for all age groups except those aged 50 to 64, where p < 0.05). Overall means were 33.7u/l for men and 18.6u/l for women (p < 0.01). *(Table 17.51)*

Age and sex distributions for *serum calcium* and *serum creatinine* are given in Tables 17.52 and 17.53.
(Tables 17.52 & 17.53)

None of the differences observed between subjects living in different areas in Great Britain were statistically significant (p > 0.05). *(Table 17.56)*

Mean levels of alkaline phosphatase were higher in the specimens obtained from economically inactive and unemployed men compared with working men (p < 0.01). Mean levels of γ-glutamyl transpeptidase showed the same trend, but the differences were not statistically significant (p>0.05). Economically inactive women also had significantly higher levels of alkaline phosphatase than working women (p<0.01), but there was no significant association between women's economic status and γ-glutamyl transpeptidase.

(*Table 17.57*)

For both male and female subjects mean values of alkaline phosphatase were lowest in the highest social classes (I and II), gradually increasing to their highest mean values for subjects from Social Classes IV and V (p<0.01). Mean levels of γ-glutamyl transpeptidase were lowest among men in Social Classes I and II and highest for those in Social Class III manual (p<0.05).

(*Table 17.59*)

Male non-smokers had lower levels of γ-glutamyl transpeptidase than light smokers (p<0.05), and lower levels of alkaline phosphatase than heavy smokers (p<0.05). There was no systematic relationship between these analytes and smoking behaviour among women.

(*Table 17.61*)

In men γ-glutamyl transpeptidase was significantly lower in non-drinkers compared with the heaviest drinkers (p<0.01), but the similar difference observed in the data for women was not significant (p>0.05). Alkaline phosphatase was highest in male and female non-drinkers and lowest in those reporting drinking a moderate amount of alcohol (for men, p<0.05, for women, p<0.01).

(*Table 17.62*)

17.6 Vitamin A, carotenoids, vitamin E and the tocopherol: cholesterol ratio

Plasma vitamin A (retinol)
Plasma vitamin A (retinol) is not related to short-term dietary intake. A very low level is suggestive of long-term dietary restriction.

Adequate intakes of vitamin A are necessary for the maintenance of epithelial cell integrity and for vision in dim light.

Carotenoids
Of the carotenoids only β-carotene is an important precursor of retinol, but all the carotenoids have been shown to contribute to antioxidant status.

β-carotene
Dietary β-carotene is partially cleaved in the intestine to form retinol. A proportion of the remaining β-carotene is absorbed and this is reflected in circulating levels.

β-cryptoxanthin, lycopene, α-carotene
β-cryptoxanthin, lycopene and α-carotene are not major contributors to vitamin A status (lycopene has no pro-vitamin A activity). Results of these analyses are given for information without any further comment.

Vitamin E (tocopherol)
Circulating levels reflect intakes of vitamin E. Vitamin E is a fat soluble vitamin, and a major contributor to antioxidant status.

Tocopherol:cholesterol ratio
Plasma vitamin E concentration is related to the level of serum cholesterol. Plasma vitamin E (tocopherol) and serum cholesterol both rise with age. The tocopherol:cholesterol ratio gives an estimate of vitamin E status corrected for serum cholesterol.

Values for *vitamin A* (*retinol*) for men showed little variation with age except for the youngest group of men, where the mean was significantly lower— 1.9µmol/l (p<0.01, for all age groups). Among women mean values were the same across the age ranges, until age 50 to 64, when there was a significant increase (p<0.01, for all age groups). (*Table 17.63*)

Mean levels of β-carotene were significantly lower for male and female subjects aged 18 to 34 than for those aged 35 to 64 (p<0.01). The overall mean value for β-carotene was higher for women than for men, 0.38µmol/l compared with 0.29µmol/l (p<0.01).

(*Table 17.64*)

Tables 17.65 to 17.67 show age and sex distributions for β-cryptoxanthin, lycopene, α-carotene.

(*Tables 17.65 to 17.67*)

For both sexes mean levels of *vitamin E* (*tocopherol*) increased significantly between each age group (p<0.01, except between women aged 18 to 24, and 25 to 34, where p<0.05). (*Table 17.68*)

The mean values for the *tocopherol:cholesterol ratio* were not significantly associated with age or sex.

(*Table 17.69*)

None of the analytes showed any association with whether or not a slimming diet was being followed.

(*Table 17.70*)

Among men living in London and the South East levels of β-carotene, vitamin E and the tocopherol:cholesterol ratio were significantly higher than those for men living in the Northern region (p<0.05, except for β-carotene, where p<0.01). For women living in London and the South East, levels of β-carotene were also above those of women living elsewhere (p<0.01), but there were no other significant differences associated with area of residence. (*Table 17.72*)

When the employment status of the subject was taken into account for all these analytes, including the tocopherol:cholesterol ratio, unemployed men had significantly lower mean levels than working men (p<0.01, except for vitamin A, where p<0.05); the same was also true for women in respect of mean levels of plasma vitamin A (p<0.01), vitamin E (p<0.01), and the tocopherol:cholesterol ratio (p<0.05). The data also showed that economically inactive women, who were mainly housewives, had higher average levels of plasma vitamin A than working women (p < 0.05).

(*Table 17.73*)

Associations with social class were found for both men and women in relation to β-carotene, vitamin E and the tocopherol:cholesterol ratio. The mean values of these analytes were lower for subjects living in households where the head was in a manual occupation than where the head was in a non-manual occupation. Mean values for β-carotene in men for example, ranged from 0.33 μmol/l for those in Social Classes I and II to 0.24 μmol/l for men from Social Classes IV and V (p < 0.01 for men and women). For vitamin E the mean values for men ranged from 28.5 μmol/l to 24.8 μmol/l across the social class gradient (p < 0.01 for men and women). Mean values for the tocopherol:cholesterol ratio were associated with social class for both men and women. For men, mean ratios ranged from 4.87 (Social Classes I and II) to 4.42 (Social Classes IV and V); for women the comparable mean ratios were 4.83 and 4.41 (p < 0.01). (*Table 17.75*)

Men living with other adults but no spouse had the lowest mean levels of vitamin A, β-carotene, vitamin E and for the tocopherol:cholesterol ratio. These values were significantly below the highest values for vitamin E (p < 0.01), and the tocopherol:cholesterol ratio (p < 0.05), which were recorded for married men with children, and for vitamin A which was for married men without dependent children (p < 0.01). Among women, lone mothers had the lowest average levels of β-carotene, vitamin E and for the tocopherol:cholesterol ratio. Married women without dependent children had the highest mean levels of β-carotene and vitamin E (p < 0.01, compared with lone mothers) and women living alone had higher vitamin A levels than married women with children (p < 0.01). (*Table 17.76*)

Male and female non-smokers had higher levels of all these analytes, except vitamin A, than heavy smokers (p < 0.01). Among men, but not women mean levels of plasma vitamin A were also higher in non-smokers compared to light smokers (p < 0.05). (*Table 17.77*)

For male subjects mean plasma vitamin A was higher in the heaviest drinkers compared with non-drinkers (p < 0.01), and β-carotene was lower in the heaviest drinkers, again compared with non-drinkers (p < 0.01). For men, other analytes, and for women, all these analytes show no significant association with drinking behaviour. (*Table 17.78*)

17.6.1 Correlation with dietary intakes
Table 17.79 shows correlation coefficients between dietary retinol and carotene and serum retinol and carotenes obtained from the analysis of the blood samples.

Among both men and women intakes of carotene showed a significant positive correlation with plasma α-carotene and β-carotene (p < 0.01). Intakes of retinol,

from food sources alone, and from food plus food supplements were positively correlated with plasma vitamin A for men (p < 0.01), but the correlation was not significant for women. (*Table 17.79*)

Plasma vitamin E and the tocopherol:cholesterol ratio showed significant positive correlations with intakes of vitamin E for both men and women (p < 0.01).

(*Table 17.80*)

17.7 The erythrocyte glutathione reductase activation coefficient
The *erythrocyte glutathione reductase activation coefficient* (EGRAC) is a measure of biochemical saturation with riboflavin (vitamin B2). The enzyme glutathione reductase requires riboflavin as a cofactor. Its activity in red blood cells is measured before and after the addition of flavin adenine dinucleotide. The coefficient is expressed as the ratio of the two activity measurements, and the higher the coefficient the lower the saturation. A coefficient of less than 1.30 is generally regarded as normal. Riboflavin is essential for the utilization of energy from food.

The mean value for EGRAC for male subjects was 1.09 and for female subjects 1.10. Mean EGRAC for samples from men and women aged between 50 and 64 were significantly lower than for other age groups (p < 0.01), but between the younger age groups there was little variation. (*Table 17.81*)

For 1% of males and 2% of females EGRAC was 1.3 or higher, but this difference was not statistically significant.

Females who were on a slimming diet during the dietary recording period had a lower EGRAC than women who were not dieting, 1.08 compared with 1.10 (p < 0.05).

(*Table 17.70*)

Associations between EGRAC and area of residence, economic status, social class and household composition were weak for male subjects and generally not found in the data for women.

Male subjects living in Scotland, unemployed men and men in Social Classes IV and V had a higher EGRAC than men living elsewhere in Great Britain, economically inactive men, and men in non-manual social classes (p < 0.05). Unemployed women also had a higher EGRAC than economically inactive women (p < 0.05).

(*Tables 17.72, 17.73 & 17.75*)

EGRAC was lower for married men without children compared to men not living with a spouse and was higher for lone mothers as compared to married women without dependent children (p < 0.05). (*Table 17.76*)

For both males and females there was a consistent tendency for EGRAC to rise with the number of cigarettes smoked. For male non-smokers mean EGRAC was 1.09 and for the heaviest smokers, 1.11 (p < 0.05). For the comparable groups of women mean EGRACs were 1.09 and 1.12 (p < 0.05). (*Table 17.77*)

There was no clear association between EGRAC and drinking behaviour for either men or women.

(*Table 17.78*)

EGRAC was significantly negatively correlated with intake of riboflavin, both from food sources alone, and from all sources (p < 0.01); this was true for both men and women. (*Table 17.82*)

17.8 Summary
This chapter presents the results from the analyses of the specimens of blood given by co-operating male and female subjects aged 18 and over.

Less than 1% of men and 4% of women had haemoglobin concentrations below 11.0g/dl, and there was little variation with age.

Mean serum ferritin concentration in men was 106.9µg/l, and increased steadily with age. Mean serum ferritin concentration in women was 46.8µg/l, being 31.3µg/l in those aged 18 to 24 but 76.2µg/l in those aged 50 to 64. Overall 4% of men and 33% of women had a serum ferritin concentration of less than 25µg/l, but this proportion rose from 12% in women aged 50 to 64 to 46% in women aged 18 to 24.

Mean corpuscular volumes were higher for men and women living in Scotland, and also rose with increasing consumption of alcohol. Serum ferritin and haemoglobin concentrations were higher in the heaviest male drinkers compared with non-drinkers, but there was no such association for women.

For men, but not women, serum ferritin was positively correlated with dietary intakes of folate and vitamin B12.

The blood samples were analysed for total serum and HDL cholesterol; LDL cholesterol was estimated as serum total cholesterol minus HDL cholesterol.

The mean serum total cholesterol concentration for both men and women was 5.8mmol/l, and for both sexes concentrations increased with age. Of men aged 18 to 24, 75% had a mean concentration below 5.2mmol/l, but for those aged 50 to 64, this fell to only 13%. Four per cent of men aged 25 to 34 had a serum total cholesterol of 7.8mmol/l or higher, rising to 10% among those aged 50 to 64. In women the age effect was most marked in those over age 50; two thirds of the youngest group of women had a total cholesterol level below 5.2mmol/l, compared with only one in ten of those aged between 50 and 64. Between the ages of 18 and 49 no more than 3% of women had a total cholesterol at or above 7.8mmol/l, but among those aged 50 to 64, nearly one in five had a level this high.

Body mass index was significantly associated with serum total cholesterol concentrations for both men and women, concentration increasing with increasing body mass index; the proportion of energy derived from saturated fatty acids and the intake of dietary cholesterol also had a significant positive correlation with serum total cholesterol for both men and women.

Serum total cholesterol levels were higher in men consuming the largest amounts of alcohol, but there was no such association for women, nor, for either sex, was total cholesterol significantly associated with smoking behaviour, area of residence, social class or economic status.

Mean HDL cholesterol concentrations were lower in men than women, 1.2mmol/l compared with 1.4mmol/l, but there was no age effect. For both men and women there was a significant positive correlation between the proportion of food energy derived from fat and HDL cholesterol concentrations, and those who smoked or had a higher body mass index were more likely to have a lower HDL cholesterol concentration than others. Concentrations also increased significantly with increasing consumption of alcohol. As with serum total cholesterol there were no differences in HDL cholesterol concentrations for either men or women associated with region, social class or economic status.

Mean values for γ-glutamyl transpeptidase were 33.7u/l for men and 18.6u/l for women. The highest values were found for men aged between 35 and 49. Male non-smokers had lower levels than males who smoked, and non-drinkers had lower levels than the heaviest consumers of alcohol, but these differences were not found for women.

Mean values of vitamin A were 2.2µmol/l for men and 1.9µmol/l for women and there was little variation associated with age for either sex. Women had higher mean levels of β-carotene than men and for both sexes levels were lower for those aged 18 to 34 than for those aged 35 to 64. Dietary intakes of retinol were positively correlated with plasma vitamin A levels for men, as were intakes of carotene with plasma α-carotene and β-carotene levels for both men and women. Mean levels of β-carotene were lower for both men and women who smoked, and where the head of the household was in a manual occupation. Men and women living in London and the South East had higher concentrations of β-carotene than those living in the Northern region of England. Among men, but not women, significantly lower mean values for β-carotene were also found for the unemployed and the heaviest drinkers.

Mean levels of vitamin E were 27.1µmol/l for men and 26.2µmol/l for women, and levels generally increased with age in both sexes, being about 50% higher for those aged 50 to 64 than for those aged 18 to 24. The tocopherol:cholesterol ratio was 4.65 for men and 4.58 for women; these values did not vary significantly with age. For both men and women the tocopherol:cholesterol ratio was significantly lower for those who were unemployed, where the head of the household was in a manual occupation and for the heaviest smokers.

The mean value for the erythrocyte glutathione reductase activation coefficient (EGRAC) was 1.09 for men and 1.10 for women; for 1% of men and 2% of women EGRAC was 1.3 or higher. For both men and women EGRAC rose with the number of cigarettes smoked, and EGRAC was higher for men in Social Classes IV and V than for other men.

References and notes

1. Life Sciences Research Office. *Suggested measures of nutritional status and health conditions for NHANES III*. Bethesda: Federation of American Societies for Experimental Biology (FASEB) (1985).
2. Miller G J, Miller N E. Plasma high density lipoprotein concentration and development of ischaemic heart disease. *Lancet* 1975; i: 16–19.
3. Handbook of coronary heart disease prevention. Ed. Lewis B, Assmann G, Mancini M, Stein Y. *Current Medical Literature.* (London, 1989).
4. US Department of Health and Human Services. *National Cholesterol Education Program. Report of the Expert Panel on detection, evaluation and treatment of high blood cholesterol in adults.* National Institutes of Health. No 88–2925 (1988).
5. Among men 56% of the economically inactive were aged between 50 and 64; for working and unemployed men the proportions in this age group were 21% and 24% respectively (p<0.01). Among women 38% of the economically inactive group were aged between 50 and 64; for working and unemployed women the proportions in this age group were 19% and 16% respectively (p<0.01).
6. For definitions of the economic status and drinking behaviour variables used in the analysis of variance see Chapter 12 (12.2).

Table 17.1 Percentage distribution of haemoglobin concentration by age and sex

Haemoglobin concentration (g/dl)	Men				All ages 18–64	Women				All ages 18–64
	18–24	25–34	35–49	50–64	18–64	18–24	25–34	35–49	50–64	18–64
	cum %	cum %	cum %	cum %	cum %	cum %	cum %	cum %	cum %	cum %
Less than 11.0	1	1	0	–	0	6	4	4	4	4
Less than 12.5	2	2	2	2	2	21	24	23	13	20
Less than 14.0	16	18	17	20	18	79	79	75	69	75
Less than 17.0	75	78	72	79	76	97	98	98	97	98
All	100	100	100	100	100	100	100	100	100	100
Base	*129*	*197*	*289*	*231*	*846*	*110*	*199*	*315*	*232*	*856*
Mean (average) value	14.9	14.8	14.9	14.7	14.8	13.2	13.1	13.1	13.4	13.2
Median value	14.9	14.8	14.8	14.7	14.8	13.3	13.1	13.2	13.4	13.3
Lower 5.0 percentile	13.4	13.3	13.2	13.0	13.2	10.8	11.1	11.0	11.1	11.1
Upper 5.0 percentile	16.8	16.5	16.8	16.3	16.6	14.6	14.9	15.1	15.2	15.1
Standard error of the mean	0.10	0.07	0.07	0.07	0.04	0.11	0.09	0.07	0.08	0.04

Table 17.2 Percentage distribution of mean corpuscular volume by age and sex

Mean corpuscular volume (fl)	Men				All ages 18–64	Women				All ages 18–64
	18–24	25–34	35–49	50–64	18–64	18–24	25–34	35–49	50–64	18–64
	cum %	cum %	cum %	cum %	cum %	cum %	cum %	cum %	cum %	cum %
Less than 79	–	2	1	–	1	5	3	3	4	3
Less than 89	34	31	22	18	25	34	28	28	22	27
Less than 99	95	95	93	90	93	94	94	92	94	94
All	100	100	100	100	100	100	100	100	100	100
Base	*129*	*197*	*289*	*231*	*846*	*110*	*199*	*315*	*232*	*856*
Mean (average) value	91.0	90.6	91.9	93.0	91.8	90.4	91.3	91.6	91.4	91.3
Median value	90.5	90.3	91.6	92.8	91.5	90.6	91.3	92.1	91.4	91.4
Lower 5.0 percentile	84.4	85.1	85.3	85.9	85.1	80.3	82.3	81.2	83.9	81.7
Upper 5.0 percentile	99.0	98.3	99.9	101.5	100.1	99.1	99.4	99.7	99.9	99.5
Standard error of the mean	0.37	0.38	0.29	0.30	0.17	0.55	0.38	0.34	0.37	0.20

Table 17.3 Percentage distribution of haematocrit by age and sex

Haematocrit	Men				All ages	Women				All ages
	18–24	25–34	35–49	50–64	18–64	18–24	25–34	35–49	50–64	18–64
	cum %	cum %	cum %	cum %	cum %	cum %	cum %	cum %	cum %	cum %
Less than 0.375	2	3	2	4	3	24	31	30	16	26
Less than 0.400	9	11	9	10	10	57	62	58	47	56
Less than 0.425	25	36	30	33	32	85	87	85	78	64
Less than 0.450	67	71	63	67	66	97	97	96	91	75
All	100	100	100	100	100	100	100	100	100	100
Base	129	197	289	230	845	110	200	315	232	857
Mean (average) value	0.44	0.44	0.44	0.44	0.44	0.39	0.39	0.39	0.40	0.39
Median value	0.44	0.44	0.44	0.44	0.44	0.39	0.39	0.39	0.40	0.39
Lower 5.0 percentile	0.39	0.39	0.39	0.38	0.39	0.34	0.33	0.33	0.34	0.33
Upper 5.0 percentile	0.49	0.49	0.50	0.50	0.50	0.44	0.44	0.45	0.46	0.45
Standard error of the mean	0.003	0.002	0.002	0.002	0.001	0.003	0.003	0.002	0.002	0.001

Table 17.4 Percentage distribution of mean corpuscular haemoglobin concentration by age and sex

Mean corpuscular haemoglobin concentration (g/dl)	Men				All ages	Women				All ages
	18–24	25–34	35–49	50–64	18–64	18–24	25–34	35–49	50–64	18–64
	cum %	cum %	cum %	cum %	cum %	cum %	cum %	cum %	cum %	cum %
Less than 33.0	14	13	20	19	17	27	24	22	29	25
Less than 33.5	32	28	41	39	36	41	40	41	47	43
Less than 34.0	61	52	61	61	59	68	57	66	69	65
Less than 34.5	78	74	80	82	79	87	82	82	84	83
All	100	100	100	100	100	100	100	100	100	100
Base	129	197	289	230	845	110	199	315	231	855
Mean (average) value	33.7	33.9	33.7	33.7	33.8	33.4	33.7	33.6	33.5	33.6
Median value	33.8	33.9	33.7	33.8	33.8	33.6	33.8	33.7	33.5	33.6
Lower 5.0 percentile	31.8	32.6	32.1	31.9	32.1	31.5	32.1	31.9	31.6	31.9
Upper 5.0 percentile	35.0	35.3	35.2	35.0	35.1	34.7	35.0	35.2	35.1	35.1
Standard error of the mean	0.08	0.06	0.06	0.09	0.04	0.09	0.06	0.06	0.07	0.03

Table 17.5 Percentage distribution of vitamin B12 concentration by age and sex

Vitamin B12 concentration (ng/l)	Men				All ages	Women				All ages
	18–24	25–34	35–49	50–64	18–64	18–24	25–34	35–49	50–64	18–64
	cum %	cum %	cum %	cum %	cum %	cum %	cum %	cum %	cum %	cum %
Less than 300	20	20	23	25	23	24	22	19	18	20
Less than 360	36	33	40	44	39	42	37	31	29	33
Less than 420	56	50	56	47	55	61	48	50	44	49
Less than 480	78	73	77	71	77	71	75	71	72	72
All	100	100	100	100	100	100	100	100	100	100
Base	128	207	309	245	889	76	159	313	239	787
Mean (average) value	403.5	413.9	397.9	392.5	400.9	415.4	417.8	422.8	428.9	422.9
Median value	380.0	390.0	370.0	370.0	380.0	360.0	400.0	400.0	420.0	400.0
Lower 5.0 percentile	210.0	200.0	200.0	190.0	200.0	200.0	200.0	210.0	210.0	210.0
Upper 5.0 percentile	700.0	660.0	650.0	640.0	650.0	720.0	750.0	690.0	680.0	700.0
Standard error of the mean	12.82	9.77	8.27	9.30	4.84	19.33	12.68	8.48	9.61	5.46

Table 17.6 Percentage distribution of ferritin by age and sex

Ferritin (µg/l)	Men				All ages 18–64	Women				All ages 18–64
	18–24	25–34	35–49	50–64		18–24	25–34	35–49	50–64	
	cum %	cum %	cum %	cum %	cum %	cum %	cum %	cum %	cum %	cum %
Less than 13	2	1	2	2	1	13	13	21	5	14
Less than 25	4	4	4	5	4	46	39	42	12	33
Less than 50	38	21	14	13	19	84	84	73	37	67
Less than 75	74	41	34	33	41	96	94	91	64	85
Less than 100	86	62	55	50	60	99	97	97	80	92
All	100	100	100	100	100	100	100	100	100	100
Base	128	209	291	221	849	76	155	289	199	719
Mean (average) value	63.4	99.1	114.4	129.8	106.9	31.3	34.6	37.1	76.2	46.8
Median value	55.0	85.0	91.0	99.0	85.0	29.0	27.0	29.0	58.0	35.0
Lower 5.0 percentile	25.0	27.0	26.0	28.0	26.0	5.0	6.0	5.0	15.0	6.0
Upper 5.0 percentile	127.0	228.0	263.0	303.0	266.0	71.0	78.0	96.0	205.0	128.0
Standard error of the mean	2.97	4.77	5.20	8.08	3.11	2.30	2.35	1.80	4.58	1.70

Table 17.7 Results for the haematological profile, serum ferritin and vitamin B12 by sex of informant and whether on a slimming diet

Blood analytes (units)	Whether on a slimming diet							
	Dieting				Not dieting			
	Mean	Median	SE	Base	Mean	Median	SE	Base
Men								
Haematology								
Hacmoglobin concentration (g/dl)	14.7	14.8	0.20	37	14.8	14.8	0.04	809
Mean corpuscular haemoglobin concentration (g/dl)	33.9	33.8	0.18	37	33.7	33.8	0.04	808
Mean corpuscular volume (fl)	91.9	91.2	0.71	37	91.8	91.5	0.17	809
Red cell folate concentration (µg/l)	232.8	197.3	20.51	31	213.0	199.0	3.44	698
Haematocrit	0.43	0.42	0.01	37	0.44	0.44	0.00	808
Ferritin (µg/l)	118.0	100.5	15.16	34	106.5	85.0	3.18	815
Vitamin B12 concentration (ng/l)	409.7	400.0	28.89	34	400.6	380.0	4.90	855
Women								
Haematology								
Haemoglobin concentration (g/dl)	13.3	13.4	0.12	99	13.2	13.2	0.04	757
Mean corpuscular haemoglobin concentration (g/dl)	33.5	33.7	0.11	99	33.6	33.6	0.04	756
Mean corpuscular volume (fl)	91.5	91.3	0.54	99	91.3	91.4	0.21	757
Red cell folate concentration (µg/l)	218.0	200.2	11.71	71	186.4	172.6	3.91	566
Haematocrit	0.40	0.40	0.00	99	0.39	0.37	0.00	758
Ferritin (µg/l)	52.4	42.5	5.10	84	46.0	34.0	1.81	635
Vitamin B12 concentration (ng/l)	409.1	400.0	13.89	92	424.8	400.0	5.91	695

Table 17.8 Results for the haematological profile, serum ferritin and vitamin B12 by sex of informant and whether unwell during seven-day dietary recording period

Blood analytes (units)	Whether unwell during seven-day dietary recording period											
	Completed food diary									No food diary		
	Not unwell			Unwell								
				Eating affected			Eating not affected					
	Mean	Median	SE	Mean	Median	SE	Mean	Median	SE	Mean	Median	SE
Men												
Haematology												
Haemoglobin concentration (g/dl)	14.8	14.8	0.04	15.0	14.8	0.17	14.5	14.5	0.17	14.6	14.8	0.14
Mean corpuscular haemoglobin concentration (g/dl)	33.7	33.8	0.04	33.8	33.8	0.23	33.8	33.8	0.11	34.0	34.0	0.21
Mean corpuscular volume (fl)	91.9	91.6	0.18	92.2	91.7	1.00	90.3	90.6	0.63	91.9	92.1	0.78
Red cell folate concentration (μg/l)	211.8	195.0	3.79	207.5	175.5	20.0	241.2	229.0	11.79	212.5	207.0	11.59
Haematocrit	0.44	0.44	0.00	0.45	0.45	0.01	0.43	0.43	0.01	0.43	0.44	0.00
Ferritin (μg/l)	104.0	84.0	3.28	128.2	100.5	19.15	115.7	85.0	14.03	123.7	99.5	13.94
Vitamin B12 concentration (ng/l)	403.5	380.0	5.37	431.6	415.0	20.0	387.4	370.0	16.79	370.1	350.0	19.54
Women												
Haematology												
Haemoglobin concentration (g/dl)	13.2	13.3	0.05	13.1	13.1	0.16	13.3	13.3	0.13	13.4	13.6	0.19
Mean corpuscular haemoglobin concentration (g/dl)	33.6	33.6	0.04	33.6	33.6	0.10	33.5	33.6	0.10	33.5	33.6	0.15
Mean corpuscular volume (fl)	91.3	91.6	0.23	90.6	90.6	0.62	92.3	92.9	0.58	90.7	90.0	0.90
Red cell folate concentration (μg/l)	189.5	173.0	4.25	190.7	179.5	13.02	192.9	192.0	11.72	189.4	198.4	17.14
Haematocrit	0.39	0.40	0.00	0.39	0.39	0.01	0.40	0.40	0.00	0.40	0.40	0.01
Ferritin (μg/l)	47.1	36.0	1.74	37.6	25.0	4.22	52.2	36.0	11.11	49.3	27.5	10.90
Vitamin B12 concentration (ng/l)	425.4	400.0	6.09	403.0	380.0	19.47	430.6	420.0	19.60	403.3	365.0	26.68
Base numbers	*Men*	*Women*		*Men*	*Women*		*Men*	*Women*		*Men*	*Women*	
Haematology												
Haemoglobin concentration	*688*	*650*		*33*	*85*		*67*	*86*		*58*	*35*	
Mean corpuscular haemoglobin	*687*	*650*		*33*	*84*		*67*	*86*		*58*	*35*	
Mean corpuscular volume	*688*	*650*		*33*	*85*		*67*	*86*		*58*	*35*	
Red cell folate	*605*	*495*		*22*	*58*		*53*	*59*		*49*	*25*	
Haematocrit	*687*	*651*		*33*	*85*		*67*	*86*		*58*	*35*	
Ferritin	*704*	*581*		*28*	*57*		*61*	*51*		*56*	*30*	
Vitamin B12 concentration	*727*	*612*		*32*	*71*		*66*	*72*		*64*	*32*	

Table 17.9 Results for the haematological profile, serum ferritin and vitamin B12 by sex of informant and region

Blood analytes (units)	Region											
	Scotland			Northern			Central, South West and Wales			London and South East		
	Mean	Median	SE	Mean	Median	SE	Mean	Median	SE	Mean	Median	SE
Men												
Haematology												
Haemoglobin concentration (g/dl)	14.6	14.6	0.13	14.9	14.8	0.09	14.8	14.8	0.06	14.8	14.8	0.06
Mean corpuscular haemoglobin concentration (g/dl)	33.8	33.8	0.19	33.8	33.9	0.08	33.7	33.7	0.05	33.7	33.8	0.06
Mean corpuscular volume (fl)	93.0	92.1	0.63	91.4	91.2	0.35	91.4	91.1	0.28	92.2	92.1	0.29
Red cell folate concentration (μg/l)	192.0	181.5	10.38	222.7	198.5	7.67	211.5	198.5	5.54	214.7	202.3	5.77
Haematocrit	0.43	0.44	0.00	0.44	0.44	0.00	0.44	0.44	0.00	0.44	0.44	0.00
Ferritin (μg/l)	118.9	83.0	18.58	111.7	87.5	6.44	100.3	81.0	4.38	106.7	87.0	4.63
Vitamin B12 concentration (ng/l)	410.3	370.0	15.39	387.8	360.0	9.99	391.7	370.0	8.74	418.1	410.0	7.88
Women												
Haematology												
Haemoglobin concentration (g/dl)	13.3	13.3	0.13	13.3	13.4	0.08	13.1	13.2	0.08	13.2	13.3	0.07
Mean corpuscular haemoglobin concentration (g/dl)	33.4	33.5	0.12	33.6	33.7	0.07	33.6	33.7	0.06	33.5	33.5	0.06
Mean corpuscular volume (fl)	93.3	93.2	0.54	92.0	92.0	0.36	90.5	90.8	0.33	91.2	91.3	0.38
Red cell folate concentration (μg/l)	183.5	174.0	11.26	195.9	180.5	7.18	181.8	168.2	6.32	195.9	189.0	6.98
Haematocrit	0.40	0.40	0.00	0.40	0.40	0.00	0.39	0.39	0.00	0.39	0.40	0.00
Ferritin (μg/l)	41.3	33.0	4.51	53.1	37.0	4.67	44.2	33.0	2.46	46.0	35.0	2.57
Vitamin B12 concentration (ng/l)	391.9	370.0	17.17	423.2	400.0	12.06	416.4	390.0	8.70	438.3	410.0	9.69
Base numbers	*Men*	*Women*		*Men*	*Women*		*Men*	*Women*		*Men*	*Women*	
Haematology												
Haemoglobin concentration	69	77		214	208		288	300		275	271	
Mean corpuscular haemoglobin concentration	69	77		213	207		288	300		275	271	
Mean corpuscular volume	69	77		214	208		288	300		275	271	
Red cell folate concentration	58	51		188	162		250	225		233	199	
Haematocrit	69	77		213	209		288	300		275	271	
Ferritin	73	63		220	179		279	245		277	232	
Vitamin B12 concentration	77	68		288	193		293	275		291	251	

Table 17.10 Results for the haematological profile, serum ferritin and vitamin B12 by sex and employment status of informant

Blood analytes (units)	Employment status of informant								
	Working			Unemployed			Economically inactive		
	Mean	Median	SE	Mean	Median	SE	Mean	Median	SE
Men									
Haematology									
Haemoglobin concentration (g/dl)	14.8	14.8	0.04	15.0	14.9	0.13	14.8	14.9	0.15
Mean corpuscular haemoglobin concentration (g/dl)	33.8	33.8	0.04	33.6	33.7	0.11	33.8	33.8	0.16
Mean corpuscular volume (fl)	91.5	91.3	0.18	93.1	93.1	0.63	92.8	92.7	0.54
Red cell folate concentration (µg/l)	213.9	200.0	3.78	204.6	186.5	11.16	222.9	206.0	11.27
Haematocrit	0.44	0.44	0.00	0.45	0.45	0.00	0.44	0.44	0.01
Ferritin (µg/l)	105.5	86.0	3.05	120.2	82.5	17.50	107.0	73.0	10.96
Vitamin B12 concentration (ng/l)	404.2	380.0	5.34	382.2	355.0	14.49	389.9	360.0	17.92
Women									
Haematology									
Haemoglobin concentration (g/dl)	13.2	13.2	0.05	13.4	13.4	0.17	13.3	13.3	0.08
Mean corpuscular haemoglobin concentration (g/dl)	33.6	33.7	0.04	33.4	33.5	0.15	33.5	33.6	0.06
Mean corpuscular volume (fl)	91.5	91.7	0.26	90.7	91.9	0.83	91.1	91.2	0.32
Red cell folate concentration (µg/l)	181.7	167.5	4.55	171.8	152.0	11.88	207.8	192.0	7.20
Haematocrit	0.39	0.39	0.00	0.40	0.40	0.01	0.40	0.40	0.00
Ferritin (µg/l)	43.2	34.0	1.73	43.2	39.5	4.35	55.3	36.0	4.21
Vitamin B12 concentration (ng/l)	420.3	400.0	6.45	357.1	330.0	20.80	441.1	410.0	10.88
Base numbers	*Men*	*Women*		*Men*	*Women*		*Men*	*Women*	
Haematology									
Haemoglobin concentration	*686*	*530*		*80*	*42*		*80*	*276*	
Mean corpuscular haemoglobin concentration	*686*	*530*		*80*	*42*		*79*	*275*	
Mean corpuscular volume	*686*	*530*		*80*	*42*		*80*	*276*	
Red cell folate concentration	*598*	*390*		*66*	*31*		*65*	*208*	
Haematocrit	*686*	*531*		*80*	*42*		*79*	*276*	
Ferritin	*707*	*456*		*78*	*40*		*64*	*216*	
Vitamin B12 concentration	*728*	*481*		*82*	*42*		*79*	*256*	

Table 17.11 Results for the haematological profile, serum ferritin and vitamin B12 by sex of informant and whether receiving benefits

Blood analytes (units)	Whether benefits received							
	Receiving				Not receiving			
	Mean	Median	SE	*Base*	Mean	Median	SE	*Base*
Men								
Haematology								
Haemoglobin concentration (g/dl)	15.1	15.1	0.12	*94*	14.8	14.8	0.04	*748*
Mean corpuscular haemoglobin concentration (g/dl)	33.8	33.7	0.14	*94*	33.8	33.8	0.04	*747*
Mean corpuscular volume (fl)	92.7	93.0	0.60	*94*	91.7	91.4	0.18	*748*
Red cell folate concentration (μg/l)	223.4	194.0	10.43	*79*	212.9	199.3	3.62	*646*
Haematocrit	0.45	0.45	0.00	*94*	0.44	0.44	0.00	*747*
Ferritin (μg/l)	110.5	80.0	14.97	*89*	106.2	85.0	2.99	*755*
Vitamin B12 concentration (ng/l)	387.1	360.0	13.75	*99*	403.2	380.0	5.18	*786*
Women								
Haematology								
Haemoglobin concentration (g/dl)	13.2	13.3	0.13	*108*	13.2	13.3	0.04	*747*
Mean corpuscular haemoglobin concentration (g/dl)	33.6	33.7	0.09	*108*	33.5	33.6	0.04	*746*
Mean corpuscular volume (fl)	90.9	91.0	0.54	*108*	91.4	91.6	0.21	*747*
Red cell folate concentration (μg/l)	179.4	172.0	8.46	*83*	191.0	179.0	4.07	*553*
Haematocrit	0.39	0.39	0.00	*108*	0.39	0.40	0.00	*748*
Ferritin (μg/l)	46.1	37.0	4.54	*97*	46.8	35.0	1.84	*621*
Vitamin B12 concentration (ng/l)	412.6	360.0	18.85	*109*	424.4	400.0	5.58	*677*

Table 17.12 Results for the haematological profile, serum ferritin and vitamin B12 by sex of informant and social class of head of household

Blood analytes (units)	Social class of head of household											
	I and II			III non-manual			III manual			IV and V		
	Mean	Median	SE	Mean	Median	SE	Mean	Median	SE	Mean	Median	SE
Men												
Haematology												
Haemoglobin concentration (g/dl)	14.7	14.7	0.06	14.9	14.9	0.10	14.8	14.7	0.06	14.9	14.8	0.12
Mean corpuscular haemoglobin concentration (g/dl)	33.8	33.8	0.53	33.9	34.0	0.08	33.7	33.7	0.74	33.6	33.7	0.08
Mean corpuscular volume (fl)	91.6	91.8	0.28	91.3	91.1	0.44	92.2	91.8	0.29	91.5	91.2	0.43
Red cell folate concentration (µg/l)	214.5	202.5	5.82	209.5	191.0	10.05	216.9	203.0	5.13	208.3	188.0	9.69
Haematocrit	0.44	0.44	0.00	0.44	0.44	0.00	0.44	0.44	0.00	0.44	0.44	0.00
Ferritin (µg/l)	103.6	88.0	4.18	101.2	85.0	6.77	111.1	80.0	5.67	112.8	83.5	10.63
Vitamin B12 concentration (ng/l)	423.6	400.0	8.11	408.3	390.0	14.16	385.4	360.0	8.14	378.2	350.0	11.36
Women												
Haematology												
Haemoglobin concentration (g/dl)	13.1	13.2	0.07	13.3	13.2	0.11	13.3	13.4	0.08	13.3	13.3	0.09
Mean corpuscular haemoglobin concentration (g/dl)	33.6	33.6	0.06	33.4	33.5	0.10	33.6	33.6	0.06	33.6	33.6	0.07
Mean corpuscular volume (fl)	91.5	91.6	0.31	91.9	91.4	0.47	90.7	91.3	0.41	91.4	91.4	0.42
Red cell folate concentration (µg/l)	200.5	185.5	6.23	186.3	179.0	10.81	183.7	165.0	6.51	185.3	169.0	8.44
Haematocrit	0.39	0.39	0.00	0.40	0.40	0.00	0.40	0.40	0.00	0.39	0.39	0.00
Ferritin (µg/l)	50.1	35.0	3.34	45.3	37.5	3.02	40.4	30.0	2.48	49.0	38.0	3.83
Vitamin B12 concentration (ng/l)	458.1	430.0	9.25	442.3	400.0	17.36	411.3	400.0	8.66	363.8	350.0	11.11
Base numbers	*Men*	*Women*		*Men*	*Women*		*Men*	*Women*		*Men*	*Women*	
Haematology												
Haemoglobin concentration	*306*	*294*		*102*	*111*		*283*	*260*		*141*	*181*	
Mean corpuscular haemoglobin concentration	*306*	*294*		*102*	*111*		*282*	*259*		*141*	*181*	
Mean corpuscular volume	*306*	*294*		*102*	*111*		*283*	*260*		*141*	*181*	
Red cell folate concentration	*270*	*226*		*94*	*84*		*239*	*183*		*114*	*139*	
Haematocrit	*306*	*294*		*102*	*111*		*282*	*261*		*141*	*181*	
Ferritin	*307*	*265*		*101*	*94*		*286*	*208*		*140*	*145*	
Vitamin B12 concentration	*318*	*284*		*112*	*102*		*300*	*227*		*144*	*166*	

Table 17.13 Results for the haematological profile, serum ferritin and vitamin B12 by sex of informant and household composition

Blood analytes (units)	Household composition											
	Informant alone			With others, no dependent children						With dependent child		
				With spouse			No spouse					
	Mean	Median	SE	Mean	Median	SE	Mean	Median	SE	Mean	Median	SE
Men												
Haematology												
Haemoglobin concentration (g/dl)	15.1	15.1	0.19	14.7	14.6	0.06	14.9	14.9	0.08	14.8	14.8	0.06
Mean corpuscular haemoglobin concentration (g/dl)	33.7	33.8	0.13	33.7	33.8	0.08	33.7	33.7	0.07	33.8	33.8	0.05
Mean corpuscular volume (fl)	92.1	92.8	0.93	92.7	92.7	0.27	91.6	91.4	0.36	91.0	90.8	0.26
Red cell folate concentration (µg/l)	193.1	179.5	12.85	220.3	203.5	6.21	215.6	194.0	7.06	210.9	199.3	5.37
Haematocrit	0.45	0.44	0.01	0.44	0.43	0.00	0.44	0.44	0.00	0.44	0.44	0.00
Ferritin (µg/l)	131.6	77.0	25.01	123.8	97.0	5.47	77.1	65.0	3.73	104.3	85.5	4.34
Vitamin B12 concentration (ng/l)	384.0	365.0	19.34	404.6	380.0	8.13	387.8	370.0	10.52	407.8	380.0	7.93

	Informant alone			With others, no dependent children						With dependent child					
				With spouse			No spouse			With spouse			Lone mother		
	Mean	Median	SE	Mean	Median	SE	Mean	Median	SE	Mean	Median	SE	Mean	Median	SE
Women															
Haematology															
Haemoglobin concentration (g/dl)	13.3	13.20	0.12	13.4	13.5	0.07	13.3	13.4	0.11	13.0	13.1	0.07	13.2	13.3	0.15
Mean corpuscular haemoglobin concentration (g/dl)	33.6	33.8	0.13	33.6	33.6	0.06	33.4	33.6	0.09	33.5	33.6	0.06	33.7	33.7	0.11
Mean corpuscular volume (fl)	92.5	92.7	0.55	91.7	91.5	0.32	91.2	91.1	0.59	90.6	91.2	0.34	92.0	91.4	0.60
Red cell folate concentration (µg/l)	203.9	178.0	18.40	200.5	188.5	5.84	164.2	157.1	8.99	187.9	168.0	6.40	169.8	162.0	10.38
Haematocrit	0.39	0.39	0.00	0.40	0.40	0.00	0.40	0.40	0.00	0.39	0.39	0.00	0.39	0.39	0.00
Ferritin (µg/l)	56.2	38.5	6.66	64.1	53.0	3.56	41.8	30.0	4.38	31.1	25.0	1.63	39.7	34.5	3.95
Vitamin B12 concentration (ng/l)	421.9	380.0	23.91	430.4	410.0	8.49	423.8	390.0	16.44	418.0	400.0	8.53	408.5	350.0	26.41

Base numbers	Men	Women	Men	Women	Men	Women	Men	Women	Women
Haematology									
Haemoglobin concentration	58	66	290	300	177	109	321	318	63
Mean corpuscular haemoglobin concentration	58	66	289	299	177	109	321	318	63
Mean corpuscular volume	58	66	290	300	177	109	321	318	63
Red cell folate concentration	48	47	246	240	151	66	284	234	50
Haematocrit	58	66	289	300	177	109	321	319	63
Ferritin	53	56	295	259	183	82	318	274	48
Vitamin B12 concentration	60	59	310	298	183	84	336	291	55

Table 17.14 Results for the haematological profile, serum ferritin and vitamin B12 by sex of informant and smoking behaviour

Blood analytes (units)	Smoking behaviour								
	None			Fewer than 20 cigarettes a day			20 or more cigarettes a day		
	Mean	Median	SE	Mean	Median	SE	Mean	Median	SE
Men									
Haematology									
Haemoglobin concentration (g/dl)	14.7	14.7	0.05	14.8	14.8	0.10	15.1	15.0	0.09
Mean corpuscular haemoglobin concentration (g/dl)	33.8	33.8	0.04	33.8	33.8	0.11	33.7	33.7	0.07
Mean corpuscular volume (fl)	90.9	90.9	0.19	93.0	92.4	0.45	93.9	93.8	0.41
Red cell folate concentration (µg/l)	220.6	205.8	4.40	198.6	185.0	7.25	203.6	190.0	7.52
Haematocrit	0.44	0.44	0.00	0.44	0.44	0.00	0.45	0.45	0.00
Ferritin (µg/l)	112.0	87.5	4.13	98.0	77.0	6.79	95.4	78.0	5.41
Vitamin B12 concentration (ng/l)	413.7	390.0	6.24	389.8	375.0	11.68	364.1	350.0	8.90
Women									
Haematology									
Haemoglobin concentration (g/dl)	13.1	13.2	0.05	13.4	13.4	0.08	13.7	13.7	0.11
Mean corpuscular haemoglobin concentration (g/dl)	33.6	33.6	0.04	33.5	33.6	0.07	33.6	33.7	0.10
Mean corpuscular volume (fl)	90.3	90.6	0.24	92.9	93.2	0.38	93.7	93.8	0.58
Red cell folate concentration (µg/l)	199.5	187.0	4.79	173.2	155.0	7.44	167.3	154.0	8.26
Haematocrit	0.39	0.39	0.00	0.40	0.40	0.00	0.41	0.41	0.00
Ferritin (µg/l)	48.6	33.0	2.37	43.0	37.0	2.35	43.9	36.5	3.71
Vitamin B12 concentration (ng/l)	443.5	420.0	6.78	393.1	370.0	11.19	370.3	360.0	14.07
Base numbers	*Men*	*Women*		*Men*	*Women*		*Men*	*Women*	
Haematology									
Haemoglobin concentration	*551*	*559*		*146*	*190*		*149*	*107*	
Mean corpuscular haemoglobin concentration	*550*	*559*		*146*	*189*		*149*	*107*	
Mean corpuscular volume	*551*	*559*		*146*	*190*		*149*	*107*	
Red cell folate concentration	*477*	*423*		*125*	*137*		*127*	*77*	
Haematocrit	*550*	*559*		*146*	*190*		*149*	*108*	
Ferritin	*568*	*472*		*132*	*157*		*149*	*90*	
Vitamin B12 concentration	*582*	*512*		*150*	*173*		*157*	*102*	

Table 17.15 Results for the haematological profile, serum ferritin and vitamin B12 by sex of informant and alcohol consumption during seven-day dietary recording period

Blood analytes (units)	Alcohol consumption during seven-day dietary recording period											
	Nil			Less than 168g			168g—less than 400g			400g or more		
	Mean	Median	SE	Mean	Median	SE	Mean	Median	SE	Mean	Median	SE
Men												
Haematology												
Haemoglobin concentration (g/dl)	14.7	14.6	0.10	14.8	14.8	0.06	14.8	14.9	0.07	15.0	14.9	0.11
Mean corpuscular haemoglobin concentration (g/dl)	33.7	33.7	0.07	33.8	33.8	0.05	33.6	33.7	0.06	33.9	33.9	0.16
Mean corpuscular volume (fl)	91.0	90.5	0.41	91.3	91.1	0.22	92.0	91.8	0.36	93.9	93.1	0.53
Red cell folate concentration (μg/l)	191.4	183.0	6.84	207.5	188.1	5.46	226.4	210.7	6.93	240.7	224.0	11.21
Haematocrit	0.44	0.44	0.00	0.44	0.44	0.00	0.44	0.44	0.00	0.45	0.44	0.00
Ferritin (μg/l)	90.5	74.0	5.60	101.0	83.0	5.08	106.5	86.0	5.10	138.4	100.0	11.74
Vitamin B12 concentration (ng/l)	414.3	375.0	13.09	414.4	390.0	8.05	395.3	390.0	8.74	369.5	360.0	11.25

	Nil			Less than 112g			112g—less than 280g			280g or more		
	Mean	Median	SE	Mean	Median	SE	Mean	Median	SE	Mean	Median	SE
Women												
Haematology												
Haemoglobin concentration (g/dl)	13.3	13.4	0.08	13.1	13.2	0.05	13.2	13.2	0.12	13.4	13.5	0.31
Mean corpuscular haemoglobin concentration (g/dl)	33.5	33.6	0.06	33.6	33.7	0.05	33.6	33.7	0.09	33.7	34.0	0.30
Mean corpuscular volume (fl)	90.8	91.0	0.35	91.3	91.4	0.27	93.0	93.1	0.57	92.6	93.3	1.56
Red cell folate concentration (μg/l)	192.1	174.0	7.55	189.7	176.5	5.11	180.6	171.0	8.33	232.8	242.0	33.26
Haematocrit	0.40	0.40	0.00	0.39	0.39	0.00	0.39	0.39	0.00	0.40	0.40	0.01
Ferritin (μg/l)	45.8	35.0	2.53	44.0	35.0	2.34	55.9	38.0	6.19	75.1	58.5	14.74
Vitamin B12 concentration (ng/l)	422.5	390.0	10.82	429.8	410.0	7.19	417.0	400.0	15.42	315.4	300.0	23.90

Base numbers	Men				Women			
	Nil	Less than 168g	168g—less than 400g	400g or more	Nil	Less than 112g	112g—less than 280g	280g or more
Haematology								
Haemoglobin concentration	143	330	218	97	264	434	109	14
Mean corpuscular haemoglobin concentration	143	330	217	97	264	433	109	14
Mean corpuscular volume	143	330	218	97	264	434	109	14
Red cell folate concentration	121	288	185	86	189	328	84	11
Haematocrit	143	330	217	97	264	435	109	14
Ferritin	137	331	218	107	223	365	89	12
Vitamin B12 concentration	148	342	230	105	246	398	98	13

Table 17.16 Correlation coefficients between blood analytes and dietary intakes—haemoglobin, ferritin, and red cell folate

Dietary intake	Blood analyte		
	Haemoglobin	Ferritin	Red cell folate
Men			
Total dietary iron (inc. supplements)	−0.07 (p<0.05)	−0.00 (NS)	−
Iron from food sources	−0.04 (NS)	0.02 (NS)	−
Total dietary vitamin B12 (inc. supplements)	0.03 (NS)	0.07 (p<0.05)	−
Vitamin B12 from food sources	0.03 (NS)	0.07 (p<0.05)	−
Total dietary folate (inc. supplements)	0.03 (NS)	0.10 (p<0.01)	0.22 (p<0.01)
Folate from food sources	0.05 (NS)	0.11 (p<0.01)	0.22 (p<0.01)
Base	*788*	*793*	*745*
Women			
Total dietary iron (inc. supplements)	−0.05 (NS)	−0.02 (NS)	−
Iron from food sources	−0.02 (NS)	0.04 (NS)	−
Total dietary vitamin B12 (inc. supplements)	0.04 (NS)	0.07 (NS)	−
Vitamin B12 from food sources	0.07 (p<0.05)	0.07 (NS)	−
Total dietary folate (inc. supplements)	0.00 (NS)	0.07 (NS)	0.19 (p<0.01)
Folate from food sources	0.01 (NS)	0.07 (NS)	0.18 (p<0.01)
Base	*821*	*689*	*673*

Table 17.17 Correlation coefficients between vitamin B12 and dietary intakes of vitamin B12

Dietary intakes	Men	Women
Total dietary vitamin B12 (inc. supplements)	0.12 (p<0.01)	0.09 (p<0.05)
Vitamin B12 from food sources	0.11 (p<0.01)	0.10 (p<0.01)
Base	*825*	*755*

Table 17.18 Percentage distribution of total cholesterol by age and sex

Total cholesterol (mmol/l)	Men				All ages 18–64	Women				All ages 18–64
	18–24	25–34	35–49	50–64		18–24	25–34	35–49	50–64	
	cum %	cum %	cum %	cum %	cum %	cum %	cum %	cum %	cum %	cum %
Less than 5.2	75	41	21	13	32	66	61	35	10	36
Less than 6.5	96	84	66	58	72	94	98	79	41	74
Less than 7.8	100	96	91	90	94	98	99	97	79	92
All		100	100	100	100	100	100	100	100	100
Base	*139*	*216*	*317*	*251*	*923*	*84*	*170*	*315*	*240*	*809*
Mean (average) value	4.7	5.5	6.1	6.4	5.8	4.9	5.1	5.7	6.8	5.8
Median value	4.6	5.5	6.0	6.3	5.8	4.8	5.0	5.6	6.8	5.6
Lower 5.0 percentile	3.4	4.0	4.6	4.8	4.0	3.6	3.9	4.1	4.9	4.0
Upper 5.0 percentile	6.4	7.4	8.1	8.3	8.0	6.7	6.3	7.4	9.0	8.1
Standard error of the mean	0.08	0.08	0.06	0.07	0.04	0.12	0.06	0.06	0.08	0.05

Table 17.19 Percentage distribution of high density lipoprotein cholesterol by age and sex

High density lipoprotein cholesterol (mmol/l)	Men				All ages 18–64	Women				All ages 18–64
	18–24	25–34	35–49	50–64		18–24	25–34	35–49	50–64	
	cum %	cum %	cum %	cum %	cum %	cum %	cum %	cum %	cum %	cum %
Less than 1.0	27	36	31	39	34	15	9	12	10	11
Less than 1.2	63	58	64	65	63	35	29	32	29	31
Less than 1.4	85	76	81	81	81	66	50	52	50	52
Less than 1.6	94	89	90	91	91	84	72	71	70	72
All	100	100	100	100	100	100	100	100	100	100
Base	139	214	315	251	919	82	170	314	240	806
Mean (average) value	1.1	1.2	1.2	1.1	1.2	1.3	1.4	1.4	1.4	1.4
Median value	1.1	1.1	1.1	1.1	1.1	1.3	1.4	1.4	1.4	1.4
Lower 5.0 percentile	0.74	0.73	0.73	0.63	0.68	0.88	0.92	0.89	0.83	0.88
Upper 5.0 percentile	1.62	1.76	1.84	1.76	1.76	1.80	2.01	2.09	2.19	2.07
Standard error of the mean	0.02	0.02	0.02	0.02	0.01	0.03	0.03	0.02	0.03	0.01

Table 17.20 Percentage distribution of LDL cholesterol concentration by age and sex*

LDL cholesterol concentration (mmol/l)	Men				All ages 18–64	Women				All ages 18–64
	18–24	25–34	35–49	50–64		18–24	25–34	35–49	50–64	
	cum %	cum %	cum %	cum %	cum %	cum %	cum %	cum %	cum %	cum %
Less than 3.4	45	22	8	3	16	47	40	19	5	22
Less than 4.1	75	44	25	16	36	79	75	46	16	47
All	100	100	100	100	100	100	100	100	100	100
Base	139	214	315	251	919	82	170	314	240	806
Mean (average) value	3.5	4.3	5.0	5.3	4.7	3.6	3.7	4.3	5.4	4.4
Median value	3.5	4.3	4.8	5.3	4.6	3.5	3.5	4.2	5.3	4.2
Lower 5.0 percentile	2.2	2.7	3.2	3.5	2.8	2.3	2.6	2.8	3.4	2.7
Upper 5.0 percentile	5.2	6.4	7.2	7.3	6.9	5.4	5.1	6.1	7.7	6.8
Standard error of the mean	0.08	0.08	0.07	0.07	0.04	0.10	0.06	0.06	0.09	0.05

* Not all samples were analysed for total and HDL cholesterol; mean LDL cholesterol concentrations apply only to samples from subjects for whom both total and HDL cholesterol concentrations were obtained.

Table 17.21 Serum cholesterol concentrations by sex of informant and whether on a slimming diet*

Blood analytes (units)	Whether on a slimming diet							
	Dieting				Not dieting			
	Mean	Median	SE	Base	Mean	Median	SE	Base
Men								
Serum concentration								
Total cholesterol (mmol/l)	6.03	5.96	0.20	40	5.83	5.74	0.04	883
LDL cholesterol (mmol/l)	5.02	4.78	0.22	40	4.67	4.63	0.04	879
HDL cholesterol (mmol/l)	1.02	0.95	0.05	40	1.16	1.10	0.01	879
Women								
Serum concentration								
Total cholesterol (mmol/l)	5.72	5.63	0.11	96	5.84	5.63	0.05	713
LDL cholesterol (mmol/l)	4.39	4.44	0.11	96	4.41	4.16	0.05	710
HDL cholesterol (mmol/l)	1.33	1.31	0.03	96	1.42	1.39	0.01	710

* Not all samples were analysed for total and HDL cholesterol; mean LDL cholesterol concentrations apply only to samples from subjects for whom both total and HDL cholesterol concentrations were obtained.

Table 17.22 Serum cholesterol concentrations by sex of informant and whether unwell during seven-day dietary recording period*

Blood analytes (units)	Whether unwell during seven-day dietary recording period											
	Completed food diary									No food diary		
	Not unwell			Unwell								
				Eating affected			Eating not affected					
	Mean	Median	SE	Mean	Median	SE	Mean	Median	SE	Mean	Median	SE
Men												
Serum concentration												
Total cholesterol												
(mmol/l)	5.86	5.79	0.04	5.39	5.32	0.17	5.64	5.57	0.13	5.95	5.93	0.17
LDL cholesterol												
(mmol/l)	4.71	4.66	0.05	4.32	4.29	0.17	4.52	4.51	0.14	4.77	4.80	0.19
HDL cholesterol												
(mmol/l)	1.15	1.09	0.01	1.08	1.06	0.04	1.12	1.11	0.04	1.18	1.14	0.05
Women												
Serum concentration												
Total cholesterol												
(mmol/l)	5.85	5.63	0.05	5.66	5.56	0.13	5.67	5.38	0.12	5.97	5.79	0.22
LDL cholesterol												
(mmol/l)	4.43	4.19	0.05	4.32	4.17	0.13	4.26	4.10	0.13	4.59	4.39	0.23
HDL cholesterol												
(mmol/l)	1.42	1.39	0.01	1.35	1.34	0.04	1.41	1.37	0.04	1.39	1.33	0.06
Base numbers	*Men*	*Women*		*Men*	*Women*		*Men*	*Women*		*Men*	*Women*	
Serum concentration												
Total cholesterol	*752*	*620*		*35*	*77*		*73*	*79*		*63*	*33*	
LDL cholesterol	*748*	*618*		*35*	*77*		*73*	*78*		*63*	*33*	
HDL cholesterol	*748*	*618*		*35*	*77*		*73*	*78*		*63*	*33*	

* Not all samples were analysed for total and HDL cholesterol; mean LDL cholesterol concentrations apply only to samples from subjects for whom both total and HDL cholesterol concentrations were obtained.

Table 17.23 Serum cholesterol concentrations by sex of informant and region*

Blood analytes (units)	Region											
	Scotland			Northern			Central, South West and Wales			London and South East		
	Mean	Median	SE	Mean	Median	SE	Mean	Median	SE	Mean	Median	SE
Men												
Serum concentration												
Total cholesterol												
(mmol/l)	5.78	5.72	0.14	5.74	5.61	0.08	5.87	5.79	0.07	5.89	5.82	0.07
LDL cholesterol												
(mmol/l)	4.58	4.63	0.15	4.62	4.57	0.09	4.72	4.64	0.07	4.73	4.68	0.07
HDL cholesterol												
(mmol/l)	1.20	1.15	0.04	1.12	1.07	0.02	1.14	1.09	0.02	1.16	1.10	0.02
Women												
Serum concentration												
Total cholesterol												
(mmol/l)	5.65	5.58	0.12	5.86	5.68	0.10	5.92	5.70	0.07	5.74	5.48	0.08
LDL cholesterol												
(mmol/l)	4.23	4.18	0.12	4.45	4.28	0.10	4.53	4.27	0.08	4.30	4.01	0.08
HDL cholesterol												
(mmol/l)	1.41	1.31	0.05	1.38	1.31	0.03	1.39	1.37	0.02	1.44	1.45	0.02
Base numbers	*Men*	*Women*		*Men*	*Women*		*Men*	*Women*		*Men*	*Women*	
Serum concentration												
Total cholesterol	*83*	*69*		*233*	*199*		*313*	*283*		*294*	*258*	
LDL cholesterol	*82*	*68*		*233*	*198*		*310*	*282*		*294*	*258*	
HDL cholesterol	*82*	*68*		*233*	*198*		*310*	*282*		*294*	*258*	

* Not all samples were analysed for total and HDL cholesterol; mean LDL cholesterol concentrations apply only to samples from subjects for whom both total and HDL cholesterol concentrations were obtained.

Table 17.24 Serum cholesterol concentrations by sex and employment status of informant*

Blood analytes (units)	Employment status of informant								
	Working			Unemployed			Economically inactive		
	Mean	Median	SE	Mean	Median	SE	Mean	Median	SE
Men									
Serum concentration									
Total cholesterol (mmol/l)	5.79	5.71	0.04	5.79	5.57	0.15	6.31	6.31	0.14
LDL cholesterol (mmol/l)	4.63	4.58	0.04	4.63	4.42	0.15	5.23	5.38	0.16
HDL cholesterol (mmol/l)	1.16	1.10	0.01	1.16	1.10	0.04	1.07	1.04	0.04
Women									
Serum concentration									
Total cholesterol (mmol/l)	5.71	5.54	0.05	5.52	5.13	0.22	6.06	5.94	0.09
LDL cholesterol (mmol/l)	4.30	4.10	0.05	4.06	3.87	0.19	4.66	4.51	0.09
HDL cholesterol (mmol/l)	1.41	1.40	0.02	1.34	1.31	0.05	1.41	1.36	0.02
Base numbers	*Men*	*Women*		*Men*	*Women*		*Men*	*Women*	
Serum concentration									
Total cholesterol	*754*	*498*		*88*	*40*		*81*	*263*	
LDL cholesterol	*750*	*497*		*88*	*39*		*81*	*262*	
HDL cholesterol	*750*	*497*		*88*	*39*		*81*	*262*	

* *Not all samples were analysed for total and HDL cholesterol; mean LDL cholesterol concentrations apply only to samples from subjects for whom both total and HDL cholesterol concentrations were obtained.*

Table 17.25 Serum cholesterol concentrations by sex of informant and whether receiving benefits*

Blood analytes (units)	Whether received benefits							
	Received				Not received			
	Mean	Median	SE	*Base*	Mean	Median	SE	*Base*
Men								
Serum concentration								
Total cholesterol (mmol/l)	5.92	5.72	0.14	*102*	5.82	5.76	0.04	*816*
LDL cholesterol (mmol/l)	4.76	4.69	0.14	*102*	4.68	4.63	0.04	*812*
HDL cholesterol (mmol/l)	1.16	1.13	0.03	*102*	1.15	1.09	0.01	*812*
Women								
Serum concentration								
Total cholesterol (mmol/l)	5.59	5.32	0.12	*116*	5.86	5.68	0.05	*692*
LDL cholesterol (mmol/l)	4.24	4.12	0.12	*115*	4.43	4.20	0.05	*690*
HDL cholesterol (mmol/l)	1.31	1.29	0.03	*115*	1.42	1.39	0.01	*690*

* *Not all samples were analysed for total and HDL cholesterol; mean LDL cholesterol concentrations apply only to samples from subjects for whom both total and HDL cholesterol concentrations were obtained.*

Table 17.26 Serum cholesterol concentrations by sex of informant and social class of head of household*

Blood analytes (units)	Social class of head of household											
	I and II			III non-manual			III manual			IV and V		
	Mean	Median	SE	Mean	Median	SE	Mean	Median	SE	Mean	Median	SE
Men												
Serum concentration												
Total cholesterol												
(mmol/l)	5.86	5.79	0.07	6.02	6.04	0.12	5.84	5.68	0.07	5.64	5.50	0.11
LDL cholesterol												
(mmol/l)	4.70	4.63	0.07	4.86	4.86	0.12	4.72	4.62	0.07	4.49	4.40	0.11
HDL cholesterol												
(mmol/l)	1.16	1.11	0.02	1.16	1.10	0.03	1.13	1.06	0.02	1.15	1.08	0.03
Women												
Serum concentration												
Total cholesterol												
(mmol/l)	5.80	5.66	0.07	5.92	5.68	0.14	5.83	5.63	0.08	5.82	5.54	0.10
LDL cholesterol												
(mmol/l)	4.31	4.16	0.07	4.51	4.17	0.14	4.43	4.16	0.08	4.50	4.29	0.10
HDL cholesterol												
(mmol/l)	1.49	1.47	0.02	1.41	1.38	0.03	1.37	1.36	0.02	1.32	1.28	0.03
Base numbers	*Men*	*Women*		*Men*	*Women*		*Men*	*Women*		*Men*	*Women*	
Serum concentration												
Total cholesterol	*323*	*283*		*111*	*104*		*319*	*242*		*154*	*172*	
LDL cholesterol	*323*	*283*		*111*	*103*		*316*	*241*		*153*	*171*	
HDL cholesterol	*323*	*283*		*111*	*103*		*316*	*241*		*153*	*171*	

* Not all samples were analysed for total and HDL cholesterol; mean LDL cholesterol concentrations apply only to samples from subjects for whom both total and HDL cholesterol concentrations were obtained.

Table 17.27   Serum cholesterol concentrations by sex of informant and household composition*

Blood analytes (units)	Household composition											
	Informant alone			With others, no dependent children						With dependent child		
				With spouse			No spouse					
	Mean	Median	SE	Mean	Median	SE	Mean	Median	SE	Mean	Median	SE
Men												
Serum concentration												
Total cholesterol (mmol/l)	5.83	5.88	0.13	6.21	6.13	0.07	5.10	5.05	0.08	5.91	5.82	0.06
LDL cholesterol (mmol/l)	4.65	4.66	0.14	5.07	4.93	0.07	3.93	3.81	0.08	4.77	4.73	0.07
HDL cholesterol (mmol/l)	1.21	1.12	0.05	1.14	1.07	0.02	1.17	1.13	0.02	1.13	1.09	0.02

Blood analytes (units)	Informant alone			With others, no dependent children						With dependent child					
				With spouse			No spouse			With spouse			Lone mother		
	Mean	Median	SE	Mean	Median	SE	Mean	Median	SE	Mean	Median	SE	Mean	Median	SE
Women															
Serum concentration															
Total cholesterol (mmol/l)	6.12	5.85	0.18	6.40	6.35	0.07	5.37	5.07	0.14	5.45	5.34	0.06	5.14	5.01	0.13
LDL cholesterol (mmol/l)	4.76	4.52	0.19	4.95	4.84	0.08	3.98	3.57	0.14	4.03	3.95	0.06	3.84	3.64	0.13
HDL cholesterol (mmol/l)	1.37	1.39	0.05	1.45	1.41	0.02	1.38	1.39	0.04	1.40	1.37	0.02	1.30	1.29	0.04

Base numbers	*Men*	*Women*		*Men*	*Women*		*Men*	*Women*		*Men*	*Women*		*Women*		
Serum concentration															
Total cholesterol	63	57		324	305		198	88		338	299		60		
LDL cholesterol	62	57		324	305		197	87		336	297		60		
HDL cholesterol	62	57		324	305		197	87		336	297		60		

* *Not all samples were analysed for total and HDL cholesterol; mean LDL cholesterol concentrations apply only to samples from subjects for whom both total and HDL cholesterol concentrations were obtained.*

Table 17.28   Serum cholesterol concentrations by sex of informant and smoking behaviour*

Blood analytes (units)	Smoking behaviour								
	None			Fewer than 20 cigarettes a day			20 or more cigarettes a day		
	Mean	Median	SE	Mean	Median	SE	Mean	Median	SE
Men									
Serum concentration									
Total cholesterol (mmol/l)	5.85	5.78	0.05	5.60	5.33	0.10	5.99	5.97	0.10
LDL cholesterol (mmol/l)	4.68	4.57	0.05	4.49	4.53	0.11	4.89	4.86	0.10
HDL cholesterol (mmol/l)	1.17	1.11	0.01	1.13	1.06	0.03	1.10	1.06	0.03
Women									
Serum concentration									
Total cholesterol (mmol/l)	5.85	5.64	0.06	5.67	5.52	0.10	5.94	5.70	0.12
LDL cholesterol (mmol/l)	4.39	4.19	0.06	4.29	4.10	0.09	4.71	4.36	0.13
HDL cholesterol (mmol/l)	1.46	1.43	0.02	1.35	1.30	0.03	1.24	1.23	0.03
Base numbers	*Men*	*Women*		*Men*	*Women*		*Men*	*Women*	
Serum concentration									
Total cholesterol	608	528		149	176		166	105	
LDL cholesterol	606	528		147	175		166	103	
HDL cholesterol	606	528		147	175		166	103	

* *Not all samples were analysed for total and HDL cholesterol; mean LDL cholesterol concentrations apply only to samples from subjects for whom both total and HDL cholesterol concentrations were obtained.*

Table 17.29 Serum cholesterol concentrations by sex of informant and alcohol consumption during seven-day dietary recording period*

Blood analytes (units)	Alcohol consumption during seven-day dietary recording period											
	Nil			Less than 168g			168g—less than 400g			400g or more		
	Mean	Median	SE	Mean	Median	SE	Mean	Median	SE	Mean	Median	SE
Men												
Serum concentration												
Total cholesterol												
(mmol/l)	5.76	5.66	0.10	5.81	5.69	0.06	5.78	5.71	0.08	6.06	6.07	0.11
LDL cholesterol												
(mmol/l)	4.71	4.65	0.10	4.68	4.57	0.07	4.59	4.58	0.08	4.81	4.82	0.12
HDL cholesterol												
(mmol/l)	1.06	1.02	0.02	1.12	1.07	0.02	1.18	1.15	0.02	1.27	1.22	0.04
	Nil			Less than 112g			112g—less than 280g			280g or more		
	Mean	Median	SE	Mean	Median	SE	Mean	Median	SE	Mean	Median	SE
Women												
Serum concentration												
Total cholesterol												
(mmol/l)	5.92	5.68	0.09	5.83	5.71	0.06	5.50	5.28	0.11	5.84	5.59	0.34
LDL cholesterol												
(mmol/l)	4.56	4.33	0.09	4.42	4.24	0.06	3.95	3.80	0.10	4.32	3.89	0.34
HDL cholesterol												
(mmol/l)	1.34	1.30	0.02	1.41	1.39	0.02	1.55	1.53	0.03	1.53	1.61	0.12

Base numbers	Men				Women			
	Nil	*Less than 168g*	*168g—less than 400g*	*400g or more*	*Nil*	*Less than 112g*	*112g—less than 280g*	*280g or more*
Serum concentration								
Total cholesterol	*155*	*353*	*238*	*114*	*252*	*411*	*100*	*13*
LDL cholesterol	*154*	*353*	*237*	*112*	*251*	*409*	*100*	*13*
HDL cholesterol	*154*	*353*	*237*	*112*	*251*	*409*	*100*	*13*

* *Not all samples were analysed for total and HDL cholesterol; mean LDL cholesterol concentrations apply only to samples from subjects for whom both total and HDL cholesterol concentrations were obtained.*

Table 17.30 Men—analysis of variance for serum total cholesterol concentrations and HDL cholesterol concentrations

Characteristics	No. of cases	Adjusted deviations from grand mean and significance of F ratios for:	
		Total serum cholesterol (mmol/l)	HDL cholesterol (mmol/l)
Grand mean		5.83	1.14
Covariate—Age		**	NS
Correlation coefficient		0.44	−0.02
Region		NS	NS
Scotland	67	−0.11	0.06
Northern	208	−0.06	−0.04
Central, South West & Wales	290	0.02	0.00
London & South East	272	0.06	0.02
Social class of HOH		NS	NS
I and II	304	−0.01	0.00
IIINM	103	0.19	0.02
IIIM	294	0.01	−0.02
IV and V	136	−0.15	0.03
Economic status		NS	NS
Receiving benefits	86	0.09	0.01
Working	681	−0.02	0.00
Not working	70	0.07	−0.06
Household type		**	NS
Informant alone	54	−0.06	0.09
Informant, spouse, no dep. children	297	0.05	−0.01
Informant, adults, no dep. children	166	−0.34	0.01
Informant, spouse, dep. children	320	0.14	−0.01
Smoking behaviour		NS	*
Non-smoker	558	0.01	0.03
Less than 20 per day	129	−0.13	−0.05
20 or more per day	150	0.07	−0.06
Whether on a slimming diet		NS	**
Slimming	35	0.16	−0.14
Not slimming	802	−0.01	0.01
Unwell and eating affected		NS	NS
Unwell & eating affected	35	−0.11	−0.03
Eating not affected	72	−0.20	−0.01
Not unwell	730	0.03	0.00
Drinking behaviour		**	**
Non-drinker	147	−0.04	−0.09
Lowest intakes	348	−0.08	−0.03
Medium intakes	233	−0.03	0.04
Highest intakes	109	0.37	0.13
% of variance explained		*26%*	*8%*

** *F ratio $p < 0.01$*   NS *F ratio $p > 0.05$*
* *F ratio $p < 0.05$*

Table 17.31 Women—analysis of variance for serum total cholesterol concentrations and HDL cholesterol concentrations

Characteristics	No. of cases	Adjusted deviations from grand mean and significance of F ratios for:	
		Total serum cholesterol (mmol/l)	HDL cholesterol (mmol/l)
Grand mean		5.80	1.41
Covariate—Age		**	NS
Correlation coefficient		0.58	0.06
Region		NS	NS
Scotland	63	−0.14	0.02
Northern	187	0.00	−0.02
Central, South West & Wales	266	0.05	−0.02
London & South East	241	−0.02	0.03
Social class of HOH		NS	NS
I and II	271	−0.04	0.04
IIINM	96	0.04	0.02
IIIM	231	0.06	−0.03
IV and V	159	−0.05	−0.03
Economic status		NS	NS
Receiving benefits	103	−0.15	−0.06
Working	438	−0.02	0.01
Not working	216	0.12	0.01
Household type		NS	NS
Informant alone	51	0.15	−0.04
Informant, spouse, no dep. children	284	0.06	0.02
Informant, adults, no dep. children	82	0.09	−0.05
Informant, spouse, dep. children	286	−0.09	0.00
Lone mother	54	−0.12	0.01
Smoking behaviour		NS	*
Non-smoker	498	−0.04	0.05
Less than 20 per day	165	0.01	−0.05
20 or more per day	94	0.19	−0.16
Whether on a slimming diet		NS	*
Slimming	92	−0.12	−0.08
Not slimming	665	0.02	0.01
Unwell and eating affected		NS	NS
Unwell & eating affected	74	0.09	−0.04
Eating not affected	77	−0.19	0.02
Not unwell	606	0.01	0.00
Drinking behaviour		NS	*
Non-drinker	244	0.06	−0.05
Lowest intakes	404	0.01	−0.01
Medium intakes	97	−0.20	0.13
Highest intakes	12	0.19	0.23
% of variance explained		*37%*	*12%*

** F ratio $p < 0.01$ NS F ratio $p > 0.05$
*   F ratio $p < 0.05$

Table 17.32 Men—multiple regression analysis for serum total cholesterol concentrations

Variables in regression	Serum total cholesterol		
	Standard regression coefficient*	T-value	Significance of T-value
Alcohol intake (*log value*)		1.789	(NS)
Age	0.4102	13.143	(p<0.01)
Body mass index	0.2041	6.511	(p<0.01)
If smokes: *yes = 1; no = 0*		0.249	(NS)
If head of household in manual occupation: *yes = 1; no = 0*		−1.575	(NS)
Total energy intake		0.924	(NS)
Fat as a % of food energy		0.710	(NS)
Ratio of polyunsaturated: saturated fatty acids		−0.027	(NS)
% of variance explained	24.7%		

* the standard regression coefficient is given only for those variables where $p < 0.05$.

Table 17.33 Women—multiple regression analysis for serum total cholesterol concentrations

Variables in regression	Serum total cholesterol		
	Standard regression coefficient*	T-value	Significance of T-value
Body mass index	0.0706	2.338	(p<0.05)
Ratio of polyunsaturated: saturated fatty acids	−0.1116	−3.740	(p<0.05)
Age	0.5534	18.364	(p<0.01)
If smokes: *yes = 1; no = 0*		0.819	(NS)
If head of household in manual occupation: *yes = 1; no = 0*		−0.075	(NS)
Total energy intake		−0.896	(NS)
Fat as a % of food energy		1.124	(NS)
Alcohol intake (*log value*)		−0.789	(NS)
% of variance explained	35.1%		

* the standard regression coefficient is given only for those variables where $p < 0.05$.

Table 17.34 Men—multiple regression analysis for HDL cholesterol concentrations

Variables in regression	HDL cholesterol		
	Standard regression coefficient*	T-value	Significance of T-value
Alcohol intake (*log value*)	0.2295	6.575	(p<0.01)
Age		1.759	(NS)
If smokes: *yes = 1; no = 0*	−0.1077	−3.251	(p<0.01)
Fat as a % of food energy	0.0957	2.834	(p<0.05)
Body mass index	−0.2871	−8.337	(p<0.01)
Total energy intake	−0.0807	−2.336	(p<0.05)
If head of household in manual occupation: *yes = 1; no = 0*		0.924	(NS)
Ratio of polyunsaturated: saturated fatty acids		0.562	(NS)
% of variance explained	11.58%		

* the standard regression coefficient is given only for those variables where $p < 0.05$.

Table 17.35 Women—multiple regression anaylsis for HDL cholesterol concentrations

Variables in regression	HDL cholesterol		
	Standard regression coefficient*	T-value	Significance of T-value
Alcohol intake (*log value*)	0.1597	4.541	(p<0.01)
If smokes: *yes = 1; no = 0*	−0.2005	5.675	(p<0.01)
Body mass index	−0.1651	−4.673	(p<0.01)
Fat as a % of food energy	0.1254	3.594	(p<0.01)
Age	0.0695	1.970	(p<0.05)
If head of household in manual occupation: *yes = 1; no = 0*	−0.0771	−2.162	(p<0.05)
Total energy intake		−0.107	(NS)
Ratio of polyunsaturated: saturated fatty acids		0.741	(NS)
% of variance explained	12.72%		

* the standard regression coefficient is given only for those variables where $p < 0.05$

Table 17.36 Correlation coefficients between blood analytes and dietary intakes—serum total cholesterol, HDL cholesterol, and LDL cholesterol

Dietary intake	Blood analyte		
	Total cholesterol	HDL cholesterol	LDL cholesterol
Men			
Fat (g)	−0.02 (NS)	−0.04 (NS)	−0.01 (NS)
Saturated fatty acids (g)	0.01 (NS)	−0.05 (NS)	0.03 (NS)
Saturated plus trans fatty acids (g)	0.00 (NS)	−0.06 (NS)	0.02 (NS)
Monounsaturated fatty acids (g)	−0.02 (NS)	−0.03 (NS)	−0.01 (NS)
Cholesterol (mg)	0.09 (p<0.01)	0.03 (NS)	0.08 (p<0.05)
Total fat as % food energy	0.02 (NS)	0.08 (p<0.05)	−0.00 (NS)
Saturated fatty acids as % food energy	0.07 (p<0.05)	0.02 (NS)	0.06 (NS)
Saturated plus trans fatty acids as % food energy	0.06 (NS)	−0.00 (NS)	0.06 (NS)
Base	*860*	*856*	*856*
Women			
Fat (g)	−0.02 (NS)	0.13 (p<0.01)	−0.05 (NS)
Saturated fatty acids (g)	0.06 (NS)	0.11 (p<0.01)	0.03 (NS)
Saturated plus trans fatty acids (g)	0.05 (NS)	0.11 (p<0.01)	0.02 (NS)
Monounsaturated fatty acids (g)	−0.03 (NS)	0.12 (p<0.01)	−0.06 (NS)
Cholesterol (mg)	0.09 (p<0.05)	0.12 (p<0.01)	0.06 (NS)
Total fat as % food energy	0.05 (NS)	0.13 (p<0.01)	0.01 (NS)
Saturated fatty acids as % food energy	0.17 (p<0.05)	0.08 (p<0.05)	0.15 (p<0.01)
Saturated plus trans fatty acids as % food energy	0.16 (p<0.05)	0.07 (p<0.05)	0.13 (p<0.01)
Base	*776*	*773*	*773*

Table 17.37 Percentage distribution of albumin by age and sex

Albumin (g/1)	Men				All ages	Women				All ages
	18–24	25–34	35–49	50–64	18–64	18–24	25–34	35–49	50–64	18–64
	cum %	*cum* %	*cum* %	*cum* %	*cum* %	*cum* %	*cum* %	*cum* %	*cum* %	*cum* %
Less than 42	4	1	8	24	10	12	13	15	22	16
Less than 44	14	6	27	53	28	31	31	40	50	39
Less than 46	35	30	55	76	52	60	61	67	76	67
Less than 48	68	62	77	95	77	80	84	89	93	88
All	100	100	100	100	100	100	100	100	100	100
Base	*139*	*218*	*319*	*260*	*936*	*121*	*224*	*337*	*255*	*937*
Mean (average) value	46.3	46.8	45.3	43.3	45.3	44.9	44.7	44.3	43.5	44.2
Median value	46.0	47.0	45.0	43.0	45.0	45.0	45.0	44.0	44.0	44.0
Lower 5.0 percentile	42.0	43.0	41.0	39.0	40.0	40.0	40.0	39.0	39.0	39.0
Upper 5.0 percentile	51.0	51.0	50.0	48.0	50.0	50.0	49.0	49.0	48.0	49.0
Standard error of the mean	0.23	0.16	0.16	0.18	0.10	0.27	0.20	0.15	0.18	0.09

Table 17.38 Percentage distribution of serum total protein by age and sex

Serum total protein (g/l)	Men				All ages	Women				All ages
	18–24	25–34	35–49	50–64	18–64	18–24	25–34	35–49	50–64	18–64
	cum %	*cum* %	*cum* %	*cum* %	*cum* %	*cum* %	*cum* %	*cum* %	*cum* %	*cum* %
Less than 68	9	4	11	21	12	7	13	15	18	14
Less than 70	26	11	24	42	26	24	29	35	36	32
Less than 72	42	34	42	62	46	40	46	56	57	52
Less than 74	61	53	65	81	66	64	69	74	75	72
Less than 76	81	76	82	91	83	78	84	90	88	87
All	100	100	100	100	100	100	100	100	100	100
Base	*139*	*218*	*319*	*260*	*936*	*121*	*224*	*337*	*255*	*937*
Mean (average) value	72.3	73.2	72.2	70.4	71.9	72.5	71.8	71.1	71.0	71.4
Median value	72.0	73.0	72.0	70.0	72.0	72.0	72.0	71.0	71.0	71.0
Lower 5.0 percentile	67.0	68.0	66.0	65.0	66.0	67.0	65.0	66.0	65.0	65.0
Upper 5.0 percentile	80.0	79.0	79.0	77.0	78.0	78.0	78.0	77.0	77.0	77.0
Standard error of the mean	0.34	0.23	0.21	0.23	0.12	0.33	0.25	0.20	0.25	0.12

Table 17.39 Percentage distribution of globulin by age and sex

Globulin (g/l)	Men				All ages	Women				All ages
	18–24	25–34	35–49	50–64	18–64	18–24	25–34	35–49	50–64	18–64
	cum %	*cum* %	*cum* %	*cum* %	*cum* %	*cum* %	*cum* %	*cum* %	*cum* %	*cum* %
Less than 24	21	15	17	13	16	7	13	10	9	10
Less than 26	43	36	34	33	35	30	34	34	30	33
Less than 28	68	69	60	57	62	48	57	61	56	57
Less than 30	89	86	81	83	83	75	77	82	75	78
All	100	100	100	100	100	100	100	100	100	100
Base	*139*	*218*	*319*	*260*	*936*	*121*	*224*	*337*	*255*	*937*
Mean (average) value	26.0	26.3	26.9	27.1	26.7	27.6	27.1	26.8	27.6	27.2
Median value	26.0	26.0	27.0	27.0	27.0	28.0	27.0	27.0	27.0	27.0
Lower 5.0 percentile	21.0	22.0	22.0	22.0	22.0	23.0	22.0	22.0	23.0	22.0
Upper 5.0 percentile	31.0	32.0	33.0	32.0	32.0	33.0	33.0	31.0	34.0	33.0
Standard error of the mean	0.27	0.20	0.18	0.20	0.10	0.29	0.23	0.16	0.24	0.11

Table 17.40 Serum albumin, serum globulin and serum total protein by sex of informant and whether on a slimming diet

Blood analytes (units)	Whether on a slimming diet								
	Dieting				Not dieting			
	Mean	Median	SE	Base	Mean	Median	SE	Base
Men								
Total protein (g/l)	72.1	72.0	0.58	40	71.9	72.0	0.13	896
Albumin (g/l)	44.8	45.0	0.43	40	45.3	45.0	0.10	896
Globulin (g/l)	27.4	27.0	0.48	40	26.6	26.0	0.11	896
Women								
Total protein (g/l)	71.4	72.0	0.30	116	71.4	71.0	0.13	821
Albumin (g/l)	44.3	44.0	0.26	116	44.2	44.0	0.10	821
Globulin (g/l)	27.1	27.0	0.27	116	27.2	27.0	0.12	821

Table 17.41 Serum albumin, serum globulin and serum total protein by sex of informant and whether unwell during seven-day dietary recording period

Blood analytes (units)	Whether unwell during seven-day dietary recording period											
	Completed food diary									No food diary		
	Not unwell			Unwell								
				Eating affected			Eating not affected					
	Mean	Median	SE	Mean	Median	SE	Mean	Median	SE	Mean	Median	SE
Men												
Total protein (g/l)	72.0	72.0	0.14	72.3	72.0	0.64	71.2	71.0	0.44	72.0	72.0	0.45
Albumin (g/l)	45.3	45.0	0.11	45.9	46.0	0.60	44.4	45.0	0.41	45.0	45.0	0.35
Globulin (g/l)	26.6	26.0	0.12	26.5	26.0	0.61	26.8	27.0	0.37	27.0	27.0	0.40
Women												
Total protein (g/l)	71.4	71.0	0.14	71.7	72.0	0.39	71.0	71.0	0.45	71.8	72.0	0.68
Albumin (g/l)	44.3	44.0	0.11	44.0	44.0	0.31	43.9	44.0	0.33	44.1	45.0	0.55
Globulin (g/l)	27.1	27.0	0.12	27.7	27.0	0.37	27.1	27.0	0.38	27.7	28.0	0.66
Base numbers	*Men*	*Women*		*Men*	*Women*		*Men*	*Women*		*Men*	*Women*	
Total protein	*763*	*719*		*35*	*90*		*74*	*91*		*64*	*37*	
Albumin	*763*	*719*		*35*	*90*		*74*	*91*		*64*	*37*	
Globulin	*763*	*719*		*35*	*90*		*74*	*91*		*64*	*37*	

Table 17.42 Serum albumin, serum globulin and serum total protein by sex of informant and region

Blood analytes (units)	Region											
	Scotland			Northern			Central, South West and Wales			London and South East		
	Mean	Median	SE	Mean	Median	SE	Mean	Median	SE	Mean	Median	SE
Men												
Total protein (g/l)	71.9	72.0	0.47	71.7	72.0	0.24	71.9	72.0	0.21	72.2	72.0	0.22
Albumin (g/l)	45.1	45.0	0.35	44.7	45.0	0.20	45.3	45.0	0.17	45.7	46.0	0.18
Globulin (g/l)	26.8	27.0	0.38	27.0	27.0	0.20	26.6	26.0	0.17	26.5	26.0	0.20
Women												
Total protein (g/l)	70.8	71.0	0.40	71.1	71.0	0.25	71.3	71.0	0.21	71.9	72.0	0.22
Albumin (g/l)	44.4	45.0	0.30	43.7	44.0	0.19	44.1	44.0	0.17	44.7	45.0	0.16
Globulin (g/l)	26.5	26.0	0.34	27.4	27.0	0.21	27.2	27.0	0.19	27.2	27.0	0.20
Base numbers	*Men*	*Women*		*Men*	*Women*		*Men*	*Women*		*Men*	*Women*	
Total protein	*84*	*83*		*238*	*227*		*317*	*324*		*297*	*303*	
Albumin	*84*	*83*		*238*	*227*		*317*	*324*		*297*	*303*	
Globulin	*84*	*83*		*238*	*227*		*317*	*324*		*297*	*303*	

Table 17.43 Serum albumin, serum globulin and serum total protein by sex and employment status of informant

Blood analytes (units)	Employment status of informant								
	Working			Unemployed			Economically inactive		
	Mean	Median	SE	Mean	Median	SE	Mean	Median	SE
Men									
Total protein (g/l)	72.0	72.0	0.14	71.9	72.0	0.40	71.4	71.0	0.45
Albumin (g/l)	45.5	46.0	0.11	44.6	45.0	0.33	43.4	44.0	0.37
Globulin (g/l)	26.4	26.0	0.11	27.3	27.0	0.34	28.0	28.0	0.38
Women									
Total protein (g/l)	71.4	71.0	0.15	71.8	71.0	0.71	71.4	71.0	0.22
Albumin (g/l)	44.4	44.0	0.12	44.4	44.0	0.44	43.9	44.0	0.18
Globulin (g/l)	27.0	27.0	0.13	27.5	27.0	0.57	27.5	27.0	0.20
Base numbers	*Men*	*Women*		*Men*	*Women*		*Men*	*Women*	
Total protein	*762*	*582*		*89*	*44*		*85*	*303*	
Albumin	*762*	*582*		*89*	*44*		*85*	*303*	
Globulin	*762*	*582*		*89*	*44*		*85*	*303*	

Table 17.44 Serum albumin, serum globulin and serum total protein by sex of informant and whether receiving benefits

Blood analytes (units)	Whether received benefits							
	Received				Not received			
	Mean	Median	SE	*Base*	Mean	Median	SE	*Base*
Men								
Total protein (g/l)	72.0	72.0	0.39	*104*	71.9	72.0	0.13	*827*
Albumin (g/l)	44.4	44.0	0.28	*104*	45.4	45.0	0.11	*827*
Globulin (g/l)	27.6	27.0	0.33	*104*	26.5	26.0	0.11	*827*
Women								
Total protein (g/l)	71.3	71.0	0.39	*127*	71.4	71.0	0.13	*809*
Albumin (g/l)	43.5	43.0	0.29	*127*	44.3	44.0	0.10	*809*
Globulin (g/l)	27.8	27.0	0.33	*127*	27.1	27.0	0.11	*809*

Table 17.45 Serum albumin, serum globulin and serum total protein by sex of informant and social class of head of household

Blood analytes (units)	Social class of head of household											
	I and II			III non-manual			III manual			IV and V		
	Mean	Median	SE	Mean	Median	SE	Mean	Median	SE	Mean	Median	SE
Men												
Total protein (g/l)	72.1	72.0	0.21	71.1	71.0	0.38	71.9	72.0	0.21	72.2	72.0	0.30
Albumin (g/l)	45.8	46.0	0.16	45.1	47.0	0.30	44.9	45.0	0.17	44.8	45.0	0.25
Globulin (g/l)	26.3	26.0	0.18	26.0	26.0	0.30	27.0	27.0	0.17	27.4	27.0	0.26
Women												
Total protein (g/l)	71.5	71.0	0.20	71.6	71.0	0.36	71.6	72.0	0.23	70.8	71.0	0.28
Albumin (g/l)	44.7	45.0	0.15	44.6	45.0	0.29	44.2	44.0	0.17	43.1	43.0	0.21
Globulin (g/l)	26.8	27.0	0.18	27.0	27.0	0.33	27.4	27.0	0.20	27.7	27.0	0.24
Base numbers	*Men*	*Women*		*Men*	*Women*		*Men*	*Women*		*Men*	*Women*	
Total protein	*328*	*327*		*114*	*121*		*321*	*284*		*157*	*194*	
Albumin	*328*	*327*		*114*	*121*		*321*	*284*		*157*	*194*	
Globulin	*328*	*327*		*114*	*121*		*321*	*284*		*157*	*194*	

Table 17.46 Serum albumin, serum globulin and serum total protein by sex of informant and household composition

Blood analytes (units)	Household composition														
	Informant alone			With others, no dependent children						With dependent child					
				With spouse			No spouse								
	Mean	Median	SE	Mean	Median	SE	Mean	Median	SE	Mean	Median	SE			
Men															
Total protein (g/l)	71.8	72.0	0.47	71.4	71.0	0.22	72.1	72.0	0.28	72.4	72.0	0.19			
Albumin (g/l)	44.7	45.0	0.39	45.6	44.5	0.19	45.7	46.0	0.20	45.8	46.0	0.14			
Globulin (g/l)	27.1	27.0	0.39	26.8	27.0	0.18	26.4	26.0	0.24	26.7	26.0	0.17			
	Informant alone			With others, no dependent children						With dependent child					
				With spouse			No spouse			With spouse			Lone mother		
	Mean	Median	SE	Mean	Median	SE	Mean	Median	SE	Mean	Median	SE	Mean	Median	SE
Women															
Total protein (g/l)	71.4	72.0	0.36	71.1	71.0	0.21	72.2	72.0	0.37	71.5	71.0	0.20	71.3	71.0	0.49
Albumin (g/l)	43.9	44.0	0.32	44.1	44.0	0.15	44.8	45.0	0.32	44.4	45.0	0.15	43.7	44.0	0.34
Globulin (g/l)	27.6	27.0	0.34	27.0	27.0	0.19	27.5	27.0	0.29	27.1	27.0	0.18	27.6	27.0	0.38
Base numbers	*Men*	*Women*		*Men*	*Women*		*Men*	*Women*		*Men*	*Women*		*Women*		
Total protein	*65*	*76*		*330*	*331*		*198*	*116*		*343*	*347*		*67*		
Albumin	*65*	*76*		*330*	*331*		*198*	*116*		*343*	*347*		*67*		
Globulin	*65*	*76*		*330*	*331*		*198*	*116*		*343*	*347*		*67*		

Table 17.47 Serum albumin, serum globulin and serum total protein by sex of informant and smoking behaviour

Blood analytes (units)	Smoking behaviour								
	None			Fewer than 20 cigarettes a day			20 or more cigarettes a day		
	Mean	Median	SE	Mean	Median	SE	Mean	Median	SE
Men									
Total protein (g/l)	72.1	72.0	0.16	71.6	72.0	0.28	71.4	71.0	0.28
Albumin (g/l)	45.5	46.0	0.12	44.9	45.0	0.24	44.5	45.0	0.23
Globulin (g/l)	26.6	26.0	0.13	26.7	27.0	0.26	26.8	27.0	0.24
Women									
Total protein (g/l)	71.8	72.0	0.15	71.3	71.5	0.27	69.7	69.0	0.34
Albumin (g/l)	44.4	44.0	0.11	44.4	44.0	0.20	43.1	43.0	0.29
Globulin (g/l)	27.4	27.0	0.14	26.9	27.0	0.24	26.6	26.0	0.26
Base numbers	*Men*	*Women*		*Men*	*Women*		*Men*	*Women*	
Total protein	*618*	*606*		*152*	*208*		*166*	*123*	
Albumin	*618*	*606*		*152*	*208*		*166*	*123*	
Globulin	*618*	*606*		*152*	*208*		*166*	*123*	

Table 17.48 Serum albumin, serum globulin and serum total protein by sex of informant and alcohol consumption during seven-day dietary recording period

Blood analytes (units)	Alcohol consumption during seven-day dietary recording period											
	Nil			Less than 168g			168g—less than 400g			400g or more		
	Mean	Median	SE	Mean	Median	SE	Mean	Median	SE	Mean	Median	SE
Men												
Total protein (g/l)	71.6	71.0	0.30	71.7	72.0	0.20	72.1	72.0	0.26	72.7	73.0	0.35
Albumin (g/l)	44.7	45.0	0.23	45.5	46.0	0.17	45.4	46.0	0.20	45.2	45.0	0.27
Globulin (g/l)	27.0	27.0	0.26	26.2	26.0	0.16	26.7	27.0	0.20	27.6	27.0	0.31
	Nil			Less than 112g			112g—less than 280g			280g or more		
	Mean	Median	SE	Mean	Median	SE	Mean	Median	SE	Mean	Median	SE
Women												
Total protein (g/l)	71.2	71.0	0.22	71.5	71.0	0.17	71.5	71.0	0.33	73.0	72.0	1.13
Albumin (g/l)	43.7	44.0	0.18	44.4	45.0	0.13	44.7	44.0	0.22	46.3	46.0	0.91
Globulin (g/l)	27.4	27.0	0.19	27.1	27.0	0.15	26.9	26.0	0.29	26.7	27.0	1.13

Base numbers	Men				Women			
	Nil	Less than 168g	168g—less than 400g	400g or more	Nil	Less than 112g	112g—less than 280g	280g or more
Total protein	158	360	239	115	295	466	124	15
Albumin	158	360	239	115	295	466	124	15
Globulin	158	360	239	115	295	466	124	15

Table 17.49 Correlation coefficients between serum albumin and dietary protein intake for men and women

	Men	Women
Correlation coefficients	0.04 (NS)	0.07 (NS)
Base	872	900

Table 17.50 Percentage distribution of alkaline phosphatase by age and sex

Alkaline phosphatase (u/l)	Men				All ages	Women				All ages
	18–24	25–34	35–49	50–64	18–64	18–24	25–34	35–49	50–64	18–64
	cum %	cum %	cum %	cum %	cum %	cum %	cum %	cum %	cum %	cum %
Less than 125	4	17	12	12	12	34	48	42	11	34
Less than 150	18	30	31	32	32	59	70	68	25	56
Less than 175	30	57	56	57	55	77	84	83	49	73
Less than 200	55	72	78	73	74	93	92	93	69	86
All	100	100	100	100	100	100	100	100	100	100
Base	139	218	318	260	935	121	224	337	255	937
Mean (average) value	204.0	162.8	172.1	177.6	176.2	145.0	137.3	138.9	185.4	152.0
Median value	196.0	157.0	168.0	168.0	169.0	140.0	126.5	129.0	175.0	142.0
Lower 5.0 percentile	125.0	102.0	110.0	109.0	109.0	94.0	84.0	85.0	108.0	90.0
Upper 5.0 percentile	315.0	247.0	247.0	271.0	266.0	206.0	224.0	219.0	293.0	238.0
Standard error of the mean	5.60	2.97	2.49	3.67	1.76	3.38	2.90	2.33	4.35	1.79

Table 17.51 Percentage distribution of γ-glutamyl transpeptidase by age and sex

γ-glutamyl transpeptidase (u/l)	Men				All ages 18–64	Women				All ages 18–64
	18–24	25–34	35–49	50–64		18–24	25–34	35–49	50–64	
	cum %	cum %	cum %	cum %	cum %	cum %	cum %	cum %	cum %	cum %
Less than 30	85	79	63	60	69	93	92	92	86	90
Less than 40	94	86	75	76	81	97	96	94	93	95
Less than 100	100	98	95	97	97	99	99	99	98	99
All		100	100	100	100	100	100	100	100	100
Base	139	218	318	260	935	121	224	337	255	937
Mean (average) value	21.0	26.5	44.8	32.7	33.7	15.2	17.1	17.3	23.2	18.6
Median value	16.0	20.0	25.0	25.0	22.0	13.0	13.0	13.0	15.0	14.0
Lower 5.0 percentile	10.0	11.0	12.0	13.0	11.0	7.0	7.0	8.0	9.0	8.0
Upper 5.0 percentile	55.0	73.0	102.0	82.0	81.0	31.0	36.0	45.0	48.0	41.0
Standard error of the mean	1.20	1.58	5.46	1.49	1.97	1.14	1.27	0.79	2.21	0.75

Table 17.52 Percentage distribution of calcium by age and sex

Calcium (mmol/l)	Men				All ages 18–64	Women				All ages 18–64
	18–24	25–34	35–49	50–64		18–24	25–34	35–49	50–64	
	cum %	cum %	cum %	cum %	cum %	cum %	cum %	cum %	cum %	cum %
Less than 2.2	9	5	8	15	9	9	19	21	9	16
Less than 2.3	39	41	48	63	49	57	59	61	50	57
Less than 2.4	72	78	84	89	82	90	91	92	82	89
Less than 2.5	97	95	98	99	97	99	99	99	94	98
Less than 2.6	100	100	99	99	99	100	100	100	99	99
All			100	100	100				100	100
Base	139	218	318	260	935	121	224	337	255	937
Mean (average) value	2.33	2.33	2.31	2.28	2.31	2.29	2.28	2.28	2.32	2.29
Median value	2.35	2.32	2.31	2.27	2.31	2.29	2.29	2.28	2.30	2.29
Lower 5.0 percentile	2.16	2.19	2.18	2.14	2.17	2.17	2.12	2.14	2.17	2.14
Upper 5.0 percentile	2.48	2.49	2.46	2.44	2.46	2.45	2.43	2.42	2.51	2.45
Standard error of the mean	0.008	0.006	0.005	0.005	0.003	0.008	0.006	0.005	0.008	0.003

Table 17.53 Percentage distribution of creatinine by age and sex

Creatinine (μmol/l)	Men				All ages 18–64	Women				All ages 18–64
	18–24	25–34	35–49	50–64		18–24	25–34	35–49	50–64	
	cum %	cum %	cum %	cum %	cum %	cum %	cum %	cum %	cum %	cum %
Less than 120	95	94	92	85	91	100	100	99	95	99
Less than 500	100	100	100	99	99			100	100	100
All				100	100					
Base	139	218	319	260	936	121	224	337	255	937
Mean (average) value	97.8	100.4	102.4	109.8	103.3	80.6	83.3	85.3	91.6	85.9
Median value	96.0	100.0	101.0	104.0	101.0	81.0	83.0	84.0	88.0	84.0
Lower 5.0 percentile	79.0	84.0	83.0	88.0	84.0	66.0	68.0	70.0	73.0	69.0
Upper 5.0 percentile	121.0	122.0	123.0	134.5	126.0	96.0	102.0	105.0	118.0	106.0
Standard error of the mean	1.15	0.79	0.83	3.51	1.05	0.84	0.67	0.61	1.14	0.44

Table 17.54 γ-glutamyl transpeptidase, serum calcium, serum creatinine and alkaline phosphatase by sex of informant and whether on a slimming diet

Blood analytes (units)	Whether on a slimming diet							
	Dieting				Not dieting			
	Mean	Median	SE	*Base*	Mean	Median	SE	*Base*
Men								
γ-glutamyl transpeptidase (u/l)	29.7	24.0	3.24	*39*	33.8	22.0	2.05	*896*
Calcium (mmol/l)	2.30	2.31	0.01	*39*	2.31	2.31	0.00	*886*
Creatinine (μmol/l)	103.4	101.0	2.15	*40*	103.3	101.0	1.10	*896*
Alkaline phosphatase (u/l)	170.2	160.0	5.79	*40*	176.5	170.0	1.82	*895*
Women								
γ-glutamyl transpeptidase (u/l)	18.0	14.5	1.21	*116*	18.7	13.0	0.84	*821*
Calcium (mmol/l)	2.29	2.30	0.01	*112*	2.29	2.29	0.00	*797*
Creatinine (μmol/l)	87.9	86.0	1.45	*116*	85.6	84.0	0.46	*821*
Alkaline phosphatase (u/l)	151.7	140.5	5.18	*116*	152.0	142.0	1.91	*821*

Table 17.55 γ-glutamyl transpeptidase, serum calcium, serum creatinine and alkaline phosphatase by sex of informant and whether unwell during seven-day dietary recording period

Blood analytes (units)	Whether unwell during seven-day dietary recording period											
	Completed food diary									No food diary		
	Not unwell			Unwell								
				Eating affected			Eating not affected					
	Mean	Median	SE	Mean	Median	SE	Mean	Median	SE	Mean	Median	SE
Men												
γ-glutamyl transpeptidase (u/l)	32.6	22.0	2.02	25.2	20.0	2.55	40.8	23.5	11.56	42.4	22.0	8.24
Calcium (mmol/l)	2.31	2.31	0.00	2.30	2.28	0.02	2.31	2.32	0.01	2.32	2.31	0.01
Creatinine (μmol/l)	103.4	100.0	1.27	100.2	98.0	2.00	105.3	107.0	1.49	101.6	100.0	2.10
Alkaline phosphatase (u/l)	175.4	169.0	1.88	180.1	172.0	9.97	180.9	167.0	8.58	178.4	172.0	5.55
Women												
γ-glutamyl transpeptidase (u/l)	18.4	13.0	0.92	19.3	14.0	1.79	19.4	14.0	1.86	18.7	17.0	1.62
Calcium (mmol/l)	2.29	2.29	0.00	2.32	2.30	0.02	2.29	2.28	0.01	2.29	2.30	0.01
Creatinine (μmol/l)	86.1	84.0	0.53	85.8	85.0	1.21	84.7	82.0	1.23	85.8	84.0	1.77
Alkaline phosphatase (u/l)	152.3	144.0	2.07	146.9	137.0	5.08	151.2	140.0	5.62	160.9	141.0	10.09

Base numbers	Men	Women		Men	Women		Men	Women		Men	Women	
γ-glutamyl transpeptidase	*762*	*719*		*35*	*90*		*74*	*91*		*64*	*37*	
Calcium	*756*	*701*		*33*	*86*		*72*	*85*		*64*	*37*	
Creatinine	*763*	*719*		*35*	*90*		*74*	*91*		*64*	*37*	
Alkaline phosphatase	*762*	*719*		*35*	*90*		*74*	*91*		*64*	*37*	

Table 17.56 γ-glutamyl transpeptidase, serum calcium, serum creatinine and alkaline phosphatase by sex of informant and region

Blood analytes (units)	Region											
	Scotland			Northern			Central, South West and Wales			London and South East		
	Mean	Median	SE	Mean	Median	SE	Mean	Median	SE	Mean	Median	SE
Men												
γ-glutamyl transpeptidase (u/l)	56.0	24.0	15.23	32.2	22.0	3.02	32.1	22.0	3.17	30.2	22.0	1.51
Calcium (mmol/l)	2.30	2.29	0.01	2.30	2.29	0.01	2.33	2.33	0.01	2.30	2.30	0.01
Creatinine (µmol/l)	102.2	99.0	2.14	101.6	100.0	0.84	103.0	101.0	0.90	105.3	102.0	3.05
Alkaline phosphatase (u/l)	184.4	182.0	6.15	174.7	170.5	2.96	176.4	169.0	3.06	174.8	166.0	3.38
Women												
γ-glutamyl transpeptidase (u/l)	19.1	14.0	1.60	18.5	14.0	1.13	19.0	13.0	1.68	18.1	14.0	1.12
Calcium (mmol/l)	2.28	2.28	0.01	2.28	2.28	0.01	2.30	2.29	0.01	2.30	2.30	0.01
Creatinine (µmol/l)	86.8	85.0	1.49	85.9	85.0	1.14	85.8	84.0	0.73	85.8	84.0	0.61
Alkaline phosphatase (u/l)	156.8	142.0	6.05	150.2	141.0	3.13	154.4	145.0	3.67	149.4	142.0	2.68
Base numbers	*Men*	*Women*		*Men*	*Women*		*Men*	*Women*		*Men*	*Women*	
γ-glutamyl transpeptidase	*84*	*83*		*238*	*227*		*316*	*324*		*297*	*303*	
Calcium	*82*	*81*		*236*	*223*		*313*	*316*		*294*	*289*	
Creatinine	*84*	*83*		*238*	*227*		*317*	*324*		*297*	*303*	
Alkaline phosphatase	*84*	*83*		*238*	*227*		*317*	*324*		*296*	*303*	

Table 17.57 γ-glutamyl transpeptidase, serum calcium, serum creatinine and alkaline phosphatase by sex and employment status of informant

Blood analytes (units)	Employment status of informant								
	Working			Unemployed			Economically inactive		
	Mean	Median	SE	Mean	Median	SE	Mean	Median	SE
Men									
γ-glutamyl transpeptidase (u/l)	32.4	22.0	2.28	34.7	24.0	3.68	43.6	29.0	5.93
Calcium (mmol/l)	2.31	2.31	0.00	2.32	2.32	0.01	2.31	2.30	0.01
Creatinine (µmol/l)	102.1	101.0	0.50	102.0	97.0	1.99	116.0	105.0	10.45
Alkaline phosphatase (u/l)	171.4	166.0	1.68	190.2	190.0	5.12	204.4	181.0	10.35
Women									
γ-glutamyl transpeptidase (u/l)	16.5	13.0	0.61	19.2	14.0	2.74	22.5	15.0	1.95
Calcium (mmol/l)	2.28	2.29	0.00	2.30	2.29	0.01	2.30	2.30	0.01
Creatinine (µmol/l)	85.6	84.0	0.55	82.1	80.0	1.67	87.0	85.0	0.81
Alkaline phosphatase (u/l)	143.8	135.0	1.81	159.9	150.5	8.19	166.0	153.0	3.99
Base numbers	*Men*	*Women*		*Men*	*Women*		*Men*	*Women*	
γ-glutamyl transpeptidase	*761*	*582*		*89*	*44*		*85*	*303*	
Calcium	*757*	*565*		*87*	*44*		*81*	*292*	
Creatinine	*762*	*582*		*89*	*44*		*85*	*303*	
Alkaline phosphatase	*761*	*582*		*89*	*44*		*85*	*303*	

Table 17.58 γ-glutamyl transpeptidase, serum calcium, serum creatinine and alkaline phosphatase by sex of informant and whether receiving benefits

Blood analytes (units)	Whether received benefits							
	Received				Not received			
	Mean	Median	SE	Base	Mean	Median	SE	Base
Men								
γ-glutamyl transpeptidase (u/l)	36.6	24.5	3.33	104	33.0	22.0	2.17	826
Calcium (mmol/l)	2.32	2.32	0.01	103	2.31	2.31	0.00	817
Creatinine (μmol/l)	101.4	98.5	1.73	104	103.5	101.0	1.17	827
Alkaline phosphatase (u/l)	194.3	194.0	4.75	104	173.6	166.0	1.87	826
Women								
γ-glutamyl transpeptidase (u/l)	21.6	14.0	2.51	127	18.1	14.0	0.78	809
Calcium (mmol/l)	2.29	2.28	0.01	122	2.29	2.29	0.00	786
Creatinine (μmol/l)	83.5	81.0	1.10	127	86.3	85.0	0.48	809
Alkaline phosphatase (u/l)	162.4	149.0	5.42	127	150.4	141.0	1.89	809

Table 17.59 γ-glutamyl transpeptidase, serum calcium, serum creatinine and alkaline phosphatase by sex of informant and social class of head of household

Blood analytes (units)	Social class of head of household											
	I and II			III non-manual			III manual			IV and V		
	Mean	Median	SE	Mean	Median	SE	Mean	Median	SE	Mean	Median	SE
Men												
γ-glutamyl transpeptidase (u/l)	28.0	22.0	1.28	36.0	24.5	4.50	38.5	23.0	5.00	31.7	21.0	2.50
Calcium (mmol/l)	2.30	2.30	0.01	2.30	2.29	0.01	2.32	2.32	0.01	2.32	2.32	0.01
Creatinine (μmol/l)	103.0	102.0	0.80	103.5	100.5	1.64	101.4	100.0	0.72	108.0	100.0	5.74
Alkaline phosphatase (u/l)	163.2	157.5	2.71	171.7	166.0	4.70	183.3	178.0	2.74	189.3	180.5	5.33
Women												
γ-glutamyl transpeptidase (u/l)	20.0	13.0	1.74	19.0	13.0	2.26	17.1	13.0	0.86	18.4	14.0	1.01
Calcium (mmol/l)	2.29	2.29	0.01	2.30	2.31	0.01	2.29	2.29	0.01	2.29	2.29	0.01
Creatinine (μmol/l)	85.6	84.0	0.78	85.6	84.0	1.02	86.2	85.5	0.76	86.3	84.0	1.09
Alkaline phosphatase (u/l)	146.4	134.0	3.30	149.7	144.0	4.89	153.6	146.0	3.01	161.3	151.0	3.78
Base numbers	*Men*	*Women*		*Men*	*Women*		*Men*	*Women*		*Men*	*Women*	
γ-glutamyl transpeptidase	327	327		114	121		321	284		157	194	
Calcium	325	319		113	114		318	278		153	187	
Creatinine	328	327		114	121		321	284		157	194	
Alkaline phosphatase	328	327		114	121		321	284		156	194	

Table 17.60 γ-glutamyl transpeptidase, serum calcium, serum creatinine and alkaline phosphatase by sex of informant and household composition

Males

Blood analytes (units)	Household composition											
	Informant alone			With others, no dependent children						With dependent child		
				With spouse			No spouse					
	Mean	Median	SE	Mean	Median	SE	Mean	Median	SE	Mean	Median	SE
γ-glutamyl transpeptidase (u/l)	49.6	24.0	11.98	33.9	24.0	2.87	29.1	18.0	2.86	33.1	34.0	3.64
Calcium (mmol/l)	2.30	2.30	0.01	2.30	2.30	0.01	2.32	2.33	0.01	2.31	2.31	0.01
Creatinine (μmol/l)	99.4	97.0	1.51	108.6	104.0	2.80	99.5	99.0	0.97	101.2	100.0	0.71
Alkaline phosphatase (u/l)	187.6	181.0	7.90	171.2	164.0	3.04	191.8	186.0	4.52	169.9	166.0	2.20

Women

	Informant alone			With others, no dependent children						With dependent child					
				With spouse			No spouse			With spouse			Lone mother		
	Mean	Median	SE	Mean	Median	SE	Mean	Median	SE	Mean	Median	SE	Mean	Median	SE
γ-glutamyl transpeptidase (u/l)	17.2	14.0	1.14	21.3	15.0	1.77	16.0	13.0	0.92	16.9	13.0	0.93	19.9	15.0	2.43
Calcium (mmol/l)	2.31	2.29	0.01	2.30	2.30	0.01	2.29	2.29	0.01	2.28	2.28	0.01	2.27	2.27	0.01
Creatinine (μmol/l)	85.1	84.5	1.41	89.7	87.0	0.93	83.8	82.0	1.01	84.0	84.0	0.55	81.7	81.0	1.34
Alkaline phosphatase (u/l)	153.8	133.5	6.92	165.7	159.0	3.42	151.7	143.0	4.53	137.9	129.0	2.34	155.9	146.0	6.82

Base numbers	Men	Women		Men	Women		Men	Women		Men	Women			Women	
γ-glutamyl transpeptidase	65	76		330	331		198	116		342	347			67	
Calcium	65	75		324	318		195	116		341	336			64	
Creatinine	65	76		330	331		198	116		343	347			67	
Alkaline phosphatase	65	76		330	331		197	116		343	347			67	

Table 17.61 γ-glutamyl transpeptidase, serum calcium, serum creatinine and alkaline phosphatase by sex of informant and smoking behaviour

Blood analytes (units)	Smoking behaviour								
	None			Fewer than 20 cigarettes a day			20 or more cigarettes a day		
	Mean	Median	SE	Mean	Median	SE	Mean	Median	SE
Men									
γ-glutamyl transpeptidase (u/l)	30.3	22.0	1.65	38.3	23.0	7.91	41.7	25.0	5.68
Calcium (mmol/l)	2.31	2.31	0.00	2.32	2.31	0.01	2.31	2.30	0.01
Creatinine (μmol/l)	103.4	102.0	0.63	105.9	98.0	5.87	100.8	100.0	0.94
Alkaline phosphatase (u/l)	170.5	164.0	2.00	187.2	177.0	5.81	187.5	186.5	3.52
Women									
γ-glutamyl transpeptidase (u/l)	18.6	13.0	1.08	18.2	15.0	1.04	19.4	15.0	1.17
Calcium (mmol/l)	2.29	2.29	0.00	2.29	2.29	0.01	2.28	2.27	0.01
Creatinine (μmol/l)	86.7	85.0	0.51	84.0	83.0	1.13	85.1	84.0	1.16
Alkaline phosphatase (u/l)	149.8	138.0	2.32	155.6	146.0	3.79	156.9	152.0	3.89

Base numbers	*Men*	*Women*		*Men*	*Women*		*Men*	*Women*	
γ-glutamyl transpeptidase	618	606		152	208		166	123	
Calcium	610	585		150	207		165	117	
Creatinine	618	606		152	208		166	123	
Alkaline phosphatase	617	606		152	208		166	123	

Table 17.62 γ-glutamyl transpeptidase, serum calcium, serum creatinine and alkaline phosphatase by sex of informant and alcohol consumption during seven-day dietary recording period

Blood analytes (units)	Alcohol consumption during seven-day dietary recording period											
	Nil			Less than 168g			168g—less than 400g			400g or more		
	Mean	Median	SE	Mean	Median	SE	Mean	Median	SE	Mean	Median	SE
Men												
γ-glutamyl transpeptidase (u/l)	29.3	21.0	3.08	25.4	20.0	1.11	34.2	23.0	3.82	59.3	34.0	11.63
Calcium (mmol/l)	2.30	2.31	0.01	2.30	2.30	0.01	2.32	2.31	0.01	2.32	2.32	0.01
Creatinine (μmol/l)	102.8	100.0	1.25	104.8	101.0	2.52	102.6	101.0	0.96	102.0	99.0	1.69
Alkaline phosphatase (u/l)	186.3	174.5	5.09	173.2	165.5	2.90	171.9	166.0	3.04	179.5	176.0	4.77

	Nil			Less than 112g			112g—less than 280g			280g or more		
	Mean	Median	SE	Mean	Median	SE	Mean	Median	SE	Mean	Median	SE
Women												
γ-glutamyl transpeptidase (u/l)	19.3	14.0	0.95	17.7	13.0	1.23	18.8	15.0	1.85	31.3	20.0	8.77
Calcium (mmol/l)	2.30	2.29	0.01	2.29	2.29	0.01	2.28	2.28	0.01	2.36	2.37	0.03
Creatinine (μmol/l)	86.6	85.0	0.83	85.8	84.0	0.65	85.0	84.0	0.97	84.8	86.0	1.65
Alkaline phosphatase (u/l)	162.1	154.0	3.13	149.4	140.0	2.66	134.4	125.5	3.50	158.6	154.0	13.7

Base numbers	*Men*				*Women*			
	Nil	*Less than 168g*	*168g—less than 400g*	*400g or more*	*Nil*	*Less than 112g*	*112g—less than 280g*	*280g or more*
γ-glutamyl transpeptidase	158	359	239	115	295	466	124	15
Calcium	157	352	237	115	283	453	121	15
Creatinine	158	360	239	115	295	466	124	15
Alkaline phosphatase	152	360	238	115	295	466	124	15

Table 17.63 Percentage distribution of vitamin A (retinol) by age and sex

Vitamin A (retinol) (μmol/l)	Men				All ages	Women				All ages
	18–24	25–34	35–49	50–64	18–64	18–24	25–34	35–49	50–64	18–64
	cum %	*cum %*	*cum %*	*cum %*	*cum %*	*cum %*	*cum %*	*cum %*	*cum %*	*cum %*
Less than 1.19	2	1	1	0	1	11	5	5	2	5
Less than 1.51	20	8	6	6	9	32	33	27	11	25
Less than 1.83	47	26	19	19	25	52	56	56	35	50
Less than 2.15	67	55	42	43	49	81	77	77	62	73
Less than 2.47	89	75	67	69	73	92	92	89	79	87
Less than 2.79	96	88	84	84	87	97	96	97	90	95
All	100	100	100	100	100	100	100	100	100	100
Base	*142*	*221*	*321*	*262*	*946*	*121*	*223*	*342*	*257*	*943*
Mean (average) value	1.9	2.2	2.3	2.3	2.2	1.8	1.8	1.8	2.1	1.9
Median value	1.9	2.1	2.3	2.2	2.2	1.8	1.8	1.8	2.0	1.8
Lower 5.0 percentile	1.3	1.5	1.5	1.5	1.4	1.1	1.2	1.2	1.4	1.2
Upper 5.0 percentile	2.7	3.2	3.3	3.4	3.2	2.6	2.7	2.7	3.1	2.8
Standard error of the mean	0.04	0.04	0.03	0.04	0.02	0.04	0.03	0.03	0.04	0.02

Table 17.64 Percentage distribution of β-carotene by age and sex

β-carotene (μmol/l)	Men				All ages	Women				All ages
	18–24	25–34	35–49	50–64	18–64	18–24	25–34	35–49	50–64	18–64
	cum %	*cum %*	*cum %*	*cum %*	*cum %*	*cum %*	*cum %*	*cum %*	*cum %*	*cum %*
Less than 0.15	35	29	24	18	25	18	14	7	6	10
Less than 0.25	68	58	47	43	52	55	39	26	27	33
Less than 0.35	83	75	68	70	72	79	62	55	49	58
Less than 0.45	94	85	82	82	84	86	75	72	65	73
Less than 0.55	95	90	90	88	90	95	86	82	78	83
All	100	100	100	100	100	100	100	100	100	100
Base	*142*	*221*	*320*	*262*	*945*	*121*	*222*	*340*	*256*	*939*
Mean (average) value	0.23	0.26	0.32	0.31	0.29	0.26	0.35	0.40	0.44	0.38
Median value	0.19	0.22	0.26	0.27	0.24	0.23	0.29	0.33	0.36	0.32
Lower 5.0 percentile	0.07	0.06	0.07	0.08	0.07	0.08	0.10	0.12	0.14	0.11
Upper 5.0 percentile	0.47	0.60	0.69	0.71	0.66	0.54	0.81	0.77	0.95	0.84
Standard error of the mean	0.015	0.011	0.022	0.013	0.009	0.013	0.015	0.016	0.019	0.009

Table 17.65 Percentage distribution of β-cryptoxanthin by age and sex

β-cryptoxanthin (μmol/l)	Men				All ages	Women				All ages
	18–24	25–34	35–49	50–64	18–64	18–24	25–34	35–49	50–64	18–64
	cum %	*cum %*	*cum %*	*cum %*	*cum %*	*cum %*	*cum %*	*cum %*	*cum %*	*cum %*
Less than 0.075	20	21	21	24	22	11	13	18	12	14
Less than 0.150	62	50	57	57	56	44	43	50	39	44
Less than 0.225	83	78	76	79	79	67	68	70	65	68
Less than 0.300	92	87	88	87	88	80	83	82	74	79
All	100	100	100	100	100	100	100	100	100	100
Base	*142*	*221*	*321*	*262*	*946*	*121*	*223*	*342*	*257*	*943*
Mean (average) value	0.16	0.17	0.17	0.17	0.16	0.20	0.20	0.20	0.23	0.21
Median value	0.12	0.14	0.13	0.13	0.13	0.16	0.17	0.15	0.18	0.16
Lower 5.0 percentile	0.04	0.04	0.03	0.03	0.03	0.05	0.04	0.04	0.05	0.05
Upper 5.0 percentile	0.37	0.39	0.43	0.40	0.41	0.44	0.45	0.51	0.58	0.51
Standard error of the mean	0.011	0.008	0.007	0.009	0.004	0.012	0.010	0.009	0.012	0.006

Table 17.66 Percentage distribution of lycopene by age and sex

Lycopene (μmol/l)	Men				All ages 18–64	Women				All ages 18–64
	18–24	25–34	35–49	50–64		18–24	25–34	35–49	50–64	
	cum %	cum %	cum %	cum %	cum %	cum %	cum %	cum %	cum %	cum %
Less than 0.125	11	13	19	33	20	8	13	18	33	20
Less than 0.250	38	37	46	65	48	31	39	51	64	49
Less than 0.375	64	59	71	81	70	65	62	76	83	73
Less than 0.500	78	76	83	92	83	85	79	88	93	87
All	100	100	100	100	100	100	100	100	100	100
Base	142	221	321	262	946	121	223	342	257	943
Mean (average) value	0.37	0.35	0.30	0.23	0.30	0.33	0.34	0.28	0.23	0.28
Median value	0.30	0.31	0.26	0.19	0.25	0.31	0.31	0.24	0.18	0.25
Lower 5.0 percentile	0.08	0.07	0.07	0.05	0.06	0.10	0.07	0.07	0.04	0.06
Upper 5.0 percentile	0.74	0.74	0.66	0.55	0.68	0.58	0.68	0.58	0.55	0.60
Standard error of the mean	0.04	0.02	0.01	0.01	0.01	0.02	0.01	0.01	0.01	0.00

Table 17.67 Percentage distribution of α-carotene by age and sex

α-carotene (μmol/1)	Men				All ages 18–64	Women				All ages 18–64
	18–24	25–34	35–49	50–64		18–24	25–34	35–49	50–64	
	cum %	cum %	cum %	cum %	cum %	cum %	cum %	cum %	cum %	cum %
Less than 0.02	8	11	8	10	9	5	5	3	6	5
Less than 0.04	35	31	28	30	30	28	23	18	19	21
Less than 0.06	63	54	45	51	52	52	44	39	41	42
Less than 0.08	79	72	64	71	70	74	61	57	56	60
Less than 0.10	86	75	70	75	75	82	68	63	62	66
Less than 0.12	92	88	87	89	89	91	83	80	76	81
All	100	100	100	100	100	100	100	100	100	100
Base	142	221	320	262	945	121	222	340	256	939
Mean (average) value	0.07	0.07	0.08	0.08	0.08	0.07	0.09	0.09	0.10	0.09
Median value	0.05	0.06	0.07	0.06	0.06	0.06	0.07	0.08	0.08	0.07
Lower 5.0 percentile	0.02	0.02	0.02	0.02	0.02	0.03	0.02	0.03	0.02	0.03
Upper 5.0 percentile	0.14	0.15	0.16	0.17	0.16	0.15	0.19	0.20	0.23	0.21
Standard error of the mean	0.005	0.003	0.003	0.005	0.002	0.004	0.004	0.004	0.008	0.003

Table 17.68 Percentage distribution of vitamin E (tocopherol) by age and sex

Vitamin E (tocopherol) (μmol/1)	Men				All ages 18–64	Women				All ages 18–64
	18–24	25–34	35–49	50–64		18–24	25–34	35–49	50–64	
	cum %	cum %	cum %	cum %	cum %	cum %	cum %	cum %	cum %	cum %
Less than 20	40	23	15	12	20	41	34	18	9	22
Less than 25	77	56	41	31	47	76	73	48	28	52
Less than 30	96	78	66	56	71	94	90	76	50	75
Less than 35	100	90	80	74	84	99	98	91	69	88
All		100	100	100	100	100	100	100	100	100
Base	142	221	321	262	946	121	223	342	257	943
Mean (average) value	21.2	25.5	28.2	30.4	27.1	21.5	22.7	26.0	31.6	26.2
Median value	21.1	23.8	26.7	28.7	25.5	21.5	21.8	25.3	30.1	24.7
Lower 5.0 percentile	13.1	15.7	16.8	17.5	15.5	13.9	15.3	15.1	18.9	15.3
Upper 5.0 percentile	29.5	39.6	42.8	46.1	43.1	30.4	33.4	38.6	50.2	42.1
Standard error of the mean	0.43	0.54	0.49	0.63	0.29	0.49	0.38	0.41	0.62	0.28

Table 17.69   Percentage distribution of tocopherol:cholesterol ratio by age and sex

Tocopherol:cholesterol ratio	Men				All ages 18–64	Women				All ages 18–64
	18–24	25–34	35–49	50–64		18–24	25–34	35–49	50–64	
	cum %	cum %	cum %	cum %	cum %	cum %	cum %	cum %	cum %	cum %
Less than 2.21	—	0	1	1	1	1	—	0	—	0
Less than 3.21	6	7	8	8	7	11	7	7	9	8
Less than 4.21	38	38	36	33	36	45	39	39	38	39
Less than 5.21	79	72	75	72	74	83	78	78	72	77
Less than 6.21	94	93	93	91	93	98	95	92	90	93
All	100	100	100	100	100	100	100	100	100	100
Base	139	216	314	250	919	83	170	314	239	806
Mean (average) value	4.59	4.68	4.60	4.71	4.65	4.38	4.51	4.61	4.66	4.58
Median value	4.49	4.57	4.45	4.67	4.54	4.28	4.44	4.55	4.54	4.50
Lower 5.0 percentile	3.09	3.10	2.94	2.85	3.01	2.85	3.06	3.04	2.96	3.00
Upper 5.0 percentile	6.52	6.48	6.57	6.99	6.59	5.95	6.02	6.51	7.29	6.51
Standard error of the mean	0.084	0.079	0.061	0.076	0.037	0.126	0.074	0.067	0.082	0.041

Table 17.70   Vitamin A, carotenoids, the erythrocyte glutathione reductase activation coefficient, vitamin E and the tocopherol:cholesterol ratio by sex of informant and whether on a slimming diet

Blood analytes (units)	Whether on a slimming diet							
	Dieting				Not dieting			
	Mean	Median	SE	Base	Mean	Median	SE	Base
Men								
Vitamins								
Vitamin A (retinol) (μmol/l)	2.11	2.07	0.09	40	2.21	2.16	0.02	906
α-carotene (μmol/l)	0.09	0.08	0.01	40	0.07	0.06	0.00	905
β-carotene (μmol/l)	0.32	0.30	0.03	40	0.29	0.24	0.01	905
Lycopene (μmol/l)	0.29	0.25	0.03	40	0.30	0.25	0.01	906
β-cryptoxanthin (μmol/l)	0.19	0.15	0.02	40	0.16	0.13	0.00	906
Erythrocyte glutathione reductase activation coefficient	1.08	1.07	0.01	39	1.09	1.08	0.00	898
Vitamin E (tocopherol) (μmol/l)	28.7	26.8	1.37	40	27.0	25.5	0.30	906
Tocopherol:cholesterol ratio	4.75	4.67	0.14	40	4.64	4.52	0.04	879
Women								
Vitamins								
Vitamin A (retinol) (μmol/l)	1.95	1.92	0.04	116	1.88	1.82	0.02	827
α-carotene (μmol/l)	0.09	0.08	0.01	115	0.09	0.07	0.00	824
β-carotene (μmol/l)	0.36	0.32	0.02	115	0.38	0.32	0.01	824
Lycopene (μmol/l)	0.27	0.26	0.02	116	0.29	0.25	0.01	827
β-cryptoxanthin (μmol/l)	0.22	0.19	0.02	116	0.21	0.15	0.01	827
Erythrocyte glutathione reductase activation coefficient	1.08	1.07	0.00	112	1.10	1.09	0.00	814
Vitamin E (tocopherol) (μmol/l)	26.1	24.2	0.67	116	26.2	24.7	0.30	827
Tocopherol:cholesterol ratio	4.67	4.53	0.12	96	4.57	4.49	0.04	710

Table 17.71 Vitamin A, carotenoids, the erythrocyte glutathione reductase activation coefficient, vitamin E and the tocopherol:cholesterol ratio by sex of informant and whether unwell during seven-day dietary recording period

Blood analytes (units)	Whether unwell during seven-day dietary recording period											
	Completed food diary									No food diary		
	Not unwell			Unwell								
				Eating affected			Eating not affected					
	Mean	Median	SE	Mean	Median	SE	Mean	Median	SE	Mean	Median	SE
Men												
Vitamins												
Vitamin A (retinol)												
(μmol/l)	2.21	2.15	0.02	2.13	2.04	0.10	2.18	2.10	0.06	2.26	2.24	0.07
α-carotene (μmol/l)	0.08	0.06	0.00	0.06	0.05	0.01	0.07	0.05	0.01	0.07	0.07	0.00
β-carotene (μmol/l)	0.29	0.24	0.01	0.28	0.21	0.04	0.30	0.24	0.03	0.24	0.23	0.02
Lycopene (μmol/l)	0.31	0.26	0.01	0.27	0.26	0.03	0.26	0.20	0.02	0.31	0.23	0.03
β-cryptoxanthin (μmol/l)	0.17	0.13	0.01	0.19	0.11	0.04	0.15	0.12	0.14	0.11	0.01	0.01
Erythrocyte glutathione reductase activation coefficient	1.09	1.08	0.00	1.11	1.10	0.01	1.09	1.08	0.01	1.10	1.09	0.01
Vitamin E (tocopherol) (μmol/l)	27.3	25.7	0.32	25.3	23.0	1.69	26.5	25.4	1.11	26.9	24.8	1.02
Tocopherol:cholesterol ratio	4.65	4.55	0.04	4.62	4.39	0.18	4.67	4.36	0.15	4.63	4.60	0.14
Women												
Vitamins												
Vitamin A (retinol)												
(μmol/l)	1.88	1.83	0.02	1.93	1.80	0.08	1.91	1.87	0.05	1.89	1.70	0.10
α-carotene (μmol/l)	0.09	0.07	0.00	0.08	0.07	0.01	0.09	0.08	0.01	0.07	0.05	0.01
β-carotene (μmol/l)	0.38	0.32	0.01	0.35	0.32	0.02	0.38	0.33	0.02	0.31	0.26	0.03
Lycopene (μmol/l)	0.29	0.25	0.01	0.29	0.24	0.02	0.28	0.25	0.02	0.24	0.23	0.03
β-cryptoxanthin (μmol/l)	0.21	0.16	0.01	0.19	0.16	0.02	0.20	0.16	0.02	0.16	0.13	0.02
Erythrocyte glutathione reductase activation coefficient	1.10	1.08	0.00	1.10	1.10	0.01	1.09	1.09	0.01	1.09	1.09	0.01
Vitamin E (tocopherol) (μmol/l)	26.4	24.7	0.33	24.2	23.7	0.72	26.4	26.0	0.79	25.5	23.8	1.42
Tocopherol:cholesterol ratio	4.62	4.54	0.05	4.29	4.28	0.11	4.63	4.49	0.14	4.28	4.32	0.16
Base numbers	*Men*	*Women*		*Men*	*Women*		*Men*	*Women*		*Men*	*Women*	
Vitamins												
Vitamin A (retinol)	770	723		36	90		75	93		65	37	
α-carotene	769	721		36	89		75	92		65	37	
β-carotene	769	721		36	89		75	92		65	37	
Lycopene	770	723		36	90		75	93		65	37	
β-cryptoxanthin	770	723		36	90		75	93		65	37	
Erythrocyte glutathione reductase activation coefficient	763	712		36	89		75	87		63	38	
Vitamin E (tocopherol)	770	723		36	90		75	93		65	37	
Tocopherol:cholesterol ratio	748	618		35	76		73	79		63	33	

Table 17.72 Vitamin A, carotenoids, the erythrocyte glutathione reductase activation coefficient, vitamin E and the tocopherol:cholesterol ratio by sex of informant and region

Blood analytes (units)	Region											
	Scotland			Northern			Central, South West and Wales			London and South East		
	Mean	Median	SE	Mean	Median	SE	Mean	Median	SE	Mean	Median	SE
Men												
Vitamins												
Vitamin A (retinol) (μmol/l)	2.27	2.17	0.07	2.16	2.10	0.04	2.22	2.18	0.03	2.21	2.16	0.03
α-carotene (μmol/l)	0.07	0.05	0.01	0.07	0.05	0.00	0.08	0.07	0.00	0.08	0.07	0.00
β-carotene (μmol/l)	0.31	0.17	0.08	0.23	0.18	0.01	0.31	0.26	0.01	0.32	0.28	0.01
Lycopene (μmol/l)	0.25	0.20	0.02	0.28	0.22	0.03	0.30	0.26	0.01	0.34	0.29	0.01
β-cryptoxanthin (μmol/l)	0.15	0.11	0.01	0.13	0.10	0.01	0.17	0.14	0.01	0.19	0.15	0.01
Erythrocyte glutathione reductase activation coefficient	1.12	1.11	0.01	1.09	1.08	0.00	1.09	1.08	0.00	1.09	1.08	0.00
Vitamin E (tocopherol) (μmol/l)	26.2	25.4	0.98	26.1	24.3	0.57	27.6	25.5	0.54	27.6	26.1	0.49
Tocopherol:cholesterol ratio	4.56	4.57	0.13	4.52	4.42	0.08	4.70	4.61	0.06	4.72	4.57	0.06
Women												
Vitamins												
Vitamin A (retinol) (μmol/l)	1.91	1.86	0.06	1.84	1.77	0.34	1.89	1.81	0.03	1.93	1.87	0.03
α-carotene (μmol/l)	0.09	0.08	0.01	0.09	0.07	0.01	0.09	0.07	0.00	0.10	0.08	0.00
β-carotene (μmol/l)	0.32	0.28	0.02	0.34	0.28	0.02	0.38	0.33	0.01	0.42	0.34	0.02
Lycopene (μmol/l)	0.32	0.27	0.03	0.25	0.21	0.01	0.27	0.25	0.01	0.32	0.29	0.01
β-cryptoxanthin (μmol/l)	0.21	0.14	0.03	0.18	0.14	0.01	0.20	0.15	0.01	0.23	0.20	0.01
Erythrocyte glutathione reductase activation coefficient	1.10	1.09	0.01	1.09	1.08	0.00	1.10	1.09	0.00	1.10	1.09	0.00
Vitamin E (tocopherol) (μmol/l)	25.8	23.2	0.92	25.7	24.5	0.56	26.7	25.7	0.48	26.0	24.3	0.48
Tocopherol:cholesterol ratio	4.57	4.28	0.15	4.53	4.40	0.08	4.62	4.56	0.07	4.57	4.54	0.07
Base numbers	*Men*	*Women*		*Men*	*Women*		*Men*	*Women*		*Men*	*Women*	
Vitamins												
Vitamin A (retinol)	83	85		242	230		319	327		302	301	
α-carotene	83	83		241	230		319	326		302	300	
β-carotene	83	83		241	230		319	326		302	300	
Lycopene	83	85		242	230		319	327		302	301	
β-cryptoxanthin	83	85		242	230		319	327		302	301	
Erythrocyte glutathione reductase activation coefficient	82	84		237	227		319	319		299	296	
Vitamin E (tocopherol)	83	85		242	230		319	327		302	301	
Tocopherol:cholesterol ratio	82	68		232	200		313	282		292	256	

Table 17.73 Vitamin A, carotenoids, the erythrocyte glutathione reductase activation coefficient, vitamin E and the tocopherol:cholesterol ratio by sex and employment status of informant

Blood analytes (units)	Employment status of informant								
	Working			Unemployed			Economically inactive		
	Mean	Median	SE	Mean	Median	SE	Mean	Median	SE
Men									
Vitamins									
Vitamin A (retinol) (μmol/l)	2.21	2.16	0.02	2.08	2.01	0.06	2.32	2.25	0.07
α-carotene (μmol/l)	0.08	0.07	0.00	0.06	0.04	0.01	0.06	0.05	0.00
β-carotene (μmol/l)	0.31	0.25	0.01	0.21	0.18	0.02	0.25	0.23	0.02
Lycopene (μmol/l)	0.32	0.27	0.10	0.27	0.20	0.02	0.22	0.18	0.02
β-cryptoxanthin (μmol/l)	0.17	0.14	0.01	0.12	0.08	0.01	0.12	0.10	0.01
Erythrocyte glutathione reductase activation coefficient	1.09	1.08	0.00	1.11	1.10	0.01	1.08	1.07	0.01
Vitamin E (tocopherol) (μmol/l)	27.4	25.8	0.32	23.3	21.6	0.76	28.6	27.2	1.09
Tocopherol:cholesterol ratio	4.73	4.63	0.04	4.08	4.01	0.10	4.47	4.32	0.13
Women									
Vitamins									
Vitamin A (retinol) (μmol/l)	1.87	1.81	0.02	1.71	1.75	0.06	1.95	1.91	0.04
α-carotene (μmol/l)	0.09	0.07	0.00	0.09	0.06	0.01	0.10	0.08	0.01
β-carotene (μmol/l)	0.37	0.32	0.01	0.36	0.28	0.04	0.39	0.31	0.02
Lycopene (μmol/l)	0.30	0.27	0.01	0.27	0.25	0.02	0.26	0.22	0.01
β-cryptoxanthin (μmol/l)	0.22	0.17	0.01	0.16	0.13	0.02	0.20	0.15	0.01
Erythrocyte glutathione reductase activation coefficient	1.10	1.08	0.00	1.11	1.09	0.01	1.09	1.09	0.00
Vitamin E (tocopherol) (μmol/l)	26.0	24.8	0.32	22.7	20.6	1.19	26.9	24.9	0.54
Tocopherol:cholesterol ratio	4.63	4.56	0.05	4.21	4.18	0.16	4.52	4.37	0.08
Base numbers	*Men*	*Women*		*Men*	*Women*		*Men*	*Women*	
Vitamins									
Vitamin A (retinol)	*766*	*584*		*90*	*44*		*90*	*307*	
α-carotene	*765*	*581*		*90*	*44*		*90*	*306*	
β-carotene	*765*	*581*		*90*	*44*		*90*	*306*	
Lycopene	*766*	*584*		*90*	*44*		*90*	*307*	
β-cryptoxanthin	*766*	*584*		*90*	*44*		*90*	*307*	
Erythrocyte glutathione reductase activation coefficient	*758*	*572*		*89*	*43*		*90*	*303*	
Vitamin E (tocopherol)	*766*	*584*		*90*	*44*		*90*	*307*	
Tocopherol:cholesterol ratio	*751*	*496*		*87*	*40*		*81*	*262*	

Table 17.74 Vitamin A, carotenoids, the erythrocyte glutathione reductase activation coefficient, vitamin E and the tocopherol:cholesterol ratio by sex of informant and whether receiving benefits

Blood analytes (units)	Whether received benefits							
	Received				Not received			
	Mean	Median	SE	*Base*	Mean	Median	SE	*Base*
Men								
Vitamins								
Vitamin A (retinol) (μmol/l)	2.14	2.10	0.06	*106*	2.22	2.16	0.02	*835*
α-carotene (μmol/l)	0.06	0.05	0.01	*106*	0.08	0.07	0.00	*834*
β-carotene (μmol/l)	0.19	0.15	0.02	*106*	0.30	0.25	0.01	*834*
Lycopene (μmol/l)	0.24	0.19	0.02	*106*	0.31	0.26	0.01	*835*
β-cryptoxanthin (μmol/l)	0.12	0.08	0.01	*106*	0.17	0.14	0.01	*835*
Erythrocyte glutathione reductase activation coefficient	1.11	1.10	0.01	*105*	1.09	1.08	0.00	*827*
Vitamin E (tocopherol) (μmol/l)	24.1	21.9	0.85	*106*	27.5	25.9	0.31	*835*
Tocopherol:cholesterol ratio	4.35	3.96	0.09	*101*	4.73	4.60	0.04	*813*
Women								
Vitamins								
Vitamin A (retinol) (μmol/l)	1.79	1.70	0.06	*128*	1.91	1.83	0.02	*814*
α-carotene (μmol/l)	0.07	0.05	0.01	*127*	0.10	0.08	0.00	*811*
β-carotene (μmol/l)	0.30	0.23	0.02	*127*	0.39	0.33	0.01	*811*
Lycopene (μmol/l)	0.24	0.21	0.01	*128*	0.29	0.26	0.01	*814*
β-cryptoxanthin (μmol/l)	0.14	0.11	0.01	*128*	0.22	0.17	0.01	*814*
Erythrocyte glutathione reductase activation coefficient	1.11	1.10	0.01	*127*	1.09	1.08	0.00	*798*
Vitamin E (tocopherol) (μmol/l)	23.9	21.5	0.80	*128*	26.5	25.0	0.29	*814*
Tocopherol:cholesterol ratio	4.35	4.19	0.13	*116*	4.62	4.54	0.04	*689*

Table 17.75 Vitamin A, carotenoids, the erythrocyte glutathione reductase activation coefficient, vitamin E and the tocopherol:cholesterol ratio by sex of informant and social class of head of household

Blood analytes (units)	Social class of head of household											
	I and II			III non-manual			III manual			IV and V		
	Mean	Median	SE	Mean	Median	SE	Mean	Median	SE	Mean	Median	SE
Men												
Vitamins												
Vitamin A (retinol) (μmol/l)	2.21	2.17	0.03	2.23	2.20	0.06	2.23	2.15	0.03	2.15	2.09	0.05
α-carotene (μmol/l)	0.09	0.07	0.00	0.08	0.07	0.01	0.07	0.06	0.00	0.07	0.05	0.00
β-carotene (μmol/l)	0.33	0.29	0.01	0.29	0.26	0.02	0.28	0.20	0.02	0.24	0.20	0.01
Lycopene (μmol/l)	0.34	0.30	0.01	0.30	0.25	0.02	0.30	0.24	0.02	0.23	0.18	0.01
β-cryptoxanthin (μmol/l)	0.20	0.16	0.01	0.15	0.13	0.01	0.15	0.12	0.01	0.13	0.10	0.01
Erythrocyte glutathione reductase activation coefficient	1.08	1.07	0.00	1.08	1.07	0.00	1.10	1.09	0.00	1.11	1.10	0.01
Vitamin E (tocopherol) (μmol/l)	28.5	26.9	0.51	27.6	26.0	0.84	26.9	25.0	0.50	24.8	23.7	0.65
Tocopherol:cholesterol ratio	4.87	4.72	0.06	4.58	4.45	0.09	4.58	4.50	0.06	4.42	4.29	0.10
Women												
Vitamins												
Vitamin A (retinol) (μmol/l)	1.91	1.82	0.03	1.88	1.78	0.05	1.83	1.80	0.03	1.96	1.91	0.05
α-carotene (μmol/l)	0.11	0.10	0.01	0.10	0.08	0.01	0.08	0.07	0.00	0.07	0.06	0.00
β-carotene (μmol/l)	0.43	0.38	0.01	0.41	0.34	0.03	0.34	0.28	0.02	0.32	0.26	0.02
Lycopene (μmol/l)	0.32	0.29	0.01	0.29	0.26	0.02	0.27	0.23	0.01	0.24	0.21	0.01
β-cryptoxanthin (μmol/l)	0.25	0.20	0.01	0.23	0.20	0.02	0.19	0.14	0.01	0.16	0.12	0.01
Erythrocyte glutathione reductase activation coefficient	1.09	1.08	0.00	1.10	1.09	0.01	1.10	1.09	0.00	1.10	1.09	0.00
Vitamin E (tocopherol) (μmol/l)	27.4	26.1	0.50	27.1	25.4	0.82	24.8	23.2	0.43	25.4	23.8	0.58
Tocopherol:cholesterol ratio	4.83	4.67	0.07	4.64	4.52	0.12	4.35	4.37	0.06	4.41	4.28	0.08

Base numbers	Men	Women		Men	Women		Men	Women		Men	Women	
Vitamins												
Vitamin A (retinol)	329	327		120	123		326	286		155	196	
α-carotene	328	326		120	122		326	285		155	195	
β-carotene	328	326		120	122		326	285		155	195	
Lycopene	329	327		120	123		326	286		155	196	
β-cryptoxanthin	329	327		120	123		326	286		155	196	
Erythrocyte glutathione reductase activation coefficient	324	318		119	123		325	280		153	194	
Vitamin E (tocopherol)	329	327		120	123		326	286		155	196	
Tocopherol:cholesterol ratio	322	281		111	104		319	241		151	172	

Table 17.76   Vitamin A, carotenoids, the erythrocyte glutathione reductase activation coefficient, vitamin E and the tocopherol:cholesterol ratio by sex of informant and household composition

Blood analytes (units)	Household composition											
	Informant alone			With others, no dependent children						With dependent child		
				With spouse			No spouse					
	Mean	Median	SE	Mean	Median	SE	Mean	Median	SE	Mean	Median	SE
Men												
Vitamins												
Vitamin A (retinol) (μmol/l)	2.23	2.19	0.07	2.29	2.21	0.03	2.05	1.98	0.04	2.23	2.16	0.03
α-carotene (μmol/l)	0.08	0.06	0.01	0.08	0.07	0.00	0.07	0.05	0.00	0.07	0.07	0.00
β-carotene (μmol/l)	0.35	0.21	0.10	0.31	0.27	0.01	0.24	0.19	0.01	0.29	0.25	0.01
Lycopene (μmol/l)	0.28	0.25	0.03	0.28	0.23	0.01	0.32	0.23	0.03	0.32	0.27	0.01
β-cryptoxanthin (μmol/l)	0.16	0.12	0.02	0.17	0.13	0.01	0.15	0.11	0.01	0.17	0.14	0.01
Erythrocyte glutathione reductase activation coefficient	1.10	1.10	0.01	1.08	1.07	0.00	1.10	1.09	0.00	1.09	1.09	0.00
Vitamin E (tocopherol) (μmol/l)	26.4	25.6	0.99	29.0	27.3	0.53	22.8	21.9	0.50	28.0	26.0	0.48
Tocopherol:cholesterol ratio	4.57	4.55	0.13	4.66	4.56	0.06	4.51	4.40	0.07	4.73	4.62	0.06

Blood analytes (units)	Informant alone			With others, no dependent children						With dependent child					
				With spouse			No spouse			With spouse			Lone mother		
	Mean	Median	SE	Mean	Median	SE	Mean	Median	SE	Mean	Median	SE	Mean	Median	SE
Women															
Vitamins															
Vitamin A (retinol) (μmol/l)	2.05	1.95	0.07	2.02	1.96	0.03	1.85	1.86	0.05	1.77	1.71	0.02	1.80	1.64	0.09
α-carotene (μmol/l)	0.09	0.07	0.01	0.10	0.08	0.01	0.09	0.07	0.01	0.09	0.07	0.00	0.07	0.06	0.00
β-carotene (μmol/l)	0.36	0.31	0.03	0.42	0.37	0.02	0.33	0.29	0.02	0.37	0.31	0.01	0.29	0.23	0.02
Lycopene (μmol/l)	0.28	0.23	0.02	0.25	0.21	0.01	0.35	0.32	0.02	0.30	0.27	0.01	0.27	0.23	0.02
β-cryptoxanthin (μmol/l)	0.22	0.19	0.02	0.22	0.16	0.01	0.23	0.20	0.02	0.20	0.15	0.01	0.15	0.12	0.01
Erythrocyte glutathione reductase activation coefficient	1.09	1.08	0.01	1.08	1.07	0.00	1.10	1.08	0.00	1.10	1.09	0.00	1.12	1.10	0.01
Vitamin E (tocopherol) (μmol/l)	27.9	25.7	1.06	29.5	27.3	0.53	24.6	23.3	0.76	23.8	23.2	0.31	22.2	21.0	0.98
Tocopherol:cholesterol ratio	4.55	4.48	0.16	4.69	4.58	0.07	4.70	4.63	0.13	4.47	4.42	0.06	4.40	4.24	0.18

Base numbers	Men	Women	Men	Women	Men	Women	Men	Women	Women
Vitamins									
Vitamin A (retinol)	64	76	329	333	203	115	350	352	67
α-carotene	64	76	329	330	203	115	349	351	67
β-carotene	64	76	329	330	203	115	349	351	67
Lycopene	64	76	329	333	203	115	350	352	67
β-cryptoxanthin	64	76	329	333	203	115	350	352	67
Erythrocyte glutathione reductase activation coefficient	64	76	329	326	201	116	343	341	67
Vitamin E (tocopherol)	64	76	329	333	203	115	350	352	67
Tocopherol:cholesterol ratio	62	57	321	302	198	88	338	299	60

Table 17.77   Vitamin A, carotenoids, the erythrocyte glutathione reductase activation coefficient, vitamin E and the tocopherol:cholesterol ratio by sex of informant and smoking behaviour

Blood analytes (units)	Smoking behaviour								
	None			Fewer than 20 cigarettes a day			20 or more cigarettes a day		
	Mean	Median	SE	Mean	Median	SE	Mean	Median	SE
Men									
Vitamins									
Vitamin A (retinol)									
(μmol/l)	2.24	2.18	0.02	2.15	2.05	0.05	2.16	2.12	0.04
α-carotene (μmol/l)	0.08	0.07	0.00	0.06	0.05	0.00	0.06	0.04	0.00
β-carotene (μmol/l)	0.31	0.27	0.01	0.26	0.19	0.04	0.23	0.18	0.01
Lycopene (μmol/l)	0.31	0.26	0.01	0.30	0.24	0.04	0.29	0.23	0.02
β-cryptoxanthin (μmol/l)	0.19	0.15	0.01	0.13	0.11	0.01	0.11	0.09	0.01
Erythrocyte glutathione reductase activation coefficient	1.09	1.08	0.00	1.10	1.09	0.00	1.11	1.11	0.00
Vitamin E (tocopherol) (μmol/l)	28.3	26.5	0.37	24.5	22.6	0.67	25.3	24.0	0.64
Tocopherol:cholesterol ratio	4.82	4.69	0.05	4.41	4.36	0.09	4.22	4.06	0.08
Women									
Vitamins									
Vitamin A (retinol)									
(μmol/l)	1.91	1.85	0.02	1.87	1.81	0.04	1.84	1.74	0.05
α-carotene (μmol/l)	0.11	0.08	0.00	0.07	0.06	0.00	0.06	0.05	0.00
β-carotene (μmol/l)	0.42	0.36	0.01	0.32	0.27	0.02	0.27	0.25	0.01
Lycopene (μmol/l)	0.29	0.26	0.01	0.28	0.24	0.01	0.27	0.21	0.02
β-cryptoxanthin (μmol/l)	0.23	0.19	0.01	0.18	0.13	0.01	0.15	0.10	0.02
Erythrocyte glutathione reductase activation coefficient	1.09	1.08	0.00	1.11	1.10	0.00	1.12	1.11	0.01
Vitamin E (tocopherol) (μmol/l)	27.1	25.6	0.36	24.2	22.9	0.52	24.5	23.2	0.67
Tocopherol:cholesterol ratio	4.75	4.60	0.05	4.37	4.39	0.08	4.08	3.96	0.10
Base numbers	*Men*	*Women*		*Men*	*Women*		*Men*	*Women*	
Vitamins									
Vitamin A (retinol)	*622*	*609*		*158*	*208*		*166*	*126*	
α-carotene	*621*	*608*		*158*	*208*		*166*	*123*	
β-carotene	*621*	*608*		*158*	*208*		*166*	*123*	
Lycopene	*622*	*609*		*158*	*208*		*166*	*126*	
β-cryptoxanthin	*622*	*609*		*158*	*208*		*166*	*126*	
Erythrocyte glutathione reductase activation coefficient	*615*	*595*		*158*	*206*		*164*	*125*	
Vitamin E (tocopherol)	*622*	*609*		*158*	*208*		*166*	*126*	
Tocopherol:cholesterol ratio	*606*	*525*		*148*	*176*		*165*	*105*	

Table 17.78 Vitamin A, carotenoids, the erythrocyte glutathione reductase activation coefficient, vitamin E and the tocopherol:cholesterol ratio by sex of informant and consumption of alcohol during seven-day dietary recording period

Blood analytes (units)	Alcohol consumption during seven-day dietary recording period											
	Nil			Less than 168g			168g–less than 400g			400g or more		
	Mean	Median	SE	Mean	Median	SE	Mean	Median	SE	Mean	Median	SE
Men												
Vitamins												
Vitamin A (retinol) (μmol/l)	2.05	2.02	0.04	2.18	2.13	0.03	2.23	2.18	0.03	2.47	2.40	0.06
α-carotene (μmol/l)	0.08	0.06	0.01	0.08	0.07	0.00	0.07	0.06	0.00	0.06	0.05	0.01
β-carotene (μmol/l)	0.34	0.24	0.04	0.32	0.28	0.01	0.27	0.23	0.01	0.20	0.14	0.02
Lycopene (μmol/l)	0.24	0.21	0.01	0.31	0.27	0.01	0.34	0.27	0.03	0.29	0.25	0.02
β-cryptoxanthin (μmol/l)	0.16	0.12	0.01	0.18	0.15	0.01	0.17	0.13	0.01	0.13	0.11	0.01
Erythrocyte glutathione reductase activation coefficient	1.10	1.08	0.01	1.09	1.08	0.00	1.09	1.08	0.00	1.10	1.09	0.01
Vitamin E (tocopherol) (μmol/l)	26.8	25.8	0.69	27.6	25.6	0.50	26.8	25.1	0.56	26.7	25.9	0.85
Tocopherol:cholesterol ratio	4.60	4.54	0.08	4.78	4.60	0.06	4.63	4.52	0.07	4.37	4.41	0.10
	Nil			Less than 112g			112g–less than 280g			280g or more		
	Mean	Median	SE	Mean	Median	SE	Mean	Median	SE	Mean	Median	SE
Women												
Vitamins												
Vitamin A (retinol) (μmol/l)	1.88	1.86	0.03	1.86	1.80	0.02	1.96	1.87	0.05	2.39	2.24	0.32
α-carotene (μmol/l)	0.09	0.06	0.01	0.09	0.08	0.00	0.10	0.07	0.01	0.09	0.08	0.02
β-carotene (μmol/l)	0.36	0.29	0.02	0.39	0.34	0.01	0.39	0.31	0.03	0.34	0.18	0.05
Lycopene (μmol/l)	0.27	0.22	0.01	0.29	0.25	0.01	0.32	0.29	0.02	0.33	0.32	0.06
β-cryptoxanthin (μmol/l)	0.20	0.14	0.01	0.22	0.17	0.01	0.20	0.16	0.02	0.18	0.13	0.04
Erythrocyte glutathione reductase activation coefficient	1.10	1.09	0.00	1.09	1.08	0.00	1.09	1.09	0.01	1.10	1.11	0.01
Vitamin E (tocopherol) (μmol/l)	25.6	23.7	0.48	26.7	25.5	0.39	25.9	24.7	0.83	24.6	24.2	1.82
Tocopherol:cholesterol ratio	4.43	4.31	0.08	4.64	4.54	0.05	4.82	4.71	0.12	4.32	4.56	0.39

Base numbers	Men				Women			
	Nil	*Less than 168g*	*168g–less than 400g*	*400g or more*	*Nil*	*Less than 112g*	*112g–less than 280g*	*280g or more*
Vitamins								
Vitamin A (retinol)	160	365	241	115	301	466	124	15
α-carotene	159	365	241	115	301	463	123	15
β-carotene	159	365	241	115	301	463	123	15
Lycopene	160	365	241	115	301	466	124	15
β-cryptoxanthin	160	365	241	115	301	466	124	15
Erythrocyte glutathione reductase activation coefficient	157	363	239	115	296	453	124	15
Vitamin E (tocopherol)	160	365	241	115	301	466	124	15
Tocopherol:cholesterol ratio	155	351	237	113	252	409	99	13

Table 17.79 Correlation coefficients between blood analytes and dietary intakes—vitamin A (pre-formed retinol) and carotenoids

Dietary intake	Blood analyte		
	Vitamin A	α-carotene	β-carotene
Men			
Total dietary pre-formed retinol (inc. supplements)	0.09 (p<0.01)	—	—
Pre-formed retinol from food sources	0.10 (p<0.01)	—	—
Total dietary carotene (inc. supplements)	—	0.41 (p<0.01)	0.20 (p<0.01)
Carotenes from food sources	—	0.41 (p<0.01)	0.20 (p<0.01)
Base	*881*	*880*	*880*
Women			
Total dietary pre-formed retinol (inc. supplements)	0.02 (NS)	—	—
Pre-formed retinol from food sources	0.01 (NS)	—	—
Total dietary carotene (inc. supplements)	—	0.43 (p<0.01)	0.38 (p<0.01)
Carotenes from food sources	—	0.43 (p<0.01)	0.38 (p<0.01)
Base	*906*	*902*	*902*

Table 17.80 Correlation coefficients between blood analytes and dietary intakes—vitamin E and tocopherol:cholesterol ratio

Dietary intake	Men		Women	
	Blood analyte		Blood analyte	
	Vitamin E	Tocopherol: cholesterol ratio	Vitamin E	Tocopherol: cholesterol ratio
Total dietary vitamin E (inc. supplements)	0.19 (p<0.01)	0.31 (p<0.01)	0.25 (p<0.01)	0.29 (p<0.01)
Vitamin E from food sources	0.20 (p<0.01)	0.29 (p<0.01)	0.14 (p<0.01)	0.27 (p<0.01)
Base	*881*	*856*	*906*	*773*

Table 17.81 Percentage distribution of erythrocyte glutathione reductase activation coefficient by age and sex

Erythrocyte glutathione reductase activation coefficient	Men				All ages 18–64	Women				All ages 18–64
	18–24	25–34	35–49	50–64		18–24	25–34	35–49	50–64	
	cum %	*cum %*	*cum %*	*cum %*	*cum %*	*cum %*	*cum %*	*cum %*	*cum %*	*cum %*
Less than 1.1	51	56	57	73	60	56	48	60	69	59
Less than 1.2	94	95	96	95	95	92	92	95	97	94
Less than 1.3	99	99	99	100	99	97	99	98	100	98
All	100	100	100		100	100	100	100		100
Base	*141*	*218*	*317*	*261*	*937*	*119*	*218*	*337*	*252*	*926*
Mean (average) value	1.10	1.09	1.10	1.08	1.09	1.11	1.11	1.10	1.08	1.10
Median value	1.09	1.09	1.09	1.07	1.08	1.09	1.10	1.09	1.07	1.09
Lower 5.0 percentile	1.02	1.03	1.02	1.02	1.02	1.02	1.03	1.02	1.01	1.02
Upper 5.0 percentile	1.20	1.20	1.19	1.19	1.19	1.25	1.22	1.20	1.16	1.20
Standard error of the mean	0.005	0.004	0.003	0.003	0.002	0.007	0.004	0.003	0.003	0.002

Table 17.82 Correlation coefficients between the erythrocyte glutathione reductase activation coefficient and dietary intakes of riboflavin

Dietary intake	Erythrocyte glutathione reductase activation coefficient	
	Men	Women
Total dietary riboflavin (inc. supplements)	−0.13 (p<0.01)	−0.24 (p<0.01)
Riboflavin from food sources	−0.23 (p<0.01)	−0.31 (p<0.01)
Base	*874*	*888*

Appendices

Appendix A Fieldwork documents

A1   Letter sent in advance to sampled addresses

Purpose leaflet

S1   Interview questionnaire
S2   Self-completion forms for men and women—clothing being worn when weighed
S3   Self-completion form—home grown fruit and vegetables

Cards A–F prompt cards

Visual aid to demonstrate correct position of head for measurement of height (Frankfort plane)

D1   Food diary—foods eaten or prepared at home
D2   Food diary—foods eaten outside the home
D3   Transcription sheet for foods eaten outside the home
D5   Meals check sheet for interviewers' use
D6   Classification of fats and oils for cooking by brand name
D7   Prompt card—details required for foods recorded in the diary
D8   Guide weights—card for interviewers' use

BP1   Letter to subject's GP explaining purpose of survey and blood pressure measurement
BP2a Blood pressure results—form sent to subject's GP
B1   Appointment sheet—calls for taking specimens of blood and urine
B2   Instructions for making a 24-hour urine collection

Instruction sheet—venepuncture procedure

Instruction sheet—taking a specimen of urine from the 24-hour collection

Analysis request cards sent to laboratories with specimens of blood and urine

B4   Authorisation of payment to 'doctors' taking blood specimens

THE ADULT DIETARY SURVEY

This survey is being carried out by the Social Survey Division of the Office of Population Censuses and Surveys, for the Ministry of Agriculture, Fisheries and Food and the Department of Health. This leaflet tells you more about why the survey is being done.

1. What is it about?

Over the past fifteen years or so there has been a considerable increase in the range of foods available in the shops, and, for many people, this has meant changes in the kinds of foods they eat. This is the first large national survey of dietary habits for many years, and it will find out, in detail, about the eating habits of men and women in Great Britain. The survey will also collect information about the individuals themselves, not only their age, sex, whether they are in paid employment and so on, but also some physical measurements, such as their height, weight and blood pressure. This information together with the detail about foods eaten will help provide a better understanding of the relationship between diet and health. Government is particularly interested in having this information, because, at the present time, Great Britain has one of the highest rates in the world for heart disease; they hope that data from the survey will help in understanding why this might be.

A1

Office of Population Censuses and Surveys
Social Survey Division
St Catherines House 10 Kingsway London WC2 6JP
Telephone 01-242 0262 ext 2315

Your reference

Our reference S1241

Date

Date as postmark

Dear Householder

ADULT DIETARY SURVEY

I am writing to tell you about a survey that this Office will shortly be carrying out for the Ministry of Agriculture, Fisheries and Food in consultation with the Department of Health. The main aim of the survey is to find out exactly what adults in Great Britain eat each week, and to relate this information to characteristics such as their age, sex, height, weight and social class. The results of the survey will provide a better understanding of the relationship between diet and health.

The sample for the survey is of addresses chosen at random from the Electoral Register. Your address is one of those included in the sample and one of our interviewers will be calling on you within the next four weeks. The interviewer will be able to tell you much more about the survey and may also select, again at random, one adult from your household whom we would like to take part in the survey. Any information that any member of your household gives us will be kept in strictest confidence; the names and addresses of the people who take part in the survey will not be passed to anyone outside this Office without their permission, and the results from the survey will be presented in such a way that no individual can be identified.

I do hope that you will be able to help us in this survey; the results will be of great value to both the Ministry of Food and the Department of Health, and I am sure that your household would find it interesting to take part. If you have any questions in advance of our interviewer calling please contact me at the address and telephone number given at the head of this letter. Thanking you in anticipation of your kind co-operation.

Yours faithfully

Janet Gregory
Principal Social Survey Officer

2. Why have we come to your household?

To visit every household in Great Britain would take too long and cost far too much money. Therefore we selected a sample of addresses from the Official Electoral Registers and called only on them. We chose the addresses in a way that gives every one the same chance of being selected: this is how your address was selected. We did not know anything in advance about you or your household, and as the survey is looking at the eating habits of men and women aged 16 to 64, the interviewer must select the one adult in your household to be interviewed. Again it is a matter of chance who is selected, and everyone aged 16 to 64 has an equal chance. If there is no-one in your household between these ages then the interviewer will not be able to invite anyone from your household to take part. However, once an address and an individual are selected we must contact them; we cannot substitute anyone else. In this way we know that all types of people will be represented in the survey.

Some people think either that they are not typical enough to be of any help in the survey, or that they are very different from other people and would distort the findings. The important thing to remember is that the community consists of a great many different types of people and we need to represent them all in our sample survey. Everyone has information to give which is needed. It is therefore vital that everyone we approach agrees to take part.

3. Is the survey confidential?

Yes; we take very great care to protect the confidentiality of the information we are given. All our interviewers are covered by the Official Secrets Act, and the information we collect is not released to other government departments or to members of the public in any way in which an individual, a household or an address could be identified. The survey results will be published in a form which contains no information about individuals; the results will be shown as statistics only.

4. Is the survey compulsory?

In all our surveys we rely on voluntary co-operation, which is essential if our work is to be successful.

We hope this leaflet answers some of the questions you might have, and that it shows how important the survey is.

Your co-operation is very much appreciated.

Social Survey Division
Office of Population Censuses and Surveys
St Catherines House
10 Kingsway
London WC2B 6JP
01-242 0262

S1

S1241

IN CONFIDENCE

Serial no. label

Interviewer number

Date of interview

	8	7

ADULT DIETARY SURVEY : MAINSTAGE ROUND 4

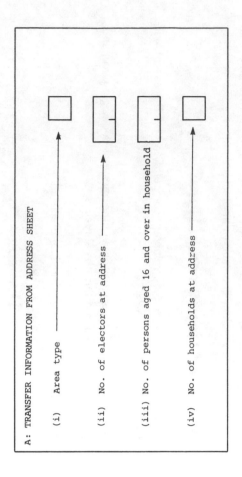

A: TRANSFER INFORMATION FROM ADDRESS SHEET

(i)   Area type

(ii)   No. of electors at address

(iii) No. of persons aged 16 and over in household

(iv)   No. of households at address

HOUSEHOLD COMPOSITION

1. List all persons in household aged 16 and over in relationship to INFORMANT

PER NO	RELATIONSHIP TO INFORMANT	OFF USE	HOH RING →	AGE	SEX M F	MARITAL STATUS M S W/D/S	EMPLOYMENT F/t P/t None	FAM UNIT	A C W N
01	INFORMANT		1		1 2	1 2 3	1 2 3	①	1 2 3 4
02			1		1 2	1 2 3	1 2 3		1 2 3 4
03			1		1 2	1 2 3	1 2 3		1 2 3 4
04			1		1 2	1 2 3	1 2 3		1 2 3 4
05			1		1 2	1 2 3	1 2 3		1 2 3 4
06			1		1 2	1 2 3	1 2 3		1 2 3 4
07			1		1 2	1 2 3	1 2 3		1 2 3 4
08			1		1 2	1 2 3	1 2 3		1 2 3 4
09			1		1 2	1 2 3	1 2 3		1 2 3 4
10			1		1 2	1 2 3	1 2 3		1 2 3 4

2. List all persons in household aged under 16 in relationship to INFORMANT

PER NO	RELATIONSHIP TO INFORMANT	OFF USE	AGE	FAM UNIT	A C W E
11					1 2 3 4
12					1 2 3 4
13					1 2 3 4
14					1 2 3 4
15					1 2 3 4
16					1 2 3 4

1

3. How many years have you lived at this address?

[IF UNDER 1, CODE AS '00']

No. of years ——>

4. How old is this building; was this building first built

RUNNING PROMPT

before 1919	1
between 1919 and 1944	2
or after 1944? → between 1945 and 1964	3
1965 or later	4
DK but after 1944	5

IF DK CODE YOUR ESTIMATE

DK, neither informant nor interviewer able to estimate	6
DNA, caravan, houseboat	7

5. Do you have a kitchen, that is a separate room in which you cook?

Yes	1
No	2

(a)-(c)
Q6

IF CODED (1)

(a) Is the narrower side of the kitchen less than 6½ feet wide from wall to wall?

Less than 6½ feet	1
6½ feet or more	2

(b) Do (any of) you ever eat meals in it or use it as a sitting room?

Yes	1
No	2

(c) Do you share the use of the kitchen with any other household?

Yes, shares kitchen	1
No, not shared	2

2

9. OCCUPATION OF INFORMANT

Record current or most recent job if under retirement age, main job in working life if over retirement age.

DNA, never worked......... 1   SEE Q14

JOB TITLE:

DESCRIBE FULLY WORK DONE:

INDUSTRY:

Employee..........1   (a)
Self-employed.......2   SEE Q14

(a) IF EMPLOYEE:
ASK OR RECORD

Manager............1
Foreman/supervisor....2   SEE Q10
Other employee......3

10. IS INFORMANT AN EMPLOYEE CURRENTLY WORKING FULL OR PART TIME?

Yes X   Q11
No .....Y   SEE Q14

11. Does the total number of hours you work tend to vary from week to week?

Yes 1
No 2

12. Do you do shiftwork at all?

Yes 1   Q13
No 2   SEE Q14

13. SHOW CARD A

Which of the categories on this card describes the shiftwork that you do?

CODE FIRST THAT APPLIES

Three shift working	01
Continental shifts	02
Two-shift system with 'earlies' and 'lates'/ double day shifts	03
Sometimes night and sometimes day shifts	04
Split shifts	05
Morning shifts	06
Afternoon shifts	07
Evening or twilight shifts	08
Night shifts	09
Weekend shifts	10
Other type of shiftwork (SPECIFY)	11

4

---

6. APPLIES IF (INFORMANT) NOT IN F/T OR P/T EMPLOYMENT

DNA others.......X

(Are you) currently:

CODE FIRST THAT APPLIES

	INFORMANT	HOH
	Q8	
off-sick with a job to go back to?.........	1	1
waiting to take up a job (you have) already obtained?.........	2	2
looking for work?.........	3 (a)	3 (a)
or intending to look for work but prevented by temporary sickness or injury?.........	4	4
NONE OF THESE.........	5 Q7	5 Q7

(a) How many weeks (have you) been away from work?

SPECIFY ————

7. (Are you) currently:

CODE FIRST THAT APPLIES

	INFORMANT	HOH
	Q8	
sick or injured and NOT intending to seek work?.........	1	1
at school or college full-time?.........	2	2
retired?.........	3	3
keeping house?.........	4	4
OTHER (SPECIFY).........	5 Q9	5 Q9

8. IS INFORMANT THE HOH?

Yes............W   Q9
No............X   (a)

(a) IS HOH CURRENTLY IN F/T OR P/T EMPLOYMENT?

Yes............Y   Q9
No............Z

ASK Q6 AND Q7 ABOUT HOH AND RECORD IN HOH COLUMN

3

EATING HABITS: INTRODUCE

17. ASK ABOUT INFORMANT

Are you on a slimming diet now?

Yes........	1	(a)
No.........	2	Q18

IF CODED (1)
(a) How long have you been on a slimming diet?

SPECIFY PERIOD – NUMBER OF
WEEKS/MONTHS ETC

– – – – – – –

18. Are there any foods which you do not eat because you do not like them?

Yes.........1		SPECIFY
No.........2		Q19

IF YES, SPECIFY WHICH FOODS

19. (Apart from these) Are there any (other) foods which you do not eat because you are on a diet or for health or other reasons?

Yes.........1		SPECIFY
No.........2		Q2O

Food type	Reason

---

14. IS INFORMANT THE HOH?

Yes X		Q16
No ....Y		Q15

15. OCCUPATION OF HOH
Record current or most recent job if under retirement age,
record main job in working life if over retirement age.

DNA, never worked 1   Q16

JOB TITLE:

DESCRIBE FULLY WORK DONE:

Employee 1		(a)
Self-employed 2		Q16

INDUSTRY:

Manager 1
Foreman/supervisor ..2   Q16
Other employee 3

(a) IF EMPLOYEE:
ASK OR RECORD

16. Are you, or is anyone in your household currently receiving:

	Yes	No
unemployment benefit?	1	2
supplementary benefit?	1	2
family income supplement (FIS)?	1	2

INDIVIDUAL PROMPT

5

20. On weekdays do you usually have breakfast or don't you bother?

    Usually has breakfast 1

    Doesn't bother 2

21. At weekends do you usually have breakfast, or don't you bother?

    Usually has breakfast 1

    Doesn't bother 2

22. Do you usually take sugar in tea, do you use an artificial sweetener, or do you drink it without sugar or sweetener?

    Sugar in tea 1

    Artificial sweetener in tea 2

    Drinks tea without (either) 3

    Does not drink tea 4

23. Do you usually take sugar in coffee, do you use an artificial sweetener, or do you drink it without sugar or sweetener?

    Sugar in coffee 1

    Artificial sweetener in coffee 2

    Drinks coffee without (either) 3

    Does not drink coffee 4

24. APPLIES IF USES ARTIFICIAL SWEETENER IN TEA OR COFFEE - Q22 OR Q23 CODED 2

    DNA, others ....X --- Q25

SHOW CARD C
What brand of artificial sweetener do you usually use?

  Sweeteners with calorie value 1
  includes: Sweet'n'Slim, Sweet'n'Low, Sprinkle
  Sweet, Sugatwin, Sugarlite, Dietade, Sorbital,
  Sucron powder, Sweetex powder, Sweetex
  granulated, Canderel sugar substitute,
  Canderel Spoonful

CODE AND RECORD BRAND NAME

  Non-calorie sweeteners 2
  includes: Hermesetas Gold, Slender,
  Hermesetas, Sweetex Liquid, Saxin, Sucron tablets,
  Sweetex, Natrena, Canderel tablets, Bisk's Slim Sweet,
  Sionon

  Other(SPECIFY)................ 3

RECORD BRAND NAME _ _ _ _ _ _ _ _ _ _ _

25. Has salt generally been added to your food during cooking?

    Yes, includes sea salt 1

    No 2

    Yes, uses 'Lo Salt'/salt alternative (not sea salt) 3

    Other (SPECIFY) 4

26. SHOW CARD D
At the table do you:

    generally add salt to your food without tasting it first? 1

CODE FIRST THAT APPLIES

    taste the food, but then generally add salt? 2

    taste the food, but only occasionally add salt? .. 3

    rarely, or never, add salt at the table? 4

IF USES 'LO SALT' OR SALT ALTERNATIVE (NOT SEA SALT) RING CODE 1-3 AND RING CODE 5

27. When you have meat with fat on, has the fat generally been trimmed off before serving?

    Yes, fat trimmed off .... 1 — Q28

    No, fat left on .... 2 — (a)

    Does not buy meat with fat on ..... 3 — Q28

    Does not eat meat .... 4 — Q30

SPONTANEOUS

IF CODED (2)
(a) Generally do you:

    eat the lean meat and the fat 1

RUNNING PROMPT

    or eat the lean meat and leave the fat? 2

28. When you have casseroles, stews or mince, has the fat usually been skimmed off the top before serving the food out, or do you prefer the fat left in the food?

    Fat skimmed 1

    Fat left in food 2

    Does not eat stews, casseroles, mince (which need skimming) 3

SPONTANEOUS

29. When you have gravy, has it usually had thickening or flavouring added?

    Thickening added e.g. cornflour, flour. 1

    Flavour added e.g. Oxo, Bovril........ 2

    Both added e.g. Bisto, gravy granules.. 3

    Neither 4

    Does not use gravy 5

Page 9

30. When you have foods which are deep fried, what kind of fat or oil are the foods generally cooked in?

    REFER TO BLUE 'FATS AND OILS' CARD

    CODE ONE ONLY

    Blended vegetable oil, NOT polyunsaturated 1
    Dripping 2
    Lard 3
    Polyunsaturated oil 4
    Other(SPECIFY) 5

    Does not eat deep fried foods 9

31. When you have foods which are shallow fried, what kind of fat or oil are the foods generally cooked in?

    REFER TO BLUE 'FATS AND OILS' CARD

    CODE ONE ONLY

    Blended vegetable oil, NOT polyunsaturated 1
    Butter 2
    Dripping 3
    Lard 4
    Margarine NOT polyunsaturated 5
    Polyunsaturated margarine or oil .. 6
    Other(SPECIFY) 7
    Does not use any fat or oil 8
    Does not eat shallow fried foods .. 9

32. Do you always have the same kind of bread, or do you have more than one kind of bread?

    Always the same kind 1
    More than one kind 2

33. Which kind(s) of bread do you have?

    CODE ALL THAT APPLY

    White 1
    Hovis 2
    Wholemeal 3
    Slimcea/Procea 4
    Other (SPECIFY) 5

34. Do you usually buy sliced bread or unsliced bread?

    Sliced bread 1
    Unsliced bread 2
    Both 3

9

Page 10

35. What kind(s) of milk do you usually have?

    CODE ALL THAT APPLY

    Whole 1
    Semi-skimmed 2
    Skimmed 3
    Other (SPECIFY) 4

36. I would now like to ask you about some foods which you may eat only occasionally, or perhaps not at all.

    PROMPT EACH FOOD LISTED BELOW, ASK (a) AND CODE IN GRID

    (a) About how often, on average, do you eat (ITEM)? ....

Frequency: PROMPT AS NECESSARY	Liver	Carrots	Free range eggs, in any form	Fresh fish, NOT frozen	Kidney, includes in a chop or as steak and kidney	Fresh shellfish - mussels, crab, prawns, etc	Canned or frozen shellfish
not at all	1	1	1	1	1	1	1
every day............	2	2	2	2	2	2	2
at least once a week.....	3	3	3	3	3	3	3
at least once a fortnight but less than once a week	4	4	4	4	4	4	4
at least once a month, but less than once a fortnight	5	5	5	5	5	5	5
less often than once a month (SPECIFY)	6	6	6	6	6	6	6
IF (ITEM) EATEN AT ALL (CODED 2-6) ASK (b) (b) About how much do you eat when you have it? (SPECIFY)		Number (per wk)					

10

37. TO ALL

At present, are you taking any tablets, pills, powders or drops to supplement your diet?

Yes	1	(a)
No	2	SEE Q38

(a) FOR EACH FOOD SUPPLEMENT TAKEN, RECORD FULL DESCRIPTION, INCLUDING BRAND NAME, STRENGTH, DOSE, AND HOW OFTEN TAKEN

(i) Description and brand name:

– – – – – – – – – –

Strength: Dose; no of tablets, drops, 5 ml spoons: – – – – – – – –

How often taken; no of times and period; eg 3 x a day

– – – – – – – – – –

(ii) Description and brand name:

– – – – – – – – – –

Strength: Dose; no of tablets, drops, 5 ml spoons: – – – – – – – –

How often taken; no of times and period; eg 3 x a day

– – – – – – – – – –

(iii) Description and brand name:

– – – – – – – – – –

Strength: Dose; no of tablets, drops, 5 ml spoons: – – – – – – – –

How often taken; no of times and period; eg 3 x a day

– – – – – – – – – –

OFF. USE ONLY

	(i)	(ii)	(iii)	(iv)
A:	☐	☐	☐	☐
B:	☐	☐	☐	☐

38. TO WOMEN AGED 16-45 ONLY

(May I check) Are you pregnant now?

DNA Others X		SEE Q39
Yes	1	
No	2	
Not sure	3	

39. TO MOTHERS WITH CHILDREN AGED UNDER 1 YEAR IN HOUSEHOLD

(May I check) Are you currently breastfeeding your (younger) baby?

DNA Others X		
Yes	1	Q41
No	2	

40. Are you getting tokens to exchange for free vitamin tablets for yourself, from your baby clinic or welfare centre?

EXCLUDE VITAMIN DROPS FOR BABY

IF YES, CHECK THAT TABLETS ARE RECORDED AT Q37

Yes	1
No	2

41. TO ALL

Do you smoke cigarettes at all?

Yes	1	(a)
No	2	Q42

IF CODED (1)

(a) About how many cigarettes a day do you usually smoke?

Less than 1	0 0
No. smoked a day ⟶	

42.

Now can you tell me what you usually have to eat and drink in a day, starting with when you get up and going right through the day to the time you go to bed? RECORD APPROXIMATE TIMES, FOOD DESCRIPTIONS.

In bed or before breakfast

Breakfast

During the morning

Mid-day

During the afternoon

When you get home from work (if working)

During the evening

Before going to bed/in bed

43. NOW PLACE DIARY. IF DIARY REFUSED, CONTINUE WITH THIS QUESTIONNAIRE (SEE NEXT PAGE)

PREGNANT WOMEN: END INTERVIEW (THANK AND WITHDRAW)

13

PICK-UP INTERVIEW: to be completed at end of dietary recording period

DNA, no dietary record   9   Q8

1. Have you been unwell at any time in the past seven days?

Yes   1   (a)-(c)
No   2   SEE Q2

IF CODED (1)

* (a) What has been the matter with you?

(b) On how many days in the past seven days have you been unwell?   SPECIFY NO. OF DAYS →

(c) Did your being unwell affect your eating habits on these days?

Yes   1
No   2

RECORD COMMENTS AND
PROBE ANY AMBIGUITIES

2. APPLIES IF CURRENTLY IN EMPLOYMENT

DNA others   9   Q3

Apart from days when you would not normally work, have you been away from work on any day in the past seven days, through illness, or for any other reason?

Yes   1   (a)
No   2   Q3

IF CODED (1)

(a) On how many days in the past seven days were you away from work through illness or for some other reason?   SPECIFY NO. OF DAYS →

3. TO ALL

Have there been any (other) unusual circumstances which may have affected your eating habits during the last seven days?

Yes   1   (a)
No   2   SEE Q4

IF CODED (1)

* (a) What has been different about your eating habits over the past seven days?

14

329

4. APPLIES IF INFORMANT DOES SHIFTWORK (Q12 CODED 1)

DNA, others 9 Q5

Can you tell me the times you started and finished work on each of the seven days that you have been keeping the diary. You started keeping the diary last ....; What time did you start work that day?

RECORD THE TIMES INFORMANT STARTED AND FINISHED WORK ON EACH OF THE 7 DAYS DURING THE RECORDING PERIOD

DAY ORDER	DAY - WRITE IN:	STARTED WORK AT (24 HRS): HRS	MINS	ENDED WORK AT (24 HRS): HRS	MINS	DIDN'T WORK/REST DAY, ETC	SAME HRS AS PREVIOUS DAY
☐	----------- day	☐	☐	☐	☐	8	☐
☐	----------- day	☐	☐	☐	☐	8	9
☐	----------- day	☐	☐	☐	☐	8	9
☐	----------- day	☐	☐	☐	☐	8	9
☐	----------- day	☐	☐	☐	☐	8	9
☐	----------- day	☐	☐	☐	☐	8	9
☐	----------- day	☐	☐	☐	☐	8	9
☐	----------- day	☐	☐	☐	☐	8	9
☐	----------- day	☐	☐	☐	☐	8	9
☐	----------- day	☐	☐	☐	☐	8	9
☐	----------- day	☐	☐	☐	☐	8	9
☐	----------- day	☐	☐	☐	☐	8	9
☐	----------- day	☐	☐	☐	☐	8	5

15

5. TO ALL

Sometimes differences in local soils, lead to different mineral contents in some foods. We are therefore interested in knowing whether you eat any home grown fruit or vegetables. During the seven days that you kept the food diary were any of the vegetables or fruit that you ate home grown?

Yes ...... 1 (a)
No 2 Q6

INCLUDE HOME GROWN AND DEEP FROZEN HOME GROWN BY LOCAL FRIENDS, NEIGHBOURS, ETC

IF CODED (1)

(a) HAND SELF-COMPLETION SHEET TO INFORMANT (S3) AND EXPLAIN:

Please would you list any vegetables or fruit you ate while you were keeping the food record diaries, that were home grown by you, or by local friends or neighbours. Please also include anything that was originally home grown and then deep frozen.

The headings are to remind you of things to include:
COLLECT SELF COMPLETION S3 AND TAG TO END OF SCHEDULE

6. TO BE COMPLETED IN EVERY CASE

Interviewer's assessment of the quality of weighing and recording, and notes on any special circumstances affecting eating habits during the recording period:

7.

CHECK   TICK

(a) Collect weighing scales, plate, diary and pocket diary ....

(b) Complete incentive payment forms, D4 ....

16

ANTHROPOMETRIC AND PHYSIOLOGICAL MEASUREMENTS

8. No dietary record and Q8-Q30 refused............. 9

   Date [8] [7] [ ] [ ]

   (a) Personal height (cms) [ ]

       Ring code if height measurement affected by:
       Hairstyle 1
       Turban 2
       Posture 3

   (b) Personal weight (kilograms) [ ]
       [Hand informant self completion S2 when complete tag to end of schedule]

       Ring code if scales placed on:
       Carpet 1

   (c) Wrist diameter (cms) (left arm) [ ]

   (d) Upper arm length (cms) (left arm) [ ]

   (e) Upper mid-arm circumference (mms) (left arm) [ ]

   (f) MALES ONLY: Calf circumference (mms) (left leg) [ ]

9. IF ALL MEASUREMENTS (a)-(e)/(f) REFUSED RING CODE 9 →Q11

10. RECORD ANY SPECIAL CIRCUMSTANCES THAT MIGHT HAVE AFFECTED
    MEASUREMENTS (a)-(e)/(f):
    None 9
    Other (SPECIFY). 1

17

11. Blood pressure and heart rate readings: Time (24 hrs) [ ] [ ]

    [Take three measurements from left arm and record readings below]

Measurement	Systolic	Mean	Diastolic	Heart rate
1 →				
2 →				
3 →				

    BLOOD PRESSURE MEASUREMENT REFUSED: Ring code ——→ SEE Q14
    SPECIFY REASONS. RECORD ANY DIFFICULTIES IN TAKING READINGS
    No difficulties 9
    Difficulties (SPECIFY). 1

12. Record the name and address of the informant's GP:

    No GP 1   SEE Q14
    Name refused 2

    Dr _____

    Address _____

13. COMPLETE BLOOD PRESSURE CONSENT FORMS (BP 2a, 2b and 2c)

    (a) Obtain informant's signature on consent form

    (b) Send: Top copy (BP 2a) and letter (BP 1) to informant's GP
             Carbon copy - BP 2b] return to HQ
             Back copy   - BP 2c

    (c) Ring code:
        GP consent form signed 1
        Consent refused (SPECIFY REASONS) 2

18

331

332

14. BLOOD SAMPLE: APPLIES TO THOSE AGED 18 AND OVER

DNA, aged 16/17 ...... X ------- Q15

EXPLAIN PURPOSE AND PROCEDURE
FOR TAKING BLOOD SAMPLE

Would you be willing to have a blood
sample taken?

Yes 1
No 2
Conditional 3

GIVE REASONS FOR REFUSAL
AND SPECIFY CONDITIONAL ANSWERS

15. URINE COLLECTION AND URINE SAMPLES: APPLIES TO ALL

EXPLAIN PURPOSE AND OUTLINE PROCEDURE
FOR MAKING 24-HOUR URINE COLLECTION

Would you be willing to make a 24-hour
urine collection?

Yes 1
No 2
Conditional 3

GIVE REASONS FOR REFUSAL
AND SPECIFY CONDITIONAL ANSWERS

16. To all agreeing to have blood sample taken,
and/or make a 24-hour urine collection

DNA others ...... X ------- Q28

Tick

(a) Leave explanatory note: B 1 ....

(b) Make an appointment for calling with doctor to take
blood sample/urine samples ....

(c) Leave instructions and equipment for making 24-hour
urine collection:

    Leaflet: B 2 ....
    Collection container(s) with clip, serial no.
    labels and added preservative ....
    Plastic jug (to be kept in plastic bag) ......
    Safety pin ....
    Plastic carrier bag ....

(d) Go through procedure for making 24-hour urine
collection ....

(e) Check that letter to informant's GP is correct: BP1 ..

19

COLLECTION OF BLOOD SAMPLE

17. Outcome: ring code

DNA, did not agree to provide
sample, or aged 16/17 ...... 1 Q21
Blood sample taken 2 Q18
Blood sample not taken 3 Q21

GIVE REASONS FOR NOT
TAKING SAMPLE

18. Date blood sample taken → | 8 | 7 | | |

19. RECORD ANY DIFFICULTIES
IN TAKING SAMPLE

No difficulties 9
Difficulties (SPECIFY) 1

20. CHECK:

Tick

(a) Are all the specimen tubes labelled? ....

(b) Are the blood analysis request forms complete? ...

(c) Complete the doctor's payment authorisation: B 4 ..

20

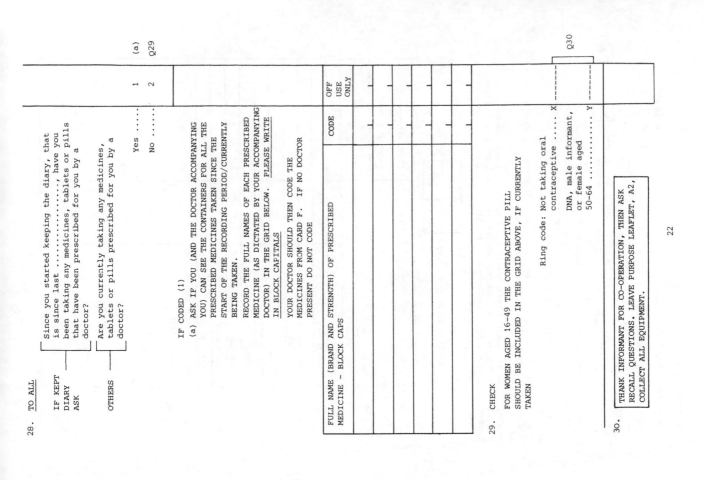

COLLECTION OF URINE SAMPLES

21. Outcome: ring code

DNA, did not agree to make collection 1   Q28

24-hour collection made and samples taken 2   Q22

24-hour collection not made ... 3   Q28

GIVE REASONS FOR INFORMANT NOT MAKING 24-HOUR COLLECTION

22. Date and time collection:

	Date		Hrs	Mins
started:	8 7			
ended:	8 7			

23. Date urine samples taken: → 8 7

24. Total volume of urine collected in 24 hours (mls) →

25. Were any collections missed?

Yes 1   (a) (b)
No 2   Q26

IF CODED (1)

(a) Estimated no. of collections missed: ↑

(b) Estimated volume of urine lost (mls) ↑

26. RECORD ANY DIFFICULTIES IN MAKING 24-HOUR COLLECTION

No difficulties 9

Difficulties (SPECIFY) 1

27. CHECK: Tick

(a) Are all the specimen tubes labelled? ....

(b) Is the urine analysis request form complete? ....

(c) Is the doctor's payment authorisation complete (B 4)? ....

21

---

28. TO ALL

IF KEPT DIARY ASK — Since you started keeping the diary, that is since last ...., have you been taking any medicines, tablets or pills that have been prescribed for you by a doctor?

(a)
Yes 1
No 2   Q29

OTHERS — Are you currently taking any medicines, tablets or pills prescribed for you by a doctor?

IF CODED (1)

(a) ASK IF YOU (AND THE DOCTOR ACCOMPANYING YOU) CAN SEE THE CONTAINERS FOR ALL THE PRESCRIBED MEDICINES TAKEN SINCE THE START OF THE RECORDING PERIOD/CURRENTLY BEING TAKEN.

RECORD THE FULL NAMES OF EACH PRESCRIBED MEDICINE (AS DICTATED BY YOUR ACCOMPANYING DOCTOR) IN THE GRID BELOW. PLEASE WRITE IN BLOCK CAPITALS

YOUR DOCTOR SHOULD THEN CODE THE MEDICINES FROM CARD F. IF NO DOCTOR PRESENT DO NOT CODE

FULL NAME (BRAND AND STRENGTH) OF PRESCRIBED MEDICINE – BLOCK CAPS	CODE	OFF USE ONLY

29. CHECK

FOR WOMEN AGED 16-49 THE CONTRACEPTIVE PILL SHOULD BE INCLUDED IN THE GRID ABOVE, IF CURRENTLY TAKEN

Ring code: Not taking oral contraceptive X

DNA, male informant, or female aged 50-64 .... Y   Q30

30. THANK INFORMANT FOR CO-OPERATION, THEN ASK RECALL QUESTIONS, LEAVE PURPOSE LEAFLET, A2, COLLECT ALL EQUIPMENT.

22

Form for Men

IN CONFIDENCE

SELF COMPLETION FORM FOR MEN

ADULT DIETARY SURVEY S1241

Serial no label

Date [ ][8][ ][ ]

Interviewer number [ ][ ][▨]

People's clothing will obviously make a difference to their weight; so to help us allow for this we would like you to put a tick by any item that you will be wearing when you are weighed. If you will be wearing any item which is not on the list please add it at the end.

As shoes and jackets or coats are likely to be the heaviest items would you mind taking them off just before you are weighed.

Also if you are wearing heavy jewellery or have much loose change in your pocket please give these into the safe keeping of another member of your family whilst you are being weighed. If this is not possible please make a note of these items on the list.

Tick each item being worn   eg.

Shirt	✓
Kilt	✓

ITEMS WORN WHILST BEING WEIGHED	TICK	If you are wearing more than one please record how many
Pair of socks		
Pants/Briefs		
Vest		
T-Shirt		
Shirt		
Trousers		
Kilt		
Belt/Braces		
Jumper		
Cardigan		
Tie/Cravat		
Corset		
Something else not on list		
Please write down		

W2603B OPCS 6/86

Form for Women

IN CONFIDENCE

SELF COMPLETION FORM FOR WOMEN

ADULT DIETARY SURVEY S1241

Serial no label

Date [ ][8][ ][ ]

Interviewer number [ ][ ][▨]

People's clothing will obviously make a difference to their weight; so to help us allow for this we would like you to put a tick by any item that you will be wearing when you are weighed. If you will be wearing any item which is not on the list please add it at the end.

As shoes and jackets or coats are likely to be the heaviest items would you mind taking them off just before you are weighed.

Also if you are wearing heavy jewellery or have much loose change in your pocket please give these into the safe keeping of another member of your family whilst you are being weighed. If this is not possible please make a note of these items on the list.

Tick each item being worn   eg.

Blouse	✓
Skirt	✓

ITEMS WORN WHILST BEING WEIGHED	TICK	If you are wearing more than one please record how many
Pair of socks		
Stockings/Tights		
Suspender Belt		
Pants/Briefs		
Corset/Girdle		
Bra		
Slip/Underskirt		
Vest		
Blouse		
T-Shirt		
Skirt		
Trousers		
Belt		
Dress		
Jumper		
Cardigan		
Waistcoat/Jerkin		
Something else not on list		
Please write down		

334

S3

S1241 ADULT DIETARY SURVEY

Serial no. label

HOME GROWN FRUIT AND VEGETABLES

Please list any vegetables or fruit that you ate while you were keeping
your food record diaries that were home grown by you, or by local
friends or neighbours. Please also include anything that was
originally home grown and then deep frozen.

The headings are to remind you of things to include.

Salad vegetables - lettuce, tomatoes, radish, spring onions, beetroot, etc

Other green vegetables - cabbage, beans, peas, spinach, etc

Other vegetables, including potatoes

Soft fruit - strawberries, raspberries, gooseberries, currants, etc

Other fruit - apples, pears, plums, etc

OFFICE USE ONLY

S1241

Reference Card

SHIFTWORK

Three-shift working
(code **01**)

The 24-hour day is divided into three working periods, eg morning, afternoon and night. Someone doing this kind of shiftwork will usually, but not always, do one or more weeks of mornings, followed by one or more weeks of afternoons, followed by one or more weeks of nights.

Continental shifts
(code **02**)

A continuous three-shift system that **rotates rapidly** – eg three mornings, then two afternoons, then two nights. Usually there is a break between shift changes. Sometimes called **metropolitan shifts**.

Two-shift system with earlies and lates or double day shifts
(code **03**)

Normally two shifts of eight hours each, eg 0600-1400 and 1400-2200. The worker usually alternates between shifts, often weekly, but it can be at longer intervals.

Sometimes night and sometimes day shifts
(code **04**)

Use this code for any other pattern of working which involves working shifts both during the hours of daylight and at night. See also the definition of night shifts, below.

Split shifts
(code **05**)

Full shifts divided into two distinct parts with a gap of several hours in between. Used in passenger transport, catering, and service industries, where there is a need to meet peak demands at different times of the day.

Morning shifts
(code **06**)

Usually 0600-1400. Use if the morning shift is the only shift worked. It can be part time.

Afternoon shifts
(code **07**)

Usually 1400-2200 if full time.
Can be part time between 1200 and 1800.

Evening or twilight shifts
(code **08**)

Usually 1500-2400 if full time.
Can be part time between 1700 and 2200.
Twilight shift is a term for part-time evening shifts.

Night shifts
(code **09**)

Full time, usually 1800-0600.
Use only for permanent night work, as any rotating system should be coded 01-04.

Weekend shifts
(code **10**)

Work during the day on Friday-Sunday (0600-1800).

S1241

Shiftwork

Three-shift working 1

Continental shifts 2

Two-shift system with 'earlies' and 'lates'/double-day shifts 3

Sometimes night and sometimes day shifts 4

Split shifts 5

Morning shifts 6

Afternoon shifts 7

Evening or twilight shifts 8

Night shifts 9

Weekend shifts 10

Other type of shiftwork 11

E/W
S

B38

336

S1241

CARD C

ARTIFICIAL SWEETENERS

Sweeteners with calorie value 1

includes: Sweet'n'Slim, Sweet'n'Low, Sprinkle Sweet,

Sugatwin, Sugarlite, Dietade, Sorbital, Sucron

powder, Sweetex powder, Sweetex granulated,

Canderel sugar substitute, Canderel Spoonful

Non-calorie sweeteners 2

includes: Hermesetas, Hermesetas Gold, Slender,

Sweetex, Sweetex Liquid, Saxin, Sucron

tablets, Natrena, Canderel tablets,

Bisk's Slim Sweet, Sionon

Other (specify) 3

ARTIFICIAL SWEETENERS: alphabetical list

	Code
Bisk's Slim Sweet	2
Canderel Spoonful	1
Canderel Sugar Substitute	1
Canderel Tablets	2
Dietade	1
Hermesetas	2
Hermesetas Gold	2
Natrena	2
Saxin	2
Sionon	2
Slender	2
Sorbital	1
Sucron powder	1
Sucron tablets	2
Sugarlite	1
Sugatwin	1
Sprinkle sweet	1
Sweetex	2
Sweetex liquid	2
Sweetex granulated	1
Sweetex powder	1
Sweet'n'low	1
Sweet'n'slim	1

337

S1241

CARD D

At the table:

I generally add salt to my food,
without tasting it first: 1

I taste the food, but then generally
add salt: 2

I taste the food, but only occasionally
add salt: 3

I rarely, or never, add salt at the table: 4

S1241

ADULT DIETARY SURVEY
CONVERSION CHART

CARD E

HEIGHT: to nearest ½"		PERSONAL WEIGHT: to nearest whole pound					
cms	ft/ins	kg	st	lbs	kg	st	lbs
135	4 5⅜	40	6	4	86	13	8
136	4 5½	41	6	6	87	13	10
137	4 5¾	42	6	9	88	13	12
138	4 6⅛	43	6	11	89	14	0
139	4 6¾	44	6	13	90	14	2
140	4 7⅛	45	7	1	91	14	5
141	4 7½	46	7	3	92	14	7
142	4 7⅞	47	7	6	93	14	9
143	4 8¼	48	7	8	94	14	11
144	4 8⅝	49	7	10	95	14	13
145	4 9⅛	50	7	12	96	15	2
146	4 9½	51	8	0	97	15	4
147	4 9⅞	52	8	3	98	15	6
148	4 10¼	53	8	5	99	15	8
149	4 10¾	54	8	7	100	15	10
150	4 11	55	8	9	101	15	13
151	4 11⅜	56	8	11	102	16	1
152	4 11¾	57	9	0	103	16	3
153	5 0¼	58	9	2	104	16	5
154	5 0⅞	59	9	4	105	16	7
155	5 1	60	9	6	106	16	10
156	5 1⅜	61	9	8	107	16	12
157	5 1¾	62	9	11	108	17	0
158	5 2¼	63	9	13	109	17	2
159	5 2⅝	64	10	1	110	17	5
160	5 3	65	10	3	111	17	7
161	5 3⅜	66	10	6	112	17	9
162	5 3¾	67	10	8	113	17	11
163	5 4⅛	68	10	10	114	17	13
164	5 4⅝	69	10	12	115	18	2
165	5 5	70	11	0	116	18	4
166	5 5⅜	71	11	3	117	18	6
167	5 5¾	72	11	5	118	18	8
168	5 6⅛	73	11	7	119	18	10
169	5 6½	74	11	9	120	18	13
170	5 6⅞	75	11	11	121	19	1
171	5 7⅜	76	12	0	122	19	3
172	5 7¾	77	12	2	123	19	5
173	5 8⅛	78	12	4	124	19	7
174	5 8⅝	79	12	6	125	19	10
175	5 8⅞	80	12	8	126	19	12
176	5 9¼	81	12	11	127	20	0
177	5 9⅝	82	12	13	128	20	2
178	5 10⅛	83	13	1	129	20	4
179	5 10½	84	13	3	130	20	7
180	5 10⅞	85	13	5			
181	5 11¼						
182	5 11⅝						
183	6 0						
184	6 0⅜						
185	6 0⅞						
186	6 1⅜						
187	6 1⅝						
188	6 2						
189	6 2¼						
190	6 2⅝						

1 cm = 0.3937 ins   1 kilogram = 2.2046 lbs

S1241

CARD F

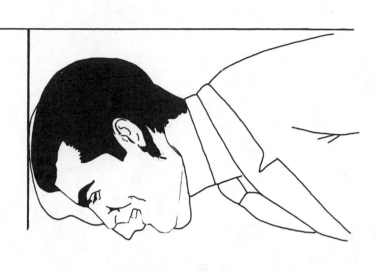

PRESCRIBED MEDICINES CODE LIST

Drug group	Code
Antacids, including H_2 receptor blockers	01
Laxatives	02
Anticoagulants	03
Anti-hypertensives, including β blockers	04
Lipid-lowering drugs	05
Analgesics and non-steroidal anti-inflammatory drugs	06
Drugs used in Parkinsonism	07
Antidiabetic drugs, including insulin	08
Corticosteroids; steroids	09
Thyroid and antithyroid drugs	10
Diuretics	11
Antibiotics	12
Antimalarials	13
Antituberculous drugs; anti-TB drugs	14
Drugs for anaemia: iron, folate, B_{12}	15
Vitamin and mineral supplements excluding iron, folate and B_{12}	16
Oral contraceptives	17
Cytotoxics	18
Other drugs, or drug group not known	19

W889 OPCS 1/80

339

D1

Serial no. label

Interviewer number

CONFIDENTIAL

S1241 ADULT DIETARY SURVEY

Sex	
M	F

Age [ ]

HOME RECORD BOOK

**Please record all food and drink
as shown inside.   Thank you**

Office of Population Censuses and Surveys
Social Survey Division
St Catherines House
10 Kingsway London WC2B 6JP

The interviewer will call again on:

Day	Date	Time

THE FOOD RECORD BOOKS

The instructions at the front of this book tell you how to use the food weighing scales, and how to describe the food and drink items in this book and in the blue pocket notebook.

Please read through these notes carefully before starting your seven days of weighing and recording. The interviewer will go over the main points with you, and can help you with any difficulties you might have.

REMEMBER :   -   write down everything you eat or drink, whether at mealtimes or in between; medicines, tablets and drinks of water must be included.

                        -     start each day on a new sheet; you can use more than one sheet a day, if necessary.

                        -     write in the day and date at the top of each sheet.

HOW TO WEIGH

Press button on scales to switch on and make the green or red zero show.

Weigh container (plate, cup or bowl) and write the weight in column E.

Leave plate on scales and press button to set scale back to zero.

Write down the brand name and a full description of first food in columns C and D, then put it on the plate and write weight in column E.

Leave plate on scales and set scale back to zero (press button).

Write down brand name and description of second food in columns C and D, then put it on the plate and write weight down in column E.

Leave plate on scales and set scale back to zero.

Repeat for each item of food or drink.

NOW EAT IT!

Weigh plate with any leftovers (if there are any), write the weight against the plate entry in column F and tick in column F to show which foods were leftover.

DESCRIBING FOOD AND DRINK: as full a description of each food, together with its brand name is needed

Column A: Write down the time the food will be eaten, indicating whether the time was a.m. or p.m.; if you prefer, you can use the 24 hour clock. If you are preparing food for lunch or work tomorrow, record the information on tomorrow's sheet.

Column B: Ring code 1 if the food is being eaten at home; ring code 2 if the food was, or will be eaten away from home.

Column C: Write down the brand or product name of the food. Please give as much information as possible. Describe EACH ITEM ON A SEPARATE LINE. Fresh meat, fresh fish, fresh fruit and vegetables, doorstep milk, unwrapped bread and cakes and other unwrapped fresh foods (eg unwrapped cheese, cooked meats, and pasta) do not need brand or product names. In these cases no information is required, so leave the space in this column blank. Do not write in the name of the shop where the item was purchased. However, remember to record 'own brand' names in this column, for example, 'Sainsbury's baked beans'.

Column D: Put down the description of the food. Please give as much information as possible - type of food, name, and how it was cooked. If the food was fried or roasted, please write down the type of fat or oil it was cooked in. If the food includes homemade pastry please write down the type of fat used to make the pastry. If you need to, you may use more than one line, but please put EACH ITEM ON A SEPARATE LINE. If the item was a cooked dish made from several items, for example, Shepherd's pie, weigh the portion and write in the information as described above, against a single entry. Do not try to weigh the potato and meat parts separately; when the interviewer calls she will record more information about the cooked dish.

Column E: Write in the weight of the food or drink.

Column F: Write down the weight of the plate with leftovers on it and tick which items were left.

After everything on your plate is written down, leave a line blank before your next plate.

342

(ii)

Whenever you weigh anything always start with a plate, bowl or cup, please never put food directly onto the scales.

For foods that already come in containers like yoghurt or trifles you can weigh the full container and then weigh the container again when you have eaten the food. Or, if you prefer, you can tip out the food into a bowl which you have just weighed.

To weigh bread and butter or anything else you spread on bread, start by weighing the plate as usual. Press the button again to set scale back to zero and weigh the bread. Press the button again to set the scale back to zero then remove the bread and quickly spread the butter. Put the bread back on the scales and it will show the weight of the butter or margarine you have just spread. Now set the scale back to zero and then remove the bread again to quickly spread the jam or marmalade. Put the bread back on the scale and it will show the weight of the jam you have put on. If the scales switch off before you have buttered your bread, or spread the filling, do not worry. Switch the scales on again and record the total weight of plate, bread, butter etc. However, please make a note against the entry to show what happened, for example, 'total wt. of plate, one slice of toast, butter and marmalade'.

If there are any leftovers we need to know about them. You should weigh the plate with the leftovers on it and put the weight in column F next to the weight you wrote down for the empty plate. Then be sure to put a tick next to each type of food that was left over.

If something was spilt write into the leftovers column about how much you think was lost; for example "about ½ spilt".

USING THE BLUE POCKET NOTEBOOK

If you are eating somewhere that you cannot weigh the food, then write down the most information you can, including brand names, if possible, in your blue pocket notebook.

For example a meal in a cafe like this:

11.30 am		In Rainbow Cafe, High Street :
	H P	Bacon Sandwich - two rashers, streaky bacon, in 2 slices buttered white bread 85p Brown Sauce
	Maxwell House	Large mug of coffee, made with water and a dash of whole milk, 2 teaspoons white sugar. 40p
	Lyon's	Individual apple pie, shortcrust pastry top and bottom Custard 65p
		Left ¼ sandwich

(iv)

A COMPLETE PAGE IN THIS HOME RECORD BOOK SHOULD LOOK LIKE THIS

Remember to write in day and date at top of each page

Day .... TUES..day   Date

Day	Month	Year
2	1 0	8 6

If you do not eat everything you have put on the plate, remember to weigh the plate with leftovers.

And show what you left.

Always weigh everything on a plate or cup. Remember to weigh the plate first.

Leave a line before starting a new plate or cupful of something

A	B	C	D	E	F
12.15 pm	①		Plate	200	240
	1		Steak pie, homemade, 1 crust, shortcrust pastry made with Blue Band	140	✓
	1 2	Bejam	Crinkle cut frozen chips: deep fried in corn oil	100	✓
	1 2	Birds Eye	Frozen peas: boiled	60	
	1 2				
12.15	①		Plate	100	120
	1 2	Hovis sliced loaf	2 slices bread	60	✓
	1 2	Blue Band	Margarine	10	✓
	1 2				
12.25 pm	①		Bowl	120	
	1 2	Whitworth's rice	Rice pudding, made with whole milk, no sugar	104	
	1 2		Homemade plum jam	24	

Please remember to put each food item on a separate line.

A	B	C	D	E	F
12.30 pm	①		Cup	150	
	1 2	Nescafe Gold Blend	Coffee powder	2	
			Hot water (no milk)	120	
	1 2	Silver Spoon	Sugar - white	8	
1.00 pm	①		Plate	110	126
	1 2		Apple (v)	110	✓ core

Serial number ☐ ☐ ☐

Day ....*day*   Date

	Day	Month	Year	Day order	OFF USE
	☐	☐	8	☐	☐

Please use a separate line for each item eaten; write in weight of plate; leave a line between different 'plate' entries

A	B		C	D	E	F	OFFICE USE ONLY	
Time eaten am/pm	Food eaten at home	away	Brand name of each item, in full, (except for fresh produce)	Full description of each item including: - whether fresh, frozen, dried, canned - how cooked; what type of fat food fried in gms.	Weight of served gms.	Weight of leftovers TICK ITEMS	Brand	Food
	1	2						
	1	2						
	1	2						
	1	2						
	1	2						
	1	2						
	1	2						
	1	2						
	1	2						
	1	2						
	1	2						
	1	2						

D2

Serial no label

Pocket Book

Please use this notebook to write down any food or drink you have away from home, and hand it back to the interviewer

Day............................ **Date** ....

Time eaten am/pm	Brand name, in full, unless fresh produce	Description, including price where it was bought, and quantity.	Any leftovers?

TRANSFERS FROM POCKET BOOK

Serial number

OFFICE USE ONLY

Brand	Food

Day .... *day* Date

Day	Month	Year
		8

Day order

OFF USE

Please use a separate line for each item eaten; leave a line between different 'plate' entries

A	B		C	D	E	F
Time eaten am/pm	Food eaten at away	home	Brand name of each item, in full (except for fresh produce)	Full description of each item including: - whether fresh, frozen, dried, canned - how cooked; what type of fat food fried in - portion size	Weight served gms.	Weight of leftovers TICK ITEMS
	2					
	2					
	2					
	2					
	2					
	2					
	2					
	2					
	2					
	2					
	2					
	2					
	2					

ADULT DIETARY SURVEY S1241

INTERVIEWER'S MEALS CHECK SHEET

Serial number label

Complete one sheet for each dietary
record: ring code for number of
items eaten each day

Interviewer
number

D5

Day	Main meal (at least 2 foods at one time)	Other meals (at least 2 foods at one time)	Drinks with meals	Drinks NOT with meals	Crisps, snacks or sweets	Tick if a note made on diary about eating pattern that day.
...day	1 2 3	1 2 3 4	1 5 2 6 3 7 4 8	1 5 2 6 3 7 4 8	1 5 2 6 3 7 4 8	
...day	1 2 3	1 2 3 4	1 5 2 6 3 7 4 8	1 5 2 6 3 7 4 8	1 5 2 6 3 7 4 8	
...day	1 2 3	1 2 3 4	1 5 2 6 3 7 4 8	1 5 2 6 3 7 4 8	1 5 2 6 3 7 4 8	
...day	1 2 3	1 2 3 4	1 5 2 6 3 7 4 8	1 5 2 6 3 7 4 8	1 5 2 6 3 7 4 8	
...day	1 2 3	1 2 3 4	1 5 2 6 3 7 4 8	1 5 2 6 3 7 4 8	1 5 2 6 3 7 4 8	
...day	1 2 3	1 2 3 4	1 5 2 6 3 7 4 8	1 5 2 6 3 7 4 8	1 5 2 6 3 7 4 8	
...day	1 2 3	1 2 3 4	1 5 2 6 3 7 4 8	1 5 2 6 3 7 4 8	1 5 2 6 3 7 4 8	

Banquet soft margarine	Margarine, not polyunsaturated
Beef fat	Dripping
Blue Band soft margarine	Margarine, not polyunsaturated
Butter, salted or slightly salted	Butter
Butter, unsalted	Butter
Carousel soft margarine	Margarine, not polyunsaturated
Clover	Specify; flag entry
Cookeen compound cooking fat	Specify; flag entry
Corn oil	Polyunsaturated oil
Country Fare solid oil	Dripping
Delight	Specify; flag entry
Echo hard margarine	Margarine, not polyunsaturated
Flora margarine and oil	Polyunsaturated oil/margarine
Flora: white	Specify; flag entry
Fresh Fields hard margarine	Margarine, not polyunsaturated
Gold	Specify; flag entry
Golden Churn	Specify; flag entry
Golden Vale	Polyunsaturated margarine
Goodlife margarine (CWS)	Polyunsaturated oil
Grapeseed oil	Polyunsaturated oil
Groundnut oil	Polyunsaturated oil
Kraft polyunsaturated margarine	Polyunsaturated margarine
Kraft Superfine	Margarine, not polyunsaturated
Krisp and Dry oil	Blended vegetable oil
Krona	Margarine, not polyunsaturated
Lupa cooking oil	Blended vegetable oil
Luxury soft margarines	Margarine, not polyunsaturated
Maize oil	Polyunsaturated oil
Mazola	Polyunsaturated oil
Meadowcup	Specify; flag entry
Olive oil	Specify; flag entry
Outline	Specify; flag entry
Own brand – blended oil (foods NOT purchased from a takeaway)	Blended vegetable oil
– block margarine	Margarine, not polyunsaturated
– hard margarine	Margarine, not polyunsaturated
– low fat spreads	Specify; flag entry
– soft margarine, not polyunsaturated	Margarine, not polyunsaturated
– soft margarine, polyunsaturated	Polyunsaturated margarine
Palm oil, red palm oil	Specify; flag entry
Peanut oil	Polyunsaturated oil
Pork fat	Lard
Pura Big Fry solid cooking oil	Dripping
Pura solid vegetable oil	Dripping
Rape seed oil	Specify; flag entry
Safeway table margarine	Margarine, not polyunsaturated
Safflower oil	Polyunsaturated oil
Sesame oil	Polyunsaturated oil
Soya margarine and oil	Polyunsaturated margarine/oil
Tomor margarine	Margarine, not polyunsaturated
Trex compound cooking fat	Specify; flag entry
Stork hard margarine	Margarine, not polyunsaturated
Stork SB	Margarine, not polyunsaturated
Sunflower margarine and oil	Polyunsaturated margarine/oil
Summer County hard margarine	Margarine, not polyunsaturated
Spry compound cooking fat	Specify; flag entry
Vitalite margarine	Polyunsaturated margarine
Vitaquelle	Polyunsaturated margarine
Whitecap	Lard
White flora	Specify; flag entry

Fats and oils for cooking: group list

Butter: salted, slightly salted and unsalted

Blended vegetable oil (foods NOT purchased from a takeaway):

    Krisp and Dry
    Lupa cooking oil
    Own brand and other oils labelled blended vegetable oil; NOT pure vegetable oil

Dripping: beef fat
    Country Fare solid oil
    Pura Big Fry solid cooking oil
    Pura solid vegetable oil

Lard: pork fat
    Whitecap

Margarine, NOT polyunsaturated:

    Hard margarines: Echo
        Fresh Fields
        Krona
        Stork
        Summer County
        Tomor

    Soft margarines: Banquet
        Blue Band
        Carousel
        Kraft Superfine
        Luxury soft
        Safeway table
        Stork SB

    Own brands NOT labelled polyunsaturated

Margarine, polyunsaturated:

    CWS Goodlife   Soya
    Flora   Sunflower
    Kraft polyunsaturated   Vitalite
    Own brands labelled polyunsaturated   Vitaquelle

Oil, polyunsaturated

    Corn   Safflower
    Flora solid oil   Sesame
    Groundnut   Soya
    Maize   Sunflower
    Mazola

Specify, and flag entry:

    Clover   Olive oil
    Delight   Outline
    Flora: White   Own brand and other low fat spreads
    Gold   Palm oil
    Golden Churn   Rapeseed oil
    Golden Vale   Red palm oil
    Cookeen compound cooking fat   White Flora
    Spry compound cooking fat
    Trex compound cooking fat

BOUGHT FORM

Fresh
Frozen; chilled
Canned; bottled
Dried; dehydrated
Ready-meal

COOKING METHOD

Uncooked; raw
Rehydrated; reconstituted
Boiled; stewed; casseroled
Poached, in milk or water
Steamed
Baked - no added fat
Grilled - added fat? ⎤
Deep fried   ⎥ what fat?
Shallow fried   ⎦
Roasted - added fat
Microwaved - with fat = fried; grilled with fat

LEFTOVERS

Meat: fat, bones, skin
Fish: bones, skin
Fruit: skin, peel, stones, pips

COATINGS

Flour
Batter: egg, flour and milk
Crumbs: and egg?

MEAT PREPARATION

Fat trimmed before eating or cooking
Fat skimmed from meat dishes
Lean and fat eaten, or lean only

GRAVY AND SAUCES

Thickened; with flour, cornflour, Bisto
Skimmed; fat skimmed or no added fat
Casseroles: thickened; skimmed; with
        vegetables/potatoes

FATS AND OILS

Blended vegetable oil: home fried or
                              takeaway
Butter; salted or unsalted
Dripping
Lard
Margarine, NOT polyunsaturated
Polyunsaturated margarine or oil

DAIRY PRODUCTS

Low fat; full fat
Milk: skimmed; semi-skimmed; whole;
                UHT
Yoghurt: low fat; creamy; UHT
Cheese: low fat; full fat

PASTRY

One or two crusts
Type of pastry: shortcrust; flakey
Type of flour: white; wholemeal
Type of fat

SOFT DRINKS

Juice; juice drink
Pasteurised; UHT
Sweetened; unsweetened
Canned; bottled; cartons

CHIPS

Old/new potatoes; fresh/frozen
Cut
Oven ready; fried
Fat used

SWEETENERS

Sugar
Artificial sweetener: record and
        code separately

FRUIT

Canned in syrup; canned in juice
Fruit only; fruit and juice/syrup
Sweetened with sugar, artificial
sweetener, or unsweetened

S1241   ADULT DIETARY SURVEY

GUIDE WEIGHTS

Note: these weights are a guide; reported weights outside these ranges
may be correct, but should have a note to explain the circumstances.
You should only use this sheet in the early days of fieldwork. After
the first two weeks of fieldwork you should rely on your own experience.

Approximate conversion (grams ──────► pounds/ounces)

454 gms	=	1lb
228 gms	=	8oz
114 gms	=	4oz
60 gms	=	2oz
30 gms	=	1oz

Guide weights:

Milk : in tea or coffee	-	20-30 gms
as a drink, or on cereal		190 gms: third of a pint
		285 gms: half a pint
Coffee powder	-	2-4 gms
Sugar: 1 teaspoon	-	6-10 gms
1 tablespoon	-	30 gms
Canned carbonated drink	-	330 gms
Bread, white, one slice	-	20-40 gms
Bread roll	-	40-50 gms
Butter, margarine, on one slice of bread	-	4-10 gms
Preserve; jam, marmalade, on one slice of bread	-	10-16 gms
Egg; without shell	-	50 gms
with shell	-	56-66 gms
Cereal, portion	-	20-40 gms
Sausages: one large	-	40-60 gms
one chipolata-type	-	20-30 gms
Hamburger, meat only, standard size	-	44-66 gms
Chips, portion	-	80-150 gms
Baked beans: smallest can	-	75 gms
: large can	-	450 gms
Fish finger in breadcrumbs	-	20-26 gms
Apple; with core	-	120 gms; core: 6-18 gms
Crisps, packet, standard size	-	25-30 gms
Biscuit, plain	-	8-16 gms
chocolate covered	-	24-30 gms

Office of Population Censuses and Surveys
Social Survey Division
St Catherines House 10 Kingsway London WC2B 6JP

Telephone 01-242 0262 ext 2315

Your reference

Our reference
S1241
Date

Date as postmark

Dear Doctor

The person named on the enclosed form, who is one of your patients, has agreed to co-operate in a survey being carried out by this Office for the Department of Health and Social Security, and the Ministry of Agriculture, Fisheries and Food.

The survey is designed to measure the dietary intake of adults in Great Britain, and involves their keeping a weighed dietary record of all the foods they consume over a seven-day period. As part of the survey we have also recorded the person's blood pressure and are arranging for an appropriately qualified person to call and take a blood sample and a specimen of urine from a measured 24-hour collection. These will be sent to a medical laboratory for analysis. The blood is to measure lipids and estimate accurate haemoglobin levels. The particular purpose of the urine specimen is to estimate salt output. The aim of the study is to follow-up some of the recommendations in the report from the Committee on Medical Aspects of Food Policy "Diet and Cardiovascular Disease" HMSO, 1984.

Your patient agreed to our taking:

a. their blood pressure
b. a blood sample
c. a specimen of urine

We hope you have no objection to their co-operating with us.

Your patient has been told of the blood pressure readings and has consented to our passing the information to you. Three readings were taken, on the same occasion, using an automatic sphygmomanometer. The systolic and diastolic pressures are shown on the enclosed form. The reading given is based on the lowest systolic pressure measured. If asked about the meaning of the reading, the fieldworker would have told your patient to seek guidance from their GP; no suggestion would have been made that the reading was in any way unusual.

We shall not be asking you to let us have any information or feedback, as the blood pressure data are being used only for statistical purposes by this Office in conjunction with the other data collected on the survey.

Thank you for your co-operation.

Yours faithfully

Janet Gregory

Janet Gregory
Principal Social Survey Officer

Blood pressure results form

S1241 ADULT DIETARY SURVEY

Serial no. label

		8

Date of test

Name of informant: Mr/Mrs/Miss _____ _____
                         First name   Surname

Address: _____

Name of GP: Dr _____

Address: _____

**BLOOD PRESSURE READING
AND PULSE RATE**

Systolic   Diastolic   Pulse rate

I consent to the Office of Population Censuses and Surveys

informing my GP of my blood pressure reading.

Signature: _____

INTERVIEWER USE ONLY	Ring code
GP consent refused	1
No GP	2

[GP's copy]

353

S1241   ADULT DIETARY SURVEY

Instructions for making a 24-hour urine collection

We are asking you to collect all urine passed during a period of 24 hours, so that we can measure various nutrients which are present in food and show up in the urine. The timing of such a collection is started usually in the morning, immediately after you have emptied your bladder.

A special collection container, with a small amount of preservative already added, is provided in which all urine passed should be stored. To make it easier for you to collect your urine, a plastic jug is also provided into which you can pass urine directly; you can then pour the urine from the jug into the collection container.

The jug can be rinsed out with tap water - no soap, please - and drained after each use.

After you have made the 24-hour collection, the doctor who calls to take the sample of blood, or the interviewer, will measure the total amount of urine you have collected, and take the samples we need for analysis. The remainder can then be thrown away.

S1241 ADULT DIETARY SURVEY: BLOOD TEST/URINE SAMPLE

Thank you for agreeing to provide us with a blood sample and urine sample. These are important aspects of the survey as their analysis will tell us a lot about the relationship between diet and health.

The blood test

This involves taking a small amount of blood from your arm. The sample will be taken by a qualified medical person, accompanied by our interviewer, and will be sent to a medical laboratory for analysis. The analysis will tell us, for example, about the levels of cholesterol and iron in the blood, which can be related to the foods a person eats, their height, weight and age.

The urine test (please also read the instructions the interviewer will leave with you):

This involves your collecting all the urine you pass in a 24 hour period. The urine should be collected in the container the interviewer will leave with you, and should be kept in a cool place. We suggest you collect for 24 hours over a weekend. When the interviewer calls again she will have with her a qualified medical person who will measure the quantity of urine and then take a small sample of it and send it to a medical laboratory for analysis. The analysis will tell us, for example, about the level of salt in the body, which cannot be measured in any other way.

With your consent, we will let your GP know that you have agreed to co-operate with these aspects of the survey.

The interviewer will call again, with the qualified medical person, to collect your urine specimen and for the blood test on:

_____

Thank you again for your co-operation.

Office of Population Censuses and Surveys
St Catherines House
10 Kingsway
London
WC2B 6JP

01-242 0262

Please follow these instructions:

1. On the first morning empty your bladder into the toilet. Please make a note on the collection container of the date and time you did this.

2. **After this,** collect and store in the container all the urine you pass during the day and the following night.

   When you feel the need to have a bowel movement, first try to pass urine into the jug for transfer to the container (that is, try not to pass urine direct into the toilet with a bowel motion).

4. The following morning, at the same time as on the previous day, that is 24 hours after you started, complete the collection by emptying your bladder and transferring the urine into the container. Please note the date and time you did this on the container. Even if it is not exactly 24 hours later, do not worry, but please make sure the time you completed the collection is recorded.

5. Keep the top of the collection container closed with the plastic clip, and keep the container in a cool place.

Practical points

1. Many people find it easier to collect their urine while they are at home most of the time, for example during a weekend. They can then make their 24-hour collection from Saturday morning to Sunday morning, or from Sunday morning to Monday morning.

2. It will probably be easier for you not to collect urine on a day when you might be drinking a lot of beer or other liquids.

3. It is easiest to start the collection in the morning, so first thing in the morning you should empty your bladder into the toilet. Then collect all the urine you pass during that day and the following night, and collect the first urine you pass the next morning. Don't forget to note the times and dates you started and finished the collection on the container.

4. If you decide to do your collection on a day when you will be away from home, you should take the collection container and jug with you in the plain plastic carrier bag provided.

5. If you pass urine but forget to collect it, please tell the interviewer when she calls back. Keep a note of the date and time this happened, and, if possible, an estimate of how much was lost. You can do this by noting how much you collect in the plastic jug on the next occasion you pass urine. Some people find it helpful to pin their pants to their outer clothes with a safety pin for the 24-hour period, as a reminder to make a collection each time they go to the toilet.

6. Women who are having their period may make the urine collection; this will not affect the analysis of the urine samples.

7. Please use only the jug and container provided, as other containers may have various things in them which would get into the urine and affect the analysis.

8. Please ask the interviewer if you have any queries, and tell her if you had any difficulties in making the 24-hour collection.

Thank you for your help

Janet Gregory
Principal Social Survey Officer
Social Survey Division OPCS

INSTRUCTIONS FOR COLLECTING VENOUS BLOOD SPECIMENS

USE ONLY THE EQUIPMENT PROVIDED

1. The alcohol wipe must be used to swab the subject's arm. With minimum stasis, take as much blood as possible using the 20 ml syringe provided. A standard needle is provided but the interviewer will have a selection of other needles if required. She will also provide a tourniquet if required. If the subject is difficult to bleed then do not attempt more than two venepunctures.

2. Carefully remove the needle from the syringe (failure to do so will result in haemolysis of the specimen). The tubes should be supported in the rack. Dispense the blood gently as follows:-

A) Add 5 mls of blood to the pink top, EDTA tube, taking care not to contaminate the tip of the syringe with anticoagulant. Secure the cap and mix well.

B) Add 4 mls of blood to the orange top, lithium heparin tube, secure the cap and mix well.

C) Add 2 mls of blood to the smallest white top tube, secure the cap and mix well.

D) Add the remainder of the specimen to the 10 ml plain tube with beads and secure the cap.

If the required volume of blood is not obtained then (A) has priority, then (B), (C) and (D) in order.

3. The interviewer will label all the tubes, including the 5 ml plain white top tube which has not yet been used (this is for the serum obtained from the 10 ml plain tube with beads). The interviewer will complete all the details on both request cards.

4. The interviewer will wrap the pink EDTA tube in the packing material provided and place it in the plastic bag. This and one of the completed request cards will be put into the prepaid envelope addressed to Dr Leeming at the General Hospital. The envelope should be sealed and despatched immediately.

5. The doctor should take the remaining 3 tubes of blood back to the laboratory and, within three hours, centrifuge the 10 ml plain tube. All the available serum (without any red cells) should be transferred to the remaining 5 ml white top tube, using a Pasteur pipette. Ensure the cap is secure.

6. All the samples should be kept out of direct sunlight and in a cool place. If possible, refrigerate but do not freeze the two whole blood specimens while the clotted blood is being separated.

7. The interviewer will wrap the three tubes (blood in orange top tube, blood in small white top tube and serum in white top tube) in packing material and place in the plastic bag provided. These will be put into the transit carton with the request card and despatched by the interviewer immediately.

8. The doctor should dispose of all waste materials in the supply carton, according to normal laboratory practices.

INSTRUCTIONS FOR TAKING THE URINE SAMPLES FROM URINE COLLECTION BOXES

USE ONLY THE EQUIPMENT PROVIDED

1. The subject will have made a 24-hour urine collection. The interviewer will weigh the volume of urine collected.

2. The interviewer will record the following information on the urine request form.

   i.   Date and time at start of collection.

   ii.   Date and time at end of collection.

   iii. Total volume of urine collected in mls.

   iv.   Period of collection in hours.

   v.   Whether any of the collections were missed.

3. The doctor should take 4 aliquots from the collection into the urine tubes.

   i.   Ensure the urine in the collection container is well mixed. Do NOT invert the container. If the subject has filled more than one container then the contents of both containers should be mixed together.

   ii. Transfer approx 5 mls of urine into each of the 3 small urine tubes and approximately 10 mls of urine into the large urine tube. A rack, Pasteur pipettes and disposable gloves are provided in the supply carton.

   iii. Take care not to over fill the tubes since they are to be frozen later and the tubes will split if they are filled completely.

4. Ensure that the caps on the tubes are secure and that the tubes are labelled. The interviewer will wrap the tubes in the packing material provided and then place them in the plastic bag. She will replace the tubes and card in the transit carton and despatch to the Wolfson Research Laboratories immediately.

5. The subject will be asked to dispose of the remaining urine and used container. The doctor should dispose of the gloves and pipettes in the supply carton.

QUEEN ELIZABETH MEDICAL CENTRE – WOLFSON RESEARCH LABORATORIES 021 472 1311 Ext. 4553
COMPLETE ALL SECTIONS OF THIS CARD AND RETURN WITH BLOOD SAMPLES

PROJECT CODE | P | 5 | 0

SERIAL NUMBER
AFFIX LABEL HERE

DATE OF COLLECTION

TIME OF COLLECTION
(24 hr CLOCK)

AGE

SEX M/F

LAB USE ONLY
4 HEP   2 HEP
SERUM

QUEEN ELIZABETH MEDICAL CENTRE – WOLFSON RESEARCH LABORATORIES 021 472 1311 Ext. 4553
COMPLETE ALL SECTIONS OF THIS CARD AND RETURN WITH URINE SAMPLES

PROJECT CODE | P | 5 | 0

SERIAL NUMBER
AFFIX LABEL HERE

COLLECTION STARTED
DATE   TIME 24 HR CLOCK

COLLECTION FINISHED
DATE   TIME 24 HR CLOCK

TOTAL URINE VOLUME   MLS

PERIOD OF COLLECTION   HRS

WERE ANY COLLECTIONS MISSED?   Y/N

AGE

SEX M/F

LAB USE ONLY
1   3
2   4

S 1241   ADULT DIETARY SURVEY

AUTHORISATION OF PAYMENT TO DOCTORS

Serial no ⟶

Date sample was taken

	YES	NO
Was a blood sample taken?	1	2
Was a urine sample taken?	1	2

I certify that a visit was made to take a blood/urine
sample from this informant on the above date.

Doctor's signature: _____

Interviewer's
signature: _____

Authorisation no: _____

Appendix B The sample design

1 Requirements of the sample

The sampling method for the dietary and nutritional survey of British adults was designed to give a representative sample of adults aged 16 to 64 living in households in Great Britain. In determining the sample size, the critical requirement was to achieve at least 2000 seven-day food records in total, about 500 food records per round of fieldwork. The greatest constraint on the number of interviews planned was the relatively large cost per informant for fieldwork and coding on a survey of this complexity which involved both diary-keeping and physical measurements of informants. The sample size was chosen to be sufficiently large to indicate important differences between selected subgroups of the population.

It was recognised that the survey was particularly onerous for respondents, involving their commitment over a considerable period of time, and for this reason only one individual per sampled household was asked to keep a dietary record. The selection of only one individual in a household also ensured the maximum variety of diets within the relatively small sample on this survey; there may be considerable similarity between the diets of different members of the same household. The requirements of the sample were therefore that only one adult aged 16 to 64 from each selected household should be interviewed, and that households should be selected with probability proportional to their size in order that individuals living in smaller households were not over-represented. It was also necessary for the addresses to be clustered to give areas of a realistic size for interviewers to cover.

When drawing a sample of households with probability proportional to their size, the Electoral Register provides a better sampling frame than the Postcode Address File (PAF) since it includes information on the number of electors at an address. It is, however, recognised that the Electoral Register is deficient as a sampling frame in its coverage of groups such as the young and ethnic minority groups. The report on coverage of the 1981 Electoral Register by Todd and Butcher[1] indicated that about 3.6% of adults in Great Britain live in addresses which are not on the register at the start of the year for which it is in force. In that study it was suggested that use of the register as a sampling frame might exclude 8% of 20 to 24 year olds, 38% of adults who are not citizens of the Commonwealth or the Republic of Ireland, and 14% of New Commonwealth citizens. However, these groups may be difficult to contact regardless of the sampling frame which is used.

It was not possible to draw a sample of individuals from the Electoral Register for a named person sample since the register lists only those who are eligible to vote and aged 18 or over (and those who will become 18 during the year for which the register is in use), whereas all adults aged between 16 and 64 years were eligible to take part in the survey. This deficiency was overcome by sampling electors, and hence defining the household from which the informant was to be selected. After selection of the household there was, therefore, a second stage of selection.

2 Selection of households

In order to select the appropriate number of addresses, a stratified multi-stage sampling design was used. The stages in the selection of the sample were as follows:

(i) The chosen primary sampling units (psus) were local authority wards, and 120 wards were selected by a systematic sampling method from a stratified listing of wards. For this purpose, all wards in England, Wales and mainland Scotland[2] were stratified first by region and then by a socio-economic indicator, which was the proportion of the population of each ward in socio-economic groups 1 to 5 and 13. The regional stratification differentiated between metropolitan and non-metropolitan areas within standard regions, and the Scottish Highlands were defined as a separate stratum in order to ensure at least one selection from this area. A random selection of wards was then made with the chance of selection of each ward being proportional to its total electorate.

(ii) The 120 wards chosen were systematically allocated to the four rounds of the survey, ensuring as far as possible a similar distribution of all regions in each quarter. Thus, in each quarter, interviewing took place in 30 wards spread throughout England, Scotland and Wales.

(iii) The final stage of selection before addresses were issued to interviewers was to draw a random sample from the Electoral Register of 33 electors (and therefore of addresses) within each ward, with probability proportional to the number of electors at the address. The name of the selected elector was recorded on the sample sheet and, in the cases of multi-household addresses, this person defined the household of interest.

The representativeness of any selected sample can, of course, be affected by the sampling frame used being incomplete or out of date, and this sample could also be affected if the number of adults in the household differed from the number of electors on the register. A record was therefore made of the number of electors on the register at the address at which the sampled elector lived; this information was later keyed onto the database, together with other details collected by the interviewer at the address, in order to assess whether weighting of the sample was necessary.

3 Selection of an individual

The above steps defined the households which were to be visited by interviewers but a further selection procedure was necessary to determine which person within the household should be interviewed. Interviewers were issued with sampling forms which gave the name of the selected elector and the address as listed on the Electoral Register. Each form also contained a version of a selection table, based on those designed by Kish to indicate which individual within that sampled household should be interviewed.[3]

The selection procedure carried out at the household was as follows:

(i) The interviewer first identified the household containing the chosen elector whose name was given on the sampling form. In the majority of cases there was only one household at the selected address. In a minority of cases where the sampled address contained a number of households the sampled household was defined as that to which the named elector belonged; if the named elector had moved away then the required household was defined as that occupying the space previously occupied by the named individual's household.

(ii) The interviewer was asked to determine how many households there were at the address stated on the sample form and to record this information, together with the total number of adults aged 16 or over in the household. These figures were important in interpreting the information from the Electoral Register on number of electors at the address, and so in assessing whether it was necessary to weight the sample.

(iii) In order to carry out the selection procedure in the household, the interviewer needed to list all adults aged 16 or over with their sex and age. A number was then allocated to each person listed who was in the eligible age range for the survey; adults aged 65 or more were excluded from the selection process. Eligible adults were numbered in descending order of age, starting with males in the household.

(iv) The person to be interviewed was then defined by reference to the selection table which had been written onto the sample sheet for that address. The interviewer found the appropriate column for a household containing the number of eligible adults

that he or she had recorded, and read off the person number of the individual to be interviewed. An example of an address sheet and selection table is shown opposite.

The selection tables recorded on the sample sheets were based on those designed by Kish, which gave a close approximation to the proper fractional representation of each adult within the household for up to six adults.[3] For this survey selection tables for households of up to eight adults were used, which required sixteen versions to be used in a stated proportion of cases. Each of these versions of the selection table was assigned to an equal number of the total sample and to a broadly similar proportion of the addresses in each ward.

4 Ineligible addresses and individuals

The eligible population for the survey was all adults aged between 16 and 64 years inclusive living in private households. Since adults outside this age range were excluded from the sampling process, households where all members were aged 65 or over were ineligible households.

Individuals not living in private households were also ineligible for the survey. Most addresses which were obviously institutions were excluded at the sampling stage (i.e. hospitals, old people's homes, student halls of residence). Some institutions could not be recognised at the sampling stage and such addresses were considered to be ineligible if the occupants were catered for communally.

Pregnant women were also ineligible to take part in the survey. Where the individual selected by the procedure outlined at point (iv) above was a pregnant woman, no interview was carried out at that household. In some situations it was not immediately obvious that the selected woman was pregnant; the interviewer would then complete the questionnaire on dietary habits which included a question about pregnancy, and the interview was concluded at this stage.

References and notes

1. Areas of Scotland excluded from the sample were: the Orkneys, Shetlands, Western Isles and other Scottish Islands. If, however, a ward covered part of the mainland and part of an island in Scotland then that ward was included in the sampling frame. Also excluded from the sampling frame were the Channel Islands, Isle of Man and the Scilly Islands.
2. Todd J and Butcher B. *Electoral Registration in 1981*. HMSO London 1982
3. Kish L. *Survey Sampling*. J Wiley & Sons Ltd London 1965

ADULT DIETARY SURVEY (S1241)

1		
Round	Ward	Address

Interviewer's Name _____   No. of sheets _____

A D D R E S S		District
		Ward
		Name of chosen elector

List all persons in household aged 16 and over

Name of person	Relationship to HOH	Sex	Age	Person No.	Interview Person No

(i)	Met	1	Other Urban	2	Rural	3

(ii)	Number of electors at address (FOR OFFICE USE ONLY):	
(iii)	Number of persons aged 16 and over :	
(iv)	Number of households at address :	

List eligible males in descending order of age followed by eligible females in descending order of age. Then use the Selection Table on the right to choose the person for interview.	Selection Table								
	If the No. of persons 16-64 in household is	1	2	3	4	5	6	7	8 or more
	Interview the person numbered	1	1	2	3	4	4	5	6

W2603A OPCS 5/76

361

Appendix C The feasibility and pilot studies

The fieldwork methodology for recording food intake was based on methods used by Social Survey Division (SSD) with schoolchildren and published previously.[1] There are several important differences between surveys of adults and schoolchildren which might affect the quality of data. Adults might, for example, be less willing to co-operate with a survey, be more likely to consume a greater variety of foods than children, particularly prepared dishes requiring recipes, and be more likely to eat out at a wider range of places than children, who eat mainly at home or at school.

The survey of adults included a number of elements not contained in the survey of schoolchildren such as the collection and coding of brand information for the dietary record. Measurements of blood pressure and samples of blood and urine were also required.

1.1 The feasibility study

A feasibility study was carried out in June and July 1985, with the aims of assessing the level of co-operation with various aspects of the survey, testing the methodology for selecting the sample, testing procedures for taking measurements and samples, and examining the quality of the dietary information recorded.

1.2 Methodology

The feasibility study included all the elements adopted for the mainstage survey except measurements of wrist diameter and calf and mid-upper arm circumference (see Chapter 1 for a description of the elements in the mainstage survey).

Methodology for the seven-day weighed dietary record followed that of the schoolchildrens' dietary survey, and the same food code list was used in the feasibility study.

Measurement of the informant's blood pressure was carried out by the interviewer, using a portable battery-operated automatic sphygmomanometers (see Chapter 3; 3.3). The reliability of these machines under field conditions was tested in the feasibility study.

One doctor was recruited by the Department of Health in each area of fieldwork to take the blood samples. An extra visit to the respondent's household was made by the interviewer and the doctor to take the blood sample; this visit was usually arranged so that the urine specimen could be taken at the same time. The blood

sample was processed, centrifuged, where appropriate, by the doctor, at his surgery or a local hospital, and despatched by the interviewer to the laboratories for analysis.

1.3 The sample and response

The sample for the feasibility study was designed in a similar way to the final sample, although the six wards were selected to include an inner city area, other urban areas and a rural area. Interviews and seven-day records were obtained from 45 individuals in these areas, representing a response rate of 54%. This overall figure was disproportionately affected by a very low response in one of the six selected areas; if this one area is disregarded then a response rate of 65% would have been achieved.

The standard of recording in the dietary records was very high but a number of difficulties in the coding of brands became evident. In particular it was often unclear whether the brand recorded by the informant was in fact the name of the outlet rather than the correct 'own-label' brand for the food, or whether the food was actually a fresh product sold by that outlet.

Of respondents to the dietary record, 95% co-operated with the anthropometric and blood pressure measurements and 68% provided blood and urine samples.

1.4 The recommendation for a pilot study

Following the feasibility study a number of issues suggested that a pilot study should be undertaken in advance of the mainstage.

The Ministry of Agriculture, Fisheries and Food (MAFF) wished to prepare a revised food code list for use at the mainstage since the existing list did not provide sufficient detail, particularly about fats. More detailed information about foods would be needed to use the revised code list, and it was therefore recommended that it should be tested at a pilot stage. It was also decided to revise the brand code list, which would also require further testing.

Two suggestions to improve response were implemented following the feasibility study; these were the payment of a small amount of money to respondents who kept a complete dietary record, and sending a letter in advance of the interviewer calling to sampled households.

Measurement of wrist diameter and calf and mid-upper arm circumference had not been tested in the feasibility study, and the pilot study allowed the methodology for these measurements to be tested.

2.1 The pilot study

The pilot study incorporated all elements planned for the mainstage survey and was carried out in February 1986. The main aim was to test the new and altered elements listed above, but it also offered the opportunity to rehearse all the methodologies used and to test various aspects of the organisation and administration of the survey.

In addition to the anthropometric measurements mentioned above and introduced for the pilot, interviewers were also trained to take measurements of triceps skinfold thickness. This measurement technique was not adopted at the mainstage, because it was not possible to give the large numbers of interviewers working on the mainstage of the survey sufficient training and experience to produce acceptable precision; moreover the pilot showed that the technique was unacceptable to a significant proportion of informants (see Chapter 3; 3.2).

For the measurement of blood pressure on the pilot study, interviewers in half of the areas were issued with portable, battery-operated machines whilst the other interviewers used mains-powered automatic sphygmomanometers.

2.2 The sample and response

Fifteen wards were chosen for inclusion in the pilot study, ensuring a spread of metropolitan, other urban, and rural wards. Interviews and seven-day dietary records were completed by 151 individuals, a response rate of more than 70% of the eligible sample.

Anthropometric measurements were taken in 98% of cases where a dietary record had been completed, and 55% of informants who did not keep dietary record also co-operated with the measurements. Of those who had kept a dietary record and were eligible to provide samples of blood and urine, 86% agreed to provide a specimen of blood and 91% to making a 24-hour urine collection.

These improved response rates appeared to justify the introduction of an advance letter and an incentive payment for the dietary record, and confirmed the acceptability both of the anthropometric measurements and of the blood and urine samples.

In spite of the greater complexity of the food code list and of the details required from informants, the quality of record keeping and information given was at least as good as in the feasibility study. It was, however, recognised that considerable training needed to be given to interviewers on the use of both the food and brand code lists. It was also decided that, in relation to foods eaten outside the home, information should be obtained centrally on the weights of standard items of food purchased from national multiple outlets, such as Wimpy and Pizza Hut, in order to reduce the number of duplicates interviewers needed to obtain.

On the basis of the pilot study, it was also decided that measurement of skinfold thickness should not be incorporated in the mainstage package, and that the mains-operated automatic sphygmomanometer should be used in preference to the battery-operated device.

3.1 The mainstage survey

The recommendations from the feasibility and pilot studies were adopted for the survey mainstage. Details of the mainstage survey package are given in Chapter 1, and the methodologies are described in Chapters 2 to 4 and Appendices D and G.

Fieldwork for the mainstage was carried out in four rounds throughout a complete year, in order to give a representative sample of diets at different times of the year. Within each round fieldwork was spread over a two-month period, and the dates of these field periods were as follows:

round 1: 29 September—28 November 1986
round 2: 5 January—27 February 1987
round 3: 30 March—29 May 1987
round 4: 29 June—31 August 1987

Reference
1. Committee on Medical Aspects of Food Policy Subcommittee on nutritional surveillance. *The diets of British schoolchildren*. Department of Health. Report on Health and Social Subjects No 36 HMSO London 1989.

Appendix D Dietary methodology: details of the recording and coding procedures

1.1 Recording procedures

The food scales

Soehnle digital scales weighing to 2g with a maximum weight of 2.5kg, were used. The scales, which can be zeroed after each item is weighed, have a memory which enables the previous weight to be recalled when an item is removed for a short time and then replaced, for example when bread is buttered. Although weight readings are retained on the digital display for a short time, it was recommended that informants should first write in the home record book a list of the items to be weighed, and then weigh the plate and each item in quick succession, zeroing the scales after each item. The maximum cumulative weight of 2.5kg was a potential problem where the informant used a heavy plate, and therefore plastic plates were provided for use in these circumstances.

Foods eaten at home

The introduction to and pages from the home record book are included at Appendix A. Interviewers and informants were trained in a standard procedure for completion of the record book; this was designed to assist in the coding and editing of the data.

Each food or group of foods was preceded by an entry for a container, such as a plate, dish or cup which was weighed first. Each food served was then entered on a separate line with information on the brand, a full description of the food item, and the weight served. Where foods could be split the individual components were weighed and recorded separately, for example, milk, tea infusion and sugar. Where the food was a composite item which could not readily be split, such as a fruit pie or meat casserole, informants were asked to record a full description of the food, including recipe details, and the total weight served.

For some food items it was difficult to follow this recommended method for weighing and recording. Foods that are purchased in containers, such as yoghurts, were initially weighed as a complete item—container plus edible contents—and the empty container was then weighed at the end of the meal. Such entries were later rewritten by the interviewer or office coders.

Second helping at meals were treated in the same way as the first serving; the plate, with any foods remaining on it, was first re-weighed and then the scales zeroed and each new item weighed separately.

A record was also made of all leftovers, both edible and inedible, for each plate of food. At the end of each meal the plate or container was re-weighed, with the leftover items on it, the weight was recorded in the leftover column besides the entry for the container and a tick was placed in the leftovers column besides each type of food left on the plate. Informants were also encouraged to record relevant descriptions of leftovers from meat, fish and fruit, such as bone, fat, skin or stone. These details helped when coding the items since different codes applied, for example, to stoned fruits depending on whether the leftover stone had been weighed, and there were various codes for chops depending on whether the leftover bone and fat had been weighed.

Foods eaten away from home

The pocket book was designed so that informants could record all food items which were eaten away from home. A description of each item was required together with information on the portion size, the price of the item, where it was purchased, and any leftovers. At the coding stage interviewers split composite items into their components and transcribed the entries from the pocket book to pages with a similar format to those in the home record book.

Information about the weight of foods eaten away from home was added to the records in a variety of ways. For items purchased from local shops or cafes interviewers used the information given about the price and the place of purchase to buy a duplicate item; this was either weighed directly or split into its components and weighed. Duplicates of items from national chains, pre-packaged snacks, confectionery and soft drinks were bought centrally. Interviewers were also asked to find out further details of foods purchased from takeaway food outlets so that they could be correctly coded; such information included the type of fat used for frying, and the type of spread used in sandwiches.

Where no specific information was available about the weights of the components of a composite item or of items within a meal, weights were estimated by the consultant nutritionists working on the survey.

Checks by the interviewer

After the interviewer had demonstrated the use of the food scales and the procedures for completing the home record book at the placing call, the informant was asked to record all food and drink consumed from that time. The seven-day recording period started at midnight, so the remainder of the first day was used as a practice period in which informants could become accustomed to the food scales and identify any difficulties that they might have in weighing or recording food. The interviewer made his or her first checking call approximately 24 hours after the placing call. At this call the interviewer checked that the weights recorded were not cumulative, that leftovers were being weighed and recorded, that the description of the foods eaten was sufficiently detailed, and that composite items had been split before weighing.

At each subsequent visit the interviewer read through the home record book and pocket diary to check for any obvious difficulties in recording, to probe for more details of foods that were inadequately described, and to check that non-edible leftovers such as apple cores and bones of chops had been weighed where appropriate.

2.1 Coding

The coding of both of foods and of brands was carried out by interviewers so that they could refer back to informants where details of foods were missing from the record.

Food coding

The essential information required for coding foods was as follows:

(a) the form in which the food was bought, e.g. fresh, frozen, canned;

(b) whether the product was low-fat or low-calorie, and if fat had been trimmed from meat;

(c) the cooking method, e.g. grilled, braised, stewed, fried; for fried items the type of fat used;

(d) whether a coating was used for fried fish and meat, and whether thickenings were used for stews and casseroles;

(e) whether foods had been sweetened and, if so, whether sugar or artificial sweeteners had been used; and

(f) details of the type of fat and flour used in pastry and cakes.

Informants were asked to weigh separately the components of foods which could be split. If composite items eaten at home had not been split and weighed separately then the interviewer asked for an estimate of quantity for each of the constituent parts; this might be a relatively standard amount as in the case of slices of bread, or could involve a description of the quantity or of the relative proportions of each component. Using this information the consultant nutritionists apportioned the total weight recorded between the components of the dish.

While, in general, foods which could be separated to their constituent elements were split before being coded, some composite items could not readily be split to their constituent parts and were included as made-up items in the food code list. The procedure for such items differed according to whether they were classed as recipe or non-recipe dishes on the food code list.

Recipe items were identified in the food code list by an 'R' preceding the code number and their nutrient values were based on standard recipe ingredients. Where the dish was homemade, the interviewer collected details of the recipe used for the total quantity of the dish prepared. Recipes were individually checked by the consultant nutritionists and the type and proportions of ingredients used were compared with those of the standard recipe to which the food code referred. If the ingredients differed from the standard recipe in a way which was nutritionally significant the existing food code could not be used and a new food code was allocated to the item; the appropriate nutrients for the new recipe code were calculated by the MAFF Nutrition Branch and added to the nutrient databank.

Where recipe items were eaten away from home it was not always possible to establish details of the ingredients, so the standard food code for that item was used. In some cases, for example for foods from works' canteens, interviewers were able to collect details of ingredients used in recipe items, and this information enabled items to be coded to the most appropriate code available for that food item or a new recipe code to be calculated.

Non-recipe items were generally more standard items, such as fish in batter or fruit pies, for which a range of codes were provided on the code list to allow for variants in recipes. These items could be coded directly from the food code list so long as the details of the item eaten conformed to the description given, and recipes did not need to be recorded. Special codes were also included in the code list for composite items purchased from national fast-food chains (for example standard products from Wimpy) where data on the nutritional content of the foods was available.

Brand codes

Brand information was recorded and coded for all pre-packaged foods, including fresh foods, but the information was not coded for items which were sold loose. The brand code list was organised into the same sections as the food code list, with an additional section for 'own brands', and a brand code could only be used for the specific food group under which it was included. A single manufacturer could therefore have various brand codes for use with products in the different food groups.

The definition of the brand of an item varied according to the food type, and was usually the level of information which gave most detail of the specific product. Thus, for example, Diet Ski yoghurts had a different code to Ski yoghurts, and savoury snacks were coded according to the name of the product, such as *Hula Hoops* or *Monster Munch*, rather than to the name of the manufacturer.

The brand coding of biscuits, wine and bottled water differed from other food items in that the own-brand list was not used and the codes available were based on the description of the product: biscuits, for example, were coded as ginger nuts or orange creams rather than by the name of the manufacturer; similarly wines and bottled waters were coded according to the type of product, for example Cote du Rhone or Soave, and Highland Spring or Ashbourne, respectively.

Brands were also recorded for the ingredients of recipe items. For composite items which were single food codes the brand recorded was that of the 'main' ingredient; the 'main' ingredient was defined by the food group the item was ascribed to. For example, the brand code for custard powder was used for made-up custard and the code for fish used for fish in batter.

Interviewer training

Interviewers were trained at a three-day briefing and by exercises to recognise the detail required for coding foods of different types. Before the briefing each interviewer kept his or her own five-day weighed dietary record and coded the foods eaten. After the briefing each interviewer was asked to place a dietary record with someone outside their household and to code both foods and brands. The completed records were checked by the consultant nutritionists to ensure that interviewers had reached the necessary standard of coding.

Appendix E The nutrient databank, details of nutrients measured and the coding frame for dietary supplements

1 The nutrient databank

Intakes of nutrients were calculated from the records of food consumption using a specially developed nutrient databank. Past dietary surveys have largely relied upon the standard UK food composition tables, *McCance and Widdowson's The Composition of Foods*.[1] However the composition of foods changes over time—not only are new products constantly being developed and old ones reformulated, but apparently traditional foods also change. Changes in composition may result from, among other things, new plant varieties and animal breeds, importation from different countries, altered storage practices, processing techniques, fortification practices, packaging and domestic practices.

Since accepting responsibility for the revision and extension of the UK food composition tables in 1978, the Ministry of Agriculture, Fisheries and Food has conducted a major programme of nutrient analyses in foods. The groups of foods and nutrients studied are outlined in *The British Diet: Finding the Facts,* together with details of the rationale of approaches adopted for the analyses.[2]

In view of the analytical data available, the likely changes in composition and the large number of new foods available, complete revision of the food tables was undertaken for this survey.

Methods of preparation

Values for each nutrient in the databank which was included in the fourth edition of *McCance and Widdowson's The Composition of Foods*[1] and *Immigrant Foods*,[3] were evaluated and where they were considered still to be valid or where no other reliable data existed, these were used in the databank. These data were extended using the results of recent analytical surveys, manufacturers' data, published scientific literature and, where appropriate, food composition tables from other countries.

For some foods no reliable information was available for certain nutrients. These values have not been taken as zero, but a likely value has been calculated from ingredients or imputed from similar foods.

During the survey period the range of foods included in the databank was extended as new products with different nutrient contents were consumed by informants, for example, reduced fat or low sugar products.

Composite dishes and recipe calculations

A number of the foods in the databank were consumed as composite items, for example, beef stew or sponge cake.

Composite dishes with the same name, for example, beef stew, may vary in their nutrient content because they contain different ingredients. For composite items informants were asked to record the recipe used. Where this differed, in a nutritionally significant way, from the standard item on the code list, a new code was ascribed to the food. The nutrient content was calculated from the raw ingredients after allowing for likely fat or moisture losses or gains and after making standard adjustments for nutrient losses on cooking.[1]

Dietary supplements

Information was collected on brand name, strength, and quantity of each supplement taken over the seven-day recording period. Each supplement was classified into one of 28 different groups (see over).

In addition, manufacturers' data were applied to each individual supplement taken by the informants and the total nutrients provided by the supplements were calculated.

References

1. Paul A A and Southgate D A T. *McCance and Widdowson's The Composition of Foods* Fourth Edition, HMSO 1978.
2. Ministry of Agriculture, Fisheries and Food. *The British Diet: Finding the Facts*, the twenty-third report of the Steering Group on Food Surveillance, Food Surveillance Paper No 23, HMSO 1988.
3. Tan S P, Wenlock R W, Buss D H. *Immigrant Foods Second Supplement to McCance and Widdowson's The Composition of Foods*, HMSO 1985.

Appendix E Details of nutrients measured and units

Nutrient	Units	
moisture	*(g)*	
sugars	*(g)*	total sugars, expressed as monosaccharide
starch	*(g)*	expressed as monosaccharide
dietary fibre	*(g)*	expressed as modified Southgate method[1]
energy	*(kcals)*	$(4 \times \text{protein}) + (9 \times \text{fat}) + (3.75 \times \text{carbohydrate}) + (7 \times \text{alcohol})$
	(kJ)	$(17 \times \text{protein}) + (37 \times \text{fat}) + (16 \times \text{carbohydrate}) + (29 \times \text{alcohol})$
protein	*(g)*	
fat	*(g)*	
carbohydrate	*(g)*	sum of sugars plus starch, expressed as monosaccharide
alcohol	*(g)*	
sodium	*(mg)*	
potassium	*(mg)*	
calcium	*(mg)*	
magnesium	*(mg)*	
phosphorus	*(mg)*	
iron	*(mg)*	
copper	*(mg)*	
zinc	*(mg)*	
chloride	*(mg)*	
iodine	*(µg)*	
retinol	*(µg)*	sum of trans retinol + $(0.75 \times \text{cis retinol})$ $+ (0.9 \times \text{retinaldehyde}) + (0.4 \times \text{dehydroretinol})$
carotene	*(µg)*	largely as β-carotene
vitamin D	*(µg)*	sum of cholicalciferol and ergocalciferol
vitamin E	*(mg)*	α tocopherol + $(0.3 \times \beta \text{ tocopherol})$ + $(0.15 \times \gamma \text{ tocopherol})$ + $(0.3 \times \alpha \text{ tocotrienol})$
thiamin	*(mg)*	
riboflavin	*(mg)*	
niacin equivalent	*(mg)*	mg niacin + (mg tryptophan/60)
vitamin C	*(mg)*	
vitamin B6	*(mg)*	
vitamin B12	*(µg)*	
folate	*(µg)*	
pantothenic acid	*(mg)*	
biotin	*(µg)*	

fatty acids

total saturated	*(g)*
total cis mono unsaturated	*(g)*
total cis n–3 polyunsaturated	*(g)*
total cis n–6 polyunsaturated	*(g)*
cholesterol	*(mg)*

Reference

1. Southgate D A T. Dietary fibre: analysis and foods sources. *Am J Clin Nutr* 1978; 31: Suppl S107–S110.

Coding frame for dietary supplements

Code	*Dietary supplement*
01	Multivitamins (no iron or other minerals)
02	Multivitamins with iron or other minerals
03	Vitamins A, C and D
04	Vitamin C
05	Vitamin A (not cod liver oil etc)
06	Vitamin E (not wheat germ oil)
07	Vitamin B6
08	Other single vitamins
09	B complex vitamins
10	Zinc
11	Iron
12	Calcium (not bonemeal)
13	Selenium with or without other minerals or vitamins
14	Other minerals/mineral mixtures (not tissue salts)
15	Yeast
16	MAXEPA
17	Evening primrose oil, blackcurrent seed oil, γ-linolenic acid, wheat germ oil
18	Cod liver oil, halibut liver oil
19	Bonemeal
20	Kelp
21	Ginseng
22	Pollen and royal jelly
23	Lecithin
24	Garlic oil, garlic capsules
25	Fibre (not bran)
26	Other miscellaneous supplements including tissue salts, amino acids and herbal salts
27	Unknown
28	Prescribed vitamins

Appendix F Regression equations for predicting fat free mass in males and females

Males: age last birthday[1]

16 years: $(15.2 \times \text{height}) + (0.542 \times \text{weight}) + (0.186 \times \text{calf}) + (2.15 \times \text{ulna}) - 24.8$

17–19 years: $(17.4 \times \text{height}) + (0.466 \times \text{weight}) + (0.181 \times \text{calf}) + (2.75 \times \text{ulna}) - 27.6$

20–24 years: $(20.0 \times \text{height}) + (0.410 \times \text{weight}) + (0.290 \times \text{calf}) + (2.91 \times \text{ulna}) - 33.6$

25–29 years: $(22.3 \times \text{height}) + (0.387 \times \text{weight}) + (0.487 \times \text{calf}) + (2.52 \times \text{ulna}) - 40.1$

30–39 years: $(17.1 \times \text{height}) + (0.487 \times \text{weight}) + (0.219 \times \text{calf}) + (2.17 \times \text{ulna}) - 27.3$

40–49 years: $(20.5 \times \text{height}) + (0.354 \times \text{weight}) + (0.353 \times \text{calf}) + (2.39 \times \text{ulna}) - 32.3$

50–64 years: $(26.1 \times \text{height}) + (0.354 \times \text{weight}) + (0.190 \times \text{calf}) + (3.96 \times \text{ulna}) - 40.5$

Females: age last birthday[1]

16–29 years: $(10.9 \times \text{height}) - (0.51 \times \text{muac}) + (0.563 \times \text{weight}) + 5.6$

30–64 years: $(14.7 \times \text{height}) + (0.14 \times \text{muac}) + (0.397 \times \text{weight}) - 9.6$

References and notes

Units: height (mm)
weight (kg)
calf, wrist (ulna), mid-upper arm circumference (muac) (cm)
fat free mass (kg)

1. Regression equations were calculated by Durnin, McKay and Webster[2] only for males aged up to 59 years, and for females in two age groups, 17 to 29 years and 30 to 39 years. In this survey, for males aged 60 to 64 years the equation that has been used is that given for 59 years olds. In the survey, fat free mass for females aged 16 has been calculated using the equation for 17 year olds, and for females aged over 39 the equation given by Durnin for the older group of women has been used.

2. Durnin J V G A, McKay F C, Webster C I. A new method of assessing fatness and desirable weight, for use in the armed services. University of Glasgow 1985 Unpublished paper.

Appendix G Techniques for making the anthropometric measurements and protocol for taking blood pressure

1 Stature (height)
This measurement was made with the subject standing on the horizontal platform of a stadiometer, in a position that achieved maximum height.

The stadiometer used was a free-standing, fold-up model specially designed and manufactured for OPCS, which had previously been used on the survey of the heights and weights of adults in Great Britain.[1,2] Before being used on this survey all the stadiometers were inspected by the manufacturer and their accuracy checked.

The stadiometer was placed on firm, level surface before commencing to make the measurement. Subjects were than asked to remove their shoes and to stand on the baseboard of the stadiometer , with their backs towards the vertical bar, their heels against the horizontal cross bar on the baseboard and their arms hanging loosely at their side. The importance of achieving the correct posture in order to attain maximum height was explained to the subject, with the help of a visual aid, and the interviewer then positioned the subject's head such that the line between the external auditory meatus and the lower border of the orbit was horizontal and parallel to the floor; this position is known as the *Frankfort plane*.

The horizontal arm of the stadiometer was lowered to be in contact with the crown of the head and the subject was then asked to maintain the position of the Frankfort plane and at the same time to stretch to his or her fullest height. The interviewer then checked that the correct stance was being maintained and that maximum height had been achieved by observing upward movement on the horizontal plate (downward movement being prevented by means of a friction lock). The subject stepped off the stadiometer before the measurement was read. The mark on the scale was positioned parallel to the interviewer's eye before being read, to ensure accuracy. If the subject failed to maintain the correct position of the head, if there was other body movement, of if an upward movement of the horizontal plate was not seen on stretching then the whole procedure was repeated. Only if the subject was unable to maintain the correct head position unsupported was the head held by the interviewer.

2 Body weight
Body weight was measured using battery operated Soehnle personal weighing scales, calibrated in kilogram and 200g units, and with a digital display. All the scales were checked and, if necessary, recalibrated before being used on the survey.[3] The batteries were replaced at regular intervals during the fieldwork period of the survey.

The scales were placed on a hard, level surface. If only a carpeted surface was available then this was noted on the recording document by the interviewer, but subsequent experiment showed that there was no difference in measurement according to the surface that the scales were placed on, provided it was level.

Subjects were asked to remove shoes, any heavy outer garments, (jacket, jumper, etc), or heavy jewellery, and loose money and keys from any pockets. They were then asked to indicate on a self-completion form all the items of clothing being worn while the measurement was being made.[4] The scales were switched on, and when the display showed zero, subjects were asked to stand on the scales with their feet together, heels on the back edge, arms hanging loosely at the side and head facing forward. The interviewer checked that both feet were placed fully on the weighing surface.

Once the scales had stabilised, the reading 'froze' on the display, and was recorded. If the informant moved while the scales were stabilising, they were asked to step off, and the procedure was repeated.

3 Mid-upper arm circumference
The measurement was made in two stages on the subject's left arm with the arm removed from the sleeve of clothing being worn. First the mid-point of the upper arm was located and then the circumference at the mid-point was measured. To locate the mid-point of the upper arm, the subject's forearm was placed at an angle of 90 degrees across the body. Using a conventional cloth tape measure the distance between the inferior border of the acromion and the tip of the olecranon process was measured, and the mid-point marked on the subject's arm. To measure the circumference at the mid-point, the subject's arm was positioned to hang loosely at the side of the body. Using an insertion tape made of non-stretch material and specially modified for this survey, the circumference was measured, ensuring that the tape was horizontal, in contact with the arm around the entire circumference, and without pressure to compress the tissues.[5]

4 Wrist diameter
This measurement was made on the subject's left wrist using specially modified vernier callipers.[6]

The subject was seated at a table and the left arm positioned on the table, such that the whole of the lower arm, from the elbow down, was resting on a flat surface, palm down. The fingers were positioned together, flat on the surface, with the thumb close against the fingers. The breadth was measured across the styloid processes with pressure applied to the jaws of the callipers to compress the tissues.

5 Calf circumference (males only)

This measurement was made with the subject seated, and his trouser leg rolled to above the knee. The measurement was taken using the same modified insertion tape used to measure the circumference of the upper arm.

The subject was asked to sit well back in an upright chair and, with his shoe removed, the left leg was positioned such that there was a 90 degree angle between the lower and upper leg at the knee joint. To achieve this angle, the height of the foot was raised when necessary, using a step, book or other suitable object to hand. The insertion tape was positioned horizontally around the calf, and, by moving the tape up and down the calf, the maximum horizontal circumference was located and measured. As far as possible the tape was in contact with the calf throughout the circumference, although this was not always achievable because of the shape of the leg. Care was taken when making the measurement not to compress the tissues of the calf.

Note: Durnin *et al* recommended that to make this measurement the subject be seated on a table with the leg hanging freely and the back of the knee touching the table.[7] Pilot work showed that a table or similar piece of suitable furniture was not always available in the subject's home; it was therefore decided after consultation to take the measurement with the subject seated in the standardised position as described above.

6 Blood pressure

Measurements of systolic and diastolic blood pressures and heart rate were taken using a mains-powered sphygmomanometer, the Accutorr 2A monitor.[8]

Pressures are detected by the monitor by means of an oscillator and transducer, and the readings are displayed on a digital display unit. Two cuffs are supplied with the monitor, a standard adult, and a large adult size, each cuff having index markings to indicate that the appropriate size for the subject's arm is being used. The inflation pressure is automatically adjusted to take account of the size of cuff being used.

The monitor can be set to take repeated measurements at pre-set intervals, and the cuff is inflated to an appropriate pressure, determined automatically. The measurement cycle can be interrupted at any point by the operator, and the timing sequence is held until the

monitor is reactivated. An audible tone indicates that the monitor is ready to commence a measurement cycle.

Interviewers were provided with a detailed instruction manual from the manufacturers of the monitor, and additional briefing notes for interviewers were prepared by OPCS.

Each monitor was checked for correct calibration against a standard mercury column, and, if necessary, recalibrated before being issued to an interviewer. Three measurements were taken from each subject, at pre-set intervals of one minute.

The measurements were made after the end of the dietary recording period and the procedure was carried out by the interviewer in the subject's home, on a visit when the interviewer was not accompanied by the doctor or other person taking the specimen of blood. Details of all prescribed drugs being taken by the subject were recorded, and in the analysis of blood pressure those subjects taking drugs which could affect the pressures (for example, anti-hypertensive drugs and diuretics) were excluded.

Details are given elsewhere of the protocol adopted to ensure that in all cases the subject's general practitioner (GP) was informed that blood pressure measurements had been taken as part of the survey, with the subject's co-operation.[9] The diastolic and systolic pressures and heart rate associated with the lowest recorded systolic pressure of the three measurements made were passed to the subject's GP.

Before taking the blood pressure measurements efforts were made to ensure that the subject was relaxed and sitting in a quiet room, likely to remain free of interruptions. Subjects were asked to refrain from smoking, eating and drinking while the measurements were being taken, and, if possible, to have abstained from these for at least 10 to 15 minutes previously.

The measurements were made on the left arm, preferably with the arm removed from the sleeve of any clothing being worn. If this was not possible then the sleeve was rolled to above the point where the cuff would be fitted, ensuring that the sleeve was not constricting the flow of blood to the arm.

With the subject seated, and the left arm supported on the arm of a chair or other flat surface, a cuff of the appropriate size was fitted to the arm. A small adult size cuff was not supplied with the monitor, so for subjects with a relatively small arm the standard size cuff had to be used, with a note recorded on the interview questionnaire by the interviewer.

Interviewers were trained to place the cuff, with the correct degree of tension around the upper arm, (defined as being just able to get two fingers between the cuff and the arm). The lower edge of the cuff was positioned approximately one inch above the crease at the elbow joint, and with the black connection hose in line with the third finger of the left hand. This position corresponds to that used when pressure is measured using a 'microphone' system; that is, that the microphone should be sited over the point where the brachial artery is palpated.

Wrapping the cuff to the required tension for subjects with a large upper arm sometimes proved difficult. There is evidence that with a conical cuff, lower systolic and diastolic pressures are obtained than with a standard rectangular cuff, independent of arm circumference, and that in obese individuals blood pressure is probably measured more accurately with a conical cuff due to a better fit on subjects with a large upper arm.[10]

The subject was warned about the audible sound that would be emitted by the monitor when the cycle was ready to commence, and asked to remain still and silent until the cycle was completed. The interviewer then checked that the subject's upper arm was supported and approximately level with the position of the heart. Having checked that the hose connections to the monitor were secure and the machine settings corresponded to the size of cuff being used the measurement cycle was initiated, to take three sets of measurement at one-minute intervals.

At the start of each measurement the cuff inflated, and when complete the cuff deflated completely and the pressures and heart rate were displayed by the monitor and held until the next measurement began. The pressures displayed on the monitor were recorded by the interviewer on the interview questionnaire.

If, for any reason, a measurement was unsatisfactory (because for example, the subject moved, or was inter-rupted), the machine was switched off, the cuff removed or slackened, and after a few minutes wait, the whole procedure was repeated.

References and notes

1. This equipment was manufacutured, checked and calibrated by CMS Weighing Ltd, London.
2. Knight I. *The heights and weights of adults in Great Britain* HMSO London 1984.
3. The personal weighing scales were checked and recalibrated by CMS Weighing Ltd, London.
4. Copies of the self-completion forms (one for males, one for females) are given at Appendix A.
5. Insertion tapes were purchased from TALC, St Albans, Herts, and modified by OPCS.
6. The callipers were purchased from, and modified by CMS Weighing Ltd, London.
7. Durnin J V G A, McKay F C, Webster C I. A new method of assessing fatness and desirable weight, for use in the armed services. University of Glasgow 1985, Unpublished paper
8. The Accutorr 2A monitor is manufactured by Datascope Corporation, Paramus, New Jersey. UK distributor: Datascope Medical Company Ltd, Cambridge Science Park, Cambridge CB4 4WE. Accutorr monitors were kindly loaned to us, for the duration of the study, by Dr B Cox of Cambridge University School of Community Medicine, Cambridge.
9. See Chapter 3
10. Maxwell G F, Pruijt J F M, Arntzenius A C. Comparison of the conical cuff and the standard rectangular cuffs. *Int J Epidemiol* 14; 3: 468–472.

Appendix H(i) Main and subsidiary food groups

Note: The numbered food groups and food types (**bold**) have been used in the calculation of nutrients from food groups. The subsidiary food groups (*italics*) have been used only in the calculation of the quantities of foods consumed.

1 Pasta, rice and other miscellaneous cereals
—*Pasta*
—*Rice*
—*Other*

2 White bread
3 Wholemeal bread
4 Other breads
5 Wholegrain and high fibre breakfast cereals
6 Other breakfast cereals
7 Biscuits
8 Buns, cakes, pastries and fruit pies
—*Fruit pies*
—*Buns, cakes and pastries*

9 Puddings and ice cream
—*Milk puddings*
—*Ice cream*
—*Sponge type puddings*
—*Other puddings*

1–9 Total cereals and cereal products

10 Whole milk
11 Semi-skimmed milk
12 Skimmed milk
13 Other milk and cream
14 Cheese
—*Cottage cheese*
—*Other cheeses*

15 Yoghurt

10–15 Total milk and milk products

16 Egg and egg dishes

17 Butter
18 'Polyunsaturated' margarine
19 Low fat spread
20 Block margarine
21 Other margarines and spreads
—*Soft margarine (not polyunsaturated)*
—*Yellow spreads*
—*Other*

17–21 Total fats

22 Bacon and ham
23 Beef, veal and dishes
24 Lamb and dishes
25 Pork and dishes
26 Coated chicken
27 Chicken and turkey dishes
28 Liver and dishes, liver paté and liver sausage
29 Burgers and kebabs
30 Sausages
31 Meat pies and pastries (incl. chicken pies)
32 Other meat and meat products (incl. game and offal excl. liver)

22–32 Total meat and meat products

33 Fried white fish in flour, batter or breadcrumbs
34 Other white fish and dishes
—*Shellfish*
—*Other white fish and dishes*

35 Oily fish (incl. canned)

33–35 Total fish and fish dishes

36 Salad vegetables
—*Carrots (raw)*
—*Tomatoes (raw)*
—*Other salad vegetables*

37 Vegetables
—*Peas*
—*Green beans*
—*Baked beans*
—*Leafy green vegetables (incl. broccoli)*
—*Carrots (not raw)*
—*Fresh tomatoes (not raw)*
—*Other vegetables*

38 Fried potatoes (incl. chips)
—*Potato chips*
—*Other fried or roast potatoes*
—*Other potato products*

39 Other potatoes
42 Savoury snacks

36–39 & 42 Total vegetables

40 Fruit and nuts
—*Apples and pears*
—*Oranges, tangerines, etc*
—*Bananas*

—*Canned fruit in juice*
—*Canned fruit in syrup*
—*Unsalted nuts, fruit and nut mixes*
—*Other fruit*

40 Total fruit and nuts

41 Sugars and preserves
—*Sugar*
—*Preserves*
—*Other sugars*

43 Sugar confectionery
44 Chocolate confectionery

41, 43 & 44 Total sugar, preserves and confectionery

45 Fruit juice
46 Soft drinks
—*Diet soft drinks*
—*Other soft drinks*

47 Spirits and liqueurs
—*Liqueurs*
—*Spirits*

48 Wine
—*Wine*
—*Fortified wine*

49 Beer, cider and perry
—*Beers*
—*Cider and perry*

51 Tea, coffee and water
—*Coffee (made-up weight)*
—*Tea (made-up weight)*
—*Water*

45–49 & 51 Total beverages

50 Miscellaneous

Appendix H(ii) Examples of foods included in main food groups

Food groups

1. Pasta, rice and other miscellaneous cereals

   includes boiled/fried rice, pasta—all types (dried fresh and canned), Yorkshire pudding, dumplings, pizza

2. White bread

   includes sliced, unsliced, french stick, milk loaf, slimmers type, white pitta bread, white rolls

3. Wholemeal bread

   includes sliced, unsliced, high fibre white and soft grain breads, wholemeal chapatis and pitta breads, wholemeal rolls

4. Other breads

   includes brown bread, granary, rye, crumpets, muffins, pikelets, brown and granary rolls.

5. Wholegrain and high fibre breakfast cereals

   includes All Bran, Branflakes, Shredded Wheat, muesli, porridge, Weetabix

6. Other breakfast cereals

   includes cornflakes, Rice Krispies, Special K, Sugar Puffs, Honey Smacks

7. Biscuits

   all types, including sweet and savoury

8. Buns, cakes, pastries and fruit pies

   includes danish pastry, chelsea bun, doughnuts, eccles cakes, frangipane tarts, jam tarts, scones (sweet and savoury), sponge cakes, fruit cakes, meringue, fruit pies (all types)

9. Puddings including ice-cream

   includes instant whip, fruit crumbles, arctic roll, batter puddings, custard/blancmange, christmas pudding, fruit flans, fresh cream desserts, jelly, fruit fools, sponge puddings, milk puddings, sorbets, ice-cream

10. Whole milk

    all types including pasteurised, UHT, sterilised, Channel Island

11. Semi-skimmed milk

    all types including pasteurised, UHT, flavoured, canned, milk with added vitamins

12. Skimmed milk

    all types including pasteurised, UHT, sterilised, canned, milk with added vitamins

13. Other milk and cream

    includes condensed, dried milks, evaporated, goats milk, sheeps milk, soya milk, milk shakes and all creams

14. Cheese

    all types including hard types, soft cheeses, cream cheese, processed cheese, cottage and curd cheeses

15. Yoghurt

    includes low fat (fruit, flavoured), thick and creamy, 'diet' yoghurts, goats and sheep milk yoghurt and yoghurt drinks

16. Egg and egg dishes

    includes boiled, fried, scrambled, omelettes (sweet and savoury), souffle, quiche and flans, scotch egg

17. Butter

18. Polyunsaturated margarine

    margarine that can make a claim to be high in polyunsaturated fatty acids

19. Low fat spread

376

20. Block margarine

21. Other margarines and spreads   includes soft margarines not polyunsaturated and yellow spreads

22. Bacon and ham   includes bacon joints and rashers, gammon joints/steaks, ham sliced off bone

23. Beef, veal and dishes   includes beef (and veal) joints, steaks, minced beef, stewing steak, beef stews and casseroles, meat balls, lasagne, chilli con carne, beef curry dishes, bolognaise sauce

24. Lamb and dishes   includes lamb joints, chops, cutlets, lamb curries, Irish stew, lamb casseroles/stews

25. Pork and dishes   includes joints, chops, steaks, belly rashers, pork stews/casseroles, sweet and sour pork, spare ribs

26. Coated chicken   includes chicken (and turkey) drumsticks, chicken pieces, nuggetts, fingers, burgers etc coated in egg and crumb, Kentucky Fried Chicken

27. Chicken and turkey dishes   includes roast chicken (and turkey), barbecued, fried (no coating) pieces, curries, stews/casseroles, chow mein, in sauce, spread, chicken/turkey roll

28. Liver, liver paté etc   includes all types liver (fried, stewed, grilled), liver casserole, liver sausage

29. Burgers and kebabs   includes beefburgers, hamburgers, cheeseburgers (with or without roll), doner/shish/kofte kebabs (with pitta bread and salad)

30. Sausages   includes beef, pork, turkey, polony, sausage in batter, saveloy, frankfurters

31. Meat pies and pastries   includes chicken/turkey pies, vol-au-vents, beef pies, pork pies, veal and ham pie, pasties, sausage rolls, meat samosas

32. Other meat and meat products   includes game (e.g. duck, grouse, hare, pheasant), rabbit, offal (not liver), faggots, black pudding, meat paste, canned meats (e.g. tongue, luncheon meat), salami, meat loaf, moussaka, shepherds pie, chop suey

33. White fish in batter or breadcrumbs   includes cod, haddock, hake, plaice, etc, coated in egg and crumb or batter; coated fried cartilaginous fish (e.g. dogfish, skate), scampi, fillet-o-fish, fish cakes, fish fingers, cod roe fried, prawn balls

34. Other white fish and dishes   includes cod, haddock, hake, plaice etc (poached, grilled, smoked, dried), fish coated in flour, shellfish, curried fish, fish paste, fish in sauce, fish pie, kedgeree

35. Oily fish   includes herrings, kippers, mackerel, sprats, eels, herring roe (baked, fried, grilled), salmon, tuna, sardines, taramasalata, mackerel paté

36. Salad vegetables   includes leafy green vegetables (e.g. endive, lettuce, spinach, chicory), other raw vegetables (e.g. cabbage, carrots, tomatoes, radish, spring onions), coleslaw, purchased prepared salads

37. Vegetables   includes beans/pulses, cooked vegetables, vegetable casseroles/stews, vegetable curry dishes, tofu, ratatouille, cauliflower cheese

38. Fried potatoes incl. chips   chips (fresh and frozen), oven chips, potato waffles, hash browns, roast, sauteed, croquettes

39. Other potatoes   includes boiled, mashed, jacket, potato salad, canned potato, potato based curries, instant potato

40.	Fruit and nuts	includes fruit cooked (with and without sugar), raw, canned (with and without syrup), fruit pie filling (not fruit pies); nuts incl. almonds, hazelnuts, mixed nuts, peanuts, peanut butter, bombay mix, seeds (e.g. sunflower, sesame)
41.	Sugars and preserves	includes sugar (white and brown), glucose liquid/powder, black molasses, treacle, syrup, honey, jams, marmalade (incl. low sugar varieties), glace cherries, mixed peel, marzipan
42.	Savoury snacks	includes crisps, other potato products (e.g. puffs, rings), Twiglets
43.	Confectionery—sugar	includes boiled sweets, gums, pastils, fudge, chews, mints, rock, liquorice, toffees, popcorn
44.	Confectionery—chocolate	includes chocolate bars, filled bars, assortments
45.	Fruit juice	includes single fruit and mixed fruit 100% juices; canned, bottled, cartons; carbonated, still, freshly squeezed
46.	Soft drinks	includes carbonated beverages (and low calorie versions), fruit squashes, cordials, fruit drinks, syrups
47.	Spirits and liquors	includes cream liquors, Pernod, Southern Comfort, 70% proof spirits, Pimms
48.	Wine	includes white, red, rosé, sparkling, champagne, port, sherry
49.	Beer/cider/perry	includes beer and lager (both non-premium and premium), low alcohol lagers, stout, strong ale (bottled, draft and canned), cider, Babycham, perry
50.	Miscellaneous	includes sauces, ketchups, chutneys, pickles, gravy, mayonnaise, soups, beverages (not tea or coffee)
51.	Tea, coffee and water	instant and leaf/bean, also lemon tea, vending machine tea and coffee; tap water, bottled, carbonated

Appendix J Methods of biochemical analysis and quality control

1 Introduction

The methods of collection, processing and transport of blood, serum and urine samples are described in Chapter 4. The samples thus obtained were sent to the Wolfson Research Laboratories in Birmingham. A separate whole blood sample was sent from the Wolfson Laboratories to the Department of Haematology of the Birmingham General Hospital for the haematology and the analysis of red cell folic acid and vitamin B12. A separate plasma sample was prepared and sent from the Wolfson Laboratories to Dr D I Thurnham at the Nutrition Laboratory of the Dudley Road Hospital, Birmingham for the analysis of fat soluble vitamins. The following sections of this appendix give the methodology of the assays and evaluations of quality assurance throughout the year.

2 Haematology

The measurements of haemoglobin, haematocrit, mean cell volume (MCV) and mean corpuscular haemoglobin concentration were carried out on blood collected into tubes pre-treated with EDTA on the commercial Coulter counter system (Model S) located in the Department of Haematology of the Birmingham General Hospital. Samples from the survey were integrated into the normal hospital throughput. There was thus no internal quality control data but for external quality assurance (EQA) samples from the survey were included in the Regional Scheme in which the hospital participates.

The reference ranges for haemoglobin were, for males 14–18g/100ml, and for females 12–16g/100ml.

The average values for the four rounds of the survey for each haematological parameter are shown in Table J1. *(Table J1)*

There were no significant differences between rounds and no age related differences. Eighteen samples were included in the regional EQA scheme these showed no evidence of significant bias. It was concluded that the results of these haematological measurements were acceptable throughout the period of the survey.

3 Whole blood analyses
(i) Erythrocyte glutathione reductase activity coefficient (EGRAC)

The ratio of glutathione reductase activity before and after adding flavine adenine dinucleotide was deter-

mined by the method of Thurnham and Rathakette,[1] modified for use on a Kone Discrete Analyser. Two internal quality control (IQC) samples, one with low and one with normal initial activity, were analysed over each survey round. No external quality control was available. Mean EGRAC values for each round and the IQC samples means are shown in Table J2.

(Table J2)

There were no sex differences and no significant differences between the rounds. The coefficient of variation, that is, standard deviation as a proportion of the mean, for the IQC samples was 1.5% to 2.0%, and no changes over time were detected. It was concluded that the results of these analyses were acceptable throughout the survey.

(ii) Red cell folic acid (folate)

Red cell folic acid concentrations were determined by a standard microbiological assay using *lactobacillus casei*. The times of blood collection and of arrival at the laboratories were recorded. Blood samples received after more than 48 hours were not analysed. Folic acid concentrations were determined in whole blood and serum, and erythrocyte levels calculated from these. No external quality control was possible but internal quality control was carried out with three sets of IQC samples with low (below 1μg/l), medium (3μg/l) and high (9μg/l) concentrations of folic acid.

The results are shown in Table J3. *(Table J3)*

Analyses showed that there were significant differences between the rounds with round 1 having significantly higher results than rounds 2 to 4. There were also significant differences between the sexes and different age groups. However, the differences between rounds were much greater than could be accounted for by age, sex and seasonal differences. Corrections were made for outliers, antibiotic usage and for age of samples (under 24 hours, and 24 to 48 hours) but the differences between the rounds remained. Seasonal variation was discounted as there was no sign of a trend for round 4 results to rise towards those of round 1 as would be expected for a cyclical phenomenon.

It was concluded that there was a downward drift intrinsic to the analytical method over the period of the survey and that despite significant age and sex differences the results were unreliable. They are therefore quoted in this Report, but no interpretation has been attempted.

4 Routine serum analyses

Separated serum samples were analysed by standard laboratory techniques on a Hitachi 737 analyser for concentrations of total protein, albumin, alkaline phosphatase, calcium, creatinine and γ-glutamyl transpeptidase. Globulin was calculated as total protein minus albumin. Non-HDL cholesterol was calculated as total cholesterol minus HDL cholesterol. External quality assurance was obtained from participation of the laboratories in the UK consensus system (NEQASs and Wellcome). Internal quality control was obtained by analysing appropriate standards continuously. The results are given in Tables J4 and J5. It was concluded that the results of all the analyses from the Hitachi 737 analyser were acceptable throughout the survey.

(Tables J4 and J5)

5 Serum ferritin

Serum ferritin was analysed using the routine laboratory method which used a commercial two-site immunoradiometric assay (Ciba Corning). The results in each survey round are shown in Table J6. The coefficient of variation in the IQC data was 4.3% to 9.8%. The mean bias in the 24 samples analysed in the EQA scheme was -0.6%. It was concluded that the results of the measurements for serum ferritin were acceptable throughout the survey. *(Table J6)*

6 Serum HDL cholesterol

Serum HDL cholesterol was analysed by the method of phosphotungstate-magnesium precipitation followed by enzymatic assay of cholesterol on a Kone analyser. The results of the analyses for each round of the survey are shown in Table J7. *(Table J7)*

The coefficient of variation of the IQC results was 4.1% to 7.8%. The reference range for HDL cholesterol was 0.58mmol/l to 2.24mmol/1. The mean for survey subjects in round 4 was significantly higher than for round 1. Both sets of IQC data tended to rise by about 9% over the survey year, probably due to the analytical system. This was not thought high enough to disregard the results and the data on HDL cholesterol were thought to be acceptable throughout the survey.

7 Serum vitamin B12

Serum vitamin B12 was measured using *lactobacillus leichmanni* and no external quality assurance was available. Internal quality control on three control sera gave coefficients of variation of 6.7% to 13.1%. However mean values for all three sera rose during each survey round with round 4 about 16% higher than round 1. This was found to be due to a significant change in analytical accuracy over the survey period. In view of this the results for serum vitamin B12 were not considered reliable and are reported here without further comment.

8 Fat soluble vitamins in plasma

Plasma samples were analysed for α and β-carotenes, β-cryptoxanthin, lycopene, retinol (vitamin A) and vitamin E (tocopherols) by High Pressure Liquid Chromatography (HPLC) on a $3\mu m$ ODS-2 Spherisorb column after heptane extraction. Carotenoids were monitored at 450nm, retinol at 325nm and tocopherol at 392nm.[2] For β-carotene, retinol and tocopherol external quality assurance was arranged by participating in the EQA scheme organised by the National Bureau of Standards in Washington DC. However for the other fat soluble vitamins there was no external quality assurance. The results for each round of the survey are shown in Table J8. *(Table J8)*

External quality assurance from the National Bureau of Standards showed non-significant bias of $+2\%$, $+6\%$ and $+11\%$ for β-carotene, retinol and tocopherol respectively. There was a fall in IQC controls, particularly for lycopene, over the survey period which was found to be due to instability of the control serum.[3] It was concluded that the results of the analyses of the fat soluble vitamins were acceptable throughout the period of the survey.

9 Analysis of 24-hour urine samples

Urine samples were analysed for their sodium, potassium, urea and creatinine concentrations and the excretion rates per 24 hours were then calculated from the recorded urinary volumes and period of collection.

Sodium and potassium concentrations

These were measured using flame photometry. No external quality assurance was available. The results of the analyses are shown in Table J9. *(Table J9)*

The coefficient of variation for the IQC for sodium was 1.7%, and for potassium 1.0%. It was concluded that the results of these analyses were acceptable throughout the survey.

Urea and creatinine concentrations

Urea was measured by the urease method and creatinine by the Jaffé method on a Cobas Bio centrifugal analyser. No external quality assurance was available. The results of the analyses are shown in Table J10.

(Table J10)

The internal quality control coefficients of variation for urea and creatinine were 1.2% to 3.0% and 2.0% to 2.5% respectively. It was concluded that the results of these analyses were acceptable throughout the survey.

References

1. Thurnham D I, Rathakette P. Incubation of NAD(P)H: glutathione reductase (EC 1.6.4.2) with flavine adenine dinucleotide for maximal stimulation in the measurement of riboflavin status. *Br. J Nut* 1982; 48: 459–466

2. Thurnham D I, Smith E, Flora P S. Concurrent liquid chromatographic assay of retinol, α-carotene, β-carotene, lycopene, β-cryptoxanthin in plasma with tocopherol acetate as internal standard. *Clin Chem* 1988; 34: 377–381

3. Thurnham D I, Flora P S. Stability of individual carotenoids, retinol and tocopherol in stored plasma. *Clin Chem* 1988; 34: 1947

Table J1   Results of haematology

Round	Haemoglobin		Haematocrit		MCV		MCHC	
	mean (g/100ml)	n	mean	n	mean (fl)	n	mean (g/100ml)	n
1	13.94	444	0.415	445	91.70	444	33.62	444
2	14.11	408	0.423	408	90.98	408	33.43	408
3	13.92	444	0.410	443	91.27	444	33.93	442
4	14.02	414	0.419	414	92.23	414	33.58	414
Total	14.00	1710	0.417	1710	91.54	1710	33.65	1708
EQA % bias	−0.7	18	+3.5	18	+3.3	18	−4.0	18

Table J2   Quality control for erythrocyte glutathione reductase activation coefficient (EGRAC)

	Round				
	1	2	3	4	Total
Number	492	457	479	442	1870
Mean EGRAC	1.08	1.10	1.10	1.09	1.09
IQC number	58	56	52	30	216
IQC mean	1.06	1.06	1.06	1.06	1.06

Table J3   Quality control for red cell folic acid

Round	Folic acid (μg/l)							
	Survey subjects (Erythrocyte)		IQC1 (Serum)		IQC2 (Serum)		IQC3 (Serum)	
	mean	n	mean	n	mean	n	mean	n
1	247	442	0.6	13	3.2	13	9.1	13
2	191	404	0.8	10	3.5	10	9.8	10
3	184	440	0.7	14	3.3	14	9.3	14
4	176	406	0.8	10	3.5	10	9.9	10
Total	200	1692	0.7	47	3.4	47	9.5	47

Table J4   Results of serum analyses obtained on the Hitachi 737 analyser

	Round										Reference range
	1		2		3		4		Total		
	mean	n	mean	n	mean	n	mean	n	mean	n	
Albumin g/l	43.69	488	45.26	460	44.94	482	45.11	448	44.74	1878	34–50
Total protein g/l	71.50	488	71.87	460	71.73	482	71.55	448	71.66	1878	
Alkaline phosphatase u/l	157.9	488	167.9	461	165.5	484	165.4	447	164.1	1880	70–350
Calcium mmol/l	2.32	488	2.31	461	2.29	484	2.28	447	2.30	1880	2.20–2.65
Total cholesterol mmol/l	5.67**	488	5.90	458	5.90	482	5.77	445	5.81	1871	4.0–8.0
Creatinine μmol/l	94.02	488	93.79	460	94.62	482	96.11	488	94.62	1878	
γ-glutamyl transpeptidase u/l	25.14	488	28.89	461	25.38	483	25.04	446	26.10	1878	4–28

* See footnote to Table J5

Table J5 Quality control for serum analytes

Round	Albumin (g/l)				Total protein (g/l)				Alkaline phosphatase (u/l)				Calcium (mmol/l)			
	IQC1		IQC2		IQC1		IQC2		IQC1		IQC2		IQC1		IQC2	
	mean	n	mean	n	mean	n	mean	n	mean	n	mean	n	mean	n	mean	n
1	36	22	28	22	60	22	63	22	82	22	294	22	2.18	22	2.42	22
2	37	18	29	18	60	18	63	18	80	18	294	18	2.17	17	2.42	17
3	38	17	29	17	61	17	64	17	80	17	296	17	2.16	17	2.44	17
4	38	17	28	17	61	17	63	17	89	17	310	17	2.14	16	2.40	16
Total	37	74	28	74	60	74	63	74	83	74	298	74	2.16	72	2.42	72
Coefficient of variation*	1.5%–2.8%				1.3%–2.1%				3.8%–8.9%				1.6%–2.7%			
EQA % bias					−1.4 (n=38)				+10.8 (n=22) NEQAS −8.3(n=15) Wellcome				−1.4 (n=24)			

Round	Total cholesterol (mmol/l)						Creatinine (μmol/l)				γ-glutamyl transpeptidase (u/l)			
	IQC1		IQC2		IQC3		IQC1		IQC2		IQC1		IQC2	
	mean	n	mean	n	mean	n	mean	n	mean	n	mean	n	mean	n
1	3.36	22	2.26	22	7.36**	22	106	22	205	22	19	22	48	22
2	3.47	18	2.29	18	7.56	18	105	18	206	18	19	18	49	18
3	3.50	17	2.31	17	7.72	16	104	17	202	17	19	17	50	17
4	3.50	17	2.29	17	7.73	17	104	17	203	17	19	17	50	17
Total	3.45	74	2.29	74	7.57	73	105	74	203	74	19	74	49	74
Coefficient of variation*	2.0%–3.0%						2.1%–4.5%				4.0%–6.0%			
EQA % bias	+1.07 (n=39)						−2.6 (n=35)				−1.3 (n=22)			

* Coefficient of variation = $\dfrac{\text{standard deviation}}{\text{mean}}$ for each IQC in each round

** Results for round 1 about 2.4% lower than for the rest. Changes probably due to change in one reagent. Overall round 1 about 1% low, rounds 2, 3 and 4 about 1.5% high

Table J6 Quality control for serum ferritin

Round	Serum ferritin (μg/l)							
	Survey subjects		IQC1		IQC2		IQC3	
	mean	n	mean	n	mean	n	mean	n
1	74.60	480	430	20	101	21	79	21
2	77.95	459	432	17	99	17	74	16
3	75.18	477	427	13	99	13	72	13
4	70.97	445	443	14	100	13	73	14
Total	76.62	1861	443	64	100	64	75	64

Table J7 Quality control for HDL cholesterol

Round	HDL cholesterol (mmol/l)					
	Survey subjects		IQC1		IQC2	
	mean	n	mean	n	mean	n
1	1.22	487	1.45	22	1.22	18
2	1.27	456	1.41	13	1.25	11
3	1.29	482	1.49	14	1.27	11
4	1.34	447	1.55	15	1.27	16
Total	1.28	1872	1.47	64	1.25	56

Table J8 Quality control for plasma carotenoids and vitamin E

Round	α-carotene (µmol/l)				β-carotene (µmol/l)				β-cryptoxanthin (µmol/l)			
	Survey subjects		IQC1		Survey subjects		IQC1		Survey subjects		IQC1	
	mean	n	mean	n	mean	n	mean	n	mean	n	mean	n
1	0.083	493	0.066	24	0.374	493	0.152	24	0.174	493	0.305	24
2	0.007	462	0.067	24	0.295	462	0.145	24	0.244	462	0.295	24
3	0.080	488	0.067	28	0.339	488	0.141	28	0.153	488	0.202	28
4	0.095	453	0.061	26	0.328	453	0.110	26	0.177	453	0.225	26
Total	0.084	1896	0.065	102	0.335	1896	0.137	102	0.187	1896	0.254	102

EQA mean bias = + 2% (NBS)
not significant

Round	Lycopene (µmol/l)				Retinol (vitamin A) (µmol/l)				Tocopherols (vitamin E) (µmol/l)			
	Survey subjects		IQC1		Survey subjects		IQC1		Survey subjects		IQC1	
	mean	n	mean	n	mean	n	mean	n	mean	n	mean	n
1	0.324	493	0.825	24	2.021	493	2.075	24	25.48	493	23.22	24
2	0.260	462	0.710	24	2.060	462	2.228	24	26.36	462	24.80	24
3	0.252	488	0.668	28	2.051	488	2.162	28	26.49	488	23.29	28
4	0.342	453	0.457	26	2.076	453	2.035	26	28.27	453	23.58	26
Total	0.294	1896	0.661	102	2.051	1896	2.125	102	26.62	1896	23.70	102

Retinol: EQA mean bias = + 6% (NBS) not significant

Tocopherols: EQA mean bias = + 11% (NBS) not significant

Table J9 Results of analyses of sodium and potassium in 24-hour urine collection

Round	Sodium (mmol/l)				Potassium (mmol/l)			
	Survey subject		IQC1		Survey subjects		IQC1	
	mean	n	mean	n	mean	n	mean	n
1	98.6	522	103.5	4	50.70	522	57.0	4
2	115.2	494	104.7	39	49.22	494	57.1	38
3	103.4	539	103.1	50	47.74	539	57.6	50
4	109.6	485	104.2	58	47.76	485	57.5	88
Total	106.5	2040	104.0	151	48.85	2040	57.4	150

Table J10 Results of analyses of urea and creatinine in 24-hour urine collection

Round	Urea (mmol/l)				Creatinine (mmol/l)			
	Survey subjects		IQC1		Survey subjects		IQC1	
	mean	n	mean	n	mean	n	mean	n
1	228.0	522	220	18	8.34	522	8.4	18
2	247.8	494	230	39	9.01	494	8.4	39
3	236.9	539	224	46	8.42	539	8.2	51
4	248.5	484	226	59	8.48	485	8.2	59
Total	240.0	2039	226	162	8.64	2040	8.3	167

Appendix K

Table K1 Percentage distribution of red cell folate concentration by age and sex: samples arriving at the laboratory within 48 hours*

Red cell folate concentration (μg/l)	Age				All ages
	18–24	25–34	35–49	50–64	18–64
	cum %	cum %	cum %	cum %	cum %
Men					
Less than 120	12	13	15	9	13
Less than 170	37	33	39	30	35
Less than 220	66	57	62	55	59
Less than 270	79	79	77	73	76
All	100	100	100	100	100
Base	*106*	*182*	*247*	*194*	*729*
Mean (average) value	201.3	211.9	207.2	231.2	213.9
Median value	186.8	205.3	192.0	207.5	199.0
Lower 5.0 percentile	80.0	93.0	84.0	101.0	89.0
Upper 5.0 percentile	345.0	347.0	375.0	420.0	383.0
Standard error of the mean	7.65	6.16	5.93	7.40	3.41
	cum %	cum %	cum %	cum %	cum %
Women					
Less than 120	40	34	26	8	23
Less than 170	66	56	51	31	47
Less than 220	85	74	73	59	70
Less than 270	93	84	85	78	84
All	100	100	100	100	100
Base	*58*	*127*	*267*	*185*	*637*
Mean (average) value	155.2	170.8	184.1	222.3	189.9
Median value	143.0	155.0	168.0	199.0	178.5
Lower 5.0 percentile	51.0	57.0	73.0	105.0	69.0
Upper 5.0 percentile	321.0	325.0	346.4	416.2	362.1
Standard error of the mean	9.46	7.75	5.39	7.66	3.73

* see Chapter 17 (17.2)

Table K2 Percentage distribution of red cell folate concentration by age and sex: all samples*

Red cell folate concentration (μg/l)	Age				All ages
	18–24	25–34	35–49	50–64	18–64
	cum %	cum %	cum %	cum %	cum %
Men					
Less than 120	14	13	16	9	13
Less than 170	38	34	39	30	35
Less than 220	67	58	61	54	59
Less than 270	79	79	76	72	76
All	100	100	100	100	100
Base	*120*	*189*	*279*	*212*	*800*
Mean (average) value	198.8	210.7	207.0	232.9	213.5
Median value	186.3	204.0	192.0	208.5	197.9
Lower 5.0 percentile	71.5	93.0	84.0	103.0	88.5
Upper 5.0 percentile	346.2	347.0	375.6	420.0	381.5
Standard error of the mean	7.34	5.99	5.53	7.13	3.26
	cum %	cum %	cum %	cum %	cum %
Women					
Less than 120	40	35	25	8	23
Less than 170	68	57	50	32	48
Less than 220	84	74	71	61	70
Less than 270	93	85	85	80	84
All	100	100	100	100	100
Base	*68*	*142*	*289*	*203*	*702*
Mean (average) value	158.7	169.4	185.4	219.2	189.4
Median value	143.0	152.9	171.3	198.0	174.4
Lower 5.0 percentile	57.0	58.0	73.0	109.0	69.9
Upper 5.0 percentile	321.0	325.0	346.0	375.0	361.0
Standard error of the mean	10.64	7.25	5.15	7.09	3.53

* Results based on the analysis of all specimens received, including those received after 48 hours [see Chapter 17 (17.2)]

Appendix L   Glossary of abbreviations, terms and survey definitions

Benefit households	see *State benefits (receipt of)*.
BMI	see *Body mass index*.
Body mass index	A measure of body fatness which standardises weight for height: calculated as [weight(kg)/height(m)^2]. Also known as the *Quetelet index*.
Dependent children	Children of the informant under the age of 16, or aged 16 to 18 and in full-time education.
Diary sample	Informants who completed a full seven-day dietary record.
Economically active	Those working or *unemployed*.
Economically inactive	Those neither working nor *unemployed*; includes students, the retired and those looking after the home or family.
Economic status	Whether at the time of interview the informant was working, *unemployed*, or *economically inactive*.
EGRAC	The erythrocyte glutathione reductase activation coefficient.
EQA	External quality assurance.
Fat free mass	A calculated measurement, based on measurements of height, weight, calf circumference and wrist diameter for men, and height, weight and mid-upper arm circumference for women. See Appendix F for the regression equations used to calculated fat free mass for men and women in different age groups.
FFM	see *Fat free mass*.
Frankfort plane	The desired position for a subject's head when measuring height: the position is achieved when the line between the external auditory meatus and the lower border of the orbit is horizontal.
GGT	γ-glutamyl transpeptidase.
HDL cholesterol	High density lipoprotein cholesterol.
Head of household	The head of household is a member of the household and (in order of preference) either the husband of the person, or the person, who: —owns the household accommodation, or —is legally responsible for the rent of the accommodation, or —has the accommodation as an emolument or perquisite, or —has the accommodation by virtue of some relationship to the owner in cases where the owner or lessee is not a member of the household. Where two members of a different sex have equal claim, the male is taken as head of household. Where two members of the same sex have equal claim, the elder is taken as head of household.
Health-related diet	An analytic variable based on recorded intakes of specific foods which had a 'healthy image' and were particularly associated with recent advice on diet through health education. Details of the derivation are given in Chapter 12 section 12.2.

Heavy smoker	Informants smoking more than 20 cigarettes a day.
Household	The standard definition used in most surveys carried out by OPCS Social Survey Division, and comparable with the 1981 Census definition of a household, was used in this survey. A household is defined as a single person or group of people who have the address as their only or main residence and who either share one meal a day or share the living accommodation. (See L McCrossan *A Handbook for Interviewers*. HMSO London 1985.)
	A group of people would not be counted as a household solely on the basis of a shared kitchen or bathroom.
IQC	Internal quality control.
LDL cholesterol	Low density lipoprotein cholesterol. LDL cholesterol was not measured in this survey. Total serum cholesterol minus HDL cholesterol is taken as approximation of LDL cholesterol, uncorrected for triglycerides. For brevity the term LDL cholesterol is used for non-HDL cholesterol.
Light smoker	Informants smoking fewer than 20 cigarettes a day.
MAFF	Ministry of Agriculture, Fisheries and Food.
Manual social classes	Informants living in households where the head of household was in an occupation ascribed to *Social Classes III manual, IV or V*.
MCHC	Mean corpuscular haemoglobin concentration.
MCV	Mean corpuscular volume.
Median	see *Quantiles*.
Non-manual social classes	Informants living in households where the head of household was in an occupation ascribed to *Social Classes I, II or III non-manual*.
OPCS	The Office of Population Censuses and Surveys.
PCV	Packed cell volume.
Quantiles	The quantiles of a distribution divide it into equal parts. The *median* of a distribution divides it into two equal parts, such that half the cases in the distribution fall, or have a value, above the median, and the other half fall, or have a value below the median.
Quetelet index	see *Body mass index*.
Responding sample	Informants who co-operated with any aspect of the survey.
RDA	Recommended Daily Amount.
SE	Standard error of estimate; see *Notes* for method of calculation.
Social class	Based on the Registrar General's *Classification of Occupations 1980*, OPCS (HMSO, London 1980) social class was ascribed on the basis of the occupation of the head of household. The classification used in the tables is as follows:

Descriptive definition	Social class
Professional and intermediate occupations	I and II
Skilled occupations—non-manual	III non-manual
Skilled occupations—manual	III manual
Partly-skilled and unskilled occupations	IV and V

Spouse	Includes a non-married partner in the household where the informant described him or herself as married or living together.
State benefits (receipt of)	Receipt of unemployment benefit or supplementary benefit (income support), by anyone in the informant's household *except* when the head of household was in full-time work, and all cases where family income supplement (family credit) was being received.
Unemployed	Those actively seeking work, those intending to look for work but prevented by sickness, and those waiting to take up a job already obtained.

Index

Page references to tables and figures are shown in *italics*

Printed in the United Kingdom for HMSO
Dd292646 5/90 C25 G443 10170